Asian Law Series
School of Law
University of Washington
Number 12

Asian Law Series
School of Law
University of Washington

The Asian Law Series was initiated in 1969, with the cooperation of the University of Washington Press and the Institute for Comparative and Foreign Area Studies (now the Henry M. Jackson School of International Studies), in order to publish the results of several projects under way in Japanese, Chinese, and Korean law. The members of the editorial committee are Donald C. Clarke, Daniel H. Foote, John O. Haley, Nicholas R. Lardy, and Dan Fenno Henderson (chairman).

Constitutional Systems
in Late Twentieth Century Asia

Edited by
LAWRENCE W. BEER

University of Washington Press
Seattle and London

To the victims of power abuse in Asia and the United States,
and to law leaders who care

Library of Congress Cataloging-in-Publication Data
Constitutional systems in late twentieth century Asia / edited by
Lawrence W. Beer.
    p. cm. — (Asian law series ; no. 12)
  Includes index.
  ISBN 0-295-97174-6
  1. Asia—Constitutional law. I. Beer, Lawrence Ward, 1932– .
II. Series
KNC524.C66 1992
342.5'02—dc20   91–5165
[345.022]   CIP

The paper used in this publication meets the minimum requirements of American
National Standard for Information Sciences—Permanence of Paper for Printed Library
Materials, ANSI Z39.48–1984. ∞

CONTENTS

PREFACE

This book is offered at the Bicentennial commemoration of the United States Constitution and its Bill of Rights, from the signing date on September 17, 1987 to December 15, 1991 two centuries after the Bill of Rights was ratified. Most of the thirteen studies of current constitutional systems of Asia were prepared by distinguished indigenous scholars; where political circumstances dictated -- in the cases of China, North Korea, and Vietnam-- an American specialist has written the country study. Introductory and concluding chapters attempt to provide a theoretical framework and comparative perspectives, and wonder with concern about the adequacy of America's present constitutional assumptions, provisions and performance for a twenty-first century constitutionalist state. My purposes are to advance cross-cultural understanding of Asia's diverse approaches to law, rights and governance, and to set forth data, queries and ideas sufficient to suggest a need to recast some common terms and notions to better accommodate all the world's major cultural zones while reaffirming the few universal public values proposed as suitable foundations for constitutionalism in the future.

A country's performance with respect to constitutionalism seems a more valid measure of "advanced" or "high civilization" than its prowess in economic, technological, military or legalistic terms, because modern barbarism is quite compatible with all those standards. Naked power in any of these spheres more easily dominates the seats of media power than more genuine achievements for civilization of constitutionalist governance in states of whatever size and clime. Even a great contribution to constitutionalist civilization--such as the American institution of judicial review or the unique practical pacifism of Japan--can so consume its admirers' attention as to block out from consideration other essential elements of a civilized modern constitutionlism. For example, however impressive at its best in technical legal artistry and in orderly commitment to public principle, the "judicialist constitutionalism" of the United States now tends to smother a transcultural vision of law and justice-in-community that would legitimize rigorous restraint of the public and private power of those controlling the empire of law itself on behalf of human rights. In place of a positivist court-centered constitutionalism, I posit a human rights-centered constitutionalism in which systems of review analogous to U.S. courts are but one of the essential elements.

Work on this book began in 1980 with the persuasive encouragement of Professor Albert P. Blaustein of the Rutgers University Law School, a leader in helping Americans and others appreciate without exaggeration the relevance of the Constitution of the United States to constitution-making in foreign countries.   The original intent was to cover only the nations of East Asia(my primary sub-region of specialization); but I yielded to the allure of the fascinating systems in the countries of the Association of Southeast Asian Nations(ASEAN), too rarely noticed in the West. Having traveled that far, it was not hard at a later date to come to see that India's importance from a global perspective and Vietnam's deeply etched place in the American mind dictated their inclusion as well. Inclusion of all the constitutional systems in the enormous Asian area, home to over 60% of humankind and a good portion of all the world's radically diverse cultures, was never contemplated; but all Asia's countries are touched on in chapter 1.   Other books should cover, with maximum respect for indigenous scholars of law and constitutionalism, Latin America and, as they emerge, the new Europe and Africa. The present work is obviously not a "conference volume" resulting from a meeting organized and/or supported by non-Asians to pursue non-Asian analytical themes in law or social science, but the result of straightforward invitations extended to eminent scholars across the vast expanse of Asia to share understanding of their respective constitutional systems, each in a manner which he/she would find intellectually appropriate and comfortable. All were asked to take note of the relevance, if any, of the American constitutional experience to that of their own countries, but the primary focus was to be on explaining the principles, institutions, and actual working of their constitutional systems. The book thus provides what may be an unprecedented look at both national systems and the modalities of thinking about law and constitution in many Asian scholarly circles.   Although a number of the Asian authors have held high official posts, and indeed have participated in making their countries' constitutional histories, their views here are their own and not official statements of policy.   Much consultation preceded the selection of authors, but the choices are my responsibility. As will be apparent from my editorial notes and chapters, the authors' opinions are not necessarily my own.

More than the usual number of debts is incurred with such a multi-national project. My deepest indebtedness is to the Asian and American authors. In many cases the very distinction of the authors made completion of a manuscript--at different points in time during the 1980s--an impressive sign of commitment to international communication and legal education about their respective countries. Great distances, paucity of material on some Asian nations, and diversity of legal and political tradition still seriously impede communications between Asia and the United States, more precisely, and the rest of the world; but cultural barriers other than those of language translation did not obstruct the progress of the project. Rather, the expanded scope of coverage, significant changes in the personal lives of some authors, and major constitutional developments in some Asian countries during the 1980s delayed completion of the book beyond expectations. Most chapters were up-dated in 1991.

For support of related travel to and within Asia, I am very grateful to Lafayette College, the Japan Foundation, and the Fulbright Commissions of Japan and Korea. Asian colleagues too numerous to name extended warm hospitality and instructed me in the ways of their nations law and constitutionalism, in Indonesia, South Korea, Japan, Malaysia, the Philippines, Singapore, and Thailand. For assistance in translating manuscripts into English, I warmly thank Keiko H. Beer, William B. Cleary, Masako Kamiya, Herbert H.P. Ma, and Joseph H. Saunders. I am also indebted for help along the way to the late Al Mansur Adabi of Singapore, to George Gadbois(University of Kentucky) on India, to David Engel(State University of New York at Buffalo) on Thailand, and to Dan Fenno Henderson and John O. Haley(University of Washington) on Asian law more generally.

Donald Ellegood of the University of Washington Press graciously shepherded publication processes. W. Ronald Parks, Jr. was immensely helpful in the final preparations for publication. Ann Reichel of the United Nations Treaty Section kindly provided up-to-date human rights treaty data on Asian states. For typing the manuscript, with the meticulous care needed with unfamiliar languages, special thanks to "Dr. Ruth" Panovec of the Department of Government and Law, Lafayette College, and to Lenair Mulford of the Northwestern School of Law, Lewis and Clark College, in Portland, where I grew up looking across the Pacific Ocean towards Asia.

Finally, I wish to thank my wife Keiko and our children, David, Chris, Kimberley, and Larry, for the joyous family life between Asia and America, and for always being there with support.

Lawrence W. Beer
Bethlehem, Pennsylvania
1991

Constitutional Systems
in Late Twentieth Century Asia

INTRODUCTION:

Constitutionalism in Asia and the United States

Lawrence W. Beer

Introduction

The latter decades of the twentieth century will be remembered, as many times past, for wars, leaders and economic changes, and as no time past, for human entry into space, computers, and genetic codes. It may also be noticed a hundred years hence that this was an era of unprecedented experimentation in forms of government and law under written constitutions, as colonialism ended and each newly independent state sought its constitutional identity while other countries responded to challenge by revising or amending their basic laws. The trend was global, but most dramatic in 1989 and 1990 when Mikhail Gorbachev's government allowed the waves of independence and constitutionalist creativity to sweep through Mongolia, Eastern Europe, and the Soviet Union.

Three phenomena attended these historic decades of frenetic constitution-making activity: (1) a convergence in the world towards relatively few living traditions of modern law, and the beginnings of mutual comprehension among legal scholars and practitioners of these different traditions; (2) the achievement of at least formal global political consensus on the centrality--once national independence and stability are achieved--of human rights to sound and moral government and law (though with differences among nations on which rights to emphasize); and (3) at the deepest level, like the sliding together of suboceanic continental plates, convulsive interactions among profoundly different cultures, all reciprocally accepted for the first time as authentically human by educated international elites. That sometimes contradictory emphases characterize world discourse on human rights is less surprising than the level of mutual comprehension achieved (the basis for all genuine disagreements) across all seas, and the virtually universal compulsion felt by national leaders to act on the world stage as if they were responsive advocates of human rights. While the primordial observer could not see the overlapping plates change the seas and continents, we can view the wrenching clash of cultural forces in wars internal and external, in Asia's trade relations with the West, and in contrasts between religious and sociopolitical systems. But in the late twentieth century it is hard to even imagine where and with what aspect the new peaks of world civilization, law, and constitutional government will arise in the next century.

The difficulty of cross-cultural communication about constitutionalism is daunting, because constitutionalism is where national history, custom, religion, social values and assumptions about government meet positive law, economic force, and power politics, because few authors blend knowledge of such elements to render a country's constitutional life easily comprehensible to the uninitiated foreign reader, and because few legal scholars are committed to such interdisciplinary writing for a foreign audience. This book attempts to further understanding of constitutionalism in many radically diverse Asian nations while taking note of instances where United States constitutional experience has been influential or relevant. Although each writer was asked to explain his country's constitutional structure, principles, and operation in historical and sociopolitical context, care was taken not to impose a foreign analytical approach (such as the editor's) on accomplished Asian scholars, in the belief that such editorial imposition would presumptuously tamper with academic freedom and cross-cultural tolerance. Rather, for most chapters, one or two distinguished indigenous constitutional lawyers were asked to introduce their country's constitutional system as they deemed appropriate, stressing features they considered most important for the foreign reader to understand, and adopting a mode of exposition and analysis preferred in their own tradition of constitutional scholarship. The styles of thought and language in some chapters may be alien to some readers and may test their intellectual tolerance and openness. A number of chapters may administer a jolting legal culture shock, rather than a sense of flowing easily along with other chapters or in the mainstream of some American approach to law and social science writing. Such intellectual discomfiture seems inevitable now in mature dialogue on constitutionalism with colleagues in Asia and other non-Western regions. They have studied us; let us study them. After mutually chastening intercultural exchanges on how best to write about law and constitution for foreigners without culture-specific intolerance, some mix of legal and interdisciplinary discourse may become very widely accepted for comparative constitutional studies (for example, the stress on the "living constitution" suggested later). But that development awaits a later stage in scholarly history. At the bicentennial, this book offers a partial remedy for the widespread Western unfamiliarity with Asia's constitutional systems.

In the late 1980s, the bicentennial of the Constitution of the United States of America, the world's oldest single-document constitution, was an occasion for justifiable celebration of achievement. The bicentennial years commemorated a series of events, from the signing of the Constitution on September 17, 1787 to the ratification of the Bill or Rights on December 15, 1791. Unfortunately, American cups raised in toast of the Constitution and Bill of Rights sometimes ran over with unreflective self-congratulation. The 200-year record of American progress towards compliance with constitutional rights principles has been quite mixed; still, the quest for the dream of equality and freedom under a government of laws and limited power continues, and the republic stands.

The United States is one of the few countries whose basic ideas about government institutions, approach to law, and national experience commonly are taken into account when constitutionalism is debated around the world. Among America's contributions to the discourse of making and interpreting constitutions are the following: a single-document national constitution with a preamble setting forth the basic institutions of government, their interrelationships, and the relations between government and citizenry; a list of constitutional rights to be defended in laws, government administration, and independent courts;[1] the notion of a constitution as "the supreme law of the land"; the institution of a constituent or constitutional assembly representing all the people of a country which has the authority to adopt the nation's basic law; the implementation of the view that the branches of government should be separated so that the power of each is limited and counterbalanced by the power of another; a federalism uniting autonomous democracies in a sovereign union[2] with legislators representing both member states and the union; and finally, the conviction that government should be inspired and constrained "by the people and for the people" in recognition that "all men are created equal" and have inherent inviolable rights as individual humans.

The sheer present power of the United States in the planet's politics, military affairs, economics, and mass media diffusion of facts and views regarding America has drawn disproportionate attention to U.S. constitutionalism, especially since the end of the Second World War in 1945. That admitted, scholars and leaders in some Asian countries have adapted one or more elements of American constitutionalism based on freely conducted study of many alternatives. Other knowledgeable Asians have rejected either some foundation principle of U.S. constitutionalism, or its cultural particularization in American life, or both. This chapter presents a reformulation of some meanings of "constitutionalism," some instances in Asia of American influence on or relevance to local constitutionalism, and some patterns and preferences in Asia revealed by the studies in this book and elsewhere.

Constitutions in Asia

For perspective on the constitutions of the United States, Asia and the world, consider that of 167 single-document constitutions in effect as of 1991, only about twenty dated earlier than 1950(See Figure 1).[3] Very few countries, such as Norway (1814) and Columbia (1886), continue with constitutions of the nineteenth century, and only the U.S. basic law has been in force since the eighteenth century. Most thought-provoking, well over 100 of today's constitutions trace their origins only as far back as 1970. In every continent, constitutional experimentation and change continue, but in pursuit of stable order.

In Asia's constitutional chronology, only four nations have basic laws written as early as the 1940s: Japan, whose 1947 constitution has yet to be amended; the Republic of China, 1947, written for China but only in force on Taiwan and in the process of major change in 1991; Indonesia, 1945, but two other constitutions were in effect between 1949 and 1959; and India, whose constitution has been amended sixty-two times.[4] Other current constitutions were adopted as follows: Afghanistan, 1987; Bangladesh, 1972; Bhutan, 1953; Brunei, 1984; Myanmar (Burma), 1974; Cambodia, 1989; China, 1982; Laos, 1975; Malaysia, 1963; Mongolia, 1960; Nepal, 1990; North Korea, 1972; Pakistan, 1973; Papua-New Guinea, 1975; the Philippines, 1987; Singapore, 1963; South Korea, 1987; Sri Lanka (Ceylon), 1978; Thailand, 1991; and Vietnam, 1980.

Western "Constitutionalism" and Colonialism in Asia

What is "constitutionalism"? What is "a constitution"? Are all Asian countries, by virtue of having a single-document basic law, "constitutionalist"? How is "democratic" theory and practice related to "constitutionalism"? The terms "constitutionalism" and "a constitution" in the Western world have a rich and sometimes confusing content. How the words have been understood has depended in fair measure on the academic specialty, nationality, or profession of the writer. For example, many American historians have taken "constitutionalism" to be shorthand for the constitutional ideas of the founding period. Legal realists and positivists among lawyers in the United States have had trouble relating the descriptive and prescriptive elements implied by "constitutionalism." British scholars, such as Albert V. Dicey, without a one-document constitution and with "conventions of the constitution" to live with, have focused on the rule of law under an "unwritten constitution" (or a constitution in part unwritten and in part expressed in key statutes and other documents). In the same common law tradition, Edward S. Corwin analyzed the "higher law background" of American constitutional law which also contains much that is theoretical, cultural and unwritten. Continental European authors have worked within the quite different but historically parallel Western tradition of "civil law," with its coherent comprehensive "Codes," closer ties with Roman Law, and magisterial theories. More specifically, along with the pivotal French Revolution, students of French constitutionalism see before them fifteen constitutions since 1791, not all democratic. Each Western country has had its own story and slant on the meaning of constitutionalism; and each colonial power brought its own distinctive heritage to its Asian region of paramountcy between the sixteenth and twentieth centuries.

Thus, British constitutionalism and legalism found roots in the varied soils of India, Sri Lanka, Bangladesh, Myanmar, Malaysia, Singapore, Hong Kong, Pakistan, and other lands, while Dutch thought and law have left a legacy in Sri Lanka and Indonesia. France influenced its "Indochina" of Cambodia, Laos and Vietnam, while the United States began around 1900 to supplant Spanish legalism with its own in the Philippines. Japan was forcefully persuaded to adopt Western constitutional thought and legalism as a step toward regaining full independence from imposed unequal treaties, and chose European (especially German) models rather than common law approaches to modern law. In turn, Japan gained sovereignty over Taiwan in 1895 after defeating China in war. She annexed Korea in 1910 after the Russo-Japanese War (1904-05), making Japan's law Korea's. From 1842 until 1945, China was exploited and, in varying degrees, influenced by colonialists from Great Britain, France, Germany, Italy, Japan, Russia, the United States, and smaller European countries. Since 1945, almost all Asian countries have gained the independence necessary to pursue their own constitutional destinies; as they have done so, the colonialist and pre-colonialist past has cast shadows of different length and shape in each nation.

In the multi-cultural and contemporary context of the present book, it seems best to leave behind the past and to attempt to reformulate theoretical guidelines for comparing and evaluating present and future constitutional systems. Here, the goal is to sketch out a theory bridging perennial Western and modern Asian understandings of constitutionalism in a way that is transculturally persuasive and "omnidirectional."

"East" and "West," like "North" and "South" or "First," "Second," "Third" and "Fourth Worlds," have had a limited utility for identifying and analyzing clusters of nations with some shared political or economic characteristics. However, these words are inadequate pointers to the diverse geographical and cultural roots of contemporary constitutional systems and may even discourage the kind of constitutional theory that is now needed. Constitutional development does not depend on some specific type of economic development. Nor can law and constitution be adequately analyzed solely in political terms. Humans are to some degree "rational actors," but there is much more complexity, depth, diversity, and community in human motivations than suggested by economistic theories and the drive for power. Use of the term "omnidirectional" is an attempt to shatter the prism of West-dominated perspectives through which the immense variety of national constitutional systems is often viewed in the United States, implicitly or explicitly. Any theoretical account of what "constitutionalism" means is rooted historically in the particular cultural matrix of its author and usually responds most directly to the concerns and experience of that nation with a style of argumentation comfortable to indigenous colleagues. However, for a theoretical account of constitutionalism to be most useful at this stage in history, it needs to be "transculturally persuasive."

By "transcultural," I mean that the basic principles of the theory proposed--those of a very general nature which are not inherently limited in relevance by their particularity to the country of origin--must be applicable and relevant to many or all cultures, at least prescriptively, and in some cases descriptively. If the principle is nowhere concretized in a state's performance, few other nations are likely to be persuaded of its salience. On the other hand, a country's manner of formulating or implementing a sound principle may bias other people against the principle itself. For example, some American conceptions of "individualism" are neither transculturally valid nor philosophically convincing,[5] but must be taken into account to understand the strong and weak points of American constitutionalism. (This assertion in no way implies dismissal of general theories asserting the importance of human dignity and individual rights.) We do not yet have a terminology which adequately reflects awareness of and sensitivity to the multiplicity of current nation-state experiences and constitutional cultures.

Western constitutionalism developed slowly and often painfully over millennia *within* the parameters of the Greco-Roman, Judaeo-Christian, and Enlightenment traditions; it was latterly affected by such phenomena as scientific, industrial, and political revolutions and war. None of that is true of the non-Western world. Western powers superimposed principles and practices derived from their own governmental experience and reflection about law on the Asian constitutional cultures they dominated. Under colonial regimes, no time was given the Asians by history for gradual, organic, indigenous development, or for autonomous and selective adaptation of foreign ideas. With the exceptions of Japan and Thailand, Asian countries had limited options or no choice about their own law and constitution until independence was conferred some time after the Second World War. Thus, it is only in the latter half of this century that most countries of Asia have begun, at an accelerated pace, the autonomous development of a constitutional system which appropriately mingles the past and the present, the indigenous and the foreign, the traditional and the new, to meet the needs of the future. Modern constitutional traditions in Asia have just begun.

Some Meanings of "Constitutionalism" Today

Europeans and Americans still tend towards a residual chauvinism in their views of constitutionalism in Asia, while many Asian systems strain as their new traditions evolve. How in this context should one explain "constitutionalism" in a transculturally persuasive manner?

How we frame questions and discourse about constitutionalism predetermines the type and range of answers that may emerge. What do our ways of talking about constitutionalism and law include and exclude, implicitly or with firm explicitness? What questions do we tend to think most meaningful, useful, and worthy of exploration as we grope toward understandings for the future? What do we tend to assume?

American constitutional lawyers and social scientists assume a lot, and those assumptions may seriously impede the world's dialogue on constitutionalism, because they sometimes confuse the essential with the unessential, principle with culture-specific particularity, and this breeds insensitivity to contrasting cultural emphases in Asia that are compatible with principle. Many American lawyers and legal scholars exaggerate, for example, the importance of American (not Western) liberalism, capitalism, and judicial review. At best, in the midst of exaggerated claims, the American constitutional lawyer shows awareness of shortcomings in U.S. human rights performance.

> [W]hile there is probably no society, certainly no complex and pluralistic one, which has recognized a greater range of individual rights entitled to protection or fulfillment than the United States, there is also a substantial gap between rights in the abstract and their reality in practice.[6]

Many countries of great complexity in Asia and elsewhere recognize a greater range of human rights than the U.S. and arguably do a better job of rights protection and governance than America. More telling in the long run, by the standards of Asia and Europe, American "grand theory" in constitutional law, however refined within its own court-centered world, offers little grand analysis of many dimensions of "constitutionalism."[7] Some American constitutional theorists are also hamstrung by a unicultural framework while the subject area requires responsiveness to both cultural diversity and crucial principle.

Less influential in constitutional studies and the constitutional affairs of Asia than law, social science and its assumptions affect American and Asian thinking about constitutionalism:

> The social sciences are primarily products of Western civilization, and Africans, Asians, and other non-Westerners who work in the social sciences generally use the theory and methods of the Western social sciences as their framework."[8]

The field of Asian Studies mixes to unusual smoothness the disciplines of history, social sciences, and the humanities, and most of the relatively few American specialists in Asian law and constititutionalism are in this mold. Critical to the development of cross-cultural coherence in understandings of constitutionalisms, Asian Studies may be settling into a balanced middle ground between the old extremes of cultural relativism and culture-blind universalism, a third intellectual way, a result of decades of explicating the fully human within the diverse particularities of many Asian cultures. As Andrew Nathan suggests, "It is the view that holds one culture's values are not relevant to another that turns out to be insular."[9] By what standards should the quality of governance be judged? A distinction is often made in the United States, though not always with clarity, between "constitutionalism" and "democracy."[10] Useful additional distinctions can be made between these two terms and "documentary constitutionalism," "non-constitutionalism," and "human rights constitutionalism."

I would submit that human rights constitutionalism provides the most persuasive set of normative standards by which to assess the quality of a constitutional system and its day-to-day operation--the human rights of each individual in the community. Of the theories discussed below, only "human rights constitutionalism" is grounded in recognition of the equal inherent dignity and nobility of each individual and a comprehensive notion of human rights.

Human rights provide the omnidirectional, transcultural axis around which the gyroscope of constitutional government, law and politics should spin. Respect for human rights is now the best test of humane civilization, if not of great art and gentility. Human rights are not vague, abstract or culture-specific. Many of the concrete requirements of service and protection of the individual that are implied by respect for each person's dignity are spelled out in United Nations human rights documents; others regarding government structure and process are explicated below.

Article 55 of the United Nations Charter (1945) gave treaty law very general language on human rights, such as the following:

> [B]ased on respect for the principle of equal rights and self-determination of peoples, the United Nations shall promote.... (c) universal respect for, and observance of, human rights and fundamental freedoms for all without distinction as to race, sex, language, or religion.[11]

Clarification and refinement of the meaning of human rights have been provided by the thirty articles of the Universal Declaration of Human Rights--approved without dissent by the United Nations General Assembly on December 10, 1948[12]--and by the other elements in the so-called "International Bill of Human Rights," namely the 1966 "International Covenant on Economic, Social and Cultural Rights," the "International Covenant on Civil and Political Rights," and the "Optional Protocol to the International Covenant on Civil and Political Rights" which came into effect for ratifying countries in 1976.[13] Additional specificity has come in other instruments, such as the "Convention on the Elimination of All Forms of Discrimination against Women" (1979)[14] and the "Convention against Torture and Other Cruel, Inhuman, or Degrading Treatment" (1984).[15] Among the regional human rights formulations developed on all continents are the "Basic Principles of Human Rights" issued by the Human Rights Committee of the nongovernmental Law Association for Asia and the Pacific (LAWASIA).[16] What is remarkable in the late twentieth century is not the continuing failure of governments to adhere to some or most international human rights standards, but the worldwide diffusion of these standards, their transcultural acceptance, and their gradually increasing effect in the international law and constitutional law of nations. (See Figure 2)

A government of human rights constitutionalism would include the following:

(1) a constitutional division of governmental power among two or more basic organs or "branches";

(2) some form of independent judicial system, with jurisdiction including cases on civil rights and liberties;

(3) regularized limits on the amount of governmental power possessed by anyone and, generally, on the length of time power may be legitimately possessed. (A few Asian constitutional monarchies present partial exceptions.) Democratic elections using the secret ballot assure peaceful, routine passage from one national leader or group of leaders to the next, and encourage public agreement on the legitimacy and composition of the leadership;

(4) government authority and means of coercion under law sufficient to maintain public peace, security of person, and national security, within limits defined by the human rights of citizens and those of other countries. Rigorous restraints on military power and military involvement in government politics.

(5) government involvement in socioeconomic problem-solving in order to meet citizens' subsistence needs (e.g., food, clothing, shelter) and a life compatible with human dignity, insofar as the private sector fails to meet these needs. Property rights and economic freedom are protected insofar as they do not result in such inequitable distribution as to deny the socioeconomic rights of other citizens, particularly the least fortunate;

(6) legally protected and encouraged freedom of peaceful expression and a right to silence;

(7) legal tolerance and government support for expression of personal and group beliefs about the meaning of human life and the universe, insofar as such expression is compatible with respectful treatment of other people in the circumstances of the specific society;

(8) a system of local autonomy showing the maximum respect for regional desires for self-governance that is compatible with human rights claims in other affected territories;

(9) procedural rights in criminal and civil justice for each citizen equal to those of all others within the national community; the standard for treatment of the most privileged members of society is applied to the least fortunate;

(10) acceptance of the constitution and human rights as the supreme law of the land, by the government and by the general public.

The unequivocal commitment to human rights implied here is not characteristic of documentary constitutionalism, democracy, or constitutionalism. *Documentary constitutionalism* reflects the rare level of worldwide agreement achieved that a modern nation state needs a single document of basic law setting forth constitutional arrangements. "Documentary constitutionalism" refers only to the adoption by a nation state (and, by analogy in federal systems, by States or Provinces, as in Australia and

Canada) of a single document to state its fundamental formal law on the major divisions, structures, principles and powers of government, and the rights and duties of citizens. The term does not touch on the question of whether or how a government implements that constitution in whole or part. (In parallel, the formal acceptance by almost all governments of the ideals in the Universal Declaration and international Covenants on human rights may be taken as illustrating, at the very least, "international documentary constitutionalism.")

The single-document constitution may not be equated with "the constitution" of a nation, which may also include other fundamental documents, judicial decisions, speeches by a key leader (for example, Abraham Lincoln in the U.S.), theories, public values, customs, and laws. The "laws" may be statutes, administrative rules or, as in some one-party states (for example, China), the basic party rules. Nevertheless, it is not a trivial advance in civilization that after millennia of reflection and political experience, statements of basic law and some structures of modern government have become a shared part of discourse and world legal culture for the first time. In the face of human imperfection and contemporary barbarism, the substantive human accomplishment represented by worldwide documentary constitutions, a sign of and a basis for cross-cultural comprehension and communication, often goes unnoticed.

Relationships are often complex between printed provisions, government policies, and social practices. The constitutional document may be near sacred writ in one country and an object of little interest to the government or the public in another. (For the general public in the U.S., it is a rarely studied but sacred document.) A constitutional provision may accurately reflect the *serious intent* of a government and a people on a problem of governance or rights, but history, economy, and/or sociopolitics may make achievement of that goal in the short run improbable or impossible. In other cases, no linkage may exist between written constitutional principle and government intent, as in what I later refer to as "non-constitutionalist" regimes or actions. A government's intent may be obvious upon cursory investigation, or discernible only with detailed knowledge of the incident or the country. The contours of a country's ruling agencies may reflect a distinctive history or the politics of a recent coup, and may endow with more or less formal authority a legislature, an elected executive, a court system, a bureaucracy, a monarch, a general, or a local government office. National *priorities* regarding citizen rights and duties vary of course, both in documentary language and in operative policy. It is in terms of the different degrees of seriousness and comprehensiveness of a system's commitment to human rights that I distinguish between "human rights constitutionalism," other meanings of "constitutionalism," and "democracy."

In both Asia and the West, definitions of *"democracy"* often rest on a recognition of human dignity, but without insisting upon comprehensive protection of human rights. Unlike much American constitutional thought, "democracy" implies an optimistic view of political life and human nature. Democracy denotes government grounded in popular sovereignty, the right of final determination as actualized in majoritarian decision-making processes. Democracy makes *the expressed will of the majority* of voting adults the determinative political value. A human is defined in terms of individual autonomy and free will; no clear account is given of community, reason, or the satisfaction of minority needs at variance with the majority will. A "want" is accorded primacy; the "need" of another may be down played in political and legal processes, and in theory. Thus understood, democracy is not the antithesis of authoritarian government or repression of rights, because the majority may prefer very strong government, inequalities, and the repression of rights, and because democratic processes do not by themselves imply protection of human rights other than those of political participation; nor do they imply some other public value demanding restraints on public and private power, such as a stress on or a deemphasis of private property rights. Indeed, majoritarian politics did not inspire America along her tortuous path toward universal suffrage and equal voting rights, theoretically the all-important rights in this understanding of democracy. Democracy may be less preoccupied with substance than with a particular type of *process* for legitimizing acts of government and the accession of particular citizens to positions of *public authority*.

Democracy's ultimate demand seems to be that each vote be equal in weight and be cast freely for or against a policy proposition or a candidate for public office. Acts of the political community or its government are legitimate and authoritative only insofar as freely approved by the majority of sovereign voters. The "clear and distinct idea" of the mathematically precise and decisive majority vote is compelling. The sanguine implicit assumptions are that adults in appropriate numbers will vote and that they will have a reasonably equal opportunity to participate, and will be reasonably well informed, concerned, fair, and responsible. However, funds, organization and media access, rather than quality of citizen participation, seem decisive to garnering majority approval in some democratic systems (for example, the U.S.).

Neither of the following constitutes a manifestation of democracy: passive acceptance of a government or its actions--as often in authoritarian systems and sometimes in democracies--or mass participation in discussing and implementing government-made policies without a legitimizing process of direct voting or the election of leaders who vote on policy. Freedom and equality of participation in majority decision-making processes are the crucial ideals of democracy, so freedom of expression about alternatives, egalitarian election laws, and the secrecy of the ballot are essential. But most other issues of human rights (for example, in criminal and social justice) are irrelevant to democratic legitimacy. The relative wisdom or morality of a majoritarian decision or law does not affect its legitimacy.

Matters undecided by majoritarian government are left to personal choice and private competition for power. Some rights, responsibilities, and relations between the public and private sectors are left unaccounted for by such democratic theory. In some democracies, these empty spots have not been filled in by cultural sensitivity toward minorities and the poor. In the U.S. the fusion of legal positivism with democracy has strengthened theoretical underpinnings for authoritarian democracy and relativist indifference to human rights values. Stated thus, in broad theory democracy is not transculturally persuasive. In sum, democracy is an optimistic faith; democratic processes are essential but insufficient means for protecting the liberty and promoting the other human rights of the individual.

"Constitutionalism" as here defined connotes organization, division, and limitation of governmental power under law more unequivocally than does democracy. Democracy clearly limits power only with respect to majoritarian politics and decision making, and is silent on many issues regarding human rights and restraint of power. Constitutionalism mirrors less trust in democratic processes and human nature, and more reliance on laws and institutions which set the parameters of legitimate government action. Like a democracy, a constitutionalist system may become authoritarian, with or without a change in the written constitution or avowed public ideology. The configuration of laws, structures, social culture, economy, politics and public values making up each nation's "constitutional culture" is its own. In all nations, some cultural elements support while others hinder constitutionalism. Western writers sometimes refer to tolerance, to British restraint, to French or American individualism, or to some attitude towards law or authority as buttressing constitutionalism. Most other constitutional cultures also have elements on which constitutionalism is or can be built. For example, the groupism of Japanese society generally assures the limitation of government power through competitive factionalism in the political parties, bureaucracy, and society.

As used here in a transcultural setting, constitutionalism does not imply a comprehensive or overriding commitment to individual rights (as does human rights constitutionalism), or to a particular way of distributing powers and functions among government structures. It does not, for example, denote preference for a republic or a monarchy, a parliamentary prime minister or a president, a federal or a unitary system, civil law or common law, or two rather than three branches of government. "Constitutionalism" *does* assume commitment to and institutionalization of *some* basic principle(s) requiring restraint of the governmental power of all agencies and individuals. Insofar as it implies some regularized restraint of power under law, democracy is a form of constitutionalism, but some forms of constitutionalism do not include majoritarian democracy. Authority in a constitutionalist government, past or present, is defined and limited by written and/or unwritten basic rules in a way generally recognized among the populace (promulgated), and these restraints are mandated by national constitutional values and legitimized by compatible political processes.

However complex the local law and politics of voting may be, majoritarian democratic theory is remarkable for the simplicity of its appeal to all nations to adopt a mathematically clear idea: honor the majority vote. The understanding of constitutionalism suggested here offers no such simple guideline for determining whether and how a state is constitutionalist. Such determinations may prove easy or may presuppose investigation of a country's constitutional culture on its own terms, in order to learn how power is understood, organized, used, abused and restrained there, and why. (Asian examples are discussed later.) What fundamental values (i.e., state, religious, economic, familial), what decision-making processes (i.e., authoritarian, consultative, consensual, magical, or democratic), what patterns of public attitude and behavior affect the flow of power and the style of government, legal processes, and politics? What assumptions and rules govern the distribution of resources and the restraint of power? How power is exercised and limited in everyday community life and why are keys to comprehending the status of constitutionalism in a nation, because official power-holders are of their country's constitutional culture.

Although in some contexts, the state is separate from or even in opposition to society or the individual--as when rights related to eminent domain, criminal justice or free speech are at issue--Western constitutional theory may overemphasize the distinctions (and separations) between the public and the private, the state and society, the written statutory and/or judicial law and customary law, and law and the patterned manner in which a given people orders authority and propriety in community life.[17] Where constitutionalism is present, the country's "living constitution" suffuses government, society and the legal system. Government power may be limited by "checks and balances" among an executive, a legislature, a council, a court system, a military, an ombudsman, a monarch, or some other official agency. Private power centers may or may not be critically important in properly or wrongly restraining the use of government power in service of avowed constitutional values. Examples of such powerful private forces in some Asian countries include: Buddhist, Christian or Islamic religious leaders; criminal organizations; people of immense wealth; civic movements; opposition political parties; unions; a foreign government or business.

Ideally, a constitution reflects both a people's shared ideals and their weak points. A constitution should exalt public virtues emerging from a nation's history and society, but also attempt with remedial provisions to grapple with serious, even intractable problems arising from the same cultural sources. For example, slavery and its aftereffects have confronted America since the inception of U.S. constitutionalism. Cogent analysis of socially systemic anti-constitutionalist tendencies can serve as the basis for enhancing the quality of a country's constitution or at least for sharply focused constitutional debate. A few Asian examples will clarify the problem.

In some Asian political cultures, there is no old or modern national tradition of a leader relinquishing power after a set term of office. (The lack of an orderly succession system at the national level may contrast with well-established processes of leadership change and communitarian democracy in villages.) For instance, from South Korea's independence in 1948 until 1988, no President gave up office at the end of the term(s) specified by South Korea's Constitution at the time he took office. In recognition of this problem, the 1988 Korean Constitution of the Sixth Republic limited the President to one five-year term. Analogously, in response to the repeatedly extended years in office of ousted President Ferdinand Marcos, the 1987 Philippine Constitution limited the President to one six-year term. A similar provision and a restriction on the total allowable years in elective office at each level of government (to, say, twelve years) might well improve the quality of American politics and governance.

A second Asian problem has been the tendency of high officials in some countries to show extreme favoritism for members of their immediate or extended families. In admirable response, the 1987 Constitution of the Republic of the Philippines (Article 7, Section 13) prohibits presidential appointment of "spouse and relatives ... within the fourth civil degree" to public office; and a 1987 law bans the election candidacy of "relatives of high-ranking government officials within the second degree of consanguinity."[18]

Another example of remedial constitutionalism is the antimilitarist, quasi-pacifist 1947 Constitution of Japan (Article 9), which excludes the military from Cabinet posts and denies Japan the usual sovereign rights to arm at will and to resort to force to settle international disputes. In part, these popular provisions are a reaction to the aggressive and repressive military regime of the 1930s and early 1940s.[19]

As elsewhere, challenges for constitutionalism in Asia arise from social culture. The serious private obligation of a civil servant or politician to exchange favors and manifest particularistic loyalty in patron-client relations may clash with impartial performance of public duty. Striking differences of ethnic culture (for example, between the Malays, Indians, and Chinese of Malaysia, between the Tamils and Sinhalese of Sri Lanka), or religion (for example, between Sikhs, Christians, Hindus and Muslims in India) may result in deeply embedded mutual distrust and contempt inimical to stable government under law. On the other hand, diverse community identities may lend power to free speech rights and constitutionalist restraint of official power, and religious faith may provide the primary motivation for tolerance.

It seems essential to the viability of human rights as a transculturally proposed set of constitutional standards that they be secular rather than inherently religious in nature, because such standards must provide empirical tests in public law needing no reference to any specific system of ideas, or beliefs (for example, a proscription on ripping out fingernails and other torture bans only behavior), and because primary linkage with any one religion, even with one of the few great universalist religions, would invite *prima facie* rejection in too many cases by adherents of other universalist religions or local belief systems, and would add to the difficulty of precise intercultural communication. Here "secular" does not imply opposition to any or all religions but the absence of linkage to any one religion.

On the other hand, we must ask: Where do the underlying public values come from that can motivate development of "a living human rights constitution" in official and popular attitudes, institutions and actions? Of all the available ideas in any culture, those which are most essential to legitimizing, justifying human rights (or alternative public standards) can be termed that culture's "religious" ideas. [20] "Religion" here denotes the most important, most binding ideas at the heart of a culture, those which in the minds and daily lives of the people give ultimate meaning to the state community (or to a subnational portion in a weakly integrated multi-national state), with attendant institutions and customs which embody that community's way of expressing and honoring what it sees as most important. The core of a constitutional culture is a religion in that sense, the coherent (as sociopolitical force if not as concept) set of public values underlying and legitimizing government and law. Human rights standards must deal effectively with such "constitutional religion"; they must be linked with what is already seen as most important in a community, or fail.

In challenging the tendency in American law schools to isolate legal discourse from religion and moral values (which are part of "religion" in the above, broader sense), Mary Ann Glendon captures the ethos well:

> The most commonly *stated* reasons for drawing a *cordon sanitaire* around legal political discourse....are not that moral and religious beliefs are essentially arbitrary or foolish, or that ordinary men and women are unfit to rule. They are, rather, that religion has often been a source of civil strife, and that particularistic groups are often intolerant and 'illiberal.' All to frequently, what is implied is that religion and particular communities are *presumptively* intolerant and socially divisive.[21]

Besides Western ideas of secular democracy, constitution, legalism, Christianity, capitalism, and socialism, diverse Asian traditions influence current understandings of state purposes to some extent; for example:

There is no reason to *presume* today anything positive or negative *a priori* about the impact of a particular religious idea on social or governmental behavior affecting a specific human right of an individual in a given time and place; that is an empirical question. One must discover what really happened and why in each case of right protection and right violation. There is, however, good reason to assume that maximizing positive linkage between indigenous religion and human rights is an indispensable approach to mobilizing a community in favor of tolerance and a strong human rights performance.[22] *The goal is to make behavior respectful of human rights an integral part of the religious ethos in every nation's constitutional culture.* Besides western ideas, diverse Asian traditions influence current understandings of state purposes to some extent:

(1) State harmony by adherence to confucian ethics and obedience to a virtuous monarch with an extremely broad mandate from Heaven to govern (for example, the traditional kings of China, Korea, and Vietnam; recent leaders there and in Sinic Singapore);[23]

(2) The just service of Allah (for example, the heavily Islamic states of Pakistan, Bangladesh, Malaysia, and Indonesia);[24]

(3) Prosperity in state and society based on kingship in tune with the cosmos, at times by observance of astrologically legitimizing rituals (for example, the Brahmanic and Buddhist monarchies of Nepal and Thailand);[25]

(4) Sacrificial dedication to the nation as a uniquely sacred collectivity under a quasi-divine monarch (for example, Japan under the Emperor from around 1870 to 1945).[26]

These alternative state foundations seem to have in common four tendencies: (1) to relate, not separate, religion and state; (2) to conceptually and institutionally integrate, not divide, the public and the private, the economic, the social and the political, in short, to view community life organically; (3) to see the individual person as achieving fulfillment within a dense network of family and community relationships, rather than as an autonomous individual; and (4) to give the state great formal power, not without restraining responsibilities, but with vagueness about how rulers are to be held accountable. Theories of democracy and constitutionalism, indigenous traditions, religion and social culture interact in late twentieth-century Asian law and constitutional politics.

"*Human rights constitutionalism*" combines the features of majoritarian democracy and constitutionalist restraint on power. However, as here used, it goes beyond both in two respects, asserting: (1) that government is required to engage in *remedial discrimination* to promote equal treatment of all citizens under the law, and to assure all the satisfaction of such basic needs as food, clothing, shelter and personal security; and (2) that, pursuant to a constitutional attribution to each person of equal, inherent and politically transcendent value, the state's appropriate *preoccupation* is with public policies which protect and promote *all* the human rights, as comprehensively understood in the International Bill of Human Rights and some modern constitutions, not, for example, with protection of free enterprise to the neglect of worker rights or with press freedom more than criminal justice rights. Human rights constitutionalism insists upon a broader conception of rights and government responsibility than democracy, with its focus on majority rule and political liberties, or American constitutionalism, with its restraints on state power, stress on property rights and unequal assurance of criminal justice rights.

Finally, the clumsy term "*nonconstitutionalism*" is employed: (1) to refer to that substantial number of nation-state *regimes* which do not support democracy, constitutionalism, or human rights constitutionalism; and (2) to categorize *official actions in all* the world's systems which are incompatible with any reasonably constitutionalist theory. A nonconstitutionalist state is one which does not clearly limit the power of government under law and principle. It is a state where official power is absolute or vague in scope and unpredictable in its exercise, where human rights are subject to capricious violation and neglect. Insofar as the quality of government and law is an indicator of civilization, the extent of any state's nonconstitutionalism is a reliable measure of its barbarism.

Whether a country's laws, institutions and normative political attitudes, or its recent behavior in a specific issue area, manifest democracy, constitutionalism, human rights constitutionalism, or nonconstitutionalism is an *empirical question*. Precisely how and with what understandings and purposes do government personnel act with respect to affected citizens? Compliance is a matter of degrees even where constitutionalism is apparently deep-rooted. In Asia, as in the United States, the relationships between law and constitution, theory and popular myth, fact and boastful political rhetoric, ideals and practice, are inconsistent and sometimes bafflingly complex. For example, although American democratic theory places great emphasis on voting, the United States ranks very low among democracies in its voting rates.[27] Similarly contrary to myth, compared to many systems in Asia and Europe, the American constitutional order seems intolerant of free expression of diverse political ideas, witness the narrow range of ideological views institutionalized in political parties and the internal authoritarianism of private corporations. How strong is free speech in a country where employees may be fired "at will," even for revealing the criminal activities of employers (as in the United States)?

Documentary constitutionalism, democracy, constitutionalism, human rights constitutionalism, and nonconstitutionalism have been distinguished as guidelines for assessing the systems and behavior of countries in Asia and elsewhere. Applying the standards discussed to the *apparent general intent* of national leaders, as shown by recent operative policies, laws, and institutions, how might one characterize specific Asian systems? Brunei, Cambodia, China, Myanmar, North Korea and Vietnam seem among the nonconstitutionalist regimes of Asia, due in part to their systemic opposition to restraints on government power and (in most cases) their failure to establish predictable processes of leadership succession under law. Indonesia and Singapore embody limited democracy and two of many contrasting indigenous constitutionalisms, Indonesia is slowly building a theistic modern military state with limited government resources over a vast archipelago with staggering subcultural diversity. Singapore is a tiny, prosperous confucian state where socioeconomic rights and somewhat restrictive laws and policies are effectively implemented. While the operative systems of the Philippines, South Korea, Taiwan and Thailand have lent nonconstitutionalist power for substantial periods to the military and a relatively few wealthy families, the general thrust of government intent since 1978 in Thailand, and since the late 1980s in the others, was toward human rights constitutionalism. With radically different cultures and with continuing problems and exceptions, India (e.g. the caste system)and Japan, along with Sri Lanka (for Sinhalese more than Tamils), have generally pursued the ideals of human rights constitutionalism since the late 1940s.

Theory, culture and guidelines of intermediate abstraction such as the above can be brought to bear on performance. However, broad characterizations of regime are prone to chauvinism and imprecision, investigation, analysis, and reporting of specific cases of human rights violation and promotion are far more useful not only in politics but also at the intellectual foundations. Human Rights constitutionalism involves the fusing of a radical empiricism with humanistic universalism. Monitoring and measuring both general and highly specific regime behavior in terms of democracy and human rights has become the work of scholars and public and private agencies around the world.[28] Dedicated official and private activism now meshes with increased though damnably spasmodic coverage of problems by the world media, careful scholarship, and ever-more-precise debate on the meaning and observance of human rights.[29]

Constitutionalism in Asia and the United States

Among elite and populist constitutionalists in many Asian countries, the appeal and influence of United States constitutionalism lies not so much in American democracy or constitutionalism per se, or in economic or military prowess, as in America insofar as it can be perceived as a symbol and/or supporter of a full panoply of human rights and respect for each person's dignity.[30] This symbolism does not fit very well with American reality today. More common among American constitutional lawyers and other custodians of the system is commitment to democracy, constitutionalism, legal positivism, some variant of economic liberalism, and "individualism."[31] Where human rights are analyzed, the question is often: Which human rights can/should be made legal rights under positive law? The answer usually limits legal rights to civil liberties, property rights, and procedural safeguards. Sadly, relatively few seem ready for the incorporation into constitutional law of social and economic rights.

The record and prospects for human rights in the United States do not seem very bright--especially for the socioeconomic rights of the less fortunate 40% of American families and for equal treatment under the law of those with modest means.[32] In the 1980s the gap in living standards between those in the upper and lower thirds on the income scale widened, and not, as in some Asian countries, due to a shortage in aggregate national resources.[33]

David Apter argues that a low level of enjoyment of socioeconomic rights in economically developed nations will negatively affect rights stressed by democracy and constitutionalism.[34]   Other sober voices point out serious deficiencies in America's constitutional system with respect to mass media freedom, educational opportunity, election campaign law, criminal justice, economic justice, discrimination problems, and national purpose.[35]   Granted, the constitutional accomplishments of the past 200 years give grounds for pride, but humility seems especially healthy to counter an American tendency to exaggerate the positive and neglect the negative when comparing the United States favorably with foreign constitutional systems, not least those in Asia.

Relativism, Individualism, and Mutualism

Two other characteristics of American constitutional culture bear brief consideration: value relativism and "individualism." If a human rights theory is not somehow grounded in an intellectual conviction that each human being does indeed have inherent and great value, the question legitimately rises: Why bother with the human rights of others? (How pursuit of human rights constitutionalism may be *motivated* in response to personal and national experience, feelings, faith and/or convictions is a separate set of critically important issues.) If all humans are accorded equal value in constitutional theory, how much value? Are all equal in near meaninglessness, or are all to be treated "as if" each is an end in him/herself, rather than a means to be used by other individuals or the state? Or does the public value inherent in each person transcend all human categories for differentiation, based on God's alleged attribution to each of value and cosmic destiny? Or must the state and its law calibrate carefully rewards and punishments to favor the allegedly best and brightest, those with useful skills, intelligence, and/or moral quality? Or with wealth? Does hereditary position or higher education confer special public value on an individual which law and constitution should take into account? Since social hierarchy is virtually universal, why fuss with equality issues in constitutional life?

Here, the position taken is that, whatever its source in the cosmos--the most widely relied upon source is God, following the Judaeo-Christian-Islamic tradition--each person has equal and great intrinsic dignity justifying its formal recognition in state law and constitution, and that compatibility with respect for that dignity is the ultimate standard for testing the constitutionality of a law or other official act covered in a nation's constitution. That is, an intersubjectively (not subjectively or objectively) persuasive nexus must be demonstrated between the official treatment of an individual within a given community and *respect* for that individual and others affected. In reconciling this attribution of value to humans with obvious cultural diversity in symbols of respect and other matters of community standard, *"relationalism"* may be a better term than "relativism." Relativism honors diversity, but does not claim certainty about the great inherent value of each person.[36] The "relationalist" position here suggested sees humans everywhere as interrelated within communities and respects the cultural standards affecting governance and human rights performance in any given polity, with one transcultural proviso: that the indigenous standard is intersubjectively compatible with human rights as understood by the generality of local leaders committed to human rights constitutionalism.   Each country needs its own autonomous existence, has its own story to tell, and develops from within its own constitutional culture affecting human rights.

When comparing constitutionalism in the United States and in Asian countries, perhaps the most distinctive American constitutional conviction that emerges is "individualism." The individualism espoused in the United States and urged upon the world as "Western" is more American than typically Western in some respects, and is often a barrier to American communication in Asia, Europe, and elsewhere. "Individualism" is an element in the collective psyche which often affects the cross-cultural constitutional analysis of individualist constitutional lawyers. Alasdair MacIntyre, Robert Bellah and others have criticized and tried to clarify the varieties of American individualism.[37] Every year, Fulbright professors in American Studies go abroad to explain the United States to puzzled foreign university students. One of these, David Kolb, wrote insightfully as follows for group-oriented Japanese:[38]

> What is crucial for understanding American individualism as many Americans think about it is the belief in the priority of the individual and desirability in principle of having all the content of a person's life stem from his or her decision.... What is required is that we be able to think about a core person who consists of a naked chooser. I use the word "naked" to indicate that this chooser must be thought of as separated from all the content which the person's choices give to his or her life. Such a core person is not an individual member of a group, but an individual first and then a member of a group.... But if we want to describe "what" a person is we must say that first and foremost he is a free deciding person, a core naked individuality, plus the results of past decisions and commitments.   Yet the priority of freedom does mean that past

commitments never can completely define a person. There is always the possibility of change.... [I]f a person is first of all a core free decider, then no choices can be final, and commitments are sustained by continual renewal. I am not merely the sum of my commitments; I must be defined as the core freedom that has made those commitments and accepted those roles. *I must be respected as such a freedom* (emphasis added)....

(American beliefs regarding the universality of individualism) are not simple; they represent an alternative to cultural relativism based on a theory of man which makes room for diversity but also asks for certain basic realities to be respected, realities which are the foundation of the variety that does exist. Such assertions seem more strong than those of other nations based on cultural or religious grounds or on specific cultural achievements. The notion of naked core individuality may more plausibly be widely applied than other social notions such as the Japanese [or other Asian] family system, precisely because the core individual is so purified and naked. Americans may be narrowing their conceptions of what kinds of *institutions can express core individuality* (emphasis added), but their basic ideas are not naive.

If human beings are indeed such core freedoms, if all content of one's life should be created or ratified by free decision, then the universality of individualism is well established, since all cultural and national differences will be subsequent to free individuality.

Americans therefore are willing to reject the idea that another nation's culture should be left the way it is. They must repudiate such a view, if they are to be true to their own beliefs about individuality. If humans are, beyond and behind culture, pure individual choosers, then it would be wrong to connive at the avoidance of this truth and the suppression of individual freedom even among people who do not realize that they are being imposed upon.

With all due allowance made for the diversity among Americans and the difficulty of capturing in cross-culturally intelligible words a nation's core constitutional conceptions, Kolb's formulation is helpful. He states a major component of America's "constitutional religion" as that term was discussed earlier.[39] Each Asian nation and many Asian subcultures rest on core concepts of the individual, community, loyalty, authority, duty, power, law, and human destiny which affect their systems of government and law. Many allow ample room for respecting human dignity and achieving mature individuality and self-realization, while others do not. In any case, the American understanding of individualism is not a theory or cultural norm which would ever occur to most Asians as a way of comprehending social reality, or which would seem a useful way of formulating the ideal as one worked for human rights and limited government within an Asian constitutional culture.

A tyranny of terms seems to impede transcultural discourse on constitutionalism. "Individualism" is often a verbal barrier to communication. Like "collectivism," "liberalism," "conservatism," "socialism" and a few other key terms, it is brittle and burdened with overtones peculiar to a particular country, world region, time, theory, or ideology, not a transculturally suggestive way of integrating conceptions of human rights, law, government, the individual and community.

Better than "individualism," the term *"mutualism"* expresses a theoretically and transculturally valid perspective on human rights and human rights constitutionalism. In general, humans are community beings, not "naked choosers" standing alone with a high degree of autonomy. In Asia, as elsewhere, governmental power is limited and abused, human rights are enjoyed, violated and fought for, generally within the dense interpersonal relationships of a coherent, established social culture. Normally, change towards greater regard for human rights constitutionalism comes by modification over time of the value and behavior content of those relations, or not at all. Without supportive change in social foundations, governmental changes of principle, structure or process in a constitution do not take hold.

"Mutualism" is intended to reflect recognition of the non-individualist (not anti-individual) nature and the social and historical embeddedness of rights and constitutional government. Mutualism implies two people's awareness within an interpersonal relationship of the interplay, the inherent interdependence, and the equality of each other's rights; it includes acknowledgment of the mutual responsibility and rights reciprocity essential to democratic citizenship, vigorous pluralism, and responsible limited government. The term calls for more appreciation of interdependence, community and cooperation and less emphasis on competition, while fully honoring the integrity and rights of the individual. "Mutualists" seems to reflect well the high civilizational ideal of human rights constitutionalism: a people with a strong and disciplined sense of responsibility for the human rights of others as a correlative of recognizing their own individual dignity and rights.

Principle, culture, institutional structure and legal forms meet best in moderate systems, open to humane transcultural challenge but protective and proud of national tradition. As Fritz Gaenslen suggests: "[P]urely cultural accounts of human behavior portray man as *less* malleable than we suspect he really is ... [while] purely structural accounts of human behavior portray man as *more* malleable than we suspect he really is."[40] With respect to ideology, though extremes may sharpen comprehension of fundamental problems and may for a time inspire to needed revolution--a shift in basic direction--in the long run, extremes generally do not work and are transculturally repugnant. In Asian tendencies, *pragmatic democratic socialism*, for example, has been stronger than the extremes of unbridled capitalism and repressive communism. Western dominance was not a result of cultural superiority, but of severe Asian disorientation and military weakness at a time of forced confrontation with radically different peoples. Khan Marut's concluding words hint at Asia's agony and resentment: "[T]he scourge and bane of most Asian principalities [was] the takeover of the nation by a colonial power, in the name of 'progress' or 'civilization.'"[41]

Since liberation, elements of Japanese, European and American popular culture, technology, and constitutional thought have become part of daily Asian life; but pride of nation has grown, not diminished in the latter half of the century. Each polity has its distinctive view of what "progress" in "civilization" means. Constitutionalists in Asia are less inclined than American counterparts to regard their own constitutional faith as applicable in other lands; and they are conscious of the deep tensions everywhere between a moderate human rights constitutionalism and cultural, democratic or non-constitutionalist preferences. In general, notions of "natural justice" and "natural law," both indigenous and Western in origin, are accorded far more respect by law professionals and intellectuals than in the United States.

Comparisons among Asian and American constitutional features will illustrate such tensions and serve as background for discussing instances of U.S. constitutional influence in Asia.[42] Among topics touched on are legal development, preambles and policy principles, executive, legislative and judicial systems, the military, monarchy, religion and the state, individual rights, and ways of changing constitutions.

One caveat: Level of *legal and institutional development* may affect constitutional practice. Here I refer to the development of national state law, not customary, religious or traditional local law. Some Asian systems have fully elaborated statutory law and highly articulated administrative and judicial systems to implement law and constitution throughout the country; others do not, and cannot be accurately assessed on an assumption that they do. In criminal justice, for example, a reformist national government may need many trained professionals serving as police, prosecutors, judges, defense attorneys, and prison officials in many locales, or its performance--regardless of policy-- may not measure up to constitutionalist standards due to entrenched practices. On the other hand, if Japan or Singapore--states highly developed in law-- violates the rights of an accused person or censors the press, in most cases that may be taken fairly to reflect policy. Vietnam, China and Indonesia, on the other hand, have put in place relatively few criminal law professionals due to both policy and lack of resources. The less developed the system of law and legal services, the less predictable and the more difficult to interpret may be the reasons for a government act. Ironically, as in parts of the United States, a lawyer must be ready at hand to tell one what highly developed local and national law allows or requires. America may well have the world's most complex legal system; perhaps most Asians never or rarely use an attorney.

Preambles proclaim a mix of national values, history, accomplishments, ideology and aspirations. At best, they accurately reflect the country's "constitutional religion."[43] In addition, some Asian constitutional systems establish a source of law intermediate between the general provisions and preamble of a constitution and a statute. (These statements differ from the great Codes of the world's civil law systems, which comprehensively state the basic law pertaining to private relationships, crime and commerce.) They are variously referred to as a "Declaration of Principles and State Policies" (the Philippines) or "Directive Principles of State Policy" (for example, Thailand and India).[44] Analogously, every five years Indonesia's People's Consultative Assembly (*Madjelis Permusjawaratan Rakjat* or MPR) of 1,000 elects the President and passes "Resolutions" regarding "the basic outlines of state policy" (Article 3) to guide law making by presidential decree or action of Parliament (DPR).[45] This is similar to, but more general than, multi-year economic plans used by governments worldwide. In Communist states such as China, North Korea and Vietnam, speeches and party rules and policies promulgated after meetings of a Central Committee or Party Congress tell what the constitution has come to mean at a given stage in revolutionary processes. In effect, basic party policy is "the supreme law" of the constitution.

The United States Constitution is missing an adequate formal statement of what the country stands for. The Preamble of the U.S. Constitution might well be reformulated to incorporate some of the inspiring language of the Declaration of Independence, the Gettysburg Address, and other expressions of the ideal American consensus. Periodic general outlines of a few national policies--not in the mode of a plank in a party election platform but on the

Indonesian model--might add coherence and focus to national legislative debate.

Asian executive systems display one or more of five institutions in various combinations: *presidents, prime ministers* with cabinets, *monarchs, party* chiefs, *military* leaders. In the Philippines, South Korea, Taiwan, and Indonesia, a strong president also serves as ceremonial head of state, as in the United States. More commonly, parliamentary prime ministers rule, with cabinets or councils and with a president (for example, India, Singapore, China) or monarch (for example, Malaysia, Japan) fulfilling the role of head of state. Though Pakistan's President is generally only a head of state, his authority to ask someone to form a government on the basis of election results is substantial, particularly as in 1988 when no party had a parliamentary majority, and Benazir Bhutto became Prime Minister.[46]

The rich Asian tradition of kingships continues in Japan, Brunei, Malaysia, Nepal, Thailand, the Himalayan principalities (Sikkim, Bhutan), and in the influence of Prince Sihanouk in war-ravaged Cambodia. Japan's powerless imperial institution (not Emperor Akihito as a person) is occasionally caught in the swirl of controversy pitting the mainstream against minority Shinto nationalist calls for "restoring" state power to the Emperor.[47] In Nepal, the directives of King Birendra carry much more than ceremonial weight, as in his sweeping restoration of the right to form political parties and the establishment of a new democratic constitution in 1990.[48] King Bhumibol Adulyadej has ably added to stability and democratic inclinations as Thailand's constitutional monarch.[49] The Sultan of Brunei (or *Brunei Darussalam*) is virtually an absolute monarch, though English common law and the country's judges--who are brought from Hong Kong--temper his exceptional prerogatives as law-giver and executive.[50] In Malaysia, a king (*Yang di Pertuan Agong*) is elected every five years from among the nine hereditary sultans on the thirteen-member Conference of Rulers.[51]

In Asian Communist states, government is generally controlled by a small party elite. In most instances, these leaders are influenced by Confucian constitutionalist tradition under which the authoritarian king-figure (for example, Mao Zedong, Deng Xiaoping) and ruling group are accepted as legitimate as long as they manifest benevolent paternalism, the power to maintain order, and administrative ability. However, as in China intermittently since the 1950s, government, party and military positions may be juggled unpredictably in internal struggles over leadership or policy. The "pro-democracy" movement of May and June, 1989 in Beijing and elsewhere, like the 1988 student demonstrations against the twenty-six year rule of U Ne Win and his Socialist Program Party in Myanmar, resulted in draconian use of military force and illustrates the tragic tensions between democratic political aspirations and authoritarian establishments in a few Asian systems.[52]

The ruling Nationalist Party (*Kuomintang*, KMT) on Taiwan, while culturally and organizationally similar to the Chinese Communist Party, presides over a prosperous and increasingly democratic Confucian state. Its leader, Lee Teng-hui, like his predecessors Chiang K'ai-shek and Chiang Ching-kuo, is also President in the government. In power, the government has been subordinate to the party-military tandem since the 1920s: but major constitutional reform was in process in 1991.[53]

Although the military-industrial-financial complex has shaped much about America since the Cold War began in the 1940s, the armed forces themselves have remained subordinate to civilian leaders and have not engaged in administering the country. In many Asian nations, the *military* has had a deep impact on constitutional governance, for many reasons: some military men found themselves in a privileged position after international war and were loath to relinquish power. Some refused to abide by a constitution requiring political neutrality or forbidding involvement in government. In other cases, they had once filled a vacuum as the government's main source of professionalized administrators and had grown accustomed to power. Others were seen as legitimate leaders of government because of the military's role in gaining liberation from colonialism. The military may have controlled the ruling party and the means of coercion, with or without popular support. And in some instances the military assumed governmental power to cleanse a country of corruption or to end instability.

For a mix of reasons, at one time or another in recent decades, generals or retired generals have ruled Bangladesh, Burma, Indonesia, Pakistan, South Korea, and Thailand, and their roles have deeply affected government in China, the Philippines, and Taiwan. In Thailand, "The King holds the position of Head of the Thai Armed Forces" (Chapter 1, Section 8), but from 1932 onward generals have generally ruled Thailand.[54] Under Indonesia's constitution, "The President holds the highest authority over the Army, Navy, and Air Forces" (Article 10),[55] but President Soeharto is himself a general and the extra-constitutional "ABRI," a politico-military group of immense influence in government, has a "dual function":

> This key theoretical and doctrinal construct, which spells out a "sociopolitical" as well as defense and security role for the armed forces, was strongly reaffirmed in the February 22 [1988] law on military affairs. This dual role, moreover, is seen as a permanent one ... Indeed, given ... [its] legacy in the founding and the preservation of the Indonesian state,

its self-perception [is] as the institutional embodiment of Indonesian nationalism ...[56]

Elsewhere, martial law or emergencies (for example, Malaysia) have put constitutionalism on hold or at best in an ambiguous position, but demilitarized government may well be more common by the turn of the century. Taiwan was under martial law longer than any other nation, from 1949 until July 15, 1987. The rigors of control varied over time; civilian law and democratic tendencies grew in uneasy parallel with martial law. With the end of martial law, some restraints continued, but the constitution functioned more autonomously and the KMT showed increasing tolerance of political diversity and opposition.[57] South Korea's politics have often been turbulent, with government under six constitutions since 1948, and under generals since 1961. In 1988 for the first time, the party of an incumbent President (Roh Tae-woo, a retired general) failed to win a majority in the National Assembly; three civilian-controlled parties held a parliamentary majority until two joined in a coalition with the President's party in 1990.[58] The question asked by the Koreans, as by other Asians, was: Will the military permit the democratic constitutional system to function and develop? As the military is an irregular center of public power, its primacy in a government generally indicates constitutionalist weakness, as does a "military-industrial complex." It is not that military officials tend more to corruption or abuse of power than civilians, but that the skills and mental set, the criteria and processes of leader selection in a military are not those appropriate for modern governance and human rights development.

Civilian rule is preferable to military rule. On the other hand, it affects not human rights constitutionalism whether a state is federal or unitary, and whether a national *legislature* has one, two, or three houses. Asian legislative traditions owe more to British and continental European institutions than to American traditions. Most parliaments are bicameral, but those of South Korea and Singapore have one chamber. Only Malaysia and India have *federal* systems analogous to America's, but Indonesia experimented with "the United States of Indonesia" in 1950.[59] Tun Mohamed Suffian compared the U.S., India, and Malaysia:

[I]n the United States the Constitution spells out what powers "are delegated" to the centre "nor prohibited" to states and provides that anything not so delegated to the centre nor prohibited to the states is reserved to the states respectively or to the people. The Malaysian Constitution ... follows the Indian Constitution in providing for a federal

list, a state list, and a concurrent list, which spell out in great detail
federal subjects, state subjects, and concurrent subjects with respect to
which the federation, the states, and both ..., respectively, have legislative
and executive power, and further in providing in Article 77 that residual
power on subjects not in the lists shall be vested in states. (Malaysia is
a small country, and needs a strong central government; thus subjects like
the police and education ... are federal....)[60]

India looked to several precedents when developing its federal structure:
experience under the British Government of India Act (1935) and the systems
of Australia, Canada and the United States.[61] The central government can
dissolve a state government and rule directly in time of crisis. Parliament may
legislate on a *state* matter (Article 249), if the upper house has first passed by
a two-thirds majority a resolution declaring it "necessary or expedient in the
national interest."[62]

Of more critical importance to constitutionalism in Asia than the federal-
unitary question have been myriad intractable problems in balancing the
interests of central government with local territorial, religious, and ethnic
needs, and in pursuing acceptable forms of confederation or integration of
territories.   A few examples.   "Reunification" has been a persistent
constitutional demand in both the communist North and the democratic South
of the Korean peninsula, where one government ruled one people from 668
until 1945.[63] Normalcy in either sector seems unlikely until some form of
confederation has ended this most tragic of national divisions; yet, radical
differences between the constitutional systems of North and South make
prospects vague. In the late 1990s, China will absorb Hong Kong and Macao,
but with what measure of autonomy? The degree of local self-rule allowed
in these territories and in Tibet (controlled as an area of China since 1950)
may well determine whether some form of constitutional confederation
between China and Taiwan is developed, or Taiwan formally declares
"independence" from China (its de facto status since the late 1940s).

In Indonesia, tensions continue between the central government and some
of the many distinctive peoples on islands across its vast archipelago. For
example, tiny East Timor was forcibly incorporated into Indonesia in 1976
when Portugal suddenly ended its colonialism; it continues to desire its
measure of autonomy. In Sri Lanka, a constitutional democracy, endemic
conflict between the majority Sinhalese and the Tamils exploded into large-
scale violence in the 1980s. With the help of India under the Indo-Lankan
Accord of July, 1987, Sri Lanka's government has kept the unitary state intact,
but has also sought ethno-territorial reconciliation by creating a "federal-style"

devolution of functions to elected "Provincial Councils."[64] Perhaps only in the Civil War and in relations with Native Americans has the United States faced challenges analogous to some of the Asian problems touched on above.

The *judiciaries* of Asia have not been co-equal with the executive or legislative branches of government except where the United States tradition of judicial review has been at work, directly or indirectly. In general, English and European legalisms are the key foreign influences. Soviet law has provided a partial model for China, North Korea, Mongolia and Vietnam. Courts are commonly located under a justice ministry. In the non-communist Asian systems, many courts enjoy a high degree of independence, others do not. The legacy of British law in some South and Southeast Asian nations is profound. German, Swiss and French approaches to judicial thinking have affected Japan, Taiwan, Thailand, and South Korea, while Dutch law has contributed to jurisprudence in Indonesia and Sri Lanka.

English common law parliamentarism and/or civil law deference to statutes passed by democratically elected legislatures have in some countries added to the local political factors restraining judges from applying constitutional provisions to court cases. Yet, America's most appreciated contribution to constitutional cultures in Asia may be the example of a fully independent judicial system with the power to determine the constitutionality of laws and other official acts. Judicial review powers are constitutionally conferred on the courts of India, Japan, and the Philippines, and on South Korea's "Constitution Court."[65] Elsewhere, they are viewed as a respected possibility or as undemocratic. The Philippine Supreme Court--especially before the 1972 imposition of martial law and after the 1986 "People's Revolution"--has been the most prestigious organ of that country's government. In Japan as well, the Supreme Court and the 1947 Constitution are by far the most trusted and respected national political institutions. In India, and through India's influence in Malaysia, Singapore, Sri Lanka, and other countries, judicial review generally reinforces limited, responsible government and human rights.[66] The general logic of human rights constitutionalism suggests judicial review in some form as a necessary check on executive, legislative, and private violations of human rights.

To compare *individual rights* in one country (here, the United States) with rights in an immense multi-national region containing about 60% of humankind and hundreds of cultures is admittedly presumptuous and a daunting task. One needs to clarify who one is talking about; one must differentiate within a given country, for example, between the economically powerful and the poor, the highly educated and the illiterate, the urban and the remote rural, the authoritarian and the democratic. That admitted, even the briefest of comparisons must touch on basic differences of emphasis as much as upon specific rights issues.

In Asia, *freedom* has been valued highly by many governments and peoples. To a meaningful degree, *voting rights* have been institutionalized in most non-communist countries and have been discussed seriously with respect to China, Vietnam, and Cambodia. However, the freedom of the individual is commonly seen as inextricably linked with and even dependent upon the freedom of one's family (nuclear or extended) or work unit, ethnic and/or religious group, local or regional subculture, or even one's country. But *equality* has been stressed even more strongly than freedom, both as an individual and as a nationalist matter. This is based on general principle among the educated, and because many citizens have suffered severely from poverty, maldistribution of wealth, lack of opportunity, and national and international economic exploitation. Generally, economic justice and national development have had higher priority than individual property rights among Asian friends of human rights constitutionalism. In Singapore press freedom is limited; more unusual, no right to real property is constitutionally recognized.[67] While business prospers, as in some other Asian states, stronger concern for socioeconomic rights is manifest in Singapore than in the United States.

What Asians ask is respect for their civilizations, and a fair measure of national benefit from economic activity carried on by domestic and international business interests in the country. Elites in and out of government find weak evidence of a linkage between free enterprise and individual rights and freedoms generally, and so disagree with a common American assumption. Anti-communist Asians inclined toward human rights constitutionalism separate clearly economic liberty from political and social freedoms, giving the latter more vigilant attention. Like democracy, capitalism can co-exist with both strong and weak protection of key human rights, such as *freedom of expression, religious liberty,* and *criminal justice rights.*

Freedom of the press and other forms of expression in Asia generally became more vigorous during the 1980s, in its exercise if not in its legal protection.[68] The freedom of the mass media is more often restricted in some Asian countries than in the United States; but the range of views in the free Asian press is much broader than in the United States. Advertising is generally a less dominant factor in Asian than in American serial publication; political advertisements are less crucial to Asian than to U.S. democratic processes. Occasionally, repressive governments which claim commitment to press freedom allege that controls are necessary for public peace, security and/or national development. Some such appeals manifest nonconstitutionalist authoritarianism; others do not, as when communal violence would surely result from insensitive media coverage (for example, in India or Malaysia).

Legal technicalities abound in the area of criminal justice, from the moment of contact with a policeman until sentencing and incarceration or release. Differential treatment based on economic means as in the United States, or torture or prolonged detention without trial for peaceable political dissent as in a number of Asian countries, are always contrary to human rights constitutionalism. Discrimination on the basis of ethnic group, race, religion, and sex vary less with constitutional system than with local culture, but problems are endemic as in America.

Full *religious liberty* presupposes official and societal tolerance for the public existence of diverse belief systems, not simply for the private and silent adherence of an individual to a faith or idea system. With a public, institutionalized, officially protected existence, a religion first enjoys freedom to speak to issues and to influence society, law and policy. How to protect and moderate by law the free individual and institutional expression of belief systems in a pluralist society or a secularist state so that the rights of all are honored? In a country where one persuasion (whether religious, secular, or anti-religious) is dominant? The answers proffered by Asian constitutional systems and the United States differ.

America would protect religious liberty by strictly maintaining distance between the state and all religion (in theory), by prohibiting laws which either establish one religion or interfere with the free public exercise of any religion. Yet, American public life abounds with "in God we trust" and other signs of "civil religion." Many Asians, like many Europeans and others, have found the American understanding of the "separation of church and state," as concretized in judicial decisions and commentary, sometimes strained, convoluted, inconsistent and more compatible at times with rigid secularism than with a neutral or friendly attitude toward religion in general. Be that as it may, United States doctrine does express movement towards tolerance in a distinctive history of religious politics and deep intolerance; great progress has been made, especially since the presidential election of a Catholic, John F. Kennedy, in 1960.

A multitude of ethnic and religious divisions and harsh history have made enforcement of tolerance a higher priority of constitutionalism in many South and Southeast Asian nations than in America. However, religion, taken seriously, can generally be a powerful motivational force for rather than an obstacle to "modernization."[69] A great majority of the world's Muslims and Buddhists live in Asia. The Islamic countries, the Philippines, and Christian minorities in almost all Asian countries adhere to monotheism. Hinduism, Buddhism, Taoism, Confucianism, nation-specific belief systems, and animism add to this broadest of the world's continental arrays of religions. In South and Southeast Asia, the Islamic revolution has sharpened religio-political debate among Muslims, and has led to efforts to establish Islam more firmly in constitution and/or law. For example, Islam became the state religion of Bangladesh under the 1988 Constitution (8th Amendment) Act, but without restricting other religions.[70]

Some Muslim countries establish Islam, others, like Indonesia, do not. Indonesia instead makes belief in God one of its five constitutional pillars (*Pancasila*).[71] A large majority of Asia's Muslims are moderates (generally Sunni) rather than "Fundamentalists." In a few countries people continue to die over their religious differences. Examples include the recurrent communal violence in India involving Hindus, Muslims, and Sikhs, and in Malaysia between Muslim Malays and Chinese-Malaysians. Buddhism is the major religion, in a few cases established, in countries such as Sri Lanka, Burma, Thailand, Kampuchea, Laos, Vietnam and Japan.[72] In Japan's constitutional thinking, the quasi-pacifist human rights constitutionalism embodied in the basic law, rather than Buddhism or Shinto, has become virtually the national faith.[73] India is a secular multi-religious state. Singapore, Taiwan and South Korea have become secular confucianist democratic states, but the large Christian minority in the latter has continued a leadership role in democratic nationalism since the 1919 "March First (independence) Movement."[74] Thailand's Constitution provides: "The King is a Buddhist and Upholder of religions."[75] In general, religious liberty is honored in practice by Asian constitutional systems. The consensus, apart from the Communist states, may be: The wisdom or danger of establishing a religion depends on local factors. Law and constitution should assure tolerance, prevent religious discrimination, and foster respect for all religions.

All Asian states have *changed their constitutions* by amendment or replacement since the Second World War, but all except the Communist countries have aspired to a constitutional document that is relatively stable and permanent in its substance,[76] like the United States. A few examples. Since readopting its short 1945 Constitution in 1959, Indonesia has passed no amendments. Japan did not once amend its 1889 constitution and has yet to amend the 1947 constitution, but that displeases only a small minority. On the other hand, Thailand's fourth constitution since 1932 came into effect in 1978 and a fifth was being written in 1991; South Korea's sixth came in 1988.[77] India's constitution, the world's longest, is of book length and had been expanded by sixty-two amendments as of 1991. Amendment requires only a simple majority with "a majority of not less than two-thirds of the members" of each house "present and voting."[78]   Malaysia's amendment processes, used twenty times, are modeled on India's, but establish different levels of difficulty for amending provisions of different subject matter.

Such are some of the similarities and differences between constitutionalism in the United States and Asia with respect to executive, legislative, judicial, military and party powers, individual rights, and the place of religion.   With exceptions, Asians, like Americans, support freedom of expression, elections, and limited government.   Among American systemic characteristics that seem to contrast with Asian patterns are: Clarity about military subordination to civilian leaders; incomprehension of long-term government planning; little apprehension about government stability; an extraordinarily elaborate system of written law; courts which are not only independent but have a decisive power of judicial review; overemphasis on economic freedom and underemphasis on basic socioeconomic rights; muddled and rigid law on religion and the state; and a consensual belief that the Constitution is really *supreme* over all laws and leaders. How equality and hierarchy mesh and contend in both regions defies simple formulation.

American Influence on Constitutionalism in Asia

Since 1945, the United States has affected constitutionalism in many countries of East, Southeast and South Asia. Subsequent chapters indicate the nature and limits of American influence and its absence in some cases. Here the contexts of influence and some instances not cited in the country studies are presented.

American constitutionalism has influenced many Asian countries during U.S. occupations and by their free consultation of America's constitutional experience. America occupied the Philippines (1898-1946, except 1942-1945), Japan (1945-1952), and South Korea (1945-1948) and encouraged democratic revolution there, with quite different policies and results. The more common context of U.S. influence has been free consultation by Asian constitution-makers, politicians and scholars, of seminal American documents, constitutional law scholarship, and judicial decisions.   Many Asian constitutional lawyers, judges, and leaders have been for decades *au courant* with major developments in American case law, by reading case reporters, professional journals, newspapers, or American news weeklies. In some cases reading has been supplemented by ongoing associations with American colleagues. At the origins of some constitutions, consultations with American scholars and public figures have taken place in Asia and in the United States.

In addition, judges in some Asian countries have used and sometimes cited in their decision-making the doctrines of American courts, particularly the U.S. Supreme Court. Numerous Asian scholars and students, and some judges, have spent short or long periods in the United States, studying and experiencing American constitutionalism, and American counterparts have studied in Asia. (Relatively few Asian professors have taught about their countries' law in America.) In some cases, impact has depended on the intensity of the exposure, not on the length of a stay. More weighty than any particular documents, books, or judicial decisions, has been the degree to which the United States has been perceived by the Asian as deeply committed to human rights constitutionalism in law and policy.

The United States Constitution has been less relevant to American influence in Asia than other documents such as the 1776 "Declaration of Independence" and Abraham Lincoln's "Gettysburg Address." Before 1945, American ideas might inspire, but to subjugated Asian leaders as to most Europeans, simply as part of the Western political heritage, not as a model for possible imitation. For example, the Indonesian Nationalist Party (PNI) was proclaimed on July 4, 1927 in conscious commemoration of the U.S. Declaration of Independence. In the decades that followed before independence, Indonesian speeches and political posters abounded with phrases from the Declaration and the Gettysburg Address. They were seen as appropriate for people everywhere who supported the cause of anti-colonialist democracy.[79] Later, framers of the 1945 Constitution of Indonesia, such as Mohamed Yamin, consulted American documents:[80]

> Before me is the structure of the Republic of the United States of America, which time and again has been used as an example for several constitutions in the world, for this is the oldest constitution existing in the world, and contains three elements: (1) the Declaration of Rights in the city of Philadelphia (1774); (2) the Declaration of Independence of July 4, 1776; (3) and finally, the Constitution of the United States of America (1787).

At the end of the last century, the United States reimposed colonial control on the Filipinos just as they were gaining freedom from Spain. By the time independence came on July 4, 1946, America had institutionalized its own ideas of law and constitution in the island nation. Public health and education were also promoted, but wealth was left in the hands of an exploitive few families. The constitution approved by both the United States government and the Filipinos in 1935 became the "supreme law" of the land from 1946 until martial law was declared in 1972 by President Ferdinand Marcos.[81] The 1987 Constitution of the Philippines, explained by Professors Fernando in this book, goes beyond the American tradition in its emphasis on socioeconomic rights and other features.[82]

At times, America's constitutional wisdom has been explicitly rejected, as by Sir Ivor Jennings when drafting Sri Lanka's "Soulbury Constitution" in the 1940s. He opposed an American-style Bill of Rights as superfluous, noting that Britain has "no Bill of Rights: we merely have liberty according to law, and we think--truly, I believe--that we do the job better than any country."[83] After independence, in the absence of rights provisions, Sri Lankan judges relied on law and on judicial precedents to affirm individual rights. They drew some precedents from India and the United States.[84] However, the later Constitutions of 1972 and 1978 contain declarations of rights which represent "a radical break from the British tradition .... [They are] reminiscent of the Constitutions of the United States, Ireland and India and of certain countries of Europe."[85]

Asian constitution-makers have on occasion solicited the views of American constitution scholars and judges. For example, leaders such as A.S. Chowdhury and Kamal Hossein consulted with Professor Albert P. Blaustein of Rutgers University and other Americans as they drafted a constitution for Bangladesh in the early 1970s.[86] By bloody rebellion, Bangladesh, the former East Pakistan, had detached itself from federation with West Pakistan. Abu Sayeed Chowdhury, the first President, said of individual rights in the Bangladesh Constitution:

> A study of these rights would at once make it clear that in their formulation, Magna Carta (1215), the Petition of Right (1628), the Bill of Rights (1689), and the Constitution of the United States of America, together with its amendments, were kept in mind. It is in this part of the Constitution that the full benefit of the written Constitution of the United States was taken as a model, and in fact, in dealing with these provisions the courts of Bangladesh freely refer to the judicial pronouncements of the Superior Courts of Britain, America, and the Commonwealth countries.[87]

American influence on judicial review, federalism and rights in Indian constitutionalism has been substantial, and through the Indian filter it has extended to other former British possessions such as Bangladesh, Sri Lanka, Malaysia and Singapore.[88] During the long drafting process, "Sir B.N. Rau, the Constitutional Adviser to the Constituent Assembly, and Sir Alladi

Krishnaswamy Ayyar, one of the ... most respected lawyer members of the
[Assembly committees] ..., frequently relied on the Constitution of the United
States."[89]   Rau also consulted President Harry Truman, American
constitutional lawyers, and judges Felix Frankfurter and Learned Hand, and
cited such documents as the Articles of Confederation and John Marshall's
opinion in *McCulloch v. Maryland*.[90] Since India's Constitution came into
force in 1950, American judicial precedents have been cited in over 1,000
Indian court cases.[91]

Although China's search for stable modern statehood has taken her down
quite different paths, Nationalist leaders in the 1920s seriously proposed the
establishment of "united autonomous provinces" of China with a federal
government analogous to the United States.[92] Moreover, the ideology of
KMT leader Dr. Sun Yat-sen, still prevailing on Taiwan, has been compared
to Lincoln's view on "government of the people, by the people and for the
people."[93]   Those words were heard again in the student democracy
movements of Myanmar (Burma) and China in 1988 and 1989.

The influence of the United States during and since the occupations of
South Korea and Japan are covered by our authors, below.[94]   A few
comparisons may be added. The "USAMGIK" (U.S.A. Military Government
in Korea) directly governed southern Korea from its liberation in 1945 until
independence began under the 1948 Constitution. USAMGIK had little
preparation or expertise for the task. In 1948, Americans did not participate
in drafting the Constitution; but USAMGIK gave its essential backing to the
autonomy of Korea's constitution-making progress. In Japan, on the other
hand, General MacArthur's offices ruled indirectly through Japan's
government apparatus, wartime planning had yielded useful guidance for the
Occupation, and Americans drafted a good deal of Japan's Constitution.
MacArthur, Charles Kades and a few others are among the principal pioneers
of Japan's human rights constitutionalism. Except for the many years of
colonial rule in the Philippines, this constitution-writing may be the most
significant extension of United States governance into a foreign land in
American history.

Conclusion

Asia's post-colonial constitutional history is brief, but, with exceptions,
impressive. Besides unexcelled competence, many of Asia's constitutional
lawyers display great learning about foreign systems and creative openness to
adapting constitutional and legal devices of others to their own nations' needs.
By emulating them, more American counterparts can learn to think in a

transculturally comparative manner, and freshen perspective on U.S. constitutional problems. Harold Berman contends that for about 1,000 years, revolutionary challenges from within the West have recurrently revitalized its legal tradition, but that now this legal tradition is in crisis:

> A social theory of law must move beyond the study of Western legal systems, and the Western legal tradition, to a study of non-Western legal systems and traditions, and of the development of a common legal language for mankind. For only in that direction lies the way out of the crisis of the Western legal tradition in the late twentieth century.[95]

The authors here manifest a common language of constitutional discourse. Consideration of Asian experiences of government and law can revitalize and broaden the West's understanding of its own transcultural principles and may serve as a corrective to ossified thinking about constitutional issues. One would hope that if the United States celebrates a tercentenary, it will be joined by many Asian countries feting their constitutional centennials, and that Americans may have enriched their own heritage by learning of other traditions of human rights constitutionalism, where community lives with individuality and equality with freedom.

Figure 1

THE 167 NATIONAL CONSTITUTIONS—LATEST REVISION DATES

1788 U.S.A.	1968 Maldives	Ecuador	Chad
1814 Norway	Mauritius	Iran	Iran
1831 Belgium	Nauru	Kiribati	Lebanon
1853 Argentina	1969 Kenya	Nigeria	Portugal
1868 Luxembourg	1970 Gambia	Peru	Tunisia
1874 Switzerland	Iraq	St. Lucia	1990 Benin
1901 Australia	Qatar	St. Vincent	Burkina Faso
1917 Mexico	1971 Bulgaria	Seychelles	Fiji
1919 Finland	Egypt	Somalia	Mozambique
1920 Austria	U.A.E.	Togo	Namibia
1921 Liechtenstein	1972 Bangladesh	Zimbabwe	Nepal
1937 Ireland	Cameroon	1980 Angola	Sao-Tome Principe
1944 Iceland	Hungary	Chile	Yemen
1945 Indonesia	Korea (PDR)	Guyana	1991 Thailand
1947 China (Rep.)	Morocco	Vanuatu	Cambodia
Italy	1973 Bahamas	Vietnam	*NO ONE DOC. CON.*
Japan	Bahrain	1981 Antigua & Barbuda	Israel
1949 Costa Rica	Pakistan	Belize	Libya
Germany	Swaziland	Cape Verde	New Zealand
India	Syria	1982 Canada	Oman
1952 Jordan	Zambia	China (PRC)	Saudi Arabia
Poland	1974 Grenada	Equatorial Guinea	United Kingdom
1953 Bhutan	Mali	Ghana	*NOT INCLUDED*
Denmark	Myanmar	Guinea	Andorra
1958 France	Niger	Honduras	San Marino
1960 Côte d'Ivoire	Romania	Turkey	
Cyprus	Turkey	1983 El Salvador	
Czechoslovakia	Yugoslavia	Lesotho	
Mongolia	1975 Gabon	Netherlands	
West Samoa	Greece	St. Chris.-Nevis	
1961 Malta	Laos	1984 Brunei	
Venezuela	Madagascar	Guinea-Bissau	
1962 El Salvador	Mozambique	Liberia	
Jamaica	Papua New Guinea	South Africa	
Kuwait	Sweden	Vatican City State	
Monaco	1976 Albania	1985 Guatemala	
1963 Malaysia	Cuba	Mauritania	
Senegal	Dem. Kampuchea	Sudan	
Singapore	Trinidad & Tobago	1986 U. Rep. Tanzania	
1966 Barbados	1977 Djibouti	Central African Rep.	
Botswana	U.S.S.R	Nicaragua	
Dominican Rep.	1978 Comores	Tuvala	
Malawi	Dominica	1987 Afghanistan	
1967 Bolivia	Mauritania	Burundi	
Paraguay	Panama	Ethiopia	
Tonga	Rwanda	Haiti	
Uganda	Sierra Leone	Korea (Rep.)	
Uruguay	Solomon Islands	Philippines	
	Spain	Surinam	
	Sri Lanka	1988 Brazil	
	Zaire	1989 Algeria	
	1979 Congo	Cambodia	

Figure 2

Human Rights International Instruments
Signatures, Ratifications, Accessions, etc.
June, 1991

States	1	2	3	4	5	6	7	8	9	10	11	12	13	14	15	16	17	18	19	20	21	22
Afghanistan	x	x		x	x		s	x	x	x	x	x	x	x						x		x
Australia	x	x		x			x	x		x	x	x	x		x	x	x	x	x	x		
Bangladesh				x	x		x			x	x	x	x	x								
Bhutan				s			x															
Burma								x		x	x	x		s						s		
China				x	x		x	x		x	x				x	x						s
Dem. Kampuchea	s	s		x	x		s	x					x									
North Korea	x	x					x	x														
Fiji				x			x			x	x	x	x		x	x		x	x	x	x	
India	x	x		x	x	x	s	x	x	x	x	x	x	x					s	x		
Indonesia					s	x														x		s
Iran	x	x		x	x	s		x		x		x	s	x	x	x						
Japan	x	x					x						x	x	x					x		
Kiribati																	x	x				
Laos				x	x		x	x	x				x	x						x		
Malaysia						x							x						x			
Maldives				x	x	s	s	x														
Mongolia	x	x	x	x	x	s	x	x	x		x	x	x							x		
Nauru																						
Nepal				x	x	s	x	x				x	x							x		
New Zealand	x	xa		x			x	x		x	x	x	x		x	x			x	x	x	s
Pakistan				x	x		x					x	x	x					s	x		
Papua New Guinea				x			x					x			x	x				x		
Philippines	x	xa	s	x	x	x	x	x	x		x	x	x	x	x	x		s		x	x	x
Republic of Korea	x	xa	x	x			x	x	x					x				x		x		
Samoa																					x	
Singapore													x	x					x			
Solomon Islands	x			x						x	x	x	x							x		
Sri Lanka	x	xa		x	x		x	x				x	x	x					x		s	
Thailand								x												x		
Tonga				x			x															
Tuvalu															x	x						
Vanuatu																						
Vietnam	x	x		x	x		x	x	x													

Notes to Figure 2

x Ratification, accession, notification of succession, acceptance or definitive signature
s Signature not yet followed by ratification
a Declaration recognizing the competence of the Human Rights Committee under article 41
   of the International Covenant on Civil and Political Rights
b Declaration recognizing the competence of the Committee on the Elimination of Racial
   Discrimination under article 14 of the International Convention on the Elimination All
   Forms of Racial Discrimination

1.	International Covenant on Economic, Social, and Cultural Rights
2.	International Covenant on Civil and Political Rights
3.	Optional Protocol to the International Covenant on Civil and Political Rights
4.	International Covenant on the Elimination of all forms of Racial Discrimination
5.	International Covenant on the Suppression and Punishment of the Crime of *Apartheid*
6.	International Convention Against Apartheid in Sports
7.	Convention on the Elimination of All Forms of Discrimination Against Women
8.	Convention on the Prevention and Punishment of the Crime of Genocide
9.	Convention on the Non-Applicability of Statutory Limitations to War Crimes and Crimes Against Humanity
10.	Slavery Convention of 1926
11.	1953 Protocol amending the 1926 Convention
12.	Slavery Convention of 1926 as amended
13.	Supplementary Convention on the Abolition of Slavery, the Slave Trade, and Institutions and Practices Similar to Slavery
14.	Convention for the Suppression of the Traffic in Persons and of the Exploitation of the Prostitution of Others
15.	Convention relating to the Status of Refugees
16.	Protocol Relating to the Status of Refugees
17.	Convention on the Reduction of Statelessness
18.	Convention relating to the Status of Stateless Persons
19.	Convention on the Nationality of Married Women
20.	Convention on the Political Rights of Women
21.	Convention on the Consent to Marriage, Minimum Age for Marriage and Registration of Marriages
22.	Convention Against Torture and other Cruel, Inhuman, or Degrading Treatment or Punishment

Sources: *The LAWASIA Human Rights Bulletin*, Vol. 6, Nos. 1 & 2, Jan., 1988, 137;
Multilateral Treaties Deposited with the Secretary-General: Status as at December 1989, New York United Nations, 1990; and Ann Reichel, Treaty Section, United Nations, May, 1991.

NOTES

1.   Klaus Stern, "The Genesis and Evolution of European-American Constitutionalism," Berlin Conference on the Law of the World, World Peace Through Law Center, July, 1985, 8. The American theory and list of rights is more an indigenous product than a derivation from English common law. The U.S. Bill of Rights can be traced to early state constitutions and very early colonial documents such as the Massachusetts Body of Liberties (1641). Donald S. Lutz, "U.S. Bill of Rights in Historical Perspective," presented at the American Political Science Association meeting, Atlanta, September, 1989.

2.   Thomas Fleiner-Gerster, "Federalism, Decentralization and Rights," in Louis Henkin and Albert Rosenthal, eds., *Constitutionalism and Rights: The Influence of the United States Constitution Abroad*, New York, Columbia University Press, 1990, 19.

3.   Albert P. Blaustein provided the latest revision dates of constitutions. See his *Constitutions of the Countries of the World*, 17 volumes Dobbs Ferry, NY, Oceana Publications, 1988. The first constitution to establish a sovereign entity was the Fundamental Orders of Connecticut, 1638. Albert P. Blaustein and Jay A. Sigler eds. and comps., *Constitutions That Made History*, New York, Paragon House Publishers, 1988, 1.

4.   On India's Constitution, *see infra* note 69 and ch. 5.

5.   See, for example, Robert N. Bellah *et al.*, *Habits of the Heart: Individualism and Commitment in American Life*, Berkeley, University of California Press, 1985.

6.   Joel B. Grossman, "Teaching Civil Liberties in the Bicentennial Year," *Focus on Law Studies*, Vol. 6, No.2, spring, 1991, 9. see also American Society of Learned Societies, *The ACLS Comparative Constitutionalism Project*, ALCS Occasional Paper No.13, 1990, especially 5-16.

7.   Mark Tushnet, *Red, White, and Blue: Critical Analysis of Constitutional Law*, Cambridge: Harvard University Press, 1988, the "Introduction".

8.   David L. Sills and Robert K. Merton, "Social Science Quotations: Who Said What, When and Where," *Items: Social Science Research Council*, Vol.45, No. 1, March, 1991, 3.

9.   As quoted in David D. Buck, "Forum on Universalism and Relativism in Asian Studies: Editor's Introduction, "*The Journal of Asian Studies*, Vol.50, No.1, February, 1991, 32.

10.   The best analysis of democracy and constitutionalism as found in U.S. constitutional law may be Walter F. Murphy, James E. Fleming, and William F. Harris, II, *American Constitutional Interpretation*, Mineola, NY, Foundation Press, 1986.

11.   United Nations, *United Nations Actions in the Field of Human Rights*, New York, United Nations, 1980, 5-6 [hereinafter *UN*]; David R. Forsythe, *Human Rights and World Politics*, Lincoln, University of Nebraska Press, 1981, 8.

12. Resolution 217 A(III) of the General Assembly, December 10, 1948, in UNIFO ed., *International Human Rights Instruments of the United Nations, 1948-1982,_* Pleasantville, NY, UNIFO Publishers, 1983, 5-7 [hereinafter, *UNIFO*].

13. *UNIFO*, 86-100; *UN*, 8-10, 12-14. For a thoughtful analysis of the comparative context of current democratic theorizing, see John E. Lent, "Thoughts on Political Thought: An Introduction," *International Political Science Review*, Vol. 11, No. 1, 1990, 5. A second Optional Protocal to the International Covenant on Civil and Political Rights to abolish the death penalty, was adopted by the General Assembly in 1990. G.A. Res. 44/128, U.N. Press Release GA/7977, at 406, 1990. For a concise account of the historical and regional development of international human rights instruments, and a summary of the content of human rights of the three "generations," see Burns H. Weston, "Human Rights," in R.P. Claude and B.H. Weston eds., *Human Rights in the World Community: Issues and Action*, Philadelphia, University of Pennsylvania Press, 1989, 17-28.

14. Resolution 34/180 of the General Assembly, December 18, 1979, in effect on September 3, 1981; *UNIFO*, 150-154.

15. Resolution 39/46 of the General Assembly, December 10, 1984; *Amnesty International Report 1985*, 10-11, 353-357. United States policy is *not* to ratify international human rights agreements.

16. This 1985 LAWASIA statement deals only with civil rights and liberties, the preoccupation of democratic law elites in a number of Asian countries.

"Basic Principles of Human Rights"
(LAWASIA Human Rights Committee, 1985)

Principle 1
(a) Everyone has the inherent right to life, and shall not be arbitrarily deprived of his life.
(b) The death penalty may be imposed only for the most serious crimes and after fair public trial on evidence presented to a legally competent, independent and impartial tribunal.

Principle 2
(a) Everyone has the inherent right to liberty and security of person and shall not be subjected to arbitrary arrest or detention.
(b) Anyone who is arrested or detained shall be informed of the reasons therefore at the time of his arrest and shall be entitled to communicate the fact of his arrest to a person of his choice.
(c) Anyone arrested shall be entitled to access to counsel of his choice.
(d) Anyone charged with an offence is entitled to a fair and public trial within a reasonable time by a legally competent, independent and impartial tribunal.

Principle 3
Everyone is equal before the law and is entitled without any discrimination to the equal protection of the law.
Principle 4
No one shall be held guilty of any criminal offence for any act or omission which did not constitute a criminal offence when it was committed.
Principle 5
(a) Anyone deprived of his liberty shall be treated with respect for his inherent dignity as a human person.
(b) No one shall be subjected to torture, or to cruel, inhuman or degrading punishment or treatment.
Principle 6
No one should be subject to preventive detention but in those countries where preventive detention exists, everyone so detained shall be entitled to prompt periodic review of his detention by a legally competent, independent and impartial tribunal.
Principle 7
(a) No one shall be arbitrarily deprived of the right to enter his own country.
(b) Anyone who is an alien, lawfully in a country, shall not be expelled except pursuant to a decision reached in accordance with the law in force at the time he entered the country.
Principle 8
No one shall be subject to coercion which would restrict his choice of religion or belief. Freedom to manifest one's religion or beliefs may be subject only to such limitations as are prescribed by law and are necessary to protect public safety, order, health or morals or the fundamental rights and freedoms of others.
Principle 9
To ensure the enjoyment of these minimum standards everyone is entitled to have legal assistance available to him.
Principle 10
These principles have been formulated on the basis that they are the minimum standards to be observed at all times after allowing for the fact that emergencies threatening the life of a nation may occur from time to time."
For further information on the Human Rights Committee and its Human Rights Bulletin, contact: LAWASIA Human Rights Committee, Law School, Ateneo de Manila University, Salcedo Village, Makati, Metro Manila 3116, Philippines. A broader conception of human rights applying only to ASEAN countries, is contained in the "Declaration of the Basic Duties of ASEAN Peoples and Governments," adopted on December 9, 1983, Jakarta, Indonesia. A.P. Blaustein, R.S. Clark, and J.A. Sigler, eds., *Human Rights Sourcebook*, New York:Paragon House Publishers, 1987, 646.
17. Although "cultural fluidity" and change may well be more noteworthy in Asia than in most Western countries since 1945, perennial understandings of social obligations, religion, public authority and power continue to influence government

and politics. See Lucian Pye, *Asian Power and Politics*, Cambridge, Harvard University Press, 1985; John T. Noonan, *Bribes*, Berkeley, University of California Press, 1987; Crawford Young, *The Politics of Cultural Pluralism*, Madison, University of Wisconsin Press, 1974; S.N. Eisenstadt, M. Abitol, and H. Chazan, "Cultural Premises, Political Structures and Dynamics," *International Political Science Review*, Vol. 8, No. 4, 1987, 291; Larry Diamond, Juan J. Linz, and S.M. Lipset eds., *Democracy in Developing Countries: Volume 3, Asia*, Boulder, Westview Press, 1988; and John R. Bowen, "On the Political Construction of Tradition: *Gotong Royong* in Indonesia," *Journal of Asian Studies*, Vol. 45, No. 3, May, 1988, 545.

18. *The Constitution of the Republic of the Philippines*, Quezon City, 1987.

19. *The Constitution of Japan*, Tokyo, 1947. For a translation, see Hiroshi Itoh and Lawrence W. Beer, *The Constitutional Case Law of Japan: Selected Supreme Court Decisions, 1961-70*, Seattle, University of Washington Press, 1978, 258.

20. This perspective borrows from Richard John Neuhaus, Editor of *First Things*, Institute on Religion and Public Life, New York.

21. Mary Ann Glendon, "Notes on the Culture Struggle: Dr. King in the Law Schools," *First Things*, No. 7, November, 1990, 9.

22. On the salience of religion to Asian development, see David E. Apter, *Rethinking Development: Modernization, Dependency, and Postmodern Politics*, Beverly Hills, Sage Publications, 1987.

23. I.W. Mabbett, ed., *Patterns of Kingship and Authority in Traditional Asia*, London, Croon Helm, 1985; James C. Hsiung ed., *Human Rights in East Asia*, New York, Paragon House Publishers, 1986.

24. John L. Esposito, ed., *Islam in Asia: Religion, Politics and Society*, New York, Oxford University Press, 1987; Majid Khadduri, *The Islamic Conception of Justice*, Baltimore, Johns Hopkins University Press, 1985; M.B. Hooker, *Islamic Law in Southeast Asia*, Singapore, Oxford University Press, 1984; and R. Israeli and A.H. Johns, eds., *Islam in Asia: Vol. II, Southeast and East Asia*, Boulder, Westview Press, 1984.

25. I.W. Mabbett, *Patterns of Kingship*; Robert Heine-Geldern, *Conceptions of State and Kingship in Southeast Asia*, Data Paper No. 18, Southeast Asia Program, Cornell University, Ithaca, April, 1976.

26. Lawrence Ward Beer, *Freedom of Expression in Japan: A Study in Comparative Law, Politics and Society*, Tokyo, Kodansha International, 1984, chapter 2.

27. Bingham Powell, Jr., "American Voter Turnout in Comparative Perspective," *American Political Science Review*, Vol. 80, No. 1, March, 1986, 35.

28. Among the periodic surveys of human rights performance are: *The Lawasia Human Rights Bulletin*, Human Rights Committee, *supra* note 16; U.S. Department of State, *Country Reports on Human Rights Practices* (annual), Washington, D.C., U.S. Government Printing Office; Raymond D. Gastil, ed., *Freedom in the World: Political Rights and Civil Liberties* (annual), New York, Freedom House; *Amnesty International Report* (annual), London, Amnesty International; *World Survey of Press Freedom* (annual), Columbia, Journalism School, University of Missouri; *Report on Science and*

Human Rights (newsletter), Washington, D.C., American Association for the Advancement of Science.

In addition, some of the above and other agencies issue reports on individual countries and problems; for example: the United Nations Human Rights Committee, the International Commission of Jurists, *Article 19* (freedom of expression), and Asiawatch.

On problems of assessment and measurement, see Jack Donnelly and Rhoda E. Howard, "Assessing National Human Rights Performance: A Theoretical Framework," *Human Rights Quarterly*, Vol. 10, No. 2, May 1987, 214, and their edited work *International Handbook of Human Rights*, Westport, CT, Greenwood Press, 1987; and David Hollenbach, *Claims in Conflict*, New York, Paulist Press, 1979. Donnelly's earlier analysis of human rights conceptions in the non-Western world is valuable but not very well grounded in precise understanding of Asia; see "Human Rights and Human Dignity: An Analytic Critique of Non-Western Conception of Human Rights," *American Political Science Review*, Vol. 76, No. 2, June, 1982, 303.

29. Milestones were the 1979 founding by Richard Pierre Claude of *Universal Human Rights*, now *Human Rights Quarterly*, Johns Hopkins University Press, and the 1981 establishment of the International Association of Constitutional Law (IACL); see *Years of IACL, 1981-1986*, IACL, Beograd, Yugoslavia, 1987, 3-11.

30. C.G. Weeramantry, *Equality and Freedom: Some Third World Perspectives*, Colombo, Hansa Publishers, 1976.

31. Bellah, *Habits of the Heart*; Walter F. Murphy, "Constitutions, Constitutionalism, and Democracy," a paper for the American Council of Learned Societies, September, 1988.

32. A Congressional Budget Office Report, 1989, indicates the following trends in after-tax family income, adjusted for inflation in constant 1987 dollars, and including food and housing benefits:

Families	*1979*	*1987*	*Difference*
Lowest 20%	$ 6,692	$ 6,178	- 7.7%
Second 20%	$14,742	$13,986	- 5.1%
Middle 20%	$21,742	$22,035	+ 1.3%
Fourth 20%	$29,293	$30,997	+ 5.8%
Top 20%	$45,404	$52,584	+15.8%

See David Ellwood, *Poor Support: Poverty in the American Family*, New York, Basic Books, 1988; and Michael B. Katz, *The Undeserving Poor: From the War on Poverty to the War on Welfare*, New York, Pantheon Books, 1989.

33. See *The Forgotten Half: Non-College Youth in America*, Washington, D.C., William T. Grant Foundation Commission on Work, Family and Citizenship, January, 1988. The proportion of jobs that are low paying will continue to increase rapidly in the years ahead. *See also* the U.S. Census Bureau report to the House Committee on Children, Youth, and Families, Washington, D.C., March, 1990. For

detail on socioeconomic conditions in Asia, see "Regional Performance Figures," *Asia Yearbook 1991*, Hong Kong, Far Eastern Economic Review, 1991, 6-9.

34. David E. Apter, *Rethinking Development: Modernization, Dependency, and Postmodern Politics*, Beverly Hills, Sage Publications, 1987.

35. For example, Gary J. Jacobson, *The Supreme Court and the Decline of Constitutional Aspiration*, Totowa, N.J., Rowman & Littlefield, 1986; Michael Harrington, *The New American Poverty*, New York, Holt, Reinhart & Winston, 1984; Jerold Auerbach, *Unequal Justice: Lawyers and Social Change in Modern America*, New York, Oxford University Press, 1976; Norman E. Isaacs, *Untended Gates: The Mismanaged Press*, New York, Columbia University Press, 1986; Nathan Glazer, *Affirmative Discrimination: Ethnic Inequality and Public Policy*, Cambridge, Harvard University Press, 1987; and U.S. Bishops, *Economic Justice for All: Catholic Social Teaching and the U.S. Economy*, Washington, D.C., U.S. Catholic Conference, 1985.

36. See Buck, *supra*, n. 9; Alison Dundee Renteln, "The Unanswered Challenge of Relativism and the Consequences for Human Rights," *Human Rights Quarterly*, Vol. 7, No. 4, November, 1985, 514; and James H. Mittelman, "Opening the American Mind: International Political Science," *PS: Political Science and Politics*, March, 1989, 52.

37. Bellah, *Habits of the Heart*; Alasdair MacIntyre, *After Virtue: A Study in Moral Theory*, Notre Dame, University of Notre Dame Press, 1981, especially 233-237; Amatai Etzioni, "The 'Me First' Model in Social Sciences Is Too Narrow," *Chronicle of Higher Education*, February 1, 1989; "Crisis in Political Thought: In Search of New Directions," *Participation*, International Political Science Association, fall, 1986, 6; and James A. Bill, "Area Studies and Theory-Building in Comparative Politics: A Stocktaking," *PS*, fall, 1985, 810.

38. David Kolb, "American Individualism: Does It Exist?" *Nanzan Review of American Studies*, Vol. 6, 1984, Nanzan University, Nagoya, Japan, 25-26, 30-31. The quite different perspectives of Europe, and their scholarly effects, are succinctly stated in David McKay, "Why Is There a European Political Science?," *PS: Political Science and Politics*, fall, 1988, 1051. U.S. individualism does not seem to translate into excessive use of law for rights protection; see Marc Galanter, "Reading the Landscape of Disputes: What We Know and Don't Know (and Think We Know) about Our Allegedly Contentious and Litigious Society," *UCLA Law Review*, Vol. 31, No. 1, October, 1983, 4.

39. See *supra*, text at n. 20.

40. Fritz Gaenslen, "Culture and Decision-making in China, Japan, Russia and the United States," *World Politics*, October, 1986, 78.

41. See *infra* chapter 13, last sentence.

42. Besides the country studies here, see my *Constitutionalism in Asia: Asian Views of the American Influence*, 1988 edition, Baltimore, OP/Reprint Series in Contemporary Asian Studies, University of Maryland Law School, 1988; Vernon Bogdanor, ed., *Constitutions in Democratic Politics*, Aldershot, U.K., Gower

Publishing Co., 1988; Jack Donnelly and Rhoda Howard, eds., *International Handbook of Human Rights*, Henkin and Rosenthal, *Constitutionalism and Rights*.
43. See *supra* text at n. 20.
44. See Article 2, The Constitution of the Republic of the Philippines, 1987; Chapter 5, Constitution of the Kingdom of Thailand, 1978.
45. Article 3, the Indonesian Constitution of 1945; *see infra* "Appendix" to chapter 6.
46. Rasul B. Rais, "Pakistan in 1988: From Command to Conciliation Politics," *Asian Survey*, February, 1989, 199; P.M. Bhutto was removed by coup in 1990 in a regression to military government. See Lawrence Ziring, "Pakistan in 1990: The Fall of Benazir Bhutto, "*Asian Survey*, February, 1991, 113.
47. *See infra* chapter 7, and Lawrence Beer, *Freedom of Expression in Japan*, chapter 7.
48. Dor Bahadur Bista, "Nepal in 1988: Many Losses, Some Gains," *Asian Survey*, February, 1989, 223; B.N. Aziz, "Nepal's Monarch Is Teetering," *Christian Science Monitor*, March 21, 1990; *New York Times*, April 7-10, 1990; and Hiranjan Koirala, "Nepal in 1990: End of an Era, "*Asian Survey*, February, 1991, 134.
49. *See infra* chapter 13.
50. *See infra* chapter 8, and K.U. Menon, "Brunei Darussalam in 1988: Aging in the Wood," *Asian Survey*, February, 1989, 140.
51. *See infra*, chapter 10, and K.S. Nathan, "Malaysia in 1988: The Politics of Survival," *Asian Survey*, February, 1989, 129; Fred R. von der Mehden, "Malaysia in 1990: Another Electorial Victory," *Asian Survey*, February, 1991, 164.
52. Lowell Dittmer, "China in 1988: the Continuing Dilemma of Socialist Reform," *Asian Survey*, January, 1989, 12, and "China in 1989: The Crisis of Incomplete Reform," *Asian Survey*, January, 1990, 25; *New York Times* and *Far Eastern Economic Review*, July and August, 1988, May and June, 1989; Burma Watcher, "Burma in 1988: There Came a Whirlwind," *Asian Survey*, February, 1989, 174. When the democratic opposition in 1990 swept to easy election victory, the Burmese military disregarded the results and continued its regime. See James F. Guyot, "Myanmar in 1990: The Unconsummated Election," *Asian Survey*, February, 1991, 205.
53. See *infra*, chapter 3; James D. Seymour, "Taiwan in 1988: No More Bandits," *Asian Survey*, January, 1989, especially 56-60; June T. Dreyer, "Taiwan in 1989: Democratization and Economic Growth," *Asian Survey*, January, 1990, 52, and "Taiwan in 1990: Finetuning the System," *Asian Survey*, January, 1991, 57.
54. *Infra*, chapter 13, "Appendix 4." See Larry A. Niksch, "Thailand in 1988: The Economic Surge," *Asian Survey*, February, 1989, 165; Scott Christensen, "Thailand in 1990: Political Tangles," *Asian Survey*, February, 1991, 196; and David Morell and Chai-anan Samudvanija, *Political Conflict in Thailand*, Cambridge, Oelgeschlager, Gunn, and Hain, 1982. More generally, see Clark D. Neher, *Politics in Southeast Asia*, Cambridge, Schenkman Publishing Co., 1981.
55. *Infra*, chapter 10, "Appendix."

56. Gordon R. Hein, "Indonesia in 1988: Another Five Years for Soeharto, *Asian Survey*, February, 1989, 119; and Hans thoolen, ed., *Indonesia and the Rule of Law: Twenty Years of New Order Government*, London, Frances Pinter, Publishers, 1987.
57. James Seymour, "Taiwan in 1988;" June T. Dreyer, "Taiwan in 1990."
58. William Shaw, ed., *Human Rights in Korea: History and Policy Perspectives*, Cambridge, Harvard Council on East Asian Studies Publications, 1991; Donald Macdonald, *The Koreans*, Boulder, Westview Press, 2d ed. 1990; and Young Whan Kihl, "South Korea in 1989: Slow Progress Toward Democracy," *Asian Survey*, January, 1990, 67.
59. Oemar Seno Adji, "An Indonesian Perspective on the American Constitutional Influence," in Lawrence Beer, *Constitutionalism in Asia*, 102. See generally Chung-5: Ahn, ed., *The Local Political System in Asia*, Seoul: Seoul National University Press, 1987.
60. Tun Mohamed Suffian, "The Malaysian Constitution and the United States Constitution," in *id.*, 136; *infra*, chapter 10; and Tun Mohamed Suffian, H.R. Lee & F.A. Tindale, eds., *The Constitution of Malaysia, 1957-1977*, Kuala Lumpur, Oxford University Press, 1978, 101-122.
61. P.K. Tripathi, "Perspectives on the American Constitutional Influence on the Constitution of India," in Lawrence Beer, *Constitutionalism in Asia*, 62-63.
62. *Id.* 57-71.
63. Donald Macdonald, *The Koreans*.
64. Bruce Matthew, "Sri Lanka in 1988: Seeds of the Accord," *Asian Survey*, February, 1989, 229; and annual articles on Sri Lanka in February issues of *Asian Survey*.
65. *Infra* chapters 2 and 7.
66. *Infra*, chapters 10 and 12.
67. *Infra*, chapter 12. As John Lent contends:

"[T]he definition of values must go beyond property or *raison d'Etat*. Humans are a moral force, not just an economic one. We think as well as produce and consume. We desire, we are moral creatures. For its part, if the state is to receive our allegiance, if it is to be legitimate, it must also serve basic human needs, including those of the impoverished. Nor is it sufficient for leadership to be by technique--by opinion polls, imagery, thought control and manipulation."

Lent, *supra* note 13, at 17.
68. For example, consider the periods of more open political expression during the years 1986-1989 in Bangladesh, Myanmar, China, the Philippines, Pakistan, and Taiwan. See *Asian Survey*, January and February, 1985-1990.
69. Fred von der Mehden, *Religion and Modernization in Southeast Asia*, Syracuse, Syracuse University Press, 1986; and Leroy Rouner, ed., *Human Rights and World*

Religions, Vol. 9, Boston University Studies in Philosophy and Religion Series, Notre Dame, Notre Dame University Press, 1988.

70. Syedur Rahman, "Bangladesh in 1988: Precarious Institution Building Amid Crisis Management," *Asian Survey*, February, 1989, 218; Craig Baxter, "Bangladesh in 1990: Another New Beginning?" *Asian Survey*, February, 1991, 146.

71. *Infra* chapter 10.

72. Fred von der Mehden, *Religion and Modernization in Southeast Asia*.

73. Lawrence W. Beer, "Japan (1947): Forty Years of the Post-War Constitution," in Vernon Bogdanor, *Constitutions in Democratic Politics*, 174-183.

74. William Shaw, *Human Rights in Korea*.

75. Constitution of the Kingdom of Thailand, 1978, Chapter 1, Section 7, *infra*, chapter 13, Appendix 4.

76. On current constitutions and their ratification dates, see *supra*, Figure 1.

77. *Infra* chapters 9 and 13.

78. Jagdish Lal, *The Constitution of India as Amended* ... Delhi, Delhi Law House, 1977, 173. W.D. Morris-Jones explains: "The Constitution has been amended 55 times [62 as of 1991] ... It is doubtful, however, that this has had any ill effect on the extent of respect for the Constitution. The relevant public understands quite well the reasons for change. The very length (22 Parts, comprising nearly 400 Articles plus 10 Schedules) and detail of the documents invites 'adjustment' amendments. An examination of the first 42 amendments reveals ... 15 were occasioned simply by changes in the status or boundaries of the States or other constituent units and ... 14 were concerned with minor and virtually routine adjustments. 11 can be identified as significant responses to interpretations of the document made in Supreme Court Judgments." In "The Politics of the Indian Constitution (1950)," in Bogdanor, *Constitutions in Democratic Politics*, 149-150.

79. Adam Malik, *In the Service of the Republic*, Jakarta, Gunung Agung, 1980, 8-9, 129.

80. M. Yamin, as quoted in Lawrence Beer, *Constitutionalism in Asia*, 104. The Preamble of the 1945 "Constitution of the Proclamation State," as it is called by Indonesians, is reminiscent of the Declaration of Independence; *see infra* chapter 6, Appendix.

81. James L. Magavern and Enrique M. Fernando in Lawrence Beer, *Constitutionalism in Asia*, 141-148. *See also* Robert Pringle, *Indonesia and the Philippines*, New York, Columbia University Press, 1980; and Harry M. Scoble and Laurie S. Wiseberg, eds., *Access to Justice*, London, Zed Books, 1985, 101-105.

82. *Infra* chapter 11.

83. Joseph A.L. Cooray, *Constitutional and Administrative Law of Sri Lanka*, Colombo, Hansa Publishers, 1973, 509-511.

84. Discussion in March, 1985 with past Justice C.G. Weeramantry, Supreme Court of Sri Lanka.

85. Joseph Cooray, *Law of Sri Lanka*, 510-511.

86. Albert P. Blaustein, "The United States Constitution: A Model in Nation Building," *National Forum*, fall, 1984, 17.

87. Abu Sayeed Chowdhury, "The Bangladesh Constitution in American Perspective," in Lawrence Beer, *Constitutionalism in Asia*, 30.

88. Even where a British or indigenous precedent has been of primary importance, as in Malaysia, legal scholars have been aware of American commentary and alternative views on an issue. For relevant references, see Tun Mohamed Suffian *et al.*, *The Constitution of Malaysia*, 10, 31, 34, 37, 126, 136, 177, 181.

89. P.K. Tripathi in Lawrence Beer, *Constitutionalism in Asia*, 64.

90. *Id.* 64-71.

91. Communication from George Gadbois, University of Kentucky, 1984.

92. Herbert H.P. Ma in Lawrence Beer, *Constitutionalism in Asia*, 39-55.

93. *Id.* 42-50.

94. *Infra*, chapters 7 and 9. *See also* Lawrence W. Beer, "Constitutionalism and Rights in Japan and Korea," in L. Henkin and A. Rosenthal, *Constitutionalism and Rights*.

95. Harold J. Berman, *Law and Revolution: The Formation of the Western Legal Tradition*, Cambridge, Harvard University Press, 1983, 1-4.

EASTERN ASIA

PEOPLE'S REPUBLIC OF CHINA

The Constitution of the People's Republic of China

William C. Jones

Introduction

The 1982 Constitution of the People's Republic of China,[1] like its many predecessors, purports to establish a government that appears quite recognizable to Westerners. It bears an obvious relation to both the United States[2] and Soviet Constitutions,[3] though it has some unusual characteristics. Power is said to belong to the people, but it is exercised by what looks like an indirectly elected parliament, the National People's Congress.[4] Congress enacts--or formally approves--legislation. But in addition, it elects the President, who is the head of state; the Premier, who is head of the government, that is, the bureaucracy; and the top officials in the courts, the procuracy, and a number of other organizations.[5] Congresses at lower levels, such as the provinces and counties, exercise similar powers at their levels. That is, they choose the local administrative chiefs such as governors in the case of provinces, mayors, county heads, and so on. They also choose the presidents of the courts and the chief procurators at their levels.[6] Citizens are guaranteed the usual political rights such as freedom of speech, assembly and religion,[7] as well as the new social and economic rights such as the right to remunerative employment, retirement benefits and the like.[8]

The most unusual feature is Congress. It is not really a parliament in the usual sense, both because it is too large (around 3,000 members)[9] and because it meets too seldom (once a year) actually to initiate legislation on its own.[10] In fact, it is not intended to initiate legislation. Its primary function is to elect and remove the important officials of government, including a standing committee that can act as Congress when the latter is not in session.[11] The actual control of the government is in the hands of the Premier and the top officials of the ministries. Legislation is supposedly the task of the standing Committee of the National People's Congress.[12] The Premier, government officials and Standing Committee are responsible to Congress, but only in an ultimate sense: Congress selects them and can remove them from office.[13] There is no parliamentary responsibility in the sense of a system whereby a government that fails to get a majority in parliament on a vote of confidence falls. The process of election of Congress is unusual. The Constitution provides that citizens elect representatives to local people's congresses directly.[14] These congresses elect delegates to the congress of the next superior level and so on up the line to the National People's Congress. At present there are only three levels in the process: the local congresses, provincial congresses (or the equivalent), and the National People's Congress.[15] Thus, citizens vote directly for members of local congresses. These congresses elect the members of the provincial congresses, and the latter choose the members of the National People's Congress.

In other words, the Constitution purports to establish a rather interesting system of government. One might wonder how a large number of problems that seem to be presented will be resolved. For instance, how will the Chinese solve the problem of divided control between the local congresses and top level officials in Peking? The problem is most obvious in the case of the courts. While, as indicated, local courts are appointed by local congresses and are responsible to them,[16] appeals from their decisions lie to the higher courts and in some cases to the Supreme People's Court in Peking. These higher courts are charged with supervising the lower courts.[17] Who controls? The courts or the Congresses? The same problem exists in all ministries because all ministries exercise ultimate control over local levels, and yet local officials are said to be responsible to the local congresses that appoint them.

Such questions, and many others, are interesting for students of government, but unless there are some radical changes in China, we shall never know the answers. The Constitution seems to bear no relation to the actual government of China. Citizens enjoy neither civil[18] nor economic rights.[19] Congresses are in fact rubber stamps that do as they are told by whoever is in power at their level.[20] The meetings of a congress are ceremonial occasions. No doubt they afford a welcome opportunity for their members to travel, see friends, and make contacts. Perhaps they are significant as meeting places for important people because congress members are normally persons of some significance. In that way they may serve as significant parts of the actual government of China.

But it is fairly clear which governmental structures exercise power in China, at least in a formal sense, and the National People's Congress and the local congresses are not among them. China is a country that is governed by a highly centralized bureaucracy that is more or less under the control of the Communist Party.[21] The Army remains a great power that is not usually directly involved either in the government or party, but that may become so at any time. Of course, it is not clear at all just how control is exercised either within the Party or by the Party on external organizations such as ministries, to say nothing of the Army. The situation at the lower levels is especially murky, but it is difficult to understand how things work even at the more visible top levels. Deng Xiaoping is nominally an official who is chairman of a committee that supervises the Army; he is subordinate, on paper, to Congress. He has never held the very top posts in either the government or Party. Yet it is quite clear that if Deng were to go to E Mei Shan to contemplate nature and observe the sacred monkeys for an extended time, E Mei Shan is where the government of China would be. Congress could continue to hold performances in Peking or not. It would not affect the way things ran. For that matter, the Politburo could continue to hold its meetings and make pronouncements, but unless it was clear that Deng agreed, it would not be wise to rely on these actions.[22]

The Roles of China's Constitutions

What is true of the 1982 Constitution was also true of its predecessors. The written Constitution was not the place to start if one wanted to know what the government of China was really like. One might say that the written Constitution had little to do with the actual Constitution, that is, the real structure of government. Though it should be said that the 1975 and 1978 Constitutions were a little closer to reality than the rest, because they both emphasized the importance of the Communist Party.[23] In other respects, however, they shared the remoteness from reality of their fellows. In view of this, it is tempting simply to dismiss Chinese constitutions as trumpery designed to provide an occasion for flights of oratory at the time of their adoption.[24] There is much to be said for this point of view. Indeed, it may be the only rational position to take on the question of the content of Chinese constitutions.

This is not to say that written constitutions play no role in the Chinese polity. They clearly have one function: The adoption of a constitution is a signal that a significant change has taken place in the government or in society, and that it is conceived to be long-lasting. The first constitution, the so-called "Common Program" in 1949, signified that the Communists had won the civil war against the Nationalists and had formed a completely new government for China.   The 1954 Constitution showed that the new government regarded itself as firmly established. Military and political control were complete. There was no significant problem with foreign or domestic enemies, and the foundations of a socialist state had been laid. The 1975 Constitution indicated that what might be called the leftist faction believed that it had won decisively the bitter intra-party struggle of the Cultural Revolution and was in a position where the adoption of a new constitution would solidify its control. The 1978 Constitution indicated how mistaken the leftist faction was, and affirmed what was apparently believed to be the permanence of the coalition that overturned the "Gang of Four." This belief was in turn pretty firmly exploded by the end of the same year in the Third Plenum of the Eleventh Session of the Central Committee. This signaled the establishment of Deng's primacy. The change was confirmed by the 1982 Constitution whose promulgation purports to indicate a complete rejection of the Cultural Revolution and all "leftist" ideas and a return to the good old days of the 1950s. If the former pattern continues, then the failure to promulgate a new constitution when Deng passes from the scene might indicate a belief--or perhaps just a hope--of the ruling powers that they would continue to govern. Or it might mean that a fight was going on and it was not yet clear who had won. Of course, something might have happened to the Chinese polity and it might mean that a more impersonal and permanent system of government had been established.   Whatever happens, the promulgation of the next constitution will be an event of great political significance.

There is not much question that constitutions play this role in China. The question is, do they have any other significance, since they do not establish or describe the apparatus of government nor determine the rights of citizens. It seems pretty clear that they perform at least one additional, though related, function. Apart from merely signaling a change in power or in the political and economic conditions of the country, constitutions also tend to show the direction that their promulgators plan to take in governing China. This will take the form both of indications of actions that the new government plans to take and of a basic ideological statement. The result is that constitutions can indeed be regarded as the course of law in the People's Republic of China just as they are declared to be.[25] But the term "constitution" has a different meaning from the one normally given to it in the West. The constitution is not written for the ages. It is a statement of current policy. When the policy changes, the law ipso facto changes. Indeed, the change in the operative rule may antedate the change in the wording of the constitution. For instance, when in the 1950s, the ownership of agricultural land was converted from cooperative and individual property to commune or collective property, and then in the late 1970s and 1980s was changed back again, it was because the rulers of China believed that collective or individual operation of the land, as the case might be, was the best way to solve the problem of increasing agricultural production at that time. Once this decision was made, an appropriate system of land ownership was adopted. Eventually the constitutions were changed to reflect the new policy, but the law in an operative sense had changed long before. Policy in China is law. It does not merely influence law.[26]

Presumably this is a perfectly correct way of looking at law and the constitution in a Marxist society. Law is an instrument that the ruling class uses to exert social control. It is an aspect of the superstructure.[27] The only real law is dialectical materialism. The governing structure in a country like China is the Communist Party, which establishes--and disestablishes--institutions as seems desirable in order to achieve the ultimate goal of communism. A constitution is a general summary of present policy. Laws are more particularized statements of policy. For this reason, an ideological statement is even more important than a concrete statement of economic or social policy because it serves as the basis of such policies. Particular policies must be appropriate to the current stage of society's development. This stage will be made clear in the ideological statement. For example, the most important change in the 1975 Constitution from the 1954 Constitution was the change in the phrase "China is a people's democratic state"[28] to "China is a state of the dictatorship of the proletariat."[29] This indicated that there had been a change in the nature of the state and society. Even more important, it was regarded as emphasizing the fact that there would be a continuation of the class struggle against, among others, enemies at home. And in turn this meant a continuation of the Cultural Revolution. On the other hand, the switch to the phrase "people's democratic dictatorship" in the 1982 Constitution[30] signals the elimination of the class struggle, and that indicates that the Cultural Revolution will not be revived. At least in the current stage of development, the policy of advancing the Four Modernizations rests on this foundation. The various measures in furtherance of foreign trade, including the Joint Venture Law[31] and the individual responsibility system, are aspects of the Four Modernizations campaign. Thus the ideological statement is the basis of a general statement, which serves as the basis of concrete statutes.

Of course, one cannot regard any of these ideological or policy statements as permanently binding, but if a statement is fairly recent and seems to be in accord with current conditions and attitudes, it is a good indication of where the leadership expects to go. A clear statement of policy may, in consequence, be of considerably more value than a more detailed set of rules. As a result, the preamble is generally the most important part of the constitution. Thus the statements in the preamble to the 1982 Constitution that emphasize the importance of modernization and the necessity to make use of foreign capital and almost to eliminate class struggle[32] may be rather more significant to a person who is contemplating a joint venture than a whole portfolio of legal materials of the usual type.

A description of Chinese constitutions is, therefore, a description of the way the documents called constitutions relate to the social, economic and political conditions that existed when they were promulgated and to the actions taken and contemplated by those who promulgated them. It has a continuing relationship with those conditions, and changes accordingly. A Chinese constitution must, in consequence, be seen as part of a process and can only be understood if one has some sense of this development. This has been true since the very beginning of the People's Republic of China.

Earlier Constitutions

The People's Republic of China came into existence formally in 1949 immediately after the enactment of the Common Program.[33] The Common Program was, as indicated above, a response to the victory of the Communists in their long war with the Nationalists. Its purpose was to solemnize this victory and to indicate where the country was to go. The main task of the new government was to assure its control and to eliminate the effects of decades of war and neglect. At the same time, the government was committed to Marxism-Leninism-Mao Zedong Thought. It wished to establish the basis for socialism in China, but without scaring people. The program began by declaring that China was a people's democratic dictatorship on the basis of an alliance of workers and peasants.[34] The tasks of the new nation were to complete the war of liberation,[35] to destroy the special rights of imperialist countries in China, and to confiscate bureaucratic capital and return it to the ownership of the democratic society. The nation should gradually change feudal and semifeudal ownership into a system whereby the farmers owned the land. It should protect rights and advance China from an agricultural into an industrial country.[36] It must establish equality of the sexes[37] and eliminate counter-revolutionary and imperialist Guomindang [Nationalist Party] antirevolutionary activity. In necessary cases, it must, according to law, take away the political rights of persons involved in such activities.[38] In foreign affairs, China is united with those countries which love peace and freedom and particularly the Soviet Union and the People's Democracies.[39] There were a number of more particular provisions connected with the establishment of new social conditions such as the necessity for workers to participate in management.[40]

The policy was carried out pretty much as written. By 1954, all significant opposition was quelled except in Taiwan; a successful war had been fought against the United States [in Korea]; the economy was rehabilitated and progressing; nationalization had begun.[41] As the preamble to the 1954

Constitution announced, "the necessary conditions have been created for planned economic construction and gradual transition to socialism." Thus the time was ripe for a new constitution--the first to be given the name of "constitution." The preamble stated that during this time of transition to socialism, there was to be a "broad people's democratic united front." State ownership, cooperative ownership, individual ownership, and capitalism could all exist, though it was implied that capitalism was only temporary. In foreign affairs, "China has already built an indestructible friendship with the great Union of Soviet Socialist Republics and the People's Democracies."

In the body of the constitution, China was again defined as a "people's democratic state led by the working class and based on the alliance of workers and peasants."[42] Article 4 is perhaps the most significant. It provides: "The People's Republic of China, by relying on the organs of state and the social forces, and by means of socialist industrialization and socialist transformation, ensures the gradual abolition of systems of exploitation and the building of a socialist society." Several sections follow in which it is stated that different groups, such as individual workers and capitalists, will be "helped and guided" to enter into cooperatives or state-controlled activity.[43] Capitalists are forbidden to engage in "unlawful activities which injure the public interest, disrupt the social-economic order or undermine the economic plan of the state."[44] "Feudal landlords" and bureaucratic landlords continue to be deprived of political rights. Treasonable and counterrevolutionary activities are suppressed.[45]

Socialist transformation, in the sense of a change in ownership relations, came very quickly thereafter. By 1958, almost all agricultural land had been collectivized and all industry had come under state control. The individual sector of the economy had ceased to be of much importance.[46] In some ways, it was time for a new constitution. Indeed, the issue was raised by Mao Zedong.[47] But the completion of the transition to socialism (if that is an accurate description of what happened) was almost immediately succeeded by a number of disturbances that delayed the adoption of a new constitution.

The two most important occurrences were the Great Leap Forward in 1958[48] and the Cultural Revolution in 1966.[49] These two events were very complex. Opinions vary enormously as to what caused them and what they mean. There is no space to discuss these matters here. There is, however, one element that is common to both of these events that has been very important for Chinese constitutional development. This is the issue of the persistence of and the necessity for the class struggle in China after the goals of nationalization of the economy and the establishment of political and military control have been achieved.

There is no question that the exploiting classes in the usual sense of the term had been eliminated. Many members of those classes--landlords, capitalists, officials in the former government, an so on--had been killed or imprisoned. Their ownership rights in the means of production had been confiscated and their organizations were destroyed. But China's revolution was not complete. Both agricultural and industrial production were far too low. What should be done to improve them? If one believed that the class struggle was essentially over, then the emphasis would be on physical conditions. One might feel that the chief obstacles to China's march towards socialism were essentially the objective material conditions of poor transportation, a low educational level, poor technology, and lack of skilled personnel and of capital to make improvements and the like. In short, one might concentrate on what could be called "productive forces."

On the other hand, if one believed that the basic problem was always political and that development comes from changing ownership relationships, or, one might say, the class struggle, then the problem was to locate the class that must be struggled against. One could, of course, continue to badger the survivors of the old exploiting groups and their descendants. And, as a matter of fact, the constant harassment of persons with a bad class background was a feature of Chinese life until quite recently. But it is obvious that this was not enough because these people had little power. Who did? High officials and members of the Communist Party. If these people were harboring feudal or bourgeois thoughts, they must be struggled against. They had become an exploiting class.[50] But ultimately--according to one very influential view--the battle was subjective. We must all struggle to rid ourselves of the ego.[51] If these political problems were attacked first, the solution to economic and social problems would appear.

Of course, it does not do to regard the upholders of these views as completely separate. All Marxists believe in the importance of the class struggle and that political questions, as they understand the term, are very important. No one in China questions the necessity for improved irrigation and the use of computers. But there are great differences in emphasis and these differences are reflected in the constitutions that have been promulgated since 1975.

It is not clear just who was in control of China in 1975, but it is pretty clear that the group favoring emphasis on the class struggle was in control of the media. Apparently this group also controlled the government sufficiently to cause a new constitution reflecting their views to be promulgated, because the preamble made it very clear that this constitution was the product of those who emphasized the class struggle. It provided:

Society covers a considerably long historical period. Throughout this historical period, there are classes, class contradictions and class struggle, there is the struggle between the socialist road and the capitalist road, there is the threat of subversion and aggression by imperialism and social-imperialism. These contradictions can be resolved only by depending on the theory of continued revolution under the dictatorship of the proletariat and on practice under its guidance.[52]

These ideas are pervasive in the 1975 Constitution. It is what might be called a very Maoist document.[53] Almost all traces of the former social system had disappeared.[54] The Communist Party is the core of leadership of the whole Chinese people. "The working class exercises leadership over the state through its vanguard, the Communist Party of China."[55] References to capitalists and other parties had disappeared. Essentially the only property relationships that are recognized are collective or state property,[56] though very grudging permission is given for private plots and handicrafts.[57] The emphasis is on struggle. Administrators must "put proletarian politics in command, combat bureaucracy, maintain close ties with the masses and wholeheartedly serve the people. Cadres at all levels must participate in collective productive labour."[58] "The proletariat must exercise all-round dictatorship over the bourgeoisie in the superstructure, including all spheres of culture."[59] Article 13 more or less describes and endorses the Cultural Revolution. It provides:

Speaking out freely, airing views fully, holding great debates and writing big-character posters are new forms of carrying on socialist revolution created by the masses of the people. The state shall ensure to the masses the right to use these forms to create a political situation in which there are both centralism and democracy, both discipline and freedom, both unity of will and personal ease of mind and liveliness, and so help consolidate the leadership of the Communist Party of China over the state and consolidate the dictatorship of the proletariat.[60]

The standing committees of local congresses are replaced by "revolutionary committees."[61] In regard to legal procedures, the constitution provided that: "The mass line must be applied in procuratorial work and in trying cases. In major counter-revolutionary criminal cases the masses should be mobilized for discussion and criticism."[62]

It is difficult to determine the extent to which China was actually governed by these precepts, but there is no question that between the time when the constitution was adopted in 1975 and the death of Mao in September 1976, the "leftists" who, as indicated above, seem to have controlled the media, made strenuous efforts to promote these views. During the summer before Mao's death, there was a vigorous campaign against Deng Xiaoping and his doctrine of emphasizing "productive forces."[63] There was a lot of favorable publicity given to the Cultural Revolution with perhaps a hint at its revival.[64] This period is included in what the present government calls ten years of turmoil. It could also be classified as a period in which the doctrine of viewing the class struggle as the key link was the keystone of official government policy.[65]

Almost immediately upon Mao's death, things began to change. The group--later characterized as "the Gang of Four"--who had presumably been behind this constitution were imprisoned and new people began to take over.[66] One of the first notable changes in policy involved education.[67] The entire system of university admissions was changed. In the early 1970s admission was, in theory, based primarily on work experience and political reliability and not on academic qualifications as we understand the term. The course of study emphasized practice more than theory and the length of time spent in the university was shortened. In 1977, soon after the fall of the Gang of Four, this was changed to a system that based admission on an extremely competitive examination more or less of the Western type. The courses of study became much more academic and longer. There were changes in other fields as well. Foreign contacts were encouraged and imports increased.[68] There were purges of those who had sided with the Gang of Four, and there was a "reversal of verdicts" of those who were said to have been unjustly accused of various things--usually counterrevolutionary activity--during the Cultural Revolution.[69] The government was a rather strange alliance. It included both Deng Xiaoping and Hua Guofong, the man who had replaced him after his downfall in April 1976.[70] In the midst of all this, the 1978 Constitution was promulgated.[71] It reflected the unresolved conflicts in the government.

The new constitution retained the general ideological line of the 1975 Constitution, but there were some modifications. Thus, in the preamble, China is still said to be a country under the dictatorship of the proletariat and the Cultural Revolution is still a great victory. But there is a slight relaxation in the cry for the class struggle. Intellectuals are now included in the worker-peasant alliance by means of the "mass line," which was to be expanded and strengthened as a sort of united front. The big task is to preserve the revolution and to make China a modern country by the end of the century by achieving the Four Modernizations.

In the text there is the same compromise. Most of the language is the same as in the 1975 Constitution, but some changes have been made. For instance, the rural people's commune is no longer defined as "an organization which integrates government, administration and economic management."[72] Instead, it is a "socialist sector" of the economy.[73] In the article on improving production, instead of saying that the state by "grasping revolution ... improves the people's material and cultural life step by step ...,"[74] the 1978 Constitution says that the state "adheres to the general line of going all out, aiming high and achieving greater, faster, better and more economical results in building socialism ... and it continuously develops the productive forces so as to consolidate the country's independence and security and improve the people's material and cultural life step by step."[75] The term "productive forces" was anathema to the Gang of Four because it indicated that one was not emphasizing the importance of the class struggle as the key to development.

The 1978 document also eliminated the statement that the proletariat must "exercise all-round dictatorship over the bourgeoisie in the superstructure."[76] Education and science again became primary aims of the state.[77]

There were some structural changes as well. The procuracy was restored[78] as well as the use of "people's assessors" in the trial of cases.[79] The accused had a right to a defense, and while the masses were to be drawn in for discussion and suggestions in major counter-revolutionary or criminal cases,[80] there was no statement that the mass line must be generally used.[81] In the part dealing with the legislature, the powers given to the National People's Congress and to its Standing Committee are set out in much more detail[82] than in the 1975 Constitution.[83] It was believed by some that these provisions strengthened Congress.[84]

It is hard to say whether any of these changes in the language of the constitution would have had any effect whatever on the actual government of China even if the constitution had remained in effect. But as it happens, before the year 1978 was out, the political situation changed radically. The Third Plenum of the Eleventh Central Committee Meeting of the Party was held in December.[85] Its report announced the end of the class struggle and made the Four Modernizations the country's main task. This meeting signaled the basic victory of Deng Xiaoping and his group in the struggle for control of the Party--though mopping-up operations still go on. In August 1980, the Central Committee of the Communist Party recommended the establishment of a committee to revise the constitution.[86] Soon thereafter, the National People's Congress established a constitutional revision committee.[87] The

1982 Constitution is what they came up with. In June 1982, at the Sixth
Plenum of the Central Committee, Hua Guofong resigned as Party Chairman
and Hu Yaobang, a follower of Deng, was selected to replace him.[88] These
events indicated that the Deng group was in firm control of both the Party
and the government, at least at the top levels.

Political Change and the 1982 Constitution

In the period since Deng took power, the most visible aspect of political
life in China has been the emphasis on the Four Modernizations. Or, one
might say, industrialization at almost any cost. This campaign, if one can call
it that, pervades every aspect of Chinese life. In fact, though not in name,
collective ownership of agricultural land is being scrapped in favor of a sort
of limited individual ownership under the label of the "individual responsibility
system."[89] Foreign investment is sought eagerly and foreigners are even
permitted to develop and, in effect, to own China's natural resources such as
oil.[90] Internally, private capitalism at a low level, such as handicraft industry,
hauling, restaurants, etc., is permitted.[91] It is reported that shares will soon
be sold in Chinese enterprises and that both Chinese and foreigners will be
permitted to buy them.[92] In other words, private and even foreign
ownership of the means of production is now permitted (although
considerable intellectual energy is expended to deny this). Education is also
being emphasized and changed. Its chief goal now is to produce high-quality
experts in large numbers. Education is now based on an elite system that
relies on competitive examinations, foreign experts and foreign training for its
staff, a complete reversal of the radical egalitarian theories of Chairman Mao.
The new officials in the Party and government, at least at the top levels, tend
to be people with university educations.[93]
In evaluating these changes, it is instructive to look back at the campaign
that was conducted against Deng Xiaoping during late 1975 and 1976.[94]
That is roughly the period between the promulgation of the 1975 Constitution
and the death of Mao. This campaign began with the attack on Deng's
theories of education. It was alleged that he advocated that there be more
attention to theory, less to practice. He advocated downplaying the worker-
peasant teams. He was accused of having said, "The greatest tragedy of these
years is that study has been abandoned and everything is work and trade."[95]
He is supposed to have said that universities should train scientists and cadres
and "universities" which train people to become peasants and workers should
be abolished.

The general attack on Deng's ideas that followed in the next few months quoted speeches in which Deng is alleged to have criticized campaigns as a waste of time that harmed old Party members who were falsely accused of being revisionists. He objected to the criticism of intellectuals. He emphasized science and technology. In general he advocated the development of productive forces as opposed to the class struggle. He said, quoting Mao, "The criterion of good or bad is whether production force is released or tied down."[96] He advocated purchasing foreign technology on credit, using Chinese resources to pay for it. He advocated the use of material incentives both in industry and agriculture to raise production.

Thus the positions for which Deng was criticized have become the official program of the Chinese government and the basis of the 1982 Constitution. This could have been predicted: So long as Deng and his group are in power, this will continue to be the program (unless they change their minds). If what have been his opposition are in power, one can expect a shift in emphasis from productive forces to the class struggle. At any rate, these are the principles that govern China now and they form the basis of the new constitution just as the ideology of previous groups has governed the constitutions they promulgated and the policies they followed.

The ideological message of the 1982 Constitution is very clear. The preamble begins with the usual history of the struggle of the Chinese people against feudalism and imperialism. However, it emphasizes China's long and glorious history and the role of Sun Yat-sen in overthrowing the Manchus. These are both new features of the standard history. Then there is a summary of the history of the People's Republic of China. The Cultural Revolution--emphasized in the 1975 and 1978 Constitutions--is ignored. In sum, the "people's democratic dictatorship led by the working class and based on the alliance of workers and peasants, which is, in essence, the dictatorship of the proletariat, has been consolidated and developed."[97] The basic task at this stage is to achieve the Four Modernizations.[98] The class struggle is basically over. It is essential to rely on workers, peasants and intellectuals in achieving modernization; there must be a "broad patriotic united front."

In the constitution's text, this message is continued. Article 1 states that China is a people's democratic dictatorship. This phrase is apparently a code term that means that the class struggle is downplayed. It is especially valuable for intellectuals and former capitalists--two groups very important for the Four Modernizations--who can be classified as "people" or even "workers," but who are a little difficult to characterize as "the proletariat." If these groups participate in the dictatorship, then they are less likely to be targets of it. In the case of the dictatorship of the proletariat, anyone who is not a member of the proletariat is a likely target for the dictatorship. The consequences can range from inability to get work or an education to execution as an enemy.

The Four Modernizations are not mentioned by name in the text, but their spirit governs. In the 1975 and 1978 Constitutions, the state administers the individual economy in an effort to eliminate it. Now the individual economy is a complement to the "socialist public economy," and "the state protects the lawful rights and interests of the individual economy."[99] Article 14 summarizes the present economic program:

> The state continuously raises labour productivity, improves economic results and develops the productive forces by enhancing the enthusiasm of the working people, raising the level of their technical skill, disseminating advanced science and technology, improving the system of economic administration and enterprise operation and management, instituting the socialist system of responsibility in various forms and improving organization of work.[100]

State and collective enterprises are given some independence.[101] Foreign investment is allowed.[102] The state awards achievements in scientific discoveries. Article 25 provides: "The state increases the number of intellectuals and creates conditions to give full scope to their role in socialist modernization."[103]

All of this is in line with the preamble and with what Deng preached before he got to power and practices thereafter. In other words, China is a state that is dedicated to the principles of Marxism-Leninism-Mao Zedong Thought, but which at the present time must concentrate on building up its productive forces. When the aims of the Four Modernizations are achieved, China will presumably be able to advance to a stage closer to socialism. Because the intellectuals by that time will be in control of both Party and state, their positions would seem to be assured, so that this would be socialism with a very different face from that contemplated in 1975 and 1978.

The activities of the government since the 1982 Constitution was promulgated are in accordance with these aims. And that is perhaps one of the points to notice about Chinese constitutions. To say that policy is law is not to say that China's political system is lawless, or unpredictable, or subject to the whim and caprice of its leaders. The official policy of a country like China is normally hammered out after lengthy discussions. Once established, it is likely to continue for a long while. If a group that is in power wishes to change policy, there will probably be many signals. And if an opposing group comes to power, it is likely that one will know beforehand much of what it plans to do. Still, there is more uncertainty and more change than there is in a system such as that of the United States, in which policy tends to be crystallized into "law." The policy against over-concentration in industry is held in varying degrees of esteem by different administrations, but none has felt it possible formally to repeal the antitrust laws. But in China, every policy, every law, can be completely changed within a very short time.

Such changes are now going on. What will happen next? If past practice continues, then this constitution will remain in force as long as the present group remains in power, unless its policies should change considerably. In the event of a significant political or policy change, there would be a formal constitutional change. This would presumably be of no surprise to the Chinese, who are at least as aware as we are of the transitory nature of their constitutions. Indeed, they sometimes say as much. A member of the Chinese People's Political Consultative Conferences is supposed to have said in regard to the 1982 Constitution: "Will the new constitution become a mere scrap of paper as the 1954 constitution became ...?"[104] The Chinese must also be aware of the fact that institutions of government such as the courts and congresses have no real power and that a constitutional guarantee such as a guarantee of freedom of the person or the right to have a trial uninfluenced by "Administrative organs, public organization or individuals"[105] and the like, is pretty empty. Officials must, in other words, be aware of the facts that not only can all their policies and laws change if they lose out in a power struggle, but also they themselves run a serious risk of personal harm if this should happen. It has already happened to these officials during the Cultural Revolution--and before, for that matter. It seems reasonable to assume that they do not wish it to happen again. Consequently, they seem to have a great desire for stability, and they have attempted to make this constitution different from its predecessors in order to get that stability. They have attempted to substitute law, as we understand the term, for policy. They have done this by means of certain provisions in the constitution itself,[106] and by means of a vigorous campaign for the "rule of law" in China.[107]

It is difficult to know what significance to give to these or any other institutional changes in Chinese constitutions, because all we have to go on are the constitutions themselves and the Chinese commentaries. The Chinese commentaries make no effort to ask how things will actually work. Instead, they write about Chinese constitutions in the way an American might write about a new state constitution. They discuss every institution as if it functioned exactly as one would expect from reading the text. This is almost never true. It often seems that none of the institutions that are dealt with at length in the constitutions have any importance at all. Consequently, what does it matter if there are changes in the functions that are supposedly given to the institutions? It would matter, of course, if there were a strong desire on the part of very powerful people to have the changes mean something. There are hints in the new constitution and its official commentary that this may be the case now. What seems to be intended is to create a government that is at least distanced from the Party, if not completely removed from its control.[108]

The outlines of such a government are anything but clear. They may not always be clear to the authors. One clue to what is intended may be found in the seven changes in governmental institutions in the new constitution that are said by the draftsmen in their official commentary to be particularly significant.[109] These changes were:

1. The power of the National People's Congress is increased. Because the Standing Committee can meet frequently and is much smaller than the Congress as a whole, it can exercise power effectively. This is something that the Congress cannot do.

2. The position of President of the Republic is restored.

3. A Military Affairs Control Committee is established. It is appointed by the Congress and responsible to it. Formerly the armed forces were under the Party's control (at least that is what the constitution said).

4. The Premier is made responsible to Congress for the actions of the government. Each ministry operates under a system whereby the minister is responsible for the action of his ministry to the Premier. A system of auditing is instituted both at the national and local levels in order to strengthen the supervision of fiscal matters.

5. The local government authorities have been strengthened under central leadership. The congresses of provinces and cities under direct rule exercise supervisory authority over local governments, which operate under a system whereby the chief administrator is responsible.

6. The communes have been deprived of all political functions, which now go to the "township." This clarifies political responsibility.

7. Certain high officials, such as the President and members of the Standing Committee of the National People's Congress, may not serve more than two terms.

These provisions seem to be designed to create an hierarchical system of government with the apex in the Premier. Each unit has a head who is responsible to the next higher level and so on up to the top. The Premier is in turn nominally responsible to the National People's Congress, but in fact this means that he is responsible to the Standing Committee. The Committee will, in all probability, be more or less self-perpetuating because, in view of the indirect nature of the electoral process, radical changes in the composition of the Congress are unlikely, and the Standing Committee is clearly intended to control Congress. Hence, what one has is very similar to the system of government in an American corporation. The organization is run by its permanent bureaucracy, the President and his subordinates, but there is a very real power of ultimate supervision by a self-perpetuating board of directors. In China, however, there is the troublesome memory of a long-term power holder--Mao Zedong--that is no doubt fresh in people's minds. So no one is permitted to stay in a top job for more than two terms. One curious aspect to this system is that it is, in some ways, more in harmony with the theories of Sun Yat-sen than the government that now exists in Taiwan.[110]

Dr. Sun believed that political power should be distinguished from governmental power. A strong government was not to be feared so long as the government is ultimately controlled by the people in the exercise of their political power. Government consists of making, enforcing and interpreting rules as well as recruiting personnel for government and investigating its work. The mass of the people cannot do these things. But the people can control the government by exercising four political powers: suffrage, initiative, referendum and recall. in a country as large as China, they cannot exercise powers directly as they might, perhaps, in a Swiss canton. Hence they act through the people's Congress. The Congress is not a legislature. It does not make laws in the usual way. Rather, it elects the leaders of the government, one branch of which makes laws (the legislative yuan). The people, acting through their representatives, the Congress, can elect or remove all top officials. The people can initiate legislation or have it referred to them for approval (referendum). But the initiative and referendum are as extraordinary in China as they are in the United States. Normally people simply elect top officials of the government and supervise their work by getting periodic reports. This is, of course, the way the National People's Congress is supposed to work.

There are also, to be sure, many differences between the 1982 Constitution and the ideas of Dr. Sun and his followers.[111] Still, if one looks only at what the constitution says about the political as opposed to the economic institutions of China and at what it says about international relations, one cannot help wondering about the possible influences of Dr. Sun--who has never been repudiated by the Communists. At the present time, even those economic provisions of the constitution that encourage individual farmers to control the land they farm and benefit from it seem to be a sort of echo of Dr. Sun's famous program of giving land to the tiller. Dr.

Sun attempted to assimilate Western democratic ideas and institutions into traditional Chinese ideas and institutions in order to create a system that would work in China. If the present constitution is in fact influenced by Dr. Sun, its draftsmen are emphasizing the Chinese tradition as the foundation of their government. There seems to be some hint of this in the Preamble in the midst of many protestations of loyalty to Marxism-Leninism.[112] Connecting the present government to Chinese tradition is an obvious way of giving the government a basis for existing independent of the Party.

Regardless, however, of whether the leaders of China are the ardent followers of Marxism-Leninism-Mao Zedong Thought that they purport to be, or closet devotees of Sun's Three People's Principles, it is still not clear that the governmental institutions described in the constitution will ever operate independently of the Party. The Party at the present time is not, after all, a small band of enthusiastic revolutionaries. It is an enormous bureaucracy with tens of millions of members. For thirty-five years, membership in the Party has been the principal road to power and the perquisites of power such as housing, food, education, health care, travel, and the like.[113] The vast majority of persons now living in China have never known anything else. All of the persons who are in the top positions in the government are also important Party members. The two things go together. It is hard to see those Party members who are, for example, Standing Committee members, getting rid of Party control of the electoral process. However, it was suggested recently by one of the most authoritative observers of China that the current Chairman of the National People's Congress, Peng Zhen, who was vice-chairman of the committee that was said to have drafted the constitution, is attempting to make the Standing Committee of the National People's Congress a rival power-center to the Politburo of the Communist Party because Zhen is not a member of the Politburo. He is said to have significant support.[114] If this is an accurate assessment, it is interesting. Even if it does not mean that power has shifted from the Party to governmental institutions, Zhen's attempt would mean that they, particularly the Standing Committee, have become fora in which battles for Party control might be fought. Hence they would acquire some real life as opposed to the merely formal existence they have had heretofore. Of course such importance, even if it exists, may be short-lived. Mao Zedong created extra-Party organizations, notably the Cultural Revolution Small Group and the Red Guards, when he had apparently lost control of the Party apparatus. He used these new organizations to destroy the leaders of the Party (sometimes in a very literal sense).[115] But once this was accomplished, he simply put his men into control of the Party. The new organizations disappeared or ceased to have much power. Moreover, if there is some sort of struggle for power going on now between Deng and Peng, it is a struggle between two octogenarians. It is not clear that its outcome will have any long-term significance. Although, of course, it may.

There is another development that might make the institutions created by this constitution different from those created by its predecessors. That is the development of a legal profession. China has never had a significant legal profession in the Western sense outside of the Treaty Ports such as Shanghai where there were extraterritorial courts. Even the vestiges of a Western (or even Soviet) system pretty much disappeared after 1958. There were courts, but it is not clear what function they fulfilled. There was clearly no general system of criminal courts in a Western sense. Nor were there lawyers.[116] Beginning in the late 1970s, however, there has been a determined movement to change this situation. Laws and law books proliferate. Law departments are being established or reestablished in universities. University-level institutions and special courses are being formed to give training in law to judges, most of whom were military men and had no legal training.[117] If this activity continues, it will mean that there will be a very large number of people in a well-entrenched bureaucracy--the courts and procuracy (though will the security administration continue to dominate?)--who have been trained to think in terms of law as something independent of policy. There will be other trained lawyers throughout the bureaucracy. This is already true of the foreign trade organs.

It would be foolish to suppose that all of these individuals will have acquired a passionate fondness for civil rights and due process, although it is clear that at least those who have studied law in law departments have had access to Western legal materials, including constitutional law materials.[118] It does seem possible, however, that they will serve to form a core of resistance to rapid change outside the normal channels, such as to something like the Cultural Revolution. If one wished to rid oneself of an opponent, a "trial" for counterrevolutionary acts would be used rather than a mass meeting. the "trial" of the Gang of Four is of interest in this context because previously trials were not used in purges of Party leaders.[119]

Despite this apparent desire for change and the measures that seem to have been taken to bring it about, it is far too early to say whether the new constitution will in fact effect some changes or simply go the way of its predecessors. Much depends on how long Deng stays in power and on who succeeds him. To make any predictions on how the Chinese constitution will fare in the midst of these events, one must be able to predict the immediate future of Chinese politics, and few would wish to attempt that.[120] All that one can say is that from 1949 to the present, Chinese constitutions have not played a Western role of describing and prescribing the forms and powers of governmental institutions and the rights of citizens, although they purport to do so. Rather, they have signaled political and ideological change. The more recent changes have involved a bitter and violent dispute over the issue of continuation of the class struggle thirty years or so after liberation. Those who oppose continuation of the struggle are now in power. They have attempted in every possible way to prevent a reversal of their programs. Doubtless the most important method that they have used is the traditional one of purging the party and replacing supporters of the old group with their own people.[121] They have devoted much attention to building up mass support. But they have also attempted to make some institutional changes in the Chinese government that may make it more resistant to change. And they constantly emphasize the importance of law as opposed to policy, and have sponsored the development of a legal system and a legal profession. Only time will tell what they have accomplished.

Afterword

This article was written in 1985, and the question arises whether anything has happened between then and now (1991) that requires any adjustments or changes to be made in it. The answer is, unfortunately, no. There have been minor adjustments to the Constitution. Under article 11 it is now provided explicitly that the private economy is permitted "to exist and to develop within the limits prescribed by law." Article 10 has been amended to permit the transfer of "land-use rights."[122] These represent a significant change in the official policy, but ist was a change that had taken place in fact prior to the change in the Constitution. Hence the position taken by this article that the Constitution is primarily significant as a statement of existing policy is reaffirmed. The Constitution does not describe the real institutions of government nor the way they actually function.

The only significant event in the development of constitutional law and practice did not consist of any changes in the wording of the constitution, nor in the decisions of the courts or promulgation of laws and regulations. It consisted rather of the student movement of spring, 1989, and the way handled by the government.[123] The movement itself is important because it indicates that at least among the urban educated elite--and perhaps among the urban workers as well--there is a passionate desire for "democracy". It is not clear that the term had a very definite meaning to those who used it, but it is clear that there was a great hostility to the present system. The actions of the government in dealing with the movement are of much less interest in this connection since thay are in many ways simply a continuation of practices developed in the forty years procedeing that event. Massacres are nothing new in the history of the People's Republic of China. The legal structures set up by and under the Constitution obviously have no significance to the government--a fact that is not lost on the citizens of Hong Kong who have been re-evaluating their guarantees under the Basic Law. The actions of the government depend on the shifting power alliance of top leaders. The most important leader by far is still Deng Xiaoping. He now has no official position whatever in either government or Party, but he remains China's dominant figure. China seems to be marking time until he dies. What happens then will determine the shape of the real operative constitution and government of China. It is impossible to predict with any assurance what that will be.

NOTES

1. I have used the following sources for the Chinese texts of the constitutions: 1949 Common Program, 1 XIAN FA ZELIAO XUANBIAN, SELECTED MATERIALS ON CONSTITUTIONAL LAW [hereinafter CONSTITUTIONAL MATERIALS]; the 1954 Constitution is found in id. at 150; the 1975 Constitution is found in id. at 293; the 1978 Constitution is found in id. at 303; and the 1982 Constitution is found in the official pamphlet edition, which contains the report of the drafting committee. I have used the following English translations from which all translations in the text are taken: Common Program, FUNDAMENTAL LEGAL DOCUMENTS OF COMMUNIST CHINA 34 (A.P. Plaustein ed. 1962); 1954 Constitution, SELECTED LEGAL DOCUMENTS OF THE PEOPLE'S REPUBLIC OF CHINA 1 (J. En-pao Wang ed. 1976); 1975 Constitution, id. at 65; 1978 Constitution, official translation in separate booklet published by Foreign Languages Press (1978); 1982 Constitution, official translation in separate booklet published by Foreign Languages Press (1982).
2. Most constitutions are modeled to some extent on the United States Constitution because it is one of the oldest and easily the best known. The similarities with the Chinese constitution lie primarily in the structure of the constitution. In both, the powers of the most important organs of government are set out in general terms, and the organs are similar: Congress, the Administration and the Judiciary. Yet there are differences, particularly in the Administration where, in China, the existence of the bureaucracy is recognized (arts. 30-32).   And there are some additional institutions in China such as the Central Military Commission (art. 93) and the Procuracy (arts. 129-133).   China is a unitary rather than a federal state, so the treatment of local matters is quite different. Still the document as a whole is close to the form of the United States Constitution and it includes a Bill of Rights. See infra note 7.
3. The principal similarity of the Chinese constitution to that of the Soviet Union seems to me to lie in the presence of ideological statements and the prominence of economics, in other words, the clear recognition of Marxism as the official doctrine of the state. Thus, the preambles in both constitutions refer to the struggle to overturn capitalism and to establish socialism. Both define themselves as socialist states. China: "The People's Republic of China is a socialist state under the people's democratic dictatorship led by the working class and based on the alliance of workers and peasants." Art. 1. The U.S.S.R.: "The Union of Soviet Socialist Republics is a socialist all-people's state expressing the will and the interests of the workers, the peasants, and the intelligentsia, and of the working people of all the nations and nationalities of the country." Art. 1. The Soviet Constitution devotes Chapter II to the "Economic System." The Chinese Constitution devotes thirteen articles in its first chapter, "General Principles," to economics. Arts. 6-18.

There are also institutional similarities. The Chinese procuracy is obviously of Soviet origin. *See* Ginsburgs & Stahnke, "The Genesis of the People's Procuracy Procuratorate in the People's Republic of China," THE CHINA Q. 1 (1964); "The

People's Procuratorate in Communist China: The Period of Maturation, 1951-1955," *id.* at 53 (1965); "The People's Procuratorate in Communist China: The Institution Ascendant, 1954-1957," *id.* at 82 (1968). The use of standing committees of larger bodies, such as a congress, to do the real work of those bodies, is also a common feature of the two constitutions. *See* the provisions on the Presidium of the Supreme Soviet, arts. 119-124. The Standing Committee of the National People's Congress is dealt with primarily in articles 65-69.

4. Art. 59. The actual process of election is controlled by the Election Law for the National People's Congress and Local Congress of 1979. CONSTITUTIONAL MATERIALS, *supra* note 1, at 336, amended by Fifth National People's Congress, Dec. 10, 1982, translated in SUMMARY OF WORLD BROADCASTS, PART III: THE FAR EAST (Dec. 18, 1982 FE/7212/C/1) [hereinafter SWB].

5. Arts. 62 and 79. The term that the Chinese now translate as "President" [*Zhuxi*] is normally translated as "Chairman," as in "Chairman Mao." I do not know the reason for the change.

6. Art. 101.

7. Article 33 provides that all citizens are equal before the law; article 34 gives the right to vote, and to be elected, to all citizens over 18 years old, except to those "deprived of political rights according to law"; article 35 gives rights of "freedom of speech, of the press, of assembly, of association, of procession and of demonstration"; article 36 gives freedom of religious belief; article 37 declares that the freedom of persons is inviolable, that no one can be arrested except by order of the court of procuracy, and that unlawful searches of the person are prohibited; article 38 guarantees personal dignity; article 39 protects against unlawful searches of houses; article 40 guarantees the confidentiality of correspondence; article 41 gives the right to criticize and make complaints to officials.

8. Article 42 declares that citizens have the right and duty to work; article 43 declares working people have the right to rest; article 44 says the state will prescribe a system of retirement for workers and staff in enterprises and organs of the state; article 45 declares that citizens have the right to material assistance from the state and provides for the blind and other disabled persons; article 46 declares that citizens have a right to an education.

9. The number varies from session to session. *See* C.E. Weng, CONTEMPORARY CHINESE POLITICS 109 (2d ed. 1958) [hereinafter WENG].

10. The time varies from session to session. *See, e.g.*, Wang, "The New Constitution Strengthens the Standing Committee of the National People's Congress," in A GUIDE TO THE CONSTITUTION OF THE PEOPLE'S REPUBLIC OF CHINA [*Zhonghua Renmin Gonheguo Xian Fa Jianghua*] 110 (1983) [hereinafter CHINESE CONSTITUTION].

11. Arts. 61 and 67.

12. Art. 67. There are some statutes that only Congress can enact--notably amendments to the constitution, arts. 62(1) and 64.

13. Art. 62(5)-(8) (power to appoint); art. 63 (power to dismiss).

14. Art. 59.
15. Article 5 lists the level below the national level; article 97 sets out the election process. *See also* FOREIGN BROADCAST INFORMATION SERVICE (FBIS), Electoral Law of the PRC for the NPC and Local People's Congresses of All Levels, in DAILY REPORT 12 (July 27, 1979).
16. Arts. 101 and 128.
17. Art. 127.
18. It is perhaps enough to cite the case of Wei Jingsheng, one of the leaders of the short-lived "Peking Spring" movement, when some young people expressed themselves very freely in making criticisms of the government. Wei was sentenced to 15 years on what seems to me to have been trumped-up charges. *See* Jones, "Due Process in China: The Trial of Wei Jingsheng," 9 REV. OF SOC. L. 55 (1983). To be sure, this was before the 1982 Constitution, but freedom of speech was also guaranteed in the 1978 Constitution, article 45 and the people who put Wei in prison are the people who still govern China and who promulgated the 1982 Constitution. Wei is still imprisoned. For reports on a number of political prisoners, *see* AMNESTY INTERNATIONAL, CHINA: VIOLATIONS OF HUMAN RIGHTS 5-51 (1984). One might also note the "Cultural Pollution" campaign of 1983-84. *See* Schram, "Economics in Command? Ideology and Policy Since the Third Plenum," THE CHINA Q. 418, 437-48 (1984). This was used to dampen discussion in at least one university. But citation is otiose. Some of the "freedoms" are so qualified in the text that they are meaningless. Thus, article 36 guarantees freedom of religion but states that "Religious bodies and religious affairs are not subject to any foreign domination ...." In practice, this means that many persons cannot practice their religion, notably Roman Catholics and Tibetan Buddhists.
19. China is a poor country and does well to keep its citizens from starving to death. It does not always succeed in that. "Retirement" as such is not guaranteed to farmers and perhaps some kinds of workers. All are supposed to get material assistance when they are old. Art. 45. But one hears that one of the reasons peasants are not cooperating with the birth-control program is that they believe sons are the only dependable social security. It might be added that China has a significant unemployment problem, although it is disguised by such terms as "youth waiting for assignment". *See, e.g.,* WENG, *supra* note 9, at 255.
20. The Chinese would, of course, deny this. I can only say that I have never seen any evidence of independence. Even Professor Weng who has tried to find examples of independent action regards Congress as pretty subservient. *See* WENG, *supra* note 9, at III.
21. This does not mean that every order from the center is automatically obeyed nor that local organizations have no independence. As a matter of fact, they are often quite resistant and hard to control. But the organizational chart is quite clear. And by and large, the center gets what it wants.

22. He is Chairman of the Central Military Commission, which was created by the 1982 Constitution, art. 93. This position is subject to the National People's Congress. Art. 63(3).

23. 1975 CONST. art. 2; 1978 CONST. art. 2(24).

24. There is quite a lot of that. *See, e.g.,* "PLA Delegates Discuss New Constitution," SWB (Dec. 3, 1982, FE/7199/C/99:

> ... said that inclusions of provisions for building socialist spiritual civilization is of great significance. He said communist ideology is the core of socialist spiritual civilization of which Lei Feng was an exemplar ... every PLA fighter should emulate Lei Feng, foster a deep love for the motherland and the people, and for labour, science and socialism, display the communist spirit and be a vanguard in building socialist spiritual civilization ....

See also the reactions of Chinese People's Political Consultative Conference observers at the National People's Congress: "all an historic event ..., an achievement gained through a struggle and a summary of experience. It is paid for with blood." FBIS, Report CPPCC meeting in Renmin Rih Bao, in DAILY REPORT K8 (Dec. 9, 1982). Peng Zhen in presenting the constitution to Congress said, "When our one billion people all cultivate the consciousness and habit of observing and upholding the constitution and fight against all acts violating and undermining the Constitution this will become a mighty force." SWB (Dec. 7, 1982, FE/7202/C/16).

25. The preamble, in its last paragraph, states that the constitution "is the fundamental law of the state." It must be taken by all as "the basic norm of conduct." Wang Zhengzhao and Lin Yuhui, in "The New Constitution Is Our Country's Basic Law" (Chinese Constitution, People's Daily Press, *supra* note 10, at 12) say that the constitution is the basic law because (1) its content sets out the basic principles of law such as the necessity for constructing socialist modernization, the nature of the state, and the economy, but it does not go into detail; (2) any law that is in conflict with it is without effect; and (3) it is enacted and amended in a different way.

26. The 1954 Constitution recognized the existence of state, cooperative, individual, and capitalist ownership, art. 5. The formation of cooperatives was encouraged, arts. 7 and 8. But individual ownership of land by peasants is protected, art. 8. It was anticipated that no more than one-third of the peasant households would form "lower-level producer cooperatives," in which the individuals retained ownership but farmed cooperatively and split the profits, by the end of 1957. However, in 1955 Mao decided that the pace should be accelerated and the country was almost completely collectivized by 1957, having passed through cooperatives into socialist collectives in which there was no individual ownership and peasants were regarded for their work. Communes that unified political and economic control appeared in 1958. *See* M. Meissner, MAO'S CHINA 140-60, 230-41 (1977) [hereinafter MEISSNER]. But the constitutional provisions on land ownership were not changed until 1975. The 1978 Constitution stated that there were two types of ownership of

the means of production: state ownership and collective ownership (communes), art. 5. Within the commune, there was ownership by: the commune, the production brigade and the production team. Farming of private plots for personal needs subject to predominance of the collective economy was permitted, art. 7. In 1977, prior to the time the constitution was promulgated, "household contracting" had begun in some areas. Under this system, the procurement contract was made with an individual household rather than a team or brigade. Once its quota was met, it could dispose of the surplus for its own benefit. The system has many variations. By 1982, it dominated in China. The changes were effected by a series of Central Committee Documents. The constitutional change recognizing (more or less) individual responsibility was promulgated in December 1982. 1982 CONST. art. 14. For a summary of these developments, see Walker, "Chinese Agriculture During the Period of Readjustment 1978-83," THE CHINA Q. 783, 786-89 (1984).

27. *See* Wang Shuwen, "The Basic Characteristics of the New Constitution," CHINESE CONSTITUTION, *supra* note 10, at 21. He states that constitutions are important component parts of the superstructure. According to Lenin, there are two types: the "real constitution" and the "written constitution." The real constitution determines the nature, content and character of the written constitution. Wang then indicates how the four written constitutions (the Chinese never call the Common Program a constitution) reflect their real constitutions. The only good ones are those of 1954 and 1982. The latter reflects the conclusions of the Third Plenum such as the four basic policies and the Four Modernizations [of industry, the military, argriculture, and science and technology].

28. 1954 CONST. art. 1.

29. 1975 CONST. art. 1. This change in phrasing was the principal subject of the publicity in favor of the 1975 Constitution when it was promulgated. *See* Cohen, "China's Changing Constitution," 76 THE CHINA Q. 794 (1978) [hereinafter Cohen].

30. Art. 1.

31. Enacted July 1, 1979, translated in SWB (July 16, 1979, FE6/63/C/222).

32. The preamble to the 1982 Constitution keeps the concept of the class struggle, but only just. After making it clear that the exploiting classes no longer exist as a class, it states that the class struggle will have to go on for a long time against foreign and domestic enemies. However, in the official commentary, it is pointed out that according to the 1981 census, 99.97% of those over 18 years old had the right to vote and be elected. In other words, they were not "exploiters" who had been deprived of their political rights. The exploiting classes have diminished greatly in size. Still the country has to fight the enemy within and without. So, dictatorship is preserved. *Id.* at 56.

33. The Common Program was enacted by the Chinese People's Political Consultative Conference on September 29, 1949. 1 COLLECTED LAWS AND REGULATIONS OF THE CHINESE CENTRAL PEOPLE'S GOVERNMENT [*Zhongyang Renmin Zhengfu Faling Huipian*] 17 (1945-50). The People's Republic

of China came into being on October 1, 1949. Central People's Government Announcement of the People's Republic of China, *id.* at 28.

34. Art. 1.

35. Art. 2.

36. Art. 3.

37. Art. 6.

38. Art. 7.

39. Art. 11.

40. Part IV, Economic Policy, arts. 26-40, sets out the government's policy, which is, essentially, to permit and encourage capitalism under state control, while making the state economy the principal factor. Art. 32 deals with workers' participation in management.

41. MEISSNER, *supra* note 26, at 59, 60, 73-80, 92-97.

42. Art. 1.

43. Article 7 states that the state encourages, "guides and helps" the development of cooperatives, which are "the chief means for the transformation of individual farming and individual handicrafts." Article 8 provides that the state "guides and helps" individual peasants to form cooperatives. The policy of the state in regard to the rich peasant economy is to eliminate it. Under article 9, handicraft workers are to be "guide[d] and help[ed]" into cooperatives. Under article 10, the good aspects of capitalist industry and commerce are permitted but the state "encourages and guides their transformation into various forms of state-capitalist economy."

44. Art. 10.

45. Art. 19.

46. D. Perkins, MARKET CONTROL AND PLANNING IN COMMUNIST CHINA 13-17 (1966).

47. JOINT PUBLICATIONS RESEARCH SERVICE, MISCELLANY OF MAO TSE-TUNG THOUGHT [*Maoze dong sixiang wan suui*] (1949-1968), Pt. I, 138 (Feb. 20, 1974). It is reported that Mao said on December 12, 1958, "The issue of integrating politics and the commune, for example, was not passed by the People's Congress, nor is it in the constitution. Many parts of the constitution are obsolete, but it cannot be revised now. As for surpassing the U.S., we will formulate a written constitution."

48. The Great Leap is discussed in MEISSNER, *supra* note 26, at 204-52.

49. The Cultural Revolution is discussed in MEISSNER, *supra* note 26, at 309-58.

50. *See* the discussion of "old classes" in Whyte, "Inequality and Stratification in China," 64 THE CHINA Q, 698-705 (1976).

51. *See* report on Jiang Qing by Roxanne Witke in COMRADE CHIANG CH'ING 339 (1977):

Chiang Ch'ing concluded her remarks on a cherished subject, the problem of Ego. That subjective aspect of revolutionary transformation was always (and most emphatically in our interview) at the forefront of her consciousness, and seemingly was her sense of the heart of the Cultural Revolution. Making revolution, she said in effect, was simultaneously an introverted and extroverted experience, a personal and public affair. Conflicts were not only external-- between the enemy and ourselves--or internal--among ourselves, as Chairman Mao had argued. They must be waged *within* oneself--*against* the so-called Ego.

52. 1975 CONST. preamble.

53. There is some question whether or not Mao approved of it since he did not attend either the meeting of the Party Central Committee prior to the meeting of the National People's Congress at which the constitution was promulgated, or the Congress itself. *See* M-H Yao, "The Fourth National People's Congress and Peiping's Future Direction," THE NEW CONSTITUTION OF COMMUNIST CHINA 3245, 327-28 (M. Lindsay ed. 1976).

54. There is no reference to capitalism or, for that matter, to landlords except as persons deprived of political rights. Art. 14.

55. Art. 2.

56. Art. 5.

57. Art. 7. Private plots are permitted so long as the "development and absolute predominance of the collective economy of the people's commune are ensured." Article 9 permits ownership of income from work, savings, houses, and "other means of livelihood."

58. Art. 11.

59. Art. 12.

60. Art. 13.

61. Art. 22.

62. Art. 25.

63. The discussion of the campaign against Deng Xiaoping is based upon "Two Systems, Lessons of Teng's Crimes," CHINA NEWS ANALYSIS (1976). *See also* B. Brugger, CHINA: RADICALISM TO REVISION 1962-1979, 170-96 (1981).

64. *See, e.g.*, "The Great Cultural Revolution Will Shine Forever," PEKING REV., at 14 (July 2, 1976); "The Making of a Young Actress," *id.*; "Advance Along the Road of the Great Proletarian Cultural Revolution," *id.* at 16.

65. *see, e.g.*, the translation of the official commentary to the 1975 Constitution in SELECTED LEGAL DOCUMENTS OF THE PEOPLE'S REPUBLIC OF CHINA 93-95 (J. En-Pao Wang ed. 1976), where it is said that "our main task is to ... persist in continued revolution ..." and a statement of Mao Zedong is quoted: "... there are still classes, class contradictions and class struggles ..."

66. *See* B. BRUGGER, *supra* note 63, at 194-96, 201-02.

67. *See* Pepper, "Chinese Education After Mao: Two Steps Forward, Two Steps Back and Begin Again?," THE CHINA Q. 1 (1980).

68. *See*, for instance, the statement about a 26.8% increase in exports in the first half of 1979 and the establishment of new institutions to encourage trade and the import of technology, in *Quarterly Chronicle and Documentation*, THE CHINA Q. 881, 886 (1979).

69. *See* "Quarterly Chronicle and Documentation: (b) The Campaign Against Lin Piao and the 'Gang of Four'," and *id.* (c) "The Leadership," THE CHINA Q. 157-58, 173 (1979).
70. Deng was rehabilitated and reappeared as Vice-Chairman of the Party by mid-1977. B. BRUGGER, *supra* note 63, at 202-03.
71. The 1978 Constitution is discussed in detail, Cohen, *supra* note 29.
72. 1975 CONST. art. 7.
73. 1978 CONST. art. 7.
74. 1975 CONST. art. 10.
75. 1975 CONST. art. 11
76. 1975 CONST. art. 12.
77. 1978 CONST. art. 13.
78. 1978 CONST. art. 43.
79. 1979 CONST. art. 41.
80. *Id.*
81. 1978 CONST. art. 22.
82. 1978 CONST. art. 25.
83. 1975 CONST. arts. 17 and 18.
84. Cohen, *supra* note 29, at 809-12.
85. The Third Plenum is discussed in B. BRUGGER, *supra* note 63, at 218-19.
86. Proposal of the Central Committee of the Chinese Communist Party Regarding the Revision of the Constitution and the Establishment of a Constitutional Revision Committee [*Zhongguo Gongzhan Dang Zhongyang Weiyuanhui Guanyu Xingai Xianfa He Changli Xianfa Zingai Weiyuanhui*] of August 30, 1980, in CONSTITUTIONAL MATERIALS, *supra* note 1, at 375.
87. Resolution of the Third Session of the Fifth National People's Congress of the People's Republic of China Regarding the Revision of the Constitution and the Establishment of a Constitution Revision Committee [*Zhonghua Renmin Gongheguo Ti Wu Ji Quanguo Renmin Daibiao Da Hui Ti San Ze Huiyi Guanyu Xingai Xianfa He Changle Xianfa Xiugai Weihuanhui*] of September 10, 1980, CONSTITUTIONAL MATERIALS, *supra* note 1, at 379.
88. *See* "Quarterly Chronicle and Documentation," THE CHINA Q. 547, 548 (1981).
89. *See* Schell, "A Reporter at Large: The Wind of Wanting to Go It Alone," THE NEW YORKER 65-73 (Jan. 23, 1984) [hereinafter Schell]. *See also supra* note 26. The Chinese would, of course, deny that land farmed under the individual responsibility system is "owned" by the cultivator because it cannot be sold or even rented. Even if the peasants were not busy finding ways around these prohibitions-- as one assumes they are--the rights they do have constitute ownership as this term is defined in the RESTATEMENT OF PROPERTY § 10 comment b (1936). The recent "Circular of the Central Committee of the Chinese Communist Party on Rural Work During 1984," THE CHINA Q. 132 (1985), allows households to enter into contracts to use land for 15 years or more. This is "ownership" by almost any definition. While land "may not be bought or sold, may not be leased to a third

party and may not be transferred as building plots for housing or for any other non-agricultural use," *id.*, the contract can be transferred with the consent of the collective. *Id.* It is said that the peasants expect the leasehold to become "property" after 15 years and in the meantime there is a brisk trade in them. Kueh, "The Economics of the 'Second Land Reform' in China," THE CHINA Q. 122, 128 nn.10-12 (1985).

90. The Joint Venture Law is available in both English and Chinese in 1 CHINA'S FOREIGN ECONOMIC LEGISLATION 1 (1982).

91. *See* Schell, *supra* note 89, at 43-58.

92. As to possible foreign ownership of shares in Chinese concerns, see "Peking firms may seek Hong Kong listing," SOUTH CHINA MORNING POST, July 6, 1984, at 1.

93. *See* WENG, *supra* note 9, at 251-54.

94. This is based on CHINA NEWS ANALYSIS No. 1044 (June 18, 1976). *See also* B. BRUGGER, *supra* note 63, at 177-95.

95. CHINA NEWS ANALYSIS, No. 1044 (June 18, 1976).

96. *Id.*

97. 1982 CONST. preamble.

98. The Four Modernizations are: industry, agriculture, defense, and science and technology.

99. 1982 CONST. art. 11.

100. 1982 CONST. art. 14.

101. 1982 CONST. art. 16.

102. 1982 CONST. art. 18.

103. 1982 CONST. art. 25.

104. FBIS, DAILY REPORT K8 (Dec. 9, 1982).

105. Art. 126.

106. Consider, for example, the treatment of article 5, which provides that "no law ... shall contravene the Constitution" and all "state organs, the armed forces," etc., "must abide by the Constitution and the law." Both the Congress, art. 62(2), and its Standing Committee, art. 67(1), are to enforce this apparently. The problem of constitutionality is discussed in one standard commentary under the chapter heading "The new constitution strengthens the stipulations for defining the constitution" [*Xin Xianfa Zhajiangle Xianfa Bao Zhangde Guiding*]. The authors list four ways in which the new constitution provides this protection: (1) it strengthens the supervisory power of the Congress and its Standing Committee; (2) it gives the Standing Committee power to declare acts and regulations unconstitutional; (3) it provides that all agencies and citizens must respect the constitution; and (4) it requires a super-majority of Congress to amend the constitution. There is no discussion of how all this will work. There seems to be a feeling that if there are words in a statute that say someone has a "right," then he does. *See* W. Zhaozhe and C. Yunsheng, GUIDE TO THE NEW CONSTITUTION [*Xin Xinfa Jianghua*] 224-27 (1983).

107. *See supra* note 19. *See also* "The Use of the Legal Weapon," CHINA NEWS ANALYSIS (June 18, 1984).

108. The 1982 Party Constitution, adopted three months before the State Constitution, is in harmony with this view. It provides in the preamble that "The Party must conduct its activities within the limits permitted by the Constitution and the laws of the state." 25 BEIJING REV. at 8 (1982). In 1980 when this constitution was being drafted, Deng Xiaoping, in a speech delivered to the Political Bureau of the Party, stated that the Party should be separated from the government. The Party would establish general principles but would strengthen the state structure. Policy would not be a substitute for government. Hsia and Johnson, THE CHINESE COMMUNIST PARTY CONSTITUTION OF 1982: DENG ZIAOPING'S PROGRAM FOR MODERNIZATION (1984).

109. Speech by Peng Zhen printed in Chinese edition of 1982 Constitution, *supra* note 1, at 66-69.

110. The Constitution of the Republic of China (Taiwan) provides for direct election to the Legislative Yuan--the body that actually legislates, art. 64, as well as to the Congress, art. 26. As indicated in the text, Dr. Sun wanted elections only to the Congress, which was to elect the Legislative Yuan. *See* P. Linebarger, THE POLITICAL DOCTRINES OF SUN YATSEN 89-121, 209-23 (1937) and W.Y. Tsao, THE CONSTITUTIONAL STRUCTURE OF MODERN CHINA 96-113, 130-45 (1947). The Tsao book reprints the translations of the texts of the Chinese Constitution of 1946 (in force in Taiwan), *id.* at 275, and the draft constitution of 1937, much closer to Dr. Sun's ideas, *id.* at 238. See *infra*, Chapter 3.

111. The most obvious difference is that Dr. Sun proposed to have the government administration divided into five divisions, or *Yuan*: Legislative, Judicial Administrative, Examination and Control. Y-S Sun, *SAN MIN CHU-I* 144-49 [Lecture Six]. The first three divisions are taken from the U.S. Constitution and the last two from traditional Chinese institutions. The table of organization for the government established by the 1982 Constitution of the People's Republic of China envisages a Congress which formally enacts legislation that is actually drafted by its Standing Committee and special committees subordinate to it, not by a Legislative Yuan that is quite separate. The government supervised by the Congress has three or four parts: the State Council (equivalent to Dr. Sun's Administrative Yuan); the Central Military Commission; the People's Courts; and the People's Procuracy. (The last two are treated together.) On the other hand, one of the principal features of Dr. Sun's program for China was the idea of "tutelage." China was not yet ready for direct elections nationwide because it had no experience with democracy. Hence, the Guomindang controlled the country and conducted elections first at the local or county level. When all the counties in a province were electing their local government, the province was then ready to have province-wide elections. When half the provinces were democratic, there could be elections to Congress. LINEBARGER, *supra* note 104, at 210-14. The system of indirect elections established in the 1982 Constitution is certainly compatible with this, although it is

not exactly the same. It is curious that the idea of a standing committee of the People's Congress, which was rejected by the drafters of the Guomindang constitution, was strongly advocated--for much the same reasons as given by Peng Zhen--by Professor Tsao, who seems clearly to be a disciple of Dr. Sun. Tsao, *supra* note 110, at 112-13.

112. *See* Preamble provisions on China's long history and Sun's role in overthrowing the Manchus.

113. *See* WENG, *supra* note 9, at 135.

114. L. LaDanay, "China's New Power Centre?," FAR EASTERN ECON. REV. 38 (1984).

115. *See* H-Y Lee, THE POLITICS OF THE CHINESE CULTURAL REVOLUTION 1-10 (1978).

116. For my views on the system as of 1975, see Jones, "A Possible Model for the Criminal Trial in the People's Republic of China," 24 AM. J. COMP. L. 229 (1976). *See* Peng, *Importance of Improving China's Legislation*, BEIJING REV. no. 35, 16 (1984), for an official view of the legal situation in China since liberation.

117. *See, e.g.*, Li, "Legal Education Surges Ahead," 26 BEIJING REV. 22 (1985); "Spare-time college helps train judges," CHINA DAILY, Feb. 18, 1983; "Socialist legal system making good progress," *id.*, Dec. 12, 1983; "Major plan adopted to train jurists," *id.*, Jan. 7, 1984.

118. For example, CONSTITUTIONAL MATERIALS consists of five volumes and includes most of the major constitutional documents of the Western world, including the Magna Carta, The Petition of Right, the U.S. Declaration of Independence and Constitution, and the Declaration of the Rights of Man. It had an initial press run of 15,000 copies and was freely available throughout the country.

119. As a "trial," it was a farce, but it was interesting that the Chinese used a public show trial to get rid of defeated opponents. Previously, people just disappeared. Sometimes they were publicly attacked, but there was no trial-like proceeding. For the early purge of Gao Gang and Rao Shushi, see F. Teiwes, POLITICS AND PURGES IN CHINA 166-210 (1979). Two prominent leaders were accused primarily of "factionalism" and trying to seize power. They were accused anonymously at the Fourth Plenum of the Seventh Central Committee Meeting in 1954, and were publicly attacked at the National Conference of the Party in 1955. Sometime in between, Gao committed suicide. There was a "verdict," but no trial. The Teiwes book discusses all of the important purges up to the Cultural Revolution.

120. Of course, if one had to guess, it would be that what is likely to emerge is something like the system in the Soviet Union: stable, but very authoritarian and controlled, and rather corrupt. The Soviets are said to believe that China will have to adopt their system, though of course, they do not characterize it as I have. *See* T. Oka, "China charts its own course," the *CHRISTIAN SCIENCE MONITOR*, June 30-July 6, 1984, at 14 (int'l. ed.).

121. This campaign to "consolidate" the Party has in fact been characterized as a purge by one well-informed observer. *See* HSIA & JOHNSON, *supra* note 108, at 30-31.

122. "Amendments to the Constitution of the People's Republic of China," enacted by the National People's Congress on 12 April 1988, contained in *COLLECTED LAWS OF THE PEOPLE'S REPUBLIC OF CHINA* [*Zhonghua renmen gongheguo fa Lu quan shu*] (1989) at 17.

123. *Editor's Note.* In the spring of 1989, policy conflicts among top Chinese leaders culminating in the purge of Zhao Ziyang, the historical visit of Soviet President Mikhail Gorbachev (May 15-18), and a dramatic student led Democracy Movement initially tolerated by the regime, drew transfixed world media attention to Beijing's political life. Events climaxed in Tienanmen Square on the night of June 3-4 when martial law troops called in by Li Peng and Deng Xiaoping massacred about 1,000 civilians and returned China to "hard line" rule. In mid-1991 this policy seemed to continue compatibly with a semi-capitalist approach to ecconomic issues. For detail and perspective, see Lowell Dittmer, "China in 1989: The Crisis of Incomplete Reform," ASIAN SURVEY, April, 1990, 331; and Ann Kent, "Waiting for Rights: China's Human Rights and China's Constitutions, 1949-1989," HUMAN RIGHTS QUARTERLY, Vol.13, No.2, May, 1991, 170.

THE REPUBLIC OF CHINA (TAIWAN)

The Constitution and Government
of The Republic of China*

Chi-tung Lin

Herbert H. P. Ma

Introduction

A constitution is the fundamental law that stipulates the basic organization of a country and the rights and duties of its people. This concept of constitution originated in ancient Greece and Rome, and was well developed in England during the Middle Ages. In the late eighteenth century individualists and liberals strenuously advocated respecting the individual, especially his or her liberties. And in the wake of the Industrial Revolution, the people urgently wanted a free economy and opposed autocratic politics. Thus the movement for the people's rights spread throughout Europe and America. Constitutions in those countries were mainly laws regarding the structure of government and guarantees of people's rights. The formation and functions of a government were stipulated by the constitution. Rights and duties of citizens were also stipulated by the constitution; the former were not to be improperly restricted, while the latter were not to be improperly increased. Therefore, constitutions in this sense, were a development of Western culture. They resulted from Western political thought and economic situations. The Republic of China, on the other hand, did not have the same cultural tradition as the West. Chinese political thought and economic development have been quite different from those of the West. Therefore, for the Republic of China, a constitution is a cultural transplant. Though there are some elements of Chinese national culture in its constitutionalism, they are far less than the transplanted components.

Secondly, the Republic of China was the first country in the East to adopt a democratic form of government. Through the efforts of numerous people inspired by lofty ideals, it was established only after a revolution terminating a thousands-of-years-long tradition of autocratic politics. Ideally, when the old autocratic regime was overthrown, realizing democratic constitutionalism and laying down a constitution should have been straightforward and easy.

However, the influence of thousands of years of autocratic traditions was hard to eradicate and the establishment of democratic constitutionalism had not yet become the desire of all the people. Moreover, to maintain their vested interests and authority, the warlord bureaucrats made every effort to obstruct the constitutional movement. The imperialists also did not want China to establish democratic constitutionalism and become a prosperous and powerful country. So they too sabotaged constitutionalist efforts. As a result, although Chinese people with a broad vision led the constitutionalist movement as early as the late nineteenth century, and the voice of constitutionalism got ever louder and louder, the few informal constitutions written after the Republic was established in 1912 were basically nominal and rarely implemented. After China had endured many ups and downs, China and the Allies defeated Japan in 1945; there was great hope of restabilizing the social order. The Constitution of the Republic of China was finally adopted by the National Assembly on December 25, 1946, and became effective on December 25, 1947. Although the Chinese constitutionalist movement began long ago, the current Chinese constitution is the first constitution worthy of the name. Therefore, the Constitution of the Republic of China, less than half a century old, is a constitution that remains to be tested and developed.

Finally, when reviewing the Constitution and the government of the Republic of China, one should notice the following facts. When the Constitution was first being made, the Communist armed forces, opposing the government, already held cities and towns in many parts of the country. Not long after the Constitution became effective, the Communists with the help of the Russians expanded day by day and seized almost the whole of Mainland China by the summer of 1949. Then the government retreated to Taiwan. Since the Constitution was the fundamental law of the whole country, the ruling party Kuomintang would not slight it because of the fall of the Mainland. It was true that to ensure the security of the last bastion against the Chinese Communists, the National Assembly adopted the Temporary Provisions Effective During the Period of Mobilization for Suppression of the Communist Rebellion [hereafter referred to as the Temporary Provisions] which restrict the application of certain parts of the Constitution, and martial law was also declared over the area of Taiwan and neighboring islands. In fact, however, except in a few special circumstances, to be dealt with later, the formation of governmental organizations, the appointment of government functionaries, and the conducting of governmental administration continued to be based on the Constitution. The prevailing peace and stability enjoyed by the society in Taiwan as a whole has also made it unnecessary to apply such measures as authorized by martial law. In other words, for more than thirty-five years, even though Taiwan has faced a threatening Communist regime across the Taiwan Straits, and often found herself on the brink of war, the Constitution has never been revised and the operation of the government has generally been conformable to the Constitution. It is significant that, although living under extraordinary circumstances, the democratic constitutional government of the Republic of China has nevertheless progressed gradually and steadily. Among other things, the implementation of local self-government of the *hsien* or countries and municipalities, the strengthening of the guarantee of the freedom of person, the putting into effect of a system of state damage-indemnity, and the rearrangement of the judicial courts and the procuracies are all particularly important measures carried out in accordance with the Constitution. Above all, the government's recent decision to life martial law over Taiwan on July 15, 1987, marked a further stride towards the realization of a constitutional democracy.

The History of the Constitution of the Republic of China

The history of the Chinese constitutional movement is quite long.[1] During the last stage of the Ching dynasty (1644-1912), the government was very corrupt and incompetent, and the people suffered untold hardships. Imperialists' aggression was so increasingly serious that the state faced the possibility of being conquered. In the late 1800s, Kang You-wei, Liang Chi-Chiao, and others began to advocate making a constitution to restrict the monarch's power, to guarantee the people's rights, and to provide a basis for all government measures. At first, the Ching government ignored such demands. But later, it became difficult for the government to hold back the mammoth and repeated anti-government movements led by Dr. Sun Yat-sen (1866-1925). To mitigate the people's opposition, the Ching government pretended that it would draw up a constitution in a timely fashion to limit the monarch's power and guarantee the people's rights. However, the irresistible anti-government democratic movement grew like wildfire, and in 1912, the Revolution overthrew the Ching government and founded the Republic of China.

After the establishment of the Republic of China, the great founding fathers of the new state, keenly aware of the importance of making a constitution, drew up a provisional Constitution, elected an interim President, and organized a national congress. The Congress then made great efforts in the drafting of the constitution, but the then President Yuan Shih-kai, attempting to establish an empire with himself as the emperor, disbanded the uncooperative congress and drove out the antimonarchial congressmen.

Though Yuan Shih-kai's monarchy campaign did not succeed because of opposition from all circles, the movement to draw up a constitution suffered a grave reverse. Later on, tangled fighting between [regional] warlords make the political situation unstable for years, thereby interrupting the making of a constitution. Though a constitution was hastily drawn up in 1927 at the instigation of the warlords, it was not accepted by all sides concerned. Therefore, before the Northern Expedition of the National Revolutionary Army (in 1926-27), there was no formal constitution.

In 1927, aiming at overthrowing the warlords' political power and putting into practice the Three Principles of the People, the National Revolutionary Army took a mass pledge and launched the Northern Expedition. In one year it drove out the warlords of the southern provinces and founded the National Government in Nanking. According to the teaching of Dr. Sun Yat-sen, the whole process for reconstructing the state was to be divided into three periods: the military period, the period of political tutelage, and the constitutional period. In the military period, the key task would be sweeping away all anti-revolutionary forces. During the second period of political tutelage, the key task would be the institution of local self-government and training the people to exercise the four powers of election, recall, initiative, and referendum. When more than half the provinces had realized local self-government, a National Assembly would be convened and a constitution would be laid down. With this the state would enter its constitutional period. This plan was well-conceived and provided for an orderly and step-by-step procedure. It was very suitable for a China with a long-standing tradition of autocracy. In the beginning, in accordance with Dr. Sun Yat-sen's teachings, the National Government did not attempt to draw up a formal constitution. But eventually, the National Assembly met and in 1937 drew up a Provisional Constitution for the Period of Political Tutelage. This was promulgated by the National Government and became effective on July 1, 1937.

Unexpectedly, Japanese warlords invaded the provinces in Northeast China (Manchuria) and seized cities and towns, beginning on September 18, 1931. Since the local authorities thought that the League of Nations could handle this situation, and took the policy of non-resistance, all of the Northeast Provinces were lost. Japanese warlords then became more swollen with arrogance and accelerated their intrusion into North China. In the face of such strong enemy pressure, there was a public outcry throughout the country, demanding an effective response. Some people advocated drawing up a formal constitution earlier than planned, practicing constitutionalism, and using this to unify the people of the whole nation to resist Japanese aggression. The authorities accepted this idea, and the Legislative Yuan of the

National Government started drawing up the constitution. After being revised several times over the years, the Draft Constitution of the Republic of China was promulgated by the National Government on May 5, 1936. Thus, this document is usually called "the May 5th Draft Constitution." The plan was to convene the National Assembly on November 12, 1937, and lay down a formal constitution based on the May 5th Draft. But with the Japanese invasion of Lugochiao and some other places in Hopei Province on July 7, 1937, a full-scale Anti-Japanese War erupted, and the planned convocation of the National Assembly and the making of the constitution were postponed.

With the defeat of Japan in September 1945, China recovered its lost territories. The government hoped to convene promptly the National Assembly to draft a constitution, thus beginning to put constitutionalism into practice. But the Communists, seizing the opportunity of the Anti-Japanese War, had captured a large territory, had improved their military equipment, and had become quite powerful. Thus war between the Communists and the government became an imminent danger. Since neither the government nor the people wanted a civil war after the eight-year-long anti-Japanese War, and since friendly countries wished that all important post-war issues could be settled through political consultations, a Political Consultative Conference was convened on January 10, 1946, in Chungking. Representatives from the Kuomintang (Nationalist Party, KMT), the Youth Party, the Democratic League, and the Communist Party, along with a number of other prominent personages were present at the conference. The resolutions for a draft constitution agreed to by the Consultative Conference read as follows:

1. *The National Assembly*: The whole people exercise the Four Powers of election, recall, initiative and referendum. There will be a National Assembly. Before instituting election of the President by a general election, the President is to be elected by an electoral organ composed of people from legislative assemblies at the central, provincial, and *hsien* levels. The recall of the President is to be done the same way as the election of the President. The exercise of the powers of initiative and referendum were to be stipulated by law.

2. *The Legislative Yuan*: The Legislative Yuan will be the highest legislative organ of the state. It is to be elected directly by the people. Its function and powers are equivalent to those of the legislative assemblies in other democratic countries.

3. *The Control Yuan*: The Control Yuan will be the highest control organ of the state. It is to be elected by the legislative assemblies of the provinces and the autonomous regions of different peoples. Its functions and powers are consent, impeachment and control.

4. *The Judicial Yuan*: The Judicial Yuan is to be the highest court of the state. However, it is not itself in charge of judicial administration. It shall have a number of Grand Justices nominated by the President of the Republic and appointed by him with the consent of the Control Yuan. All levels of judges shall be independent of party affiliations.

5. *The Examination Yuan*: The Examination Yuan will function in a collective fashion. The Examination Yuan Members shall be nominated by the President and appointed by him with the consent of the Control Yuan. It is chiefly in charge of examinations of government functionaries and professional workers. The Examination Yuan Members shall be independent of party affiliations.

6. *The Executive Yuan*: The Executive Yuan is to be the highest executive organ of the state. The President of the Executive Yuan will be nominated by the President of the Republic and appointed by him with the consent of the Legislative Yuan. The Executive Yuan is responsible to the Legislative Yuan. If the Legislative Yuan loses confidence in the Executive Yuan, the President of the Executive Yuan shall either resign or ask the President of the Republic to disband the Legislative Yuan. But no President of the Executive Yuan may ask twice for the disbanding of the Legislative Yuan.

7. *Emergency Decrees*: By resolution of the Executive Yuan, the President of the Republic may issue emergency decrees in accordance with law. Such a decree shall be presented to the Legislative Yuan within one month after issuance. The power of the President of the Republic to convene meetings of the Presidents of all the Yuans need not be stipulated.

8. *Local Government*: The province is the highest unit of local self-government. The governor of a province is elected by the people of the province. A province may make a constitution, but it may not contravene the constitution of the Republic.

On this basis, the Draft Constitution of the Republic of China was drawn up, and the National Government submitted it to the Constitution-making National Assembly for examination and approval. The resolutions concerning the Draft Constitution agreed to by the Political Consultative Conference became the principles of the Constitution of the Republic of China. Most of these principles represented points of view common in Western countries with parliamentary systems and were not particularly suited to China's conditions or in line with Dr. Sun Yat-sen's teachings. Therefore, when the Draft Constitution was first brought up, it was strongly opposed by the representatives of the Constitution-making National Assembly. However, at that time, war clouds were gathering; the Communist armed forces were already advancing south. Under these circumstances, the National Assembly did not want to disband without results, and so adopted the Constitution of the Republic of China on December 25, 1946 after much negotiation and compromise. The Constitution was to become effective on December 25, 1947.

With this brief review of constitutional history, we must now consider the "Temporary Provisions Effective During the Period of Mobilization for Suppression of Communist Rebellion" [the Temporary Provisions], because these Provisions are closely related to the powers of the government and the rights of the people during the period of Communist rebellion. Some stipulations of the Constitution were temporarily not put into practice owing to the effects of the Temporary Provisions.

As stated above, under the influence of the Political Consultative Conference, the Constitution of the Republic of China was at many points not suited to China's conditions and Dr. Sun Yat-sen's teachings. Even while the Constitution was being made, many delegates to the Constitution-making National Assembly pointed to shortcomings in of the Constitution, and proposed that it be amended. However, since the Constitution had just been implemented, most delegates thought that amendment at that time, would diminish the sanctity of the cardinal law and that chaos might result. On the other hand, the Communists had already launched an armed rebellion. Thus, if the provisions of the Constitution excessively restricted government powers, the government would be hard put to deal with dangerous situations. Weighing the advantages and disadvantages, the government finally decided to keep the Constitution intact, only to be amended within the next two years. Instead, some other way would be found, by which the government could have the power to adapt to changing circumstances without being restricted by the Constitution. Thus, with the understanding of the delegates, the Temporary Provisions were adopted by the First Meeting of the National Assembly and promulgated by the National Government on May 10, 1948. As the Temporary Provisions were amended several times later, these were called the "First Temporary Provisions." They read as follows:

> In accordance with Article 174, Section 1 of the Constitution, (the National Assembly) hereby lays down Temporary Provisions Effective During the Period of Communist Rebellion as follows. During the Period of Mobilization for Suppression of Communist Rebellion to prevent the nation or the people from suffering imminent dangers or to deal with serious unforeseen economic or financial crisis, the President may, by the resolution of the council of the Executive Yuan, take emergency measures without being restricted by Articles 39 or 43 of the Constitution. The Legislative Yuan may modify or cancel the above-stated emergency measures in accordance with Article 57, Section 2 of the Constitution. The termination of the Period of Communist Rebellion is to be announced by the President himself or upon the request of the Legislative Yuan. The President shall convene a temporary meeting of the First National Assembly by December 25, 1950 at the latest to discuss the proposals on the amendment of the Constitution. If at this time the termination of the Period for Mobilization for Suppression of Communist Rebellion is not announced according to the above stipulation, the Temporary meeting of the First National Assembly shall decide whether to prolong or to cancel the Temporary Provisions.

According to these stipulations, the Temporary Provisions were merely of a transient nature; they were not intended to be permanent. However, the government suffered setbacks in the war of suppressing the Communists, lost the Mainland of China, and the Central Government had to move to Taiwan. For the past forty years, the nation has been in an unusual situation and has not been able to reestablish the normal constitutional order. Therefore, the Temporary Provisions were not abolished until 1991. Rather, to meet the needs of the nation's unusual situation, they were amended four times. The latest amendment was made on March 23, 1970, and reads as follows:

> In accordance with Article 174, Section 1 of the Constitution, (the National Assembly) hereby lays down the Temporary Provisions Effective During the Period of Mobilization for Suppression of Communist Rebellion (hereafter, the Period of Mobilization) as follows:

1. During the Period of Mobilization, to prevent the nation or the people from suffering imminent dangers to deal with serious unforeseen economic or financial crisis, the President may, by resolution of the council of the executive Yuan, take emergency measures without being restricted by Articles 39 and 43 of the Constitution.

2. The Legislative Yuan may modify or cancel the above stated emergency measures in accordance with Article 57, Section 2 of the Constitution.

3. During the Period of Mobilization, the President and the Vice President are eligible for reelection without being subject to the restriction of two terms as prescribed by Article 47 of the Constitution.

4. During the Period of Mobilization on the basis of the constitutional system, the President is authorized to set up an *ad hoc* organ to determine policies concerning national mobilization and the suppression of the rebellion, and to deal with governmental affairs in zones of combat.

5. To meet the needs for suppressing the communist rebellion, the President may make adjustments in the central government's administrative and personnel organizations and their structure.

6. During the Period of Mobilization, the President may, in accordance with the following provisions, issue measures to strengthen the central parliamentary bodies of people's representatives without being restricted by Articles 26, 64, and 91 of the Constitution.

(1)   In the free regions, the allotted number of people's representatives in central parliamentary bodies shall be increased, and the representatives shall be elected at regular intervals; in case the Legislative Yuan Members and Control Yuan Members that should be elected by the Chinese nationals residing abroad, cannot in fact be elected, the President may issue measures to choose them.

(2)   The people's representatives in central parliamentary bodies of the first term shall be elected by the people of the whole nation and shall exercise their powers in accordance with law. This provision also applies to such representatives who are chosen by extra election or by-election. The delegates to the National Assembly who are chosen by extra election shall be elected every six years. The Legislative Yuan Members shall serve a term of three years and the Control Yuan Members shall serve a term of six years.

7. During the Period of Mobilization, the National Assembly may, without being restricted by Article 27, Section 2 of the Constitution, issue

measures regarding the exercise of the initiative and the referendum of central law.

8. When the National Assembly is not in session, a research organ shall be set up to deliberate on constitutional matters.

9. The termination of the Period of Mobilization shall be announced by the President.

10. The amendment and the abolishment of the Temporary Provisions shall be determined by the National Assembly."

From the above description, it is apparent that the amended Temporary Provisions were more extensive than the first Temporary Provisions, and that there were many differences regarding the exercise of government powers and the rights of the people between these amended Temporary Provisions and the Constitution. This was because of the special situation of the Period of Mobilization. However, owing to the very stable situation in Taiwan over the last ten years or more, although the Temporary Provisions entrusted great powers to the President, successive Presidents have exercised their powers quite discretely in order to guard the sanctity of the Constitution.

The Safeguard of the Rights of the People

The Constitution of the Republic of China consists of fourteen chapters; there are 175 Articles in all. Chapter 1, General Provisions, deals with the national polity, citizenship, the territory of the state, and so on. Chapter 2 treats the rights and duties of the people. Chapter 3 deals with the National Assembly; Chapter 4 the President; Chapter 5, the administration; Chapter 6, legislation; Chapter 7, the judiciary; Chapter 8, the examination system; and Chapter 9, the control system. Chapter 10 treats the powers of the central and local governments. Chapter 11 sets up the system of local government. Chapter 12 deals with elections, recall, initiative, and referendum. Chapter 14 is on enforcement and amendment of the Constitution. Although the Constitution has many chapters totaling 175 Articles, the key points are the safeguarding of the rights of the people, the main government organs and their powers, and the system of local government. This chapter will, therefore, deal with these points only.[2]

In the Chinese Constitution, there are quite a number of articles safeguarding the people's rights, and these articles are very similar to those in the constitutions of many countries after World War II. Some of the more significant ones are as follows:

The guarantee of freedom of person.

The freedom of person is the basis of many other freedoms. Only if the freedom of person is well guaranteed, may the people enjoy other freedoms. Hence, Article 8 of the Constitution has the following detailed provisions:

Freedom of person shall be guaranteed to the people. Except in case of *flagrante delicto* as otherwise provided for by law, no person shall be arrested or detained except by a judicial or a police organ in compliance with legal procedure. No person may be tried or punished except by a law court in accordance with legal procedure. Any arrest, detention, trial, or punishment, if not conducted in accordance with legal procedure, may be refused.

When a person is arrested or detained on suspicion of having committed a crime, the organ making the arrest or detention shall in writing inform the said person and his designated relatives or friends of the grounds for the arrest or detention, and shall, within twenty-four hours, turn him over to a competent court for trial. The said person or any other person, may petition the competent court that a writ be served within twenty-four hours on the organ making the arrest for the surrender of the said person for trial.

The court may not reject the petition mentioned in the preceding section, nor shall it order the organ concerned to make an investigation and report first. The organ concerned may not refuse to execute or delay in executing the writ of the court for surrender of the said person for trial.

When a person is arrested or detained illegally, he or any other person may petition the court for investigation. The court may not reject such a petition, and shall, within twenty-four hours, make the investigation with the organ concerned, and proceed with the case in accordance with law.

Article 9 stipulates that "Except for those in active military service, no person may be subject to trial by a military court." The Constitution attaches great importance to the protection of the freedom of person. In addition, the Council of Grand Justices of the Judicial Yuan, which is the guardian of the Constitution, has elaborated the meaning of Article 8 in its Interpretations *Shih Tsu* Nos. 130, 166, and 251 so that the protection of freedom of person is even more effective.[3]

The guarantee of the right of existence.

What is called the right of existence is the right of citizens to ask the state to guarantee their existence. The state should not merely passively avoid infringing upon this right of existence, but should actively take measures to insure that citizens can enjoy a healthy and cultured life.

In the twentieth century, the theory of the welfare state is prevalent in many countries which hold that the purpose of the state is to work for the welfare of the people. Therefore, many of the new constitutions of different countries guarantee the right of existence. In the Constitution, it is also stipulated in Article 176 that "the right of existence, the right of work, and the right of property shall be guaranteed to the people." What is more, the guarantee of the right of existence is put before the guarantee of the right of work and property. As described in its Preamble, the Constitution is made in accordance with Dr. Sun Yat-sen's teachings about the foundation of the Republic of China. Since the Principle of People's Livelihood is one of Dr. Sun's chief teachings, to carry out this principle, the right of existence must necessarily be valued. In the Constitution, stipulations guaranteeing the right of existence are found not only in Article 15, but also in Chapter 13--Fundamental National Policies--which has many articles concerning the right of existence. Some of these are as follows:

Article 153. The state, in order to improve the livelihood of laborers and farmers and to increase their technical skill for production, shall enact laws and carry out policies for their protection.

Article 155. The state, in order to promote social welfare, shall enforce a social insurance system. To the aged, the infirm, and the disabled who are unable to earn a living, and to victims of unusual calamities, the state shall extend appropriate assistance and relief.

Article 156. The state, in order to secure the foundation of national existence and development, shall protect motherhood and carry out the policy of promoting the welfare of women and children.

Article 157. The state, in order to improve national health, shall establish extensive sanitation and health protection enterprises and socialized medical services.

Article 160. All children of school age from six to twelve years shall receive free primary education and those who are poor shall be supplied with textbooks by the government. All citizens beyond school age, who have not received primary education shall receive free supplementary education and shall also be supplied with textbooks by the government.

The Constitution not only abstractly guarantees the right of existence, but also has many concrete stipulations to that effect. The government promulgates and executes laws distributing land to the tillers, protecting laborers, guaranteeing the welfare of the aged and children, and so on, and establishes various institutions for realizing social security.

A direct guarantee approach to the guarantee of the people's rights.

The constitutions of some countries use direct guarantee schemes, while others use indirect guarantees. In the former, neither executive, judicial, nor legislative organs may restrict on their own authority the people's rights which are guaranteed directly by the constitution. In the latter, the legislative organs, when necessary, may make laws to restrict the people's rights. Of the two, direct guarantee schemes are, of course, more thorough in their guarantee of the people's rights. The Constitution of the Republic of China takes this approach and stipulates in Article 23 that "No one of the freedoms and rights enumerated in the preceding articles may be restricted by law, except as warranted by reason of preventing infringements of the freedom of other persons, averting an imminent crisis, maintaining social order, or advancing the public interest."

The institution of a state damage-indemnity system.

The old idea was that the relation between the state and the people was a relation between ruler and the ruled, and that there could not be a problem of indemnity by the ruler for damage to the ruled. Therefore, when a public functionary was in violation of the law while he was performing his duties and if he infringed upon the rights of any person, the injured person could claim indemnity only from the functionary and not from the state. However, the modern idea is that the relation between the state and the people is a relationship of rights and duties under law. Therefore, on the one hand, the state, within the limits permitted by law, has the rights to issue mandatory orders to the people. On the other hand, when a state-employed functionary violates the law while performing his duties and infringes upon the rights of a person, the injured person can claim indemnity from the state because the functionary is employed by the state. After World War I, the German "Weimar Constitution" of 1919 took the lead in incorporating this modern idea. Many of the constitutions made after World War II followed this example and instituted a system of state damage-indemnity; one was the Constitution of the Republic of China. Article 24 stipulates:

Any public functionary who, in violation of law, infringes upon the freedom or right of any person shall, besides being subject to disciplinary measures in accordance with law, be responsible under criminal and civil laws.   The injured person may, in accordance with law, also claim indemnity from the state for damage sustained.

As a result of the above stipulation, a state damage-indemnity system was adopted with many laws. However, unity was lacking. To make the system more complete, the government promulgated a State-Indemnity Law on June 2, 1980, which provides in detail the grounds for and the means of indemnity, the duty of indemnity and its limits, the procedure for claiming indemnity, and other related matters.[4]

The Central Government

The National Assembly

One of the differences between the Constitution of the Republic of China and those of other countries is that, in the organization of the central government, there is a National Assembly, and besides the usual legislative, executive, and judicial organs, there are also organs of Examination and Control.

The setting up of the National Assembly is based on Dr. Sun Yat-sen's theory of division of political and administrative powers. Dr. Sun held that under the allegedly democratic parliamentary system of many countries, after the election of legislators the people could attend to nothing and in fact they did not have any real power. On the other hand, the government, restrained at every turn by the parliament, could not play its role of bringing benefits to the people. Therefore, Dr. Sun deemed it necessary to institute a division of powers and functions so that consideration could be given to both democracy and effective government. That is, the people would have powers and the government would be able to perform its functions. On the part of the people, besides the power to elect and to be elected, they have also the powers of recall, initiative, and referendum. When a legislator or important government official is in violation of law or derelict of duty, the people may recall him. When the parliament does not make laws that it should make, the people may practice their power of initiative to impel it to make such laws. When the parliament makes improper laws, the people may practice their power of referendum to abolish them, to redress the shortcomings of the parliamentary system and carry out democratic politics more thoroughly. As for the government, it can perform its functions without being unreasonably constrained by the parliament, because it has the people as its support. With the above theory of division of powers and functions, the people have powers to make the most of democratic politics, while the government can best function to bring benefits to the people, thus in keeping with the demands of current welfare states.

In local political affairs, this theory is not difficult to put into practice because the area and population are not large. But in central political affairs, because of the very large area and population of the whole country, there would be many difficulties for the citizens of the country in the exercise of their four powers of election, recall, initiative, and referendum. In fact these four powers could hardly be put into real practice. It is especially difficult in China to achieve such democracy because of the extremely large area and population of the country. Therefore, the "Outline of National Reconstruction" drafted by Dr. Sun Yat-sen, stipulates in Article 9 that "In a completely autonomous *hsien* (county), citizens shall have the powers of direct election, direct recall, direct initiative, and direct referendum" so that people's powers will be put into effect more thoroughly. In central political affairs, however, the Outline stipulates in Article 14 that "After the setting up of the local autonomous government of a *hsien*, a National Assembly delegate shall be elected to participate in a deputation and attend to central public affairs." Article 24 stipulates that "After the promulgation of the Constitution, the National Assembly shall have the powers of election and recall over central government officials, and the powers of initiative and referendum towards central laws." It is thus clear that, according to the Outline of National Reconstruction, the central political powers are exercised by the National Assembly representing citizens of the whole nation and are not exercised directly by the citizens. Hence, under the system of division of powers and functions, the National Assembly is set up to exercise central political powers.

In accordance with Dr. Sun Yat-sen's teachings, the May 5th Draft (1936) of the Constitution of the Republic of China set up a National Assembly. On its organization and powers, the Draft read as follows:[5]

1. The election of the delegates to the National Assembly "The National Assembly shall be composed of the following delegates: (1) One delegate to be elected by every *hsien*, municipality or area of an equivalent status. In case the population exceeds 300,000, an additional delegate for every 500,000. (2) The number of delegates to be elected from Mongolia and Tibet shall be determined by law" (Art. 27). "The election of the delegates to the National Assembly shall be through universal, equal, and direct suffrage by secret ballot" (Art. 28). "Any citizen of the Republic of China who has attained the age of twenty years shall have the right to vote in accordance with   law. Any citizen having attained the age of twenty-five shall have the right of being elected in accordance with law" (Art. 30).

2. *The term of office and convocation of the delegates to the National Assembly.* "The delegates to the National Assembly shall be elected for a term of six years. A delegate to the National Assembly may, when in violation of the law or derelict of duty, be recalled by his constituency in accordance with the law" (Art. 30). "The National Assembly shall be summoned by the President to meet every three years and every session shall last one month. When necessary, sessions may be extended for an additional month. Upon the petition of more than two-fifths of the delegates, the National Assembly itself may hold an extraordinary session. The President may convene an extraordinary session of the National Assembly." (Art. 31).

3. *The functions and powers of the National Assembly.* (1) Election of the President and the Vice-President, the President and the Vice-President of the Legislative Yuan, the President and the Vice-President of the Control Yuan, Legislative Yuan members, and Control Yuan members. (2) Recall of the President and the Vice-President, the Presidents and the Vice-Presidents of the Legislative Yuan, the Judicial Yuan, the Examination Yuan, and the Control Yuan, Legislative Yuan members, and Control Yuan members. (3)Initiation of laws. (4) Referendum on laws. (5) Amendment of laws. (6) Other functions and powers given by the Constitution, e.g., resolutions on alterations national territory. (Art. 32).

Though the May 5th Draft's stipulations on the National Assembly were quite in keeping with Dr. Sun Yat-sen's teachings, it had significant shortcomings. First, because the number of the delegates to the National Assembly was nearly 2,000, it would face many difficulties in convening and exercising its powers. Second, because the National Assembly was to hold its sessions as infrequently as every three years, and since every session was to be as brief as one month, there would again be many difficulties in the actual exercise of its powers.

Because of these shortcomings in the May 5th Draft, many people put forward proposals for improvement. When the Political Consultative Conference discussed the principles of the draft of the Constitution, some people advocated abandoning the concept of a National Assembly. But because of the firm position of the ruling Kuomintang, it was decided to institute such an Assembly, as mentioned earlier. Since the other political parties and groups did not favor the institution of a National Assembly, and since the current Constitution is largely the outcome of compromises among the opinions of various quarters, the National Assembly as instituted in the current Constitution was very limited in its powers. The stipulations of the current Constitution regarding the organization, functions and powers of the National Assembly are as follows:

> The National Assembly shall be composed of the following delegates: (2) Delegates to be elected by each *hsien*, municipality, or area of equivalent states; (2) delegates to be elected by Mongolia; (3) delegates to be elected by Tibet; (4) delegates to be elected by various racial groups in the border regions; (5) delegates to be elected by Chinese nationals residing abroad; (6) delegates to be elected by occupational groups; (7) delegates to be elected by women's organizations. (Art. 26).

As a result, the composition of the National Assembly is very complicated and the total number as stipulated by law may be as large as 3,000.

The functions and powers of the National Assembly are: (1) to elect the President and the Vice-President; (2) to recall the President and Vice-President; (3) to amend the Constitution; and (4) to exercise referendum on amendments to the Constitution proposed by the Legislative Yuan.

> With respect to the exercise of the powers of initiative and referendum, except as stipulated in items three and four of the preceding paragraph, the National Assembly shall institute measures pertaining thereto and enforce them, after the said two powers shall have been exercised in one-half of the *hsien* and municipalities of the whole country. (Art. 27).

According to Article 4 of the Constitution, the territory of the Republic of China shall not be altered except by resolution of the National Assembly. "The National Assembly shall be summoned by the President ninety days prior to the date of expiration of each presidential term" (Art. 29). According to Article 47 of the Constitution, the term of office of the President shall be six years; that is why the National Assembly shall meet just once every six years. According to Article 30 of the Constitution, "The National Assembly may in any of the following circumstances, convene an extraordinary session: (1) When, in accordance with the provisions of Article 49 of this Constitution, it is necessary to elect a new President and a new Vice-President. (2) When, in accordance with a resolution of the Control Yuan, an impeachment against the President or the Vice-President is instituted. (3) When in accordance with a resolution of the Legislative Yuan, an amendment to the Constitution is proposed. (4) When such a session is requested by over two-fifths of the delegates to the National Assembly.

Delegates to the National Assembly shall be elected every six years. The term of office of the delegates to each National Assembly shall terminate on the day of convocation of the next National Assembly." (Art. 28).

The National Assembly in the Chinese Constitution is a very large organization and represents a very wide cross-section of the nation. But the opportunities for the National Assembly to exercise its functions and powers are very limited because it convenes just once every six years. Moreover, with regard to the nature of functions and powers exercised, under normal conditions, the chances of exercising such important powers as amendment of the Constitution, alteration of national territory, and recall of the President or Vice-President are very rare. The powers which the National Assembly routinely exercises are no more than the election of the President and the Vice-President. This is not only not in keeping with Dr. Sun Yat-sen's teachings which place great importance on the National Assembly, but also obviously unreasonable, judging from the organization, powers and functions of the National Assembly. It is widely held that when the Constitution is amended in the future, the section dealing with the National Assembly will be in particular need of amendment.

Nevertheless, soon after the Constitution was implemented, the nation entered a period of communist rebellion. Under such unusual conditions, the National Assembly actually gave full play to some of its functions. In addition to electing the President and the Vice-President every six years in accordance with the Constitution, what is most notable is that, in accordance with the procedure of amendment of the Constitution stipulated in Article 174 of the Constitution, the National Assembly enacted the Temporary Provisions (described earlier) on May 10, 1948, and later, amended them to suit the unusual needs of this Period of Mobilization without contravening the original systems of the Constitution.[6]

The President[7]

The Constitution of the Republic of China, before dealing with the administrative, legislative, and judicial powers, devotes Chapter 4 to the office of the President. What are the President's powers? According to the Constitution, he is similar to the President in a presidential system of government in some ways and also similar to the head of state of a cabinet system of government in other ways. He has a style of his own. The President has quite a few powers though not as many as the President in a presidential system of government.

The President of the Republic of China is similar to the head of state of a cabinet system of government. For instance, Article 37 stipulates: "The President shall, in accordance with law, promulgate laws and issue ordinances with the counter-signature of the President of the Executive Yuan." Article 55 stipulates: "The President of the Executive Yuan shall be appointed by the President of the Republic with the consent of the Legislative Yuan." Article 56 provides: "The Vice-President, the heads of the various ministries and commissions, and the ministers without portfolio of the Executive Yuan, shall be appointed by the President of the Executive Yuan." Article 57 stipulates: "The Executive Yuan shall be responsible to the Legislative Yuan in accordance with the following provisions: The Executive Yuan has the responsibility to present to the Legislative Yuan a statement of its administrative policies and a report on its administration. Legislative Yuan members have, in the sessions of the Legislative Yuan, the right to interpolate the President of the Executive Yuan and the heads of the various ministries and commissions of the Executive Yuan."

There are also differences between the President of the Republic of China and the head of state of a cabinet system of government. First, in a cabinet system, most cabinet members are legislators. At the same time, members of the legislative organ may also hold posts in the executive organ and vice versa. In a presidential system of government, legislators may not concurrently hold an executive office. In this regard, the Constitution follows the presidential system of government and stipulates in Article 75 that no Legislative Yuan member may concurrently hold an executive office. Second, in a cabinet system of government, when a deadlock is reached between the legislative and executive organs, either the legislature casts a vote of no-confidence towards the cabinet, or the executive organ disbands the parliament. The Constitution of the Republic of China is more similar to that of the United States in this regard: "If the Legislative Yuan dissents to any important policy of the Executive Yuan, it may by resolution, ask the Executive Yuan to alter such policy. With respect to such a resolution, the Executive Yuan may, with the approval of the President of the Republic, request that the Legislative Yuan reconsider. If, upon reconsideration, two-thirds of the members of the Legislative Yuan attending the meeting uphold the original resolution, the President of the Executive Yuan shall either abide by the same or resign from office." "If the Executive Yuan deems a resolution passed by the Legislative Yuan on a statutory, budgetary, or treaty bill difficult of execution, it may, with the approval of the President of the Republic, request within ten days after its delivery to the Executive Yuan, that the Legislative Yuan reconsider the said resolution. If upon reconsideration, two-thirds of the members of the Legislative Yuan attending the meeting uphold the original resolution, the President of the Executive Yuan shall either abide by the same or resign from office." (Art. 57).

From the above provisions it is apparent that when there are significant divergences between the Executive Yuan and the Legislative Yuan, that is when significant political conflicts arise, the method of reconsideration is used to settle them. Only when approved by the President of the Republic can the Executive Yuan request that the Legislative Yuan reconsider, and once reconsideration is requested, if the Executive Yuan is upheld by just one-third of the members of the Legislative Yuan attending the meeting, the Executive Yuan can win. The success or failure of the Executive Yuan in requesting such reconsideration depends largely on whether or not it is approved by the President of the Republic. Therefore, the President of the Republic holds a decisive power when a significant political issue arises. In this regard, the President also differs from the head of state in a cabinet form of government.

The President in the Constitution of the Republic of China has quite substantial powers. Furthermore, as mentioned earlier, according to the Temporary Provisions, the President is given larger powers. Nevertheless, determined to carry out the national policy of advancing democratic constitutionalism, successive Presidents have exercised powers given by the Temporary Provisions with great restraint and in few cases. There are also similarities between the functions and powers of the President of the Republic of China and those of the head of state of many countries:

1. The President is the head of the state and represents the Republic of China in official foreign relations (Art. 25).
2. The President commands the land, sea, and air forces of the whole country (Art. 36).
3. The President shall, in accordance with law, promulgate laws and issue ordinances with the counter-signature of the President of the Executive Yuan (Art. 37).
4. The President, in accordance with the provisions of this Constitution, exercises the power to conclude treaties, to declare war, and to make peace (Art. 38).
5. The President may, in accordance with law, declare martial law with the approval or confirmation of the Legislative Yuan. When the

Legislative Yuan deems it necessary, it may by resolution request the President to rescind such martial law (Art. 39).

6. The President exercises under law the power to grant general amnesties, pardons, remission of sentences, and restitution of civil rights (Art. 40).

7. The President, in accordance with law, appoints and removes civil and military officers (Article 41).

8. In case of natural calamity, epidemic, or a serious national financial or economic crisis necessitating emergency actions, the President, during the recess of the Legislative Yuan, may by resolution of the Executive Yuan Council and in accordance with the Emergency Decrees Law, issue an emergency decree to effect expedient and necessary measures. Such a decree shall, within one month after issuance, be presented to the Legislative Yuan for confirmation. In case the Legislative Yuan dissents, the said decree shall immediately become null and void (Art. 43).

9. In case of any differences of opinion arising among the different Yuans which are not covered by this Constitution, the President of the Republic may summon a meeting of the Presidents of the Yuans concerned for consultation and settlement of such differences
(Art. 44).

There is a Vice-President under the President: "Any citizen of the Republic of China having attained the age of forty years may be eligible for the office of President or Vice-President" (Art. 45). "The terms of office of the President and the Vice-President shall be six years. They may be reelected for a second term" (Art. 47). But, as mentioned earlier, this article, in accordance with Article 3 of the Temporary Provisions, is not applicable in the Period of Mobilization.

The Executive Yuan

Although the President has quite extensive powers, the Executive Yuan is also an important organ of the state: "The Executive Yuan is the highest administrative organ of the state" (Article 53). The President of the Executive Yuan is appointed by the President of the Republic with the consent of the Legislative Yuan and the President, in accordance with law, promulgates laws and issues ordinances with the countersignature of the

President of the Executive Yuan. The Executive Yuan is somewhat like the cabinet of a cabinet government and is very important.

The importance of the Executive Yuan can also be seen from its organization. According to the Constitution, "The Executive Yuan shall be made up of a President, a Vice-President, a number of heads of various ministries and commissions, and a number of ministers without portfolio" (Art. 54), who together form the Executive Yuan Council with the Yuan President serving as Chairman" (Art. 58, Section 1). The organization of the Executive Yuan is very large. Under it are such ministries and commissions as the Foreign Affairs Ministry, the National Defense Ministry, the Finance Ministry, the Commission of Affairs concerning Nationals Living Abroad, and so on.

The Executive Yuan is the highest administrative organ of the state. The connotation of "administration" is quite broad, and so are the functions and powers of the Executive Yuan. Administration of internal affairs, diplomatic affairs, financial affairs, defense affairs, and educational affairs, all come within the jurisdiction of the Executive Yuan. The major function, however, is not the administration of daily affairs, but decision-making regarding important affairs. Article 58, Section 2 of the Constitution stipulates as follows:

Prior to the submission to the Legislative Yuan of any statutory or budgetary bill or any bill concerning declaration of martial law, granting of general amnesty, declaration of war, conclusion of peace, treaties, or other important affairs, or concerning matters of common concern to the various ministries and commissions, the President of the Executive Yuan and the heads of the various ministries and commissions of the Executive Yuan shall present the same to the Executive Yuan Council for discussion and decision.

The first section of the Temporary Provisions for the Period of Mobilization for Suppression of Communist Rebellion provides that with the approval of the Council of the Executive Yuan, the President may take emergency measures. On the surface, these stipulations concern the functions and powers of the Council of the Executive Yuan, but in fact they apply to the Executive Yuan itself. Especially if seen in light of Article 57, the key position of the Executive Yuan in the central government becomes even clearer. While the Executive Yuan is headed by a President, it has council meetings to decide on all important affairs. Is the Executive Yuan, then, an organ of one-man leadership in which the President has the final power of decision-making, or is it a collective organ in which important affairs are decided by a meeting of the Executive Yuan? This is a problem to be studied. Judging by actual operation, this matter depends largely on the President's seniority and prestige and his individual character. If the President of the Executive Yuan has high seniority and prestige and a strong character, most issues will be decided by him. Otherwise, more often then not, matters will be decided by members attending the council meeting of the Executive Yuan.

As the highest administrative organ of the state, the Executive Yuan makes administrative policies and is in charge of general administrative affairs. But it does not deal with specific administrative issues, which are the concern of the various ministries and commissions. At present, under the Executive Yuan, there are ministries of Internal Affairs, Finance, Education, of Justice, of Economic Affairs, Communications, and so on, as well as commissions of Mongolian and Tibetan affairs and of Overseas Chinese.

The Legislative Yuan

The Legislative Yuan in the Constitution is the same as the parliaments of many countries: "The highest legislative organ of the state, to be constituted of Legislative Yuan Members elected by the People. It shall exercise legislative powers on behalf of the people" (Art. 62). The legislative powers are, under Article 63 of the Constitution, "the powers to decide upon statutory or budgetary bills or bills concerning martial law, general amnesty, declaration of war, conclusion of peace, treaties, and other important matters of the state." The Legislative Yuan has other powers. According to Article 43, an emergency decree issued by the President shall, within one month of issuance, be presented to the Legislative Yuan for confirmation. Under Article 55, the President of the Executive Yuan is appointed by the President of the Republic with the consent of the Legislative Yuan. And Article 57, makes the Executive Yuan responsible to the Legislative Yuan in certain areas.

Therefore, the Legislative Yuan in the Constitution of the Republic of China has substantial powers. In recent years, as the people of the Republic of China have achieved a better understanding of the functioning of democratic constitutionalism, the powers of the Legislative Yuan have increased.

Article 64 of the Constitution stipulates that Members of the Legislative Yuan shall be elected by the people in accordance with the following provisions:

1. Those elected by provinces and by municipalities under the direct jurisdiction of the Executive Yuan shall be five from each province or municipality with a population of less than 3,000,000 and one additional member for every additional 1,000,000 persons in a province or municipality with a population exceeding 3,000,000.
2. Those elected from Mongolian Leagues and Banners;
3. Those elected from Tibet;
4. Those elected by various racial groups in frontier regions;
5. Those elected by Chinese nationals residing abroad;
6. Those elected by occupational groups.

The 773 Legislative Yuan Members are widely representative of regions, Chinese nationals residing abroad, and different occupational groups.

Members of the Legislative Yuan serve a term of three years and may be reelected (Art. 65)s. The current legislators were elected in 1948; their terms should have expired on May 7, 1951. At that time, however, almost all of the China Mainland was in Communist hands. In fact it was impossible to hold elections for new legislators. Since the exercise of the legislative power must not stop, the then-incumbent Legislative Yuan Members continued to exercise their functions and powers of the Legislative Yuan, as an expedient measure. This measure was not quite sound, however, because it did not have constitutional grounds. Therefore, once the Council of Grand Justices of the Judicial Yuan--which has the power to interpret the Constitution--resumed their sessions in Taipei, the Executive Yuan submitted this problem to the said Justices for an interpretation. The Council of Grand Justices in its interpretation *Shih Tsu* No. 31, rendered on January 29, 1954, ruled as follows:

Article 65 of the Constitution stipulates that members of the Legislative Yuan shall serve a term of three years. Article 93 stipulates that Control Yuan members serve a term of six years. Their terms were originally fixed as beginning on the day they assumed office and ending on the day stipulated in the Constitution. However, when a grave crisis arose in the nation and prevented the conducting of the next election, it would run counter to the purpose of the Constitution in setting up five Yuans, if the functions and powers of the Legislative Yuan and the Control Yuan were suspended. Therefore, until members for the second term have been elected and convened in accordance with law, the Legislative Yuan Members and Control Yuan Members of the first term shall continue to exercise their functions and powers.[8]

The above interpretation may sound rational on the basis of *rebus sic stantibus*. However, much time elapsed since the making of that interpretation. The Mainland was still not recovered from the Communists, and new Legislative Yuan Members still could not be reelected. As many as 400 of the legislators elected in 1948 had either failed to come to Taiwan or had died, and many of those who were still holding office could no longer exercise their powers and functions because of poor health. As a result, the legislative power was greatly affected. On the other hand, the fact that the Legislative Yuan Members held office for as long as thirty years without election left the younger generation, come of age, without the opportunity to exercise the power of election and the power to be elected. This was not only unfair but also detrimental to the state because the legislative organ had been denied fresh blood. Consequently, the whole country was loud in demanding remedial measures. As mentioned earlier, the current remedial measure is stipulated in the Temporary Provisions for the Period of Mobilization: The President may take measures to increase the allotted number of people's representatives from the free regions to the central parliamentary bodies and to conduct elections at regular intervals. Indeed, this is merely an expedient measure and cannot solve the problem thoroughly. However, since its practice, the Legislative Yuan has recruited much fresh blood which has lowered the average age of the legislators and increased the efficiency of the operations of the Legislative Yuan. As of March 1991, the total number of Legislative Yuan Members was 218, of which 85 were originally elected.[9] What is more significant is the fact that the Council of Grand Justices in a more recent interpretation (No. 26, rendered on June 21, 1990) ruled that all National Assembly Delegates, and Members of the Legislative Yuan and Control Yuan, who were elected for the first term, should cease to exercise their powers and functions before December 31, 1991, so that new delegates and members may be elected as the present circumstances allow. This will certainly further the operation of a constitutional government.

The protection guaranteed Members of the Legislative Yuan is the same as that given legislators of other countries: "No Member of the Legislative Yuan shall be held responsible outside of the Yuan for opinions he may express and votes he may cast in sessions of the Yuan" (Art. 73). "No Member of the Legislative Yuan may, except in case of *flagrante delicto*, be arrested or detained without the permission of the Legislative Yuan" (Article 74). But as mentioned earlier, "No Member of the Legislative Yuan may concurrently hold a government office" (Art. 75).

The Legislative Yuan has a President and a Vice-President elected by and from among the Legislative Yuan Members (Art. 66). the President shall be the chairman at meetings of the Legislative Yuan. He is in charge of administrative affairs within the Legislative Yuan and represents it in external relations. The Vice-President, as is the case in other countries, assists the President. Like the parliaments of other countries, the Legislative Yuan has various committees. Statutory bills, budgetary bills and other bills are generally examined by a specific committee concerned before being submitted to a plenary session. At present, there are twelve committees: Internal Affairs, Diplomatic Affairs, National Defense, Economic Affairs, Finance, Budget, Education, Communication, Frontier Affairs, Overseas Chinese Affairs, Judicial Affairs, and Legal Institutions.

The Legislative Yuan functions in a collective fashion exercising its powers with meetings. Hence the duration of the Yuan's sessions significantly affects its political influence. In this regard, the sessions of the Legislative Yuan are quite long: "The Legislative Yuan shall hold two regular sessions every year to be convened by itself. The first session shall last from February to the end of May, and the second session from September to the end of December. When necessary, a session may be extended" (Art. 68). In other words, the Legislative Yuan meets as long as eight months every year. Furthermore, "In the following circumstances, the Legislative Yuan may hold an extra ordinary session: 1. At the request of the President of the Republic; 2. Upon the petition of more than one-fourth of the Legislative Yuan Members" (Art. 69). In recent years, with legislative bills have been on the increase, the Legislative Yuan has often had to extend its sessions, thus making its political impact felt even more.

The Judicial Yuan

The powers of the Judicial Yuan are no less than those of the highest judicial organs of other countries, under Articles 77 And 78 of the Constitution. Article 77 stipulates that "The Judicial Yuan is the highest judicial organ of the state and shall attend to the adjudication of civil, criminal, and administrative suits and to disciplinary measures against public functionaries." Thus, the Judicial Yuan has full judicial authority, as the final court for civil, criminal, and administrative suits, and is concurrently in charge of the discipline of public functionaries. On the other hand, under the present system, which was based on the original system adopted during the period of political tutelage, there are instituted under the Judicial Yuan the Supreme Court, the High Court, and District Courts which adjudicate civil and criminal suits; the Adminsitrative Court which decides administrative suits, and a Committee on the Discipline of Public Functionaries. The Judicial Yuan itself, therefore, is not an adjudicative organ, but an organ to supervise the adjudicative organs. However, the above system has only been created by statute. Whether it accords with the original meaning of the Constitution is still a question. But even with the present system, it is undoubted that the Judicial Yuan doubtless remains the highest judicial organ of the State. Most judicial laws and regulations are initiated or made by the Judicial Yuan; Judges are nominated by the Judicial Yuan before appointment; and the Judicial Yuan has the power to supervise courts at all levels.

Article 78 of the Constitution also confers important powers: "The Judicial Yuan shall have the power to interpret the Constitution and the power to unify the interpretation of laws and ordinances." The Constitution is the fundamental law of the land; it seeks to govern national policies and matters of vital importance with relatively few articles with little detail. Questions about what certain articles really mean often arise and interpretations are needed. There are also laws passed by the legislative organs, ordinances promulgated by the executive organs, and local regulations made by local autonomous governments. If these should contravene the Constitution, the authority of the fundamental law would be affected and the legal system would be in disaray. Divergent views on whether a contravention in fact exists may also arise. Therefore, there must be an organ empowered to interpret the Constitution and settle disputes among various organs so that the authority of the Constitution can be upheld. This is, of course, a very important power in a nation's political system; its connection with the power of judicial review established by American constitutional law is obvious. The Constitution of the Republic of China entrusts this power with the Judicial Yuan.

Moreover, different organs of the state sometimes have different opinions of certain laws or ordinances. When one organ is subordinate to the other, or when they have a common higher authority, of course the opinion of the higher authority prevails. When this is not the case, however, there must be an organ that has the power to make a final decision, to unify the interpretation of laws and ordinances, and to settle disputes among organs of the state. This power is also given to the Judicial Yuan.

Besides the power to supervise courts at all levels, the powers to interpret the Constitution and to unify the interpretation of laws and ordinances are the main power of the Judicial Yuan. To exercise these powers, the Constitution stipulates in Article 79: "The Judicial Yuan shall have a President and a Vice-President, who shall be nominated and, with the consent of the Control Yuan, appointed by the President of the Republic." The second section of the same article provides: "The Judicial Yuan shall have a number of Grand Justices to attend to matters stipulated in Article 78 of the Constitution, who shall be nominated and with the consent of the Control Yuan, appointed by the President of the Republic."

According to the Organization Law of the Judicial Yuan, "The Judicial Yuan shall have a Council of Grand Justices consisting of seventeen Grand Justices, which shall exercise the power of interpreting the Constitution and unifying the interpretation of laws and ordinances. The President of the Judicial Yuan shall be the Chairman of the Council of Grand Justices."[10] The appointment of the Grand Justices must be consented to by the Control Yuan to ensure that they meet very high qualifications. For example, a person who has previously served as a judge of the Supreme Court for more than ten years with outstanding record may become a Grand Justice.[11] The term of office of Grand Justices is nine years.[12]

The powers and functions of Grand Justices are exercised by the Council acting through a carefully defined procedure. Before 1958, such a procedure was designed by the Council of Grand Justices themselves. In July 1958, the Law of the Council of Grand Justices of the Judicial Yuan was passed by the Legislative Yuan, detailing their procedures.[13] For example, Article 13 places strict restraints on their exercise of power: "By a resolution of three-fourths of the Grand Justices present at a Council having a quorum of three-fourths of all the Grand Justices, an interpretation of the Constitution may be made." From January, 1949, the year the first interpretation was rendered through December 1990, the Council of Grand Justices made a total of 127 Interpretations of the Constitution. Many of these were of grave significance. For example, Interpretation *Shih Tsu* No. 86 said that the high courts and lower courts should be subordinate to the Judicial Yuan and not to the Executive Yuan.[14] Interpretations *Shih Tsu* Nos. 166 and 251 ruled that the Law governing Punishment for Violation of Police Regulations, in providing that the police office may detain people who are in violation of police regulations or force them to do physical labor or commit them to certain places for correction or learning to make a living, contravenes the stipulation of Article 8 of the Constitution, which guarantees the freedom of person, and should soon be amended to ensure that punishment shall be handed down only by a court of law in accordance with legal procedure. Of greater political significance is Interpretation *Shih-Tsu* No. 261 which set December 31, 1991 as the deadline for all first-term National Assembly Delegates and Members of the Legislative Yuan and Control Yuan to leave their office to make room for new delegates and members. [15] From these examples, it is clear that the government organs concerned are making every effort to promote constitutionalism even when the Republic of China is in the Period of Suppressing Communist Rebellion.

In Chapter 7 regarding the Judiciary, the Constitution also guarantees the inviolability of the judges: Article 80 "Judges shall be independent of party affiliations and shall, in accordance with law, hold trials independently, subject to no interference of any kind."

Article 81 "Judges shall hold office for life. No judge shall be removed from office unless he has been found guilty of a criminal offense or subjected to disciplinary punishment or declared to be under interdiction. No judge shall, except in accordance with law, be suspended, transferred, or have his salary reduced" Like similar provisions in the constitutions of other countries, these indicate that the independence of judges in the Republic of China is effectively protected by law.

The Examination Yuan

Unique to the Constitution of the Republic of China is the institution of an Examination Yuan and a Control Yuan in addition to the Executive Yuan, Legislative Yuan, and Judicial Yuan. This characteristic derives from Dr. Sun Yat-sen's teachings.

First, an introduction to the Examination Yuan. In the past, public functionaries in Western countries were all examined and appointed by executive organs. Owing to partisan considerations, the people in authority in the executive organs usually would appoint those of their own party and keep out others who held different political views. Thus it was difficult to implement an equitable system of examinations and appointments. Not only did the government lose very able people, many able people also felt depressed because they could not have an opportunity to put their abilities to use. In China, on the other hand, the system of examination by open competition began during the Western Han Dynasty (706 B.C. - 8 A.D.) and was maintained by successive dynasties. In most periods, an examination organ was specially set up outside of the executive organ so that able and talented people could be selected objectively and fairly. To carry forward this fine traditional system of China, and to avoid the problems in past Western practices, Dr. Sun Yat-sen strongly advocated that the examination power should be independent of the administrative power and that an Examination Yuan should be set up outside the Executive Yuan. In keeping with Dr. Sun Yat-sen's teachings, and following the precedent of many countries in the twentieth century, which set up an independent general personnel administrative organ to administer the examination, appointment, and evaluation of public functionaries, the Constitution of the Republic of China established the Examination Yuan.

According to the Constitution, "the Examination Yuan is the highest examination organ of the state and shall attend to matters relating to examination, employment, registration, service rating, scale of salaries, promotion and transfer, safeguarding of tenure, commendation, pecuniary aid in case of death, retirement, old age pension, and so forth" (Article 83). The Constitution clearly stipulates that the principle governing personnel recruiting is that, "In the selection of public functionaries, a system of examination by open competition shall be enforced, quotas of candidates shall be prescribed severally according to provinces and areas, and examinations shall be held in designated districts. No person may be appointed to a public office without having passed an examination" (Art. 85).

With regard to the organization of the Examination Yuan, "The Examination Yuan shall have a President and a Vice-President and a certain number of Members, who shall be nominated and, with the consent of the Control Yuan, appointed by the President of the Republic" (Art. 84) and "Members of the Examination Yuan shall be independent of party affiliation and shall independently exercise their functions in accordance with law" (Art. 88).

Thus, the Constitution institutes the Examination Yuan as the general organ of personnel administration. However, according to Article 5 of the Temporary Provisions, "To meet the needs of Mobilizing for the Suppression of Communist Rebellion, the President may make adjustments in the central government's organizations of administration and personnel and their structure." The President, in accordance with this stipulation, issued the organization regulations for the Central Personnel Administration of the Executive Yuan on July 27, 1967:

> To unify and strengthen the personnel administration of the administrative organs at all levels and that of public enterprises, and to reserve various kinds of talents, the Executive Yuan shall, during the Period of Mobilization ... institute a Central Personnel Administration which shall be in charge of matters concerning personnel recruiting and registration, and which shall be commanded and supervised by the Examination Yuan.

Naturally, the exercise of the powers and functions of the Examination Yuan is impaired by these stipulations. Yet, over the years, the Examination Yuan has held various kinds of examinations every year and has quite effectively selected a great number of able and talented public functionaries.

The Control Yuan

The creation of the Control Yuan is another unique characteristic of the Constitution of the Republic of China. "The Control Yuan is the highest organ of control of the state and shall exercise the powers of consent, impeachment, censure, and auditing" (Art. 90). To elaborate, the Control Yuan has the following powers:

1. *The power of consent..* The President and the Vice-President of the Judicial Yuan, the Grand Justices, the President and the Vice-President of the Examination Yuan, and its Members are all appointed by the President of the Republic with the consent of the Control Yuan.

2. *The power of impeachment and censure.* When the Control Yuan deems a public functionary in the central or local government guilty of neglect of duty or violation of law, it may propose measures of censure or impeachment. Censure differs from impeachment, Censure occurs when the control Yuan deems a public functionary guilty of significant neglect of duty or violation of law and concludes that it is necessary to suspend him from his duties. In this case the Control Yuan will contact the official's superior and request the person's immediate suspension. Impeachment occurs when the Control Yuan requests the organization with the power to recall or discipline a public functionary to do so.[16]

3. *The power of auditing.* the Control Yuan has the power to audit the final statement presented by the Executive Yuan. The Ministry of Audit under the Control Yuan shall have the power to supervise the implementation of the budgets of various organs and to investigate their illegal or unfaithful financial activities.

In addition to these powers, the Constitution also states: Article 96 The Control Yuan, according to the nature of the work of the Executive Yuan and its ministries and commissions, may set up a number of committees to investigate their activities with a view to finding out whether or not there is any violation of law or neglect of duty on the part of the Executive Yuan and its ministries and commissions. Article 97,1. The Control Yuan may, on the basis of the investigations and resolutions of its committees, propose corrective measures to be forwarded to the Executive Yuan and its ministries and commissions concerned, directing their attention to effecting improvements.

The Control Yuan has very substantial powers and these powers are exercised in a collective fashion by the Control Yuan Members.
Article 91 provides for indirect election of members of local legislatures:

The Control Yuan shall be composed of Members, to be elected by provincial and municipal councils, the local councils of Mongolia and Tibet, and Overseas Chinese communities.   The allotment of their respective members shall be in accord with the following provisions:

1. Five Members from each province,
2. Two Members from each municipality under the direct
      jurisdiction of the Executive Yuan,
3. Eight Members from the Mongolian leagues and banners,
4. Eight Members from Tibet, and
5. Eight Members from Chinese nationals residing abroad"

This method of election is different from that used to select delegates to the National Assembly and members of the Legislative Yuan, but is rather similar to the election of Senators in the United States of America. Scholars seriously doubt whether this method is adequate.

The Constitution provides that "Control Yuan Members shall serve a term of six years and are eligible for reelection"
(Art.93).   Originally, an election should have been held in 1954, but as mentioned earlier, because the China Mainland had fallen into Communist hands, it was impossible to hold an election at that time. As in the case of Legislative Yuan Members, the first-term Control Yuan Members, on the basis of an interpretation of the Council of Grand Justices, continued to exercise their functions and powers.   Then, with the stipulations of the Temporary Provisions, the President was empowered to issue measures to increase the allotted number of people's representatives from the free regions, to the central Parliamentary bodies and to elect such representatives at regular intervals. However, as a result of a more recent Interpretation of the Council of Grand Justices, the first-term Control Yuan members will have to leave office before December 31, 1991, and new members will be elected.

Because the Control Yuan Members are among the people's representatives and because they have such important responsibilities as impeachment and censure, they must be protected, the Constitution thus provides that "No Control Yuan Member shall be held responsible outside the

Yuan for opinions expressed or votes cast in session of the Yuan" (Art. 101). "Without the permission of the Control Yuan, no Control Yuan Member may be arrested or detained except in case of *flagrante delicto*" (Art. 102). Since the duties of the Control Yuan Members are unique, the Constitution stipulates that "No Member of the Control Yuan may concurrently hold a public office or engage in any profession" (Art. 103).

The Control Yuan has a President and a Vice-president elected by and from among the Control Yuan Members (Art. 92). Their functions are limited. The President is only in charge of the administrative affairs within the Control Yuan and represents the Control Yuan in external relations. The Vice-President merely assists the President. The functions and powers of the Control Yuan are exercised by Control Yuan Members, some collectively by all Control Yuan Members, such as the power of consent; some by the committees of the Control Yuan, as is the case with the institution of measures for censure. The institution of an impeachment is exercised by several Members of the Control Yuan. The impeachment of the President or the Vice-President of the Republic is different from that of an ordinary public functionary, requiring "no less than one-fourth of the whole body of Control Yuan Members, and the endorsement, after due consideration, of a majority of the whole body of the control Yuan Members, and the same shall be brought before the National Assembly" (Art. 100). By contrast, "Any impeachment by the Control Yuan against a public functionary of the central or a local government shall be instituted upon the proposal of one or more than one Control Yuan Member and the endorsement, after due consideration, of no less than nine Control Yuan Members"
(Arts. 98 and 99). It is a shortcoming that the Constitution does not specially lay out stricter procedures regarding the impeachment of judges, auditors, and other officials whose independence and integrity in carrying out their duties must be ensured.

The Constitution also fails to provide a procedure for exercising the power to censure. Article 19 of the Control Law stipulates that "When a Control Yuan Member deems a public functionary guilty of neglect of duty or other prompt measures, he or she may, with a written censure order examined and consented to by at least three other Control Yuan Members, have the case forwarded through the Control Yuan, to the responsible official supervising the said public functionary ..." It is obvious that the procedure for instituting a censure is simpler than that for an impeachment.

The above is a brief description of the functions and powers of the Control Yuan.[17] Although not long after the promulgation of the Constitution, the nation entered the difficult Period of Mobilization, nevertheless, the Control Yuan has, generally speaking, exercised its functions and powers in a proper fashion. It has no doubt contributed to the development of a clean and efficient government.

The Local Government System

The system of local government described in chapters 10 and 11 of the Constitution resembles a federal system in some ways and a unitary system in other ways. Chapter 10 deals with matters legislated upon and executed by the central government, the matters which may be delegated by the central government to the provincial and *hsien* or county governments, the matters legislated upon by the provinces and acted on either by the provinces or the *hsien*, and matters legislated upon and executed by the *hsien* (Arts. 101 through 107). Chapter 11 provides,"A province may convene a provincial assembly to enact, in accordance with the General Principles of Provincial and *Hsien* Self-Government, a Provincial Self-Government Law, provided that the same shall not contravene the Constitution" (Art. 112). It also provides, "The *hsien* shall enforce *hsien* self-government." "The hsien may convene a *hsien* assembly and enact, in accordance with the General Principles of Provincial and Hsien Self-Government, a *Hsien* Self-Government Law, provided that the same shall not contravene the Constitution and the Provincial Self-Government Law" (Arts. 121 and 122).

Both the province and the *hsien* are communities with quite substantial powers of self-government. The province may enact a Provincial Self-Government Law equivalent to a provincial constitution and a *hsien* constitution. The Constitution spells out matters that may be legislated upon by the province or the *hsien*. The central government may not enact laws that encroach on the powers of the province or the *hsien* other than by amending the Constitution. Inasmuch as the provinces and *hsien* exercise self-government and their power of legislation and execution is guaranteed by the Constitution, the provinces and *hsien* are quite similar to the individual states and their subordinate autonomous bodies in a federal system.

On the other hand, local government in the Republic of China also resembles that in a unitary system. While the province may enact the Provincial Self-Government Law and enforce local self-government, and the *hsien* may enact a *Hsien* Self-Government Law and enforce local self-government, both the Provincial Self-Government Law and the *Hsien* Self-Government Law must accord with the General Principles of Provincial and *Hsien* Self-Government laid down by the central government (Art. 108, Section 1). Therefore, the contents of self-government laws are restricted by central legislation and thus are not completely autonomous. Furthermore, according to Article 114 of the Constitution, "The Provincial Self-Government Law, after enactment, shall be immediately submitted to the Judicial Yuan. The Judicial Yuan, if it deems any part thereof unconstitutional, shall declare null and void the article or articles repugnant to the Constitution." So the contents of the Provincial Self-Government Law are also restricted by the central judicial organ. For these reasons, the local government system of the Republic of China may be regarded as *sui generis*--one with characteristics of both a federal system and a unitary system.

Under the Constitution, all the provinces and *hsien* in China exercises powers of local self-government. However, the Mainland has occupied by the Communists since 1949, and only Taiwan Province and the islands of Quemoy and Matsu have remained as the Republic of China. As the General Principles of Provincial and *Hsien* Self-Government were originally intended to apply to all the provinces and *hsien* of the country, it is not proper to apply them to only one province, Taiwan, in such an unusual period as that of mobilizing for the suppression of Communist rebellion. In other words, this is not the right time for local self-government. As a result, the detailed provisions for all stipulations of local self-government in the Constitution have not been implemented except on a trial basis in Taiwan Province, for the following reasons:

When Taiwan Province was first restored to China by Japan after World War II, the central government intended to practice constitutionalism for all the people of China. With a restoration of freedom, after long years of rule and exploitation by a foreign country, the people of Taiwan did request that local self-government be allowed in Taiwan, the sooner the better. The central government complied with the request in a generous manner because the conditions for implementing local government were generally adequate. Education was widespread, transportation was convenient, agriculture and mining were developed, and the system of household registration was in order. However, because the General Principles of Provincial and *Hsien* Self-Government and related election laws were not enacted in time, the implementation of local self-government was delayed.

By the fall of 1949, most provinces on the Mainland were occupied by the Communists and the position of Taiwan Province became even more important. To ensure popular support and strengthen the bastion for a continuous fight against communism, the government decided that all *hsien* and municipalities of Taiwan Province should enjoy local self-government and that the government of Taiwan Province should engage experts to form a Local Self-Government Research Society which would, in accordance with the needs of the situation and the spirit of the Constitution, draw up various local self-government regulations as the standards for local self-government. This Society drew up the "Outlines for Implementing Self-Government in *Hsien* and Municipalities of Taiwan Province" and other regulations which, after being ratified by the Executive Yuan, were promulgated and made effective on April 22, 1950.[18] These regulations were amended slightly later, but their basic principles have not been altered. Thus, for more than thirty-five years the *hsien* and municipalities of Taiwan Province have had local self-government.

The Outlines mentioned above were designed in compliance with the spirit of the Constitution. For example, (1) All citizens of the *hsien* and municipalities in accordance with law, enjoy the powers of election, recall, initiative, and referendum; (2) the *Hsien* Council and Municipal Council are instituted in *hsien* and municipalities, with their members elected by the citizens and exercising the power to decide matters concerning the self-government, legislation and budget of the *hsien* and municipality; (3) in *hsien* a *hsien* government with a magistrate is elected by the people of the *hsien*. Municipal governments with a mayor are elected by the people of the municipality. All these measures are in accord with provisions in the Constitution.

The local self-government now exercised in Taiwan Province is based on the above-mentioned Outlines, with no *hsien* and municipality self-government law constitutional provisions as its basis. Although it is an expedient measure for an unusual period, it does not contravene the spirit of the Constitution. As a matter of fact, in the past thirty-five years, the local government system has contributed much to the effective exercise of election rights by the citizens of *hsien* and municipalities, and also to the efficient exercise of powers by the *hsien* and municipal governments.

At present in Taiwan Province, only the *hsien* and municipalities have local self-government. The Province itself and the municipalities directly under the Executive Yuan--Taipei and Kao hsiung--do not have local self-government. The Governor of the Province, the members of the provincial government, and the mayors of the municipalities directly under the Executive Yuan are all appointed by the central government. However, both in the Province and in the municipalities directly under the Executive Yuan, there is a Council with members elected by the people and exercising the power to decide on special regulations of the Province or municipalities related to the rights and duties of the people. These Councils also have the power to approve budgetary reports and auditing reports. Thus Taiwan Province and the two Municipalities directly under the Executive Yuan--Taipei and

Kaohsiung--are striding forward towards the implementation of self-government and the early realization of the provisions of the Constitution.

Conclusion

The Constitution of the Republic of China was made on the China was made on the China mainland in 1947, and brought to Taiwan intact by the Nationalist government in 1949 when the Communists overran the Mainland. To meet the unusual situation of Taiwan, temporary provisions were adopted by the National Assembly and Martial Law was also imposed.   These restricted the operation of certain parts of the Constitution. However, as a result of continuous economic, social, and political developments during the past three decades, the country's democratization has been accelerated in recent years, Martial Law was lifted in 1987. The Civil Organization Law of 1989 made it possible for new political parties to be formed. In particular, the Democratic Progressive Party won seats in the Legislative Yuan, the National Assembly and all levels of local councils, and played the role of an opposition party.

In June 1990, the Council of Grand Justices rendered an Interpretation to the effect that all first-term National Assembly Delegates and Members of the Legislative Yuan and Control Yuan, most of them elected in 1948, should cease to exercise their powers and functions before December 31, 1991, so that new delegates and members may be elected as the present circumstances allow. In the same month, Lee Tung-Hui, President of the Republic , called a Conference on National Affairs, composed of representatives from all walks of life, to study the reformation of the parliament, central and local governments and, above all, the amendment of the Constitution and relations between the two sides of the Taiwan Straits.   In fact, and extraordinary session of the A National Assembly was convened by the President of the Republic in April 1991. The Temporary Provisions were abolished on April 22, and ten articles were added to the Constitution proper to deal with matters discussed at the Conference on National Affairs, mainly the election of new delegates and members of the above organs of government. All these developments have led the Republic of China further towards conformity with constitutional government and democratic constitutionalism.

NOTES

*Translated by John W. Garver and Herbert H.P. Ma.

1. For a general history of the formation of the Chinese Constitution (1908-1934) in English, see W.Y. Tsao, *The Constitutional Structure of Modern China*, Melbourne University Press, Melbourne, 1947.
2. For a general explanation of the Constitution of the Republic of China in English, see Kwan-sheng Hsieh, *A Brief Survey of the Chinese Constitution*, Central Cultural Works Supply House, Taipei, 1954. A detailed treatment of the Constitution in Chinese is found in Chi-tung Lin, *An Article by Article Commentary of the Constitution of the Republic of China*, 4 volumes, San Min Book Company, Taipei, 1981. For an inquiry in English into American influence on the Constitution of the Republic of China, see, Herbert H.P. Ma, "American Influence on the Formation of the Constitution and Constitutional Law of the Republic of China: Past History and Future Prospects," in Lawrence Ward Beer (ed.), *Constitutionalism in Asia: Asian Views of the American Influence*, Berkeley, University of California Press, 1979. Among other noteworthy sources on this Constitution in Chinese are: Meng-wu Sah, *A New View on the Constitution of China*, San Min Book Company, Taipei, n.d.; Ying-chao Hung, *A New View of the Constitution of the Republic of China*, printed and published by the author, Taipei, n.d.; *The Collected Works of the Father of the Republic*, The Central Cultural Works Supply House, Taipei, n.d.; Ching-ray Liu, *The Essential Points of the Constitution of the Republic of China*, printed and published by the author, Taipei, n.d.; Chih-yuan Luo, *The History of the Constitution of China*, The Commercial Press, Taipei, n.d.; Ru-hsuan Chen, *The History of the Constitution of the Republic of China*, The World Book Company, Taipei, n.d.; Ying-chou Hsieh, *On the Constitution of the Republic of China*, printed and published by the author, Taipei, n.d.; Ou Kuan, *On the Constitution of the Republic of China*, San Min Book Company, Taipei, n.d.; and *The Records of the National Assembly*, The Secretariat of the National Assembly, Taipei. In English, see Herbert H.P. Ma, *Trade and Investment in Taiwan: The Legal and Economic Environment in the Republic of China*, 2d edition, Institute of American Culture, Academia Sinica, Taipei, 1985.
3. Interpretation Shih-Tsu No. 130 mainly defined the expression "within 24 hours," found in Section Two of Article 8 of the Constitution as not including the delay caused by traffic or other reasons beyond control. For Interpretaions *Shi-Tsu* Nos. 166 and 251, see *infra* Judicial Yuan. Also, see, *A Collection of Interpretations of the Council of Grand Justices of the Judicial Yuan*, published by the Judicial Yuan, Taipei.
4. This Law is found in *Current Book of the Six Laws*, Wu-nan Book Company, Taipei, 1985.
5. For a detailed analysis of the May 5th Draft Constitution, see, W.Y. Tsao, *The Constitutional Structure of Modern China*, op. cit.

6. *Editor's Note:* The enactment of the Temporary Provisions the number of delegates changed greatly over the years. By April, 1991 when an extraordinary session of the National Assembly was convened by President Lee Tung-hui, there were in all 593 delegates, of whom 581 registered to attend. Their party affiliations were as follows: *Kuomintang* (KMT, Nationalist Party), 519, Democratic Progressive Party (DPP), 8; no party affiliation, 24; three minor, paries, 30. Statistics provided by the Secretariat of the National Assembly, 1991.

7. *Editor's Note:*   Generalissimo Chiang Kai-shek (1887-1975) headed the Kuomintang (KMT: Nationalist Party) from 1926 until his death, and was President of the Republic of China from 1948. His son Chiang Ching-kuo (1910-1988) became President of the Republic in 1978, after the interim succession to the presidency of Vice President C.K. Yen. After Chiang's death on January 13, 1988, a Taiwanese technocrat, Vice President Lee Teng-hui succeeded to the presidency in an increasingly democratic system ready to give the 85% native Taiwanese among the island's 20 million a larger role in governance. Under the Constitution, President Lee served out the remainder of Chiang's term until March, 1990 elections, when he was elected. *China Yearbook*, Taipei, 1991; *Asia 1989 Yearbook*, Far Eastern Economic Review, Hong Kong, 1989, 230-231.

8. *See A Collection of Interpretations of the Council of Grand Justices, supra* note 3.

9. *Editor's Note:* On the historic developments of 1987-1991, see the article on Taiwan each January in *Asian Survey*; *Asia 1988 Yearbook* and *Asia 1989 Yearbook*, *supra* note 6. Although opposition parties were technically illegal at the time under the Civic Organizations Law, the Democratic Progressive Party (DPP), founded in September 1986, was allowed to exist and to participate in December 1986 Legislative Yuan elections. The DPP won 13 seats, a tiny but significant minority. Martial law, in force since 1949, ended on July 15, 1987; but dissidents could be restricted under a new National Security Law. Statistics provided by the Secretariat of the legislative Yuan.

The Civic Organization Law was amended in 1989 to allow formation of new political parties; 34 parties soon registered. After the December 1989 elections, the DPP had 22 seats (31% of the popular vote) in the Legislative Yuan; the KMT retained its majority with 61% of the vote.

10. Article 3, Organization Law of the Judicial Yuan, found in *Current Book of the Six Laws, supra* note 4.

11. For details on this matter, see Article 4, Organization Law of the Judicial Yuan, *id.*

12. Article 5, the Organization Law of the Judicial Yuan, *id.*

13. This Law is found in *Current Book of the Six Laws, supra* note 4.

14. Until 1980, the high courts and district courts of the Republic of China were under the supervision of the   Ministry of Justice of the Executive Yuan. As a result of an Interpretation of the Council of Grand Justices, these courts have since been placed under the jurisdiction of the Judicial Yuan which, according to the Constitution, is the highest judicial organ of the state. For a description of the

judicial system of the Republic of China, in English, see, Herbert H.P. Ma, "General Features of the Law and Legal System of the Republic of China," in Herbert H.P. Ma (ed.), *Trade and Investment in Taiwan--The Legal and Economic Environment in the Republic of China, supra* note 1.

15. *See A Collection of Interpretations of the Council of Grand Justices of the Judicial Yuan, supra* note 3.

16. From June 1948 through November 1990, the Control Yuan instituted 415 cases of impeachment and 579 cases of censure. Among the impeachment cases, one was against a Vice President of the Republic, on e against a Minister of Economic Affairs. Statistics provided by the Secretariat of the Control Yuan.

17. For an introduction of the Chinese Control Yuan, in English, see, Herbert H.P. Ma, "The Chinese Control Yuan: An Independent Supervisory Organ of the State," *Washington University Law Quarterly*, Dec. 19634, No. 4.

18. These Outlines and Regulations are found in *Current Book of the Six Laws, supra* note 4.

4

JAPAN

The United States Constitution and Japan's Constitutional Law

I. The Modern Development of Law and Constitution in Japan
Masami Ito
Translated by Keiko Beer and Masako Kamiya

II. The Present Constitutional System of Japan
Lawrence W. Beer

III. Human Rights and Judicial Power
Nobuyoshi Ashibe
Translated by William B. Cleary

This study is a collaborative effort of the three authors, although the primary responsibility for each section lies with the author listed below the section title. Lawrence W. Beer has had overall editorial responsibility.

I. The Modern Development of Law and Constitution in Japan

(Masami Ito)

The Formation of Modern Law in Japan

Law before the Meiji Restoration

Modern Japanese law began during the Meiji Period (1868-1912). The Emperor Meiji's "Restoration" (Meiji Restoration) in 1868 raised him to a central position in cult and government not enjoyed by his predecessors and was symbolized by his movement of the imperial court from Kyoto to Tokyo, Japan's administrative and political capital. Steps were then taken to dissolve the old feudal system and replace it with a modern centralized state.[1] This new modern system was heavily influenced by Western law and state theory and was intended to establish Japan as a modern nation-state in all respects equal to those of Europe and America. Modern Japanese law differs dramatically from the prior legal system.[2]

Japan's first formalized national legal system was developed early in the Seventh Century with a centralized state headed by the Emperor. Previously, the heads of various clans (*buzoku*) had made rules according to the will of the gods. National statutory law began with the "Seventeen Article Constitution" of Prince Shotoku in 604 A.D. [3] and the Taika Reforms of 645 A.D.[3] Later, in 701 A.D. the laws in the *Taiho code* (Taihō Ritsuryō), modeled on the Tang Dynasty law of China, consolidated the national legal system. This written law was modified and amended over time to fit social need until the beginning of the Middle Ages late in the Tenth Century. At that point, imperial power and centralized government gave way to the ascendancy of the Fujiwaras family and its long-lasting Regency system. The Emperor system was reduced to a formalism, centralized government was weakened, power became divided, and unified law applicable throughout the nation virtually ceased to exist. There was some written law. However, the law which emerged in each area as the basis for the manorial (*shōen*) life of medieval society derived principally from local custom and precedent and had lost its original linkage with the Chinese law of the Taiho Code.[4]

Towards the end of the Middle Ages, during the "Warring Nations Period" (*sengoku jidai*, 1477-1582) of complex feudal wars, feudal lords were independent and each established his own "House Law" based on local custom. In other words, the nation's governmental structure was based on a feudal system of highly decentralized authority. This decentralized system

129

yielded to the control of the Tokugawa House from about 1600 to 1868. The Tokugawa Shoguns were the most powerful by far among hundreds of feudal lords (*daimyō*) and developed a sort of federal law for dealing with problems not locally settled. Written law consisted of both Tokugawa law and clan law (*hanpō*) established by each feudal lord based on customary law and related precedent.[5]

In sum, in the history of Japanese law before the Meiji Restoration, the early influence of Chinese law gradually lost its effect; then came a period of decentralized feudal house law based on local custom; this was in turn succeeded by the long era of international isolation and Tokugawa restrictions on the power of other feudal houses.

The Reception of Western Law during the Meiji Period

The goal of the new Meiji government in 1868 was to reform a legal system based on a feudal social, political and economic order, and to replace it with modern Western law and capitalism. Modern law was needed with the development of centralized administration and a new local government system modeled on the structures of advanced Western nations. Especially important, only with a new legal system based on Western law could Japan hope for elimination of international law provisions granting foreigners extraterritorial rights under unequal treaties, a legacy of the late Tokugawa period. It was the treaty law part of Western law that forced Japan to pay heed to Western law in general. The Tokugawa government had rigidly enforced Japan's international isolation for centuries when the American "black ships" under Commodore Matthew Perry arrived in 1853 with their superior armament and began the process of forcing Japan open to Western access. In the 1850s, Japan was compelled to sign a series of treaties with Western countries which seriously encroached on her independence and rights. Some Japanese called for early revision of the treaties, but revision was an impossible dream without understanding of Western systems of law and government.[6] Japan's leaders soon realized that the education of specialists on Western law was a necessity, along with other far-reaching reforms, if independence were to be regained.

To facilitate this educational process, many foreign law professors were invited to Japan and institutes were established where Western law might be learned. Among these, leading schools were the *Kaisei Gakkō* (which later became the Faculty of Law, Tokyo University) and the *Meihō Ryō* (later, the Justice Ministry Law School or *Shihōsho Hōgakkō*). *Kaisei* taught English law and *Meihō* taught French law. Naturally enough, graduates of the *Kaisei* school tended to favor English law, while those from the *Shihōsho* school leaned toward French law. Thus, early in the Meiji period, both the English and the French legal systems greatly influenced Japanese law and legal thinking.

However, Japanese law was mainly modeled on the French system during the early modern period, because Anglo-American law based on precedents in case law (*hanrei hō*) was too complicated to learn and too technical to adopt. Yet legal principles drawn from the study of Anglo-American precedent gained respect; and we must not overlook the English law faction and its use of legal history, which meshed with the conservative nationalists' treatment of Japan's ancient traditions.[7] This is evident in the so-called "Code Dispute" (*Hōten Ronso*) which delayed enforcement of the Boissonade's Civil Code (*Mimpōten*).[8]

The Reception of German Law

For a relatively short period, the laws of England and France, the leading capitalist nations and the most developed countries at that time, greatly influenced Japanese law. In the end, it was German law that Japan adopted as a model for its modern legal system. This may be explained by the fact that the laws of Prussia, the region which eventually unified Germany, were considered to be the most suitable model for Japan's laws. Prussia was a developing country in Europe, itself struggling to build a capitalist economy and at the same time maintaining an absolute monarchy. Japan was even less developed and was endeavoring to match the more developed countries. In addition to this, Germany, at that time, was able to provide an example of the most recent codes in the form of the German Civil Code (*Burgerliches Gesetzbuch*). In Japan, a constitution was modeled after the Prussian Constitution and promulgated by the Emperor (*Tennō*), and the commercial and civil procedure codes were drafted by Germans. The first or Old Civil Code was drafted by Gustave Emile Boissonade de Fontarabie, but its enforcement was postponed. Meanwhile, a new civil code, taken from the first draft of the German Civil Code, was promulgated and became law.[9] Japan modernized her legal system during the Meiji period mainly by reception of German laws.

It became the dominant perception in Japan's academe that legislation, especially the major codes, was to be modeled after German law. The German way of legal interpretation was known to be logical and precise in its structure. That approach came to be relied on as the only standard to interpret and apply Japanese law. Even practicing lawyers had a strong tendency to consider it more important to pursue logical consistency like that of German law than to achieve appropriate and practical solutions to conflicts in society. The general attitude of Japanese lawyers and academics after the mid-Meiji period was that "any law other than German law is not law."[10] The development of legal studies in Japan eventually enabled her to avoid uncritical adoption of German law, and to receive selectively and consciously those parts of law which would suit Japanese society at the time. Nevertheless, the fundamental characteristics of Japanese law and legal studies continued to be patterned after the civil law system, especially that of German law.

Pre-War Studies of Anglo-American Law and Their Influence

The enactment of major codes was completed before 1900. Thereafter, German laws showed the way for Japanese laws. Japan became less concerned with English and American law both in legislation and in its interpretation and application, as these legal systems shared too few features in common with her own. Furthermore, the common law approach was not responsive to the demands of Japanese law at that time. The common law tends to place importance upon seeking a just or sound solution in each concrete case more than to pursue systematic coherence and logical consistency. Thus, English law specialists gradually disappeared from the scene and the prestige of English legal studies naturally diminished. Although Anglo-American law continued to be taught in universities, it was taught only as part of general legal education and not directly associated with practically useful interpretation of Japanese laws. The study of Anglo-American law was isolated even in academe, as part of comparative legal studies deemed to have nothing to do with Japanese laws. There was some highly respected scholarly research by a few students of Anglo-American law, but none contributed directly to the development of Japanese law in pre-war days.

Yet one cannot simply state that Anglo-American law had no influence whatsoever on Japanese law or legal studies. The first important form of influence appeared among lawyers. Although German law and legal approaches were useful to legal officers in the executive branch and to judges, some leading figures among practicing lawyers[11] studied Anglo-American law and applied Anglo-American legal approaches in their activities. Second, during the Taisho period (1912-1926), some influential scholars[12] reflected upon the all-too-powerful impact of the so-called conceptual legal approach of German law, and used the common law approach to revise it. Evidence of this can be seen in widespread studies on court decisions. The influence of the common law and affinity to it may be seen in the fact that those studies tended to emphasize the law-making function of a court decision and emphasized the living law of society, rather than the logical structure of law itself. Third, although the legal system as a whole was modeled after European civil law, especially German law, certain legislation originated from the common law. This may be due to the fact that stronger economic ties developed with the United Kingdom and the United States than with Germany. During the period of "Taisho Democracy," the political atmosphere was congenial to things Anglo-American. The two most important pieces of such legislation were the Trust Law[13] and the Jury Law.[14] But the basic character of the Japanese legal system was not influenced by these phenomena[15] and remained unchanged until the reforms which followed World War II.[16]

The Introduction of American Law after World War II

The defeat in World War II and the Occupation (1945-52) by the Allied Powers brought enormous changes comparable in degree to the Meiji Restoration changes in Japanese politics and society. It also affected the legal system. Because the United States was the central power among the Allies in the administration of the Occupation, many aspects of the legal reorganization and reconstruction were naturally modeled after American law. This was the turning point when a great deal of American law was introduced into Japan during the post-war period.

The Occupation policies of the General Headquarters (GHQ), Supreme Commander of the Allied Powers (SCAP) were not intended to reject completely Japan's past and completely remake the legal system. The legal system was to maintain some continuity. Though the content of the laws was fundamentally reformed, procedurally speaking, Japan could choose to amend previously existing laws or to enact new legislation. During the Occupation, no new legislation or amendments and revisions could be made against the wishes of GHQ; so naturally American law was brought to Japan.

Occupation policies determined the areas of law in which American law would be introduced. The most important among these policies were to demilitarize Japan forever, to democratize its politics, and to guarantee human rights. The Code of Criminal Procedure of 1948 may be the most notable law passed pursuant to acceptance of the 1945 Potsdam Declaration.[17]

Next in importance among Occupation policies was the thorough democratization of the economy, carried out with recognition that militarism was closely intertwined with the economic dominance of large corporations, especially the "*Zaibatsu*" (Financial Cliques). The best example of legislation to achieve this purpose is the Antimonopoly Law,[18] based on American laws and judicial decisions which apply them, which has reinforced the regulation of monopolies more than its American counterparts. Another example is the Securities Exchange Law,[19] which has attempted to prevent the concentration of economic power by providing for widely and publicly owned shares and stocks. This law was modeled directly on the Securities Act of 1933 and the Securities Exchange Act of 1934 of the United States. The two agencies to enforce the above-mentioned statutes, the Fair Trade Commission (*Kōsei Torihiki Iinkai*) and the Securities Exchange Commission (*Shoken Torihiki Iinkai*) are also modeled, respectively, after the Federal Trade Commission (FTC) and the Securities Exchange Commission (SEC) of the United States. In 1950, the Company Law[20] was completely revised, particularly to strengthen the status of shareholders. The whole revision was guided by American corporation law; the Illinois Corporation Law may have been most influential.

Enactment of new labor law was another measure used to achieve the democratization in Japan; the rights of workers, which had been inadequately protected before the war, were secured in law. The "three basic labor statutes" were all passed under strong SCAP guidance, and still form the fundamental structure of labor law in Japan. One cannot see much American influence in the first Labor Union Law,[21] enacted at the start of the Occupation; but it was totally amended in 1949. The new Labor Union Law[22] is a direct import or translation of the Wagner Act of 1935. The Labor Relations Law[23] was also heavily influenced by American law. The Labor Standards Law[24] draws much from the American Labor Standards Act in its structure and theory, but because of conditions in Japan at that time, the standards prescribed in the law were rather inadequate.

American law stimulated the interest of lawyers in American law as it was brought into important areas of Japan's legal system. Moreover, the study of American law was no longer simply a study of foreign law, but became practical and applicable to Japanese law in a manner similar to German law before World War II. Before the war, with few exceptions, lawyers did not go to the United States for their study abroad. Since 1945, the United States has been the principal foreign country in which Japanese study, not only young judges and practicing lawyers, but also legal academics. American law has played a leading role in legal studies to an extent unimaginable before the war. As the years have gone by, we have also seen great progress in studies of Japanese law in the United States, an increase in the number of people engaged in research and in resulting publications. Thus, a remarkable exchange of legal studies has developed between the two countries.[25]

Later reflection led to questioning the hasty grafting onto Japanese law of American law during the Occupation. For example, numerous administrative committees established during the Occupation were abolished immediately after Japan regained its independence in 1952, with a few exceptions like the Fair Trade Commission. Most were eventually replaced by newly established deliberative councils which were less independent and more easily controlled by the bureaucracy. The relaxation of the anti-monopoly law, which was more restrictive than that of the United States when enacted, began before the end of the Occupation, and continued after Japan achieved independence. In spite of these transitions, American law's influence permeates Japanese law.

The Characteristics of the Contemporary Legal System

With the exception of such areas as family law and inheritance law where elements of indigenous law have been retained, contemporary law in Japan is a mixture of civil law and common law. Comparative law scholars usually enumerate the civil law, the common law and socialist law as the main universal legal traditions of the world,[26] disseminated beyond their original boundaries and not committed to a specific religious belief. At one time considered inherently different in nature, civil law and common law are today grouped together, with the possibility of future integration as le droit occidental or western law. They can be contrasted with socialist law which has been based on a totally different ideology.[27] Since the reception of Chinese law in very ancient times, the Japanese legal system has been successful in the reception of foreign laws and their adaptation to domestic situations. The present legal system is no exception, in that Japan has developed its own unique system by learning from the abundant experiences of various foreign countries.

The Constitution of the Empire of Japan (Dai Nippon Teikoku Kempō) of 1889 and the Constitution of Japan (Nihonkoku Kempō) of 1946

The Making of the 1889 Constitution

Japan always had a constitution in the substantive sense of a fundamental law of the realm; but it was not until the Meiji Revolution (Meiji Ishin) that she had a constitution in the formal sense i.e., a written constitution. During the Meiji Period (1868-1912), demand arose for a modern constitution, a fundamental law based on constitutionalism and restricting the powers of the state by law.

By the Imperial Restoration (*Ōsei Fukkō*, 1869) and the Abolition of Fiefs and the Establishment of Prefectures (*Haihan Chiken*, 1871), the feudal political system was dissolved, and Japan started to organize itself as a modern state. Opportunities for participating in politics and governance were increased backed by theories of politics responsive to public opinion. This led to calls for a national assembly under a constitutionalism similar to that in the developed countries of the West. The Petition to Establish an Elected Assembly (*Minsen Giin Setsuritsu Kenpakusho of 1874*) by Taisuke Itagaki and other influential politicians is a well-known example. The Meiji Government eventually issued the Edict to Hold Councils of Local Officers (*Chihōkan Kaigi Kaisai no Fukoku*) in 1874, and later enacted the Rules and Regulations for Prefectural Assemblies (*Fukenkai Kisoku*) of 1878 and the Local Assembly Law (*Kuchosonkai Ho*) of 1880, all as means to provide for elected local assemblies.

The Government also began to draft a written constitution. In 1873, the task of drafting a constitution was assigned to the *Sa-in* [a deliberative body to discuss and report on legislation to the *Sei-in*, the main department of government. When the *Sa-in* was abolished in 1875, the Emperor issued an edict ordering the chairman of the *Genrōin* (Council of Elders) to draft a constitution (1876). Within that Council, Research Members for Constitutional Law (*Kokken Torishirabe Iin*) wrote drafts. The first was titled a Constitutional Proposal for Japan (*Nihonkoku Ken-an*) and the second, the National Constitution (*Kokken*). Both were rejected by Tomomi Iwakura and other prominent leaders as too democratic. At that time, various privately drafted constitutions were also made public. Many recommended adoption of a parliamentary cabinet system and guaranteed rights and liberties for the people, due to the influence of the then-active People's Rights Movement (*Jiyu Minken Undō*). Their declarations stood clearly for the basic principles of democratic government. The government responded by toughening its attitude and suppressing the freedom of political activities under the Assembly Ordinance (*Shūkai Jōrei*) of 1880. At the same time, this conflict accelerated the urgent efforts to make a constitution.

In 1881, the Emperor issued the Edict to Establish a National Assembly announcing that a Diet [parliament] would be held by 1890 and that a constitution would be promulgated by them. The next year, Hirobumi Ito was sent to Europe to conduct the research necessary to serve as the basis for writing a constitution. He studied mainly German constitutional law under Rudolf von Gneist and Lorenz von Stein. The German constitutional monarchy, rather than the British parliamentary system, was considered most appropriate by those controlling the Government at that time. Although the German monarchical system allowed an elected legislative body, it limited the powers of that body. Such a system supported a powerful and centralized executive branch which would maximize the power and authority of the Emperor at its apex. After Ito's return to Japan, the enactment of the Peerage Ordinance (1884) and the establishment of the Cabinet (1885) and the Privy Council (1888) prepared the stage for the coming constitution and the national assembly. Ito, with the help of Kowashi Inoue, Hermann Roesler and a few others, drafted the constitution--often called the Meiji Constitution--which the reigning Emperor (*Tennō*) Meiji promulgated on February 11, 1889. At the same time, the Rules of the Imperial Household (*Kōshitsu Tenpan*) of 1889, which were considered part of the Constitution, also came into effect. Japan thus came to have a modern constitution and began to live under constitutional government.

The Duality of the Meiji Constitution

The Meiji Constitution adopted both the absolutistic theory that the sovereignty of the Emperor is based on the divine will of a god similar in theory to the divine right of kings on the one hand, and various principles of modern constitutionalism on the other. The Meiji Constitution may be unique in that it was a mixture of two contradictory momenta. In the background explaining this dualistic nature were the aims of the mainstream of the ruling elite, during the period between the Meiji Restoration and the making of the Constitution, to strengthen the rights of sovereignty, to establish a powerful central government whose authority was based on those rights of sovereignty, and to pursue the basic policy of enriching and strengthening the nation as a whole. The underlying purpose of all these measures was to bring Japan even with the Western powers. Furthermore, the Constitution was made with a Government inclined towards absolutism.

Nevertheless, the Government could not simply ignore the public opinion which strongly supported constitutionalism; it had to present at least the appearance of a modern political and legal system comparable to those of Western countries. The former was evidenced by the rise of the people's rights movement. The latter was necessitated by the wish to revise the unequal treaties with Western Powers. A more fundamental factor was that Japan could not spare the time to go through the long historical process of development that the European nations had experienced, a process during which absolute monarchy did away with feudal regimes, and then the citizens overthrew the monarchy to establish modern constitutionalism upholding freedom and equality. Instead, Japan had to establish an absolutist structure of authority which would wipe out the feudal fiefdoms and, at the same time, introduce modern constitutional principles. Thus, the Meiji Constitution allowed the democratic elements of modern constitutionalism and the feudal and anti-democratic elements to co-exist. This duality made it possible for future politics under the same constitution to be contradictory in tendency at different times. Politics under the Meiji Constitution (1889-1947) depended very much on which features were highlighted in the interpretation and application of the Constitution.[28]

The Meiji Constitution and the British and American Constitutions

Prior to the making of the Meiji Constitution, the British and American Constitutions, especially that of the United Kingdom, were introduced as examples of constitutions of developed and democratic countries. This is illustrated by the fact that the works of Sir Maurice Sheldon Amos, Walter Bagehot, Jean Louis De Lolme and Albert Venn Dicey, which are known as the representative authorities on the British Constitution at that time, were translated into Japanese quite early. The "Constitution of England" was among the lectures included in the curriculum of the Faculty of Law at the University of Tokyo when it was established in 1877. It should also be noted that, at that time, there was an active movement for an elected assembly. The fact that the works of Sir Thomas Erskine May and Hadley on the parliament of the United Kingdom, the mother country of parliamentary systems were translated shows the degree of interest that people had in a parliamentary system.

Once the Meiji Constitution modeled after the German Constitution was promulgated, studies of the British and American Constitutions were never employed for interpretation or application. Generally speaking, there was no noticeable influence from the British and American Constitutions.[29] During the Taisho period (1912-1926), the majority party of the House of Representatives began to control the Cabinet under "regular procedures of a constitutional government." As this type of polity was in part modeled after British parliamentary democracy, the British Constitution may well have been referred to from time to time, but with no implication that studies of the British and American Constitutions were used as a basis for interpreting and applying the Meiji Constitution. Before World War II, scholarly studies by

Japanese academics on British and American constitutional laws did not have much influence.[30]

The Rise and Decline of Constitutionalism

Within the Meiji Constitution, the contradictory principles of absolutism and modern constitutionalism co-existed. The Meiji Constitution had relatively few and briefly worded provisions, which allowed a wide variety of interpretations. Conflicts appeared between "the theory of the Emperor as an organ of the state" (*Tennō Kikan Setsu*) and "the theory of imperial sovereignty" (*Tennō Shuken Setsu*). The former adopted and modified a theory then prevalent among German public lawyers that sovereignty resides in or is incorporated into the state with the monarch as its highest organ. The latter was associated with militant nationalism. Tatsukichi Minobe[31] was the representative scholar propounding the Emperor-as-Organ Theory, maintaining that the state is a legal entity capable of exercising its rights, and that the Emperor is one of its organs and capable of performing acts prescribed for it in the Constitution. This theory denied that the imperial prerogatives were unlimited and interpreted the Constitution so as to stress the importance of the Diet, especially the House of Representatives, as the organ representing the subjects. In contrast, according to the Imperial Sovereignty Theory, with Yatsuka Hozumi as the representative scholar, the most fundamental principle of the Meiji Constitution was that the Emperor possessed the highest authority and the power of the state. Because the sovereignty of the Emperor derived from the will of the gods, it was absolute and could not possibly be limited.

This conflict was not merely a theoretical issue of legal interpretation. The choice of theory and its application to the Constitution had tremendous impact on the course of politics. Whenever the democratic elements of constitutionalism were considered important, the status of the Diet, especially the elected House of Representatives, was enhanced. Whenever the anti-democratic factor of absolutism was emphasized, the authority of the Diet was weakened and the powers of the Emperor increased--in practice, the power of the executive branch which ruled in his name. The course of politics under the Meiji Constitution was determined by the weight placed upon one or the other of these two conflicting aspects of the Constitution.

Between the period of promulgation and the Sino-Japanese War (1894-95), the intent of the authors of the Constitution, who endorsed a weak elected assembly, prevailed. The Government was the Emperor's, independent from all political parties and factions, and not to be influenced by the Diet. This was referred to as the period of "*Chozen Shugi*" or "Transcendentalism." However, this caused confrontation between the various political parties in the House of Representatives and the Government, and the Government was forced to compromise. After victory in the Sino-Japanese War, the Transcendentalists tended to soften their stand. The Government began to cooperate, in varying degrees, with one or the other of the influential parties in the House of Representatives. This gradually led to increased Diet power and implementation of a system similar to that of the British parliamentary cabinet. The short-lived first term of the [shigenobu] Okuma Government (1898) was the first party cabinet in Japan.

During the Taisho period (in 1912 and in 1924), there was a movement to promote constitutional government by establishing a party cabinet system. Efforts to modernize politics in line with the rise of capitalism took the form of reinforcing the authority and powers of the Diet. In the second wave of the movement, the Kato Government was formed and from that time on the majority party in the House of Representatives formed the government. One of the defects of the Meiji constitutional system was that the Imperial Household and the military were beyond the control of the Diet and political parties. Nevertheless, the democratic elements in the Constitution were influential during the period of Taisho Democracy (1912-1925). During this time, political scientist Sakuzo Yoshino's theory of the sovereignty of the Japanese people (*Minponshugi*)[32] and the constitutional theory of Tatsukichi Minobe that the Emperor was a state organ (*Tennō Kikansetsu*) were respected by many as authoritative.

From 1926 on, political tensions rose in the international atmosphere of East Asia and uncertainty in Japan's domestic economy. None of the political parties were effective in dealing with the situation, and some politicians were attacked as corrupt. The people lost trust in party politics, and reform movements emerged from both ends of the ideological spectrum. Due to governmental suppression, the reformism of the Left never had much impact, but the totalitarian vanguard of the Right took control of politics by making the most of the anti-democratic elements of the Meiji Constitution. Thus, parliamentary politics, which stood on shaky democratic legs, went into decline. The Manchurian Incident (September, 1931) was the turning point; thereafter, the military and militarism dominated politics. The constitutionalist elements in the Meiji Constitution were almost totally overshadowed. The suppression of Minobe's Emperor-as-Organ Theory in the 1930s illustrates this trend. With the surrender of 1945, the Meiji Constitution was forcibly changed in character.

The Making of the Constitution of Japan of 1946 and the British and American Constitutions

The Drafting of a New Constitution

The process of drafting the 1947 Constitution will be dealt with in detail in section II. Here, I would briefly recount the relationship between the 1947 Constitution and the British and American Constitutions.

On July 26, 1945, the United States, the United Kingdom and the Republic of China in the Declaration at Potsdam set forth the conditions for the surrender of Japan and demanded fundamental reform of the Meiji Constitution system. Because of her acceptance of the Declaration, Japan assumed responsibility for reforming the whole system to meet the requirements of democracy, liberty and peace. This meant abolishing the anti-democratic and feudal elements of the Meiji constitutional system. However, immediately after surrender, the Japanese Government did not show itself willing to revise the Constitution. The reasons were as follows: People were not sufficiently aware of the fact that, by the very acceptance of the Potsdam Declaration, the constitutional structure of Japan underwent a reformation which was almost the equivalent of a revolution. Even among those who believed in liberalism, many thought the democratic elements in the Meiji Constitution were enough and that changes in its application would be sufficient to meet the reform demands. Even Tatsukichi Minobe, who had been persecuted and had suffered under the Meiji Constitution felt that revision was unnecessary. Some considered it undesirable to revise in haste the fundamental law of the land under the abnormal circumstances immediately following defeat and while under occupation by foreign forces. Above all, as suggested, many people were suffering from inadequate food supplies and some were starving; for the general population, revision of the Constitution was not as pressing a preoccupation as survival; "rice rather than constitution," as the slogan of the time put it. In these circumstances, the Government did not anticipate a thorough revision of the Meiji Constitution. The Government draft (called the "Matsumoto Draft") of February, 1946 preserved the principles of the Meiji Constitution such as the sovereignty of the Emperor, and was unacceptable to SCAP. The international and domestic political circumstances left SCAP no alternative but to take the drastic step of presenting the Government with a new document embodying democratic principles. Some conservatives opposed to the fundamental principles of the 1947 Constitution, long argued for revision on grounds it was forced upon Japan and does not reflect the free will of the people. Today, even among conservatives, the view that the Constitution should be amended because forced on us has virtually disappeared.

Factors Which Contributed to the Draft of the Constitution

Since the Constitution was drafted in an extremely brief period primarily by SCAP American lawyers, one might reasonably suppose that most of it was a direct translation and importation of American (federal and state) Constitutions with which they were very familiar. Indeed, the provisions about those accused of crime are very similar to provisions of the United States Constitution. But on the whole, the draft Constitution included many elements which are not in American law, in contrast to some other legislation during the Occupation (for example, the Securities Exchange Law). Longer was spent in enacting some legislation considered a direct importation of American law than in writing the Constitution. The drafters understood that a constitution is the fundamental law of the state and did not think it appropriate to impose American law. They paid much attention to the likelihood of its acceptance by the Japanese people, because it would determine the future direction of Japan. They also were aware that the making of an appropriate constitution was a serious concern to many outside Japan, such as the member nations of the Far Eastern Commission (FEC).[33]

Here are some of the factors which affected the drafting of the Constitution.

(1)   General Douglas MacArthur gave notes (the so-called "MacArthur Notes") to the drafters on a few basic principles not to be ignored in the drafting process: maintenance of the Emperor institution (he had explicitly written that the Emperor was to be at the head of the state and that succession was to be dynastic); renunciation of war; and abolition of aristocracy and feudalism. These principles revealed Occupation policies, conditions peculiar to Japan, and General MacArthur's idealism in making the Constitution. In fact, apart from reference to adoption of the British budgetary system, one cannot find any linkage in the Notes with the British or American Constitutions.

(2)   The draft reflected the strong influence of political theories underlying American federal and state constitutions. The political theory behind the U.S. Declaration of Independence, the Preamble to the United States Constitution, the Federalist Papers, addresses of Abraham Lincoln and others--the modern theory of natural law and the theory of democracy based on the idea of social contract--was alive throughout the whole draft. Although these ideas may seem to some a little dated in a contemporary constitution,

they appealed to the Japanese people as refreshing after the dominance of anti-democratic elements at the end of the Meiji Constitution regime.

(3)   The draft also paid some attention to Japan's traditional system. It is well documented that the strengths as well as the weaknesses of the Meiji Constitution were analyzed in the drafting process.   The fact that the draft followed the Meiji Constitution with respect to the formal structure of the whole constitution, the titles of each chapter, their sequence, and the wording of the text, may be due to the attempts to maintain continuity.   Such respect for the Meiji Constitution may be counted as one of the factors which prevented any direct importation of the British and American Constitutions in substance.   Retention of the Emperor institution and hereditary succession is a prominent example.   Other illustrations may be the rejection of a presidency and continuation of a parliamentary cabinet as the executive branch.   Moreover, SCAP wished to implement Occupation policies without inviting obstruction or more radical suggestions for reform.

(4)   Attention was paid to recent European constitutions, such as the German Weimar Constitution (1919).   During the drafting process, comparisons were made between constitutions.[34]   In particular, the inclusion of explicit provisions to guarantee social rights was influenced by constitutions of Europe, though strong and influential opposition felt that these rights should be guaranteed by Diet legislation and not by the Constitution.

(5)   From the time SCAP indicated the need to revise the Constitution, each political party published its own proposal for a draft constitution. Private citizens and groups also came out with numerous proposals and drafts. SCAP seems to have paid some attention to these private drafts, as well as to revisions by the Government task force, as expressions of ideas of the Japanese people.   Among these, the one published on December 26, 1945 by the Study Group on the Constitution (*Kempō Kenkyūkai*), composed of Iwasaburo Takano and six others, contained epoch-making provisions for that time, proposing that sovereignty should reside with the people, that the Emperor should perform only ceremonial acts, and that the people should have the "right to maintain standards of living which are wholesome and decent," as well as other social rights. These proposals significantly influenced SCAP's draft.[35]

(6)   The Charter of the United Nations came into effect in October, 1945 shortly before the writing of the draft constitution. It was considered the primary document providing for a new international order. The Constitution of Japan presupposes this international order. Before the actual drafting began, the drafters were told that the principles of the Charter should be kept in mind, but that the Charter need not be explicitly referred to.[36]

The Adoption of British and American Constitutionalism in the (1947) Constitution

Some factors dissuaded SCAP in the drafting process from simply transplanting British or American constitutionalism, while others favored consideration of other constitutions. Nothing was impossible for SCAP at that time, including the direct import of American federal and state constitutional ideas. However, SCAP actually took a broad view in order to integrate all factors and their impacts, and avoided direct induction during the drafting process. It was exactly the attitude an occupation force should take in making the constitution or the basic law of an occupied country. Even though it was drafted by foreigners, the Constitution of 1947 has enjoyed the general support of the public and is considered the most suitable post-war constitution for Japan, preferable to all the other constitutional drafts by Japanese, including that of the Japanese Government. With the consent of the people, it has survived without being amended even once until this day. Under this constitutional regime, Japan has managed to rise from the ruins of war and defeat, and to achieve high international status. Considering all these facts, one cannot but be struck by the wisdom of the drafters. Had they been forced by time pressures to hastily draft a direct importation of British or American constitutionalism, the resulting document would most likely have had a different fate from that of the present Constitution.

Undeniably, in the Preamble, in the theoretical background of the fundamental provisions and principles of the Constitution, and in the text, the institutions and principles of British and American constitutionalism had tremendous influence. My first impression of the draft was that one could trace back the origins of many of the provisions to British or American constitutionalism. Here is an attempt to see the relationship between specific provisions of the Constitution of Japan and the British and American Constitutions.

Constitutionalism

The Concept of a Higher Law

Broadly speaking, constitutionalism means that a state is restricted by constitutional law in the use of its powers, and that government is conducted in accordance with the constitution and all pursuant laws and orders. In earlier times, absolute monarchs were not bound by law, but constitutionalism has come to be accepted as the fundamental principle for governance of a modern state. The modern era has been marked by popular overthrow of various forms of despotism in recognition of the individual's dignity. Citizens have gained political power and civil liberties have become a prevailing social value in the West. A constitution not based on constitutionalism is not considered a true constitution. Moreover, constitutions based on constitutionalism have become widely accepted among countries outside Europe and America.

The historical and social circumstances of a state when its constitution is made seriously affect the actual state of its constitutionalism. For example, the Meiji Constitution embodied modern constitutionalism only partially and inconclusively. The following are a few features of a modern constitution which restrains state power.

(1)   Popular participation in politics and government. Citizens are not merely the object of governance. Many people actively participate directly or indirectly in the formation of the national will [e.g., voting] and take part in government.

(2)   Separation of powers. The effective way to combat abuse or arbitrary exercise of power is to prevent the concentration of power in one entity. Power should be divided among different authorities so that each restrains the others from abuse and misuse, as among the legislature, the executive and the judiciary, or between federal authority and the authority of states, or between central and local offices of government.

(3)   The guarantee of human rights. In modern constitutionalism, it is essential to prevent state power from interfering with the rights and liberties of individuals and to place some limits on the exercise of rights. One might even say that this guarantee of human rights is the central feature of constitutionalism.

Compared with the Meiji Constitution, the Constitution of 1947 is more thorough in the embodiment of constitutionalism as outlined above. (The details are explained in section II.) Such constitutionalism manifests common characteristics of a modern constitution rather than the influence of the British and American Constitutions.

A modern constitution guarantees the rule "by government" not "by a person." The constitutions of the common law countries and the civil law countries do not differ on this point. In the European civil law countries, it is the principle of "*Rechtsstaat*" or constitutional state, especially "*Gesetzmassigkeit der Verwaltung*" or administration according to law. The principle is based on liberalism, as opposed to the absolutism of a police state. A statute enacted by a legislature representing the people binds the operation of the state through its executive and judiciary. An executive, however despotic it attempts to be, must base its administration on law and execute its policies according to law. This sign of constitutionalism, a liberal principle of government, was important in Germany and elsewhere, including Japan under the Meiji Constitution. Here, it is precisely the legislative body and its judgment which controls the content and adequacy of legislation. When a legislature is dominated by despotic elements, there is danger of an empty constitutionalism. Under the Meiji Constitution, the history of oppression of the freedoms of thought and expression with the Peace Preservation Law (*Chian Iji Hō*) well illustrates the point.[37]

The words of Bracton in the English middle ages that "The King should not be under the authority of man, but of God and the law" illustrates the essence of the rule of law. This principle--which is also called the "supremacy of law," a "higher law" or "government according to law"--is the core of the British and American Constitutions as handed down to this day. The Bractonian rule of medieval law, which was also that of natural law, became the rule of common law with the words of Sir Edward Coke. Those rules served as the harbinger of modern revolution and were eventually incorporated into the various American Constitutions. In nineteenth-century Great Britain, under Whig dominance, Albert Venn Dicey analyzed the rule of law as a constitutional principle.[38] The importance of the constitutional principle of "rule of law" rests not only on the rule that legislation enacted by Parliament restricts all state functions, but also on the furtherance of constitutionalism. That is to say, there is a higher law which binds parliamentary statutes. Although this principle was transformed in Great Britain by the establishment of the principle of parliamentary sovereignty, it still is part of the jurisprudence which forms the basis for British and American constitutionalism and common law in general.

Three concrete examples can be used as standards to judge whether the "rule of law" is incorporated in a specific constitution: (1) a thorough guarantee of the individual's human rights;[39] (2) a legitimacy in the procedures and content of law, what is called due process of law in the United States and natural justice in Great Britain; (3) respect for the judiciary which gives institutional expression to the rule of law by restricting state operations.

The Constitution of Japan and the Rule of Law

The concepts of constitutionalism and the state under the Meiji Constitution did not include the "rule of law," as described above. The rule of law is not explicated as such in the text of the 1947 Constitution--that would be inappropriate. Nevertheless, the rule of law is fundamental to the whole constitution and serves as the basis for important institutions such as the following:

(1) Chapter 10 of the Constitution is entitled the "Supreme Law." In the United States, because of federalism, it is necessary to determine the relationship between federal and state laws. The Supremacy Clause of Article VI of the United States Constitution plays a significant role as the keystone of federalism. Some people consider the three articles [Articles 97 to 99] of Chapter 10 in Japan's Constitution legally meaningless and unnecessary, as they only state obvious legal and moral obligation. However, it is more appropriate to read them as clearly stating that the "rule of law" is the fundamental principle of the Constitution, probably placed at the very end, just before the supplementary provisions, as a summation of the whole Constitution. Here one may see the influence of the long history of the British and American Constitutions.

The three articles of chapter 10 are a coherent expression of the "rule of law." Article 97 reconfirms the eternity, the inviolability, and the historical origin of human rights. The fact that this article is placed at the head of the chapter on supreme law makes clear that the guarantee of human rights is at the core of this Constitution. Human rights under Article 97 are central to the "rule of law." Article 98 explicitly states the supremacy of the Constitution; based on the idea of the supremacy of law, all acts of state power in violation of this higher law shall be null and void, and all acts of the state are to comply with the Constitution. Article 99 declares the obligation of all those who exercise the powers of the state to respect and uphold the Constitution. This is also a straightforward expression of British and American constitutionalism and the rule of law, not man.

(2) Chapter 3 of the Constitution of Japan provides for the guarantee of human rights. It fully responds to the demands of the "rule of law" to guarantee human rights in both substance and form. Most of the guaranteed human rights are, like those in the United States Constitution, unaccompanied by any qualification which allows restrictions by law. In most cases, human rights are guaranteed absolutely. The text does not necessarily mean that human rights should not be limited in any way. The idea is that even legislation enacted by the Diet, representing the people, may not restrict human rights, which are an expression of a higher law.

The Constitution does not have any provisions regarding martial law or emergency powers, and does not recognize any exceptional restriction of human rights in times of emergency. This leaves open the issue of how to apply the Constitution in an extraordinary situation.[40] The lack of any emergency provisions is noteworthy as an indication of the rule of "ordinary law."

(3)   There is controversy as to whether or not Article 31 of the Constitution is modeled after the due process of law, an American expression for the "rule of law." Because it is worded "except according to procedure established by law," and is different from "without due process of law" in the United States Constitution, the drafters of the Constitution, in all likelihood, intended to avoid a direct importation of the American concept of the due process of law. The activist interpretation of the American due process clause by the United States Supreme Court, especially in order to secure economic freedom and property rights, had a number of times held social legislation and New Deal legislation unconstitutional. In my opinion, the basic idea contained in the concept of American due process is incorporated in Article 31. This has been recognized subsequently in principle, by court decisions and scholarly opinion. This point will be touched on later; suffice it to state here that the concept of due process of law was brought into the Constitution and that it adds life to the "rule of law."

(4)   A clear institutional indication of the "rule of law" is strong judicial power. The judiciary under the Meiji Constitution was supposedly independent, but had far less power and a lower status than the courts under the Constitution of Japan. The new Constitution gives the judiciary enlarged powers, institutionalizing the "rule of law" of British and American constitutionalism. Under the Court Organization Law, the judicial power now is not limited to civil and criminal proceedings, but extends to all kinds of cases and controversies in law, including administrative law.[41] The whole judicial power is concentrated in the judiciary. No extraordinary tribunal may be established. An executive agency may exercise an adjudicative function but cannot have the final judicial power. There must always be means provided for resort to courts from decisions of an executive organ.[42]

Under the Meiji Constitution, the Administrative Tribunal (*Gyōsei Saibansha*) belonging to the executive branch, not courts of general jurisdiction, had jurisdiction over litigation between the executive and subjects. Moreover, controversies defined as administrative cases were narrowly limited. That is not compatible with the concept of the "rule of law." Under the Constitution of 1947, the Administrative tribunals was abolished and all administrative cases now come under the jurisdiction of the courts. Of course, numerous problems remain, such as defining the scope and extent or special procedures of judicial review of administrative acts.[43] In a welfare state, a wide variety of acts comes under administrative discretion, raising questions about strict judicial review and the control of administrative acts. (The issue is not unfamiliar to common law countries.) Only a "rule of law" basis enables the courts to substantially guarantee compliance of the state to law.

Even statutes enacted by the Diet, the highest organ of state power, are subject to the power of courts to review for constitutionality. The ultimate manifestation of the "rule of law" is to entrust to the ordinary courts of law the role of substantially guaranteeing the supremacy of the Constitution. The forerunner was an attempt by Sir Edward Coke to apply the "rule of law" to a particular case.[44] In the United States, this claim, under the influence of natural law and higher law, bore fruit as judicial review of unconstitutional legislation. Instead of adopting the constitutional court system that prevailed in the European continent,[45] the Constitution of 1947 follows the American model, directly following the tradition of the "rule of law" and British and American constitutionalism. (This matter shall also be dealt with later, especially in section III.)

The Influence of the British Constitution

I will now note examples of influence on the 1947 Constitution, first of the British Constitution and then of the American Constitution.[46] Although the principal drafters of the Constitution were American lawyers, the text and the institutions suggest more elements derive from the British Constitution than from the various American Constitutions. Of course, many rules of the British Constitution are, like constitutional conventions, unwritten and this allows flexibility. Many of these same rules are spelled out in the Constitution of Japan, and in statutes and orders enacted and issued under the Constitution. On the whole, the influence of the British Constitution is significant. The main reasons for this may be that the United States Constitution has many provisions peculiar to a federal system, and that both the United Kingdom and Japan are unitary states, making it easier for Japan to use British institutions as a model. In some respects, the constitutional structure under the Meiji Constitution honored democracy and a parliamentary cabinet system similar to that of the United Kingdom. Where appropriate, the drafters wanted to maintain continuity with the Meiji regime.

The Emperor Institution

Based on the MacArthur Notes, the Emperor was retained as an institution, but made subject to popular sovereignty. Of course, some countries in Europe have maintained both popular sovereignty and a monarchy (for example, Belgium and Sweden); so the problem was not insoluble. In 1946, the status of the Emperor had to be so defined as to fit with popular sovereignty and two different demands. The Constitution had to reject the historical institution of the Emperor as the locus of sovereign power under the Meiji Constitution. (Actually, of course, the Emperor did not exercise these rights.) The solution also had to respond to powerful voices among the Allied Powers calling for the Emperor institution to be abolished. The best model available seemed to be the British monarchy. The institution of the Emperor in the Constitution of Japan often is said to resemble the British monarchy in that "the King (Queen) reigns but does not rule."[47]

The resulting accommodation is in Article 1 which regards the Emperor as the symbol of Japan, the state, and the unity of the Japanese people. This indicates that the Emperor, as a specific human, represents something as abstract and intangible as the state and the unity of the people.[48] The meaning in law of the word "symbol" is not clear. The preamble of the Statute of Westminster of 1931 states that "the Crown is the symbol of the free association of the members of the British Commonwealth of Nations, and as they are united by a common allegiance to the Crown." The Constitution of Japan may take after this famous passage. The present institution of the Emperor may have some resemblance to the relationship between the British Crown and the Commonwealth.

Of course, legally speaking, the Crown still has important powers in the form of royal prerogatives; but the exercise of royal prerogatives is strictly limited by numerous constitutional conventions. If, as is likely, these limitations are observed, the power and authority of the Crown are almost the same as those of the Japanese Emperor. Because these limitations are conventions, there are uncertain occasions, for example, in the appointment of the prime minister, where the Crown may have some room to make her personal will politically decisive, whereas in the case of the Emperor, the Constitution makes clear who appoints the prime minister. The Emperor can have no substantive power at all in matters of state.[49] There are differences between the Emperor and the British monarch as constitutional institutions[50] and as historical, traditional institutions. For example, all property of the Imperial Household belongs to the state and not to the Imperial Household (Article 88), and the Imperial Household Law[51] is no longer part of the Constitution, but merely a statute, with no provision on abdication and with exclusion of succession by a female.

The Diet as the Highest Governmental Body

Article 41 defines the Diet as the highest organ of state power, but the meaning of this article is not clear. A court may declare a statute, an expression of the will of the Diet, unconstitutional. Therefore, it might have been wiser to state that the Diet is an important organ at the core of the state, as it represents the people and, relatively speaking, is predominant among other organs. This means that the executive and the judiciary shall observe and administer the law, and that, in principle, an act of legislation is by its nature predominant among the official acts of state power. Under the Meiji Constitution, the executive tended to control the Diet; many contemporary states have "a weak legislature and a strong executive." Thus, there is a need to emphasize the importance of the Diet, and to have a constitutional provision making a political pronouncement to that effect. One may well suspect that the drafters meant to refer to the idea of "parliamentary supremacy," an important principle in British constitutional law.[52] Of course, the Constitution of Japan did not adopt the legal implication of "parliamentary supremacy," that an act of parliament is superior to all other sources of law and that other organs cannot review its substance. The supreme law in Japan's legal system is the Constitution, not a statute. The Constitution acknowledges the supremacy of the judiciary in a way similar to that of the United States. But taken as a whole, the Diet system resembles that of British legislative supremacy rather than the American system of checks and balances. For example, a bill passed by both Houses of the Diet becomes, without further action, a statute. No veto power is entrusted to the executive as in the United States.[53]

Various rules and regulations on the powers, status and procedures of the Diet are modeled after British law and custom, or derive from the Meiji Constitution. Following the British system are the collective responsibility of the Cabinet to the Diet, the dissolution of the House of Representatives, the status and privileges of members of the Diet, and the convocation of the Diet. However, the Diet system differs significantly from the the Imperial Diet of the Meiji Constitution and the British Parliament. Peerage and other special status are no longer recognized, so a House of Peers or of Lords does not exist; the second chamber, the House of Councillors (or *Sangiin*), is constituted of elected representatives of the people. Under the Meiji Constitution, the Imperial Diet adopted the British system of requiring three readings of a bill, whereas the 1947 Constitution follows the American committee system.

Some differences and similarities between the powers of the House of Representatives and the Commons, and in relationships with the other chamber should be noted. Basically, the 1947 Constitution recognizes that of

the two Houses, the House of Representatives more directly represents the people, and accords it superior authority. On certain occasions, it can ignore the will of the House of Councillors in forming the will of the Diet. In such instances it has the same authority as the British House of Commons. The Parliament Acts of 1911 and 1949 state that a money bill, which has been passed by the House of Commons and not passed by the House of Lords within one month after being sent there from the House of Commons, shall be an Act of Parliament on the Royal Assent, notwithstanding that the House of Lords has not consented to the bill. These laws also state that a bill other than a money bill passed by the House of Commons shall be an Act of Parliament on the Royal Assent notwithstanding that the House of Lords has not consented to it, if it was passed in two successive sessions, and if one year has elapsed between the second reading of the first session and the passage of the identical bill at the second session. In the case of Japan's present Constitution the unicameral legislature proposed in the original SCAP draft was changed to a bicameral system at the insistence of Japan's Government. On that occasion, the Government suggested adoption of a relationship between the two Houses identical to that in the British Parliament. The issue was finally settled with a provision allowing a bill to become a statute without the consent of the House of Councillors when it has been passed a second time by the House of Representatives by a majority of two-thirds or more of the members present
(Art. 59(2)).[54] The requirement of a majority of two-thirds or more is more restrictive than that for British Parliament Acts, and more like requirement in the United States Constitution that Congress pass a bill a second time by a two-thirds majority to override a presidential veto.[55]

A Parliamentary Cabinet

In the 1947 Constitution the Cabinet is charged with the executive power under a parliamentary cabinet system. The parliamentary cabinet developed through long political experience in Great Britain, and its structure and operation are governed by constitutional conventions.[56] The Constitution of Japan provides for a cabinet system reflecting both British constitutional institutions and experience under the Meiji Constitution. Some provisions regarding the Cabinet and its practices evidence strong influence from the British Constitution.

The usual form of a parliamentary cabinet is that it be composed by the party or parties of majority in the lower house, which is deemed to represent the will of the people better than the second chamber. The Cabinet continues in charge as long as it has the confidence of the lower house.

These are the main characteristics of a system which recognizes liaison between legislature and cabinet. Parliament (the House of Commons) controls the government with the power to pass a no-confidence resolution, but the Cabinet can dissolve the House of Commons. A parliamentary cabinet differs from a presidency separate from the legislature in that its checks and balances are built into that liaison. The central issue is the occasions in which the House can be dissolved. The drafters apparently intended to give great power to the Diet, and expected that the House of Representatives could be dissolved only by passing a no-confidence resolution or by rejecting a confidence resolution (Art. 69).[57] After the restoration of Japan's independence in 1952, this theory was rejected in favor of the British interpretation of the dissolution power. There is no legal limitation on the power to dissolve and the Cabinet can dissolve the House of Representatives whenever it wishes to seek the will of the people. Most scholarly opinion seems to support that interpretation.

The text of the Constitution is not clear on whether the Cabinet has the power to present bills to the Diet. Article 72 appears to place its emphasis on the fact that a Prime Minister is the representative of the Cabinet. Judging from the provisions stating that the Diet is the sole law-making organ (Art. 41) and that the Cabinet presents the budget (Arts. 86 and 73(5)), one might suspect that the original intent was that the presentation or submission of bills be confined to members of the Diet, as in the United States. However, Japan has consistently adopted the British procedure. Article 5 of the Cabinet Law[58] clearly provides to that effect and most bills are government bills as in the United Kingdom.

Of course, the parliamentary cabinet in Japan is not identical to that of the United Kingdom. One profound difference in law is the status of a Prime Minister in the Cabinet. In the United Kingdom, apart from the *de facto* power, a Prime Minister is merely "*primus inter pares*," the first among equals, in relation to his Cabinet colleagues (a Prime Minister under the Meiji Constitution had the same status). A Prime Minister under the Constitution of Japan not only has the power to appoint his ministers but also the power to remove them at will (Art. 68). The power belongs only to him and does not require a resolution of a Cabinet meeting. The power of dismissal secures the status of a Prime Minister as the head of the Cabinet. When a Minister's view is contrary to that of the Prime Minister, the whole Cabinet need not resign; the dismissal of that single Minister suffices to solve the problem. Only thrice has a Minister been thus dismissed,[59] so the power is rarely exercised. Nevertheless, this power suggests the Prime Minister may be even more powerful in constitutional terms than the British Prime Minister.

The Influence of the United States Constitution

Numerous provisions in the Constitution of Japan can be traced logically to the United States Constitution. While the influence of the British Constitution is mainly structural organization and the powers of state organs such as the Emperor, the Diet and the Cabinet, the United States Constitution is more influential in areas closely associated with the lives of the people. This makes the interpretation and application of provisions related to the United States Constitution frequently practical issues. Reference to the United States Constitution in the course of litigation or in other contexts of practical application of the Constitution can be very important. This factor, along with the fact that many aspects of the political theory underlying the United States Constitution are in the 1947 Constitution, make most people think of the United States Constitution when the impact of foreign constitutions on the Constitution of Japan is mentioned. Many consider the 1947 Constitution as an inheritance from the United States Constitution. It is not far fetched to say that one cannot discuss the former without referring to the latter. The American influence is most prominent in Chapter 3, which deals with the guarantee of fundamental human rights, and in Chapter 6 on the judiciary. The content of these provisions is described in section II and the impact of the United States Constitution on particular cases in section III; here, I would only make a few points.[60]

The Guarantee of Human Rights

Chapter 3 guaranteeing fundamental human rights is the heart of the Constitution. The Potsdam Declaration (July 26, 1945), which set the terms for ending the war and which the Japanese Government accepted, demanded in its eleventh clause the establishment of fundamental human rights. The Constitution prescribes in minute detail human rights that cannot be infringed upon by law. Among these human rights are the so-called "social rights" (*shakaiken*) appropriate to a twentieth-century constitution. These include the right to maintain a decent standard of living (Art. 25), the right to receive an education (Art. 26), and the right of workers to organize (Art. 28). These rights are not in the United States Constitution, but reflect in part the influence of America's twentieth-century New Deal experience. Most of the other provisions in Chapter 3 are logically connected with the United States Constitution.

(1)   *Personal freedoms*--The provisions for the human rights of suspects and defendants in criminal justice are detailed. From a traditional legal standpoint, they might appropriately have been prescribed in a statute, such as the Code of Criminal Procedure rather than in the Constitution. The main reason for including these articles, which may seem disproportionately detailed compared to other rights provisions, reflects on the extensive violations of related personal freedoms under the Meiji Constitution. A further reason is the influence of the numerous provisions on this kind of personal freedom in the U.S. Bill of Rights. The text and wording of some provisions are so similar that they appear to be direct importations from the Bill of Rights; for example, the prohibition on involuntary servitude, except as a punishment for crime (Art. 18 of the Constitution of Japan and Amendment 13 of the United States Constitution), the prohibition on cruel punishments (Art. 36 and Amendment 8), the right to a speedy and public trial by an impartial tribunal (Art. 37(1)) and (Amendment 6), the right to examine or confront all witnesses and the right of compulsory process for obtaining witnesses (Art. 37(2) and Amendment 6), the right to have the assistance of counsel (Art. 37(3) and Amendment 6), the prohibition on compulsory testimony against oneself (Art. 38(1) and Amendment 5), and finally the ban on double jeopardy (Art. 39 and Amendment 5).[61] American constitutional cases and scholarly opinions have undoubtedly been suggestive in the interpretation and application of these provisions.[62]

(2)   *Procedure Established by Law*--As mentioned earlier in relation to the "rule of law," the question of whether Article 31 adopted the American due process clause is debated. The prevalent view in academe and the courts at present is that Article 31 includes a certain part of the notion of due process as developed in the United States. Even though the text of Article 31 seems to allow any procedure so long as it was established by law, the common understanding disputes that. The content of the procedure established by law must meet the test of fundamental principles of liberty and justice. For instance, it is considered necessary to give notice and an opportunity for a hearing to those who would be adversely affected by an act. The text may be read to limit application to criminal procedure; but it also allows the interpretation that an appropriate procedure is required in administrative proceedings as well as in criminal proceedings. An administrative procedure requires appropriate content because an administrative action may have an adverse effect, such as a revocation of business license or permit, similar to criminal proceedings in which criminal

penalties may be imposed. The so-called substantive due process of Amendment 14 necessitates a wider application than in Japan because of the federal system. The meaning of Article 31 includes the vagueness doctrine, in that it would be unconstitutional if the constitutive factors of a crime or standards for administrative decision-making were too vague, and not comprehensible by an average person with a normal ability to judged. All these interpretations have developed under the influence of the United States Constitution.

(3)   *Freedom of Expression*--In many countries, including countries which highly appreciate the value of freedom of expression, constitutions explicitly state the grounds for restricting freedom (e.g., the Basic Law of West Germany [*Grundgesetz fur die Bundersrepublik Deutschland*] Article 5, Section 2). Article 21 of the 1947 Constitution, in guaranteeing freedom of speech, press, assembly, association and all other forms of expression, did not use any restrictive wording and takes the form of an unconditional guarantee. One may say that it follows the First Amendment of the United States Constitution. To the apprehension expressed by Japanese that this might become an absolute guarantee, the drafters answered that even though no limitation is indicated in the wording, that does not signify absolute freedom and that is clear from the operation of the United States Constitution. With such a background, the abundant constitutional cases on freedom of expression in the United States have had a powerful impact upon studies of Japanese constitutional law, and upon the courts through these scholarly works. The decision of courts have clarified the occasions when freedom of expression may be restricted (major cases are analyzed in section III).[63]

(4)   *The Separation of State and Religion*--The Meiji Constitution also guaranteed freedom of religion. However, the Japanese were not as aware of the need to uphold this freedom as those in Europe and America. Moreover, Shinto shrine worship, which was derived from ancestral worship of the Emperor as a god, was made an obligation of subjects under Meiji law. This freedom was significantly limited in that it was allowed only insofar as other beliefs were not incompatible with Shinto, the established state religion at that time. In the wartime 1930s and 1940s, Shinto worship also served as the spiritual foundation for an eccentric nationalism and militarism. SCAP issued a directive on Shinto (*Shintō Shirei*) on December 15, 1945, requiring the separation of the state from Shrine Shinto and abolishing the established status of Shinto shrines. This position was accepted and incorporated into the Constitution of Japan.

Article 20 guarantees the freedom of religion (paragraph 1), the freedom to have or not to have a religious belief, to choose a religion if one chooses to have a belief, to perform religious acts such as prayers, to form a religious association, and to propagate a belief to others. Moreover, the Constitution prohibits compulsory attendance at or participation in religious ceremonies and practices, such as were forced upon people under the Shinto establishment (paragraph 2). These provisions derived from the guarantee of the free exercise of religion of the First Amendment of the United States Constitution. In addition, Article 20 provides for the separation of the state and religion, which derives from the establishment clause of the First Amendment, and intends to eliminate the dangers of unifying the state and religion. Religious organizations are prohibited from receiving privileges from the state or exercising any political authority (paragraph 1). The state and its organs may not engage in any religious education or other religious activities (paragraph 3). Although this thorough separation of the state and religion very much follows the spirit of the United States Constitution, the Constitution goes beyond the U.S. position, in that it not only guarantees freedom of religion as a human right, but also includes an article in the chapter on finance which prohibits the spending or appropriation of public money and other properties for any religious institution or association (Art. 89). The intent is a more perfect separation of the state and religion in fiscal matters of the state. In the United States, a succession of Supreme Court cases has strengthened or refined the separation of church and state. We might say that the Constitution of Japan anticipated that trend in the United States.[64]

The Judicial System

The chapter titled "the Judiciary," defining the organization and powers of the courts, manifests extensive influence from the American judicial system. As noted earlier, the judicial power of the courts extends to all cases and controversies in law, including administrative cases; even in cases where an administrative organ or agency has performed an adjudicative function, the courts have the power to review its decision. This feature is characteristic of judicial power in the U.S. and the United Kingdom and is related to the "rule of law" principle. Also, the ordinary courts have the power to decide the constitutionality of law and orders in adjudicating a particular case. This important function derives from American constitutional law in the famous case of *Marbury v. Madison*.[65] The fact that the 1947 Constitution adopted the power of judicial review in its text means that Japan has chosen to use the American form of constitutional guarantees. (Japan's judicial review carries the deepest imprint of the United States Constitution. Section III compares the Japanese and American systems in detail. The following are a few notable features not dealt with there.)

First, the Supreme Court is made an organ whose establishment is constitutionally required. The establishment of other inferior courts is left to law enacted by the Diet (Art. 76(1)). This follows Article 3, section 1 of the United States Constitution. Three features of the present judicial system did not exist under the Meiji Constitution. None are expressly defined in the United States Constitution; but they are modeled after systems recognized in American (especially state) courts.

The first feature is the rule-making power of the courts. Under the Meiji Constitution, the courts could make law through cases, but were not vested with the power to formulate abstract and general law. The 1947 Constitution vests the courts with the power to administer the judiciary[66] and the Supreme Court with the power to determine the rules of procedure and other matters by court regulations (Art. 77(1)). Such a system was developed in the United Kingdom and the United States. Of course, procedures for the federal courts of the United States are regulated by the rules of courts. The role of these rules is extensive in the United States, whereas in Japan most of the procedures are defined by statutes such as the Code of Civil Procedure.[67]

The second matter is popular review of Supreme Court Justices. A Justice of the Supreme Court is reviewed at the first general election of members of the House of Representatives following his appointment, and again at the first general election after a lapse of ten years (and in the same manner thereafter). When the majority of votes are in favor of dismissal (an X marked above the list of judges printed is a vote in favor of dismissal; no mark above the list is considered a vote against dismissal), the judge shall be dismissed (Art. 79(1) and (2)). This system of popular control of judges was taken from the state of Missouri in the United States. In many states, judges are elected; the number of states adopting a popular review system is increasing. In Japan, where people had no experience with the popular election of judges, the reasonableness and rationale of this system have been questioned. It is impossible to imagine a case in which a majority of voters would favor dismissal (past examples show at most about 10% of voters favoring dismissal). However, because Supreme Court Justices have the ultimate power to review the constitutionality [of official acts including legislation] and to make political decisions, it is appropriate that their status be reviewed by the sovereign people. Although there are controversies concerning forms, many consider this popular review quite meaningful.

The third feature is the privilege of reappointment of lower court judges. Judges other than Supreme Court Justices are appointed and hold office for a term of ten years with the privilege of reappointment (Art. 80(1)). The term of ten years corresponds to the period after which Justices of the Supreme Court (who have no limit on their terms but must retire at age 70) become subject to popular review. The existence of a term probably is patterned after some state court systems in the United States. But where judges are not elected, and where, unlike the United Kingdom and the United States, a system of career judgeships is established, set terms seem inappropriate. The current system usually recruits a qualified graduate of the Legal Training and Research Institute at a young age to be appointed as an Assistant Judge (*hanji ho*); he continues to be a judge until retirement at sixty-five. On the one hand, it seems better to appoint judges for life, without terms like judges of the U.S. federal judiciary, even when there is a specific retirement age. On the other hand, setting a term may be one way to eliminate unfit judges since their status is otherwise so secure. The only means of removing a judge is public impeachment and trial to declare mental or physical incompetence to perform official duties (Art. 78). The principle is reappointment, not resignation at the end of one term.[68]

Conclusion

The Influence of American Constitutional Theory

The influence of the British and American Constitutions on the text of the 1947 Constitution of Japan and on institutions established by the Constitution has been enormous. But more important is influence upon the interpretation and application of the Constitution. Even when similar provisions and institutions exist, a totally different constitutional system may emerge because of a totally different interpretation and application. Especially in the case of a constitution, generally speaking, most provisions are concise and admit of a wide choice of possible interpretations. The actual applications might easily create a different constitution.

On looking back over the forty-four years of the 1947 Constitution, one sees a process of eagerly absorbing cases and theories of American constitutional law.[69] American constitutional theories have been referred to with amazing frequency in the interpretation and application of Japan's Constitution, particularly in the fields of constitutional litigation, procedure established by law, and freedom of speech. (For cases and theory, see section III.) As a conclusion, I would briefly examine the reception of American constitutional theories in court decisions, scholarly opinions, and legal education.

(1)   *Decisions of the Courts*--A typical decision of a court in Japan would cite cases of the past, but would rarely quote academic writings, far less decisions and authorities of foreign countries. Even when certain suggestions apparently came from a certain American constitutional theory, there is no direct evidence in the decision to show that. But this is not to deny their influence. The same is true in the Supreme Court. Although a decision would not refer to an American constitutional theory as such, parties to a litigation and their counsels frequently cite decisions of the United States Supreme Court to support their claims or statements for appeal to our Supreme Court. In cases where foreign authorities have been cited, judges naturally examine and consider those cases and determine their applicability to the issues in question. When decisions of the Supreme Court of Japan, especially those in constitutional cases, are scrutinized, quite often those who have some understanding of the American Constitution can easily detect one or the other American constitutional theory in them. A recent example is a case of malapportionment of Diet seats among election districts. The Supreme Court declared the serious malapportionment in question unconstitutional, although it did not declare the election itself null and void.[70] One could easily detect ideas from cases following *Baker v. Carr*[71] in this decision. In a litigation concerning the legitimacy of a preliminary injunction order by a court to prohibit the publication of defamatory documents regarding a candidate for public office, the Supreme Court decided that such prior restraint would be permitted only under very limited conditions, and that in principle such publication cannot be restricted.[72] In this decision, one can detect the influence of prior restraint theory developed since *Near v. Minnesota*.[73]

To make these references possible, the Supreme Court Library has a complete collection of American federal and state law reports and an extensive collection of monographs and law reviews. These are easily accessible not only to the Supreme Court Justices and research judges assigned to the Supreme Court, but also to other judges of lower courts. At an early stage of their career, many judges expected to have a particularly bright future are allowed to spend time studying abroad, most often in the United States, where they are exposed to American law.[74] The fact that judges learn American law in the United States when they are still young makes it natural for them to introduce American approaches to law. It is not mysterious if some of those judges employ American legal theories (especially constitutional theory) in the Japanese adjudication process. One must not overlook the influence of such American experience on those competent and promising judges.

Academic Theories--The influence of American constitutional theory on the study of constitutional law in Japan is far more obvious than in the case of court decisions. Japan's modern legal system started with the reception of European and American law. Since the nineteenth century, much of the energy and effort in Japanese legal studies has been spent in comparative law, and constitutional law has been no exception. Although comprehensive comparative studies of constitutional law have not been especially fruitful, constitutional law scholars have published studies about foreign constitutional law.[75] Most profound has been the development of studies on the American Constitution.

Many constitutional law scholars have examined in depth the United States Constitution and common law, and have endeavored to employ the results in interpreting our Constitution. Works of brilliant research have been published. A series on constitutional litigation by Nobuyoshi Ashibe, our co-author, is a typical example. My works on freedom of speech might be included in the list. Some works analyze American cases (especially decisions of the Warren Court) on personal freedom and criminal proceedings, on equality, on privacy, on environmental rights, on the right to know and other new rights, all of which deserve much attention. There is also widespread interest in the study of the most recent decisions of the United States Supreme Court.[76] These have the direct effect of introducing and clarifying the American Constitution. Because of circumstances mentioned before, academic theories on the United States Constitution are considered relevant to the interpretation and application of our Constitution. As we have already seen, the isolation of American legal studies within Japan that Kenzo Takayanagi had deplored before the war does not exist. The results of scholarly research may not be directly incorporated into decisions of the courts. Yet one cannot ignore the fact that influential theories actually have an impact on the courts, especially perhaps because academic theory is accorded relatively high status in Japan.

Legal Education--One factor determining the thought patterns of a lawyer is the kind of legal education given during the process or legal nurturing. Here, I would only indicate the importance of comparative law education. Legal education in Japan takes place at the Legal Training and Research Institute (LTRI) of the Supreme Court and at universities. After passing an extremely difficult National Law Examination (*Shihō Shiken*), those who wish to qualify as professional lawyers (*i.e.*, judges, prosecutors and practicing attorneys) enter the LTRI and receive two years of legal training. The education at LTRI places emphasis on the practical training needed for legal practice. This does not mean that comparative law is ignored. Seminars on constitutional litigation have been held as well as lectures on American law.

Legal education at the universities is for the most part undergraduate education, not intended to train professional lawyers, but to educate widely on matters pertaining to law those who will work as public officials and in private businesses. Since the Meiji period, courses on comparative law have always occupied an important place in legal education. For example, in the Faculty of Law at Tokyo University, apart from students who major in political science, all are required to earn credit from at least one Anglo-American, German or French law course. Since World War II, the majority of students have tended to choose Anglo-American law. Courses entitled "Anglo-American Public Law" mainly cover the United States Constitution. Seminars on the United States Constitution are popular.[77] Courses on constitutional law also cover American constitutional theories. Generally speaking, a fairly large majority of undergraduate law students are exposed to American constitutional theories. In this way, the fact that many law students are interested in the United States Constitution may be one of the important foundations for the influence of the United States Constitution on the Constitution of Japan, even though many of them may not engage in legal careers after graduation.

Current Trends and the Future of the 1947 Constitution

It is difficult to predict the future of the Constitution of Japan. It depends very much on political, economical and social conditions. Nevertheless, a fairly accurate prognostication may be possible in certain areas.

No matter how static a society is, reality is in flux. In contemporary society which is so changeable, gaps between constitutional text and reality are inevitable. When there is such a gap and if effort to close the gap is neglected, there is danger that the normal development of society may be obstructed or that the Constitution may be reduced to mere form without substance. The means for closing this gap differ from country to country. In many countries, the major method used might be to amend their constitutions, so that they correspond to reality through formal amending procedures. In the case of the United States Constitution, the formal amending procedure is not often invoked. In spite of the fact that the society has changed drastically in the 200 years since the time of the making of the Constitution, there are only a few formal amendments, especially when one takes into consideration the fact that the first ten amendments, called the Bill of Rights, can be treated as part of the original Constitution. If those are excluded, only sixteen amendments have been adopted during the past two hundred years. One may say that the work to close the gap has been done not by amendment of the Constitution, but mainly by changes in the interpretation and application of the Constitution, especially through Supreme Court decisions.

In the case of Japan, during nearly sixty years of history under the Meiji Constitution, the reality of the Constitution changed drastically, but the formal text was never altered. The Constitution was considered a code of permanent effect or a sacred law that ought not to be changed. The 1947 Constitution also has not experienced any amendment throughout its forty-four years of history. The Constitution is also a kind of law. It is true that because it is the fundamental law, one has to be prudent if not cautious in amending (in fact, it contains amendment procedures such as a requirement of ratification by the people, which makes it difficult to pass any amending proposals), but it is not necessary to regard it as so sacred and inviolable that no one should touch it. In reality, the gap between the Constitution and the society has been filled by decisions of the courts, by the enactment of statutes, and by conventions of the executive through interpretation and application, so that reality better reflects the norms of the Constitution. This method will probably be the way to close the gaps in the future as well. On this point, as on others, it is most likely that Japan will choose the way that the United States has taken.

It is true that, unlike the Meiji Constitution, the 1947 Constitution has always been the object of criticism from some quarters calling for amendment. Among those in the amend-the-Constitution movement, some claim that certain parts of the text are not responsive enough to the circumstances of Japan or to the demands of modern society. Examples are the popular review of Supreme Court Justices, the extreme separation of state and religion, the House of Councillors which functions in the shadow of the House of Representatives. However, the major opinions in the revision movement are based either on emotional or allegedly "realistic" grounds. The former claim that this is a Constitution whose draft was "forced upon the people" when the will of the people could not be freely expressed, and that the process of making it was not desirable for a fundamental law of a nation state. The latter maintain that even by the most far-fetched interpretation, one has to admit that reality is in conflict with the Constitution. The major example given is that the Self Defense Forces cannot possibly be judged constitutional under the pacifist provisions of Article 9.[78]

The Commission on the Constitution (*Kempō Chōsakai*) was established in 1957 and examined extensively the issue of amendment.[79] Nevertheless, no amendment has materialized and the Constitution has been left as it is until this day. There seems little likelihood that the Constitution will be amended in the near future. If this is the case, the Constitution will have to make the most out of flexible interpretation and application to suit our society and its needs. We may expect that the American way of interpreting and applying the Constitution will continue to influence the Constitution of Japan. Of course, our two countries are not identical in historical background or political, economical and social circumstances, and our interpretation and application of constitutions will not necessarily be identical. But among the countries of the world, the United States and Japan have societies which are comparatively similar in character. Therefore, I trust that basically the two constitutions will go forward in more or less the same direction.

NOTES: I

1. The Edict of Imperial Restoration (*Osei Fukko Rei*) of 1867 was followed by the dissolution of the feudal domain system, the acceleration of the modernization process, the promotion of a centralized national government, the encouragement of capitalism by the state, and a reduction of local armament.

2. See Ryosuke Ishii, *A History of Political Institutions in Japan* (1980) for a concise description of the development of Japan's law and state system since ancient times.

3. This was the first written law in Japan. It consisted of moral rules based on Confucianism and Buddhism. At that time, no distinction was made between law and morality. Thus, the promulgation of disciplinary measures was an effective means of government.

4. "*Ritsu*" defines criminal penalties and "*ryo*" consists mainly of rules of administrative law. Comparing Japan's with the original Chinese law, one finds very little difference with respect to Japanese "*ritsu*" (except that penalties are somewhat less severe) but that Japan's "*ryo*" were much modified to meet her conditions.

5. John Henry Wigmore, who studied Japanese law of the Tokugawa period (1600-1868), pointed out long ago the significance of case law in Japanese law: "From the 1600s onward, the highly organized judiciary system began to develop by judicial precedent a body of national law and practice, which can only be compared with the English independent development after the 1400s." John Henry Wigmore, *A Panorama of the World's Legal Systems* (1928), 504.

6. Shinpei Eto played a major role in the codification and in the completion of the judicial system in the early days of the Meiji Period. The story is that when Eto ordered Rinsho Mitsukuri to translate the French codes, he said, "Just translate quickly. Do not hesitate to translate incorrectly because of haste." This may illustrate the impatient attitude of the day. The translation of the five *Codes napoleoniens* by Mitsukuri was the first step in the massive reception of Western law into Japan.

7. Yatsuka Hozumi's words, "Loyalty and filial piety disappear as the [French] civil code appears" represented this school of thought.

8. Civil Code (*Minpoten*), Laws No. 28 and No. 98 of 1890. Boissonade's Civil Code, which was based on French law, was opposed by a school of common law specialists on the grounds that the law of a nation should reflect its own history and ethnological characteristics. As a result of this controversy, enforcement of this Civil Code was postponed in 1890.

9. The German influence on the structure and form of the Civil Code was profound, but some scholars believe Boissonade's Civil Code influenced the content of most provisions.

10. Underlying this tendency was the belief that it was important to emphasize the usefulness of legal studies to the bureaucrats and to the bureaucratically inclined judges. German legal studies served those interests best.

11. Prominent among practicing lawyers at that time were Chu Egi, Kiyokazu/Seiichi Kishi, Takuzo Hanai, Kado Hara.

12. Shigeto Hozumi and Izutaro Suehiro represented this movement.

13. Trust Law (*Shintaku Hō*), Law No. 62 of 1922.

14. Jury Law (*Baishinhō*), Law No. 50 of 1923.

15. First, the activities of practicing lawyers took place within a trial structure that was modelled after German law. Apart from affecting patterns of legal thought, such legal activities could not have a positive influence on Japanese law or legal studies. Second, even though some influential scholars may have had some affinity for the common law approach to law, that did not induce widespread reception of common law. Nor was there any collaboration with specialists of common law. Thus, common law had very little impact on the interpretation of Japanese law. Third, laws modeled after British or American law were not effectively utilized.

16. From 1926, an extreme right-wing ultranationalism surged to the surface. In the area of law, some asserted a unique jurisprudence peculiar to Japanese law which was supposed to be different from Western law. But such jurisprudence was either a reflection of Nazi jurisprudence or a theory of "revision to the old days" held by a select few which could not stand up to any serious criticism and did not bring any changes in the character of law and legal studies.

17. Code of Criminal Procedure (*Keiji Soshōhō*), Law No. 131 of 1948. The Habeas Corpus Law (*Jinshin Hogo Hō*, Law No. 199 of 1948) was enacted at Japanese initiative, with the support of SCAP. Though it was modeled after the Writ of Habeas Corpus, this law has not played as large a role in the protection of personal freedom as its counterpart in common law.

18. Law to Prohibit Private Monopoly and Guarantee Fair Trade (*Shiteki Dokusen no Kinshi oyobi Kōsei Torihiki no Kakuho ni Kansuru Hōritsu*), Law No. 54 of 1947.

19. Securities Exchange Law (*Shoken Torihiki Hō*), Law No. 25 of 1948.

20. Company Law (*Kaisha Hō*), Law No. 167 of 1950, which constitutes Book 2 of the Commercial Code (*Shōhō*), originally Law No. 48 of 1899.

21. Labor Union Law (*Rōdō Kumiai Hō*), Law No. 51 of 1945.

22. Labor Union Law (*Rōdō Kumiai Hō*), Law No. 174 of 1994.

23. Labor Relations Adjustment Law (*Rōdō Kankei Chōseihō*), Law No. 25 of 1946.

24. Labor Standards Law (*Rōdō Kijunhō*), Law No. 49 of 1947.

25. The Japanese American Society for Legal Studies (*Nichi Bei Hōgakkai*) was established in 1964 with branches in both the United States and Japan today. It has promoted exchanges between American and Japanese legal scholars, and has

published *Law in Japan: An Annual* and *AMERIKA HŌ* (American Law); *see* notes 76 and 77, *infra*.

26. Rene David and John E.C. Brierley, *Major Legal Systems in the World Today* (2d ed. 1978), 17.

27. *Id.* at 24; Rene David, *English Law and French Law* (1980).

28. The following are some examples of the duality of the Meiji Constitution:

(1) The Emperor was sovereign (Art. 4), allegedly based on the will of the gods, which is *"Tenjō Mukyū"* or "everlasting in the universe." Neither the Emperors nor their subjects could alter the Emperor institution. The Emperor was above the three powers of the state, namely the legislative, administrative and judicial powers, but he exercised his rights of sovereignty with the assistance of the state's organs. The authority to make a constitution belonged to him and he was the only person who could initiate the amending process. He also had the status of a priest of Shrine (*Jinja*) Shinto, the established religion which subjects were forced to observe.

(2) The Meiji Constitution established the bicameral Imperial Diet, one chamber of which was the elected House of Representatives. Without its participation, statutes and the budget could not take effect. The rights of individuals were guaranteed under statutes enacted with the consent of the Imperial Diet. This was a sign of government by law, but the powers and authority of the Imperial Diet were not those of a genuinely democratic legislature. The pattern of separation of powers followed German theory which emphasized the independence of the executive from the legislature, and was totally different from the British parliamentary cabinet system and the American model of strict separation of powers.

(3) The Emperor performed all acts of government with the advice of Ministers of State (Art. 55). In reality, the Emperor was expected to act according to the will of his ministers. The ministerial advisory system places the acts of the monarch under a democratic control and check, as long as a legislature is able to control the ministers. Under the Meiji Constitution, the legislature did not control the Ministers. Also, the Constitution left gaps. For example, the military's Supreme Command operated independently, without any interference from the Cabinet and the Diet.

(4) The Meiji Constitution's guarantee of human rights represented tremendous progress over the feudal system but those rights did not belong to individuals as human beings; they were gifts granted to subjects by the Emperor. Even in theory, the guarantee applied only against intrusions by the executive; there was no recourse when the state violated human rights under statutes passed by the Diet (*Vonbehalt des Gesetzes*, qualification by statute).

29. Masamichi Aikawa, who had studied English law, listed as the "two features of a constitution:" "to explicitly state the proper uses of government powers and authority and to prevent their abuse," and "to proclaim the rights of those who are governed against those who govern and to preserve these rights." He considered these principles of the "rule of law" to be the basic principles of a constitution. He was one of the very few to apply studies of the British Constitution to the Meiji Constitution.

30. Kenzo Takayanagi wrote an outstanding study of American judicial review. When his book was published after World War II, he wrote, "At the time when I conducted research on the constitutional guarantees by the judiciary in the United States, there was not one scholar of public law in this country who had studied this aspect of the United States Constitution.... And I suspect that probably no more than a couple of scholars had read any of the articles that I had published on the topic." Kenzo Takayanagi, *Shihō Ken No Yui* (rev. ed. 1958), 3. This illustrates well the irrelevance of the British and American Constitutions to the Meiji Constitution before the war.

31. See Frank O. Miller, *Minobe Tatsukichi: Interpreter of Constitutionalism in Japan* (1965).

32. "*Minpon shugi*" originally meant democracy. Because the Meiji Constitution explicitly stated that the Emperor was the sovereign, Yoshino used the word not to mean that sovereignty rests in the people, but, as an "ism," that state authority should pursue and fulfill the happiness of the people. He coined the word so as to signify the centrality of the people in the governance of state. This theory was influential in promoting and supporting Taisho democracy, and protecting those in favor of constitutional government.

33. One of the reasons may be that the drafters and others involved in the drafting process were critical of some aspects of the United States Constitution, because they were sympathetic to the difficulties New Deal legislation had had to face.

34. General Whitney pointed out the influence of factors listed in (2) to (4) in the making of the Constitution. See Takayanagi, *supra* note 30, at 258.

35. This point is expressly stated in a report by Lieutenant Colonel Rowell. See Takayanagi, 2.

36. *Id.* at 104.

37. See Lawrence W. Beer, *Freedom of Expression in Japan: A Study in Comparative Law, Politics, and Society* (1984) on the Peace Preservation Law (Law No. 46 of 1925), 65.

38. Albert V. Dicey, *An Introduction to the Study of the Law of the Constitution* (10th ed. 1959), 184.

39. "It must be conceded that there are such rights in every free government beyond the control of the State. A government which recognized no such rights, which held the lives, the liberty and the property of its citizens subject at all times to the absolute disposition and unlimited control of even the most democratic depository of powers, is after all but a despotism. It is true it is a despotism of the many, of the

majority, if you choose to call it so, but it is nonetheless a despotism," per Miller J. in *The Citizens' Savings & Loan Association v. City of Topeka*, 20 *Wall.* 655, 662 (U.S. 1875).

40. The 1947 Constitution lacks provisions defining the measures to be taken in case of emergency and where it becomes necessary to take steps which would be unconstitutional under normal circumstances. Possibly the Diet will enact a statute empowering or delegating broad authority to the Government without a specified mandate, but to take necessary means to handle the situation. After the Cabinet had taken possibly unconstitutional emergency measures, the Diet would examine them and confirm the measures taken, giving immunity, if necessary. This is the choice that the United Kingdom took to deal with the two world wars. The drafters seemed to expect this as the way to deal with emergencies. *See* Takayanagi *et al.*, *supra* note 24, at 205.

41. Article 3, Court Organization Law (*Saibansho Hō*), Law No. 59 of 1947.

42. Article 76(2), Constitution of Japan, Itoh and Beer, 265.

43. Administrative Case Litigation Law (*Gyōsei Jiken Soshōhō*), Law No. 139 of 1962.

44. Dr. Bonham's Case, 8 *Coke Rep.* 114a, (1610). Cf. Haines, *The American Doctrine of Judicial Supremacy* (2nd ed., 1959), 227.

45. Some scholars alleged that Article 81 gave the Supreme Court the power to adjudicate the unconstitutionality of legislation and orders in the abstract, as well as to exercise the power of judicial review in concrete cases. This would have given the Supreme Court the character of an European-type constitutional court. The majority of scholars maintain that Article 81 adopts the American model of judicial review of constitutionality. The Supreme Court also holds the latter view.

46. Here, the focus is on noteworthy features for comparison with the British and American Constitutions. A more detailed explanation of the Constitution is given in section II.

47. Use of the word "reign" was avoided in the Constitution lest it might connote even the slightest power to govern.

48. In almost all countries, national flags and national anthems play a symbolic role. A symbol does not integrate a nation or a people by itself, but reinforces the existing integrity and discourage divisions among people. These functions cannot be ignored. A monarch is said to have all the functions mentioned above. Yet a symbol acquires meaning as a symbol by actually fulfilling the role of integration. When the symbol no longer satisfies the role, it loses its status as a symbol regardless of the fact that it is so defined in the Constitution. The fact that a high percentage of the people in Japan have supported the symbolic institution of the Emperor since the establishment of the Constitution may be due to the fact that the Emperor has occupied a significant role in the integrating process.

49. The British monarch has the legal power and authority to administer the affairs of the state and is a monarch in the true sense of the word, and is the sovereign (head of the State). In comparison, there is a theoretical argument as to whether the

Emperor is a monarch or a head of the state, because he does not have any substantial power to administer affairs of state. Today, the concepts of monarch and head of the state have so changed that the Emperor may be classified as such, even though he has no power whatsoever in matters of state. Therefore, it is not necessary to call Japan a republic. International convention also treats the Emperor as a monarch and as the head of the state (for example, letters of attestation from foreign ambassadors are addressed to the Emperor). *See also infra*, section II, at notes 42-49.

50. Because the Constitution lists only a limited number of acts as matters of state that the Emperor may perform, it gives the impression that all other acts of the Emperor are purely private. This gave rise to problems regarding some acts the Emperor performs as a symbol which do not fit the description of permissible matters of state. For example, the Emperor presents himself at the opening of a new Diet and makes speeches. He makes official visits to foreign countries and exchanges letters with other heads of state. These are neither an exercise of power on matters of state nor purely private acts. Some allege that he is not entitled to engage in these acts; but the majority accept these as official or formal acts incidental to his status of symbol, and thus are not forbidden by the Constitution. Custom follows the majority opinion. Needless to say, these official and formal acts do not and should not have any political significance. For instance, the speech at the opening of a Diet must be politically neutral and merely ceremonial. There is here a tremendous difference from the Queen's speech at the commencement of parliament which states the basic policies of Her Majesty's Government.

51. Imperial Household Law, Law No. 3 of 1947; see *infra* II, note 42.

52. In the SCAP draft, the character of the Diet as supreme organ was apparent in the limited power given the Cabinet to dissolve parliament, in the need for the Diet's consent to the Prime Minister's appointment of Ministers, and in the power of the Diet to override by a two-third majority certain court decisions holding laws and other official acts unconstitutional.

53. It is widely acknowledged that the British monarch's veto power has disappeared by constitutional convention.

54. In ratifying treaties and passing budget bills, the power of the House of Representatives is even greater (Art.s 60(2) and 61).

55. The Constitution places fiscal affairs under the control of the Diet. This is called "fiscal democracy," and is more or less faithful to the British fiscal system. The major exception is that in the United Kingdom, a budget takes the form of a regular act of parliament, known as an appropriation act or a finance act, whereas in Japan, a budget bill is considered a special form of legislation that also existed under the Meiji Constitution.

56. Dicey lists the abundance of constitutional conventions as one of the features of the British Constitution, Dicey, *supra* note 38, Part III. The most important among those conventions concern the cabinet system.

57. The first dissolution during the Occupation (1948) followed a no-confidence resolution in the House of Representatives, at SCAP's suggestion.

58. The Cabinet Law (*Naikakuho*), Law No. 5 of 1947.

59. The three cases are the dismissal of Hirano as the Minister of Agriculture from the Katayama Government (1947) and of Hirokawa, also from the position of Minister of Agriculture, during the fourth Yoshida Government (1953), and of Fujio as the Minister of Education from the third Nakasone Government (1986). On other occasions, when a Minister has confronted his Prime Minister, the Minister has normally resigned before being dismissed. In that sense, the power of dismissal is a trump card that a Prime Minister may rely upon.

60. Two features in the chapter on the Diet indicate ties with the United States Constitution, the investigative power of the Diet (Art. 62) and the impeachment of judges. The investigative powers of Congress are unique to the United States Constitution, allowing each House to investigate a wide variety of matters as it deems necessary and to exercise related contempt powers. This power is also inherent in the British Parliament. Under the Meiji Constitution, the Imperial Diet's power in this area was too limited to deserve mention. Under the 1947 Constitution, the Diet now has considerable investigative powers. Like congressional power to investigate (*McGrain v. Daugherty*, 273 *U.S.* 135 (1929)), it is supplemental to all the powers and authority of the Diet. As the highest organ of state power, the Diet has power in numerous areas as natural extensions of general power, and this may conflict with the exercise of other powers. In the *Urawa* case (1949), the Legal Affairs Committee of the House of Councillors confronted the Supreme Court on an inquiry into the outcome of a specific criminal proceeding. Impeachment has its origin in England but there it has disappeared as constitutional convention. In the United States, it is maintained as a constitutional institution, and has been used most often to remove judges whose status is otherwise beyond the powers of the other branches. In the United States, the House of Representatives may indict and the Senate may hold an impeachment trial. In Japan, a Committee of Indictment and a Committee of Trial, both of which are composed of members selected from members of both chambers, have separate roles as an impeachment court.

Another significant difference from the Meiji Constitution is that the 1947 Constitution includes a chapter on local government. This reflects the American way of thinking that local government is the basis for democratic politics. This emphasis on the importance of local government meaningfully balances the centralizing tendency in politics, administration and general society. Especially in the arena of local government, institutions have developed as an essential part of direct democracy in the United States. The 1947 Constitution provides for a holding referendum on a local ordinance applicable only to one municipality (Art. 95). In the Local Autonomy Law (*Chihō Jichi Hō*), Law No. 67 of 1947), direct democracy is honored by mention of petitions to make, amend and abolish local ordinances, petitions to dissolve a local assembly, and petitions to recall governors, mayors, assembly members and other public officials. These are institutions that exist as part of local government in the United States.

61. The greatest difference between the Constitutions of the United States and Japan on criminal proceedings is the absence in Japan's of the right to trial by jury (grand jury and petit jury; Amendments 5 and 6). In Japan in 1923, a Jury Law was introduced, but the law was not much used and was later suspended because it was seen as unsuitable in Japan. The people trusted and preferred judges who were trained and experienced, and the system itself contained defects as a jury system. The present Court Law (Law No. 59 of 1947) states that nothing in this statute prevents the establishment of a jury system by another statute (Art. 3). There is influential opinion that introduction of a jury system in which jury verdicts would bind judges might violate the Constitution (Art. 76), and that it would require a constitutional amendment. Recently, some in the Japan Federation of Bar Associations have been urging adoption or revival of a jury system, as an alternative to the present system. This movement is mainly due to a number of recent cases, some involving death sentences, in which convictions have been overturned on retrial. The defendants were acquitted many years after their original sentences were handed down. [The proponents allege that the present system has contributed to prolonged trials and erroneous findings of fact supported only by improperly encouraged confessions.]

62. For example, the United States Supreme Court has developed important case law on the issue of the exclusionary rule. The Japanese Supreme Court has been responsive to the same consideration, holding that evidence is not admissible if there is significant illegality in the process of gathering evidence contrary to the spirit of Article 35 of the Constitution, and if the admission of such evidence would tend to encourage illegal search and seizure in the future. Article 35 demands writs for search and seizure. 32 *KEISHŪ* (No. 6) 1672 (Sup. Ct., 1st P.B., Sept. 7, 1978).

63. See L.W. Beer, *Freedom*, *supra* note 37 for a detailed study of freedom of expression in Japan. Article 21(2) expressly prohibits censorship. The origin of this clause can be traced back to the English common law in which the essence of freedom of speech was considered to be the prohibition of censorship. Article 21 also incorporates the theory of prior restraint of the United States Constitution. The Supreme Court has held that censorship is absolutely prohibited (Supreme Court, Grand Bench, December 12, 1984, 38 *MINSHŪ* (No. 12) 1308).

64. Some aspects of religion may have lost their religious connotation or significance, and may have become custom. In Japan, the Christmas tree is totally devoid of religious implication or association with Christianity, but has become a seasonal custom. In such situations, a strict separation of state and religion may pose a difficult problem. The Shinto ceremony to purify building sites (*Jichinsai*) raised one such controversial case (Supreme Court, Grand Bench, July 13, 1977, 31 MINSHŪ (4) 533); see III, 6(7) for the details of this case. For a different perspective on Shinto and the State, see section II text, at notes 115-125.

65. 1 *Cranch* 37 (1803).

66. In this respect, the Supreme Court's power to administer the judiciary is important. This power is exercised by the Conference of Judges (*Saibankan Kaigi; Saibansho Hō*, Article 12). The General Secretariat of the Supreme Court carries

out the details of the actual administration. Among administrative tasks are: (1) preparation of the list of lower court judges to be appointed and reappointed (Art. 80(1)); (2) appointment and dismissal of staff and officers of the court and other employees (*Saibansho Hō*, Article 64); (3) preparation of the budget to cover expenses for the administration of the judiciary (Art. 83); and (4) supervision of the administration of the judiciary (Art. 80).

67. Code of Civil Procedure (*Minji Sosho Hō*), Law No. 131 of 1948.

68. Denial of judicial reappointment by the Supreme Court is extremely rare. The reappointment process does serve as an opportunity to sort out those who are not thought suitable to the task. In 1971 the Supreme Court denied Assistant Judge Yasuaki Miyamoto a place on the list for reappointment. Because the Supreme Court refused to disclose the reason for denial, there was suspicion that it was due to his beliefs or his membership in a somewhat political association, and that he had been denied reappointment without any substantial reason. On this and related controversies, see H. Ito and L. Beer, *The Constitutional Case Law of Japan* (1978), 16-20.

69. The influence of the British Constitution on constitutional theory and constitutional interpretation has been less than that of the United States. The study of constitutional law in Japan since 1947 has focused on the Constitution as the basis for litigation, and many theoretical studies use the Constitution as a source of standards for adjudication. Naturally, this has increased interest in American constitutional theories.

70. Supreme Court, Grand Bench, July 17, 1985, 39 *MINSHŪ* (5) 1100. The Grand Bench of the Supreme Court had earlier held to the same effect on April 14, 1976 (30 *MINSHŪ* (3) 223) and on November 7, 1983 (37 *MINSHŪ* (9) 1243).

71. *Baker v. Carr*, 369 U.S. 186 (1962).

72. Supreme Court, Grand Bench, June 11, 1986, 40 *MINSHŪ* (4) 872.

73. *Near v. Minnesota*, 283 *U.S.* 697 (1931).

74. Before 1945, it was almost impossible to imagine that a judge might spend time studying abroad. The number of judges who have studied abroad for a year or more since the end of World War II, according to the research of the Personnel Office of the Supreme Court, totals 174; 112 of those judges studied in the United States; the other 62 went to West Germany, the United Kingdom, France or Australia. Of those who have studied in the United States, 83 went to universities and 29 were guests of courts.

75. Many study the constitutional law of West Germany, France and the United Kingdom. There are also studies of the Soviet Union, the People's Republic of China, and other East European socialist countries. Japan has always been interested in learning from the leading countries or well-developed countries of the West in all fields of knowledge. It is therefore sad to notice that we are devoid of studies of constitutions and law in general of countries other than those developed countries. I hope and trust that in the future legal studies in Japan will emphasize

the study of countries which I have not mentioned above, especially the countries of Asia.

76. The Japan Branch of the Japanese American Society for Legal Studies regularly holds workshops on new American cases and publishes these case comments in its publication *AMERIKAHŌ*. (The American Branch, based in the Asian Law Program of the University of Washington, Seattle, publishes the journal *LAW IN JAPAN*, now in its twenty-second volume.) The Kansai Study Group (Osaka-Kyoto area) on American Public Law (*Kansai Amerika Kōhō Kenkyū Kai*) has studied public law cases of the United States Supreme Court each term and has published the results in the journal *HANREI TAIMUZU*.

77. One should not forget that many leading American scholars have given lectures and seminars on the American Constitution as visiting professors at Japanese universities. A few examples from the University of Tokyo are Nathaniel Nathanson (Northwestern University Law School), Walter Gellhorn (Columbia University Law School), and Thomas Emerson (Yale University Law School) have visited the Faculty of Law. Professor Gellhorn's lectures were published as *Kihonteki Jinken* (trans., 1959 by Takeo Hayakawa & Yukio Yamada, Yuhikaku, 1959. The American version is *American Rights: The Constitution in Action* (1960)). Professor Emerson's lectures were published as T.I. Emerson & K. Kinoshita, *Gendai Amerika Kempō* (the University of Tokyo Press, 1978).

78. On the "no war, no armament" provisions of Article 9, see *infra* II, at notes 69-79.

79. John M. Maki, *Japan's Commission on the Constitution* (1981); Lawrence W. Beer, "Japan (1947): Forty Years of the Postwar Constitution," in V. Bogdanor (ed.) *Constitutions in Democratic Politics* (1988), 173.

II. The Present Constitutional System of Japan

(Lawrence W. Beer)

The Establishment Process, 1945-47

During her period of ultranationalist militarism--especially between 1936 and 1945--Japan inflicted great suffering upon many peoples in East and Southeast Asia, but also broke the back of European colonialism in Asia. At her surrender to the Allied Powers on August 14, 1945, Japan was a numb, defeated and devastated nation while the rest of the world rejoiced at the end of World War II. The humiliating shock of unprecedented defeat gave way to preoccupation with food and other survival needs, as rubble was cleared away, as millions of overseas Japanese military and colonial personnel came home to stay, as the leadership of war collapsed. In the aftermath, upheaval continued in China, Korea, and other Asian nations with the end of colonialism and the remaking of the political order.[1] Japan's last war to date ended in 1945.

With help in the early days from the remarkably benevolent American victors, Japan has rebuilt in peace her political and economic structures and has risen to a high position among democratic leaders of the world. To this writer, it seems probable that Japan's constitutional revolution towards freedom, individual rights, and democratic government would not have occurred without the catalytic effect of reforms instigated by Americans in the Occupation apparatus. (In the quite separate area of economy, Japan's current leadership was attainable in good part because of partnership with the United States.) Historical origins are not in themselves important as a determinant of the legitimacy of a country's constitution and its pursuant systems of law and government. Thus, what is crucial is not that the 1947 "Constitution of Japan" (the formal title of the Constitution; *Nihonkoku Kempō*) was to some degree a result of American insistence upon certain constitutional principles in 1945 and 1946, but that the document and its spirit have enjoyed free and overwhelming popular support, at its Occupation-period inception, upon the return to independence in 1952, and today. Perhaps no constitutional arrangement in Japanese history, and relatively few constitutional systems in the world today have been so strongly supported by the general citizenry of a country as the present Constitution of Japan.[2] Constitutional principles such as popular sovereignty, self-government, the rule of law, limited and divided governmental power, and individual rights had not been preoccupations of Japan's ruling elite at any time before 1945. The revolutionary changes that occurred between the signing of the surrender documents on September 2, 1945, and the coming into effect of the

Constitution of Japan on May 3, 1947, were momentous and the attendant processes historically unique.[3]

The Law and Process of Establishment

The Allied Powers assumed indirect control of Japan's government and law in early September, 1945, with the arrival in Tokyo of General MacArthur, Supreme Commander of the Allied Powers (SCAP), and the establishment of his General Headquarters (GHQ) and other institutions of the Occupation period (September 2, 1945-April 28, 1952).[4] As a defeated and occupied nation-state, Japan was subject to the Occupation's will under international law and the terms of surrender in the Potsdam Declaration (July 26, 1945) accepted by Japan. SCAP ruled through the Japanese government leadership and apparatus rather than governing the nation directly as in Germany and Southern Korea. Other nations, such as Australia and the United Kingdom, participated in Japan's occupation, but the United States' influence was dominant from start to finish.

Very few in the American apparatus were fluent in Japanese or knowledgeable about Japan's law and institutions. The United States relied heavily upon the competence of functionaries in the Japanese Government for implementation of its policies and used the Emperor to legitimize early Occupation law and a new constitution. While thousands were accused of ultranationalist taint and purged, in general, Japan's leaders, government personnel and general population cooperated in reforms with less SCAP coercion than might reasonably have been expected; there was no armed resistance. It is easy to underestimate the improbability of Occupation success, in part because there is no clear precedent or sequel elsewhere for Japan's constitutional transformation, the most impressive accomplishment of the Allied Occupation.

On August 29, 1945, General MacArthur received general instructions from President Harry S. Truman, "the United States Initial Post-Surrender Policy for Japan" [hereinafter, the Policy].[5] How to transform this Policy into Japanese law? Into law that the generality of Japanese would comprehend and Japan's government comply with? The Policy stated that Japan should be governed by SCAP directives, called "SCAPIN." SCAPIN were issued to the Imperial Japanese Government which converted them into indigenous law, by administrative action and statute, but often by means of "imperial ordinances" (chokurei).[6] Since the late nineteenth century, Japan's oligarchic leaders had at times found imperial ordinances promulgated in the name of the Emperor faster and politically more expedient than reliance on statutes passed by the Diet. Imperial Ordinance No. 542 of September 20, 1945, provided the umbrella under which SCAPIN were implemented; it reads, in part:[7]

In accordance with the acceptance of the Potsdam Declaration, in order to carry out items based on the demands made by SCAP, the Government may, when especially necessary, take the necessary steps through ordinances, and may establish necessary penal regulations.

In all, some 520 such "Potsdam Orders" (*Potsudamu meirei*) were issued by the Japanese government. Imperial ordinances as a form of law ceased to exist when the 1947 constitution came into effect; and the name of existing imperial ordinances and subsequent orders was changed to "Cabinet Orders" (*seirei*).[8]

Japan's constitutional revolution--its fundamental shift in legally legitimized sociopolitical values and government institutions toward peaceable democracy--began with the issuance of many SCAPIN in September and October, 1945. In substance, the Potsdam Declaration required that Japan start down a new road of peace, freedom and popular sovereignty. The Policy called for a broad range of individual rights and freedoms, demilitarization, punishment of war criminals, and general democratization of government and economics.[9] SCAPIN 1 of September 2 started the process of dismantling Japan's armed forces and defense industries, while other directives insisted on freedom of expression and other individual rights. Inevitably, as SCAP participated in the governance of Japan and pulled it away from chauvinistic authoritarianism, anti-democratic expression was censored; so was criticism of the Occupation and discussion of its role in constitutional change.[10] But censorship and other restraints were exceptions in the new environment of radically increased freedom and respect for individual rights.

Initially, Japan's leaders balked at freedom and popular sovereignty. Illustrative of the revolutionary circumstances was the confrontation between SCAP and the Japanese Government over the publication in newspapers of a photograph of the sovereign Emperor Hirohito standing alongside the more imposing figure of General MacArthur during his visit to GHQ on September 27, 1945. Strict *lese majeste* law was still in force; the demystification of the Emperor had not yet begun, though SCAPIN requiring press freedom had already been transmitted to the government. Japan attempted to ban the national newspapers carrying the photo. On the same day, September 27, SCAPIN 66, on "Further Steps Toward Freedom of Press and Speech," forbade all but "such restrictions as are specifically approved by the Supreme

Commander" and ordered the repeal of parts of twelve contrary laws.[11] Nevertheless, Home Minister Yamazaki continued to instruct Japanese newsmen to comply with the Peace Preservation Law which severely restricted discussion of the Emperor. On October 4, SCAPIN 93 responded to this test of SCAP resolve; the Higashikuni Cabinet resigned the next day.

SCAPIN 93 concerned the "Removal of Restrictions on Political, Civil and Religious Liberties." It ordered the Government to release and restore rights to all political prisoners, to abrogate all law contrary to freedom of expression, "including unrestricted discussion of the Emperor, the Imperial Institution" and the government system, and to "abolish all organizations and agencies" of a repressive nature (the Police Bureau, the Special Higher Police, the Protection and Surveillance Commission, and all "secret police").[12]

With American urging, the Japanese government then began serious consideration of constitutional change in October, 1945 in order to bring Japan's system into compliance with terms of the Potsdam Declaration and thus set the stage for withdrawal of the occupying forces. Prime Minister Kijuro Shidehara's Cabinet established the conservative "Matsumoto Committee" (Constitutional Problem Investigation Committee; *Naikaku Kempō Mondai Chosa Iinkai*), under the distinguished scholar-official Joji Matsumoto.[13] While the Committee worked, SCAP pushed ahead with reforms on many other fronts and awaited Japan's proposals for constitutional reform. For example, on October 11, SCAP called for Five Great Reforms: the liberation of women, the promotion of labor unions, the democratization of education, the end of repression, and more democratic economic structures.[14] SCAPIN 448 of December 15, 1945, gave all religions equal legal footing while separating government from Emperor-centered Shinto, and banned dissemination of the ultranationalist ideology.[15] For his part, Emperor Hirohito quite willingly announced on January 1, 1946, that he is an ordinary human being, not a quasi-god as modern propaganda had insisted for many decades.[16] One of the most momentous official acts taken under SCAP prodding was the revision of the House of Representatives Election Law on December 17, 1945, to confer on women for the first time the right to vote and to lower the voting age for all from 25 to 20.[17]

From December, 1945 through the following February, political parties, private organizations and individuals came forth with proposals for constitutional change. On February 1, without authorization, the *Mainichi Shinbun* newspaper published a draft constitution drawn up by the Matsumoto committee.[18] Like the proposals of the ruling Liberal and Progressive Parties, the draft manifested little intent to substantially democratize the Meiji Constitution. To SCAP readers, it seemed to be at variance with the Potsdam

Declaration, with the thrust of reforms since September, 1945, and with the reform guidelines provided by the State-War-Navy Coordinating Committee in Washington through a confidential January communication to SCAP, SWNCC 228.[19] Particularly critical to subsequent events, under the Matsumoto Draft the sovereignty of the Emperor was retained and the traditional neglect of individual rights and freedoms continued.

At this point, General MacArthur and his staff despaired of the government's capacity to break cleanly with its authoritarian past and secretly drafted a new constitution. MacArthur assigned the task of writing a model constitution to the Government Section of GHQ, which was headed by his confidant, General Courtney Whitney.[20] Whitney and his staff, not MacArthur, authored the "MacArthur Draft" constitution. However, either on his own initiative or by approval of Whitney's ideas, the General set three requirements in the "MacArthur Notes": (1) retain the Emperor system but make it subject to the will of the people; (2) include a renunciation of the nation's right of belligerency; and (3) eliminate all forms of feudalism and aristocracy.[21]

On February 3, Colonel Charles L. Kades, Whitney's Deputy Chief in the Government Section, formed a Steering Committee with two other lawyers, Alfred R. Hussey and Milo E. Rowell, to set the ground rules and divide the work of drafting different sections among small staff groups. None of the drafters was a specialist in American constitutional law or knowledgeable about Japanese public law; but all were educated and able people.[22] The Steering Committee was of central importance during the short drafting period of February 4 to February 12.

> They, individually and collectively wrote many of the provisions of the draft and rewrote, revised, or vetoed most of the provisions drawn up by their colleagues on the legislative, executive, judiciary, civil rights, local government, and finance committees into which the staff were divided.[23]

Kades, the most influential co-author of the constitution, reports that the drafting process "was a group project with group thinking and group ideas"; it involved twenty-one Americans.[24] On February 13, General Whitney and the Steering Committee presented a completed draft constitution in English to Matsumoto and other Japanese leaders at Foreign Minister Shigeru Yoshida's residence. Matsumoto had assumed the purpose of the visit was to discuss the Matsumoto Draft, as part of a long deliberative process looking toward modest amendments. All were stunned when Whitney said that draft was "wholly unacceptable to the Supreme Commander as a document of freedom and democracy," and insisted upon quick preparation of a new Japanese draft based on SCAP's.[25] Flabbergasted at this boldness--of which even Washington was unaware at the time--the Japanese government sought reconsideration in the days that followed, in vain. The Shidehara Cabinet then ordered the Bureau of Legislation to prepare a new draft constitution, in consultation with the Government Section. On wording and detail and regarding a few major issues, the Japanese influence at this and later stages was substantial. For example, SCAP accepted proposals that parliament have two Houses rather than one, and that the courts' power of judicial review not be limited to civil rights cases.[26] Following intense, sometimes bitter discussion between SCAP and Japanese representatives from 10 A.M. March 4 to 4 P.M. March 5, Japan's new "General Outline of Draft Revision of the Constitution" was released to the public along with a supportive imperial rescript. Then, as later, the constitution met with an enthusiastic welcome. While feigning uninvolvement in its drafting, SCAP publicly expressed satisfaction and exuded high praise for the document.[27]

The amending processes of Article 73 of the Meiji Constitution and a related imperial ordinance on the Privy Council were then followed:[28] the Emperor through his Cabinet presented the proposed change to the Privy Council, which approved the document on June 8 and sent it on to the House of Representatives for action. The House of Representatives which debated the new constitution was elected on April 10 in the first post-war election. Eighty-one percent of the victors were new to Diet office; women voted and held seats in parliament for the first time. On August 24, 1946, the lower House approved the Constitution of Japan by a vote of 421 to 8; on October 6 the amended Constitutional Revision Bill was passed overwhelmingly (298 to 2, according to Whitney) by the House of Peers; the House of Representatives passed the slightly amended bill without debate on October 7; and on October 29 the Privy Council in the presence of the Emperor also approved. With the issuance of the Emperor's edict of promulgation and the Constitution, the ratification process ended. Six months later, on May 3, 1947, the Constitution of Japan came into effect and stands unchanged in 1991.[29]

A fair number of Americans and Japanese made noteworthy contributions to the making of Japan's constitution in its final form; a few examples will be mentioned in relation to specific provisions.[30] Hussey was the principal author of the Preamble, which eloquently advocates popular sovereignty, peace, and freedom. General Whitney wrote Article 97: "The fundamental human rights by this constitution guaranteed to the people of Japan are fruits of the age-old struggle to be free; they ... are conferred upon this and future generations in trust, to be held for all time inviolate." Rowell and Hussey were principal drafters of provisions establishing for the first time a separate judicial branch of government with power to determine the constitutionality of laws and other official acts. Beate Sirota, Pieter K. Roest and Harry Emerson Wildes constituted the committee working on individual rights. Sirota deserves special credit for the inclusion of women's rights in the Constitution (Art.s 14 and 24)[31] and the inception of a process of radical improvement in women's status in law and society. Sirota was a young woman of twenty-two who had grown up in Japan and was fluent in the language. Along with her future husband, Joseph Gordon, she also played a major role in reconciling Japanese and English texts (e.g., at the March 4 and 5 meetings), and in searching out reference materials on other nations' constitutions for the drafters.[32]

Kades wrote Article 9, which renounces war and Japan's right of belligerency; Kades also seems to have initiated the idea of having such a provision. "Shidehara's reported suggestion to MacArthur that the Japanese constitution renounce war may have stemmed indirectly from Kades' initiative. In any event, it is clear that key figures [notably Kades, MacArthur, Shidehara, and Whitney] were thinking along very similar lines."[33] McNelly argues that, since Japan had repeatedly violated the Kellog-Briand Pact renouncing war, one purpose of Article 9 was to blunt Allied and opposition Japanese demands that the militaristic imperial institution be abolished and the Emperor put on trial, as sovereign, for war crimes. Militarism was abolished instead, and sovereignty transferred to the people, with the Emperor's cooperation and approval.

Among distinguished Japanese drafters in the Bureau of Legislation were Tatsuo Sato and Toshio Irie. Sato later became head of the National Personnel Authority and Irie served longest of anyone ever on the Supreme Court of Japan, 1952-1970. Learned constitutional lawyers, like Tatsukichi Minobe, were involved in government discussions but often not supportive of fundamental change in the Meiji Constitution.[34] With respect to specific provisions, Socialists were responsible for amendments guaranteeing "minimum standards of wholesome and cultured living" (Art. 25) and worker rights (Art.s 27 and 28). Kades and many of his colleagues shared these positions as quite congruent with New Deal ideas and with mainstream European constitutionalism.[35] Although the role of the Far Eastern Commission was severely constrained, it was responsible for a few amendments during the ratification process, such as the requirement that the majority of Cabinet members be members of the Diet (Art. 68).[36]

Before the Constitution became law in 1947, the monumental task began of making, amending and abolishing laws to conform with its requirements.

Provisions in the basic Codes had to be modified: the Civil Code (*Mimpō*), the Code of Civil Procedure (*Mimjisoshōhō*), the Criminal Code (*Keihō*), the Code of Criminal Procedure (*Keijisoshōhō*), and the Commercial Code (*Shōhō*). These codes, under the Constitution, enjoy almost quasi-constitutional status in the vast civil law world of which Japan had been a part since the late nineteenth century. Few American occupationnaires had any competence in this oldest and most widespread of the world's legal traditions. Thomas Blakemore from Oklahoma was the only trained specialist in Japanese law. Kades continued a major role. Fortunately, Alfred Oppler, a refugee judge from Germany, arrived in Tokyo on February 23, 1946, and presided over the Courts and Law Division of the Government Section:[37]

> Oppler will long be remembered for his revision of the Japanese codes of law along democratic lines. It was he who brought about the sweeping reforms of the Civil, Criminal, and Procedural Codes and the enactment of the Court Organization Law, innovations that breathed life into the new constitution...

As during the constitution ratification process, SCAP retained some veto power during the remaining years of the Occupation; but cooperative law-making characterized processes, with the Japanese Government assuming an ever larger responsibility for implementing the revolutionary Constitution of Japan. Cold War and Korean War realities did occasion SCAP interventions at times;[38] but more symbolic may be the effect of a 1947 conversation between Oppler and Yoshio Suzuki, the Justice Minister, about individual rights. Oppler mentioned the new Civil Rights Section (now the Civil Rights Division) of the U.S. Department of Justice; Suzuki "enthusiastically adopted the idea and established such a bureau in his ministry."[39] The Civil Liberties Bureau has developed into an effective instrument for human rights education and protection with the help of its many thousands of carefully selected lay Civil Rights Commissioners (*Jinken Yogo Iin*; literally, human rights protectors). Like other laws and systems introduced under the Constitution of Japan during the Occupation period, this democratic institution evolved to fit Japanese preferences, needs and mores. Japan has been responsible for the great accomplishments of constitutional democracy, as well as its weaknesses, since 1952. The remainder of this section looks at the status of Japanese constitutionalism over forty years after Constitution Day, May 3, 1947.

Popular Sovereignty

No matter how majestic its basic design, a good constitution, like the structure of a cathedral, takes on life and beauty only through quality workmanship in the details. How have the outlines of the constitutional system been filled in by law, government action, and society since 1947? What is now the state of popular sovereignty, the emperor institution, the renunciation-of-war clause, individual rights and freedoms, parliamentary democracy, the executive branch, the judiciary, and local self-government? Where are the strengths and stresses located?

The Preamble and Article 1 of the Constitution make the people (*kokumin*) sovereign for the first time in Japan's history.[40] The Preamble begins: "We, the Japanese people, acting through our duly elected representatives in the National Diet ... do proclaim that sovereign power resides with the people and do firmly establish this Constitution."[41] The Emperor's position is made subject to "the will of the people with whom resides sovereign power."[42] He has a purely ceremonial role as "the symbol of the State and of the unity of the People" (Art. 1), and is expressly denied "powers related to government" (Art. 4).[43] Article 2 continues the ancient dynastic kingship system, but Article 14(2) eliminates the aristocracy: "Peers and peerage shall not be recognized."[44] When he passed away on January 7, 1989, Emperor Hirohito had reigned since 1926, longer than any predecessor.[45] Each reign period is given a name; Hirohito's era was "*Shōwa*" (Bright Peace). "*Heisei*" (Achieving Peace) was chosen for the time of the new Emperor Akihito and Empress Michiko. Years are counted both in the international manner and from year one of an Emperor's reign; thus 1989 is year one (*gannen*) of *Heisei*.

For over 1,000 years, Emperors only very rarely exercised governmental power as national leaders; but, willingly or unwillingly, they formally confirmed the legitimacy of the dominant feudal lord of the time. The Emperor reigned in Kyoto, while the *Shogun* actually governed Japan.[46] In 1868, after the West forced Japan open to trade and diplomatic relations, radical oligarchs of the *samurai* (knight) class eliminated the Shogun system and the traditional class hierarchy (samurai, court nobles, farmers, craftsmen, merchants, and outcasts), as the way to "restore" the proper relationship between the Emperor and his subjects. The imperial and administrative functions of government were combined in Tokyo, and Europeanized law and constitutional monarchy were developed. In 1889, the "Meiji Constitution" (Constitution of the Empire of Japan) bestowed formal legal sovereignty on the Emperor (*tennō*), but others continued to rule in his name.

The government was remarkably successful in using modern techniques of control, propaganda, education, and law to transform tradition and unify the people for the first time in shared passionate loyalty to an Emperor allegedly descended from the Shinto sun goddess, *Amaterasu Omikami*. By the mid-1930s, the islands, the people, the Emperor, the State, the Shinto, the extended family system and the history of Japan were fused in an organic, nationalistic, and authoritarian entity referred to as "*kokutai*" (loosely, the imperial form of the Japanese State).[47] Yet, in 1945, the Emperor was allowed to break a leadership deadlock and accept the terms of the Potsdam Declaration; and in 1946, he publicly affirmed his humanity and his support for the Constitution of Japan.[48]

The political symbolism of the Emperor remains controversial. Small minorities favor either abolition of the system as anachronistic and dangerously manipulable, or re-mystification of the Emperor under nationalistic State Shinto. Tensions continue between supporters of popular sovereignty and tolerance on the one hand, and Emperor sovereignty in a conformist, sacralized state on the other. However, the overwhelming majority seem to prefer a powerless and depoliticized imperial family, an object of occasional curiosity or benign and respectful indifference.[49]

Popular sovereignty has been exercised in an unbroken chain of free elections under democratic law since 1946; leadership has changed hands peacefully many times at both the local and national levels. Parliamentary "elections have been conducted with virtually no violence and very little overt ill will."[50] In a world where many countries still struggle with problems of orderly leadership succession, continuity and political violence, Japan's stability is a major achievement of democratic constitutionalism.

Article 15 of the Constitution establishes "universal adult suffrage" and the people's "inalienable right" to choose and dismiss public officials by secret ballot.[51] Elections are regularly held for the National Assembly (*Kokkai*, the "Diet")[52] and for local executive and assembly positions at the village, town, city and prefectural levels. The National Assembly is composed of a House of Representatives (*Shūgiin*) with 512 seats, and a less powerful House of Councillors with 252 members.[53] One must be at least 25 years old to run for the House of Representatives, and 30 for the House of Councillors or a prefectural governorship. Article 44 prohibits discrimination against a Diet candidate on the basis of "race, creed, sex, social status, family origin, education, property or income." Article 47 of the Constitution leaves to statute the determination of "electoral districts, method of voting and other matters pertaining to the method of election," and the courts have recognized very broad parliamentary discretion in this area.[54]

From 1889 until 1925, only 25-year-old male subjects paying a designated minimum in taxes could vote in parliamentary elections. The tax requirement was dropped in 1925; in late 1945, suffrage was extended to women and the voting age was lowered to twenty.[55]   In 1950, several statutes regulating election to various offices were replaced by the present Public Offices Election Law (*Kōshoku Senkyohō*; hereafter, the Election Law).[56] Voting rates have averaged around 70% in recent decades, with a slightly higher figure for women than for men, and have gone as high as 75% in National Assembly elections and over 90% in contests for town and village positions.[57]

As under the prewar system, members of the House of Representatives are elected under an unusual system of "multi-member districts" (130 in number); depending on population, from three, four, or five seats are assigned to each district (except for one six-member, four two member, and one single seat the single-seat districts, but electors may vote for only one candidate.[58] The lower house member's term is four years, less if the House dissolves (Art. 45). A term in the House of Councillors lasts six years, with half the seats contested in elections every three years (Art. 46). Of the upper house positions, 152 are filled from prefectural districts, while 100 seats are allocated to a number of candidates on each party's list proportionate to its share of the national vote total.[59]

One of Japan's most serious unresolved constitutional problems is malapportionment of seats in parliament, especially in the House of Representatives. The 1950 Election Law provides that its "Appendix I," which apportions seats in the lower house, should be periodically revised to accord "with the results of the most recent national census every five years from the date of" the law's enforcement. However, incumbent have feared losing the support of overrepresented constituencies; so the National Assembly (Diet) has not institutionalized periodic reapportionment in response to the great population shift to Japan's cities. Until 1986, when eight seats were added to underrepresented districts and seven subtracted from others, the National Assembly simply added seats in the face of severe malapportionment.[60] Every general election is now followed by citizen suits claiming unconstitutional inequality (against Article 14) in the value of votes among election districts and seeking judicial nullification of elections.[61]

Article 34, paragraph 1 of the Election Law requires that a new election be held within forty days after the nullification of any election. But the same law (Art. 205, para. 1) stipulates that an invalid law must be revised before another election may be held, and that a Councillors election must be publicly announced eighteen days beforehand, and a House of Representatives election fifteen days before election day (Art. 34, para. 6). To fit within the forty-day and prior announcement requirements, the Diet would have to revise the election law within twenty-two (Councillors) or twenty-five (Representatives) days, which, it is claimed, would be impossible. With the House of Representatives dissolved for the election, who would revise the Election Law Appendix?

In 1976, 1983 and 1985, the Supreme Court avoided use of the "political question" basis for deference to parliament, and found unconstitutional the malapportionment prevailing at the time of three general elections (1972, 1980, 1983).[62] However, the Supreme Court has also consistently avoided nullification of an election, relying on the legal principle and the spirit behind an Administrative Litigation Law Principle (Art. 31, para. 1) which allows the courts to choose not to invalidate an *administrative* act if invalidation would seriously harm the public interest due to circumstances (*jijō*). Such judicial decisions on malapportionment have thus been referred to as "circumstantial judgments" (*jijō hanketsu*). The legal principle rather than the statutory provision itself has been applied because Article 219 of the Election Law precludes direct application of such an administrative law provision in such instances.[63]

With respect to House of Councillors malapportionment, the Supreme Court has not held unconstitutionally excessive a 5-to-1 disparity in vote values between election districts.[64] A 3-to-1 discrepancy has been adopted by the Supreme Court as the maximum tolerable for House of Representatives districts, but most constitutional lawyers and many judges believe anything more than a 2-to-1 difference violates Article 14 equality rights; some posit the "one person, one vote" standard as the appropriate legal guideline. With respect to a malapportionment of local assembly seats, the Supreme Court has let stand a Tokyo High Court decision setting 2-to-1 as the constitutional limit,[65] and warning of immediate nullification of the next election if appropriate corrective action has not been taken.

In light of parliamentary reluctance to reform apportionment, even in response to stern importuning from the Supreme Court, as in 1985, some, including a strong minority of Justices in the 1985 decision, have advocated judicial use of "prospective invalidation" of apportionment law, following the approach effectively used by the Federal Constitutional Court of West Germany to stimulate Bundestag reform.[66] "Prospective invalidation" means that the judges delay the effect of a judgment of unconstitutionality until a specific later date, by which time, it is presumed, the legislature will have completed an appropriate reapportionment. Unlike the United States Supreme Court, as in *Baker v. Carr*, and like some other courts in the continental European legal tradition, Japan's courts apparently lack injunction powers to stop an election based on unconstitutional apportionment and to order reapportionment.[67]

Constitutional Pacifism under Article 9

The Preamble proclaims: "We, the Japanese people ... [are] resolved that never again shall we be visited with the horrors of war through the action of government."[68] This is concretized in Article 9, the most unusual provision in the 1947 Constitution, the first anywhere to serve as an effective constraint on the armament and international behavior of a great power:

> Article 9. Aspiring sincerely to an international peace based on justice and order, the Japanese people forever renounce war as a sovereign right of the nation and the threat or use of force as a means of settling international disputes.
>
> 2. In order to accomplish the aim of the preceding paragraph, land, sea, and air forces, as well as other war potential, will never be maintained. The right of belligerency of the State will not be recognized."[69]

Article 9 has been such an essential element in the common Japanese conception of an appropriate constitutionalism for Japan that the 1947 document has been referred to as "the Peace Constitution," implying an inseparable linkage between commitments to international peace, and to democracy and human rights.[70] Buttressing Article 9 is Article 66(2), which requires that Cabinet members be civilians; this exclusion of military personnel from government and high politics contrasts sharply with pre-1945 modern Japanese history.[71] No legal provision is made for martial law, and the special powers granted the Prime Minister for times of "national emergency" are strictly limited.[72] The distinctive pacifist spirit of a very large proportion of Japan's people grew not from a philosophical or religious principle or from economic experience, but from a deep collective reaction to an unprecedented devastating failure in World War II, the suffering that war caused Japan and that Japanese caused other peoples, the experience of the atomic bombing of Hiroshima and Nagasaki, and the oppressiveness of mindless nationalism and authoritarian government and law in prewar Japan. Postwar civic education and mass communications and culture have reenforced the reaction and passed it on to new generations.[73] That Article 9 has brought no increase in societal suffering or external threat, but rather prosperous democracy, has naturally strengthened its legitimacy.

Under international law and Supreme Court interpretations, Japan has a right to self-defense and the "Self-Defence Forces" (SDF; *Jieitai*),[74] and a right to enter into a defensive alliance, as with the United States; but not a right to settle disputes by "threat" or "belligerency," or to have offensive military capabilities or policies.[75] In fact, Japan has not used military force in an international dispute since 1945, an exceptional phenomenon among the world's major nations. In the 1950s and 1960s especially, a substantial portion of the citizenry questioned the constitutionality of the SDF. Now, an overwhelming majority support the quasi-pacifism of Article 9, while a similar proportion matter-of-factly accepts the legitimacy of the SDF's existence. For pragmatic reasons, a strong majority also supports continuance of the 1960 United States-Japan Treaty for Mutual Cooperation and Security ("the Security Treaty," "*anpo*"), which either party may abrogate on one year's notice (Art. 10).[76] The Treaty limits use of U.S. base forces to the defense of Japan in accord with "the provisions and procedures of the Constitution" (Art. 5) or "preserving peace and security in the Far East" (Art. 6), in joint consultation.[77]

In the 1980s Japan's military budget rose to become one of the few largest in the world; but the figures could be misleading. The doubling (and more) of the yen's value against the U.S. dollar, while drastically raising the paper expenditures, did not add a bullet to Japan's munitions. Although Japan's forces and military technology achieved high quality, the SDF remained small compared to the forces of any other East Asian country (North Korea, South Korea, China or Taiwan), and were geopolitically meaningless if considered apart from the context of military cooperation with her American ally.[78] Japan paid a larger portion of U.S. costs related to base maintenance abroad than any other U.S. treaty partner.

As Japan became a world leader in the 1980s, Article 9 continued to affect constitutional debate and law as well as foreign policy. For decades the ruling Liberal-Democratic Party favored revision of Article 9 to weaken its pacifist thrust, in spite of contrary public opinion. However, by 1982 even that party came to rely not on revisionism, but on a flexible interpretation of Article 9 for moderate expansion of the SDF, and to place greater emphasis on technical and economic power than on military prowess as a basis for "comprehensive security."[79] Instead of massive military contributions which might have destabilized rather than enhanced regional security, Japan became the world's leading aid donor.[80]

Because of Article 9, Japan may not have a conscript army, and volunteer recruitment goals have never been met. Restraints on military expansion have been basic to parliamentary policy-making. Funds for conventional forces have been limited.[81] Based on a common belief that nuclear weapons can never be justified under Article 9 as defensive, none may be manufactured, possessed or introduced into Japan (the "three non-nuclear principles").[82] The manufacture and export of arms are also restricted due to Article 9, at noteworthy economic loss; yet the export of advanced technology with military applications may now be the critical test for Article 9 compliance.[83] Decades of surprisingly effective resistance to using the national flag in schools and to making "*Kimi Ga Yo*" once again the official national anthem arose in part out of concern about the possible rebirth of militarist nationalism in defiance of Article 9.[84] Until 1989, when non-military personnel were sent to assist with United Nations peace-keeping in Afghanistan and the Iran-Iraq border and with UN-supervised elections in Namibia, Japan declined to participate in United Nations efforts, in good part for Article 9 reasons.[85] In short, in these and other settings, the spirit of Article 9 found expression in concrete symbols and transcended the world's usual ideological dividing lines to assert the possibility of pragmatic pacifism. This seems Japan's important contribution to the world's wisdom on constitutionalism, but placed it at odds with Americans who supported war against Iraq in 1990-91 who thought Japan should participate in a military manner.

The Supreme Court has not directly ruled under Article 9 on the constitutionality of the SDF as "war potential," but has affirmed Japan's natural right to self-defense and the permissibility of the U.S.-Japan Security Treaties of 1952 and 1960 as "not clearly contrary" to Article 9.[86] Of lower court judgments, only the 1973 Sapporo district court decision in the *Naganuma Missile Site* case has held the SDF unconstitutional, and that decision was overturned.[87] Farmers in the village of Naganuma challenged the reclassification of a forest reserve for military use as a violation of their land-use rights and as a project of the unconstitutional SDF. The court agreed, but appellate courts in 1976 and 1982 avoided the Article 9 issue and held the farmers lacked standing to sue.[88]

Constitutional Rights, Freedoms, and Duties

Chapter 3, Articles 11 to 40 and Article 97 of the Constitution set forth a comprehensive list of individual rights rooted in affirmation of the inherent and equal dignity of each person.[89] These rights are "pre-constitutional," to be enjoyed as "eternal and inviolate" human rights (Art. 11) given by God or Nature to "this and future generations in trust, to be held for all time inviolate" (Art. 97). "All of the people are to be respected as individuals" and the individual's rights and freedoms are to be "the supreme consideration in legislation and in other governmental affairs" as long as this is consonant with "the public welfare" (Art. 13). Under Article 12 the guarantee of rights is attended by the people's duty to maintain their freedom and rights "by constant endeavor," to refrain "from any abuse," and to utilize "them for the public welfare."

With exceptions such as those pointed out, government and law have honored constitutional rights, and the education and mass media systems have given rights strong societal institutionalization. In addition, volunteer non-professionals have enhanced the status of rights at the grass roots-and-sidewalk level through a number of officially sponsored systems. For example, over 12,000 unpaid men and women meticulously selected for their human rights commitment have served locally as "Human Rights Commissioners" or "Protectors" (*Jinken Yogo Iin*)[90] under the aegis of the Justice Ministry. These Commissioners have handled over 350,000 inquiries, complaints, and disputes each year; citizen recourse to these human rights servants has steadily increased. They have no coercive authority and rely on their local prestige, education programs, conciliatory methods, and referrals to solve problems. Thousands of other laypeople (average age 60) hear citizen complaints about government officials as Local Administrative Counselors (*Gyōsei Sōdan Iin*). The Japan Civil Liberties Union (JCLU), the Human Rights Committee of the bar, and other private groups became increasingly active in promoting constitutional rights during the 1980s.

Scholars commonly cluster the comprehensive constitutional rights of a Japanese as follows: rights of participation in election politics; equality rights, socioeconomic rights; economic rights and freedoms; procedural rights; and rights and freedoms of the spirit.[91]

Equality of rights under the law.

Article 14 eliminates inherited honors and an aristocracy, and forbids "discrimination in political, economic or social relations because of race, creed, sex, social status or family origin."[92] Article 24 recognizes "the equal rights of husband and wife" in all matters, and this is implemented in private law under Article 1-2 of the Civil Code (*Mimpō*): "The dignity of individuals and the essential equality of the sexes" is the principle governing legal interpretation.[93] Men and women are usually quite free in their choice of a marriage partner, in contrast to the earlier system which allowed coercively arranged marriages. Women have equal rights to property, inheritance, and education; in practice, they bear primary responsibility for child-rearing and household finances.[94]

Most young working women have resigned to marry at around age twenty-four; more than half by 1990 reentered the work force (commonly part-time, by preference) after their children entered school. Relatively few women have sought elective office or have been readily accepted after college into management-track positions in government or (especially) large companies. When they have opted for business careers, like women in the U.S. and many other countries, they have suffered considerable discrimination in compensation and advancement opportunities. However, in 1990, the revolutionary improvement in women's status since 1945 in a traditionally male-dominated society seemed more striking then the remaining problems. When employment-related discrimination had been challenged in court, women's rights were usually upheld.

After a long legislative struggle, laws in the 1980s led up to Japan's 1985 ratification of the United Nations Convention on the Elimination of All Forms of Discrimination against Women. For example, anti-discrimination amendments to the Nationality Law (*Kokusekihō*) gave the Japanese wife of a foreigner the important right to establish a family registry (*koseki*) and Japanese citizenship at birth to their children. Prior law had given citizenship only to the illegitimate children of such Japanese wives; and wives remained in their parents' registry; on the other hand, children of a Japanese father and a foreign mother had citizenship from birth.[95] Of much broader impact on career-oriented women was the 1985 Equal Employment Opportunity Law revising parts of the Labor Standards Law and the Working Women's Welfare Law.[96] This law cut back on a few special benefits, such as menstrual leaves, but significantly strengthened provisions against differential treatment of men and women in hiring, compensation, and promotion practices. It also extended maternity leave to six weeks before and eight weeks after childbirth. Although penal sanctions against violating employers have been criticized as too weak, in practice--for reasons of legal culture--notable breakthroughs occurred in the hiring and promotion of women to prestige positions in government and the private sector. Women's starting salaries have achieved near parity with men's for the same work.

These trends dovetailed with the strongly feminist revolt in 1989 elections against the 3% consumer tax and against the financial (Recruit Cosmo Co.) and sex (e.g., Prime Minister Sosuke Uno) scandals in the Liberal-Democratic Party to draw more women into public life. Takako Doi, a Constitutional lawyer, became the first woman to head a major political party: the Japan Socialist Party; since 1990, the Democratic Party of Japan. In July, 1989 she led the opposition parties to gain a majority in the House of Councillors for the first time.[97] The LDP retained its majority in the

February 18, 1990 House of Representatives elections, in which a dozen women won seats. It was unclear in the early 1990s whether the above political and legal encouragement would in time equalize women's rights in socioeconomic and public life.

Japan is one of the most homogeneous large nations; so minority issues affect relatively few in a population of over 125 million. In general, discrimination problems have been less severe than those in the United States and many other countries; government and private efforts since the 1960s have brought some amelioration.[98] Many Japanese almost never encounter the disadvantaged minorities, which are most numerous in a few parts of a few urban areas; e.g., in Osaka and in Tokyo's Adachi-ku, which had not one institution of higher learning in 1989, in contrast to other Tokyo wards.[99] Discriminatory policies and/or attitudes of varying importance continue against the following:[100] the *Burakumin*, 1.5-to-2.5 million ethnic Japanese (depending on one's source) descended from pre-modern occupational outcastes; close to 700,000 ethnic Koreans, with varying resident status (Forced to Japan to work before 1945, they lost Japanese citizenship when Korea ceased to be part of Japan [1910-1945]); roughly 130,000 ethnic Chinese; about one million Okinawans with a distinctive subculture and accent, who were under U.S. rule from 1945 until 1972; the proto-caucasian Ainu, a tiny and virtually assimilated minority; offspring of Japanese women and U.S. military personnel left without fatherly care; foreign teachers (denied the right to hold regular public school appointments until 1983); and thousands of war refugees and imported workers from southern Asia.

Economic freedoms and property rights(Keizaiteki jiyūken).

Japanese have the rights to choose their occupations (Art. 22) and to hold and use property "in conformity with the public welfare" (Art. 29).[101] Upon "just compensation," "private property may be taken for public use." Law and policy support both private and public enterprise; pragmatic capitalism has been mixed with democratic socialist welfare concerns. Article 30 establishes the duty to pay taxes.

Rights affecting the quality of socioeconomic life ("shakaiken," lit. social rights).

Article 25 gives all the "right to maintain the minimum standards of wholesome and cultured living" and obligates the State to provide "social welfare and security, and ... public health" programs.[102] Low-cost, good quality medical care and pensions have been assured by the government; life expectancy has been among the longest in the world. Article 26 reenforces an individual right "to receive an equal education correspondent" to ability with a duty of parents or guardians to make sure every child receives the ordinary free compulsory education. Japan has long had virtually 100% literacy, and has become a world leader in pre-collegiate education (for example, in mathematics and science). Although senior high school is not compulsory, over 90% of young Japanese graduate from high school in most areas. By 1990, over 40% went on to higher education.[103]

All "have the right and the obligation to work" with reasonable "wages, hours, rest and other working conditions" and children may not be exploited (Art. 27).[104] Blue collar and white collar workers join in unions, in exercise of the Article 28 rights "to organize and to bargain and act collectively." The large union movement gained in strength with the amalgamation under *Shin Rengo* of both public and private sector unions in 1989.[105] The right to strike and the freedom of expression of public employees (*kōmuin*) have been significantly limited by law and judicial decisions.[106]

Procedural rights (Art.s 31 to 40).

The Constitution, law and policy aspire to and in many respects achieve a high quality of procedural justice under well trained and professionalized judges, prosecutors, police and prison personnel; but deficiencies with respect to the treatment of suspects seems to be one of Japan's most serious constitutional problems.[107] "No person shall be deprived of life or liberty, nor shall any other criminal penalty be imposed, except according to procedure established by law" (Art. 31). Other provisions limit what law may establish. For example, "Entries, searches and seizures" are allowed only with judicially issued warrant (Art. 35); double jeopardy (Art. 39) and cruel punishment is prohibited (Art. 36); the right to examine witnesses is guaranteed (Art. 37). Unless caught during a criminal act, a person may not be apprehended without a warrant (Art. 33). A suspect has rights of access to "speedy and public trial" and to counsel (Art.s 32, 34 and 37) ; but severe limits are often placed on defense attorney contacts with detained clients, in disregard of Article 34.[108]

Since most suspects confess (about 95%), it is particularly important for an attorney to be quickly on the scene and to strictly limit police detention of suspects for interrogation. Article 38 protects a suspect against self-incrimination; a confession received under duress may not be used as evidence, and evidence other than confession is required for a conviction. In fact, however, judges, prosecutors, and police attach a good deal of importance to confessions and a repentant attitude.

Apart from rare political cases which drag on for years, criminal cases are cleared quickly in Japan. Most cases are disposed of by prosecutors rather than by judges. Although the conviction rate is over 99%, the criminal justice system is rather lenient. To start with, Japan's crime rate is very low and a high proportion of clearly indictable suspects are given a simple "summary order" and put on probation rather than prosecuted.[109] Prosecution Review Committees (207), composed of eleven local voters picked by lot, may ask a prosecutor's superior for further investigation when a case is disposed of without trial. Sentences are generally consistent and not severe. "Delayed execution" (shikkō yūyo) of sentence is commonly preferred over actual imprisonment, so relatively few go to prison. Prisoners are safe, not in danger as in the U.S.[110] As in many democracies, plea-bargaining and jury trial are not used. Torture and "cruel punishments are absolutely forbidden" (Art. 36); but police occasionally are too forceful during interrogations. Capital punishment is generally imposed once or twice a year, and in some years not at all.[111] Involuntary servitude is allowed only "as punishment for crime" (Art. 18). An individual may sue the State for redress if "he has suffered damage through illegal act of any public official" (Art. 17) or if "arrested or detained" and then acquitted (Art. 40). On balance, B.J. George concludes that "the effective constitutional protection of the criminally-accused may justly be viewed as one of the paramount accomplishments of Japan's modern constitutional era."[112] However, before formal indictment the constitution mandates more attention to rights to counsel and personal liberty than currently granted in some cases.

Rights and freedoms of the spirit (seishinteki jiyūken).[113]

This cluster of rights includes freedom of thought and conscience (Art. 19), freedom of religious activity and from religious or anti-religious coercion (Art. 20), freedom to peacefully petition government "for redress of damage, for the removal of public officials," and for the passage or repeal of any law (Art. 16), and freedom of professional academic activity (Art. 23, the world's first such recognition of academic freedom). Article 22 recognizes rights to choose occupation, place of residence, and citizenship.

Perhaps the most demanding test of democratic constitutionalism is freedom of expression, guaranteed under Article 21: "Freedom of assembly and association as well as speech, press and all other forms of expression are guaranteed. 2. No censorship shall be maintained, nor shall the secrecy of any means of communication be violated." As Professor Ashibe explains below, freedom is protected under Japan's law and courts, but with a few problems. Mass media freedom and the freedoms of assembly and association seem especially important in promoting openness and expression in Japan's group-oriented society.[114]

Along with malapportionment and the rights of a suspect, separation of religion and the state has been a major area of constitutional concern to some. Under Article 20, "no religious organization shall receive any privilege from the State," and Article 89 prohibits the use of "public money or other property for the benefit or maintenance of any religious institution or association."[115] Although the provisions guaranteeing freedom of religion and the separation of religion and the state are framed as they might be in the constitution of a predominantly Buddhist, Christian or Islamic nation favoring separation, the issues presented by Shinto do not fit into that general mold. For purposes of understanding Japan's constitutional system, Shinto may be better viewed less as a religion than as an ideology symbolizing statism and very strong nationalism. The Shinto system combines long-established social customs and folk beliefs (for example, local shrines for heroic figures, local festivals, a sense of access to the deceased) with an ancient, powerless monarchy grounded in a sun myth. This would present no complications today were it not for a revolutionary overlay of modern statism since the latter 1800s.[116] Untraditional reverence, loyalty and obedience to the Shinto Emperor as descendant of a sun goddess--in reality, to his government--were instilled by modern methods of indoctrination and control, and became the test until 1945 of the good Japanese, as subject and as person.

The 1889 Meiji Constitution established freedom of religion within limits set by law; but "religion" in this context was so defined as to apply to *"foreign"* religions such as Christianity, not to Shinto. Shinto fused the people with a paternal Emperor in the State (*Kokka*; lit., national family).[117] In 1990, public acts and legal cases which mixed the State and politics with Shinto ceremonies, shrines, and/or the Emperor (for example, the 1989 funeral and later accession ceremonies) were still controversial symbols of unhealthy statism, nationalism and conformism at odds with freedom and tolerance.[118] What was generally at stake was not so much the sincere religious beliefs of traditionalist politicians as a passionate nationalism empty sometimes of moderating humane content and in conflict with Japan's increasing international openness and domestic freedom.

Examples include apparently unconstitutional visits by Cabinet members to the ancient Ise Shrine and to the Yasukuni Shrine for the war dead,[119] and a few widely criticized judicial decisions. For example, the Supreme Court:

held constitutional in 1977 a local government-sponsored Shinto ground-breaking ceremony (*jichinsai*) as a non-religious "custom";[120] and in 1988, overturning lower court judgments, allowed the Shinto military enshrinement by a veterans association and a local SDF office of a deceased soldier against the religion-based objections of his widow.[121] In addition, a district court approved the State's right to require state school attendance as much as seven days a week and disallowed a student's Sunday absence from extracurricular activities on religious grounds.[122] Another district court permitted the Iwate Prefectural Assembly to allocate public monies to support Yasukuni Shrine, but the Sendai High Court reversed, holding it unconstitutional. [123]

The government has been accommodating toward Shinto and unaccommodating towards other religions not historically related to the Japanese State. This stance may suggest unconstitutional State entanglement with Shinto and State insensitivity to broader religious values. In addition, political visits to Shinto Shrines and Education Ministry rewriting of textbook history have outraged Asian neighbors and complicated Japan's regional relations. The famous *Ienaga Textbook Review* cases, in the courts from 1965 into the 1990s, heightened public awareness of government efforts to gloss over Japan's wartime (1930-1945) behavior in officially certified high school textbooks.[124] While Yasukuni and some other Shinto shrines were focal points for mourning the war dead, they were also symbols, to Japan and to Asia, of arrogant nationalism, aggressive militarism and, in some countries, wartime atrocities--as are monuments to Japan's war victims elsewhere in Asia (for example, in Manila and Singapore). One of the lasting costs to Japan of World War II has been her inability to eliminate the political manipulability by nostalgic rightists and the international shame associated with places of remembrance of her war dead. None are viewed as neutral sites for the apolitical and very human activities of remembering and mourning the nation's dead.

In general, Japan's system of rights and freedoms is comprehensive and well institutionalized in law. As in other democracies, social forces favoring freedom and the rigorous refinement of rights protection continue to clash with tendencies toward coercive conformism, defensive ethnic separatism, and neglect of the less fortunate in the bureaucratic State and society.

The National Assembly (Kokkai; the Diet)

Chapter 4 of the 1947 Constitution establishes the Diet or National Assembly as the "highest organ of state power" and the "sole law-making organ" of Japan (Art. 41).[125] As noted later, the Cabinet and other agencies play major roles in legislative policy-making, but under Japan's parliamentary system "a bill becomes a law on passage by both Houses" (Art. 59), the House of Representatives and the House of Councillors.[126] The Supreme Court has judicial review "power to determine the constitutionality of any law, order, regulation or official act" (Art. 81); so it becomes "the highest organ of state power" regarding law in those rare instances when it passes judgment on an act of the legislative or executive branch challenged as unlawful or unconstitutional. In the civil law and parliamentary traditions of which Japan and most other democracies are a part, there is an even stronger tendency to defer to the legislature's judgment than is the case in the United States, where a common law Supreme Court is strongest. The Diet enjoys very broad discretion; only the Diet can pass statutory law (*horitsu*). Local ordinances (*jorei*) established by elected assemblies of prefectures, cities or towns must fall within the limited authority granted to local self-government entities (*chiho jichi dantai*) under the Local Autonomy Law (*Chiho Jichi Ho*)[127] and other statutes. Ordinances are thus not legislative acts of a State or Province with expressed or reserved powers of its own as within a federal framework. Similarly, Cabinet Orders (*seirei*) and administrative regulations are issued pursuant to Diet-passed Law.[128]

The Diet meets in ordinary session once a year, for 150 days from mid-December, and such session may be extended once.[129] The Cabinet or one-fourth of the members of either House may call for an extraordinary session (*tokubetsukai*).[130] Extraordinary or emergency sessions (*rinjikai*) may be extended twice upon a decision of both Houses; as in some other contexts, if they disagree, the wishes of the House of Representatives prevail.[131]

Sessions are public. While the Diet is in session, members enjoy immunity from arrest (Art. 50) and from liability "outside ... for speeches, debates, or votes inside the House" (Art. 51). Members enjoy franking and travel privileges while on public business.[132] Each House makes its own rules regarding meetings and discipline and has jurisdiction over disputes about member qualifications. One-third of a House's membership constitutes a quorum. All decisions are by a majority of those present (Art. 56), except that a two-thirds majority of those present is required "to deny a seat" to an elected politician (Art. 55), to expel a member (Art. 58), to call a secret meeting (Art. 57), or for the House of Representatives to override on second passage a bill rejected by the House of Councillors (Art. 59). Formal amendment of the Constitution requires concurrence of "two-thirds or more of all the members of each House" and ratification by a majority in a special referendum (Art. 96), one reason the Constitution has never been formally amended.[133]

In the Diet's legislative process, a bill is submitted by the Prime Minister on behalf of the Cabinet or by Diet members. Following the American rather than the recent English model, the Diet allows "private member bills" (*giin no hatsugi suru hōan*). However, to avoid the perceived excesses of "pork barrel legislation" on behalf of narrow constituencies of individual members ("*omiyage hōan*"; lit., "gift bills"), the Diet amended its law in 1955 to require a bill sponsorship of at least twenty members in the House of Representatives and ten in the House of Councillors. An exception is that for Diet consideration a budget-related bill needs sponsorship by fifty members and twenty members, respectively.[134] Due in part to this restraint, Diet-initiated bills account for an average of only thirty percent of those submitted, and their rate of passage is notably lower than that for Cabinet bills.[135]

Along American lines, the Diet has a system of standing committees (*jōnin iinkai*), eighteen for the Representatives and sixteen for the Councillors.[136]

The Diet has powers of investigation and may demand "the presence and testimony of witnesses and the production of records" (Art. 62). The Prime Minister and other Ministers "may at any time appear" to speak on bills, and "must appear" when "required to give answers or explanations" (Art. 63). However, Japan's committees do not play as important a role in legislative politics as in the United States. Rather, the critical actors in the legislative process have more often been the policy committee (Policy Affairs Research Committee) of the ruling Liberal Democratic Party, high-level administrators in the Ministries most affected, and, with respect to major law changes, a legal system deliberation council (*hōsei shingikai*), subject-specific advisory groups composed of public officials and private sector experts such as scholars, lawyers, and interest-group representatives.[137] Many of these may play a role, along with interest groups, in refining policy proposals and drafting Cabinet bills; but the LDP leaders, not the bureaucracy or advisors, hold the final decision-making power, as in the Diet itself. One reason for the importance of these extra-parliamentary agencies in law-making is the absence of large staffs to serve individual Diet members and their committees.[138]

In most cases, the two Houses have agreed on bills, because the LDP controlled both Houses until 1989, and voting along party lines and party discipline have been the customs as in other parliamentary systems. If there is disagreement between the two Houses, "a joint committee of both Houses" may be formed to iron out differences (Art. 59[3]). Inaction by the House of Councillors within sixty days of House of Representatives action, "times in recess excepted," constitutes "a rejection" (Art. 59[4]). The annual Budget "must first be submitted to the House of Representatives"; the fiscal year is from April 1 to March 31. If no agreement is reached on the budget by both Houses, even by a joint committee, or if the House of Councillors fails to act within thirty days after budget passage by the House of Representatives, then the "decision of the House of Representatives shall be the decision of the Diet" (Art. 60[2]).   Treaties also become the law of the land in such circumstances thirty days after lower house passage (Art. 61), and enjoy high domestic legal status under the Constitution (Art. 98).[139]

The Prime Minister and the Cabinet[140]

The first business in a Diet session is designation of the Prime Minister by Diet resolution (Art. 67). The executive power in Japan's government is "vested in the Cabinet" (Art. 65), not in "its head," the Prime Minister (Art. 66). The Cabinet is "collectively responsible to the Diet" (Art. 66[3]), but the Prime Minister is not responsible to the Diet in his selection and removal of Ministers in the Cabinet (Art. 68). Rather, in practice, the Prime Minister as President of the ruling LDP has been responsible to other faction leaders within his own party, at whose suffrance he leads and among whom he must periodically redistribute Cabinet positions, the goal of many professional politicians in the Diet; thus, the average life of a Cabinet is only about one year.[141] Besides factional balance, the LDP considers strict seniority rules in determining when a politician is eligible for a Cabinet post, not primarily age but the number of times a politician has been elected to the Diet.[142] Factional restraints and competition constitute a noteworthy element in Japan's constitutional system for limiting government power, with the Prime Minister usually a "consensus articulator"rather than a forceful leader.[143]

The Prime Minister and "a majority" of (in practice, almost all) Cabinet members must hold seats in the Diet (Art. 68[1]); all must be civilians (Art. 66[2]). In addition to their general duties of governance, the Cabinet "manages foreign affairs; concludes treaties," with prior or subsequent Diet approval; "administers the civil service"; prepares and submits the budget to the Diet; enacts Cabinet orders pursuant to the Constitution or laws; and decides about "general amnesty, special amnesty, commutation of punishment, reprieve, and restoration of rights" (Art. 73).[144]

The Cabinet (*Naikaku*) consists of the Prime Minister (*Sōri Daijin*), the heads of the twelve Ministries (*shō*), and the "State Ministers" in charge of the various agencies (*chō*) grouped under the Prime Minister's Office (*Sōrifu*) (e.g., the Environment Agency, the Economic Planning Agency, and the Defense Agency). Although many are employed by public companies (*e.g.*, the

public sector of the train industry), relatively few are in the civil service
(kōmuin):[145]

> The size of the central and local bureaucracies in Japan is the *smallest*
> per population of the democracies in the industrialized world, with 45
> government employees for every 1,000 citizens, compared to 77.5 in the
> United States, 74.4 in West Germany, and 104 in England.

Yet size is not always an indicator of influence. John Campbell suggests:
"The tradition of bureaucratic dominance is stronger in Japan than in any
other contemporary democracy."[146] From the dawn of modern government
after the Meiji Restoration in 1868, Japan's civilian and military bureaucracy
provided expertise and leadership more than professional politicians, but led
Japan to wartime disaster. After 1945, SCAP needed the civilian bureaucracy
through which to rule Japan,
 and it continues a crucial leadership function today under the democratic
1947 Constitution. In part because political appointments have been limited
to the positions of minister and parliamentary vice-minister, ministries and
agencies have maintained a good measure of internal coherence and
autonomy. The civil service generally enjoys the public's trust. In most of its
day-to-day business, career bureaucrats--the administrative vice-ministers, their
staff leaders, and bureau chiefs--have managed the government rather than
Cabinet members, who have often been more busy with political affairs during
their short ministerial tenures. Their exercise of "administrative guidance"
(gyōsei shidō), a broad use of formal and informal methods of regulation and
persuasion, has been much debated in Japan and abroad, particularly as it has
affected economic life.[147]   Administrative guidance may involve more
bureaucratic discretion than granted in some other countries, but "in all
countries bureaucrats have to interpret general laws and policy guidelines and
use various means to enforce their interpretations."[148]
    Besides implementing policy and law, leading bureaucrats have
significantly affected government policy formation. Indeed, they have often
begun the processes of making a policy or law, with a ministerial proposal
going to the LDP's Policy Affairs Research Committee (PARC) for
consideration and response.[149] In the constitutional order, the bureaucracy
is ultimately subordinate to the Cabinet, the Diet and the courts; but in the
absence of well-coordinated administrative processes and vigorous prime
ministerial or Cabinet leadership, each agency may operate somewhat as a
semi-autonomous feudal domain, at times competing with other, like domains
in government, and not always responding positively to the necessary

intrusions of elected officials. Amelioration of this problem for constitutionalist government was one major object of Prime Minister Yasuhiro Nakasone's administrative reform efforts in the 1980s.[150] Where an executive or legislative power vacuum has occurred, the able and respected bureaucratic custodians of the nation's interests have provided leadership services, usually within limits set by written law, but with some strain perhaps on the spirit of the Constitution. The earlier engrained traditions of bureaucratic power and "looking-up-to-officials-and-down-on-the-people" (*kansonminpi*) may combine with an inward-looking attitude in non-elective groups to encourage questionable presumptions of prerogative when not counterbalanced by professionalism, political neutrality, strong consciousness of constitutional rights and constitutional humility. The long continuance of one party in power may have heightened such tendencies and permeated government operations with more dependence on higher civil servants than is common in democracies. Perhaps the national bureaucracy has functioned at times as a separate quasi-constitutional branch of government, in balance with the LDP Party Cabinet, the Diet, and the Supreme Court, and yielding in its position when obviously necessary.

The Court System

As explained in sections I and III, the postwar establishment under American influence of a new Supreme Court, as an independent branch of government with broad jurisdiction and final say on legal and constitutional disputes (Arts. 76, 81), brought to Japan an unprecedented separation of constitutional powers. The Supreme Court and other judges are "independent in the exercise of their conscience and bound only by this Constitution and the laws" (Art. 76[1]); all courts share in the power of judicial review.[151] Suffice it here to briefly describe the judiciary. The Supreme Court consists of fifteen members appointed by the Cabinet, normally as recommended by the Chief Justice.[152] Justices are over sixty when appointed, by custom, and must retire at seventy; other judges step down at age sixty-five. In general, five or more Justices are career judges, four or five are attorneys, two are prosecutors, one or two professors, and one or two other "persons of learning and experience" (*e.g.*, a diplomat). Three of the attorney-members come from the three Tokyo bar associations and one represents the bar association of Osaka or other regions.

The full Supreme Court (*Saikōsaibansho*) sits as "the Grand Bench" (*Daihōtei*) only occasionally, as when deciding a constitutional issue or resolving an apparent conflict of precedents.[153] The full court also constitutes the Judicial Conference which is responsible for administering and making policies, rules and appointments for all Japan's courts. Before deciding upon a rule, the Justices receive in-put from the Advisory Committee on Rules composed of judges, prosecutors, attorneys and scholars. Most cases are decided by the Justices when sitting as three "Petty Benches" (*Shohotei*) of five members each; three constitutes a quorum.

In deciding cases, the Supreme Court is substantially helped by some twenty to thirty "Research Judges" (*Shiho chosakan*), experienced judges assigned for a few years to provide research support and advice on alternatives to the Justices. The Court is also assisted by its own independent bureaucracy, the Supreme Court General Secretariat (*Jimu Sokyoku*). Among all national institutions, the Supreme Court, after the Constitution itself, enjoys the highest repute among educated Japanese. Yet, the Court and its Secretariat are criticized by many scholars and some other analysts for bureaucratism and for approving too regularly the government's position on constitutional issues.[154]

Under the Supreme Court, both judicially and administratively, is a hierarchy of high courts (*koto saibansho*), district courts (*chiho saibansho*), family courts (*katei saibansho*), and summary courts (*kan'i saibansho*). There are eight high courts (Tokyo, Osaka, Nagoya, Hiroshima, Fukuoka, Sendai, Sapporo, and Takamatsu) with six branches. The courts of original jurisdiction for most important cases are the fifty district courts and their 242 branches. A larger number of family courts has been established to deal with family problems, juvenile delinquency (crimes by those under twenty), and adult crimes harming the young. Four hundred fifty-two summary courts handle criminal cases involving fines or lighter punishments and civil cases where no more than 900,000 yen is at issue.[155] All summary court decisions and the overwhelming majority of district court judgments are made by a single judge. When exercising appellate jurisdiction, dealing with crimes punishable by more than a year in prison, and where law otherwise requires, district courts sit as three-person collegiate bodies. Family court judges are assisted by probation officers, social workers and others.

About 2,700 judges are authorized for 125 million people. The actual number of judges deciding cases is lower, because some are engaged in research, teaching or administrative duties. Virtually all judges, prosecutors and attorneys trained since the late 1940s have been graduates of the Supreme Court's Legal Training and Research Institute, which admits fewer than 500 a year based on the National Law Examination. For ten years, judicial graduates serve as "Assistant Judges" (*hanjiho*) on collegial district courts, family courts (a few), or summary courts (after a minimum of three years experience). The courts' respective case loads are presented in Figure 3. [156]

Local Autonomy

Alongside the regional offices of the ministries and the local courts are local governments with elected governors, mayors and local assemblies. The 1947 Constitution establishes a unitary state, not a federal system; and modern systems of education, mass communication and mass transportation have heightened commonalities among an already homogeneous ethnic group living in a medium-sized island country. On the other hand, semi-autonomous villages, towns, cities, and feudal regions developed their own distinctive subcultures over many centuries before the centralization of government and law after 1868. Under Article 94 "local public entities" (*chiho kokyo dantai*) enjoy "the right to manage their property, affairs, and administration and to enact their own regulations" within limits set by law, particularly the Local Autonomy Law.[157] Local politics and self-government add vigor and variety to Japan's democracy, and a limited functional restraint on central government power.

The main administrative units are forty-three prefectures (*ken*), the special metropolitan regions of Tokyo (*to*), Osaka and Kyoto (*fu*), and the large northern island of Hokkaido (*dō*); they are collectively referred to as "*todōfuken*." Local assemblies and--unlike the Prime Minister--governors and mayors of cities, towns and villages are "elected by direct popular vote within their several communities" (Art. 93[2]).

All local governments are ultimately beholden to the center for most of their law and funding; but they have limited delegated authority to tax and to pass ordinances (*Jōrei*). Hokkaido, whose development dates from the late nineteenth century, is uniquely linked to the national government through the Hokkaido Development Agency in the Prime Minister's Office; it seems to combine some frontier spirit with more dependency on the center than other areas. The Ryukyu Islands, of which Okinawa is the largest, is the other most distinctive region, due to its possession by the United States from 1945 to 1972 and to its separate cultural traditions.[158]

Although local government powers are limited by laws, Article 92 does require that such laws be "in accordance with the principle of local autonomy."[159] Moreover, a law applicable "only to one local public entity cannot be enacted by the Diet without the consent of the majority of the voters" in the place concerned (Art. 95).[160] Examples of such "local autonomy special laws" (*chihō jichi tokubetsuhō*) are those establishing an atom bomb memorial in Hiroshima in 1949 and mandating reconstruction in Tokyo in 1950.[161] In the regulation of demonstrations and parades, local "public safety ordinances" (*koan jorei*) have served as the nation's most important form of law. Local government has also played a major role in pollution control and in the development of protection of freedom of information and privacy rights.[162] "Japan's local institutions lack the specific powers found in federal political systems such as the United States, Canada, West Germany, or Australia, but they have most or more of the powers found in centralized systems such as Sweden, France, or England."[163]

Over many years the power of the LDP in the national government has been counterbalanced by opposition-party dominance in many localities. In issue areas such as pollution and medical care for the elderly, the policies of local progressive governments have in time become the national conservative policies.[164] More broadly, local government in Japan has served constitutional democracy as a "cushion against bureaucratic arbitrariness," a place of access and influence for minorities, a promoter of citizens' rights consciousness and political participation, a training ground for national leaders, and an advocate for consumer interests.[165]

Such are the main components of Japan's constitutional system. A major test of its health is how human rights have been treated in the courts.

Figure 3
Caseload of Japan's Judiciary*

Courts	Year	Civil & Administrative Cases			Criminal Cases		
Supreme Court		Newly received	Disposed of	Pending	newly received	Disposed of	Pending
	1985	1,837	1,922	1,678	1,781	1,794	819
	1986	1,771	2,024	1,425	1,671	1,781	709
	1987	1,812	1,879	1,358	1,611	1,591	729
	1988	2,024	2,075	1,307	1,626	1,625	730
	1989	2,012	2,088	1,231	1,507	1,552	685
High Courts	1985	21,136	21,212	13,690	8,630	8,921	2,045
	1986	21,274	21,143	13,821	8,799	8,609	2,235
	1987	21,659	21,775	13,705	8,317	8,427	2,125
	1988	22,401	22,297	13,809	7,637	7,886	1,876
	1989	22,885	23,079	13,615	7,012	6,991	1,897
District Courts	1985	759,729	717,780	504,886	269,895	270,068	25,584
	1986	743,067	713,161	534,792	265,253	257,390	24,447
	1987	725,570	741,985	518,377	255,265	256,384	23,328
	1988	669,598	730,163	487,812	237,108	239,639	20,797
	1989	651,405	700,027	439,190	214,120	215,237	19.680
Summary Courts	1985	1,764,930	1,789,958	121,830	2,761,460	2,760,225	31,992
	1986	1,666,729	1,685,689	102,870	2,625,529	2,629,154	28,367
	1987	1,579,705	1.584,244	98,331	1,947,961	1,958,438	17,890
	1988	1,392,053	1,410,305	80,079	1,626,273	1,627,362	16,801
	1989	1,152,409	1,160,040	72,448	1,490,901	1,493,971	13,731
Family Courts		Family Relations Cases			Juvenile Cases		
	1985	403,230	403,038	48,526	686,514	686,969	122,370
	1986	403,992	401,793	50,725	671,973	674,405	119,938
	1987	389,480	388,731	51,474	574,467	597,891	96,514
	1988	382,814	379,358	54,930	538,919	538,832	96,601
	1989	350,542	349,837	55,635	505,226	503,462	98,365

*Statisitics on civil and family relations cases show the number of cases while those on criminal and juvenile cases show the number of defendants and juveniles. Courtesy of the General Secretariat and Justice Itsuo Sonobe, Supreme Court of Japan, July, 1991.

NOTES: II

1. See, for example, David Joel Steinberg, ed., *In Search of Southeast Asia: A Modern History*, rev. ed., Honolulu, University of Hawaii Press, 1985, especially Part V; John Fairbank, Edwin Reischauer, and Albert Craig, *East Asia: Tradition and Transformation*, Boston, Houghton-Mifflin, 1978; and Selig Harrison, *The Widening Gulf: Asian Nationalism and American Policy*, New York, Free Press, 1978; and sources infra note 3.

2. In 1991 the Constitution of Japan was arguably Japan's most trusted and respected national institution. James S. Marshall, *Japan's Successor Generation: Their Values and Attitudes*, Washington, DC, Office of Research, U.S.I.A., 1985.

3. Government Section, SCAP, *Political Reorientation of Japan*, 2 vols., Washington, DC, Government Printing Office, 1949; Robert E. Ward and Sakamoto Yoshikazu, eds., *Democratizing Japan: The Allied Occupation*, Honolulu, University of Hawaii Press, 1987, hereafter, Ward, *Democratizing Japan*--some of the best of the large body of Japanese scholarship is cited in this volume; Justin Williams, *Japan's Political Revolution Under MacArthur* (Athens, University of Georgia Press, 1978; Alfred Oppler, *Legal Reform in Occupied Japan: A Participant Looks Back*, Princeton, Princeton University Press, 1976; Peter Frost, "Occupation," *Kodansha Encyclopedia of Japan*, Vol. 6, Tokyo, Kodansha, 1983, 51-55; Kenzo Takayanagi *et al. Nihonkoku Kempō Seitei no Katei*, (1972), based on materials in Milo Rowell's collection; and O. Nishi, *Ten Days Institute General Headquaters (GHQ)*, Tokyo, Seibundo, 1989.

4. The term "SCAP" referred to either General MacArthur or to the Occupation apparatus. "The Occupation" may mean both the period of external control or the entire administrative structure of the occupiers. The Occupation ended with the coming into force of the San Francisco Peace Treaty, September, (1951) ending, in law, World War II in Asia, except between Japan and the Soviet Union.

5. SCAP, *Political Reorientation*, 192.

6. On imperial ordinances and their use, see Lawrence W. Beer, *Freedom of Expression in Japan: A Study in Comparative Law, Politics, and Society*, Tokyo, Kodansha International 1984, 55-56, 73.

7. SCAP, *Political Reorientation*, 193.

8. Beer, *Freedom*, 73. Imperial Ordinance No. 311 of June 12, 1946, established as penalties for "acts prejudicial to Occupation objectives" up to ten years imprisonment with hard labor, or a fine up to 75,0000 yen, or detention, or a minor fine. SCAP, *Political Reorientation*, 193.

9. Dramatic changes had already taken place when the more detailed "Initial Basic Directives for SCAP for the Occupation and Administration of Japan" reached General MacArthur on November 8, 1945. The Occupation structure was approved by the Moscow Agreements of December 16, 1945, and the Policy by the thirteen-nation Far Eastern Advisory Commission in Washington, DC on December 21, 1945. Technically, but not actually, SCAP was under the authority of the successor Far Eastern Commission from February, 1946 and a four-power Allied Council located

in Tokyo. The Council was to consist of representatives of the U.S., the Supreme Commander ([or his Deputy]), China, the Soviet Union and the Commonwealth countries of the United Kingdom, Australia, New Zealand, and India. The Commission members were the U.S., the U.K., the U.S.S.R., China, France, The Netherlands, Canada, Australia, New Zealand, India, and the Philippine Commonwealth. SCAP, *Political Orientation*, 421-422, 429-441.

10. Beer, *Freedom*, 77-82.

11. *Id.*, 75. The famous photograph of MacArthur and Hirohito is reproduced in Williams, *Japan's Political Revolution*, 82.

12. The complete texts of SCAPIN 66 and 93 are reproduced in Beer, *Freedom*, 95-97, notes 221 and 223.

13. For the membership and drafts of the Matsumoto Committee, see SCAP, *Political Reorientation*, 603-631. In Ward, *Democratizing Japan*, see especially the chapters by Theodore McNelly, 76, and Tanaka Hideo, 107.

14. Beer, *Freedom*, 76.

15. *Id.*, 76; SCAP, *Political Reorientation*, 195.

16. SCAP, *Political Reorientation*, 470-471; Beer, *Freedom*, 76-77.

17. Women's rights seem to have been virtually an ignored subject among most Americans and Japanese proposing constitutional changes in the fall of 1945. See especially Susan Pharr's chapter in Ward, *Democratizing Japan*, 221; the 1945 election law is in SCAP, *Political Reorientation*, 822.

18. Ward, *Democratizing Japan*, 110 and 128 n. 16.

19. The principal author of SWNCC-228 was Hugh Borton, professor emeritus now of Columbia University. On the context, content and significance of SWNCC-228, see Robert Ward's chapter in Ward, *Democratizing Japan*, especially 28-38. This document provided SCAP general guidance on constitutional principles, but SCAP was the source of initiative for provisions on some rights, the imperial institution, and the renunciation of war, as well as "the all-important details and specification that made a constitution out of what had been merely a vague and abstract set of principles." *Id.*, 36.

20. *Id.*, 81; Williams, *Japan's Political Revolution*, 104-105, and generally chapters 4 and 5; Theodore McNelly, ed. advisor, *Framing the Constitution of Japan: Primary Sources in English, 1944-1949*, Frederick, MD, University Publications of America, 1988, microfiche.

21. Ward, *Democratizing Japan*, 79-81. The various draft constitutions and related documents are in Appendix C, SCAP, *Political Reorientation*, 586-683.

22. For a participant's account, see Charles L. Kades, "The American Role in Revising Japan's Imperial Constitution," *Political Science Quarterly*, Vol. 104, No. 2, summer, 1989, 215. Rowell had submitted memoranda to SCAP in December and January on unofficial proposals for constitutional change--as from political parties and the private Constitutional Research Association, (*Kempo Kenkyūkai*)--but his activity was not part of a scheduled process for revising the Meiji Constitution. Ward, *Democratizing Japan*, 109.

23. Williams, *Japan's Political Revolution*, 39-42.

24. *Id.*, 52, and my correspondence with Charles Kades, January and February, 1986. Besides the Steering Committee and secretaries, the eight "committees" drafting parts of the constitution were: Frank Hays, Guy Swope, Osborne Hauge (Legislative Committee); Cyrus Peake, Jacob Miller, Milton Esman (Executive Committee); Pieter Roest, Harry Wildes, Beate Sirota (Civil Rights Committee); Milo Rowell, Alfred Hussey (Judiciary Committee); Cecil Tilton, Roy Malcolm (Local Government Committee); Frank Rizzo (Finance Committee); George Nelson (Committee on the Emperor, Treaties ...); Alfred Hussey (The Preamble). SCAP, *Political Reorientation*, 813.

25. Ward, *Democratizing Japan*, 82 and 121.

26. *Id.* 82-83; David J. Danelski, "Judicial Review and Democracy in Japan," paper presented at the International Political Science Association meeting, Paris, July 1985, 106.

27. Ward, *Democratizing Japan*, 84; SCAP, *Political Reorientation*, 669.

28. Ward, *Democratizing Japan*, 94-95.

29. For an account of the process and documents, see SCAP, *Political Reorientation*, 82-118, 586-683, 315-323.

30. See *supra* note 26, and *passim*; Ward, *Democratizing Japan*, and Williams, *Japan's Political Revolution*, especially chapter 3. On Article 9 origins, see Theodore McNelly, "General Douglas MacArthur and the Constitutional Disarmament of Japan," and Charles L. Kades, "Discussion of Professor Theodore McNelly's Paper ...," in *The Transactions of the Asiatic Society of Japan*, Third Series, Vol. 17, October, 1982.

31. On Beate Sirota and her role, see Pharr in Ward, *Democratizing Japan*, 230-231.

32. Williams, *Japan's Political Revolution*, 108; Dale Hellegers, panelist in *The Occupation of Japan: The Proceedings of a Seminar on the Occupation of Japan and Its Legacy to the Postwar World*, Norfolk, VA, MacArthur Memorial, 1976; 11-15.

33. Ward, *Democratizing Japan*, 80-81, 92-93, and 102; see note 30, above for McNelly and Kades views.

34. Ward, *Democratizing Japan*, 111-131; members of the Matsumoto Committee are listed in SCAP, *Political Reorientation*, 603. Frank O. Miller, *Minobe Tatsukichi: Interpreter of Constitutionalism in Japan*, Berkeley, University of California Press, 1965 is excellent in conveying the perspectives of prewar and early postwar Japanese constitutional lawyers.

35. Ward, *Democratizing Japan*, 92; Miller, *Minobe Tatsukichi*; and Beer, *Freedom*, 393-396.

36. "On July 2, 1946, the Far Eastern Commission adopted its 'Basic Principles for a New Constitution,' which was based on SWNCC-228." Ward, *Democratizing Japan*, 89. SCAP was concerned lest a larger FEC role lead to a Soviet veto of the new constitution. See the Sakamoto chapter in *id.*, 42.

37. Williams, *Japan's Political Revolution*, 64-65. For 45 laws implementing the new constitution in 1947 and 1948, see SCAP, *Political Reorientation*, 822-1283.

38. Beer, *Freedom*, 77-82.

39. Williams, *Japan's Political Revolution*, 172; Lawrence W. Beer, "Human Rights Commissioners (*Jinken Yogo Iin*) and Lay Protection of Human Rights in Japan," Occasional Paper No. 31, International Ombudsman Institute, Alberta, Canada, October, 1985. The selection process was devised during the Occupation by Kurt Steiner (now professor emeritus of Stanford Universityand remained unchanged as of 1989.

40. On the meaning of "*kokumin*" (people, nation) and "*shuken*" (sovereignty), see Masami Ito, *KEMPO*, Tokyo, Hakubundo, 1983, 93-109. On the Occupation context, see Ward, *Democratizing Japan*, 88-92, 122.

41. Ito, 93-124. The Preamble in English is in Hiroshi Itoh and Lawrence W. Beer, *The Constitutional Case Law of Japan: Selected Supreme Court Decisions, 1961-70*, Seattle, University of Washington Press, 1978, 256.

42. Itoh and Beer, 257. See Fukio Nakane (trans.), *Japanese Laws Relating to Imperial Family*, Tokyo, Eibun-Horeisha, 1958.

43. Itoh and Beer, 257. On the emperor institution early in the reign of Emperor Akihito, see *JURISUTO*, No. 933, May 1 and 15, and No. 934, June 1, 1989.

44. Itoh and Beer, 258.

45. On the passing of Emperor Hirohito and the transition to Emperor Akihito, including the controversy over funeral and accession ceremonies, see *Asahi Shimbun* and *The Japan Times*, January-May, 1989, and *JURISUTO*, Nos. 933 and 934, 1989). Many constitutional lawyers thought the ceremonies may have violated the constitutional separation of religion and the State, harkening back to the repressive prewar unity of Shinto and the State; see 4, below. Yvonne Chang, *The Funeral of Japanese Emperors in the Modern Period*, thesis, Graduate School of Comparative Culture, Sophia University, Tokyo, 1989; Robert S. Ellwood, *The Feast of Kingship: Accession Ceremonies in Ancient Japan*, Tokyo, Monumenta Nipponica, 1973. On the controversial establishment in law of the custom of naming each emperor's reign period, see Beer, *Freedom*, 251, 274 note 9.

46. David Titus, *Palace and Politics in Prewar Japan*, New York, Columbia University Press, 1974.

47. On the Emperor under the Meiji Constitution, see *supra*, I, note 28. On the importance of "*kokutai*" as the quasi-mystical union of Japan's emperor, land and people, see Beer, *Freedom*, 65-66, 75 and 190. See also S.J. Napier, "Death and the Emperor: Mishima, Oe, and the Politics of Betrayal," *Journal of Asian Studies*, Vol. 48, No. 1, Feb. 1989, 71.

48. Beer, *Freedom*, chapter 2, especially 82-85.

49. *Id.*

50. Hans Baerwald, *Party Politics in Japan*, Boston, Allen & Unwin, 1988, 37.

51. Itoh and Beer, 259.

52. "*Kokkai*" is commonly translated "the Diet," taken from a nineteenth-century German term for a two-house assembly; but, as Baerwald contends, "National

Assembly" is a more precise and appropriate rendering of "*kokkai*." Hans Baerwald, *Japan's Parliament*, New York, Cambridge University Press, 1974, Preface.
53. On the National Assembly, see Baerwald, *Parliament*. Article 43, paragraph 2 provides: "The number of the members of each House shall be fixed by law." Itoh and Beer, 261.
54. Itoh and Beer, 262.
55. For discussion of election law, see "*Senkyo*," *JURISUTO, sogo tokushu* No. 38, March 25, 1985; "Japan's Electoral System," *Liberal Star*, August 15, 1989, 6-7; Gerald L. Curtis, *Election Campaigning Japanese Style*, New York, Columbia University Press, 1971, 211-243; Beer, *Freedom*, 76, 372-378; and *infra*, III, at note 44.
56.Law No. 100 of April 15, 1950.
57. Voting rates have been as follows in recent elections:

House of Councillors   *House of Representatives*

	men	women		men	women
1976	72.8%	74.1%	*1977*	67.7%	69.3%
1979	97.4%	68.6%	*1980*	73.7%	75.3%
1980	73.7%	75.4%	*1983*	56.9%	57.1%
1983	67.6%	68.3%	*1986*	70.1%	72.4%
1986	70.2%	72.5%	source:	Ministry of Home Affairs, 1988

For comparative perspective, see G. Bingham Powell, "American Voter Turnout in Comparative Perspective," *American Political Science Review*, Vol. 80, No. 1, March, 1986, 35, and Robert W. Jackson, "Political Institutions and Voter Turnout in the Industrial Democracies," *American Political Science Review*, Vol. 81, No. 2, June, 1987, 40. The Liberal Democratic Party (LDP) controlled both Houses from its inception in late 1955 until defeated in the House of Councillors elections of July 23, 1989 by the Japan Socialist Party (JSP) and other parties. The JSP also made major gains in the February. 1990 House of Representatives elections, but the LDP kept its majority. See Hans Baerwald, "Japan's House of Councillors Election: A Mini-Revolution?" *Asian Survey*, September, 1989, 833; Kent E. Calder, "Japan in 1990: Limits to Change," *Asian Survey*, January, 1991, 25.
58. On the election system, see Baerwald, *Party Politics*, chapter 2; J.A.A. Stockwin, "Political Parties and Political Opposition," in Takashi Ishida and Ellis Krauss eds., *Democracy in Japan*, Pittsburgh, University of Pittsburgh Press, 1989, 99-109; and Curtis, *Election Campaigning*.
59. Baerwald, *Party Politics*,62-87.

60. In June, 1964, nineteen seats were added to the House of Representatives to reduce the discrepancy in vote value among districts to 2-to-1. However, the 1970 National Census revealed a ratio of 4.99-to-1 between the Third District of Osaka and the Fifth District of Hyogo. Twenty more seats were established in July, 1975, but the difference in vote value remained as high as 3.77-to-1 (Fourth District of Chiba and Fifth District of Hyogo), and was increasing. In 1986, the third reapportionment added eight seats to underrepresented urban areas while subtracting seven from overrepresented rural districts, again a stop-gap measure responding to Supreme Court pressure. Since the Supreme Court has not held House of Councillors apportionment unconstitutional, no effort to reapportion its seats has been made, although the difference in vote value among prefectural districts has risen to 5.26-to-1 between Tottori and Kanagawa Prefectures. See Hiroyuki Hata, "Malapportionment of Representation in the National Diet," and Hidenori Tomatsu, "Equal Protection of the Law," in Percy Luney, ed.), *The Constitution of Japan: The Fifth Decade*," *Law and Contemporary Problems*, 1990. Some advocate change to a single-member district system for the House of Representatives; the LDP presented a reform bill to that effect to the Diet in 1991.

61. Article 204 of the Election Law gives all voters standing to file a suit contesting the validity of an election. Although the legislative drafters of this provision envisaged grounds other than unconstitutional malapportionment for legal invalidity, the Supreme Court in 1976 affirmed extension of Article 204 to cover malapportionment suits on grounds that the Constitution requires a remedy to such problems and no other legal provision touches on the issue. Hata and Tomatsu.

62. *Kurokawa v. Chiba Prefecture Election Commission*, 30 MINSHU 223 (Sup. Ct. G.B., April 14, 1976); *Tokyo Election Commission v. Koshiyama*, 37 MINSHU 1243 (Sup. Ct., G.B., November 7, 1983); and *Kaneo et al. v. Hiroshima Election Commission*, 39 MINSHU 200 (Sup. Ct. G.B., July 17, 1985). The disparity at issue in the 1976 decision was 4.99-to-1, and in the 1983 and 1985 decisions, 4.4-to-1. Hata and Tomatsu in Luney, ed.); Lawrence W. Beer, "Japan's Constitution System and Its Judicial Interpretation," in John O. Haley, ed.), *Law and Society in Contemporary Japan*, Dubuque, Kendall/Hunt Publishers, 1988, 26-28.

63. *Id.*

64. The distribution of House of Councillors seats is presented in Appendix II of the Election Law. The Supreme Court has treated malapportionment in the upper house as a question of legislative propriety rather than constitutionality. The two leading cases on Councillor malapportionment have been *Koshiyama v. Tokyo Election Commission*, 18 MINSHU 270 (Sup. Ct. G.B., February 5, 1964), upholding a 4.09-to-1 discrepancy in vote value, and *Shimizu et al. v. Osaka Election Commission*, 37 MINSHU 345 (Sup. Ct., G.B., April 27, 1983), allowing a 5.26-to-1 disparity to stand. The former case is translated in Itoh and Beer, 53.

65. *Tokyo Election Commission v. Ishida, Asahi Shimbun* (evening ed.), February 17, 1987 (Sup. Ct., P.B., Feb. 17, 1987).

66. Hata, in Luney, ed.).

67. *Baker v. Carr*, 369 U.S. 186, 1962). This American decision has influenced Japan's malapportionment debates since 1962.

68. Itoh and Beer, 256.

69. Itoh and Beer, 258. A good alternative translation of paragraph 1 has been suggested by Theodore McNelly: "The Japanese people, aspiring sincerely to an international peace based on justice and order, renounce forever, as means of settling international disputes, war as a sovereign right of the nation and the threat or use of force." Theodore McNelly, "Disarmament and Civilian Control in Japan: A Constitutional Dilemma," *Occasional Papers/Reprint Series in Contemporary Asian Studies*, No. 4, 1982.

70. Lawrence W. Beer, "Japan, (1947): Forty Years of the Postwar Constitution," in Vernon Bogdanor, ed., *Constitutions in Democratic Politics*, Aldershot, U.K., Gower Publishing Co., (1988), 173.

71. Itoh and Beer, 264. A few have argued that Article 66(2) implies the legitimate existence of a military and thus SDF constitutionality by stating that all Cabinet members "must be civilians." This view is commonly rejected by constitutional lawyers.

72. Itoh and Beer, 262. If the House of Representatives is in dissolution at the time of a national emergency, the Cabinet may call an "emergency session" of the House of Councillors; but measures then taken are "provisional and ... null and void unless agreed to by the House of Representatives within" ten days of the opening of the next Diet session (Art. 54(2) and (3)). Article 71 of the Police Law (*Keisatsuho*) gives the Prime Minister power to proclaim a state of national emergency, on recommendation of the National Public Safety Commission, and to assume direct control over the nation's police. See Beer, *Freedom*, 167; and Osamu Nishi, *The Constitution and the National Defense Law System in Japan*, Tokyo, Seibundo Publishing Co., 1987, 138-148.

73. Beer, "Japan, (1947)."

74. Self-Defense Force Law (*Jieitaihō*), Law No. 165 of June 9, 1954.

75. On Japanese pacifism, see Tadakazu Fukase, *SENSŌ HŌKI TO HEIWATEKI SEIZONKEN*, Tokyo, Iwanami Shoten, 1987; Masami Ito, *KEMPŌ*, chap. 4; and James E. Auer, "Article 9 of Japan's Constitution," in Luney, ed.

76. Itoh and Beer, 105. Treaty of Mutual Cooperation and Security between the United States and Japan (*Nichibei Anzen Hosho Joyaku*), Treaty No. 6 of June, 1960.

77. Okinawa-based protest incidents against the flag, the anthem, and the Emperor's visit were reported in the *Japan Times*, March 11 and May 13, 15, and 24, 1987. The extraordinary combination of public and private lands leased for U.S. bases on Okinawa take up 18% of its land area, much of it among the best properties. In opposition, a local and national movement arose to acquire parcels of land and then refuse government pressures to lease them to U.S. bases. The "*Hansen Jinushi Undō*" (landholders anti-war movement), in the spirit of Article 9 and constitutional property rights. Discussions with Okinawans, November, 1986 on Okinawa.

78. Auer, in Luney, ed.; Osamu Kaihara, "Illusion of Military Power," *Japan Times*, October 3, 1989; Frank Langdon, "The Security Debate in Japan," *Pacific Affairs*, Vol. 58, No. 3, fall, 1985, 397.

79. Comments by Isao Sato, in Luney, ed. See also Seizaburo Sato, "A Constitutional Amendment for Article 9?" *Japan Echo*, Vol. 8, No. 2, 1981, 91.

80. In 1988, Japan surpassed the United States as the leading donor of Official Development Assistance (ODA) aid under OECD guidelines. For context, see Haruhiro Fukui, "Japan in 1988: At the End of an Era," *Asian Survey*, January, 1989, 1, and Bruce Koppel and Michael Plummer, "Japan's Ascendancy as a Foreign-Aid Power: Asian Perspectives," *Asian Survey*, November 1989, 1043.

81. After 1952, Japan's military budget first fell below 1% of GNP in 1967, and was at a low of .7% in 1971. Prime Minister Takeo Miki announced a temporary maximum of 1% of GNP in 1976; but this was replaced with non-quantitative standards, like the spirit of Article 9, in 1987. Nevertheless, 1% was for a decade a useful concrete symbol of constitutionally mandated restraint. J. Auer, in Luney, ed. Expenditures again fell below 1% in the 1990-91 budget.

82. Prime Minister Eisaku Sato enunciated the "three non-nuclear principles" in January, 1968; they were confirmed by Diet resolution in November, 1981. However, many officials and citizens are aware of the nuclear weaponry on U.S. craft in Seventh Fleet harbors in Japan, and they resent deeply or accept the situation based on their Article 9 views. Neither government unequivocally affirms or denies their presence on ships in port.

83. Under a 1983 U.S.-Japan agreement, "dual use" technology from Japan became a significant element in America's high-tech weaponry by 1990. Regarding the Toshiba Machine Company's export of sophisticated equipment for milling submarine propellers to the U.S.S.R., and the dispute over technology transfer in the FSX plane proposal of the U.S. and Japan, see Masaru Kohno, "Japanese Defense Policy-Making: The FSX Selection, 1985-1987," *Asian Survey*, May, 1989, 457; *Asahi Shimbun*, July 20, 1987; *Japan Times*, June 22, 24, 25, 1987. On the successful popular opposition to a succession of "State Secrets Bills" (*Kokka Himitsu Hoan*), see *Asahi Shimbun*, October 31, November 14, 19, 10, 1986 and April 6 and 21, 1987.

84. On the case of three high school students denied graduation diplomas in part for refusing to join a flag-carrying parade on campus, see *Japan Times*, February 27 and March 7, 1987; and *supra* n.77. Since the 1950s, at schools and in general society, substantial opposition has continued against giving official or even public sanction to the *de facto* national flag and anthem. The Education Ministry's use of these symbols to promote patriotism was still perceived by many in 1991 as ultimately encouraging militarist nationalism at worst, against Article 9, and at best rigid conformism.

85. *Japan Report*, 1988 and 1989.

86. Itoh and Beer, 111. See *Japan v. Sakata*, 13 KEISHŲ 3225 (Sup. Ct., G.B., December 16, 1959), translated in John M. Maki, *Court and Constitution in Japan*,

Seattle, University of Washington Press, 1964), 298; and *Japan v. Sakane et al.*, 23 KEISHŲ 685 (Sup. Ct., G.B., April 2, 1969), translated in Itoh and Beer, 103.

87. *Ito et al. v. Ministry of Agriculture and Forestry*, HANREI JIHŌ (No. 712) 26 (Sapporo dist. ct., Sept. 7, 1973), translated in Briggs, "The Self-Defense Force and the Japanese Courts: The Naganuma Nike District Court Decision," in W. Gray, ed., *Current Studies in Japanese Law*, Ann Arbor: University of Michigan, 1979, 79.

88. The appellate decisions in *Naganuma* were *Uno et al. v. Ministry*, 36 MINSHŲ 1679 (Sup. Ct., 1st P.B., Sept. 9, 1982), and *Ministry v. Ito et al.*, GYŌSAI REISHŲ 1175 (Sapporo High Ct., Aug. 5, 1976). Examples of other Article 9 cases are the *Eniwa* case [*Japan v. Nozaki*, HANREI JIHŌ (No. 476) 25 (Sapporo Dist. Ct., March 3, (1967)], and the *Hyakuri* case [43 MINSHŲ (No. 6) 385; Mito Dist. Ct., 1977; Tokyo High Ct., 1981; Sup. Ct., 3d P.B., June 20, 1989]. In a less-noticed but interesting reliance on "the spirit of the Constitution," including Article 9, the Tokyo high court denied that in time of peace a higher public interest existed in National Defense Agency (*Bōeichō*) activities than in those of civilian airports or other government agencies, and refused to excuse airplane noise pollution damaging to citizens' personal rights. *ASAHI SHIMBUN* (evening ed.), July 15, 1987, Tokyo high ct., July 15, 1987.

89. Itoh and Beer, 258-261, 268. On judicial doctrine regarding human rights, see section III, below.

90. Beer, "Human Rights Commissioners (*Jinken Yogo Iin*) and Lay Protection of Human Rights in Japan," *supra* n. 39. "Human Rights Protectors" is a literal translation of "*Jinken Yogo Iin*"; but the related agency in the Justice Ministry is called the "Civil Liberties Bureau" (*Jinken Yogokyoku*). The distinction is important because human rights under Japan's Constitution encompass much more than civil liberties. See the *JINKEN YOGO ROPPŌ* (The Six Codes on Human Rights Protection), Tokyo, Nihon Kajo Shuppan, 1983, compiled by the Civil Liberties Bureau; and Joel Rosch, "Institutionalizing Mediation: The Evolution of the Civil Liberties Bureau in Japan," *Law and Society Review*, Vol. 21, No. 2, 1987, 243.

91. See, for example, the categorization of constitutional rights in *KEMPŌ HANREI HYAKUSEN*, commentaries on leading constitutional cases published by the leading legal journal, *Jurisuto*, Tokyo, Yuhikaku Publishing Co.

92. Itoh and Beer, 258.

93. Civil Code, Law No. 89 of 1896, as amended; translated in *EHS Law Bulletin Series, Series II*, No. 2100, Tokyo, Eibun Horeisha, 1962.

94. Anne E. Imamura, *Urban Japanese Housewives:At Home and in the Community*, Honolulu, University of Hawaii Press, 1987; Catherine Brown, "Japanese Approaches to Equal Rights for Women: The Legal Framework," and Taime Bryant, "Marital Dissolution in Japan: Legal Obstacles and Their Impact," in Haley, *supra* note 62 at 197 and 221.

95. Nationality Law (*Kokuseki Hō*), Law No. 147 of 1950, as amended by Law No. 45 of 1984; Family Registry Law (*Koseki Hō*), Law No. 224 of 1947, as amended by Law No. 45 of 1984. For relevant portions of the English and Japanese texts and

explanation, see Ryoichi Yamada and Fumiaki Tuchiya (J.C. Yamanaka, (trans.), *An Easy Guide to the New Nationality Law*, Tokyo, *Japan Times*, (1985); and Sueo Ikehara, "The New Nationality Law," *Look Japan*, December 10, 1984.

96. Law to Adjust Laws for the Ministry of Labor to Promote the Assurance of Equality of Opportunity and Treatment for Employed Men and Women, Law No. 45 of June 1, 1985, in effect from April 1, 1986. For the UN Convention on women, see United Nations, *Human Rights Instruments of the United Nations, 1948-1982*, (1983), 150, 165. See sources, *supra* n.94; Frank K. Upham, *Law and Social Change in Postwar Japan*, Cambridge, Harvard University Press, 1987; and UN Committee on the Elimination of Discrimination Against Women, *Reports Submitted by States Parties under Article 18 of the Convention ... Initial Reports, Japan*, United Nations, November 3, 1987.

97. *ASAHI SHIMBUN*, July 24 and 25, 1989, and *passim*, July, 1988 to November, 1989; Fukui, *supra* n.80; *New York Times*, May 1, 1989; *New York Times*, Feb. 19, 1990.

98. Lawrence W. Beer and C.G. Weeramantry, "Human Rights in Japan: Some Protections and Problems," *Universal Human Rights* (now *Human Rights Quarterly*), Vol. 1, No. 3, 1979, 1; Upham, chap. 3; "The International Covenant on Civil and Political Rights and Human Rights in Japan," symposium in *Law in Japan: An Annual*, Vol. 20, 1987 (hereafter "Human Rights Japan"), 1-14, 30-36, 48-54.

99. Interview with Isamu Ando, Tokyo, October, 1989.

100. Sources, *supra* n.98; Yuji Iwasawa, "Legal Treatment of Koreans in Japan: The Impact of International Human Rights Law on Japanese Law," *Human Rights Quarterly*, Vol. 8, May, 1986, 131; on foreigners and refugees in Japan, see *JIYŪ TO SEIGI*, Vol. 34, No. 1, January, 1983; William R. Burkhardt, "Institutional Barriers, Marginality, and Adaptation Among the American-Japanese Mixed Bloods in Japan," *Journal of Asian Studies*, Vol. 27, May, 1983, 533; *Japan Report*, Vol. 36, No. 1, January, 1990, 3.

101. Itoh and Beer, 260; Mutsuo Nakamura, "Freedom of Economic Activity and Property Rights," in Luney, ed.

102. *Id.*; Akira Osuka, "Welfare Rights," in Luney, ed., and *SEIZONKEN*, Tokyo, Nihon Hyoronsha, 1984; Richard Rose and Rei Shiratori, eds., *The Welfare State East and West*, New York, Oxford University Press, 1986; and Social Insurance Agency, Japan, *Outline of Social Insurance in Japan*, Tokyo: Japan International Social Security Association, March, 1989). On rights problems of the mentally ill, see "Human Rights Japan," 10, 36. See also N.J.C. Vasantkumar, "The Secret 'Poverty' of Japan," *Japan Times*, September 21, 1986; and Margaret McKean, "Equality," in Ishida and Krauss, eds., 201.

103. Lawrence W. Beer, "Japan," in Jack Donnelly and Rhoda Howard, eds., *International Handbook of Human Rights*, Westport, CT, Greenwood Press, 1987, 220-221; the annual *MONBU TŌKEI YŌRAN* (Survey of Education Statistics) of Japan's Ministry of Education; and Edward Beauchamp, "Education," in Ishida and Krauss, eds., 225.

104. Itoh and Beer, 260; Beer, *Freedom*, chap. 6.

105. *Japan Labor Bulletin*, 1988 and 1989. The Japanese Private Trade Union Confederation (JPTUC)-*Rengō* was founded in November, 1987 to unify labor and virtually completed the task in two years. See JPTUC, *The Direction and Role of Rengō*, March, (1988), and the monthly *Rengō*, from December, 1987.

106. Beer, *Freedom*, chap. 6, *infra* section III.

107. Itoh and Beer, 260-261; "Human Rights Japan," 1-6, 14-28, 54-73; *JIYŪ TO SEIGI*, Vol. 38, No. 2, February, 1987 (on criminal trials); B.J. George, Jr., "Discretionary Authority of Public Prosecutors in Japan," in Haley, ed., and "Rights of the Criminally Accused," in Luney, ed.; and *Universal Principle* (Japan Civil Liberties Union), No. 1, Spring, 1989.

108. "Human Rights Japan," 14-28, 54-73. Professor Yasuo Watanabe of Hokkaido University, a former high court judge, has proposed use of tape recorders during all police interrogations to compensate for insufficient presence of counsel; "*Higisha jimmon no tepu rokuon seido*," *HANREI TAIMUZU*, No. 608, September 25, 1986. The following are useful critical descriptions of abuse: *Universal Principle*; Gavan McCormack, "Crime, Confession, and Control in Contemporary Japan," and Igarashi Futaba, "Forced to Confess," in G. McCormack and Yoshio Sugimoto, eds., *Democracy in Contemporary Japan*, Armonck, NY, M.E. Sharpe, 1986, 186-265. For balanced comparisons with U.S. prisons and police, see David H. Bayley, *Forces of Order*, Berkeley, University of California Press, 1976 and 1990.

109. Between 1977 and 1987, violent crimes in 59 American cities increased 43%, from 939/100,000 to 1,346/100,000. Police numbered 2.3/1,000 in 1987. U.S. Bureau of Justice Statistics, August 27, 1989. The rate of violent crime was significantly lower in Japan; and the incarceration rate of those convicted is five times higher in the U.S. than in Japan. Bayley, *Forces of Order*, chapter 7; Government of Japan, *White Paper on Crime*, annual.

110. James Webb, "Japan's Prisons," *Parade Magazine*, January 15, 1984. In Japan's prisons, privileges are extended or denied based on one's grade, which is determined by one's behavior. After serving one-third of a sentence, a prisoner may be released on parole for good conduct. For annual statistics, see Government of Japan, *Summary of the White Paper on Crime*, Research and Training Institute, Ministry of Justice. Malcolm Feeley, "Police Detention and Interrogation: A Comparative Perspective," International Human Rights and Environment Protection Symposium, Kobe, November 4, 1988.

111. Chin Kim and Gary D. Garcia, "Capital Punishment in the United States and Japan: Constitutionality, Justification, and Methods of Infliction," *Loyola of L.A. Intnatl. and Comp. Law Journal*, Vol. 11, No. 2, 1989, 253; Japan Civil Liberties Union, *Report concerning Present Status of Human Rights in Japan*, to the Human Rights Committee, United Nations, June, 1988, 4-6; V. Lee Hamilton and Joseph Sanders, "Punishment and the Individual in the United States and Japan," *Law and Society Review*, Vol. 22, No. 2, 1988, 301; for a case upholding the hanging method,

see Itoh and Beer, 161-164. There is no consistency on death penalty practice among U.S. states, as shown here:

Death Sentences and Executions in the United States, 1977-1989:

	Sentenced	Executed	
1st Circuit	0	0	Maine, Massachusetts, New Hampshire Rhode Island
2nd Circuit	1	0	Connecticut, New York, Vermont
3rd Circuit	47	0	Pennsylvania, New Jersey, Delaware
4th Circuit	182	12	West Virginia, Virginia, North Carolina, South Carolina
5th Circuit	372	53	Texas, Louisiana, Mississippi
6th Circuit	188	0	Michigan, Ohio, Kentucky, Tennessee
7th Circuit	170	2	Wisconsin, Illinois, Indiana
8th Circuit	114	1	North Dakota, South Dakota, Nebraska, Minnesota, Iowa, Missouri, Arkansas
9th Circuit	416	4	Alaska, Washington, Oregon, California, Hawaii, Nevada, Arizona, Iowa, Montana
10th Circuit	111	3	Wyoming, Utah, Colorado, New Mexico, Kansas, Oklahoma
11th Circuit	491	39	Alabama, Georgia, Florida

ANNUAL EXECUTION RATE IN JAPAN

Year	No.	Year	No.	Year	No.	Year	No.
1875		1906	19	1933	28	1960	39
to	1101	1907	12	1934	35	1961	6
1881		1908	51	1935	14	1962	26
1882	52	1909	18	1936	11	1963	12
1883	61	1910	39	1937	23	1964	0
1884	52	1911	40	1938	15	1965	4
1885	130	1912	24	1939	14	1966	4
1886	131	1913	60	1940	20	1967	23
1887	97	1914	5	1941	22	1968	0
1888	60	1915	94	1942	11	1969	18
1889	49	1916	63	1943	3	1970	26
1890	39	1917	53	1944	25	1971	17
1891	66	1918	56	1945	8	1972	7
1892	51	1919	41	1946	11	1973	3
1893	46	1920	41	1947	12	1974	4
1894	52	1921	25	1948	33	1975	17
1895	75	1922	32	1949	33	1976	12
1896	72	1923	32	1950	31	1977	4
1897	21	1924	13	1951	24	1978	3
1898	48	1925	19	1952	18	1979	1
1899	37	1926	29	1953	24	1980	1
1900	33	1927	12	1954	30	1981	1
1901	29	1928	21	1955	32	1982	1
1902	28	1929	13	1956	11	1983	1
1903	41	1930	15	1957	39	1984	1
1904	45	1931	19	1958	7	1985	3
1905	36	1932	22	1959	30	1986	2
						1987	2

112. B.J. George, in Luney, ed. Professor George believes it less likely for an innocent person to be convicted under Japan's system than under the American system.

113. Itoh and Beer, 259; Beer, *Freedom*.

114. Lawrence W. Beer, "Group Rights and Individual Rights in Japan," *Asian Survey*, Vol. 21, April, 1981, 437; Beer, *Freedom*, chapter 3.

115. Itoh and Beer, 259 and 267.

116. Nobuhiko Takizawa, "Religion and the State in Japan," *Journal of Church and State*, Vol. 30, No. 1, winter, 1988; Beer, *Freedom*, 46-59, 248-252. For a summation of Japan's main religion-state litigation under the current Constitution, see *Jurisuto*, No. 933, May 1 and 15, 1989, 311.

117. Professor Ishii explains: "[T]he enjoyment of religious freedom [under the Meiji Constitution] did not apply to the traditional Japanese belief of Shinto, because this belief was denied the status of an ordinary religion. Each Japanese regardless of his faith was compelled to accept Shinto, which was raised to the position of a state religion." Ryosuke Ishii (W.J. Chambliss, (trans.), *Japanese Culture in the Meiji Era: Legislation*, Tokyo, The Toyo Bunko, 1958, 400.

118. On the Emperor or "*Tennō*" system, see Titus, *Palace and Politics in Prewar Japan*; Nihon Hōshakaigakkai, ed., *TENNŌSEI NO HŌSHAKAIGAKUTEKI KOSATSU*, Tokyo: Legal Sociology Association of Japan, (1978); "*Shōchō Tennōsei*," *JURISUTO*, No. 933; and *supra* notes 42-48.

119. Takizawa; *JURISUTO*, No. 848, November 10, 1985; *Hōritsu Jihō*, January 1, 1986.,

120. *JURISUTO* No. 933, 311; *Kakunaga V. Sekiguchi*, 31 MINSHŲ 533 (Sup. Ct., G.B., July 13, (1977), on which see III, below; and Beer, in Haley, ed., 23.

121. *Veterans Association et al. v. Nakaya*, HANREI JIHŌ, No. 1277, 34 (Sup. Ct., G.B., June 1, (1988); *ASAHI SHIMBUN*, June 1 (evening ed.) and 2, 1988; *Japan Times*, June 18, 1988, 6 and 9; Beer, *Freedom*, 251; Nobuyoshi Ashibe, "*Jieikangoshi to seikyobunri gensoku*," *HOGAKU KYŌSHITSU*, No. 8, 1988, 6; and Eiichi Hoshino, "*Jieikangoshi sosho no mimpōjō no shomondai*," *HŌGAKU KYŌSHITSU*," No. 9, 1988, 12. Lt. T. Nakaya was killed in an auto accident in January, 1968 while on active duty in the SDF. Mrs. Nakaya had his ashes interred at a Christian church in Yamaguchi City. In 1972, a local SDF office and a veterans association notified the widow of their intention to jointly enshrine his soul at a Shinto "guardian of the State" (*gōkoku*) shrine, and ignored her subsequent protests. Mrs. Nakaya sued for damages and for retraction of the enshrinement and prevailed in the lower courts, 1979 and 1982. However, the Supreme Court upheld the right of the State and of a private association to override an individual's religious wishes with respect to

burial. The court denied Nakaya's claim to a "right to live a religious life ... without interference by others in regard to the death of one's intimate relations."

122. HANREI JIHŌ, No. 1185, 67 (Tokyo dist. ct., March 20, 1986).

123. HANREI JIHŌ, No. 1223, 30 (Morioka dist. ct., March 5, 1987); *ASAHI SHIMBUN* (evening ed.), March 5, 1987; and HANREI JIHŌ, No. 1370 p.3 (Sendai High Court, January 10, 1991). A Tokyo district court decision in 1979 imposed a heavier penalty for attempted murder of the Emperor than is allowed for such a crime against an ordinary person, saying the accused "had a firm intent to assassinate with bombs the Emperor, the symbol of the unity of the people of Japan." Critics pointed out the absence of a basis for such a distinction in either the Constitution or in criminal law. *Japan v. Daidoji et al.*, *ASAHI SHIMBUN* (evening ed., November 13, 1979 (Tokyo dist. ct., November 13, 1979). In 1991, the Sendai High Court held that such use of public funds was in violation of the constitutional separation of religion and the state. The Iwate Prefectural Assembly did not appeal the case to the Supreme Court.

124. Beer, *Freedom*, chap. 7, and "Freedom of Expression: The Continuing Revolution," in Luney, ed., text at n.90-93. Two examples are *Ministry of Education v. Ienaga*, HANREI JIHŌ, No. 1040, 3 (Sup. Ct., First P.B., April 8, 1982), and *Ienaga v. Ministry of Education*, *ASAHI SHIMBUN* (evening ed.), October 3, 1989 (Tokyo dist. ct., Oct. 3, 1989). Saburo Ienaga is a famous intellectual historian who has devoted himself since the 1960s to opposing in court what he sees as Ministry attempts to censor his Japanese high school history textbook in order to cover up unpleasant facts. See Teruhisa Horio (Steven Platzer, trans.), *Educational Thought and Ideology in Modern Japan*, Tokyo, University of Tokyo Press, 1988.

125. Article 41 and other provisions regarding the Diet are quoted from Itoh and Beer, 261-264. On the Diet, see Ito, *KEMPŌ*, chap. 6; and Baerwald, *Japan's Parliament*.

126. Naional Assembly (Diet) Law, Law No. 79 of April 30, 1947, as amended through Law No. 68 of 1986.

127. Local Autonomy Law, Law No. 67 of 1947.

128. The Cabinet may also issue Cabinet Orders based on the Constitution (Art. 73[6]), but they may contain no penal provisions unless authorized by statute.

129. Constitution, Article 52; Diet Law, Articles 10 and 12.

130. Constitution, Article 53, Itoh and Beer, 262.

131. Diet Law, Article 13.

132. Diet Law, Article 38.

133. On the movement to revise the Constitution, see Beer, "Japan (1947)."

134. Diet Law, Article 56; see Ito, *KEMPŌ*, 400-402.

135. Ito, *KEMPŌ*, 402; Seki, "The Drafting Process for Cabinet Bills," 19 *Law in Japan* (1986),168-187.

136. Diet Law, chap. 5, Articles 40-54. On the Diet's investigative and impeachment powers, see *supra* I, n. 60. The Diet Organization Chart is taken from the Japan Times, *Roster of Members of the Japanese National Diet, 1988,* 8-9.

137. Baerwald, *Japan's Parliament*; Ishida and Krauss, eds., 39-64, 113-137.

138. The National Diet Library (*Kokkai Toshokan*) is excellent; but Diet members do not have extensive research back-up from agencies like the committee staffs or the Congressional Research Service in the U.S.

139. Treaties are dealt with in "Chapter 10. Supreme Law" in the Constitution, Article 98: "This Constitution shall be the supreme law of the nation and no law, ordinance, imperial rescript or other act of government, or part thereof, contrary to the provisions hereof, shall have legal force or validity.

"2. The treaties concluded by Japan and established laws of nations shall be faithfully observed." Itoh and Beer, 268; Ito, *KEMPŌ*, chapter 7. The binding power of treaties has provided an increasingly strong motivation for government protection of individual rights, as Japan has ratified major UN Covenants. In furtherance of related scholarship, the Association for the Study of International Human Rights Law (*Kokusai Jinkenhō Gakkai*) was established in 1989.

140. The Cabinet Law, Law No. 5 of January 16, 1947; Constitution, chapter 5, Articles 65-75, Itoh and Beer, 264-265.

141. Ishida and Krauss, eds., 48-50.

142. Gerald L. Curtis, *The Japanese Way of Politics*, New York, Columbia University Press, 1988, 86-87. Most Cabinet members have been in their 60s or 70s.

143. Robert C. Angel, "The Prime Minister's Leadership in Japan: Recent Changes in Personal Style and Administrative Organization," *Pacific Affairs*, Vol. 61, No. 4, winter, 1988-89, 583.

144. Cabinet Law (*Naikakuho*), Law 5 of January 16, 1947, as amended.

145. Ishida and Krauss, eds., 50.

146. Ishida and Krauss, eds., 114.

147. On administrative guidance, see, for example, "*Towareru gyosei shido*," *JURISUTO*, No. 741, June 1, 1981; and chapters in Haley, ed. by Haley, Smith, Ramseyer, Young and Repeta.

148. Ishida and Krauss, eds., 51.

149. *Id.*; see *supra* text at note 137.
150. Angel.
151. Itoh and Beer, 265-266.The most comprehensive study in English of Japan's Supreme Court is Hiroshi Itoh, *The Japanese Supreme Court:Constitutional Policies*, New York, Markus Wiener Publishing, 1989.
152. Court Organization Law (*Saibansho Hō*), Law No. 59 of 1947.Formally, the Chief Justice is attested to by the Emperor as named by the Cabinet; but in practice the sitting Chief Justice and his colleagues generally dominate Supreme Court selection processes.No woman has yet been named to the highest tribunal.
153. Ito, *KEMPO*, 537; Itoh and Beer, 7-21; Itoh, *The Japanese Supreme Court*, 12-38; Supreme Court of Japan, *Outline of Japanese Judicial System*, 1985; Jiro Nomura, *Japan's Judicial System*, Foreign Press Center, Tokyo, March, 1981.
154. Marshall, *supra* n.2; and the Constitution symposium, *Jurisuto*, No. 884, May 3, 1987.
155. Supreme Court, *Outline*, 6-10, and *Supreme Court of Japan*, 1989. For Japanese critiques of Supreme Court Performance, See *Law and Contemporary Problems*, Vol. 53, Nos. 1&2, 1990. Therein, Yasugiro Okudaira notes an indirect prior restraint on lawmakers exerted by the Supreme Court through the Cabinet Bureau of Legislation:

> [B]efore submission to the majority party committee for review, the drafts undergo a strict examination by the Cabinet Bureau on legal technicalities who scrutinize the compatibility of draft bills with the existing legal system and make recommendations for modification necessary to avoid having the new laws later judged unconstitutional by the Supreme Court. This system of screening the Cabinet Bureau of Legislation is not provided for in the Constitution.

But it seems functionally analogous to constitutional courts or committees established under constitutions everywhere in Asia and other continents, and bears careful scrutiny. *Id.*, Y. Okudaira, "Forty Years of the Constitution and Its Various Influences: Japanese, American, and European," at 47.
156. *Id.* On judges and their recruitment, see Itoh, *The Japanese Supreme Court*, 19-41.
157. Itoh and Beer, 267-268; Local Autonomy Law, Law No. 67 of April 17, 1947. On local autonomy, see, for example, Ito, *Kempo*, chapter 9; Kurt

Steiner, *Local Government in Japan*, Stanford, Stanford University Press, 1965; Terry E. MacDougall, "Democracy and Local Government in Postwar Japan," in Ishida and Krauss, eds., 139; *HŌGAKU SEMINĀ, ZŌKAN No. 8*, 1979; *JŌREI HYAKUSEN, JURISUTO*, No. 800, 1983.

158. The large city of Sapporo is unique in Japan as a modern planned large city; few Japanese lived in Hokkaido prior to the latter half of the nineteenth century. Okinawa operated for centuries as an independent kingdom before its absorption by Japan during the Tokugawa period.

159. Itoh and Beer, 267; Ito, *KEMPŌ*, 575-577.

160. Itoh and Beer, 268; Ito, *KEMPŌ*, 636-637.

161. Ito, *KEMPŌ*, 637. The Diet may abolish such a special law like any ordinary law, as it did the Tokyo Reconstruction Law.

162. Beer, *Freedom*, 166-188.

163. T.J. Pempel, "Prerequisites for Democracy: Political and Social Institutions," in Ishida and Krauss, eds., 31.

164. MacDougall, p.154.

165. MacDougall, 155-168.

III. Human Rights and Judicial Power*

(Nobuyoshi Ashibe)

Differences Between the Meiji Constitution and the Constitution of Japan

The influence of the United States Constitution on the Constitution of Japan is most striking in the system relating judicial power to the Constitution's declaration of human rights, its way of making human rights justiciable under a system of constitutional review. To clarify the importance of this influence, we need first consider the basic differences between the Meiji Constitution and the Constitution of Japan in light of the constitutional thought underlying judicial review in the United States.

As is well known, no explicit provision in the U.S. Constitution recognizes in courts a power of constitutional review. For that reason, even today vigorous academic arguments abound on the issues of what the authors intended regarding a review power and where to find theoretical grounds for the legitimacy of the review power. However, despite the absence of an explicit provision, *Marbury* v. *Madison*[1] provided as theoretical grounds for recognizing in the judicial courts of the U.S. the power to review laws for constitutionality, a political ideology of distrust for legislative power rooted deeply in American society since the founding of the country. Two other constitutional concepts are noteworthy in this context, that of the constitution as the supreme law of the land and the principle of separation of powers.[2] Since the Constitution is a law which puts into positive law the fundamental values of inviolable, pre-state natural rights, it is the fundamental law of the country limiting all state powers, including the legislative power. The substantial distinction between a law and a constitution is clear if one grasps the essence of this thought. Second, the separation of powers principle, in the form loyal to Montesquieu's theory, is understood to mean that the three powers have equal position under the constitution as "coordinate" powers of equal status.

The above principles were diametrically opposed to constitutional concepts in continental Europe [and Japan] prior to World War II, where ordinary courts were denied the power of judicial review. However, these constitutional ideas of the United States now constitute the foundation principles of the Constitution of Japan. Let us look a bit more into these points, on which the present Constitution differs profoundly from the Meiji Constitution.

Differences in Constitutional Thought between the Old and New Constitutions of Japan

Human Rights

The right to freedom and the rights of citizens protected under the Meiji Constitution were rights bestowed upon subjects by the Emperor (rights of subjects), not rights one naturally enjoyed at birth (human rights). This right to freedom was a right "protected by law" (*Gesetzesvorbehalt*), a right that could not be violated "without an exception provided for by law," a right enjoyed "within the limits of law." Consequently, administrative authority was restricted while legislative powers were not. In contrast to this, the rights and freedom of the people now protected by the Constitution of Japan are pre-constitutional rights (human rights) which may not be violated by any power of the state, including its legislative power. While the Constitution may be amended, the essence of these pre-constitutional or natural rights cannot be abridged. Article 11 of the Constitution expressly provides that "the fundamental human rights" are "eternal and inviolate rights."[3] A human being, at birth, is entrusted with or granted these rights by Heaven, the Creator, or nature. This is precisely what was expressed with regard to natural rights in the American Declaration of Independence of 1776: "We hold these truths to be self-evident, that all Men are created equal, that they are endowed by their Creator with certain unalienable rights, that among these are Life, Liberty, and the Pursuit of Happiness."

The Constitution as the Supreme Law

While the Meiji Constitution was and the Constitution of Japan is the "supreme law of the nation" (Article 98), the grounds for supremacy under these two documents are completely different. With the Meiji Constitution, supremacy was based on the divinity of the Emperor and his ancestors. The Constitution could be amended through a procedure more difficult than that necessary to amend a statute. The only difference between a statute and the Constitution rested with the type of formal validity each had. Tatsukichi Minobe said, "The Constitution and ordinary laws are essentially the same in that they both express the intent of the State; it is simply that the importance of the matters dealt with in the Constitution's provisions make caution about amendment appropriate."[4] This is precisely in line with the legal positivist (*Rechtspositivismus*) way of theorizing that dominated prewar constitutional theory in the countries of continental Europe.

In contrast, the 1947 Constitution of Japan is based on the idea that human rights are inviolable in relation to all state powers, that they are themselves are the values constituting the standard for the fundamental legal order. Like the U.S. Constitution, Japan's Constitution is best thought of "not [as] a legal idea of no content, but as a concept intimately bound up with the moral notion of putting into written provisions the fundamental value called 'freedom' as [the basis for] the permanent legal order."[5] The Constitution has a higher formal effect than ordinary laws and establishes especially difficult amendment procedures because the *substantive* conception exists that the Constitution is the law which guarantees inviolable human rights.

The substantive basis for the supremacy of the Constitution can be found in the opening paragraph of Chapter X (Supreme Law) of the Constitution, where Article 97 states that fundamental human rights are "for all time" inviolable.[6]   In this way, constitutional supremacy and the guarantee of inviolable human rights in the Constitution manifest the basic principles of legal order found in Anglo-American law. These rights, the guarantee of due process discussed later, the enlargement and strengthening of judicial authority, and the establishment of constitutional review by the courts go hand in hand under the Constitution of Japan.[7]

Separation of Powers

The Meiji Constitution's system of separation of powers was modeled on constitutions embodying modern constitutionalism, but the separation was quite imperfect because of the principle of Emperor sovereignty and because the structures of governance were built on the general premise that the Emperor presided over the powers of government.   In contrast, the Constitution of Japan mixes popular sovereignty with the principle of complete separation of powers.   The structure envisaged by the entire Constitution is very similar to the American system of three separate and equal powers. This is so, even though Article 41 makes the Diet "the highest organ of State power," at the center of the scheme of separation of powers. This clause does not give the Diet ultimate authority over the other branches, but acknowledges its central role as the locus of government authority closest to the people.[8]

The above way of thinking about human rights, the Constitution, and the separation of powers in the Constitution of Japan is fundamentally in accord with that of the U.S. Constitution, and is the theoretical basis justifying the courts' judicial review powers. The 1947 Constitution establishes judicial review powers in Japan for the first time. The human rights provisions in the

Constitution of Japan are quite different in substance and form from those in the U.S. Constitution. Some of the same issues arise concerning rights and freedoms, but judicial approach and legal interpretations are often different in the two countries. Below, I focus primarily on standards applied to human rights cases in constitutional litigation.

Rights Provisions in the Constitutions of Japan and the United States

The human rights provisions of the Constitution of Japan have already been outlined (see I, and II) and the strong influence of the U.S. Constitution pointed out; but we must also note at least the following three differences:

The Substance of Rights

First, human rights provisions in Japan and the U.S. are different in substance. Rights to freedom ["civil liberties"] are central to the scheme of human rights guaranteed in the Constitution of Japan, based on serious consideration of infringement of human rights by public authorities under the Meiji Constitution. Rights to freedom are divided into three categories: freedoms of the person, freedoms of the spirit, and freedom of economic activities.

Among these three, the greatest American influence can be seen in the area of freedoms of the person in the criminal justice system, such as the prohibition against involuntary servitude (Article 18) and the provisions for procedural rights (Articles 31-39).

However, these provisions cannot always be interpreted and applied in the same way as the Fifth, Sixth, Eighth, Thirteenth, and Fourteenth Amendments of the U.S. Constitution. For example, Article 34 provides that no one "shall be detained without adequate cause; and upon demand ... such cause must be immediately shown in open court in his presence and the presence of his counsel." This is not equivalent to the system of *habeas corpus* in Anglo-American law, for in Japan it is enough that the reason for detention is shown in open court, and it is generally understood that there is no need to defend the propriety of the action.[9] A system to that affect is established by the Code of Criminal Procedure (Article 82). Japan's *Habeas Corpus* Law (*Jinshin Hogoho*) was established with the intent of giving more life to the spirit of this article. Undoubtedly, the influence of Anglo-American law on human rights provisions related to criminal affairs and on their application is striking at some points. There is the view that precedents of Japan's Supreme Court "present interpretations which, in broad principle, are in line with decisions of the American Federal Supreme Court on the various systems under the constitution, with American law as the mother law."[10] However, we find many variances from Anglo-American law in practices under the Code of Criminal Procedure established to concretize the language of the Constitution.[11]

Since Japan had adopted the continental system of criminal justice for many decades by that time, it was natural that the introduction of the sharply contrasting Anglo-American system should bring with it cases where the result is "a cross between continental law and Anglo-American law."

We can see this in Article 31: "No person shall be deprived of life or liberty, nor shall any other criminal penalty be imposed, except according to procedure established by law." This provision corresponds to the due process clause in the U.S. Constitution, and establishes the general principle for the detailed human rights provisions in criminal procedure which follow, beginning with Article 33. However, the word "*tekisai na*" (due, proper) does not appear with "procedure." The phrase "any other criminal penalty" taken together with "shall be deprived of life or liberty" limits the provision to matters of criminal procedure. These facts and the absence of the word "property" with life and liberty illustrate the differences from due process provisions in the U.S. Constitution. This situation has led to diverging scholarly opinion. One influential opinion contends that "all that is required is that procedures be established by law,"[12] but without implying that the Constitution of Japan rejects the substance of the due process clause of the U.S. Constitution. By this interpretation, the Constitution implicitly recognizes in substansive law the principle of *nulla poena sine lege* (no punishment except under written law). Retroactive punishment is prohibited is prohibited as *ex post facto* law, pursuant to Article 39; and Article 73 (6) provides that the Cabinet "cannot include penal provisions in such Cabinet orders unless authorized by such law." The main elements of appropriateness in procedure are set forth in detail from Article 33 to Article 39. Article 32 establishes the right to notice and hearing with the clause "the right of access to the courts." Regarding the substantive appropriateness of provisions, the principles of "clarity" and "reasonable content" can be drawn from constitutional guarantees of freedom of expression and property rights in Articles 21 and 29, and there is the requirement that criminal penalties be fixed by law. The principles of insisting upon "equal punishment for a crime" and "prohibiting unjust discrimination" flow from the Article 14 guarantees of equality under the law.

However, the accepted view is that *at the least* Article 31 itself requires that both substance and procedure be established in law and that in content the procedure be proper.[13] In a case where the government attempted to confiscate a ship used for smuggling but belonging to a third party, and its cargo, the Supreme Court held the owner of the ship was entitled to notice and an opportunity to defend his rights, lest there be a violation of Article 31.[14]

Since Article 31 establishes the principle of guaranteeing human rights in criminal procedure, that intent should also be applied in administrative procedures. But it is not like the Fourteenth Amendment of the U.S. Constitution a provision serving as the basis for recognizing so-called "non-enumerated fundamental rights" as new constitutionally guaranteed human rights.

Instead the "repository"[15] of basic human rights to freedom is Article 13:

> All the people shall be respected as individuals. Their right to life, liberty, and the pursuit of happiness shall, to the extent that it does not interfere with the public welfare, be the supreme consideration in legislation and in other governmental affairs.

The phrase, the people's "right to life, liberty, and the pursuit of happiness" originated with the American Declaration of Independence, and conferred extremely general and comprehensive rights. An influential minority once doubted whether any specific right could be derived from this clause in the courts. However, the dominant view has been to the contrary. In a 1969 decision, the Supreme Court as well[16] recognized as one of "the freedoms of citizens related to private life that are protected from the state in the exercise of its police power" "the freedom not to have one's face or physical appearance photographed involuntarily and without permission." Putting aside the question of whether this established a right to one's likeness (*shozoken*), this freedom is guaranteed under Article 13. Here we can see the influence of U.S. case law which established an independent constitutional right of privacy based on Article 14.[17]

The Constitution of Japan guarantees many freedoms as freedoms of spiritual activity: the freedoms of thought and conscience (Article 19), the freedom of religion (Article 20), the freedom of speech (Article 21), the freedoms of assembly and association (Article 21), the right to secrecy of communication (Article 21), and academic freedom (Article 23). The unconditional form of these guarantees came from the way of thinking in the U.S. Constitution, a direct strong influence on the specific language in these provisions.[18]

During the war years, people were essentially deprived of their political freedoms. The original drafters of the Constitution sought to incorporate the heart and soul of Section 10 of the Potsdam Declaration which called upon Japan to "remove all obstacles to the revival and strengthening of democratic tendencies" and "to establish freedom of speech, of religion, and of thought, as well as respect for the fundamental human rights."[19]

The government can actively regulate economic freedoms, within limits. One has the right to choose an occupation "to the extent it does not interfere with the public welfare" (Article 22). This clause and the property right provisions--"property rights shall be defined by law, in conformity with the public welfare" and "private property may be taken for public use upon just compensation therefor" (Article 29)--are the basis for such regulation. These provisions sprang from reflection on U.S. Supreme Court decisions holding a number of New Deal laws unconstitutional,[20] as we will see when examining Japan's Supreme Court decisions of the 1970s.

An obvious difference from rights in the U.S. Constitution is the constitutional right in Japan to maintain "minimum standards of wholesome and cultured living" (Article 25) under the new twentieth-century welfare state. There are also a right to receive education (Article 26), a right to work (Article 27), and worker rights (Article 28).

These provisions represent the great "reformist enthusiasm" of the non-lawyers in Government Section who participated in the preparation of the original draft of the Constitution.[21] These people brought with them long careers either as military men who knew from personal experiences the destitute situation of pre-war Japan, or as experts in European affairs. Though they realized these rights were incapable of judicial enforcement, they nevertheless included them into the human rights chapter to serve as an ideal. The U.S. Constitution was not a direct influence in this area.

The Limitation of Human Rights

Another major difference between the two Constitutions is in the limitation of human rights. Neither Constitution individually regulates the degree and basis of limitation for each right. However, Article 12 of the Constitution of Japan declares that the people bear the responsibility for exercising their rights "for the public welfare" (*kōkyō no fukushi*). Article 13 provides that the people's rights are to be respected by the government "to the extent that it does not interfere with the public welfare." As stated earlier, economic freedoms (the right to choose an occupation and property rights) are specifically to be regulated when it is for the "public welfare."

What is meant by the phrase "public welfare"? This issue in relation to each human right has become a major subject in the field of constitutional interpretation. Since the Constitution took effect, there has been an ever-increasing divergence of opinions and a tremendous change in case theory.

For about ten years after the enactment of the Constitution, the majority of scholars held that all rights were subject to restriction for the "public welfare" under Articles 12 and 13. No specific meaning was given to the public welfare provision of Articles 22 and 29 pertaining to economic freedoms.

Until around 1965, the Supreme Court adopted the above *external restriction idea* which allowed the general restriction of any right for "the public welfare." For example, the Supreme Court in a famous obscenity case had to decide if [a translation of] D.H. Lawrence's, *Lady Chatterley's Lover* was beyond the bounds of legitimate freedom of expression.[22] The Court stated:

> Notwithstanding the fact that each provision of the Constitution does not expressly set forth the possibility of restriction of individual fundamental human rights in the Constitution, the present Court has frequently held that the abuse of such rights is prohibited by the stipulations of Articles 12 and 13 of the Constitution, that they stand under restriction for the public welfare, and that they are not absolutely unlimited.

This view carries the danger that "the public welfare," an abstraction, could be indiscriminately used to restrict rights provided it was done according to statute. A related opinion is that of Justice Masami Ito:[23]

> These words, considered abstractly are not objectionable. However, in the Supreme Court's practice, the public-welfare test has come to be a justification for supporting the constitutionality of any law limiting freedom to express oneself. This way of thinking deprives the constitutional guarantee of free speech of its substantial significance, for whenever a law is enacted some kind of danger to the public welfare can be easily found as a legal regulation would rarely, if ever, be imposed in case no danger exists. Therefore under the public-welfare test, only extremely arbitrary restrictions upon this freedom are invalid. The attitude loses sight not only of the distinction between intellectual freedom [alternately, "freedom of the spirit"] and its external expression, on the one hand, and economic freedom, on the other, but also between the new Constitution, which guarantees the freedom of expression in absolute words, and the old Constitution which had protected it only to the extent permitted by law.

One influential emphasis in criticisms of such decisions was the following:[24] Restrictions on human rights under "the public welfare" clause should be confined to those on economic rights and freedoms where an intent to limit is clearly stated (Articles 22 and 29), and to social rights (Articles 25-28) whose realization depends on state policies for implementation.

Articles 12 and 13 are only didactic ethics provisions; "the public welfare" in Article 13 cannot serve as the basis for restriction of human rights. Other than social rights and economic freedoms regulated under positive state policies, rights and freedoms are a social reality subject only to *inherent restraints*. Such restraints contained within rights exist objectively, and are not matters of legislative control. When such restraints are disregarded, judicial control should be asserted after-the-fact. Prior restraints based on policy considerations (the public welfare) should be limited to social and economic rights.

This viewpoint, resting on welfare state principles of the Constitution, is an excellent interpretive theory taking into consideration the "double standard" idea which emerged from the 1938 decision in *U.S.* v. *Carolene Products Company*,[25] and the judgments holding New Deal legislation unconstitutional; it had great influence on subsequent academic theories. Nevertheless, doubts remained: Is it enough to interpret Article 13 as simply a statement of ethics? Or to restrict the meaning of "the public welfare" entirely to policy considerations of the state?

In response to these questions, a new theory appeared in academic circles in 1955:[26] "The public welfare" is the principle of substantial fairness for reconciling the conflicts and contradictions among human rights. Whether or not the public welfare in this sense is contained in constitutional provisions, it resides naturally in all human rights. When "the public welfare" operates together with the principles of the liberal state (the passive state)--in other words, to guarantee rights and freedoms equally to each person--we recognize only the minimum necessary restraints on rights to freedom. For example, conflicts must be moderated and both freedom of expression and a person's rights to good name and privacy must be fairly guaranteed.

However, when "the public welfare" is joined with the principles of "the social state" (the positive state), regulation as necessary of economic freedom and social rights is acceptable. That is, to effectively guarantee the rights to livelihood and the fundamental rights of workers, restrictions on property rights are imposed in some cases.

This view was highly regarded and held sway for a time among academic theories, for its limiting of the meaning of "the public welfare" and for making clear that in principle only inherent restraints are permissible; but its standards for judging the concrete limits of human rights were not clear.

In a 1966 case where the limits of public employees' fundamental rights as workers were at issue, the Supreme Court[27] stated that "such rights should be understood to be subject to inherent restriction, justified from the standpoint that the interests of the nation as a whole have to be protected." The Court set four conditions as standards for judging inherent restraints: a) that the limitation be the reasonable minimum necessary; b) that its use be confined to cases of unavoidable necessity to ward off a serious threat to the livelihood of the people; (c) that any sanctions imposed not go beyond what is necessary, with criminal sanctions restricted to cases of absolute necessity, and (d) that some sort of compensatory measures should be devised for cases of rights violation.

The freedom-oriented interpretation of this judicial decision had much influence on other Japanese constitutional decisions. However, since the 1973 Supreme Court holding in the *Zennōrin* case,[28] there has been a substantial change, and the basic flow "public welfare" theory reversed course dramatically in case law thinking.

Scholarly commentary generally took a highly critical position on this trend in the case law. I consider "the public welfare" a principle of restraint of necessity inhering in all human rights in order to fairly guarantee human rights to each person, and maintain the necessity of establishing criteria for concrete standards for restraint, constructing a case law theory based on the "double standard" theory of the United States. I have also stressed that to protect constitutionalism with the guarantee of human rights, we must give life to judicial review by adopting U.S. theories of constitutional litigation in ways that conform with Japan's legal system and legal thought.[29]

From the 1970s through the 1980s, constitutional studies in Japan made notable advances in research on theories of constitutional litigation and standards for judicial review. In this area, the influence of the U.S. Constitution has been enormous. In the 1970s, the Supreme Court also used as a general concept the "double standard" approach in a case disputing the constitutionality of legislative restraints on economic freedom; but in the sphere of freedoms of the spirit, this way of thinking remains one of the most serious problems in Japan's case law on human rights, as discussed later.

The Legal Effects of Human Rights

A major difference between the U.S. Constitution and the Constitution of Japan lies in the nature of the legal effect human rights provisions have on legal relationships at civil law between private persons. The U.S. Constitution guarantees rights in relation to governmental powers within the document itself: *Congress* shall make no law abridging the freedoms of speech, the press, religion or assembly (First Amendment); *no State* shall deprive any person of life, liberty or property without due process of law (Fourteenth Amendment).

The Constitution of Japan does not expressly provide this type of control on government power, but the "forever inviolable rights" phrases of Articles 13 and 97 have come to be understood as prohibiting government violations of right.   However, the violation of rights by "societal powers" is an ever-increasing possibility with the advance of capitalism.   Many are concerned about the possibility of human rights violations due to the creation of giant private organizations (corporations, labor unions, political groups, economic associations and so on) which exercise government-like functions and, to some extent, possess government-like structures.   Furthermore, the problem of public nuisances (*kōgai*) and pollution have accompanied the development of commerce and industry, while the mass media have increasingly threatened injury to reputation, honor and privacy.   However, traditional theory on the effect of human rights provisions as limited to relations between the people and government has never fit well with the concept of human rights itself. For historical reasons, the economic theory and the state theory of liberalism and the constitutional theory of legal positivism dominated pre-World War II Europe, especially nations in the German sphere.   These nations denied the idea of natural rights and took the rights of the people to be subjective public rights vis-a-vis the state as a juridical person.   Now, human rights are the foundation value for the whole legal order.   Consequently, to give legal effect to some form of check on human rights violation by private persons (or private organizations) would not be inconsistent with human rights concepts.

American law approaches this problem from the standpoint of asking about the degree to which government power is involved with private actions, or about the degree to which private acts have a public character or function on analogy with acts of government power.   When governmental power is very significantly involved with private acts, or when a private person performs a function of such a public nature that it amounts to a government power, those private acts are treated like "state actions" subject to regulation under the federal Constitution.   In other words, to that degree, a private action is *made into* a state action.   This theory would directly apply the Constitution to private acts.   In contrast, Japan's approach is to *indirectly* discipline acts of private persons by interpreting and applying general and summary provisions of private law in the spirit of constitutional guarantees of human rights.

Except with respect to certain human rights provisions, this is done by interpreting and directly applying to private acts a human rights provision based on its words, intent and purpose.[30] (In this matter, Japan's way of thinking is precisely the same as that of continental European systems such as Germany.)

In other words, in cases where acts violating human rights are based on legal acts such as contracts, those acts are subject to the discipline of the Constitution grounded in the principle of private autonomy and human rights values. "Public order" (public policy) in Article 90 of the Civil Code establishes that "Legal acts contrary to public order and good morals are invalid."[31]

For a long time, Japan's constitutional case law was in a state of theoretical groping, but since the 1970s the Supreme Court[32] has rather firmly established its position. However, there is no remedy under the Constitution if one adopts the indirect application theory for cases where the acts of a private organization themselves violate human rights and no mediating law or ordinance is involved. For some years, I have advocated using the "state action" theory in U.S. precedents as a reference point when devising remedies for such cases.

The Nature of Judicial Power under the Constitution of Japan: The Impact of the U.S. Constitution

The U.S. Constitution has been a major influence on the judicial power as on the rights established in the Constitution of Japan. The statement in the original SCAP draft that "the stronghold of the people's rights is a strong and independent judiciary" set forth the role and status of the judiciary under the present Constitution (see I and II, above). Here we will pay particular attention to the nature of judicial review and judicial power.

The Scope and Concept of Judicial Authority

Under the Meiji Constitution, the judicial power extended only to criminal and civil cases, and not to administrative cases. Administrative cases were tried within the executive branch in an Administrative Court separate from the ordinary courts. These were trials of disputes concerning rights and duties in public law between an administrative organ and a person whose rights or interests had been illegally damaged by an administrative disposition. This system had been adopted by continental European countries such as France and Germany.

In contrast, the present Constitution of Japan, after the model of Anglo-American law, includes the trial of administrative cases among the functions of the regular courts. Article 76, paragraphs 1 and 2, provide: "The whole judicial power is vested in the Supreme Court and in such inferior courts as are established by law. No extraordinary tribunal shall be established, nor shall any organ or agency of the Executive be given final judicial power."

Article 76 marks a major change in the Japanese court system from a continental law model to the Anglo-American model. The judicial power in Japan is almost the same as that under the U.S. Constitution, in spite of the fact that the Constitution of Japan lacks a "cases and controversies" clause as found in Article 3, section 2 of the U.S. Constitution. The Supreme Court has said: "The permissible function of the courts is limited to conclusively resolving, pursuant to legal interpretation, those disputes related to the existence of legal relationships or the concrete rights and duties of the parties concerned, that is 'legal disputes' (Art.3 of the Court Organization Law)."[33]

A "concrete dispute" is an indispensable condition for any trial under the above provision. However, we must keep in mind the following points:

Included within the Japanese concept of *a judiciary* is its independence (as well as the need for a concrete dispute), together with the requirement of fair procedures as under traditional principles of fairness, i.e., oral arguments and a public hearing.

The Constitution of Japan expressly guarantees access to the courts as a human right (Art. 32). This differs from the guarantee of trial rights which the U.S. Constitution establishes in Article 2, section 2 regarding the object of court deliberations, in the Sixth and Seventh Amendments guaranteeing trial by jury, and in the due process clauses. In Japan, the right of access to the courts is understood in case law and scholarly exegesis to require procedural guarantees, with rigorous provisions for due process set forth under Article 82:[34] "Trials shall be conducted and judgment declared publicly" with few exceptions, and "trials of political offenses, offenses involving the press, or in cases wherein the rights of the people as guaranteed in Chapter III of this Constitution are in question shall always be conducted publicly."

Since the time of the Meiji Constitution, litigation other than cases involving the rights and interests of the litigants alone has been recognized. Litigation to protect a public interest and to assure the lawfulness of administrative acts has been established in positive law; such suits are usually referred to as "a people's action" ("*minshū soshō*") or "an objective action" ("*kyakken soshō*").[35] An example is a suit in which voters challenge the validity of an election or its results. The prevailing view is that, strictly speaking, such a suit does not come under the normal judicial function, but is *an exception recognized pursuant to legislative policy.*

If such objective suits are recognized, and if they are permitted as under implied judicial powers, there will be arguments on whether this goes against the concept of judicial power, or again whether a broader understanding of plaintiff standing than is traditional should be permitted in consumer suits and environmental litigation.[36] This would happen even if the Supreme Court were given a German-style constitutional court power by law.

In the United States, such litigation exists in taxpayers' suits and citizens' suits; but the relationship between the constitutional requisite of "case and controversy" and the rule of standing is unclear, whether it is to be considered a matter of constitutional requirement or a prudential rule of judicial self-restraint.

The questions of "institutional reform litigation" or "public law litigation" and American legal theory are being hotly debated; clarification of related issues is a matter of serious concern in current Japanese legal discourse. However, Japanese case law has been rather negative about strengthening the idea of objective action or expanding the traditional understanding of the judicial function. Great importance is attached to requiring a controversy, so a liberalization of the conditions necessary for standing has not taken place to the extent found in U.S. case law. The American model of public law litigation and institutional reform litigation has come under heavy criticism in Japan, even from influential scholars.

Undoubtedly, there are limits to the liberalization of plaintiff standing requirements. Also, many problems arise with the present model of litigation recognizing direct judicial intervention into matters of public policy and politics. However, together with Archibald Cox, I think that "the hard question is one of degree."[37] With the focus on requiring a controversy while opening the door of justice as wide as possible, especially in the area of remedial law, this approach meshes with judicial power under the Constitution of Japan and is worthy of positive consideration.[38]

The Characteristics of Judicial Review

Article 81 of the Constitution of Japan reads: "The Supreme Court is the court of last resort with power to determine the constitutionality of any law, order, regulation or official act."

In *The Impact of American Constitutionalism Abroad*, Carl J. Friedrich states that "totalitarian dictatorships" clearly make useless a bill of rights in most European countries unless rights are protected against arbitrary violations by the majority party. With the institutionalization of some system for judicially guarding the Constitution, the Constitution becomes a "fundamental law" guaranteeing human rights against state power. According to Friedrich, this notion of "judicialism," rejected before by most Europeans, has made rapid headway in many countries since World War II.[39]

As Friedrich suggests, the system of judicial review has been adopted in such continental countries as West Germany, France, and Italy, as well as in post-war Japan. While this originated from strong rejection of dictatorship, we must also take notice of the great change that occurred in understandings of constitutionalism. That is to say, in the background a major turnaround came in ways of thinking about separation of powers and legislative authority, and about the Constitution and human rights. The meaning of "judicialism" varies importantly with various countries' traditions and the concrete systems they develop.

Two noteworthy characteristics of the Constitution of Japan should be mentioned: First, the Courts' power of constitutional review is the same as in the U.S., in that it is judicial review after the events, taking place in the resolution of a concrete case. There are reasons for this other than the historical circumstances surrounding the establishment of the Constitution. Article 76 authorizes the use of judicial power to resolve concrete legal disputes, and Article 81 recognizes the Supreme Court's authority as the court of last resort.

The predecessor of the Japanese Self-Defense Force (*Jieitai*) was known as the National Police Reserve when established in 1950. Not long after, Mosaburo Suzuki of the Japan Socialist Party asked the Supreme Court to declare unconstitutional the establishment of the National Police Reserve as against the renunciation-of-war clause of Article 9. In 1952, the Supreme Court, in upholding the power of judicial review, incidental to the case at hand, stated the following:

> Under the system prevailing in our country, a judgment may be sought in the courts only when there exists a concrete legal dispute between specific parties. The argument that courts have the power to determine in the abstract the constitutionality of laws, orders, and the like, in the absence of a concrete case, has no foundation in the Constitution itself or in any statute.[40]

A few claim that while Article 81 does not recognize the power of a constitutional court as found in the West German model, the granting of such a power to the Supreme Court is not in law prohibited (consequently, it is possible for the Supreme Court to act as a constitutional court if the relevant procedures are established by law).

Second, the systems of judicial review in the U.S. and Japan both function to protect constitutional democracy and are not designed simply to provide relief to private parties. In the U.S., this function of guarding the Constitution is being actualized by liberalization of the requirements for standing, by "vagueness" and "overbreadth" doctrine, "void on its face" doctrine, and attention to the "prospective effect" of decisions of unconstitutionality. To some extent, the same views are expressed in Japanese case law. Mauro Cappelletti once said there is a converging of trends between the West German and American models.[41] That can also be said with regard to judicial review in Japan. I would now like to examine in detail issues related to the method and effects of a decision declaring a law unconstitutional.

Judicial Review and Its Function of Guaranteeing the Constitution

As in the United States, there are two ways of declaring a law unconstitutional in Japan: the law itself may be considered unconstitutional, or the application of the law to a certain case may be unconstitutional. In the forty-three years since the birth of the Constitution, Supreme Court decisions have declared a law provision unconstitutional in only four cases.

The first case dealt with the killing of a parent (a lineal ascendant) and the severe penalty imposed for such a crime by Article 200 of the Criminal Code. While the gratitude and respect owed to one's direct ascendant is recognized as one of the most basic moral principles in society, and its protection by the criminal law is valued as a reasonable legislative purpose, Article 200 was declared unconstitutional by the Grand Bench of the Supreme Court in a 1973 decision.[42] The Court held that the method used to achieve this purpose was discriminatory and a violation of the "equal protection" clause (Art. 14), in that the penalty was unreasonably harsh when compared with that for ordinary homicide (a minimum three-year sentence with the possibility of a suspended sentence). Six of the liberal judges took the position that the legislature's intent was itself unconstitutional. However, the majority held the degree of disparity between the two penalties unconstitutional, while a minority felt that any disparity between the provisions should be deemed unconstitutional.

The second case concerned the licensing and opening of a new pharmacy in Hiroshima. On April 30, 1975, the Grand Bench unanimously held that a regulation requiring a certain distance between two pharmacies under the

Pharmaceuticals Law was an unconstitutional violation of the freedom to choose an occupation (Art. 22(1)).[43]

Then, in 1985 the Grand Bench held unconstitutional Table #1 of the Annex to the Public Offices Election Law, a provision which fixed the apportionment of Diet seats among election districts.[44] When the 1980 general election for the House of Representatives was held, the disparity in the value of a vote in different election districts ranged up to 1 to 4.40. Since the 1975 revision to the Public Offices Election Law, correction of disparities within a reasonable period has been required. In the absence of such a correction, this present lawsuit occurred.

In the fourth case, the Supreme Court[45] voided in April, 1987 Article 186 of the Forestry Law (*Shinrin Hō*) as counter to Article 29, paragraph 2 of the Constitution ("Property rights shall be defined by law, in conformity with the public welfare") in its treatment of jointly or communally owned forests. Article 186 negated an owner's right of petition for a division of property under Article 256, paragraph 1 of the Civil Code in cases where a joint owner has less than a half interest in the forest property. The Court held that such a limitation of rights has no reasonable connection with the legislative purposes of Article 186 of the Forestry Law to strive for stable forest management and to prevent excessive dividing up of forest lands, and exceeds the bounds of necessary regulation. Soon after this decision, the Diet took steps to abolish Article 186.

On the same day the decision on the Pharmaceuticals Law was handed down, the Welfare Ministry issued a notice to each prefectural governor which stated, "We kindly ask you, effective immediately, not to apply the proper site requirement of the ordinance when granting a license for a pharmacy." This was done as an exercise of administrative guidance (*gyōsei shidō*). On May 29, a bill was introduced in the Diet to delete the site location provision from the Pharmaceuticals Law. After passing both Houses, the bill took effect on June 13. On June 28, the Welfare Ministry sent a notice to each prefectural governor, recommending that they take appropriate measures to promptly abolish ordinance provisions imposing a placement restriction on pharmacies, due to the revised law which stemmed from the Supreme Court's decision.[46]

In Japan the effect of a decision holding a law to be unconstitutional is generally thought to have individual effect applicable only to the case in question. However, in light of what happened after the Pharmaceutical Law was held unconstitutional, we can say that Supreme Court decisions in fact have binding power actually affecting all future decisions. In the case of the unconstitutionally heavy penalty for patricide, the authorities quickly took corrective measures. There was, however, some negative reaction from the

Diet. Immediately after the 1973 decision, the Supreme Public Prosecutor's Office sent a notice to all prosecutors directing them to use Article 199, the provision on ordinary murder, when prosecuting someone for the killing of a lineal ascendant. In addition, the Ministry of Justice issued a notification on April 18, 1973 requesting all related agencies of the government to consider granting pardons (reduction of penalty or remission of sentence) to all those who were serving time in prison as a result of conviction under Article 200. These government agencies were to take these steps even without application from the prisoners themselves. Reasonable amnesty would be recognized, and prompt special corrective actions were to be taken. However, in the Diet there was no consensus as to whether or not Article 200 was still in effect. No one knew if it had been abolished or revised, and if revised, then in what form. [The debate remains unsettled].

The 1985 case, dealing with unconstitutional malapportionment of Diet seats, is more complex. The validity of an election was questioned after it was held pursuant to the Public Offices Election Law. In Japan, a request for an injunction or a declaratory judgement finding unconstitutional malapportionment, as in the U.S., is not allowed. Moreover, for a long time legal precedent hesitated over the question of whether the right to vote carries with it a right to have votes equally valued. The decision in *Baker* v. *Carr*[47] on reapportionment had a great influence on scholarly opinion in Japan. Accordingly, the question of equal vote values has been considered a subject for constitutional litigation. In 1976, the Japanese Supreme Court, in a Grand Bench decision, first recognized that equality in vote values was constitutionally demanded:

> If the degree of the inequality can in no way generally be considered reasonable, then there can be no special reason which would justify it, and if there was no correction within a reasonable period of time, as demanded by the Constitution, the apportionment in its entirety would become unconstitutional.[48]

The 1976 decision only declared that the election was unconstitutional; it did not nullify the results of the election, for to do so would have given rise to various inconvenient results not anticipated by the Constitution. Article 31 of the Administrative Case Litigation Law recognizes the so-called principle of "special circumstances" (*jijō hanketsu*). It provides, in part:

> In the event an administrative agency's disposition or ruling is illegal, the Court may, nevertheless, turn down a request which seeks to quash said

disposition or ruling, when to do otherwise would be incompatible with the public welfare. In such a case, the Court's judgment must contain a statement that the agency's disposition or ruling was illegal.

Invoking this principle as a "basic principle of general law," the Court did not invalidate the election, but merely held it to be unconstitutional. There are problems with the application of the principle of "special circumstances" to election-type litigation, and with the Supreme Court's view concerning the equality of vote values. Nevertheless, the above decision is compared to the *Baker* case, and has been highly regarded as of epoch-making significance.[49]

The solution to the apportionment problem lies with the Diet; it is their duty to take remedial measures when a situation has been declared unconstitutional. The use of the principle of special circumstances is not the final solution to the dilemma. Actually, the Diet has been very slow to react and to pass a reapportionment bill. After the 1976 decision, people groped for a method which would elicit a new decision declaring the present malapportionment unconstitutional. Two views are: (a) Even though there is no tradition of equity law in Japan, the Court itself should reapportion the electoral seats until the Diet does so, for this is a problem of remedial law, not primary law.[50] (b) Have an election enjoined and if the Diet does not immediately correct the situation, then let the Court hold the election based on its own reapportionment.[51]

In the 1985 decision mentioned above, Chief Justice Jiro Terada, along with four other Justices, argued in a concurring opinion: "Elections held without taking corrective measures after a judgement of special circumstances (*jijō hanketsu*) has declared the previous election's appointment unconstitutional should be held invalid. However, such a judgment would not take effect until after a certain period of time had elapsed." For some time, this has been the position advocated by scholars. It is noteworthy that this approach, using decisions with prospective effect,[52] was employed in a Supreme Court judgment, though in a concurring opinion.

As the above cases illustrate, many unanswered questions remain regarding the effect of and method for obtaining decisions which hold a law or governmental act unconstitutional. Nevertheless, the actualization of human rights guarantees through the power of judicial review clearly occupies an important role in preserving the Constitution and establishing the "rule of law."

We must not overlook the fact that Japan's system of judicial review is the same as that of the state supreme courts in the United States. They are courts which exercise not only powers of judicial review, but as the highest

legal organs they must also promote consistent legal interpretation. The distinguishing feature about the Japanese court system is that judges are all career judges, except for the Supreme Court. Supreme Court Justices come under Article 41 of the Court Organization Law: "Justices of the Supreme Court shall be appointed from among persons of broad vision and extensive knowledge of the law, who are not less than forty years of age."[53]   Though prosecutors, lawyers, and law professors also enter the Supreme Court, the strong tendency is to fill many
positions with career judges, and this has had a significant effect on judicial review.

The Exercise of Judicial Review

There are many points in common between Japanese and American case law concerning justiciability and the constitutional decision-making process. However, differences in structure and tradition lead to distinctive applications of constitutional doctrine.

Avoiding Constitutional Decisions

Assuming there is a case or controversy, the system of judicial review does not have as its direct purpose constitutional decision-making itself. Constitutional decision making is for the purpose of solving a specific dispute. Controlled by the rule of strict necessity "constitutional decision making is limited to the unavoidable."[54]

In the 1967 *Eniwa* case this rule was the subject of much debate.[55] Originating in the Eniwa district of Hokkaido, the case was the first to deal with the constitutionality of the Self-Defense Forces (SDF).   Many dairy farmers complained of injury to their livestock resulting from explosions, the shooting of live shells, and other effects of military exercises conducted near their property boundaries.   The farmers protested the continuation of the exercises by cutting the communication lines to the practice area.   Some of the farmers were prosecuted for violating Article 121 of the Self-Defense Forces Law which provides: "Any person who damages or destroys any possession or weapon, ammunition, aircraft, or other device used for defense shall be punished by a sentence of not more than 5 years or a fine of not more than 50,000 yen."   In the course of a three-and-a-half-year prosecution, the constitutionality under Article 9 of the Constitution of the activities of the Self-Defense Forces was an important issue.   However, side-stepping the

constitutional question, the Sapporo District Court found the defendant not
guilty as hereafter summarized:

> Article 121 of the Self-Defense Force Law provides for punishment of a
> destructive act against 'or other devices used for defense.' The same
> Article refers to 'weapon ammunition, or aircraft,' which implies that to
> be legally punishable an act must be similar in kind and in quality to
> these. The SDF's communication lines during training are not to be
> included, and the act of cutting the wire does not come within the
> prohibition of the statute. Consequently, there is no need to decide the
> constitutionality of the SDF itself.

Excluding the statutory construction issue, the technique used by the court
here is the same as that used in Justice Brandeis' opinion in *Ashwander* v.
T.V.A. in 1936.

In Japan, there are three views on when to invoke constitutional issues:
a) when it is possible to solve the case with a statutory interpretation, a court
should not resort to constitutional decision-making; b) the question of the
constitutionality of a statute should first be addressed before ruling on its
application; or c) even where a constitutional judgment can be avoided with
statutory construction, a court can boldly make a decision on constitutionality
when it finds sufficient reason after comprehensively examining the following
conditions: the degree of unconstitutionality and the scope of its influence;
the importance of the case and the nature of the rights involved; the reasons
for deciding on constitutional grounds outweigh those for using statutory
construction upon examination of the different effects of the two approaches.
The third view (c) conforms with a view of the judicial review power as a
system for upholding the Constitution, and this is the dominant view in the
academic world.   Here we see the great influence of American judicial
theory.[57]

Legal construction provides two ways of avoiding constitutional problems.
The first way, used in the *Eniwa* case, is to leave unanswered the question of
constitutionality and decide the case on other grounds, that is the construction
of a statute. The other way is to restrict the meaning of a statute so as to
exclude the unconstitutional aspects from application, usually referred to as
"a constitutionally restricted construction."   The use of constitutionally
restrictive construction raises many serious questions.[58]

In 1969 the Supreme Court handed down two landmark cases known as the Sendai Court Workers Union Incitement case (*Sendai Zenshiho Jiken*), and the Tokyo Teachers Union case (*Tokyoso Jiken*).[59] The cases involved the constitutionality of the National Public Employees Law (Art. 98 and Article 110, paragraph 1, item 17), and the Local Public Employees Law (Art. 37 and Article 61, number 4). These laws prohibit strikes or the instigation thereof by government workers. The Supreme Court in restricting the meaning of the term "instigate," said, "If these provisions are interpreted literally to prohibit all strike-related activities and to penalize anyone who conspires to effect, instigate or incite," there would be doubts about their constitutionality. Therefore, "insofar as possible the provisions should be interpreted reasonably as conforming to and capable of harmony with the spirit of the Constitution." The Court attempted to limit the meaning of strike-related activities and their instigation to those cases where there was a strong showing of illegality. That is to say, the prohibition and punishment of strike-related activities was limited to cases wherein

> the related activities themselves were strongly tainted with illegality, by deviating from the essential purposes of the employees' organization, by attendant violence or otherwise improper pressures similar in kind, or by seriously interfering with the daily life of the people by improper delays and other means contrary to the common sense of the community.

Regarding the term "instigation," the Court interpreted it so as to exclude "those activities ordinarily incidental to strikes," activities like the transmission and distribution of information concerning the aims of the strike and instructions for carrying out the strike itself. In this way, the Court avoided having to declare the statute unconstitutional. By using the narrow interpretation approach, the Court was able to uphold the constitutionality of the statute. The Court reversed the appellate court's conviction, taking the liberal position of acquitting the defendants.

However, in a 1973 decision known as the *Zennōrin* (National Union for Agriculture and Forestry Workers) case,[60] the Supreme Court overruled the 1969 decision, and held that the statute in question prohibited *all* strikes. The Court said that a narrow construction of the law was contrary to the principle of Article 31 of the Constitution that criminal penalties be prescribed in law (*zaikeihōteishugi*). In this decision we see a shift in the Court, with the minority opinion in the 1969 decision becoming the majority opinion in

Zennōrin. With much debate, this case drastically changed the course of constitutional law in Japan.

If we disregard the actual result in this case and look only at the use of the narrow construction approach, the statute undoubtedly lacks clarity, as noted in the reasoning of the 1969 decision. I wonder if it may not be appropriate for the legislature to establish a specific standard providing something less than a complete and absolute ban on strikes by public employees, thus restoring purpose and meaning to the guarantee of basic labor rights (Art. 28). However, under substantive due process, the Court overlooked the closely related problem of how narrowing construction of a statute's language is compatible with the purpose and meaning of individual human right guarantees. The Court maintained that a complete and absolute ban on strikes was a natural limitation on the rights of labor, and emphasized the clarity of the statutory definition of a violation.[61] Decisions using the narrow-interpretation approach have caused many problems with respect to legislation regulating freedom of expression, where especially careful construction is required. For example, in 1975 when the Supreme Court upheld the constitutionality of the Tokushima City Public Safety Ordinance regulating group activities in public places, the justices said that the phrase "to maintain orderly traffic" (*kōtsū chitsujo o iji suru koto*) could be read "as a standard related to interference with ordinary traffic." The Court reversed both the trial and high court decisions which had held the ordinance to be excessively vague criminal law.[62]

There may be serious difference of opinion on whether or not the Supreme Court's ruling could be said to conform with the doctrines of "void for vagueness or overbreadth". The problem with language in this case did not involve the content of speech, but the manner of regulating expression of ideas through a demonstration. However, as the Court pointed out: "Although it is quite possible to clarify obligations in an ordinance with examples of acts that would be likely to interfere with orderly traffic, no thought was given to that." "As a piece of legislation it is notably lacking." Without doubt, "the charge that its language is too abstract is inescapable." If one takes seriously the implications for law of regulating a "preferred freedom," one can say there were solid grounds for the high court's judgment that the language was too vague for an interpretation upholding its constitutionality.

A 1984 Supreme Court, Grand Bench decision on obscenity sparked serious debate when it held constitutional Article 21 of the Customs Standards Law which prohibits the import of "written materials, pictures, statues, and other articles harmful to public order and good morals."[63] The case involved imported magazines with pictures of nude females. The majority opinion held that concern about harming "good morals" should be limited to "obscene" items; and with that, the law cannot be considered invalid and unconstitutional because unclear or overly broad.

However, Justice Masami Ito and three other Justices dissented on this point, reasoning: "A statute regulating freedom of expression is subject to stricter standards of narrow interpretation than other law. Its use is limited to cases where restraints can be shown to be reasonably related to its regulatory purpose and content, and to other statutory provisions. The term (good morals) is multivocal; to confine its interpretation to mean good sexual morals goes beyond such bounds." The minority opinion is very sound; in it, we can see the influence of the doctrine of "overbreadth" found in the United States.[64]

Legislative Facts

While Japan's Constitution has been influenced by the U.S. Constitution, another contrast between the two in practice is that in Japan there is not always sufficient judicial review of legislative facts (rippō jijitsu). In Japan, proof of legislative fact was first pointed out as a case law issue, and the significance of methods of finding and social science evidence discussed, in 1960. It became clear that proof of legislative fact is necessary and indispensable in constitutional litigation.[65] This approach has had great impact on the course of constitutional litigation in Japan. From the 1960s to the 1980s, "legislative facts" have been an issue in almost all important constitutional cases. In the 1975 Supreme Court decision (discussed above) holding unconstitutional a regulation of the location of pharmacies, we first see the Court presenting a detailed argument which takes with explicit seriousness the proof of legislative facts. That is to say, in the judgment the issues were whether the means (regulation of location) were "necessary and reasonable" for achievement of legislative purpose, and whether methods "less restrictive" of the freedom to choose an occupation could be employed. On the necessity and reasonableness of the distance restriction, the prefectural governor argued that its absence "would be attended by the dangers of promoting poor distribution of pharmacies, intensifying competition, encouraging abuse of pharmaceuticals, and disrupting good business practices." The Court said, "It is hard to see this as a reasonable judgment based on sure evidence; it is simply an abstract assumption," and pointed out the possibility of less restrictive methods, such as strengthening inspections, making unannounced spot inspections, and improving consumer education. This use of legislative facts by Japan's Supreme Court closely resembles the concept of "judicial notice" used by the American Supreme Court.

A number of questions arise concerning the use of legislative facts as evidence in the courts. Do judges even have the capacity to properly evaluate general social and economic data, and if they do, to what extent should legislative facts be used? Is the use of legislative facts even necessary and how does their use relate to the burden of proof when there is no presentation of evidence? Needless to say, more than a few doubt the appropriateness of judicially recognizing legislative facts. Actually, the standards of constitutional review derived from precedent in Japan do not rely heavily on proof of legislative facts; so the role of legislative facts in judicial review is not as prominent as in the United States.

Political Questions and Legislative Discretion

In the area of justiciability of so-called "political questions," we see in Japanese case law a difference from rather than influence from United States law. In Japan, highly political legislative acts disputed in law are *outside the review authority of the courts*, and entrusted to the judgment of the political branch. This was the ordinary pre-war theory of "act of State" (*act de governement, Regierungsakt*) learned from France and Germany. In a 1960 decision, perhaps unique, Japan's Supreme Court was called upon to decide whether a dissolution of the House of Representatives had followed constitutionally prescribed procedure.[66] While there are points in common between act of state and non-justiciability, the case law distinguishes one from the other, in form and substance, with respect to acts of state in the following three ways.

First, there are acts which are entrusted to the *autonomy* of state organs on a constitutional parity with the courts. For example, in a case where the validity of a law was questioned on grounds that a Diet decision to extend its session should be nullified, the Supreme Court said, "If the law is deemed to have passed by a resolution of both Houses and to have been in force in compliance with lawful procedures, the court should respect the autonomy of the Diet and should not investigate any facts concerning legislative procedure, and should not make any judgment concerning the validity thereof."[67]

Second, there are acts entrusted to the discretion of a state organ (especially the legislative branch) on a constitutional parity with the courts. Since before the war, these acts have been explained in administrative law theory as acts of free discretion (*freies Ermessen*) which cannot be considered unconstitutional except in "cases of gross abuse of discretion or malfeasance."

An example is a case which dealt with malapportionment regarding the House of Councillors. In a 1964 judgment, the Supreme Court[68] indicated that, as long as it does not give rise to "an extreme inequality in the voter's enjoyment of the right to elect," apportionment "is a matter of legislative policy subject to the Diet's authority as the legislative branch." However, even in a case regarding a vote value ratio of 1 to 5.26 in the 1977 election, the Court recognized the broad discretion of the Diet, and stressed the special nature of the House of Councillors (with some representatives chosen on a regional basis). The Court held that no constitutional problem arises except "where a situation of unconscionably striking inequality arises, and continues for a considerable period, and it is judged that the Diet's failure to take corrective measures exceeds the permissible limits of discretion." In its recognition of court review of abuse of discretion issues, this argument differs from the act of state theory. Besides election cases, legislative discretion has been recognized as especially broad in cases dealing with social and economic rights. In Japan, this has become an object of debate as an issue in constitutional litigation.[69]

Third, there are acts distastefully dealt with by arguing for a seasoning of free discretion theory with act of state theory. In the 1959 *Sunakawa* case, the constitutionality of U.S. bases on Japanese territory under the Japan-United States Mutual Security Treaty was at issue. The Supreme Court held that the Security Treaty has a "highly political nature which possesses an extremely important relation to the basis of the existence of our country." Regarding their judgment on constitutionality, the conclusion and ratification of the treaty by the Cabinet and the Diet involved "not a few points in which [it] ... is the other side of the coin of their political or free discretionary judgment...." "Unless there is clearly obvious unconstitutionality or invalidity," such judgments "fall outside" judicial review.[70] This case differs from the case on dissolution of the House of Representatives in that with a treaty there is still a certain constitutional limit which the government must not exceed. The Court, while seeming to adhere to the theory of act of state, reviewed the question of whether the Security Treaty was obviously unconstitutional, and even recognized a highly political theory as subject to a certain degree of judicial review.

"Political questions" in the constitutional case law of the United States is a very broad concept including acts of free discretion and the exercise of autonomy by both the Cabinet and Congress. Since too easy recognition of an act as "non-justiciable" is at odds with the principles of rule of law, the prevailing view among scholars in Japan is that acts of state should be limited to rare exceptions, and problems should be approached from the standpoint of whether or not an act should be left to the autonomy or the discretionary authority of government.

Standards of Judicial Review

The Double Standard

In Japan, scholarly opinion and the case law are fundamentally in agreement on the "double standard" theory of human rights limitation which originated from U.S. constitutional case law. Each individual right must be affirmed with careful scrutiny of the concrete case. However, there are considerable differences in ways of thinking about judicial review standards regarding the same problems.

Cases Recognizing "Double Standard"

In a 1972 decision the Supreme Court made clear that there is a difference in what is constitutionally permissible restraint between freedoms of the spirit (*seishinteki jiyū*) and economic freedom. The decision upheld the licensing of retail markets under the Retail Trade and Commerce Special Measures Law, which the Court held to be constitutional.[71] In this case, the Court indicated two formulae for regulating an individual's economic activities: (a) *negative* limitations, restrictions designed to maintain public safety and order, and preventive measures (for example, to prevent danger to the life and health of the people); and (b) *positive* limitations, deriving from the concept of a welfare state (for example, planning for harmonious development to balance the overall economic state of society with stability and healthy economic progress among the people). In this regard the Court said, "The individual's freedom of economic activity differs from freedoms of the spirit. The proper construction is that the Constitution allows and expects the institution of some reasonable regulatory measures as a means of implementing socioeconomic policy." The need to obtain government permission to open a business is a reasonable condition allowed by the Constitution.

In the *Pharmacy* case (site restriction), the Court made very clear that freedoms of the spirit are superior to economic rights: "In comparison to other constitutionally guaranteed freedoms, especially freedoms of the spirit, the freedom of occupation requires regulation by public authority. Thus, Article 22(1) of the Constitution, which recognizes the freedom to choose an occupation, with the reservation, 'to the extent that it does not interfere with the public welfare,' was designed to emphasize this point in particular."

The Court upheld the constitutionality of regulating retail markets with licensing for the positive purpose of fostering medium and small businesses, yet held the distance requirement in the *Pharmacy* case to be unreasonable and unconstitutional. Nevertheless, "the general regulatory purpose of policing and restricting in order to prevent danger to the life and health of the people," was the same for both cases. Both decisions recognized that the freedom to choose an occupation is subject to a *stronger* "inherent need for regulation" than "other constitutionally guaranteed freedoms, like freedoms of the spirit."

Judicial Review of Economic Freedom

The cases attempt to clarify the difference in the standards of judicial review by separating the form of regulation dealing with occupational freedoms into two standards. The standard for constitutionally permissible regulatory legislation of economic freedom is reasonableness or rationality, as in the constitutional case law of the United States. However, in the United States, at the level of state constitutions there is a distinction in the method of judicial review between anti-competition regulation and quality-control regulation. At the federal level, this is not much of an issue. The federal courts usually take a "hands-off" approach toward legislation regulatory of economic freedom when it concerns due process and a provision; in such cases, there is a strong presumption of constitutionality and respect for legislative discretion. Typical is the 1955 case of *Williamson* v. *Lee Optical Co.*[72] After that, the Supreme Court reexamined the traditional "double standard" doctrine in the case of *Lynch* v. *Household Finance Corp.*,[73] wherein the Court specified an intermediate standard reaching a compromise between the strict separation of freedoms of the spirit from economic freedom, chiefly in cases related to the equal protection of social and economic rights (the "strict rationality" or "middle tier" standard). The 1973 case of *United States Department of Agriculture* v. *Moreno*[74] and the 1975 case of *Weinberger* v. *Wiesenfield*[75] involved disputes over equality of welfare rights, and were perhaps the first model cases to apply the new test.[76]

When I consider the realities of the legislative process and legislation under the Constitution of Japan, and the above trends in American case law, even given the presumption of constitutionality, I do not think we should expand legislative discretion in Japan as was done in the *Lee Optical* case.[77] It is worth noting that the Court did not recognize such broad legislative discretion in the *Pharmacy* case; for the standard used was one very close to that of "strict rationality" found in American law. In this case, as touched on briefly before, the Court concretely scrutinized the legislative facts in order to determine the constitutionality of a negative regulatory system: "In principle, the said regulation must not only be necessary and reasonable for an important public interest," but "it also needs to be recognized that the above purpose cannot be adequately attained by regulation of the nature and substance of business activities which is a limitation of occupational freedom less restrictive than a permit system. While maintaining the fundamental principle of respect for the discretion of the legislative branch, "the scope of reasonable discretion is likely to depend on the nature of the matter itself," so that in the case of restrictive legislation, the Court can only recognize limited legislative discretion. This is why the courts take the position that the constitutionality of such law should be reviewed in concrete detail.

In contrast, the Court recognized broader legislative discretion in the *Retail Market Licensing* case concerning the reasonableness of an affirmative regulatory system.   On this point, the standards known as "minimum rationality" found in the U.S. case law closely resemble the standard used in Japan's *Retail Market Licensing* case. "Only the discretionary judgment of the legislative branch" can determine whether the regulation is necessary or not, and whether the methods and terms of regulation in each provision are fit and appropriate.   The courts take the view that the regulation will be "*unconstitutional only*" when the regulatory measures employed to carry out legislative intent *are clearly shown to be grossly unreasonable*" (emphasis added).   This is commonly referred to in Japan as "the principle of clarity" (meikaku no gensoku).   It corresponds to what Alexander Bickel called "the rule of the clear mistake."[78]

While "the principle of clarity" may allow for greater legislative discretion, it does not imply a rule for the complete abandonment of judicial control.   In the *Retail Market Licensing* case the Court examined both the purpose of the regulation and the method of enforcement in terms of good market practices. The Court found that "both the purpose and terms of the regulation were not clearly and grossly unreasonable." As you can see, in the control of economic freedom constitutional judgments do not utilize a single standard of "reasonableness" but, depending on purpose and manner of regulation, also use the "strict rationality" standard and the "principle of clarity." This view is also generally favored by scholars. The problem lies in the area of freedoms of the spirit.

According to the *Pharmacy* case, measures regulating freedoms of the spirit must be subjected to stricter judicial review than economic freedoms. However, the present situation in most case law is fluid; stricter standards of review have not been firmly established.

The doctrines of "void for vagueness or overbreadth" and "prior restraint" are standards which have been established in the case law. However, in Japan although use of the "clear and present danger" test and the "less restrictive alternative" test has been urged by scholars and applied in some *lower courts*, the Supreme Court has rejected them. On this point, it is worth noting the *Sarufutsu* case in which restraints on the freedom of public employees to participate in political activities were hotly debated.

The freedom of public employees to engage in political activities is uniformly and entirely restricted by No. 14-7 of the National Personnel Authority's Regulations, and Article 102 of the National Public Employees Law. These regulations are stricter and broader than the restrictions of the original Hatch Act in the United States. The issue in the *Sarufutsu* case was whether restraints extended to the acts of distributing notices and putting up posters in a public place for a legislative candidate nominated by a labor union under the following: "non-managerial public employees, even temporary workers, are prohibited from using their position or government facilities outside working hours in such a way as to even unintentionally diminish their impartiality." Based on the principle of imposing only "the minimum necessary" restraints of the 1967 Supreme Court judgment in the *Tokyo Central Post Office* case (discussed above), [79] both the trial and appellate courts held that the imposition of penalties under the National Public Employees Law was *an unconstitutional application of law*. After this, ten similar decisions were handed down.

In the "expert opinion" presented at the first instance trial of the *Sarufutsu* case, I stated that, as in the constitutional case law of the United States, the Japanese courts should employ the "less restrictive alternative" standard when judging the constitutionality of a law or ordinance.[80] This standard--abbreviated in Japan to "the L.R.A. standard"--has been applied in many lower court decisions. However, in 1974 the Supreme Court overturned the lower courts' decisions and held that a complete and uniform ban on political activities was constitutional.[81]

The Supreme Court applied the "rational relationship" test in finding constitutional the ban on political activities by public employees. The Court held that to determine whether a restraint "stops at what is reasonable and unavoidable," "it is necessary to examine three points: the purpose of the prohibition, the connection between this purpose and the prohibited political activities, and the balance of benefits and losses attendant to the prohibition on these political activities."

The Court found the legislative purpose proper, so to achieve it, a uniform "ban on political activities *which might entail a fear* of diminished political neutrality" is seen "to have a reasonable connection with the purpose of the ban." There is no need expressed to consider the concrete circumstances of the employees, such as job classifications, the varied nature of their responsibilities, and the difference between times on and off the job. In other words, according to this decision, when there is a "prophylactic scheme", it is not necessary to show a real and concrete reasonable relationship between its methods and the purpose. In this way of thinking, "the collective benefit of all the people gained by this ban" outweighs the benefits lost by the merely "indirect and incidental restraint on the freedom to express opinions." The former is "more important" than the latter in the balance of interests. Consequently, this view is completely at odds with the L.R.A. standard. This decision has had a major impact on the course of constitutional litigation dealing with rights and freedoms of the spirit of Japan. It is not an exaggeration to say that this case marked a turning point in the history of Japan's constitutional case law. Much more could be said about it, but here I would only add a few comments concerning the significance of the standards for judicial review in this decision for "double standard" theory in Japan.[82]

The first thing to recognize is that the "reasonable relationship" test found in the *Sarufutsu* case was derived from the "pure speech" and "speech plus" distinction of American constitutional law during the 1970s. This view came up in the 1968 decision of *United States v. O'Brien*.[83] According to the judicial research officer in charge of the *Sarufutsu* case, the staff of Japan's Supreme Court, "the O'Brien test" was often consulted in reaching a decision.[84] According to the O'Brien test, "speech plus" is present when a speech element is mixed with a "non-speech" element in one "action"; the regulation of the non-speech element, which is "content neutral," is not unconstitutional if related to a proper legislative purpose. Such regulation only amounts to an indirect and incidental limitation of free speech.

However, the real question is whether it is possible to separate "speech" from "action" in expression. That is very doubtful. In the 1975 Supreme Court decision referred to earlier, dealing with a Tokushima City public safety ordinance, Justice Shigemitsu Dando stated in a supplementary opinion: "Speech is often accompanied by action, and in cases where it is impossible to reasonably and objectively achieve the purpose of the speech without resorting to some action, that action must be considered as speech." This opinion, as in America, has been very influential among Japanese scholars.[85] The Court in many cases finds no need to--perhaps better to say, the Court holds it must not--concretely ask the question of whether there is sufficient substantial reason for approving an indirect and incidental restriction of the speech element, even though it relies on the distinction between "speech" and "action," and the standard of reasonable connection. This presents serious problems.

The legislative purpose and its relationship to means used to achieve it, while they are supposed to be rational, may simply be an abstract concept. Moreover, even if the Supreme Court talks about balancing interests, they affirm that the benefits gained by the ban are more important than the benefits lost. This is only formalistic and nominal "balancing." This is the actual approach used in the *Sarufutsu* decision. Thus, even if there is no concrete danger of and no actual occurrence of an infringement of the legislative purpose, sanctions against any rule violation are permissible simply due to an abstract danger.

If such is the case, the rational relationship test of the *Sarufutsu* decision is actually about the same as the "rule of clarity," the previously mentioned standard for constitutionality in cases about statutes regulating economic freedom for positive purposes. This is essentially different from the search for the "less restrictive alternative" [referred to as "LRA" in Japan], the approach used in the *Pharmacy* case to reach a judgment on constitutionality.

Because the *Sarufutsu* decision dealt with the human rights of public employees, its theory might be thought inappropriate as is as a basis for considering the constitutionality of restrictions on the human rights of citizens in general. But that has not been the case. By general practical wisdom, restrictions of free speech are thought to be of two kinds: the first is that designed to restrict the content of speech in order to prevent an evil that would attend expression of a particular opinion; the second type purports to prevent an evil, unrelated to content, but attendant to an accompanying action. A concrete and direct relationship must exist between the legislative purpose and the means of achieving that purpose for the former type of restriction. Regarding the latter type of restraint, controls by the courts are limited to establishing whether or not there is a reasonable relationship with legislative purpose, as illustrated in the *Sarufutsu* case. Accordingly, the "clear and present danger" test and the "less restrictive alternative" standard can only apply to the former type of legislation, that regulating the content of speech. As for legislation regulating the time, place, and manner of speech, the reasonable relationship standard has been applied. For example, the Public Offices Election Law prohibits door-to-door visits as a method of campaigning. In 1981, the Supreme Court held that "this prohibition amounted to no more than an indirect and incidental limitation accompanying one prohibition on the manner of expressing an opinion; the interest to be protected by the ban ... was clearly greater than the benefit lost."[86] Furthermore, this decision emphasized the legislative branch's discretion: "The propriety of uniformly prohibiting door-to-door canvassing is a question of legislative policy designed to assure fairness and freedom in elections."

However, in Japan, apart from two or three cases dealing with the unconstitutionality of instigating or abetting a crime, there have been few cases in which the constitutionality of a restriction on the content of speech has been disputed. In cases where the constitutionality of laws which control sexual or defamatory expression is at issue, we cannot find model cases of directly regulating the content of expression[87] because they involve questions regarding "categorization," or "definitional balancing." Even in the *Pharmacy* case, where "the demand is strong for use of public power to regulate occupational freedom when compared to freedoms of the spirit," there is a great possibility that the "double standard" will not work on behalf of a "preferred position" for freedoms of the spirit, because the system for licensing occupations is most often based on a negative, restrictive concept. This issue remains extremely important in Japan's constitutional case law.

Finally, I would like to briefly comment on some very interesting views expressed in Japanese case law on prior restraint theory, and to compare them with U.S. constitutional law.

The prohibition of prior restraints is the heart of guaranteeing the freedom of speech and expression. In Japan, Article 21(1) of the Constitution guarantees "the freedom of speech, press, and all other forms of expression," and also contains the special provision that "no censorship shall be maintained" [Article 21(2)], a clear indication that prior restraints are forbidden.

In scholarly opinion, censorship occurs "when *public authorities* examine the content of thought before it is publicly presented, find it inappropriate, and prohibit its presentation."[88] Consequently, censorship is constituted not only in the classic circumstance of administrative imposition of censorship, but also by a court injunction against expression, excluding cases of obvious necessity. This has been the dominant view thus far. The inclusion of injunctions within the concept of censorship in Japan parallels common opinion and case law in the U.S.

Since the late 1970s, the view that the meaning of "censorship" should be limited to administrative censorship has been strong, holding that Article 21(2) of the Constitution absolutely prohibits such censorship. Except in cases of clear necessity, temporary judicial injunctive measures are seen as impermissible as prior restraint under the freedom of expression guarantees of Article 21(1).[89]

In its 1984 decision on customs investigations, referred to earlier, the Supreme Court stated: "Censorship is an exercise of administrative authority, and has as its purpose the banning, in whole or in part, of the thought content of affected materials. It is characteristic of censorship that upon inspection specific materials are found inappropriate and are banned prior to being made public."[90]   Taking the position that there is a distinction between administrative censorship and judicial censorship, the Court explained:

> Publications denied entry pursuant to a customs inspection generally originate from outside the country. The inspection takes place as one link in customs assessment procedures, and its purpose is not to review and regulate idea content. Even if importation is prohibited, this does not mean that the items are seized and destroyed by customs officials, or that all opportunity for publication is lost. A notice from the Director of the Customs Bureau denying an import permit is subject to judicial review. Thus, comprehensive consideration of customs procedures makes clear they do not constitute "censorship."

Since their consensus is that customs inspections are unconstitutional, scholars have criticized the concept of censorship in the Court's decision, for lacking clarity and for too narrowly considering limits on the means used, quite apart from problems regarding the subject of censorship.[91]

In the *Hoppō Journal* case of 1986, regarding a publication damaging to the good name of a candidate for public office, the Supreme Court[92] dealt with the issue of whether temporary injunction procedures could be used prior to the scheduled publication of the magazine containing the article in question. The Court followed the ideas regarding "censorship" expressed in the *Customs Inspection Censorship* case and held that the temporary measures *did correspond to prior restraint* but did not amount to censorship. This decision took the position that when the object of acts of expression is criticism or evaluation of a public employee or a candidate for public office, the publication becomes *a matter affecting the public interest.*[93] Since it is a social value superior to the good name of a private person, such expression is specially protected by the Constitution, and in principle injunctions are not permissible. However, there are exceptions. In the *Hoppō Journal* case the Court argued:

Even without oral argument or the occurrence of a violation on the part
of the defendant (the publishing company), when, based on materials
presented by the plaintiff (the candidate for public office), it is clear that
the content of the publication is not true or that its purpose is not solely
for the public interest, and when the court finds there is fear of serious
irreparable damage to the plaintiff, then the issuance of a temporary
injunction without oral argument or without an infringement of rights by
the defendant is not contrary to the above intent of Article 21 of the
Constitution.

In relation to defamation and freedom of expression, in the U.S. *New
York Times* v. *Sullivan* is a landmark case. In Japan, the standard of "actual
malice" has been accepted by many scholars, but only one Justice took that
position in the *Hoppō Journal* case.

Besides the elements discussed above, freedom of expression includes the
right to demand public information as an important aspect of the "right to
know." However, while national laws to protect privacy and the right to
public information have not been established, the case law strongly emphasizes
the importance of freedom of information in the news media. The posture
of the case law regarding freedom of news gathering and the freedom to
maintain the secrecy of news sources is, with exceptions, generally negative.
Decisions placing commercial speech within the system of freedom of speech
as in the U.S. have not appeared in Japan. There are numerous issues for
interesting comparisons with American law.[94] However, since U.S.
constitutional case law has not been particularly influential in this area, this
discussion stops at pointing out issues.

Freedom of Religion and the Purpose and Effect Standard

As with freedom of expression, so also in the area of freedom of religion,
U.S. judicial doctrines have been influential in Japan, but show a different
face. "Freedom of religion is guaranteed to all," and "no person shall be
compelled to take part in any religious acts, celebration, rite, or practice" (Art.
20). Detailed provisions state plainly the religious neutrality of the state, and
prohibit the state from granting privileges to religion (Art. 89).

The position of the state towards religion differs from country to country.
In Japan, the main structure of religion-state relations has been thought of in
terms of the three models of Italy, England, and America. In general, the
principle of separation of religion and state provided for in the Constitution
of Japan is modeled on the American form of complete religion-state

separation. As noted in earlier sections (I, II), this reflects a very sober change from the status of religion and Shinto nationalism under the Meiji Constitution.

However, even the American principle of separation is not so strict as to exclude all involvements of the state in religion. In the case law, we find a three-part test based on the purpose and effect of an act: a) Does the government act serve a secular purpose? b) Does that act have a primary effect of either advancing or inhibiting a religion? And c), is there excessive entanglement of religion and the state? By examining these three conditions *individually*, a court determines whether the act is permissible or a violation of the separation principle.

In Japan, in the city of Tsu, Mie Prefecture, public funds were used to support a Shinto ground-breaking ceremony in preparation for the construction of a city gymnasium. The courts discussed the possibility of violations of Articles 20 and 89. The "purpose and effect" test in American law was used but took on quite a different appearance in this case. In 1971 the Nagoya High Court interpreted strictly the separation doctrine, and held that the Shinto ground-breaking ceremony was not simply a customary ceremony, but a religious ceremony, and therefore unconstitutional. However, in 1977, the Supreme Court reversed that decision and held that it was virtually impossible, and would anyway be an unreasonable state of affairs, to have complete separation of religion and state. The Court adopted a loose notion of separation, as follows:[95]

> The principle of separation of religion and the state requires that the state take a neutral position towards religion, but the State is not prohibited from all contact with religion. In light of the effect and purpose of the act which entails involvement with religion, we should interpret it so as not to permit activities which exceed a proper limit, taking into account various conditions of society and culture of each country.

The majority of eight justices held that an activity would not be allowed "where the purpose of the act had religious significance so that its effect either aided, fostered, or encouraged religion or oppressed or interfered with it." The Court added that when judging such a matter, we must not only look at the outward appearance of the act in question, but "must also judge objectively various conditions in accord with prevailing social ideas," such as the act's influence on the average person, the presence and degree of religious consciousness, the place, the intent and purpose of those in charge, and the religious assessment of the average person. The Shinto ground-breaking ceremony, the Court concluded, "is mainly a formality of general social custom recognized as wholly secular. It has no effect which would interfere with or oppress other religions, or aid, encourage or foster Shinto."

Five justices dissented taking a strict position on the separation of church and state. The ground-breaking ceremony, they wrote, had a strong religious taint to it, with the effect of aiding and giving special treatment to a Shinto shrine, and its funding was therefore unconstitutional.

When we look at the purpose and effect test used in the U.S., we notice it gradually changing, with the criticism that it lacks consistency. However, decisions after 1970 have applied rather strict standards, adding that of avoiding "excessive entanglement." In Japan, also, some lower courts have applied a strict standard.[96] However, scholarly analysis of this standard has generally been critical. Indeed, there are problems with the considerable possibility of relativist treatment of the principle of separation of religion and the state in the purpose and effect test as discussed in the Tsu *Shinto Ground-Breaking Ceremony* case. I believe that a reconstruction of this standard with stricter separation is important to strengthen the guarantees of religious freedom in Japan.[97]

Conclusion: The Realities of Justice

The Meiji Constitution of 1889 was established on the basis of the constitutional monarchy of nineteenth-century Germany. After that and until the end of World War II, for over half a century, the legal system and jurisprudence of Japan were overwhelmingly influenced by European civil law systems, especially in constitutional law and administrative law studies. Thus, judicial decisions and scholarly analyses related to human rights in Japan have adopted such German theories as "special power relationships" (*besonderes Gewaltverhaltnis*),[98] "institutional guarantees" (*institutionelle Garantie*), and the "program rule"(*Programmsatze*). Japanese law shares many basic concepts and methods in common with continental European law.

The fact that is some areas Japan manifests distinctive development and practices, in interpreting provisions of apparently identical intent[with those in the U.S.], or in using case law theories regarding the U.S. Constitution, may be due to Japan's long cultivation of the traditions of continental law. However, since 1945, Japanese law has undergone great changes. The impact of U.S. constitutional theories and judicial decisions with respect to human rights and judicial power has been so great that it has drastically turned Japan away from the legal positivism of prewar Japan, which attached great importance to legal concepts and texts, and developed deductive methods of legal reasoning. One deep concern remains as we look back on over 45 years of constitutional developments since the end of World War II: Judicial passivity has been too great in Japan. Too much modesty has been shown and too much deference has been paid to the policy makers of the legislative and executive branches. More deference could be shown to the Constitution's mandate for full protection of human rights.

NOTES: III

Translated by William B. Cleary. To accomidate differences in English and Japanese linguistic structure, this is not at all points a word-for-word translation.

1. 1 Cranch 37 (1803).
2. Nobuyoshi Ashibe, *KEMPŌ SOSHŌ NO RIRON* (The Theory of Constitutional Litigation) (1973), 4-11.
3. Itoh & Beer, 258.
4. Tatsukichi Minobe, *KAITEI KEMPŌ SATSUYŌ* (Outline of the Revised Constitution) (1946), 74. Minobe was the leading pre-war constitutional lawyer. See Frank O. Miller, *Minobe Tatsukichi: Interpreter of Constitutionalism in Japan* (1965).
5. R.H. Grossman, *DIE STAATS-UND RECHTSIDEOLOGISCHEN GRUNDLAGEN DER VERFASSUNGS-GERICHTSBARKEIT IN DEN VEREINIGTEN STAATEN VON AMERICA UND IN DER SCHWIEZ* (1948), 39-40. Also see Nobuyoshi Ashibe, *KEMPŌ SEITEI KENRYOKU* (The Power to Establish the Constitution) (1983), 14.
6. Some have said that Article 97 was put into Chapter 10 almost by chance during the enacting process. See Tatsuo Sato, *HŌRITSU NO AKUMA* (The Evil of Law) (1969), 125. See generally, Kenzo Takayanagi, Ichiro Otomo, and Hideo Tanaka, *NIHON KOKU KEMPŌ SEITEI NO KATEI II: KAISETSU* (The Process of Establishing the Constitution II: Commentary) (1972), 283-284.
7. See Masami Ito, *supra*, I, and generally, Nobuyoshi Ashibe, *KEMPŌ NO KŌGI NŌTO I* (Lectures on the Constitution, I) (1986), 45-49.
8. In SCAP, the Diet was conceived of as the supreme organ even in law . In the understanding of the drafters, a dissolution of the House of Representations must occur under Article 69 (in case of a vote of no confidence in the Cabinet or the failure of a confidence vote) of the present Constitution. But the importance attached to the Diet is especially evident in their thought regarding the judicial review power, that the Diet could review and overturn a Supreme Court judgment of constitutionality with a two-thirds majority of the full membership, except in human rights cases. H. Tanaka, *Kempō seitei oboegaki* (Notes on the Establishment of the Constitution) (1976), at 152.
9. Article 82, Code of Criminal Procedure.
10. Toshimaro Kojo, "*Keiji Saiban to Eibeiho*" (Criminal Justice and Anglo-American Law), *JURISUTO*, No. 600, 1975, 335.
11. "Special Issue: The Theory and Reality of Criminal Procedure," 23 *JIYŲ TO SEIGI* (Liberty and Justice) 2 (1973); Shiro Sasaki, Tamio Kawakami, and Hiroshi Tamiya, "Theory and Practice of Criminal Procedure," in *Keiji Soshōhō* (Law of Criminal Procedure), *JURISUTO*, No. 600, 1975, 261. Criminal Procedure Law in Japan developed after 1945 under the influence of Anglo-American law. Now that 45 years have passed, it is time to calmly reflect upon the rich material U.S. law has provided us for comparative studies.

12. H. Tanaka, " *Kempō 31 jō*", in *Nihonkoku Kempō Taikei* (Japan's System of Constitutional Law: Essays Commemorating Professor Toshiyoshi Miyazawa's 60th Birthday), Vol. 8 (1965), 187-198.

13. Takashi Teshima, *"Tekisei Tetsuzuki No Hoshō"* (The Guarantee of Due Process), in R. Arikura and T. Kobayashi (eds.), *KEMPŌ* (Constitutional Law) (3d ed., 1986), 142.

14. *Nakamura* v. *Japan*, 16 *KEISHŪ* (No. 111), 1593 (Supreme Court, Grand Bench, November 28, 1962). For a translation, see Itoh and Beer, 58.

15. In the U.S. Constitution the Ninth Amendment is sometimes referred to as a "repository of rights"; *Griswold* v. *Connecticut*, 381 *U.S.* 479 (1965), Justice Goldberg's concurring opinion. N. Ashibe, "The 9th Amendment in the U.S. Constitution--A Provision of General Basic Rights as a Check on the Judicial Process" in *Essays Celebrating the 100th Anniversary of the Founding of Hōgaku Kyōkai*, Vol. 2, 1983, 57.

16. *Hasegawa* v. *Japan*, 22 *KEISHŪ* (No. 12) 1625 (Supreme Court, Grand Bench, December 24, 1969); for a translation, see Itoh and Beer, 178.

17. *Griswold* v. *Connecticut*, 381 *U.S.* 479 (1965). Among influential detailed studies, see in particular Masami Ito, *PURAIBASHĪ NO KENRI* (The Right of Privacy) (1963). The Supreme Court has indirectly recognized the right of privacy and has held that privacy is worthy of legal protection; but the case law does not treat it explicitly as a new right. See L. Beer, *Freedom of Expression in Japan* (1984), chapter 9, hereafter cited as Beer, *Freedom*.

18. Apparently, the Japanese Government feared this unconditional rights language when establishing the Constitution, while SCAP, judging language from a U.S. constitutional standpoint, thought any conditions on these rights would lead to restrictions.

19. In the Potsdam Declaration, see *supra*, II. Takayanagi, Otomo, and Tanaka, 165.

20. Masami Ito, "Rule of Law--A Development of Constitutional Law," in A.T. Von Mehren (ed.), *Law in Japan* (1963), 211. SCAP failed to give serious consideration to the phrase in Article 22 "to the extent that it does not interfere with the public welfare;" but they did explain that the freedoms of speech, press, belief, and assembly are more important than those of occupation and place of residence.

21. Hideo Tanaka, *KEMPŌ SEITEI KATEI OBOEGAKI*, from 130.

22. *Koyama* v. *Japan*, 11 *MINSHŪ* (No. 30), 997 (Supreme Court, Grand Bench, March 13, 1957). For a translation, see John M. Maki, *Court and Constitution in Japan* (1964), 3.

23. Masami Ito, *supra* note 20, 221-222.

24. "Notes on the Constitution of Japan," *HŌGAKU KYŌKAI ZASSHI*, 1953, 294-297, 335, 339.

25. 304 *U.S.* 144 (1938).

26. Toshiyoshi Miyazawa, *NIHON KOKU KEMPŌ* (The Constitution of Japan) (1955), 201-203, and *KEMPŌ* (The Constitution, revised edition) (1974), 228-238.

27. *Toyama et al.* v. *Japan*, 20 *KEISHŪ* (No. 8) 901 (Supreme Court, Grand Bench, October 26, 1966); for a translation, see Itoh and Beer, 85. In this case, officials of

the National Postal Service Union were prosecuted for abetting and for failing to handle the mail in violation of Article 79, Sec. 1 of the Postal Law. They incited workers at the Tokyo Central Post Office to participate in a workshop rally which extended over their duty hours, and had 38 officers leave their posts for a few hours during working hours. The majority held that "the interference in the execution of duties by actions taken in a labor dispute should not be punished provided it is done without violence." See Beer, *Freedom*, 232. For a comparison of the major opinions, see Nobushige Ukai, "The Significance of the Reception of American Constitutional Institution and Ideas in Japan," in Lawrence W. Beer ed., *Constitutionalism in Asia* (1979), 123-125. For a translation of this decision, see Itoh and Beer, at 85.

28. *Tsuruzono et al.* v. *Japan*, 27 *KEISHU* (No. 4) 547 (Supreme Court, Grand Bench, April 25, 1973). Officers of the National Union of Agriculture and Forestry Workers were prosecuted for violating Article 98, paragraph 5 of the National Public Employees Law, which prohibits certain acts taken during a labor dispute and the abetting or inciting of the same. The minority view in the Tokyo Central Post Office case was adopted as the majority opinion in this case. See Beer, *Freedom*, 235-236.

29. Nobuyoshi Ashibe, *GENDAI JINKEN RON* (Current Theory of Human Rights) (1974); *KEMPŌ SOSHŌ NO GENDAITEKI TENKA* (Current Developments in Constitutional Litigation (1981); *SHIHŌ NO ARIKATA TO JINKEN* (The Judicial Approach to Human Rights) (1983).

30. See my writings attempting to clarify this difference and examining relevant cases and theories of Japanese, American, and German law: *"Shijinkan ni okeru kihonteki jinken no hoshō,"* and *"Jinken hoshō kitei no shijinkan ni okeru kōryoku,"* in *GENDAI JINKEN RON* (1974); and *"Shijinkan ni okeru jinken no kōryoku,"* and *"Shiteki dantai ni taisuru jinken kitel no koryoku,"* in *KEMPŌ SOSHŌ NO GENDAITEKI TENKAI* (1981).

31. This view is similar to that in *Hurd* v. *Hodge*, 334 *U.S.* 24 (1948), which invalidated restrictive covenants in the District of Columbia as being against public policy. However, the theory found in *Shelly* v. *Kraemer*, 334 *U.S.* 1 (1948) is not directly applicable to Japanese law.

32. *Takano* v. *Mitsubishi Resin Inc.*, 27 *MINSHU* (No. 11) 1536 (Supreme Court, Grand Bench, December 12, 1973) and *Nissan Motor Inc.* v. *Nakamoto*, 35 *MINSHU* (No. 2) 300 (Supreme Court, Grand Bench, March 24, 1981) are important related cases. In the former case the plaintiff, Mr. Takano, who had been accepted by the company after graduating from a university, was dismissed after working only three months because he had made a false statement concerning his student political activities. The Supreme Court ruled that equality and civil liberties do not regulate relationships between private individuals in the history of establishing and developing human rights. If there is a violation of individual liberty or equality, or fear of such, the remedy lies in a tort action for damages when the violation exceeds a socially tolerable level, but such is not a crime. See "Recent Developments: Constitution Law--Applicability of Civil Rights and Freedom of Thought Clauses to the Conduct of Private Parties," 7 *Law in Japan: An Annual* 151 (1974). In the latter case, the

issue concerned the validity of office regulations which provided that men were to retire at 55 and women at 50. The Court concluded that the rule was "invalid in view of Article 90 of the Civil Code, because it amounts to irrational discrimination."

33. *Soka Gakkai* v. *Matsumoto et al.*, 35 *MINSHŪ* (No. 3) 434 (Supreme Court, April 7, 1981).

34. There are many views on the relationship between Articles 32 and 89. However, I believe that "access to the courts" (Art. 32) not only implies the presence of a case or controversy within the three principles of "being open to the public," "holding adversarial hearings," and "providing adjudication," but also includes non-contentious cases [cases in which there is no dispute, i.e., adoption, marriage, validation of a will, and so on. Translator's Note]. Also, non-contentious cases should be protected by a procedure suited to the needs of a particular case. For details, see Chapter 5 in my *KEMPŌ III, JINKEN (2) DAIGAKU SOSHO* (1981).

35. Article 5 of the Administrative Case Litigation Law provides: "'Public litigation' in this law shall mean litigation which is instituted by any person qualified as an elector, or not having his own legal interest, and which seeks to correct acts by the State or a public entity not conforming to the laws and ordinances." Also, besides public litigation, there is "agency litigation" (*Kikan sosho*) provided for in Article 6 of the same law: "litigation concerning disputes related to the existence or non-existence of authority or the exercise thereof, between agencies of the State or a public entity."

36. For example, Ichiro Ogawa, "*Uttae no rieki to minshu sosho no mondai*" in *TANAKA JIRŌ KOKI KINEN* (1976), 1259. See also "*Gyosei sosho no kyakka no keiko to genkokuteki kaku ho*" in *HŌGAKU KYŌKAI HYAKUSHŪNENKINEN RONBUNSHŪ*, Vol. 1 (1983), 633.

37. Archibald Cox, *The Role of the Supreme Court in American Government* (1976), 99 and Nobuyoshi Ashibe, *SAIBAN NO YAKUWARI* (1979), 157.

38. For my views on this, see "*Shihō ni okeru kenrisei*," *IWANAMI KIHONHŌ KŌZA*, Vol. 6 (1983), 239-43.

39. C.J. Friedrich, *The Impact of American Constitutionalism Abroad*, 1967, 78-79.

40. *Suzuki* v. *Japan*, 6 *MINSHŪ* (No. 9) 783 (Supreme Court, October 8, 1952). For a translation, see Maki, 362. Even before this decision, there were cases which advanced the American style of collateral judicial review. On Article 9, see *supra*, II.

41. M. Cappelletti, *Judicial Review in the Contemporary World* (1971), 84 (translator Y. Taniguchi in Koji Sato (ed.), *GENDAI KEMPŌ SAIBAN RON*, 1974, 126-127).

42. *Aizawa* v. *Japan*, 27 *KEISHŪ* (No. 3) 265 (Supreme Court, April 4, 1973). For a partial translation, see W. Murphy and J. Tanenhaus, *Comparative Constitutional Law* (1977), 359; see also J.O. Haley, "Recent Developments: Constitutionality of Penalty Under Article 200 of the Penal Code for Killing of Lineal Ascendant," 6 *Law in Japan: An Annual* (1973); Nobushige Ukai, "The Significance of the Reception of American Constitutional Institutions and Ideas in Japan," *Constitutionalism in Asia*, 118-119.

43. *K.K. Sumiyoshi* v. *Governor of Hiroshima Prefecture*, 29 *MINSHŲ* (No. 40) 572 (Supreme Court, April 30, 1975). See J.O. Haley, "The Freedom to Choose an Occupation and Constitutional Limits of Legislative Discretion," 8 *Law in Japan: An Annual* 188 (1975); Nobuyoshi Ashibe, *KEMPŌ SOSHŌ NO GENDAITEKI TENKAI* (Current Developments in Constitutional Litigation) (1981), 277.

44. *Kaneo* v. *Election Commission of Hiroshima Prefecture*, 39 *MINSHŲ* (No. 5) 1100 (Supreme Court, July 17, 1985). Hideki Mori, "*Shūgiin giin teisusoshō*" (Litigation Concerning the Apportionment of Diet Seats) in *JURISUTO*, No. 862, 1986, 14; and see *supra* II on popular sovereignty.

45. *Hiraguchi* v. *Hiraguchi*, 41 *MINSHŲ* (No. 3) 408 (Supreme Court, Grand Bench, April 25, 1987).

46. Hideo Wada, "*Iken hanketsu no koyoku o meguru kiron to jijutsu*," 48 *HŌRITSU RONSŌ*, Nos. 4, 5, and 6, 20-21, 1977.

47. 369 *U.S.* 186 (1962).

48. *Kurokawa* v. *Election Commission of Chiba Prefecture*, 30 *MINSHŲ* (No. 3) 223 (Supreme Court, April 14, 1976). A minority opinion held the voting itself was invalid, and that the apportionment among voting districts at the time in question was unconstitutional. Another opinion held that the voting was invalid, but only in those districts underrepresented, thus upholding the validity of the election of officials. See also *supra*, II.

49. Nobuyoshi Ashibe, *supra* note 43, at 305.

50. Hideo Tanaka, "*Teisuhaibun fubyodo ni taisuru shihōteki kyūsai*" (Judicial remedy for malapportionment, *JURISUTO*, No. 803, 1985, 41.

51. Kazuyuki Takahashi, *Teisu fukinko ikenhanketsu no mondaiten to kongo no kadai*, *JURISUTO*, No. 844, 1985, 21; Sato Koji, "*Kihonteki jinken no hoshō to kyūsai (2)*," *HŌGAKU KYŌSHITSU*, No. 56, 1985, 70.

52. Nobuyoshi Ashibe, *supra* note 43, 356-359, "*Shugiin teisu ikenhanketsu no igi to teiseian*," *HŌGAKU KYŌSHITSU*, No. 64, 1986, 8.

53. See *supra*, II.

54. *Tomabeji* v. *Japan*, 7 *MINSHŲ* (No. 7) 350 (Supreme Court, April 15, 1953). The Court said: "Regardless of what the trial court and high court have said, the power of judicial review must be exercised to the extent necessary to resolve the dispute between the parties."

55. *Japan* v. *Nozaki*, 9 *KAKYŲ KEISHŲ* (No. 3) 359 (Sapporo District Court, March 29, 1967). See Nobuyoshi Ashibe, *Shihō no arikata to jinken* (The Way of Justice and Human Rights), 1983, 193-204. See also *supra*, II.

56. 297 *U.S.* 288 (1936).

57. My own analysis of constitutional cases and doctrines in American law leads me to believe that "c" is the most reasonable view. *KEMPŌ SOSHŌ NO RIRON*, 1973, 277.

58. Nobuyoshi Ashibe, *supra* note 55, 178-192.

59. *Sakane et al.* v. *Japan*, 23 *KEISHU* (No. 5) 685 (Supreme Court, April 2, 1969); and *Hasegawa et al.* v. *Japan*, 23 *KEISHU* (No. 5) 305. See Beer, *Freedom*, 103. For a translation of the *Sakane* case, see Itoh and Beer, 232-235.

60. See *supra* note 28.

61. Nobuyoshi Ashibe, *GENDAI JINKENRON* (1974), 330-33.

62. *Japan* v. *Teramae*, 29 *KEISHU* (No. 8) 489 (Supreme Court, September 10, 1975); Beer, *Freedom*, 186.

63. *Matsue* v. *Hakodate Tax Commissioner*, 38 *MINSHU* (No. 12) 1308 (Supreme Court, December 12, 1984); Beer, *Freedom*, 337.

64. Note the cases after *Broadrick* v. *Oklahoma*, 531 *U.S.* 601 (1973), which deal with excessive breadth in American law. Nobuyoshi Ashibe, *supra* note 43, at 20-21; Koji Sato, *KEMPŌ SOSHŌ TO SHIHŌKEN* (1984), 188-197.

65. Yasuo Tokikuni, "*Kempō jijutsu*" (1963) and "*Kempō saiban no mondaiten*" (1966), both in *KEMPŌ SOSHŌ NO RIRON* (1973).

66. *Tomabeji* v. *Japan*, 14 *MINSHU* (No. 7) 1206 (Supreme Court, Grand Bench, June 8, 1960). On "act of state" (political question) doctrine in Japan, see Dan F. Henderson (ed.), *The Constitution of Japan: Its First Twenty Years*, 1947-67 (1968), 125, 145, 165; Nobuyoshi Ashibe, *supra* note 43, at 119-140.

67. *Shimizu* v. *Osaka Governor*, 16 *MINSHU* (No. 3) 445 (Supreme Court, March 7, 1962); for a translation, see Itoh and Beer, 41.

68. *Koshiyama* v. *The Tokyo Election Commission*, 18 *MINSHU* (No. 2) 270 (Supreme Court, February 5, 1964); *Shimizu* v. *The Osaka Election Commission*, 37 *MINSHU* (No. 3) 345 (Supreme Court, April 27m, 1983). For a translation of *Koshiyama*, see Itoh and Beer, 53. On the 1983 decision, see L.W. Beer, "Japan's Constitutional System and Its Judicial Interpretation," 17 *Law in Japan: An Annual* 37 (1984).

69. For example, see Tomatsu Hidenori, "*Rippō Sairyō ron*" (Legislative discretion) in Kempo Kenkyukai (ed.), *GENDAI KOKKA TO KEMPŌ NO GENRI* (1983), 187.

70. *Japan* v. *Sakata et al.*, 13 *KEISHU* (No. 13) 3225 (Supreme Court, December 16, 1959); for a translation, see Maki, 298 (quotations are from 305-306).

71. *Mamushin Sangyo Co.* v. *Japan*, 26 *KEISHU* (No. 9) 586 (Supreme Court, November 22, 1972).

72. 348 *U.S.* 483 (1955).

73. 405 *U.S.* 538 (1972).

74. 413 *U.S.* 528 (1973).

75. 420 *U.S.* 636 (1975).

76. Nobuyoshi Ashibe, "*Kempo sosho to 'niju no kijun' no riron*" in *KEMPŌ SOSHŌ NO GENDAITEKI TENKAI III* (1984).

77. *Supra* note 72, at 292.

78. Alexander Bickel, *The Least Dangerous Branch* (1962), 35.

79. *Japan* v. *Osawa*, *HANREI JIHŌ*, No. 514, 20 (Asahikawa District Court, March 25, 1968); *HANREI JIHŌ*, No. 560, 30 (Sapporo High Court, June 24, 1969).

80. I relied on American doctrines and the cases of *Bagley* v. *Washington Township Hospital District*, 421 2d 409 (1966) and *Fort* v. *Civil Service Commission*, 392 2d 385 (1964). See Nobuyoshi Ashibe, *"Kokumin no seiji katsudo kinshi no ikensei"* and *"Iwayuru sarufutsu jiken"* in *GENDAI JINKEN RON* (1974).

81. *Japan* v. *Osawa*, 28 *KEISHŪ* (No. 9) 393 (Supreme Court, November 6, 1974). See Ashibe, *supra* note 71 and Beer, *Freedom*, 236-238.

82. Nobuyoshi Ashibe, *"Kempō hanrei riron no hensen to mondaiten,"* 49 *KŌHŌ KENKYŪ* 16 (1968).

83. 391 *U.S.* 367 (1968).

84. Toshimaru Kojo, *"Saikō saibansho hanrei 'sarufutsu jiken hanketsu' kaisetsu"* in 27 *HŌSŌ JIHŌ*, No. 11, 1975, 106-109, 119-20. On judicial research officers, see *supra*, II.

85. See Ashibe, *supra* note 71, 268-270.

86. *Japan* v. *Kono et al.*, 35 *KEISHŪ* (No. 4) 205 (Supreme Court, June 15, 1981). The first appellate court decision not to prohibit door-to-door visits was of the Hiroshima High Court, Matsue Branch (*HANREI JIHŌ*, No. 923, 141); see Beer, *Freedom*, 376-378. The Supreme Court applied the standard of the *Sarufutsu* case in deciding the issue of free speech.

87. See Beer, *Freedom*, Chapters 9 and 10; regarding defamation, see also *infra*, note 91.

88. For example, Toshiyoshi Miyazawa, *KEMPŌ II* (revised edition 1974), 366; and Isao Sato, *"Kinoteki 'kenetsu' gainen no igi to genkai"* in *NIHON KOKU KEMPŌ NO KADAI* (1968), 263.

89. Koji Sato, *"Hyogen no jiyu"* in *KEMPŌ II, JINKEN* (1978), 487. See also Nobuyoshi Ashibe, *NIHON KOKU KEMPŌ GAISETSU* (3d Ed. 1983), 179. Prior restraint was distinguished from "censorship" in Masanori Sakamoto, *PURAIBASHII KENRON* (1986), 109.

90. See *supra*, note 62.

91. For example, Yasuhiro Okudaira, *"Zeikan kensa no 'ken'etsu' sei to 'hyōgen no jiyū,'"* *JURISUTO* No. 830, 1985, 12, and Masanori Sakamoto, *"Zeikan kensa soshō,"* *JURISUTO*, No. 838, 1985, 18.

92. *Hoppō Journal* v. *Igarashi*, *HANREI TAIMUZU*, No. 605, 42 (Supreme Court, June 11, 1986). For details, see the symposium on this case in *JURISUTO*, No. 867, and Hirakawa, *"Meiyo kison hyōgen no shihōteki jizen yokusei, HŌGAKU KYŌSHITSU*, No. 73, 1986, 113.

93. Article 230-2 of the Criminal Code provides: "When the act mentioned in paragraph 1 [defamation] of the preceding Article is deemed to have been committed in allegation of facts having relation to the public interest and solely for the purpose of promoting the benefit of the public, it shall not be punished, if, upon inquiry into the facts, the truth thereof is established." This provision seeks to harmonize the relationship between the rights of private individuals and free speech. Even when the defendant cannot prove the truth of his statement or when he made a good faith mistake of fact, in these cases no crime has been committed. See, *Kōchi* v. *Japan*, 23

KEISHŲ (No. 7) 975 (Supreme Court, June 25, 1969); for a translation, see Itoh and Beer, 175. This landmark decision was deeply influenced by American law; see *New York Times Co.* v. *Sullivan*, 376 *U.S.* 254 (1964), and Beer, *Freedom*, 323-324.

94. Regarding these issues, see, Beer, *Freedom*, Chapter 8.

95. *Suminaga* v. *Sekiguchi*, 31 *MINSHŲ* (No. 4) 533 (Supreme Court, July 13, 1977).

96. See Norikatsu Sasagawa, "*Shinkyō no jiyū--saikōsaiban hanrei chūshin to shita shinkyō no jiyū no dōkō*," *KŌHŌ KENKYŲ*, No. 48, 1986, 53.

97. Nobuyoshi Ashibe, "*Kokka to Shūkyō*," *HŌGAKU KYŌSHITSU*, No. 52, 1985, 13; see *supra* I, at note 64 and II, 2 and 5.

98. "Special power relationship" refers to a public civil law concept whereby the government restricts the rights of those who have a special relationship with it (e.g., public workers, prisoners), persons controlled by the government.

DEMOCRATIC PEOPLE'S REPUBLIC OF KOREA
(NORTH KOREA)

*The Constitution of the Democratic People's
Republic of Korea*

Sung Yoon Cho

Introduction to the 1972 Constitution of the DPRK

After Japan surrendered to Allied Forces on August 15, 1945, ending World War II, Japanese colonial rule of Korea, which had lasted thirty-five years, came to an end. The country was divided along the 38th parallel by U.S. and Soviet occupation troops as an expedient measure to facilitate the surrender of Japanese forces positioned on the Korean peninsula. The Soviets later refused to comply with a 1947 United Nations resolution calling for Koreans to determine their own future through elected representatives and would not allow a U.N. Temporary Commission on Korea to observe nationwide elections and carry out the terms of the resolution in North Korea. As a result, the republic of Korea was established on August 15, 1948, its first constitution having been promulgated on July 17 of that year, while the Democratic People's Republic of Korea (DPRK) was founded on September 9, 1948, along the lines of the Stalinist model of a Communist state, with a Soviet Stalinist form of constitution adopted the day before. Since that time, North Korea has been under one-party (the Korean Workers Party) and one man (Kim Il-song) rule.

This essay will focus on the salient features of the 1972 Constitution of the DPRK, namely, its fundamental principles, provisions on state structure, administration of justice, and the basic rights and duties of citizens. A special attempt will also be made to compare the 1948 and 1972 North Korean Constitutions and to point out any new developments since the adoption of the latter. The essay will conclude with some summary remarks and a consideration of the broader issue of North Korea's prospects for the future. A comparison between the North Korean Constitution and those of other socialist countries, while instructive, lies beyond the scope of this paper.[1]

The first Constitution of the Democratic People's Republic of Korea (DPRK), which was patterned after the 1936 Soviet Constitution, was enacted on September 8, 1948. It consisted of 104 Articles in 10 Chapters and underwent several minor revisions in the years 1954-1962.[1] On December 27, 1972, a new, extensively revised Constitution was adopted, which consists of 149 Articles in 11 Chapters and remains in effect today. At the first session of the Fifth Supreme People's Assembly on December 25, 1972, Kim Il-song explained the need for constitutional reform:

> Our realities today urgently demand the establishment of a new Socialist Constitution to legally consolidate the tremendous achievements of our people in the socialist revolution and in building socialism and to lay down principles for the political, economic and cultural spheres of socialist society.[2]

Thus, the new Constitution that replaced the so-called "people's democratic" Constitution of 1948 was designed to suit the needs of a socialist system of government.

As for the content of the new socialist Constitution, Kim Il-song further declared that it

> ... correctly reflects the achievements made in the socialist revolution and in building socialism in our country, defines the principles to govern activities in the political, economic and cultural fields in socialist society and the basic rights and duties of citizens, and stipulates the composition and functions of the state organs and the principles of their activities.   It is to protect by law the socialist system and dictatorship of the proletariat ...[3]

The first three Chapters, embodying 48 Articles on politics, the economy, and culture, are a kind of theoretical preface that outlines the nature of the state under the new Constitution; the 1948 Constitution covered politics, the economy, and culture in a single chapter of 10 Articles, under the rubric "Fundamental Principles."   Chapter 4 outlines the basic rights and duties of citizens (Arts. 49-72), while Chapters 5 through 10 (Arts. 73-146) spell out the formal structure of government by defining the powers, functions, and responsibilities of state organs.   Chapter 11 (Arts. 147-149) deals with the country's emblem, flag, and capital, the latter now in Pyongyang, having been in Seoul under the 1948 Constitution.

The DPRK Constitution has been influenced by the United States Constitution only in that it is a single-document national constitution, of which the American document was the first and in that structures and lists of rights and powers are referred to as in the U.S. Constitution.   This chapter will focus on the salient features of the 1972 Constitution of the DPRK, namely, its fundamental principles, provisions on state structure, administration of justice, and the basic rights and duties of citizens. A special attempt will also be made to compare the 1948 and 1972 North Korean Constitutions and to point out any new developments since the adoption of the latter. The few similarities with the United States Constitution will be pointed out. A comparison between the North Korean Constitution and those of other socialist countries, while instructive, lies beyond the scope of this chapter.[4]

Fundamental Principles

Politics

Chapter 1 of the Constitution of the DPRK deals with politics, and begins with the declaration that the DPRK is a socialist state (Art. 1). The DPRK is described as a tripartite political entity comprised of a worker-peasant alliance led by the workers, socialist production relations, and an independent national economy (Art. 2). Article 7 states that "the sovereignty of the DPRK rests with the workers, peasants, soldiers and working intellectuals." This is in contrast to Article 2 of the 1948 Constitution, which simply provided that "the sovereignty of the DPRK resides in the people."

The new Constitution reflects the many changes made in North korean society and state policy in the intervening years between 1948 and its adoption in 1972. One of its key features is the settlement of a controversy over the "transition period" and its relation to the future of the dictatorship of the proletariat.[5] The 1972 Constitution was enacted at a time when there was debate as to whether or not the transition to socialism had been completed. If the transition were complete, some argued, perhaps a proletarian dictatorship and class struggle were no longer necessary. Premier Kim Il-song considered this stance to be "rightist," yet at the same time he disagreed with those who argued that the transition period should last until a totally classless society had been created and the distinction between workers and peasants eliminated. Kim attempted to resolve the issue by stating that the establishment of a socialist system did not in itself mean that there had been a complete victory. He declared that although the cause of socialism had been advanced in the years since 1958, the proletarian dictatorship should continue because a truly classless society had not yet been achieved.[6] Kim's view was codified in Article 10 of the Constitution, which states: "The Democratic People's Republic of Korea exercises the dictatorship of the proletariat...."

The nature of relations with other socialist states is a second major area of difference in spirit between the two constitutions. The 1948 document had been based on the Soviet Constitution of 1936 and was written at a time when Soviet influence was strong. After the Sino-Soviet split, however, there were pro-Soviet and pro-People's Republic of China factions in Pyongyang. Kim Il-song decided to develop an independent Marxist program that would enable Pyongyang to stand apart from both Moscow and Peking.[7] He called his policy, formulated in 1966, *chuch'e* [self-reliance]. It is written into Article 4 of the 1972 Constitution:

> The Democratic People's Republic of Korea is guided in its activity by the Juche *chuch'e* idea of the Worker's Party of Korea, a creative application of Marxism-Leninism to the conditions of our country.

Article 4 implies that the Party is superior to the state, thereby providing the constitutional grounds for party leadership over the country and its relations with other states.

The importance of the concept of *chuch'e* was further elaborated in the following terms:

> It *chuch'e* forms the ideological, theoretical, and methodological foundations of all the lines, policies, and activities of the Republic and indicates the fundamental principles for the most correct solution of all the problems arising in the revolutionary struggle and construction work. At the same time, it serves as a sure guarantee for the thorough maintenance of the revolutionary principles of independence, self-sustenance, and self-defense in all realms of politics, economy, and military affairs of the Republic.[8]

Other related concepts incorporated into the chapter on politics are the Ch'ongsan-ni method and the Ch'ollima Movement. the *Ch'ongsan-ni* method or *Ch'ongsan-ni* spirit is to apply to every aspect of political work "to guarantee that the upper units help the lower, the masses' opinions are respected and their conscious enthusiasm is roused by giving priority to political work, work with people" (Art. 12). The Ch'ongsan-ni method is said to have been developed by Kim Il-song after he stayed at the Ch'ongsan-ni cooperative farm outside Pyongyang in February 1960. A team of scholars and students had been sent to the farm to evaluate the difficulties facing farmers there. They attributed the problems to "commandism" in local government and to the actions of Party cadres; their solution was in part

Maoist: leaders should "go to the masses" for guidance and to discuss production problems.[9]

The Ch'ollima Movement is defined by the Constitution as "the general line in the building of socialism" designed to accelerate "socialist construction to the maximum" (Art. 13). The movement was initiated by Kim Il-song after he visited the Kangson Steel Mill in South P'yongan Province in February 1956. "Ch'ollima" means "Flying Horse," a reference to a legend about a flying horse that could gallop great distances in one day. The campaign was later directed towards agricultural as well as industrial workers, and special titles were given to work units and individuals whose performance was particularly impressive. The Flying Horse Movement is similar to Stalin's "*Stakhanovite*" Movement and reflects the same faith in human accomplishment as Mao's "Great Leap Forward."[10] The movement was initially intended to help accomplish the goals of the 1957 Five-Year Plan. In May 1959, it was renamed the Ch'ollima Work Team Movement. Although it remains in the Constitution, the Ch'ollima Movement has been largely replaced by another propaganda campaign called the Three Revolutions Team Movement, which began in February 1973.[11]

Since 1973, the Three Revolutions Team Movement has been viewed as the basic method to be used for building a society based on the idea of *chuch'e*. The movement was intended to eliminate the remnants of the former society through an acceleration of ideological (Art. 11), technical (Art. 25), and cultural (Art. 36) revolution. Kim Il-song's pivotal work on the subject, "Let Us Further Accelerate Socialist Construction by Powerfully Carrying Out the Three Revolutions" of March 3, 1975, is still being quoted. For example, a March 1985 newspaper article in *Nodong sinmun* stated that the work is still significant because in it Kim expounds the historical inevitability of the three revolutions, pointing out that ideological, technological, and cultural revolution constitute the three aspects of the general line of socialist and communist construction and should be continued by future generations.

The Economy

Chapter 2 of the 1972 Constitution, in 17 Articles, deals exclusively with economic matters, in contrast to the 1948 Constitution, which lacked a separate chapter on the subject of the economy. Article 2 declares that the DPRK rests on the foundation of an independent national economy, defined by the Constitution as a planned economy based on socialist laws of economic development (Art. 31) achieved through the "historic task" of industrialization

(Art. 24). Three important features of Chapter 2 are the new definition of property, the introduction of the Taean work system, and the abolition of taxation.

The Constitution recognizes three types of ownership: state property, cooperative property, and private property. State property is the property of the entire people (Art. 19). It includes all natural resources, major factories and enterprises, harbors, banks, means of transport, and communications facilities. In theory, there is no limit on what the state may own. Thus, state property differs from cooperative property and private property which are limited. Cooperative property, or property of cooperative organizations includes land, draught animals, farm implements, fishing boats, and buildings, as well as small and medium factories and enterprises (Art. 20). Cooperative ownership is a form of ownership of transitional character; it is bound to be converted gradually into ownership by the entire people (Art. 21). Private property is property for the personal use of the working class. It primarily consists of "the products from the inhabitants' supplementary husbandry, including those from the small [vegetable] plots of cooperative farmers" (Art. 22). this property is derived mainly from socialist distribution according to work done and from additional benefits accorded by the state and society. Under the 1977 Land Law of the DPRK,[12] the size of family plots is 20-30 *p'yong* (66-99 square meters).

Since the 1972 Constitution states that all means of production are owned by the state and cooperative organizations (Art. 18), the scope of private ownership is severely limited. The 1948 Constitution allowed a certain amount of private ownership by those who worked the land or operated small-scale means of production as well as private ownership by small-scale enterprises and commercial organizations; the 1972 Constitution entirely abandoned recognition of this kind of personal property.

The Taean work system, the basic economic model for the nation, is described in Article 30, which provides:

> The State directs and manages the nation's economy through the Taean work system, an advanced socialist form of economic management whereby the economy is operated and managed scientifically and rationally on the basis of the collective strength of the producer masses....

It was implemented as the system for management of state enterprises in December 1961. Its name derives from a visit made by Kim Il-song to the Taean Electrical Appliance Plant in 1961. The Taean work system has been described as an adaptation of the Ch'ongsan-ni method (a form of management designed for agriculture) to industry. Workers are in theory to become involved in the process of management. While production goals are still set by planning officials, the methods of implementation of those goals are supposedly to be determined by collective leadership.[13]   This system is designed to replace the "one-man" management system of enterprises which preceded it. The latter had been blamed for such administrative inefficiencies as duplication of effort, delays in procurement, and excessive "bureaucratism." The Taean system has been combined with an effort to bring political control into factory leadership, so that the latter becomes a vehicle for Party control. Thus, each factory is run by a Party committee.

The third major area provided for in Chapter 2 of the North Korean Constitution is the abolition of all taxes. The first step in the process had been imposed by the Decision Concerning Agricultural Tax-in-Kind and originally set at the rate of 25 percent; it had been reduced to an average of 20.1 percent, then further reduced to 8.4 percent, and finally eliminated in 1966.[14]   North Korean authorities frequently cited the abolition of the agricultural tax-in-kind as evidence of the emancipation of the peasant. All other taxes were abolished on April 1, 1974, by virtue of a law adopted eleven days earlier. The regime then boasted that North Korea was the first country in the world to be without a taxation system.

The abolition of taxes was part of the implementation of the Constitution of 1972, which states in Article 33 that "the State abolishes taxation, a relic of the old society." Details of the implementation plan can be found in the report of the Vice-President at the time, delivered at the Third Session of the Fifth Supreme People's Assembly.[15]   It was at that session, on March 21, 1974, that the Law on the Complete Abolition of the Taxation System was adopted.[16]

Culture

Chapter 3 of the 1972 Constitution, on the subject of culture, was not in the 1948 version. It reflects the political themes of the early 1970s in North Korea by stressing the *chuch'e* principle and declaring that the DPRK "builds a true people's principle and declaring that the DPRK "builds a true people's revolutionary culture which serves the socialist working people" (Art. 37). Some of the provisions in the chapter deal with the educational system, establishing a program of one year of universal pre-school education plus 10 years of universal, compulsory, free education (Arts. 43, 41). In contrast, the one Article on education in the 1948 Constitution had only called for universal and compulsory education at the elementary level (Art. 18). Both documents mention stipends for students at higher levels (Art. 18, Constitution of 1948, and Art. 42, Constitution of 1972).

Other topics covered in the chapter on culture include strengthening scientific research and creative cooperation (Art. 44), developing "Juche-oriented, revolutionary literature and art, national in form and socialist in content" (Art. 45), and popularizing physical culture and training (Art. 47). Article 48 stipulates that the state will develop universal free medical service and stresses preventive medical care.

The chapter as a whole emphasizes nationalistic values, and Article 46 in particular invokes those values in reference to the Korean language, stating that the latter must be defended, against "the policy of the imperialists and their stooges to destroy it."

State Structure

The Supreme People's Assembly

Under the 1972 Constitution, the Supreme People's Assembly (SPA), a unicameral legislative body, is "the highest organ of State power" (Art. 73). Its deputies are elected to a four-year term by "universal, equal, and direct suffrage by secret ballot" (Arts. 74, 75). The deputies comprise representatives of the workers, peasants, soldiers, and working intellectuals.[17] Usually two regular sessions of about three to five days' duration are convened annually by the Assembly's Standing Committee. Extraordinary sessions may be convened when the Standing Committee deems it necessary, or by vote of one-third of the total number of deputies (Art. 77).

The SPA exercises legislative power by adopting or amending the Constitution, laws, and ordinances. In addition, it formulates the basic principles of domestic and foreign policy, approves the state economic plan and national budget, and decides on questions of war and peace. The SPA also elects the President of the DPRK, and elects and recalls other top government officials, such as Vice-Presidents of the DPRK, the Secretary and members of the Central People's Committee members of the SPA's Standing Committee the Premier of the Administration Council, the Vice-Chairman of the National Defense Commission, and the Presidents of the Central Court and the Central Procurator's Office. However, the Vice-Presidents of the DPRK, the Secretary and members of the Central People's Committee, the Premier, and the Vice-Chairman of the National Defense Commission can only be elected or recalled upon the recommendation of the President of the DPRK (Art. 76).

Items to be deliberated are submitted by the President, the Central People's Committee, the Standing Committee of the SPA, the Administration Council, or the Assembly's own deputies (Art. 80). Decisions are made by a majority vote of the delegates present, with the exception of constitutional amendments, which require a two-thirds vote of all SPA deputies (Art. 82). At present, a budget committee, a bill committee, and a credentials committee within the SPA assist in carrying out its work.

The SPA's constitutional powers and functions appear to be manifold, but in actual practice the SPA's legislative duty is simply to ratify decisions made by the Korean Workers' Party and the Central People's Committee.[18] Even under the 1948 Constitution, the SPA had no independent initiative; its legislative actions were always subject to Party policy.[19]

The Standing Committee of the SPA

The Standing Committee of the SPA, elected by the full Assembly, serves as its permanent body (Art. 85). It is comprised of a Chairman, three Vice-Chairmen, a Secretary and 18 members (as of April 1985).[20] The Chairman and Vice-Chairmen of the SPA Standing Committee concurrently hold the same positions in the SPA. Under the 1948 Constitution, when the Assembly was not in session, its Standing Committee was the highest government organ; the clause containing this provision was deleted from the 1972 Constitution. Among other powers, the Standing Committee under the former Constitution could promulgate laws, issue pardons, appoint and recall envoys, ratify or abrogate treaties, and receive foreign envoys. Its Chairman served as head of state. With the implementation of the 1972 Constitution, however, these powers were transferred to the newly-created office of President of the DPRK and the new Central People's Committee. Thus the 1972 Constitution reflects the reality of President Kim Il-song's strong one-man rule.

Even though the Standing Committee's power was curtailed by the creation of the office of President and the Central People's Committee, under the 1972 Constitution the Standing Committee is still to examine and decide on bills and to amend laws and ordinances when the SPA is not in session. It also interprets the laws and ordinances already in force, convenes the regular and extraordinary sessions of the SPA, works with deputies to the SPA, works with committees of the SPA when the SPA is not in session, conducts the election of deputies to the SPA, prepares for the election of deputies to the local people's assemblies, and issues its own decisions (Arts. 87, 88). In addition, it has been accorded a new power, that of electing and recalling the judges and people's assessors of the Central Court (Art. 87, item 9).

The Presidency

The office of President (*chusok*) was newly created in the Constitution, which states that the President is head of state and represents the DPRK (Art. 89). the 1948 Constitution was silent about who was head of state; following Soviet practice, the Chairman of the Standing Committee of the SPA had served concurrently as head of state. Thus under the 1972 Constitution, the separation between head of state and head of the government was eliminated. The President, elected by the SPA for a four-year term (Art. 90), is accorded all the powers normally held by a strong president.[21] Kim Il-song was elected as the first President of the DPRK immediately after the enactment of the new Constitution. Although in fact Kim Il-song also serves as head of the Workers' Party, there is no formal tie between the positions of President of the DPRK and Chairman of the Party.

The President is Supreme Commander of the Armed Forces and Chairman of the National Defense Commission. He promulgates laws and ordinances enacted by the SPA, the decrees of the Central People's Committee, and the decisions of the Standing Committee of the SPA. He directly guides the Central People's Committee and convenes and presides over the Administration Council. The President also has the authority to issue his own "orders," to grant special pardons, to ratify or abrogate treaties, and to receive foreign envoys (Arts. 91-97). As was noted earlier, some of these functions had been performed by the Standing Committee of the SPA under the 1948 Constitution.

The President is in theory accountable to the SPA for his actions (Art. 98), but there are no constitutional provisions that enable the SPA to enforce this Article. Unlike other top government officials, the President is not subject to recall or removal. Nor are there any constitutional provisions that limit the number of terms he can serve. It should be noted that at the Sixth Party Congress, held in October 1980, Kim Chong-il, the son of Kim Il-song, was installed as the second most powerful man in North Korea as part of Kim Il-song's plan to establish a dynasty, with his son as heir-apparent, without regard to constitutional provisions.[22]

Without providing any further elaboration of their role, the Constitution simply states that the Vice-Presidents "assist" the President in his work (Art. 99). Unlike their counterparts in the United States, North Korean Vice-Presidents are not to succeed the President upon the latter's incapacitation or death. The role of the Vice-President is purely ceremonial.

The Central People's Committee

The Central People's Committee (CPC), which was newly established under the 1972 Constitution, is the "highest leadership organ of State power" (Art. 100) and the top decision-making body. According to *State and Social System of the DPRK*, a 1984 North Korean publication, the CPC serves as the permanent "highest leadership organ of State power" when the SPA is not in session.[23] It consists of the President of the DPRK, three Vice-Presidents of the DPRK, a Secretary, and 13 members (as of April 1985). All of these officials and members (except the President) are elected by the SPA for a term of four years on the recommendation of the President, and they may also be recalled by the SPA on the recommendation of the President.

In addition to the powers that were transferred to it from the SPA and its Standing Committee under the 1972 Constitution, the CPC has, among other powers, the power to shape domestic and foreign policy; to direct the work of the Administration Council, local people's assemblies and committees, and judicial and procuratorial organs; to supervise the enforcement of the Constitution, laws, and ordinances of the SPA, the orders of the President of the DPRK, and the decrees, decisions, and directives of other state organs that contravene them; to institute or change administrative divisions; to declare a state of war; to issue orders for mobilization in case of emergency (Art. 103); and to adopt or issue its own decrees, decisions, and orders (Art. 104).

The CPC originally established four commissions, on domestic policy, foreign policy, national defense, and justice and security (Art. 105, para. 1). By April 1985, four more commissions, on economic policy, legislation, parliamentary groups, and state inspection, had been added.[24] The members of these commissions are appointed or recalled by the CPC (Art. 105, para. 2), with the exception of the Vice-Chairmen of the National Defense Commission, who are elected by the SPA on recommendation of the President. In general terms, the Commission resembles special assistants and their staffs who serve in the Office of the President of the United States.

The CPC is known as a "Super Cabinet" that exercises a mixture of executive, legislative, and judicial powers. According to Professor Chong-Sik Lee, it was created to supplant "the myth" of the superior role of the legislature and "the fiction" that Party and State have separate powers and authority, so that simply by doing away with duplication of effort, greater efficiency would be achieved.[25] Kim Il-song made reference to the creation of the Central People's Committee and the people's committees in a speech he delivered on December 25, 1972:

> The new State structure is built in such a way that the activities of administrative bodies are always supervised and controlled by the masses of the people. Under the new State structure ... the People's Committees are separated from administrative bodies, and the former, which are composed of representatives of the workers, peasants, soldiers and working intellectuals, are to perform the function of exercising day-to-day supervision and control over the latter's activities so that the functionaries of the administrative bodies are able to do away with bureaucracy in their work and serve the people better as their servants.[26]

A North Korean writer has commented that the separation of the people's committees from administrative organs provided for in the 1972 Constitution aimed at strengthening the monolithic leadership of Kim Il-song over state organs and all state activities, thereby accelerating control of the whole society by the *chuch'e* idea.

It should be noted that there is considerable overlap in membership between the new Central People's Committee and the Politburo of the Party, with members of the latter monopolizing membership in the former.[28] It is through this close relationship that the Party maintains its power, rather than on the basis of any direct statement made in the constitutional description of state structure.

The Administrative Council

Under the 1972 Constitution, the functions of the central government are divided between the CPC, which makes policy and supervises its implementation, and the Administration Council, which carries out the policy. Under the 1948 Constitution, the Cabinet, with Kim Il-song as its head (Premier), had exercised unlimited power by performing both the policy-making and policy-executing functions. The Cabinet was renamed the Administration Council under the 1972 Constitution.

The Council, defined by the 1972 Constitution as "the administrative and executive body of the highest organ of State power" (Art. 107), is composed of the Premier, Vice-Premiers, ministers, vice-ministers, commission

chairmen, and other necessary members (Art. 108). The Premier is elected
or recalled by the SPA on the recommendation of the President; other
members are appointed or removed by the CPC on the recommendation of
the Premier (Art. 103). The Council is responsible to the SPA, the President,
and the CPC for its work. Since its decision-making power was taken away
by the CPC, the Council is merely an administrative body that carries out
decisions made by other organs. Ultimately, the Council and Premier are
under the direct control of the President.[29]

The Council performs its day-to-day administrative functions by
directing the work of ministries and other organs directly under its authority.
Among other powers, it has the power to conclude treaties, guide defense
work, maintain public order, and safeguard the rights of citizens. It also has
the power to formulate the state plans for economic development and their
implementation and to adopt measures to strengthen the monetary and
banking systems (Art. 109). In order to carry out its work, the Council is
authorized to adopt decisions and issue directives (Art. 112).

Local Organs of State Power

In addition to performing the traditional functions of local government,
the various units of local administration in North Korea also serve as organs
of economic production and management. The 1972 Constitution provides for
the carrying out of these functions by establishing People's Assemblies,
People's Committees, and Administrative Committees in the provinces (and
in municipalities directly under central authority), cities or districts, and
counties. Thus, the county is the lowest unit of local government; local organs
that were established under the 1948 Constitution in towns and villages have
been abolished. At the village level today there are no local organs of
government;[30] each village has been placed under the supervision of a
Cooperative Farm Management Committee. Local organs at the county level
are also charged with providing administrative and other types of guidance to
the villages and to workers' settlements.

People's Assemblies have the power to approve local economic
development plans and budgets and to elect or recall local officials, including
judges and people's assessors, at the corresponding level. The Assemblies are
also empowered to supersede inappropriate decisions and directives issued by
local organs at corresponding and lower levels (Art. 118). However, the
People's Assemblies only meet in regular session once or twice a year. An
extraordinary session may be convened when the People's Committee at the

corresponding level deems it necessary or at the request of at least one-third of the total number of deputies (Art. 119).

Under the 1972 Constitution, the authority to make and to execute policy is divided between the People's Committees and the Administrative Committees, along the lines of the changes made in the central government structure. According to *State and Social System of the DPRK*, however, "The People's Committee is the local organ of state power when the People's Assembly is not in session and at the same time serves as the administrative and executive body."[31] No mention is made of the existence of the Administrative Committee, and so it appears that the People's Committee has taken over its function.[32]

According to the same source, the People's Committee has additional powers, probably as a result of the demise of the Administrative Committee.[33] Now the People's Committee implements the decisions and directives of the People's Assembly at the corresponding level and of the People's Committee at a higher level; convenes the sessions of the People's Assembly; and carries out work in connection with the election of deputies to the People's Assembly. Moreover, the People's Committee promotes adherence to the law-abiding life so that workers and all citizens will obey law and order conscientiously; organizes and carries out all administrative affairs at the local level; and prepares the local plan and adopts implementing measures as part of the development of the national economy. The Committee also compiles the local budget and adopts measures for its implementation; adopts measures to maintain public order, protect the interests of the state, and safeguard the rights of citizens; and directs the work of state institutions, enterprises, and cooperative organizations within its jurisdiction (Arts. 125 and 130).

The People's Committee is composed of a chairman, vice-chairman, secretary, and other members (Art. 124). It is accountable for its activities to the People's Assembly at the corresponding level and to the People's Committee at a higher level (Art. 127).

Elections

The 1972 Constitution provides in Article 74 that all People's Assembly representatives are to be elected by universal suffrage and by secret ballot. The elections that have been held thus far, however, have been *pro forma*, with only one Party-approved candidate running for each seat. It is reported that 100 percent of registered voters participate in the elections and that all the approved candidates win. Thus elections are simply exercises to demonstrate the Party's consolidated control rather than true political forums.

The constitutional provision for the secret ballot is essentially ignored. For example, coverage of the February 24, 1985, election of members to the provincial, municipal, and county People's Assemblies stressed the participation of Party and government and revealed which prominent members of the Korean Workers' Party Central Committee had voted for which candidates, described by district and name.[34]   Since there was only one candidate for each slot, this information could hardly be regarded as real news.   It was doubtless included in the Pyongyang domestic news service report as an indication of Party strength.

Administration of Justice

Courts

Unlike the 1948 Constitution, the 1972 Constitution specifies that the duty of the courts is to safeguard the power of the workers and peasants, the socialist system, the property of state and cooperative organizations, and the constitutional rights, lives, and property of the people (Art. 136). The courts must guarantee that all state and cooperative institutions and individuals observe the law and struggle against class enemies and lawbreakers, execute judgments, and conduct notarial work. As in other Communist countries, in addition to punishing lawbreakers, the courts are expected to educate criminals and the public in observance of the law and loyalty to the country. Moreover, the court is officially described as "a powerful weapon of the proletarian dictatorship which executes the judicial policy of the Party and the State."[35]

The Central Court (formerly the Supreme Court), located in Pyongyang, is the court of last resort and consists of criminal, civil, and arbitration chambers. Under the Code of Criminal Procedure,[36] the Central Court has original jurisdiction over cases of especially grave offenses against state power and over crimes committed in the course of duty by judges and other high-level elected officials as well as over other cases, at its discretion. It has jurisdiction over appeals or protests against decisions of provincial or special courts and may examine extraordinary appeals or petitions for retrial lodged by the President of the Central Court or the Procurator-General against cases decided by a lower court. In the case of extraordinary appeals or petitions, a panel of three judges hears the case and a procurator from the Central Procurator's Office also participates.[37] A decision or ruling of the Central Court may not be appealed except upon an extraordinary appeal lodged by the President of the Central Court or the Procurator-General at a plenary session of the Court. All the judges of the Court and the Procurator-General are required to be present at plenary sessions.[38]

The Central Court supervises the judicial work of all the courts (Art. 141, para. 2). Provisions that are new in the 1972 Constitution state that the Central Court is accountable for its activities to the Supreme People's Committee (Art. 142, para. 1) and carries out its judicial functions under the direction of the President and the Central People's Committee (Art. 103, item 3).

The provincial courts also consist of criminal, civil, and arbitration chambers and have original jurisdiction over cases involving important offenses such as crimes against the state and grave crimes against individuals. They serve as courts of second instance, hearing appeals of decisions rendered by the courts of first instance, the people's courts, which are at the city or county level. the people's courts have jurisdiction over most criminal and civil cases. Although North Korea has three levels of courts, it has adopted a two-trial system, which allows only one appeal.

The original Court Organization Law had established two kinds of special courts, military and transport, but the Transport Court, which heard cases of crimes committed against rail, land, and water transport systems, was abolished in August 1958. Under the 1972 Constitution, there are again two special courts, the military courts and the railroad courts. The military courts have jurisdiction over all crimes committed by members of the armed forces or security organs of the Ministry of Social Safety. Through a series of laws passed during the Korean War, their jurisdiction was broadened to cover nonmilitary cases in wartime. The military courts are to try cases within 24 hours after arrest and the sentences imposed are subject only to extraordinary appeal. The railroad courts have jurisdiction over criminal cases involving rail and water transport workers.[39]

The functions of the arbitration chambers of the Central Court and the provincial courts require explanation. An arbitrator assigned to each chamber hears disputes between state enterprises and/or other social organizations in matters involving the non-fulfillment of contracts as well as injuries and compensation demands arising therefrom. The arbitrator decides a case by imposing a penalty or fine for the breach of contract. However, the arbitrator is not allowed to handle disputes connected with the collection of administrative fines, which are usually settled through administrative procedures, nor is he to handle tort claim disputes that are not in regard to contracts.[40]

According to Article 134 of the 1972 Constitution, the judges and people's assessors of the Central Court are elected to terms of four years by the Standing Committee of the Supreme People's Assembly; judges and people's assessors of provincial and people's courts are elected to four-year and two-year terms, respectively, by the people's assemblies at the corresponding level. The 1948 Constitution lacked such a provision. People's assessors are laymen elected to share the bench with a professional judge in trials of first instance (Art. 137). Cases of second instance are handled by a bench of three judges.[41] In theory the people's assessors enjoy the same rights as judges and participate in deciding questions of both law and fact. The president and judges of the special court are appointed or removed by the Central Court (Art. 135). Neither legal education nor practical legal experience is required for judgeship.

The courts play an educational role in that most trials are public and may be reported in the press. When state secrets are involved, or when otherwise required by law, the trial is closed to the public (Art. 138); the decision, however, must still be announced. In some cases in which counter-revolutionary crimes are involved, demonstration trials or mass public trials are held for their propagandist effect. Since public attendance at such trials is compulsory, they are held at sites carefully chosen by the Workers' Party for maximum political advantage.[42]

Procuracy

Unlike the 1948 Constitution, the 1972 Constitution provides that "Investigation and prosecution are conducted under the coordinated leadership of the Central Procurator's Office, and all procurator's offices are subordinated to their higher offices and the Central Procurator's Office" (Art. 145). To ensure that the procurator will not be influenced by local organs of the state or by local conditions, the structure of the procuracy is completely centralized; unlike judges, who are elected by the Standing Committee of the Supreme People's Assembly and the People's Assemblies, procurators at all levels are appointed by the Central Procurator's Office. At present, there are procurators' offices in the cities and counties in which there are people's courts, provincial procurator's offices in each province, special procurator's offices, and the Central Procurator's Office in Pyongyang. Another provision that is new in the 1972 Constitution states that the Central Procurator's Office is accountable to the Supreme People's Assembly, the President and the Central People's Committee (Art. 146).

Like its counterparts in other Communist countries, the North Korean procuracy is responsible for the general supervision of legality, serving as the watchdog of the central authority. Article 144, item 1, of the 1972

Constitution provides that the procurator's office will exercise supervision to ensure that state laws are properly observed by state and corporate organizations and by individuals. Under item 2 of the same Article, the procuracy is responsible for determining that the decisions and directives of state organs are not in conflict with the Constitution or the laws, ordinances, orders, decrees, decisions, and directives issued by the Supreme People's Assembly, the President, the Central People's Committee, the Standing Committee of the Supreme People's Assembly, or the Administration Council. Under Article 144, item 3, the procuracy has the functions of judicial supervision, exposure and indictment of criminals, and prosecution of cases for the state in court proceedings against citizens accused of crimes. Procurators are to protect thereby the present social system, the property of the state and of cooperative organizations, and the constitutional rights of individuals. Article 144, it may be noted, is a totally new provision in the 1972 Constitution. The procuracy is officially described there as "a powerful weapon of the proletarian dictatorship that executes the judicial policy of the Party and the State."[43]

The procurator's powers in regard to criminal proceedings, coupled with its general supervisory power over the legality of operations of all state organs, make it potentially one of the strongest organs of the state. Although procurators are involved in all stages of the arrest, indictment, and prosecution process, they do not have any control over the actions of the secret police, and thus they have no role in the preparation of indictments or the prosecution of those arrested by the secret police on suspicion of committing political crimes.

Lawyers

Article 138 of the 1972 Constitution provides that "the accused is guaranteed the right of a defense." Without mentioning specifically how and to what extent this right is accorded in actual practice, an official publication of the North Korean Academy of Sciences stated in 1963 that the right to counsel is thoroughly guaranteed to the accused.[44]

The 1948 Regulation Concerning Lawyers, which superseded a 1947 regulation of the same title, reorganized the existing lawyers' association as a voluntary social organization in Pyongyang and each province, under the supervision of the courts.[45] Membership in the people's bar is granted by the standing committee of each association. The statutory requirements for membership are legal education or practical experience working in judicial organs.[46]

Only members of a lawyers' association can practice law. According to Article 3 of the 1948 Regulation, a lawyer has three major functions. First, he provides the public with legal assistance and interpretation of the law, in compliance with an individual client's request. Second, he prepares petitions, contracts, agreements, and other legal documents for individuals, groups, state agencies, and enterprises. Third, he acts as defense counsel for the accused, the appellant, or the petitioner in a criminal case or as the representative of the plaintiff, the defendant, or other interested parties in a civil case.

Above all, the fundamental duty of the lawyer is to cooperate with the court in discovering the truth, in promoting justice, and in safeguarding the interests of the state and the people against criminals, and thereby defend and implement the policies of the Workers' Party. In the final analysis, a lawyer must become a good Party lawyer who knows how to defend Party interests on the basis of the principle of proletarian dictatorship.[47]

In North Korea, the practice of law is not regarded as a lucrative profession. The lawyer practices in an office operated by the lawyers' association, which pays a fixed salary. The amount of a client's fee is determined on the basis of a contractual agreement with the lawyers' association and the fee is paid directly to the group.[48]

The Socialist Law-Abiding Life Guidance Committee

In the 1972 Constitution, there are two articles that deal with socialist legality:

> *Article 17.* The law of the Democratic People's Republic of Korea reflects the will and interests of the workers, peasants and other working people, and it is consciously observed by all State organs, enterprises, social cooperative organizations and citizens.

> *Article 67.* Citizens must strictly observe the laws of the State and the socialist norms of life and socialist rules of conduct.

Kim Il-song elaborated on this basic definition of socialist legality in 1977, when he delivered a speech, "Let Us Further Strengthen People's Government," which summarized the enforcement of the 1972 Socialist Constitution over the five years since its adoption, at the First Session of the Sixth Supreme People's Assembly on December 15. In discussing the elimination of bureaucracy, Kim originated the concept of the "socialist law-abiding life."[49] This refers to the policy, based on the *chuch'e* idea, of strengthening the legal system and publicizing laws through mass campaigns.

There are two aspects to the "socialist law-abiding life": respect for public authority and conformity to "socialist norms" of life. According to a North Korean writer, "socialist law-abiding life" is defined as "social life that requires all members of socialist society to thoroughly obey legal norms and rules and act accordingly."[50] In other words, all the members are required to thoroughly obey legal norms and rules enacted by the socialist state (dictatorship of the proletariat) in order to lead an orderly, socialist law-abiding life.

In 1977, socialist law-abiding life committees were established in the Central People's Committee and in the people's committees at all levels of the provinces, cities, and counties. They are ad hoc committees that meet once a month. The committees usually consist of six people, including a chairman and a vice-chairman, who are selected from the procuracy, the social safety agency (police), and the people's committee of the district concerned; no members are selected from the court. The president of the people's committee serves concurrently as the chairman of the Socialist Law-Abiding Life Guidance Committee.[51]

One of the important duties of these committees is to control by means of law the leading personnel of state and economic institutions in order to prevent them from abusing their power. The committees also work to "create a revolutionary atmosphere of observance of the law in the whole society."[52] The committee members and staff workers (called law commentators) are to make commentaries on particular laws and disseminate legal information to the citizens in the area, thereby strengthening the education of the people in the spirit of obedience to law.[53]

The socialist law-abiding life committees are further empowered to supervise and control the law-abiding status of all the organizations, work places, social groups, and citizens in their jurisdiction. They are thus a powerful means of implementing state power. All state inspection agencies, the procuracy, and the police are subject to the oversight of the committees in the execution and enforcement of the law.[54] The committees may directly handle law enforcement and inspection or entrust these functions to law-enforcement agencies. They may demand necessary data from various other agencies. They also work to strengthen education of workers in the provisions of the Constitution and laws.[55]

Since the socialist law-abiding life committees are empowered to supervise the observance of the law by all government and economic institutions, they apply strict legal sanctions against those who break laws and regulations. The committees handle all types of violations, short of crimes, and impose administrative sanctions.[56]

Basic Rights and Duties of Citizens

Basic Rights

There is a chapter on the basic rights and duties of citizens of the DPRK in both the 1948 and the 1972 Constitutions.[57] Freedoms of speech, the press, association, assembly, and demonstration are guaranteed today under Article 53 of the 1972 document. Citizens are also guaranteed inviolability of person and home, privacy of correspondence (Art. 64), and freedom of scientific, literary, and artistic pursuits (Art. 60). Able-bodied citizens have the "right to work," the right to choose occupations according to their skills, and the right to rest (Arts. 56 and 57). Free medical care and material assistance for those unable to work due to old age, illness, or handicap are also guaranteed in the Constitution (Art. 58).

There are some important differences between the 1948 and 1972 Constitutions in their provisions on rights of citizens. In the statement on the rights to vote and to stand for office in the former document, the influence of the times can be seen. Thus, while both documents extend the rights to elect and to be elected to all citizens except the insane and those deprived of political rights by court order, Article 12 of the 1948 version also excludes "pro-Japanese elements"; by 1972, such an exclusion was no longer considered necessary. The only other difference is that in the 1972 document (Art. 52) the voting age was lowered, from 18 years of age to 17.

There are provisions on religious freedom in both Constitutions, but the language used in the 1972 Constitution makes the guarantee seem less secure. Where originally Article 14 mentioned the "freedom of religious belief and of conducting religious services," Article 54 now gives citizens "freedom of religious belief and freedom to make anti-religious propaganda," leaving out any reference to the holding of services. There is thus an apparent imbalance between the passive right to believe and the active right to make propaganda against religion.

Both Constitutions mention the equal legal status of women and extend special protection to mothers, children, and the family unit. The 1972 Constitution also provides as follows:

The State affords special protection to mothers and children through maternity leave, shortened working hours for mothers of large families, a wide network of maternity hospitals, nurseries and kindergartens and other measures. The State frees women from the heavy burden of household chores and provides every condition for them to participate in public life (Art. 62).

This Constitution does not, however, include the statement that was in Article 23 of the 1948 document on the equal status of children born out of wedlock.

The 1972 Constitution (Art. 61) also extends special protection to "revolutionary fighters, the families of revolutionary and patriotic martyrs, the families of People's Army men, and disabled soldiers...."

One protection that had been included in the 1948 Constitution (Art. 19) but which was dropped in the 1972 version was the freedom to run medium and small-scale industrial enterprises and to engage in commerce. This change can most logically be attributed to Kim Il-song's position on the state of progress toward socialism. Indeed, Article 50 now includes the statement that the "rights and freedoms of citizens increase with the consolidation and development of the socialist system."[58]

Basic Duties

Both the 1948 and the 1972 Constitutions have provisions on the duties of citizens of North Korea. The difference between them can be ascribed to political developments of the intervening years. The 1948 document included the duty to pay taxes; under the 1972 Constitution, taxes were abolished. While in 1948 citizens had the duty to abide by the Constitution and the law (Art. 27), in 1972 this was expanded to include observance of "the socialist norm of life and the socialist rules of conduct" (Art. 67). Furthermore, citizens are now required to "display a high degree of collectivist spirit" and to "cherish" their collectives and organizations (Art. 68). Other new duties include preserving state and communal property (Art. 71). There is more ideological jargon in the provisions on citizens' duties in the 1972 Constitution, reflecting the slogans of the day. As a result, the duties of citizens are vaguely worded, so much so that these provisions could easily be used as a basis for suppressing opposition.[59]

Thus the Constitution outlines a wide range of rights, but in reality, with the government totally controlled by the Workers' Party, the state can freely control its citizens. Punishment of any "political crime," for instance, is severe. Free speech and freedom of the press may be guaranteed in one section of the Constitution, but elsewhere in the same document, North Koreans are required to observe "the socialist norm of life and the socialist rules of conduct." Moreover, Article 49 states that "rights and duties of citizens are based on the collectivist principle of 'one for all and all for one.'" This means that "the group or social interest is put before the individual interest, and individual benefit is subject to social benefit" in all aspects of social life.[60] Presumably, it also means that citizens are free only to the extent that they abide by the collectivist norms of life imposed by the Workers' Party.

Concluding Remarks

Constitutions of Communist states typically are summations of existing political, economic, and social systems. The 1972 North Korean Constitution is no exception; it reflects the developments in North Korean society of the preceding two decades. The Constitution contains, *interalia*, two key articles that define the nature of the state by providing that the DPRK exercises the dictatorship of the proletariat and that it is guided by the *chuch'e* idea of the Workers' Party. The Constitution also incorporates the Ch'ollima Movement, the Ch'ongsan-ni method, the Taean work system, and a new definition of property. All these programs and concepts had been developed in the years since the previous Constitution.

In addition, the Constitution contains the germs of future socioeconomic programs. For example, the Three Revolutions Team Movement, inaugurated in 1973, the year after the Constitution was adopted, is foreshadowed by several articles. The "three revolutions" are those of ideology, technology, and culture. Article 11 prescribes "intensifying the ideological revolution," Article 25 claims that the "State accelerates the technical revolution," and Article 36 provides for "carrying out the cultural revolution." This Three Revolutions Team movement has been viewed in North Korea in the last twelve years as the basic method to be used to build a society based on the idea of *chuch'e*.

The new Constitution changed the definition of the governing structure of the DPRK to more closely match reality. The central authority structure now consists of the SPA, the SPA's Standing Committee, the President of the DPRK, the CPC, a policy-making organ, and the Administration Council, a policy-executing organ. The Presidency and the CPC were new creations and the Administration Council was renamed in the 1972 document. The SPA is defined by the Constitution as "the highest organ of State power," whereas the CPC is "the highest leadership organ of State power." It is thus difficult to determine purely by constitutional definition the hierarchical order of these two bodies. *State and Social System of the DPRK*, mentioned earlier, seems to clarify the matter; it states that the CPC serves as the highest leadership organ when the SPA is not in session. Under the 1948 Constitution, the SPA Standing Committee had been the highest organ of power whenever the SPA was not in session, and its chairman served as head of state.

Under the 1972 Constitution, the supremacy of the legislature has apparently been discarded and there is no separation of powers. The new CPC is the backbone of the entire state structure and as supreme organ exercises a mixture of executive, legislative, and judicial powers. The President, who heads the CPC, is also head of state, chief of the Party, and like the President of the United States, Commander-in-Chief. The court and procuracy are each officially described as a "powerful weapon of the proletarian dictatorship which executes the judicial policy of the Party and the state." They are controlled and supervised by the CPC.

Although the authority to make and to execute policy is divided between local People's Committees and local Administrative Committees under the 1972 Constitution, according to *State and Social System of the DPRK*, it appears that the People's Committees have now taken over the functions of the Administrative Committees.

The impact of the Constitution as a whole is to further the authoritarian ends of the regime. Human rights under the 1972 Constitution are different from those provided for in a liberal democracy, as they are based on the collectivist principle. The duties of citizens as outlined in the document reinforce the idea of the value of the communal good over that of the individual. Article 67 of the Constitution reads, "Citizens must strictly observe the laws of the State and the socialist norm of life and the socialist norm of life and the socialist rules of conduct." To implement this provision, Socialist Law-Abiding Life Guidance Committees were established in 1977 in the People's Committees and in the CPC. These ad hoc committees are another powerful means of implementing state power under the direction of the President, and all law enforcement agencies, including the procuracy, are the subject of their oversight. The two programs developed pursuant to provision in the 1972 Constitution, the Three Revolutions Team Movement and the Socialist Law-Abiding Life Guidance Committees, undoubtedly aid the goal of control of the whole society by the Workers' Party through the ideological tool of *chuch'e*. Furthermore, the consolidation of the state structure allows for the concentration of power in the hands of one man, President Kim Il-song, who has ruled North Korea for over forty years.

Prospects for the Future

There are three constitutional issues that have particular bearing on North Korea's future: the problem of leadership succession, the possibility of creating a constitutional confederation with the South, and the impact of the changes in the USSR and Eastern Europe on North Korea and its constitution.

Leadership Succession

As noted above in 1980 Kim Chong-il, the son of Kim Il-song was installed as the second most powerful leader in North Korea, in order to establish the dynastic succession of his son.[61] Since, then preparations have been made for the transition and people seem to have accepted Kim Chong-il as the likely successor. Furthermore, many who were dissatisfied with the arrangement have been removed from the political scene. Structural changes were also undertaken to facilitate the succession of Kim Chong-Il. The Ninth Supreme People's Assembly, held in May 1990, reinforced the organization of the National Defense Commission, with Kim Il-song as chairman and his son as first vice-chairman, a newly-created position. At present, Kim Chong-il, as second-in-command, is believed to be in control of the military as well as of day-to-day government affairs.

Despite these preparations, a smooth transition is not necessarily assured. Potential opponents of the younger Kim may remain in the government or the military, and protests against the authoritarian regime may break out when Kim Il-song passes from the scene. Suggested scenarios range from a continuation of the present rule, with Kim Chong-il firmly in charge, to a government in which he would become a mere figurehead, with real power resting with a group of other leaders.

Constitutional Confederation with the South

Both North and South Korea are strongly interested in the possibility of reunification.[62] Talks of a substantive nature began in August of 1971, but they were broken off two years later and did not resume until 1984. The two regimes have, however, proposed different approaches to accomplishing reunification. The North suggests a single nation be formed with two different social, political, and economic systems, to be known as the "Confederal Republic of Koyro." As preconditions for reunification, however, the North consistently argued that the U.S. forces should be withdrawn from

South Korea, and the South Korean National Security Law should be abolished, and dissidents arrested in the South for visiting the North should be released. The Confederated Republic, as described by Kim Il-song, would be governed by a supreme national confederated assembly, with an equal number of representatives from the North and the South, plus members to represent overseas Koreans. The assembly would have a standing committee to guide regional governments in the two areas and to administer the affairs of the unified state. The assembly and its standing committee would handle political affairs, national defense, foreign affairs, and other matters of concern to the whole nation.

South Korea proposes a different method of rapprochement, in which steps toward unification would be taken slowly, so that mutual confidence could be built. Such actions as opening the border to exchanges and expanding trade could be initial steps. The Seoul government feels gradually reducing tensions between the two states by building a true national community is essential before actual reunification can be achieved. The South Korean regime also proposes that the two Koreas simultaneously be given full membership in the United Nations, to replace the "observer" status they have at present. North Korea opposes this, on the grounds that it would confirm the two separate governments and prolong the reunification process. Its preference is for Korea to join the U.N. as one country, with single-seat representation for the confederated republic. The South made it clear, however, that it would join the U.N. alone, should the North not agree to having two memberships at present. [Both applied to U.N. in 1991.]

The two regimes are thus still far apart in their suggestions for the future. With North Korea persisting in its goals of forcing U.S. troops form the peninsula and making other changes in the South, including the strengthening of dissident groups, and with South Korea poised to enter the U.N. separately if necessary, it would seem unlikely that real steps toward reunification can be taken in the next few years. They may have to wait for the passing of Kim Il-song form the scene.

Impact of Changes in the USSR and Eastern Europe

In 1988, and 1989, revisions of the Soviet Constitution and other legislation create contested elections for a parliament in the USSR.[63] In addition, there was extensive judicial reform, including new procedures for selection of judges, a new jury system, and affirmation of the detained person's right to an attorney. Improvement in the protection of individual rights and reforms in the laws regulating the economy also took place. Changes like these are not likely to occur in North Korea.

One of the major reforms affected article 6 of the Soviet Constitution which had stated that the Communist Party was the leading force of society and the nucleus of the political system, state organizations, and public organizations. The special predominance was eliminated in a 1990 amendment, but article 4 of North Korea's Constitution, which has a parallel statement to the original version of Soviet article 6, has not been revised. In fact, Kim Il-song, in his October 10, 1990, speech on the forty-fifth anniversary of the founding of the Worker's Party of Korea, stated "we must further strengthen the party and improve its leadership role."[64]

In the wake of changes taking place in the USSR and throughout Eastern Europe, North Korean leaders have taken steps to avoid similar developments.[65] The central power structure has been consolidated and ideological education, old slogans like the Ch'ongsan-ni spirit, the Taean work system, and the Three Revolutions Team Movement, and Chuch'e idea have been reemphasized. Kim Il-song has warned that a "fierce struggle" is taking place between socialism and imperialism, and stated "mankind must follow the road of socialism" in his 1990 New Year's address.[66] One result of all the changes in the USSR, once the model for the North Korean State, may be that there will be more uneasiness about the transfer of power to Kim Chong-il, forcing Kim Il-song to remain in control himself.[67] The chance of any real reform within his lifetime is slim.

NOTES

1. For a comparison of the 1972 North Korean Constitution with other socialist constitutions *see* Chin Kim and Timothy G. Kearley, *supra* note 3; John N. Hazard, "A Comparativist's View of the 1972 Constitution of the Democratic People's Republic of Korea," 7 *Studies in Comparative Communism* 74-82 (1974).

2. There are conflicting statements about the number of constitutional revisions made before 1972. Of four articles in English on the subject, for example, two say there were altogether four amendments made, two say there were five, and the fourth says there were six.

3. Kim, Il-song, *Let Us Further Strengthen the Socialist System of Our Country* 2 (Pyongyang, Foreign Languages Pub. House, 1972), as compared to the Korean text.

4. Kim Il-song, *supra* note 2, at 35, as compared to the Korean text. Many articles have been written on the 1972 Constitution in Korean, Japanese, and English. Two collections of essays by North Korean writers are of special interest: Chae-muk Chu (ed.), *Choson Minjujuui Inmin Konghwaguk sahoejuui honpop un sahoejuui konsolk ul him ikke taguch'ilsu ikke hanun wiryok han mugi* [The Socialist Constitution of the DPRK Is a Powerful Weapon for Strengthening the Socialist Constitution] (Pongyang, Kwahak Paekwa Sajon Ch'ulp'ansa, 1978); *Choson Minjujuui Inmin Konghwaguk sahoejuui honpop yon'gu nonmunjip* [A Collection of Essays on the Socialist Constitution of the DPRK] (Pongyang, Sahoe Kwahak Ch'ulp'ansa, 1973). The following publications in English are also worthy of note: Ku-jin Kang, "An Analytical Study on the North Korean Socialist Constitution," 2 *Korea and World Affairs* 126-157 (1978); Chin Kim and Timothy G. Kearley, "The 1972 Socialist Constitution of North Korea," 11 *Texas International Law Journal* 113-135 (1976); Ilpyong J. Kim, "Constitutional Development in North Korea," 2 *Journal of Korean Affairs* 31-38 (1973); Chong-Sik Lee, "The 1972 Constitution and Top Communist Leaders," in Dae-Sook Suh and Chae Jin Lee (eds.), *Political Leadership in Korea* 192-219 (Seattle, University of Washington Press, 1976); Chin-wee Chung, "The Evolution of a Constitutional Structure in North Korea," in Robert A. Scalapino and Jun-yop Kim (eds.), *North Korea Today: Strategic and Domestic Issues* 19-42 (Berkeley, Institute of East Asian Studies, 1983); Masao Fukushima, *On the Socialist Constitution of the DPRK* (Pyongyang, Foreign Languages Pub. House, 1975); Youn-Soo Kim, "The 1972 Socialist Constitution of the Korean Democratic People's Republic," 3 *Review of Socialist Law* 281-296 (1977).

5. Ilpyong J. Kim, *supra* note 4, at 34.

6. Kim Il-song, *On the Question of the Period of Transition from Capitalism to Socialism and the Dictatorship of the Proletariat* 17 (Pyongyang, Foreign Languages Pub. House, 1969).

7. Ilpyong J. Kim, *supra* note 4, at 33.

8. Masao Fukushima, *supra* note 4, at 190.

9. Robert A. Scalapino and Chong-Sik Lee, *Communism in Korea* 562-563 (Berkeley, University of California Press, 1972), pt. 1.

298   CHO

10. *Id.* pt. 2, at 1115.
11. For more information on the topic, *see* Song-nim Yi, "Three Revolutions for Building a Communist Society After Going Through the Transitional Stage of Socialist Society," 5 *Sahoe kwahak* 27-32 (Sept. 1983); Tai Sung An, *North Korea: A Political Handbook* 57 (Wilmington, Scholarly Resources, 1983).
12. The Land Law, Apr. 29, 1977; came into force on June 1, 1977.
13. Scalapino and Lee, *supra* note 10, at 1245-1247. *See also* Ilpyong J. Kim, "The Mobilization System in North Korean Politics," 2 *Journal of Korean Affairs* 12-14 (1972).
14. Scalapino and Lee, *supra* note 10, at 1097.
15. *Chosen Minshu Shugi Jinmin Kyowakoku juyo horeishu* [A Collection of Laws and Ordinances of the DPRK] 80-104 (Tokyo, Chosen Daigaku, 1979).
16. *Id.* at 27.
17. Sok-pong Han, *Choson Minjujuui Inmin Konghwaguk kukka sahoe chedo* [State and Social System of the Democratic People's Republic of Korea] 110 (Pyongyang, Kwahak Paekwa Sajon Ch'ulp'ansa, 1984).
18. Chin-wee Chung, *supra* note 4, at 29.
19. A North Korean reformist who advocated that the SPA, the highest organ of state power, be independent of the Workers' Party was branded as "reactionary." *See* "On 'The Problems Arising from the Administrative Act of the Democratic People's Republic of Korea,'" 6 *Pophak nonmunjip* 131 (1956).
20. *Directory of Officials of the Democratic People's Republic of Korea* 17 (Washington, Directorate of Intelligence, 1990).
21. Chong-Sik Lee, *supra* note 3, at 195.
22. Tai Sung An, *supra* note 11, at 60-61. *See also* B.C. Koh, "The Cult of Personality and the Succession Issue," in C.I. Eugene Kim and B.C. Koh, *ed.*, *Journey to North Korea: Personal Perceptions* 25-41 (Berkeley, Institute of East Asian Studies, 1983).
23. Sok-pong Han, *supra* note 17, at 113.
24. *Supra* note 20, at 25.
25. Chong-Sik Lee, *supra* note 4, at 209.
26. Kim Il-song, *supra* note 3, at 41-42.
27. Kuk-p'yo Hong, "The Constitutional Provisions That Separate People's Committees from Administrative Organs Are a Legal Guarantee for Strengthening Activities of the People's Committees," 5 *Sahoe kwahak* 31 (1977).
28. Ilpyong J. Kim, at 37; Chin-wee Chung, *supra* note 3, at 37; Youn-Soo Kim, at 288; Chong-Sik Lee, at 207-208, *supra* note 4.
29. Ku-jin Kang, *supra* note 4, at 146.
30. Rinn-Sup Shinn, "Government and Politics," *in* Frederica M. Bunge (ed.), *North Korea: A Country Study* 175 (3d ed., Washington, U.S. Gov't. Print. Off., 1981). For further discussion of the subject, *see* Chang Hyun Cho, "The System of Local Government In North Korea," in Se-jin Kim and Chang Hyun Cho, (ed.), *Korea: A*

Divided Nation 171-181 (Silver Spring, Md., The Research Institute on Korean Affairs, 1976).

31. Sok-pong Han, *supra* note 17, at 115.

32. A South Korean source reveals that the Administrative Committees at the provincial and county levels were replaced with Economic Guidance Committees at those levels in 1981. *See Pukhan ch'ongnam, 1945-1982* [General Survey of North Korea, 1945-1982] 249 (Seoul, Pukhan Yon'guso, 1983).

33. Sok-pong Han, *supra* note 17, at 115-116.

34. U.S. Foreign Broadcast Information Service, *Daily Report: Asia & Pacific*, Feb. 25, 1985, at D1.

35. *Choson Minjujuui Inmin Konghwaguk sahoejuui honpop haesol* {A Commentary on the Socialist Constitution of the Democratic People's Republic of Korea] 87 (Pyongyang, Inmin Kwahaksa, 1973).

36. It has been reported that the Code of Criminal Procedure, issued on Mar. 3, 1950, was revised on Dec. 10, 1974. See Kyu-sung Kim, *supra* note 32, at 127. For more information about the judicial system of North Korea under the 1972 Constitution, *see* Sung Yoon Cho, *The Judicial System of the Democratic People's Republic of Korea* (Washington, Library of Congress, Law Library, 1974); and Chin Kim, "The Legal System," *in* Han-Kyo Kim, (ed.), *Studies on Korea: A Scholar's Guide* 343-346 (Honolulu, The University Press of Hawaii, 1980); and kyu-sung Kim, *Chosen Minoshu Shugi Jinmin Kyowakoku no ho to shiho seido* [Law and the the Judicial system of the Democratic People's Republic of Korea], Tokyo, Nihon Hyoronsha, 1985. For information on the judicial system under the 1948 Constitution, *see* Sung Yoon Cho, "Law and Justice in North Korea," 2 *Journal of Korean Affairs* 3-23 (1973).

37. Article 37 of the 1976 Court Organization Law, as cited by Kyu-sung Kim, "The System of Courts, the Procuracy, and Lawyers in the Republic," 25 *Gekkan Chosen shiryo* 29 (1985). The original Court Organization Law, enacted on March 1, 1950, was revised on January 10, 1976.

38. Article 38 of the 1976 Court Organization Law, as cited by Kyu-sung Kim, *id.*

39. Kyu-sung Kim, *supra* note 37; Masao Fukushima, *supra* note 3, at 271-272.

40. Kyu-sung Kim, *supra* note 37, at 41. *Pophak sajon* [Legal Dictionary] 605-606 (Pyongyang, Sahoe Kwahak Yon'guso, 1961), as cited by Noriaki Ouchi, "Problems of Enacting Laws After the Enactment of the Socialist Constitution of the DPRK," 1124 *Ajia Keizai junpo* 15 (August 1979).

41. Article 36 of the 1976 Court Organization Law, as cited by Kyu-sung Kim, *supra* note 37, at 30.

42. In-fu Pang, "Structure and Operation of the Judiciary in North Korea," in *Pukhan cho'onggam*, 1945-1968 [Yearbooks on North Korea, 1945-1968] 929-931 (Seoul, 1968). For an account of mass trials, *see* Sung Yoon Cho, Senate Comm. on the Judiciary, 89th Cong., 1st Sess., *The Church and State Under Communism: Religion in North Korea* 7-9 (1965).

43. *Supra* note 35.

44. *Chosen Minshu Shugi Jinmin Kyowakoku no kokka, shakai taisei* [State and social system of the Democratic People's Republic of Korea] 164 (Tokyo, Nihon Hyoronsha, 1966).

45. Article 10 of the 1948 Regulation Concerning Lawyers, Cabinet Decision No. 59, Nov. 1, 1948, as cited by Kyu-sung Kim, *supra* note 37, at 39.

46. Article 13, *supra* note 45. For more information on bar membership, *see* Sung Yoon Cho, *The Judicial System of the Democratic People's Republic of Korea, supra* note 36, at 25.

47. Kyong-o Yi, "Certain Experiences Derived from Preparation of the Oral Defense in Criminal Cases," *Minju sabop* 21 (1959).

48. Kyu-sung Kim, *supra* note 37, at 40.

49. Kim Il-song, *Let Us Further Strengthen the People's Government* 24-25 (Pyongyang, Foreign Languages Pub. House, 1977).

50. Yong-ch'ol Kim, *Widehan suryong Kim Il-song tongji kkeso palkyo chusin sahoejuui pommu saenghwal e kwanhan iron* [Theory of the Socialist Law-Abiding Life Enunciated by the Great Leader Kim Il-song] 7 (Pyongyang, Kwahak Paekwa Sajon Ch'ulp'ansa, 1980). *Kulloja* and *Sahoe Kwahak*, two leading North Korean non-legal journals, have also carried several articles on the subject of the law-abiding life. And on December 15, 1982, Kim Chong-il, the son of Kim Il-song, announced his own thesis, "On the Strengthening of Socialist Life," which elaborates on his father's theory. *See* Kyu-sung Kim, "On the One-Year Anniversary of the Essay 'On the Strengthening of Socialist Law-Abiding Life' by Kim Chong-il," 23 *Gekkan Chosen shiryo* 48-57 (1983).

51. Atsushi Asai, "The Socialist Constitution of the Democratic People's Republic of Korea and the Development of the Principles of Legality," 52 *Horitsu jiho* 13 (1980). This article is based on the author's observations made during a visit to North Korea in July 1980. *See also* Ouchi, *supra* note 40, at 28. There are three regulations governing these committees established in the Central People's Committee and in the people's committees at all levels. *See* Kyu-sung Kim, *Supra* note 32, at 119.

52. Ch'ang-sop So, *Pop konsol kyonghom* [Experiences in the Construction of Law] 141 (Pyongyang, Sahoe Kwahak Ch'ulp'ansa, 1984).

53. *Minju Choson*, a government newspaper, regularly reports on campaign activities related to the concept of the "socialist law-abiding life." *See, e.g.*, articles appearing on June 3, June 8, and Nov. 5, 1982; July 30, Aug. 13, Aug. 18, Aug. 28, Oct. 9, Nov. 9 and Nov. 19, 1983.

54. Yong-ch'ol Kim, *supra* note 50, at 73; Kyu-sung Kim, "The Socialist Constitution and Its Incarnation in the Life of the State and Society," 22 *Gekkan Chosen shiryo* 60 (1982).

55. Ch'ang-sop So, *supra* note 52; Atsushi Asai, *supra* note 51.

56. Ch'ang-sop So, *supra* note 52, at 142.

57. For more information on basic rights and duties granted under the 1972 Constitution, see Ku-jin Kang, "Fiction of Fundamental Rights in North Korean

Constitution," 8 *Vantage Point* no. 4, 1-10 (1985); no. 5, 1-10; Tscholsu Kim, "Prospects for a Constitution for a United Korea, Based on a Comparison of the Constitutions of South and North Korea," 6 *Korea and World Affairs* 424-425 (1982); Bruce Cumings, "Human Rights in the Democratic People's Republic of Korea, *in Human Rights in Korea* 340-364 (New York, Asia Watch Committee, 1986).

58. On September 14, 1981, North Korea acceded to the International Covenant on Economic, Social, and Cultural Rights and the International Covenant on Civil and Political Rights, adopted by the General Assembly of the United Nations on December 16, 1966. How these two covenants are being implemented in North Korea is not known. However, at the March-April 1984 session of the Human Rights Committee of the International Covenant on Civil and Political Rights, "members criticized a report submitted by North Korea on its human rights practices as too short and inadequate." The North Korean response was to "[deny that the] country had any problems at all." *See* Senate Comm. on Foreign Relations and House Comm. on Foreign Affairs, 99th Cong., 1st Sess., *Country Reports on Human Rights Practices for 1984* 795 (Jt. Comm. Print 1985). The 1990 *Country Reports* (102d Cong., Jt. Comm. Print 1991) at 927, states that the North Korean government has not allowed any international organization to visit North Korea to monitor human rights practices. *See also Multilateral Treaties Deposited With the Secretary-General: Status as at 31 December 1981* 108, 117 (New York, United Nations, 1982. ST/LEG/SER.E/1). Bruce Cumings, who visited North Korea in 1981, was of the opinion that in the area on non-political human rights (health care, education, housing, women's rights, the right to employment and decent working conditions) North Korea does better than most developing countries. *See* Bruce Cumings, *supra* note 57, at 342.

59. Ku-jin Kang, *supra* note 4, at 151.

60. *Supra* note 35, at 80.

61. *For more background information, see* Daryl M. Plunk, "Recent Changes On the Korean Peninsula and U.S. Policy Toward Pyongyang," 5 Journal of East Asian Affairs 1-23 (Winter/Spring 1991); Charles S. Lee, *North Korea Country Background Report* 1-33 (CRS Report of Congress, Sept. 27, 1990).

62. *For more background informantion, see*: Dae-sook Suh, "Changes in North Korea and Inter-Korean Relations," 14 *Korea and World Affairs* 617-625 (Winter 1990); Rinn-sup Shinn, "Democratic Confederal Republic of Koryo: Motives, Contexts, and Implications," *id.* at 610-625; Byung C. Koh, "Seoul's New Unification Formula," *id.* at 657-671 (Winter 1989); Kim Il-song, *On the Proposal For Founding a Democratic Confederal Republic of Koryo* 1-55 (Pyongyang, Foreign Languages Publishing House, 1983) and his 1991 New Year's address apearing in English in Foreign Broadcast Information Service, *Daily Report: East Asia* 6-12 (Jan. 2, 1991).

63. *See generally* John Quigley, "The Soviet Union as a State Under the Rule of Law: An Overview," 23 *Cornell Int'l L. Rev.* 205 (1990).

64. *Nodong Sinmun*, Oct. 11, 1990.

65. *See generally* Yong Soon Yim, "The Impact of the Change in Eastern Europe on the Korean Peninsula," 14 *Korea and World Affairs* 528-530 (Fall 1990).

66. *Nodong Sinmun*, Jan. 1, 1990.

67. At the Ninth Supreme People's Assembly, held on May 24, 1990, Kim Il-song was elected President for another four-year term, ending in 1994, despite rumors and speculation that he might step down in 1990. *Nodong Sinmun*, May 24, 1990.

REPUBLIC OF KOREA (SOUTH KOREA)

*The Influence of U.S. Constitutional Law
Doctrines in Korea* *

Tscholsu Kim

Sang Don Lee

Introduction

Korea recovered her sovereignty at the end of World War II after thirty-six years of Japanese colonial rule. From 1945 when Japan surrendered to the Allied Forces until 1948 when the original Constitution of Korea took effect, the southern part of the Korean peninsula was administered by the U.S. Military Government in Korea (USAMGIK).   On the other hand, the northern part of Korea was ruled by a Soviet military administration. The sole purpose of dividing Korea was to help the Korean people establish their own government; but as the U.S.S.R. declined to allow free elections in the north, the effort to form a unified government in Korea was doomed to failure. Thus the U.S. decided to establish a democratic government in the south as soon as possible. Many Korean political leaders also wanted to put aside the unification problem for awhile and to form an independent government immediately. As a result, Korean politicians and the U.S. military authorities collaborated in approving the establishment of the Constitution of Korea; in this sense, the influence of the U.S. Government on the Constitution was notable.

The original Constitution of the Republic of Korea was adopted on July 12, 1948, and took effect on July 17, 1948, and the era of First Republic began. Korea has a relatively short constitutional history, though she is very proud of her cultural history of thousands of years. Moreover, during a period of forty years of constitutional history, her form of government was radically changed several times.   In the course of transformations of constitutional democracy and governmental structure of Korea, the influence of American constitutional law principles has been enormous. This is remarkable, as Korea's legal tradition has been in the civil law tradition of continental Europe since she began to import Western legal culture in the nineteenth century.   This chapter analyzes the influence of the U.S. constitutional law doctrines in Korea since 1945.

The Korean Constitution of 1948 and the Influence
of the United States

The End of the World War II and Establishment of the U.S. Military
Government in South Korea

On August 15, 1945, Japan surrendered to the Allied Forces, and so Korea won emancipation from Japanese colonial rule (1910-1945). On September 7, 1945, General Douglas MacArthur proclaimed that the area below 38 degrees North and the people residing there were under the military administration of the United States. On September 8, 1945, the U.S. Army landed on the Korean peninsula below the 38th parallel to disarm the Japanese armed forces. On September 12, Lieutenant General John R. Hodge, then the Commander of the U.S. Armed Forces in Korea, appointed Major General Arnold as Minister of Military Administration. The task of USAMGIK (U.S.A. Military Government in Korea) was to maintain peace and order, and to help the Korean people establish their own government.[1] As a first step, the USAMGIK administration repealed many notorious colonial Laws promulgated by the Japanese regime. Repealed laws included the Sedition Law, the Political Crimes Law, the Preventive Arrest Law, and the Publication Act. These laws provided indispensable machinery for the maintenance of the despised colonial regime in Korea. However, USAMGIK was cautious about allowing the Koreans political freedom and civil rights because of the turbulent political and social situation. Political parties and newspapers were required to obtain prior approval of their activities.

The USAMGIK contributed to the introduction of basic concepts of American constitutional law. Although from the late nineteenth century American ideas of democracy and human rights had been brought into Korea by Koreans educated in the U.S. and by American missionaries and teachers, most Koreans learned the meaning of constitutional democracy and the doctrine of separation of powers for the first time in history during the Occupation. USAMGIK also made several important ordinances which had about them a strong flavor of American constitutionalism. For example, on March 20, 1948, the government amended the Criminal Procedure Law. The amended law, which could rather be called a new Law, provided that no one could be arrested without a warrant issued by a judge, and that defendants were guaranteed the right to legal counsel. In addition, the USAMGIK promoted sexual equality in political and family affairs. As a result, women were given voting rights before the national election held on May 10, 1948.

Probably the most significant measure taken by the USAMGIK for Korean civil rights was "The Ordinance on the Rights of the Korean People" issued by General Hodge on April 7, 1948. The Ordinance consisted of twelve Articles guaranteeing the freedoms of religion, assembly and association, expression and publication, and the rights to legal counsel, to speedy and fair trial, and to equal protection under law. It also prohibited torture and deprivation of freedom or property without due process of law. These precious principles were obviously derived from the basic doctrines of the Constitution of the United States. The principles enumerated in this Ordinance had a consequential impact upon the political leaders of Korea who were preparing the nation for independence.

Making the Constitution of 1948

On June 30, 1947, a special committee consisting of Korean political leaders and jurists was established to draft various laws of the soon-to-be-born Republic of Korea. A subcommittee was organized to draft a constitution for the new republic, and after several months work, a draft Constitution was submitted to the National Assembly. Yet it is known that Dr. Chin-O Yu, the leading scholar of constitutional law, played a dominant role in the drafting process. It is also known that Colonel Emery J. Woodall, then legal officer of the USAMGIK in Korea prepared his own version of a draft Constitution for Korea and gave it to Dr. Yu.[2] However, there is no evidence that the so-called "Woodall Draft" had any significant influence in the making of the Constitution of Korea.

The draft Constitution of the subcommittee featured a unique mixture of the presidential and parliamentary systems of government. It provided for a bicameral Legislature, and for a President elected by the Legislature. The President was given the power to dissolve the Legislature, and on the other hand, the Legislature could cast a vote of no-confidence in the Cabinet headed by the Premier. Also, the Supreme Court had the power to declare unconstitutional and void laws found to be in conflict with the Constitution.

But as it turned out, bicameralism and judicial review were not adopted by the National Assembly. Instead, a strong presidency became the basis of the government's structure at the insistence of Dr. Syngman Rhee, who was at that time virtually the only candidate for President.

On May 10, 1948, national elections to constitute the unicameral National Assembly were held under the auspices of the United Nations. On July 12, 1948, the newly-organized National Assembly finally passed the draft Constitution, and the Constitution of the Republic of Korea took effect on

July 17, 1948. The National Assembly also elected Dr. Syngman Rhee as the first President of Korea.

Influence of American Constitutional Law on Civil Rights and Freedom

As pointed out above, "The Ordinance on the Rights of Korean People" issued by General Hodge had a strong influence on the drafting of the civil rights provisions of the Constitution of 1948. In fact, Dr. Chin-O Yu later acknowledged that he found very helpful this Ordinance which was clearly derived from the Bill of Rights of the U.S. Constitution.[3] The Constitutions of Korea since that time have preserved precious principles enunciated in the Ordinance, such as the right to a fair trial, the freedoms of religion and expression, the right of *habeas corpus*, and equal protection of all citizens under the law. It was truly a very important contribution of American concepts to constitutionalism in Korea.

Presidential Government

The Constitution of 1948 adopted a presidential system of government, but it also had several features of a parliamentary system. Dr. Chin-O Yu preferred the parliamentary system and actually wrote it into the draft Constitution. But the pressure from Dr. Syngman Rhee who had returned to his homeland after long exile in Hawaii and had then become virtually the sole candidate for first President, was so strong that the constitutional structure proposed was changed to the presidential system overnight.

The Korean Provisional Government was founded at Shanghai, China, on September, 1919. The March First Movement in the Korean peninsula, the peaceful anti-Japan movement of March, 1919 calling for independence, directly inspired the establishment of the Provisional Government. Dr. Syngman Rhee was elected its first President. However, Dr. Rhee stayed at Shanghai only briefly from December, 1920 until May, 1921; thereafter, he resided in the United States until his return to Korea in 1945. Dr. Rhee did not return to Shanghai and alienated the Koreans there. Dr. Rhee was more interested in his activities in America than in the Provisional Government in remote China. The Provisional Government finally returned to Korea after World War II but failed to play a leading role in politics during the crucial years of 1945 to 1948, because the United States sponsored Dr. Rhee as the political leader of Korea.[4]

The U.S. Military Government in Korea had recommended adoption of a presidential government system,[5] but the critical factor in Korea's adoption of presidential government was Dr. Syngman Rhee's strong personality. Dr. Syngman Rhee had been educated at Princeton University and had spent a long time in Hawaii; as a result, he became a staunch believer in American constitutionalism. He was, quite simply, more comfortable with a presidential government like that of the U.S. than with a parliamentary system. As he did not have many followers in Korea at that time, he surely might have thought he had no chance to be an effective leader within the framework of parliamentary government favored by most Korean politicians. Dr. Rhee was finally successful in getting the support of the U.S. Government in early 1948, and thus he could pressure the National Assembly to adopt a Constitution for the presidential government.

Yet the actual Constitution of 1948 carried several features of a parliamentary system because it represented a compromise between Dr. Rhee and those politicians who wanted parliamentary government. For example, the Prime Minister was appointed by the President upon approval of the National Assembly, the National Assembly could ask the Prime Minister and Cabinet Ministers to be present at National Assembly sessions for questioning, and the Government could introduce bills in the National Assembly. These mechanisms were intended to prevent any abuse of power on the part of the President. However, President Rhee later founded his own party, the Liberal Party, and as it gained control of the National Assembly, the legislature lost entirely its function of providing a check on presidential power. A pattern thus emerged of constitutional processes leading toward dictatorial government.

Under the original Constitution of 1948, the President was to be selected by the National Assembly, due to the urgency felt about prompt establishment of the government. Dr. Syngman Rhee himself said, "[A]t this time it is difficult to elect a President by general election, and thus a presidential election by the National Assembly seems inevitable."[6] In addition, Sang Il Suh, then Chairman of the Constitution Drafting Committee of the National Assembly, maintained, "The people's sovereignty does not necessarily mean that the President should be selected through popular and direct election. Even in the U.S., where constitutional democracy is most developed, the President is selected through indirect election."[7] While necessity justified indirect election of the President by the National Assembly at that time, the presidential election process of the U.S. was not widely known among Korean political leaders, as is suggested by Sang Il Suh's speech.

Legislature

During the Constitution drafting process a bicameral legislature was clearly prefered, and the U.S. Military Government in Seoul wanted the Government of Korea to have such a legislative branch, but the Constitution in the end adopted a unicameral legislature. A unicameral Legislature was adopted on grounds that it would suit better the new nation's need for efficiency, and that bicameralism was a luxury. The term of office of the Members of the National Assembly was set at four years, as the two-year term of U.S. Congressmen was thought too short.

Judiciary

The U.S. Military Government also provided Koreans with their own concept of a judicial system. The Judiciary Organization Law which was promulgated by USAMGIK provided: "Courts shall adjudicate civil actions, criminal actions, administrative litigation and all other legal actions." This meant that the judicial system of Korea would follow the model of the U.S. rather than those of France or Germany, where administrative litigation has been dealt with by separate special administrative tribunals like the *Counseil d'Etat* and the *Verwaltungsgerichthof*.

In the course of constitutional drafting, the U.S. Military Government seems to have wanted the Constitution of Korea to establish judicial review like that in the U.S. However, such expectations did not materialize, as the Constitution of 1948 established instead a Constitution Committee to exercise constitutional review powers. The Constitution Committee consisted of the Vice-President, five Justices of the Supreme Court and five Members of the National Assembly. When questions about the constitutionality of certain provisions of statutes arose in pending cases, the courts were required to submit such questions to the Constitution Committee. The reason why judicial review was rejected in the Constitution of 1948 has never been clearly known. It is generally assumed, however, that Members of the National Assembly were wary of establishing a government of judicial supremacy as they thought they saw in the U.S., and that the politicians were afraid that judges might invalidate reform legislation, such as a farmland reform act which was urgently needed at that time.[8]

Conclusion

The foregoing discussion suggests several conclusions:

First, the series of laws promulgated by the U.S. Military Government during the period between 1945 and 1948 had constructive effect in Korea.

Basic principles of American constitutionalism were introduced to a great many of the people of Korea for the first time.

Second, it is still not known whether the U.S. Military Government played any significant role in the process of drafting the Constitution of 1948, due to the lack of documents on that period in both Korea and the United States. Furthermore, it is almost impossible to get any information from the political leaders of Korea who played dominant roles at that period; most of them have died without leaving any meaningful memoirs. In fact, the only reliable source is the memoir by Dr. Chin-O Yu who is now in his eighties and in ill health.

Third, it is nevertheless clear that the constitutional law doctrines of the United States have consistently exerted influence on the constitutional development of Korea since 1948 although Korean constitutional democracy is not yet as mature as its American counterpart. How American constitutional law doctrines have been affecting the development of the constitutional system of Korea is discussed below.

Constitutional Developments During the Years of the First Republic (1948-1960) and the Second Republic (1960-1961)

The Government under President Rhee turned into a dictatorial regime after constitutional amendments were passed in 1952 and 1954. The amendments prolonged President Rhee's time in office. The amendment of 1952 changed the way of choosing the President from an indirect process of election by the National Assembly to direct election by the people. This could be regarded as a positive development, but in fact President Rhee was so unpopular among the Members of the National Assembly in 1952 that his reelection was thought to be possible only by means of a direct election. So the Constitution was amended at the demand of President Rhee and, as expected, he was reelected in 1952 in a general election.

The constitutional amendment of 1954 was also exclusively for the purpose of prolonging President Rhee's life in office. It repealed the constitutional prohibition on a third four-year term as President in the case of the First President of the Republic, Dr. Syngman Rhee. In such a way, political processes were used to transform the government into an authoritarian regime.

President Syngman Rhee was reelected in 1956, but resigned in April 1960 after a major student revolt. The Student Revolution was a response to the dictatorial and corrupt practices of the Government which had culminated in the notorious election of March, 1960. In this presidential election, the opposition party's candidate, Byung-Ok Cho ran against Dr. Rhee who was seeking his fourth term. However, Cho died quite suddenly in an American hospital just a month before the election, so Dr. Rhee was the only candidate for President.[9] On March 17, 1960, the Government declared Dr. Rhee and his political protege, Kee Bung Lee the winners in the presidential and vice-presidential races. There were nationwide charges of corruption in the electoral process; the opposition attacked the election as "void." The anti-government movement of students escalated in April. On April 19, 1960, major student demonstrations were held in Seoul, and on April 25, university professors joined in the anti-Rhee actions. Though President Rhee declared martial law, leaders in the military calmly supported the opposition demand for a change of political regime. On April 27, Dr. Rhee resigned from the Presidency and left the country for exile in Hawaii. His Party and Government were dismantled. It was the end of the First Republic of Korea.

After several months of interim government, the Constitution was amended and a new government organized based on a general election. Thus, the Second Republic was born and Myon Chang (John Chang) became Prime Minister. The Constitution of 1960, the "Constitution of the Second Republic," adopted a typical parliamentary system of government, with a Prime Minister elected by and responsible to the National Assembly. On the other hand, Prime Minister Chang could dissolve the Assembly. The power to decide on the constitutionality of statutes was given to a newly established Constitutional Court, a special tribunal modeled after the Federal Constitutional Court of West Germany. The Democratic Party, which had been the bitter foe of President Syngman Rhee, won a majority of the seats in the National Assembly.

As a result of the experience with the Rhee presidency, it was generally understood that the presidential system of government had been a complete failure in Korea. In 1960, so wrote Dr. Chin-O Yu, then President of Korea University in Seoul: "It is the common feeling among the people that we should escape from the hell of a presidential system and adopt a democratic parliamentary system of government."[10] Another constitutional law professor wrote:

> The American system of presidential government has no virtue at all except [in providing] for the stability and authority of the Executive.... Especially in the less-developed countries, it surely develops into severe corruption as has already been shown in the experience of Latin American states.[11]

Therefore, it is an irony that although the Government of the United States welcomed the revival of constitutional democracy in Korea, an American-style governmental structure was denounced as the origin of dictatorship. However, the constitutional provisions for political and civil rights were reinforced and American constitutional theories and court decisions were frequently mentioned in discourse on the Constitution. American constitutional law doctrines also exerted influence in the making of the Constitution of the Second Republic.

The Constitution of the Third Republic (1962-1972); System Based on U.S. Constitutional Principles

The Constitution of 1962

The Second Republic lived less than a year, as the Government led by Prime Minister Myon Chang was fragile. Governmental and political processes under the parliamentary system were democratic, but they failed to maintain social stability. In the midst of political and social turmoil, a *coup d'etat* led by Major General Chung Hee Park overthrew the Government of Prime Minister Chang on May 16, 1961.

The Supreme Council for National Reconstruction (a Military Revolutionary Council) established a military regime. The Supreme Council virtually scrapped the Constitution of 1960. It ruled first by martial law and later by ordinances issued under the National Reconstruction Extraordinary Measure Law which had been promulgated by the Supreme Council itself.

On August 12, 1961, General Park, then the Chairman of the Council, released a statement to the effect that the Army would return to the barracks after establishing civilian government in the spring of 1963, and that the new Constitution would provide for a presidential government with a one-house National Assembly. On July 11, 1962, a special Constitution Drafting Committee [consisting of nine members and twenty-one advisors] was organized within the Supreme Council.

The basic idea was to draft a completely new Constitution rather than to amend or modify an existing Constitution. The final draft of the Constitution was prepared in October, 1962 and was submitted to the Council. The draft was approved by the Council and won approval of the voters in a special referendum held on December 17, 1962.

Several characteristics are noteworthy about the process of making the Constitution of 1962. First, professors of constitutional law, administrative law and political science played a dominant role. Second, as is well known, the

Kennedy Administration of the U.S. was not very happy with the military regime in Korea and wanted a swift transfer of political power to a new civilian government. Third, the U.S. Government was very interested in the nature of the new Constitution. Indeed, invitations extended to two American scholars, Professor Emerson of Yale University and Professor Frantz of New York University, to visit Korea were taken as a sign that the Korean military leaders were sincere in their expressed intention to build a democratic regime.[12] However, there is no evidence that these two American professors played any significant role. It is also now known that the eminent diplomat, Philip Habib, then Political Attache of the U.S. Embassy at Seoul, was deeply concerned about the nature of the soon-to-be-born Constitution.[13]

As for the substance of the Constitution, most important was the adoption of a presidential system and the granting of judicial review powers to the courts. These are among the most distinctive characteristics of the U.S. Constitution, and therefore it would be fair to say that the Constitution of 1962 had more of an "American flavor" than its predecessors.

The System of Presidential Government

Most professors involved in the drafting of the Constitution preferred presidential government. Though they clearly understood that an American-style presidential government system was never successful in foreign soil, as shown in the Latin American states, they thought their country had no other alternative, since a tradition of party politics and bureaucracy, the prerequisites of parliamentary government, was not yet established.[14]

As for the method of electing the President, no dispute arose as all believed the President should be elected directly by the people in a general election. In the Presidential election held in August, 1963, former General Park won by a narrow margin, and his party, the Democratic Republican Party, won the majority of seats in the National Assembly. General Park and his followers obviously had changed their minds and had decided to participate in civilian government, and they got what they wanted.

At first, the regime under President Park worked in a quite fair way, and the country was able to embark on an ambitious economic development program. However, as the second four-year term of President Park was going to expire in 1971, the ruling Democratic Republican Party wanted to revise the Constitution to allow him a third term. Despite vehement opposition from the opposition New Democratic Party and students, the ruling camp finally gained passage of its amendment proposal in the National Assembly on September 1, 1969, and the proposal was subsequently approved in a referendum. However, the passage of the amendment proposal was done in a questionable manner and was denounced as "unlawful." In any case, the Constitution was again revised solely to allow an incumbent President's third term. In 1971, as expected, President Park ran for a third term; the New Democratic Party's candidate for the presidency was Dae Jung Kim. In the most hotly contested presidential election in the history of Korea, Dae Jung Kim won enormous momentum and almost won the race.[15] The election of 1971 unquestionably gave stimulus to the regime's movement to adopt a new Constitution in the Fall of 1972.

Judicial Review

Article 102 of the Constitution of 1962 provided: "In case a question arises in a pending case about whether a statute violates the Constitution or not, the Supreme Court makes the final decision." By this provision, the American constitutional doctrine of judicial review was imported into Korea. In fact, one of the most significant aspects of the Constitution of 1962 was the inclusion of constitutional review by the ordinary courts. If judicial review had been properly developed by the courts, and if decisions on constitutionality had been respected by the executive branch, judicial supremacy could have been established in Korea. However, such a hope proved to be only a dream.

It is not known for sure how judicial review came to be incorporated into the Constitution of 1962. Actually, one of the most hotly disputed issues during the drafting process was where to locate the power of constitutional review. Constitutional law professors were generally inclined to establish a special tribunal like the Federal Constitutional Court of West Germany. Judges and practicing lawyers maintained that constitutional adjudication is only an aspect of litigation and that declaring legislative acts unconstitutional should be an ordinary part of the judicial function.

Inside the Constitution Drafting Committee, the law professors clearly wanted to establish a Constitutional Court. Justice Young Sup Lee of the Supreme Court, the only member from the judiciary, showed careful interest in giving such power to the courts.[16] In the early 1960's, the United States was experiencing a high tide of judicial activism under the leadership of late Chief Justice Earl Warren, so it was not strange for the judges of Korea at the time to devoutly wish for the power of judicial review. The Constitution of 1962 was a calm victory for the judiciary in this sense.

After the Constitution of 1962 took effect in 1963, a number of statutes were challenged as unconstitutional in the courts. Even provisions of important acts such as the Anti-Communist Law (1961)[17] and the National

Assembly Election Law were challenged as void.[18] Several statutes were held unconstitutional by the trial and appellate courts in the late 1960s. However, the highest court was reluctant to hold acts of the National Assembly unconstitutional.

The only occasion on which the Supreme Court of Korea has declared statutory provisions unconstitutional was the decision on June 22, 1971, concerning the provision of the Government Tort Liability Law(1967).[19] As it was the first and last time that the highest court of Korea has held provisions of statutes promulgated by the National Assembly unconstitutional, it deserves more detailed analysis.

Article 2(1) of the Government Tort Liability Law provided:

> The National or local government is liable for damage occurring by wilful or negligent act of its officials or employees.... However, if military servicemen or civilian employees of the armed forces should be killed or wounded while performing combat, drill or other duty, or while in barracks, ships, airplanes or other craft which are used for military purposes, and if they or their bereaved family are eligible for compensation by other acts such as pensions for the disabled or dependents, they cannot claim compensation under this law.

Therefore, if a serviceman were killed during drill by a culpable comrade, his bereaved family would only be allowed a military pension which paid less money than a money judgment by civil court in comparable situations. As a result, this provision was denounced as a violation of the constitutional guarantee of equal protection of the law and of the right to file a claim for tort liability of government.

In 1968, two tribunals of Seoul District Court held the provision unconstitutional,[20] and their decisions were upheld by the Seoul High Court.[21] The Government brought this problem to the Supreme Court. The Government and the ruling Democratic Republican Party took this proceeding very seriously. A holding by the highest court that the provision was unconstitutional would be taken to mean a boost to judicial independence and a defeat for the regime. Furthermore, it would mean that the Government would have to pay one to four billion Wons (approximately U.S. $3 to $12 million dollars by the exchange rate at that time) for the accumulated claims. In fact, the major reason for the legal restriction on tort liability claims was to save the Government money. Also, if the provision were held invalid, the family of a soldier killed during drill by a negligent comrade could get more compensation than the family of a soldier killed during a combat mission.

So the Government was determined to save the provision. In July 1970, the Government and the ruling party sponsored a bill to revise a provision of the Judiciary Organization Law (1949).[22] The bill finally passed the National Assembly and became effective from August of the same year despite the vehement opposition of the bar and the New Democratic Party. The sole purpose of the revision of Article 59(1) was to add the following new provision: "For the Supreme Court to hold a statute unconstitutional, more than two-thirds of the Justices must be present and more than two-thirds of the Justices present must concur."

On June 22, 1971, the Supreme Court, by a vote of eleven-to-five, held the provision of Article 59(1) of the Judiciary Organization Law unconstitutional, and by a nine-to-seven vote, it also held Article 2(1) of the Government Tort Liability Law unconstitutional. The decision created a sensation throughout the country and had great impact on politics and law.

First, as for Article 59(1) of the Judiciary Organization Law, the majority opinion of the Supreme Court held that because of the separation of powers principle enunciated in the Constitution, an exception to using the majority rule in deciding cases could be made only by the Constitution itself. Thus, the Court held it would decide the constitutionality of the Government Tort Liability Law by simple majority rule. Second, the Court held that Article 2 (1) of the liability law violated the equal protection of law clause and also constituted an unjustifiable deprivation of basic right.

The decision was remarkable in many senses. It was the first time that provisions of statutes had been nullified by the Supreme Court of Korea. The bar and the academic community praised the Court's determined decision and expected the judiciary would continue to be more active to protect personal freedom and rights against abuses of government powers. But reactions from the Government and the ruling Democratic Republican Party were quite different. They denounced the judiciary as not understanding the situation of its own nation. As it turned out later, the decision gave President Park a reason to scrap the Constitution of 1962 and to build the so-called "*Yushin*" (Revitalization) regime in 1972 under a new Constitution.

Reflections on Judicial Review

By the Constitution of 1972, a Constitution Committee was given the power of constitutional review, and President Park the power to renominate all judges. The Judiciary Organization Law was radically amended. The shocking result of the renominating procedure was exclusion from renomination of the nine Justices of the Supreme Court who had held the

Provision of Article 2(1) of the Government Tort Liability Law unconstitutional.

And so judicial review disappeared from Korea. A series of questions arises. Was the system of judicial review in the Third Republic of Korea a failure? If it was a failure, what was the reason? If it was not a failure, could the system be readopted in Korea?

Professor Bong Keun Kal, one of the architects of the Constitution of 1972, once argued that judicial review in the Third Republic was a complete failure. By his theory, judicial review was doomed to fail in Korea for several reasons: a lack of historical background for judicial supremacy; the judges' lack of credibility or authority among the people; and a legal culture different from that of the U.S.[23]

But it is not difficult to arrive at a conclusion that Professor Kal's theory is far-fetched and wrong. True, the role of judges in the constitutional system of the U.S. is extremely important and the success of judicial review in the U.S. is much indebted to the general caliber of its federal judges and to the common law tradition. However, it should be emphasized that judicial review in the Third Republic of Korea was "destroyed" by the "Yushin" Reforms of 1972. The "Yushin" Reforms were in fact an imposed *coup d'etat* of the ruling group; the judiciary was helpless in the face of such a grim political reality. Therefore one may reasonably guess that judicial review could have been firmly developed in Korea if not for the "Yushin" Reforms.

However, it should also be emphasized that the judicial system of Korea has always been different from that of America. The critical role of federal judges in the development of judicial review is well-known. Federal judges of the U.S. are appointed by the President with the advice and consent of the Senate and hold their offices during good behavior, or in other words, for lifes.[24] The practice of judicial review was established by the great Chief Justice John Marshall in the historic decision of *Marbury v. Madisons*,[25] even though the Constitution is silent on this matter. Since then, the federal courts, especially the U.S. Supreme Court, have played a very important role in shaping the political and social life of Americans. A federal judgeship holds such honor that very few have resigned or moved to other offices.

In contrast, judges in Korea are normally recruited from among fresh young lawyers who have passed a national law examination. Therefore, it is not uncommon that young lawyers in their twenties become district court judges. Moreover, judges move or rotate frequently from one district to another under a personnel management system inside the judiciary. As a result, judicial independence in Korea is not comparable to that of federal judges of the U.S.

In short, though judicial review was adopted in the Third Republic of Korea, it did not develop as hoped: the Government under President Park was not willing to respect the decisions of the courts, and judges were not independent.

Conclusion

Several conclusions can be drawn. First, the Constitution of 1962 adopted a governmental system based on the constitutional principles of the U.S. However, in practice the government became more authoritarian because the regime of President Park was not willing to respect the constitutional principles.[26]   Second, the experience of judicial review during the Third Republic was never satisfactory. Yet the decisions of the Supreme Court in 1971 had an enormous impact and brought strong reaction from the regime. Third, the question of whether Korea's constitutional experience based on U.S. doctrines of constitutional law was a success or failure is debated, even when considered without reference to the notorious "*Yushin*" Reforms. If the answer is "success," then a governmental system with a presidency and judicial review can be readopted in Korea.

The Constitution of the Fourth Republic (1972-1979) and the Discarding of American Constitutional Doctrines

The Constitution of 1972

On October 17, 1972, President Park declared a state of emergency and took extraordinary measures, including dissolution of the National Assembly and suspension of the political and civil rights of the people. On October 27, a draft Constitution was promulgated by the Extraordinary Cabinet Meeting which was given legislative power. The proposed Constitution passed in a referendum on November 21 and went into effect on November 25, thus beginning the period of the Fourth Republic. The Constitution of 1972 or the Fourth Republic is commonly referred to as "*Yushin*" (revitalization) Constitution.   "*Yushin*," was a catch phrase of the regime to justify an extraordinary political upheaval.

Adoption of the new Constitution and reorganization of the Government came swiftly, a sign that the movement was well and secretly prepared by a handful of political advisers to President Park. The regime continued until the assassination of President Park in October 1979; the period between 1972-

1979 can be viewed as the "dark age" of constitutionalism in the recent history of Korea.

Characteristics of the Constitution

The major characteristic of the Constitution of 1972 was concentration of powers in the President. The President was elected by the National Congress for Reunification, a specially organized group consisting of some 2,300 delegates, elected for a term of six years. The Delegates were elected by popular vote. They had to be at least 30 years old and had to be eligible to become members of the National Assembly (Arts. 36 and 37 of the Constitution of the Fourth Republic).[27] The President was given powers to declare a state of emergency, to take extraordinary measures, and to dissolve the National Assembly. He was also empowered to appoint one-third of the Members of National Assembly upon approval of the National Congress for the Reunification, to appoint the Chief Justice with the approval of the National Assembly, and to designate all other judges upon the recommendation of the Chief Justice.

A Constitution Committee was newly established. The Committee consisted of nine members appointed by the President, among whom three were nominated by the Chief Justice and three selected by the National Assembly. The main function of the Committee was the constitutional review of laws submitted by the courts. The governmental structure under the Constitution of 1972 thus had nothing in common with the American counterpart.

The Fall of the Fourth Republic

The regime of the Fourth Republic could be sustained only by a series of extraordinary measures prohibiting activities arguing for or discussing the revision of the Constitution of 1972. That Constitution obviously had many undemocratic aspects which benefited only President Park and his followers. The latter part of the Fourth Republic period brought a bitter relationship with the U.S. Government as President Carter's foreign policy promoted human rights. With the second "oil shock" in the spring of 1979, Korea's economy was abruptly disrupted and civil turmoil erupted in southern cities in the Fall. October 26, 1979, President Park was shot and killed by his own right-hand man, Jae Kyu Kim, then Director of the Korean Central Intelligence Agency. With the death of President Park, the Constitution of 1972 and the "*Yushin*" system of government lost their sole *raison d'etre*.

Reflection

The most distinctive constitutional doctrines originating from the U.S. Constitution, presidential government based upon the separation of powers principle and the doctrine of judicial review, were thrown out of the constitutional system of Korea by the *"Yushin"* Reforms. The sole purpose of the *"Yushin"* Reforms was to make possible President Park's stay in office permanent. The Fourth Republic was an unfortunate and shameful episode for most of Korea's people.

The Fifth Republic (1980-1986: A Modified Presidential Government

The Constitution of 1980

On October 26, 1979, President Park was killed by Jae Kyu Kim. The next day martial law was declared throughout the nation (except in Cheju Island Province) to prevent possible attack from North Korea. The death of Park prompted debate on drafting a new Constitution. On November 10, 1979, Acting President Kyu Hah Choi announced that the Constitution should be amended as soon as possible, and on November 26, the National Assembly established the Special Committee for Constitutional Revision. On December 12, 1979, General Sung Hwa Chung, then the Commander of the Martial Law Command and Chief of Staff of the Army, was arrested by Armed Forces Security Command personnel [for alleged implication in the assassination of Park]. As a result Major General Doo Hwan Chun, the Commander of the Armed Forces Security Command emerged as Korea's strongman.

On March 13, 1980, the Government established the Advisory Committee for Constitutional Revision in the President's Office. From late March, demonstrations and mass assemblies were held throughout the nation demanding political freedom and democracy. University students asked for academic freedom; and serious labor disputes, some violent, arose in many workplaces. On May 15, immense student demonstrations were held throughout the nation. Two days later, the Government declared martial law and arrested Dae Jung Kim and other dissident leaders on charges of fomenting civil revolt.

On May 18, 1980, massive demonstrations by students and other citizens erupted in Kwangju City, the provincial capital of Chollanamdo Province where Dae Jung Kim has a strong following. Nervous about possible violence, military units dispatched by the Government a few days earlier from other regions opened fire on unarmed protesters. The Kwangju Incident resulted in heavy civilian casualties. After the incident, the anti-government movement was subdued. On August 16, President Choi resigned from the presidency, and on August 27, General Chun was selected as the new President under the Constitution of the Fourth Republic. The Government under President Chun took over the work of drafting the new Constitution. The Draft Constitution took final shape in September, was adopted by referendum, and went into effect on September 27, 1980, the Constitution of the Fifth Republic. On February 25, Chun was elected as the nation's twelfth President under the electoral procedures of the new Constitution.

Characteristics of the Constitution

The governmental structure of the Fifth Republic was a modified presidential system. The President, given strong power and authority under the Constitution, was elected for a term of seven years by a Presidential Electoral College consisting of some 5,000 electors. The President could not be reelected even once. The Prime Minister (Article 62) and Chief Justice were appointed by the President subject to the approval of the National Assembly. Ministers of the Cabinet were appointed by the Prime Minister (Article 69). The Chief Justice of the Supreme Court was appointed by the President subject to the approval of the National Assembly. Justices of the Supreme Court were appointed by the President upon recommendation by the Chief Justice, while other judges were appointed by the Chief Justice (Article 105).   A Constitution Committee was established to review the constitutionality of laws upon submission by the courts. Civil rights provisions were notably stronger than in the Constitution of 1972.

The Issue of the 1980s: Direct Election of the President

After the National Assembly elections in February, 1985, revision of the Constitution was the major political issue. The first point at issue was how to elect the President.   The New Democratic Party emerged as the major opposition party in the election of 1985 under the influence of two eminent dissident leaders Dae Jung Kim and Young Sam Kim. This party officially declared that prompt constitutional revision to allow direct election of the President by the people was necessary.

During the controversy on the presidential selection procedure, one constitutional law professor said that Korea's system was basically similar to that of the U.S.[28] More detailed analysis is needed in response to that and related issues.

The president election process under the Fifth Republic's Constitution had two phases, the election of the Presidential Electoral College by the people and the election of the President by the electors.[29] The Constitution provided only that the number of electors should be more than 5,000, and the Presidential Election Law said the number should be 5,278.   To be a candidate for elector, one had to be at least 30 years old and eligible to run for membership in the National Assembly.   On the other hand, Members of the National Assembly and government officials were not eligible to serve as electors.[30] Candidates for electors could declare their support for a particular prospective candidate for President, but they were not required to do so by the law.   Electors gathered and elected the President by secret ballot. Therefore, the Presidential selection process under the Fifth Constitution of Korea was clearly "indirect" election, and thus completely different from the presidential election system of the U.S.

Of course, the Electoral College still exists in the U.S. and is empowered to choose the President of the U.S. under the plain language of the U.S. Constitution.   But, as is well known, constitutional practice diverges from the text.   The Presidential Electoral College of the U.S., now consisting of 538 electors, was devised to elect the President of the U.S. by its own decision, but since electors came to serve as dummies for parties and later for the general electorate in the early nineteenth century, the process has been one of direct election in effect.   As a result, it is a mistake to claim basic similarity between the presidential election processes of Korea and the U.S.

The controversy on election of the President was serious because the ruling Democratic Justice Party refused to acknowledge the flaw in the system and the opposition New Democratic Party started a full-scale disobedience movement.   However, in April, 1986, the ruling party, which had persistently maintained that any constitutional change would be possible only after the 1988 Olympic Games in Seoul, modified its position and opened up the possibility of constitutional revision in the Fall of 1986.   This was in response to the increasing demands for constitutional change from the opposition party, students and dissident leaders.

It was obvious that the "undemocratic" Constitution should be replaced. The central question was whether Korea should once again adopt a presidential system allowing people to directly elect their President, or should rather switch to a parliamentary system, on grounds that the president system had never been successful in Korea.

Another important issue was how to revitalize the constitutional review mechanism.   Some constitutional scholars wanted to establish a constitutional court to replace the Constitution Committee,[31] while judges and practicing lawyers generally preferred to give the power of constitutional review to the ordinary courts.[32]

Once again virtually complete revision of the Constitution of Korea was asked for and eventually received. Opposition leaders such as Dae Jung Kim, the unsuccessful presidential candidate in 1971 election, and Young Sam Kim, former Chairman of New Democratic Party, wanted a presidential system where the doctrine of separation of powers is guaranteed and the President is directly elected by the people, a Constitution embodying principles originating from the U.S. Constitution. On the other hand, the ruling Democratic Justice Party inclined toward a parliamentary system of government. The major political parties negotiated at length the timing and the procedures for constitutional revision, and the Constitution of Korea was revised in the dramatic political sequence of 1987.

A New Constitution is Adopted

The year 1987 in Korea will be remembered as the year of a constitutional miracle.[33] Constitutional revision, which had been a hot issue since the general election in February 1985, once seemed almost impossible. But finally the impossible happened in Korea in a series of dramatic events.

On April 30, 1986, the Government under President Chun officially declared that constitutional revision would be possible during President Chun's current term (1981-1988). From that time, the major political parties began to prepare their respective versions of a new Constitution. The ruling Democratic Justice Party declared that a new Constitution would be one establishing a parliamentary system of government. However, the New Democratic Party, the major opposition party, made clear that only a Constitution which allowed direct presidential election would be acceptable to them. In fact, "direct election of the president" was a political motto for the opposition party in the 1985 election. Moreover, this motto had special meaning for many Koreans as they had been deprived of the right and opportunity to elect their President by themselves since the "*Yushin* Reform" in 1972.

As the ruling party and the opposition party each demanded its own versions, no compromise seemed possible. Thus political negotiations were stalled as the year 1986 ended. In early 1987, Chairman Min Woo Lee of the New Democratic Party said that if the Government was willing to take democratization measures first, a parliamentary governmental system might be considered acceptable to his party. But this remark brought forth furious opposition within his own party. Young Sam Kim, Dae Jung Kim and their followers broke away from the New Democratic Party and established their own party. The National Unification and Democracy Party became the major opposition party.

The new opposition party leaders declared that only a presidential system with direct election of the President would be acceptable to them, and the political confrontations between the ruling party and the opposition became more intense. On April 13, 1987, President Chun announced that constitutional revision was impossible because of the failure of a political consensus to emerge, and that the next President would be selected by the current method of indirect election by the electoral college. This pronouncement became a major target for attack from anti-government students, religious activists, and opposition politicians.

In the meantime, a very unfortunate incident occurred. On January 15, 1987, the Chief of the National Police Bureau disclosed that a student named Chong Chul Park died of a heart attack during interrogation in a security police unit's office in Seoul. However, it was soon disclosed that he died instead of torture around midnight of January 14. This incident set off a public outcry, and the Government reshuffled the Cabinet and ordered a full investigation of the incident. However, anti-government emotion and political movement was at a high tide.

Some change was called for on the side of the ruling party; so the Democratic Justice Party selected Tae Woo Roh, a colleague of President Chun in the Military Academy and also a key member of the political machine which established the Fifth Republic in 1980, as new Chairman of the Party. Generally regarded as moderate and reasonable, Roh was selected by the ruling party as its next presidential candidate on June 10, 1987. On the evening of the same day, the opposition party and dissident activists held nationwide rallies denouncing the torture death of the student and calling for a new democratic Constitution. Anti-government demonstrations were held in over twenty cities; from 45,000 (police estimate) to 300,000 (the opposition party's estimate) people attended. Though the demonstrations were generally peaceful, violence broke out and the riot police used tear gas. On several occasions, police stations and police vehicles were burned by firebombs thrown by demonstrators.

The climax came with massive demonstrations held on June 26, 1987. At least 200,000 people joined in anti-government gatherings throughout the nation calling for a new Constitution and direct election of the President.

Tae Woo Roh ended the crisis on June 29, 1987. Totally unexpectedly, Roh declared, as Chairman of the ruling party, that he would accept a direct presidential election system and would pursue major political reform towards genuine democracy. His declaration won him a place on the covers of such international news magazines as *Time* and *Newsweek*. With his declaration, most anti-government activity subsided.

After that, negotiations began between the parties for drafting a new Constitution. Though they had differences regarding many aspects of the constitutional system, the negotiators finally reached agreement on a draft Constitution on September 17. On October 12, the National Assembly approved the draft Constitution almost unanimously (254 yeas and 4 nays). The new Constitution of the Republic of Korea was finally approved in a referendum on October 25, by more than 93 percent of valid votes. As for the next presidential election, a special provision Article mandated election of a new President under the new Constitution *before* the whole document took effect on February 25, 1988. The first election under the new Constitution was held on December 16, 1987.[34] Tae Woo Roh defeated a divided opposition with a plurality of 36.6%. Since Dae Jung Kim and Young Sam Kim both ran for election as the candidates of different parties, their majority did not combine to defeat Roh voters. Moreover, it is generally recognized that Roh did fairly well in the campaign and was successful in gaining support from people who wanted a stable government able to continue economic growth.

A general election to choose members of the National Assembly was held on April 26, 1988, under a new Election Law, with surprising results. For the first time in Korea's constitutional history, the ruling party failed to win a majority of the seats. The strength of the four parties in the legislature was as follows:

Democratic Justice Party 125
Party of Peace and Democracy 70
National Unification and Democracy Party 59
New Democratic Republican Party 35
Total 289

The Kims who ran for the Presidency in 1987 were elected to the National Assembly. The general results of the election were obviously a disappointment for President Roh and his Democratic Justice Party. Therefore, serious concern continues: can this kind of "divided government" be successfully managed in Korea which does not have experience with the politics of delicate balance?

Major aspects of government under the Constitution of the new Sixth Republic are as follows:

The Presidency and the Executive Branch

The President is elected in a national election by the people (Art. 67). This is the single most important provision of the new Constitution. The people of Korea were able to elect their President directly for the first time since 1971 on December 16, 1987.

The President's term is five years and he may not stand for reelection (Art. 70). The most logical explanation for this provision seems to be that it resulted from a compromise between the ruling party and the opposition party. The Prime Minister is appointed by the President with the consent of the National Assembly (Art. 62). Ministers are appointed by the President upon recommendation of the Prime Minister (Art. 87, Art. 94). The State Council, which consists of the President, Prime Minister and Ministers, deliberates on important policies that fall within the power of the Executive (Art. 88).

The National Assembly

Members of the National Assembly are elected by universal and direct ballot (Art. 77). Their term is four years (Art. 78).

The Judiciary

The Chief Justice of the Supreme Court is appointed by the President for a non-renewable term of six years, with the consent of the National Assembly. Associate Justices of the Supreme Court are appointed for a renewable six-year term by the President upon the recommendation of the Chief Justice (Art. 104, Art. 105). All other judges are appointed by the Chief Justice with the consent of the Council of Justices for renewable terms of ten years (Art. 104, Art. 105).

The Constitutional Court

The Constitutional Court, which consists of nine judges, is empowered to decide on the constitutionality of any statute which the courts refer to it for a determination (Art. 111, Art. 112). At least six judges on the Constitutional Court must concur for a holding that provisions of a statute are unconstitutional.

The Rights of the Individual

Under the new Constitution, individual rights are reinforced. The most notable improvements in civil rights are in the areas of criminal procedure and the freedoms of expression, association and assembly. For example, a detainee has a right to be informed of the reasons for arrest and a right to be assisted by counsel (Art. 12[5]); and permits are no longer required for a public speech, publication, association or assembly (Art. 2 [2]).

Certainly, these are improvements in the constitutional text; more important is government practice in the human rights area. It is generally hoped and expected that the new government will abide by constitutional rights requirements more vigilantly than past governments.

Conclusion

The foregoing discussion has shown that the constitutional theory and practices of the United States have influenced Korea since 1945, and several main points stand out clearly as a result of our study.

First, as the U.S. Military Government (USAMGIK) ruled Korea from 1945 to 1948, many constitutional principles of the U.S. were introduced into Korea during that period. It is also widely believed in Korea that the USAMGIK did play a rather significant role in establishing the New Republic and the 1948 Constitution of Korea.

Second, the Constitution of the First Republic (1948-1960) established a presidential government, but with many differences from the U.S. system. Unfortunately, government processes became dictatorial, as the Constitution was twice amended solely for the purpose of reelecting President Syngman Rhee.

Third, the influence of the U.S. Constitution was virtually nil on the government institutions of the Second Republic (1960-1961). Rather, the governmental structure of the Second Republic was based upon European parliamentarism.

Fourth, the Constitution of the Third Republic (1962-1972) was generally based upon American concepts of government. It established presidential government with a separation of powers, and the power of judicial review was given to the courts. It is fair to say that the influence of American constitutional law doctrine was strongest during the years of the Third Republic. However, as President Park's regime became dictatorial, many constitutional limitations on power, such as judicial review, were regarded as too burdensome by the ruling party and the Government. These developments resulted in the so-called "October Revolution," the *"Yushin"* Revolution in 1972.

Fifth, political and constitutional life during the Fourth Republic years was at all times bleak. The ruling regime was only sustained by a series of extraordinary and repressive measures taken by President Park. In such a situation, the influence of American constitutional principles virtually disappeared. Moreover, some precious American constitutional doctrines were unduly criticized by several professors who supported President Park.

Sixth, the Constitution of the Fifth Republic (1980-1988) was a result of a reconciliation of the need for efficient and strong government with the people's desire for democracy. But still, this Constitution gave too much power and authority to the President. Especially criticized as undemocratic was the election of the President by the Electoral College. In addition, the Constitution Committee was under attack as ineffective; the Committee never functioned, and thus was called a "sleeping organ" of government.

One must conclude that though the current Constitution of Korea was not based upon the American model of government, Korea's experience with presidential government and judicial review during the Third Republic has continued to have great influence, and thus no discussion of constitutional revision can be conducted without considering that experience. As emphasized before, the Constitution of the Third Republic of Korea was a Constitution based on American concepts of government and constitutionalism. Though the future of constitutional democracy is not certain, it is remarkable that so many people in Korea wanted a new Constitution with a strong Bill of Rights, a separation of powers, and judicial review. Clearly, these constitute the most significant contribution of the United States Constitution to Korea.

NOTES

*This chapter draws on two previously published articles by the authors in Korean: Tscholsu Kim, "The Influence of the U.S. Constitution Upon the Korean Constitution," 25 *Seoul Law Journal*, (1985); and Sang Don Lee, "The Influence of the U.S. Constitutional Law Doctrine Upon the Constitutional Development of Korea," 14 *Public Law* (1986). Many Korean citations and notes, have been eliminated for purposes of this book, as they are not accessible to most readers. [Editor's Note: A comprehensive introduction to recent Korean affairs is Donald Stone Macdonald, *The Koreans: Contemporary Politics and Society*, 2nd ed., Boulder, Westview Press, 1990). In this chapter Korean names are given in the Western, not Korean order, with family name last.]

1. For more detailed study of the U.S. Military Administration in Korea, *see*, e.g., G. Mead, *The American Military Government* (1952); Gregory Henderson, *Korea: The Politics of the Vortex*, Cambridge, Harvard University Press, 1968; Robert Oliver, *Syngman Rhee and American Involvement in Korea, 1942-1960*, Seoul, Panmun Publishing Co., 1978; Bruce Cummings, ed., *The Child of Conflict*, Seattle, University of Washington Press, 1983.
2. Chin-O Yu, *Memoirs on Drafting the Constitution* (1980), 48-51 (in Korean).[*Editor's Note.* See W. Shaw, Ed., *Human Rights in Korea*, Cambridge, Havard University Press, 1991.]
3. *Id.* 22.
4. Tscholsu Kim, *The History of the Constitution of Korea*, Seoul, Taehak Publishing Co., 1988 (in Korean), 18-23.
5. *See* Karl Loewenstein, "The Presidency Outside the United States: A Study in Comparative Political Institution," *Journal of Politics*, Vol. VI (1949).
6. *Seoul Daily News*, June 8, 1948 (in Korean).
7. *Constitutional History: Documents*, Vol. 1 (1967) 107-108 (in Korean).
8. Chin-O Yu, *supra* note 2, at 42-43.
9. Tscholsu Kim, *The History of the Constitution of Korea*, 79-80.
10. Chin-O Yu, "Constitutional Amendment Toward the Parliamentary System and Political Prospects," *Korean University News*, June 1960 (in Korean).
11. Tae Yeon Han, "Tendency of the Constitution of the Second republic," *Sa-Sang-Kye*, June 1960, 165-173 (in Korean).
12. The first names of two American professors who visited Korea in 1962 are not recorded in Korea. People who participated to the constitution-making process only remember their last names. Some have said erroneously that Professor Emerson was from the political science department. Rather, he was Thomas I. Emerson of Yale Law School, the noted scholar of freedom of expression.
13. Statement of Dr. Chun Shik Park, then a Member of the Constitutional Drafting Committee, on February 3, 1985.

14. *Records of Constitutional Amendment*, Vol. 1 (The National Assembly Library, 1967), 197-217 (in Korean).
15. In the presidential election held on April 27, 1971, President Park won 52.68% of the valid voters nationwide, and Kim won 44.82%. However, among voters of Seoul, Kim won 59.93% while Park gained only 39.92%.
In the election of members of the National Assembly, the ruling Democratic Republican Party won 113 seats and the opposition New Democratic Party won 89 seats. However, the ruling party won only one seat from the Seoul Metropolitan Area and the remaining 18 seats went to the opposition party.
16. *Id.* 380-385.
17. The Anti-Communist Law (Law No. 643) was enacted on July 3, 1961 after the military coup in May of that year. The Law was originally intended to protect national interests from various Communist infiltrations, but it contained several vague provisions which could be misapplied to the critics of the government. The Law was amended several times and finally repealed in December, 1980. However, most of the Law was integrated into new legislation, the National Security Law of 1980 (Law No. 3318).
18. On July 15, 1968, the Supreme Court refused to review the constitutionality of the National Assembly Election Law. The Law was challenged for its "proportional representation system" which actually gave "premium seats" to the winning Party of a general election. The Court held the plaintiff lacked standing to sue. On October 23, 1969, the Supreme Court held Article 4(1) of the Anti-Communist Law constitutional. This provision punishes those who comment on, encourage or sympathize with an anti-State group by imprisonment of not more than seven years.
19. The Government Tort Liability Law(Law No. 1899) was enacted in 1967, and amended in 1973, 1980, and 1981.
20. Seoul District Court (Civil Division), May 30, 1968; Seoul District Court (Civil Division), June 11, 1968.
21. Seoul High Court (Mar. 11, 1970; Case No. 69-Na-1631).
22. The Judiciary Organization Law was first enacted in 1949 (Law No. 51) and has been amended frequently. The revision of 1970 was done by the amendment on August 7, 1980 (Law No. 2222).
23. Bong Keun Kal, *A Treatise on the Yushin Constitution* (1976), 393-394 (in Korean).
24. Art. II, Sec. 2, Art. III, Sec. 1 of the Constitution of the United States.
25. 1 *Cranch* 137 (1803).
26. For political and constitutional developments during the Third Republic of Korea, *see, e.g.*, Se Jin Kim and Chang Hyun Cho, *Government and Politics of Korea* The Research Institute of Korean Affairs, Maryland, 1972; Chi Young Park, "The Third Republic Constitution of Korea: An Analysis," 21 *Western Political Quarterly*, (1968), 110; Dai-Kwon Choi, *Law and Social Change, the Korean Experience*, Ph.D. Dissertation, University of California, Berkeley, 1976.

27. For the details of the *"Yushin"* Constitution of the Fourth Republic, *see, e.g.*, Bong Kun Kal, *Treatise on the Yushin Constitution*, Seoul, Korean Constitutional Law Association Press, 1973 (in Korean).

28. Hong Joo Moon, *Chung Ang Il Bo*, Jan. 14, 1983 (a daily newspaper in Korean).

29. Art. 40(1) of the Constitution.

30. Art. 41(1) of the Constitution.

31. Tscholsu Kim, *Constitutional Review* (1983), 545-546 (in Korean).

32.   Interview with retiring Justice Hoi Chang Lee of the Supreme Court, *Chung Ang Il Bo*, April 12, 1986, 7 (in Korean). In the interview, now retired Justice Lee said that the power of constitutional review should be returned to the courts. Justice Lee is best known for his liberal view of civil rights which was strongly stated in several famous dissenting opinions.

33. *See* Han Sung-Joo, "South Korea in 1987: The Politics of Democratization," *Asian Survey*, January, 1988, 52.

34. *Results of the Presidential Election of Dec. 16, 1987*:

Tae Woo Roh (Democratic Justice Party)
    -- 8,282,738 votes (36.6%)
Young Sam Kim (National Unification and Democracy Party)
    -- 6,337,681 votes (28.0%)
Dae Jung Kim (Party of Peace and Democracy)
    -- 6,113,375 votes (27.0%)
Jong Pil Kim (New Democratic Republican Party)
    -- 1,823,067 votes (8.1%)

SOCIALIST REPUBLIC OF VIETNAM

The Constitutional System of the Socialist Republic of Vietnam

William J. Duiker

Vietnamese Constitutions since 1946

In Communist systems, state Constitutions are not intended to serve as permanent documents reflecting the timeless political and philosophical values of a given society. Rather, they are designed to chart the progress of that society as it evolves through stages of growth to a final state of classless Communism. Normally, a separate Constitution is written at each stage in order to establish policies to be adopted at that stage and set forth objectives to be achieved in preparation for the following one.[1]

Vietnam is a case in point. Since the formation of the independent Democratic Republic of Vietnam (DRV) under the leadership of the Indochinese Communist Party in September 1945, Vietnam has had three Constitutions.[2] The first had been adopted in November 1946, at a time when the DRV (whose authority was at that time limited to the northern provinces) was preparing for an inevitable showdown with the French colonial regime, then based in the South, for control over the entire country. In keeping with the Party's needs at that time, the 1946 one was a moderate document that was specifically crafted to appeal to a broad spectrum of the population throughout Vietnam. Its political section emphasized democratic freedoms and the need for a coalition of popular forces to struggle against the restoration of French rule. Those articles dealing with economics guaranteed the sanctity of private property and included no references to the Party's ultimate objective of building a Communist society.[3]

The second Constitution was promulgated on December 31, 1959, five years after the Geneva Conference had divided Vietnam into two separate zones in North and South. The North had already begun the transition to a socialist society under the leadership of the Party. The majority of the peasants had been placed in low-level collective organizations and the Hanoi regime was about to approve its first five-year plan to lay the foundations of socialist industrialization. In ideological terms, the new document was somewhat more doctrinaire than its predecessor. The leading role of the

Party--now renamed the Vietnamese Workers' Party, or VWP--was openly stated in the Preamble, while Article 9 declared flatly that the DRV "is advancing step by step from people's democracy to socialism by developing and transforming the national economy along socialist lines."[4]

The 1959 Constitution, however, did retain some of the reticence of its predecessor about the actualities of power in the DRV and the directions that would be taken in the future. Although the VWP possessed a monopoly of power in managing the affairs of the state, nowhere, except for a brief reference to the "clearsighted leadership" of the Party in the Preamble, was its dominant role mentioned in the body of the Constitution. Nor was there any reference to the role of Marxism-Leninism as the guiding ideology of the state. Finally, an Article declared that "the state by law protects the right of national capitalists to own means of production and other capital." Socialism was clearly set forth as an ultimate goal rather than an immediate reality.[5]

Why did the Party refrain from a more direct statement of its intentions and a more rapid transition to a full state of socialism? In part, Vietnamese leaders undoubtedly recognized that because of the relatively primitive state of the Vietnamese economy, the transition to socialism would be a lengthy process. Equally important, perhaps, the regime wished to avoid alienating moderate elements in the South at the opening of what would eventually become known as the Vietnam War.

In early July 1976, the National Assembly of the DRV called for the creation of a commission to draft a third Constitution. Party General Secretary Le Duan had set the tone in his report to the Assembly on June 25th.[6]

> At present, our people have entered a new stage of the revolution, the stage in which the whole country is making socialist revolution, the north continuing to promote socialist construction, while the south actively engages in the socialist transformation of the economy and the building of socialism.The present requirement of the revolution of our state is to work out a new constitution for the whole country so as to consolidate the successes already gained and to ensure the rapid, vigorous and steady advance of our entire country to socialism.

The Constitution drafting commission indeed began its labors at a time of burgeoning optimism about the future of the Vietnamese revolution. The country, now renamed the Socialist Republic of Vietnam, or SRV, was newly reunited for the first time since before the French conquest in the late nineteenth century. Vietnamese Party leaders, understandably proud of their hard-won victory over the Saigon regime and the United States, appeared to believe that an all-out attack on the nation's internal challenges would be equally successful. At the Fourth National Congress of the Party (itself now retitled the Vietnamese Communist Party, or VCP), Party leaders decided to adopt an accelerated program to move rapidly toward socialist transformation in the South and the achievement of an essentially socialist Vietnam by the end of the decade.[7]

In the years immediately following the Fourth Party Congress, many of these enthusiastic hopes were dashed as the Vietnamese revolution entered a period of internal and external crisis. At home, economic difficulties caused by bad weather, lack of capital and experience, and the demands of postwar reconstruction led to a rising level of popular discontent. In foreign affairs, the Vietnamese invasion of Kampuchea in December 1978 led to a brief border war with China and forced the regime to devote increased funds to national defense. Faced with a serious decline in agricultural and industrial production, a plenary session of the Party Central Committee held in September 1979 decided to slow down the pace of socialist transformation in an effort to spur production and avert a further descent into crisis.

In the meantime, work on the new Constitution proceeded. In 1978, on instructions from the Party Central Committee and the Standing Committee of the National Assembly, the Constitution Drafting committee, assisted by other Party and government agencies, organized public meetings to discuss the proposed Constitution. The first phase was for senior and middle-level officials, and the second for junior cadres and the general population. According to official sources, almost twenty million people took part in the deliberations. Others sent letters or met privately with government officials.[8]

According to Truong Chinh, Chairman of the Drafting Commission and a key member of the Party Politburo, the discussions brought forth a number of useful suggestions and criticisms. Many of the latter were apparently quite blunt: the bureaucracy was cumbersome, officials were corrupt and authoritarian, and the Party had become excessively involved in day-to-day activities. Suggestions ranged from semantic issues related to the wording of specific passages in the document to broader questions concerning the degree of public participation in the governing process.[9]

The draft Constitution was presented to a plenary session of the Central Committee of the Party in September 1980. After approval by the plenum, it was brought before the National Assembly in early December. In his report to the Assembly on December 12, Truong Chinh reiterated why a new Constitution was necessary. In 1959, he said, Vietnam was divided into two zones, and the North had "just entered the period of socialist transformation."

Now the entire country was united and moving rapidly toward socialism. Thus, he concluded, our state needs a Constitution conforming to the changed economic and social relations in our country and capable of creating favorable conditions for mobilizing the force of the entire people to build socialism on a national scale.[10]

The draft Constitution unanimously approved by the National Assembly on December 18 consisted of twelve chapters and 147 articles. In form it resembled its predecessor, although it was somewhat longer, and in addition to chapters dealing with the political system, the economic system, and the basic rights and duties of citizens added two new chapters entitled "Culture, Education, Science and Technology" and "Defense of the Socialist Homeland." Like the 1959 Constitution, it opened with a preamble describing the trials and achievements of the Vietnamese people and explaining the need for a new charter.

In substance, there were relatively few basic changes from the 1959 version. But the 1980 Constitution elaborated on a number of points left ambiguous by its predecessor, and was more specific in outlining national objectives. It was clearly intended to be a document that would take the Vietnamese nation to an advanced state of socialism. As Truong Chinh noted in his opening report to the National Assembly, the new Constitution "will not confine itself to what has been and is being done ..., but also embraces some works which must be done, which will be done step by step and are sure to be accomplished in the process of the successful building of socialism."[11] The key points in the new Constitution are set out below.

The Role of the Party

In all Communist societies, the key issue is that of power--the power of the state to control and transform society according to the Party line. There is, of course, an element of paradox in this, since it was Marx's colleague Friedrich Engels who had predicted that under Communism the state, as an instrument of class oppression, would naturally "wither away". In reality, in Communist societies the state has served as a powerful weapon in the hands of the Party to eliminate the remnants of the previous ruling class in the bitter "struggle between two lines" that inevitably takes place after the revolution, and to implant the seeds of the new socialist order. The form of that weapon is called the Dictatorship of the Proletariat.

For Vietnamese Communists, the concept of the proletarian dictatorship was from the beginning complicated by the Party's need to disguise its leading role in the Vietnamese revolution in order to win support from broad elements of the population against the French and later against the United States. This was particularly the case in 1946 when the DRV was, in form, a coalition government of several political parties linked in a broad alliance to oppose the return of the French colonial regime. Although it was in practice the dominant force in the coalition, the Party formally dissolved itself in the fall of 1945 in order to allay the suspicions of moderate elements about its future intentions. The 1946 Constitution reflected this viewpoint. According to the Preamble, the new state would be based on the following principles:

> The Union of all the people without distinction of race, class, creed, wealth or sex; the guaranteeing of democratic liberties; The establishment of a true people's government. Permeated by the spirit of unity symbolized in the struggle of the entire nation and manifested in an enlarged and enlightened democratic regime, Vietnam now goes forward confidently in consonance with the progressive movements of the world and the peaceful aspirations of mankind.

The 1959 Constitution was written at a time when the role of the Party as the vanguard organization leading North Vietnamese society to socialism was well established. But, as noted above, the regime remained anxious to promote the cause of national reunification among non-communist elements in the South, and was therefore deliberately vague about that role in the new Constitution. While the Preamble referred to the "clear-sighted leadership" of the Vietnamese Workers' Party, it avoided any mention of a dictatorship of the proletariat, stating simply that the DRV was "a people's democratic state based on the alliance between the workers and peasants and led by the working class."[12]

The ambiguity was brought to an end in the 1980 Constitution, where the central role of the Communist Party was expressly underlined. Article 2, in the opening chapter dealing with the political system, declares flatly that "the Socialist Republic of Vietnam is a state of proletarian dictatorship." Article 4 elaborates: "The Communist Party of Vietnam, the vanguard and general staff of the Vietnamese working class, armed with Marxism-Leninism, is the only force leading the state and society, and the main factor determining all successes of the Vietnamese revolution."

This frank assertion of the Party's central role in the affairs of the state was apparently an issue of some sensitivity during the drafting and discussion process. In his report to the National Assembly on December 12, Truong Chinh had conceded that while the Vietnamese people as a whole "welcomed the Party's leading role", some were critical of the penchant of Party units at various echelons for overstepping their authority and encroaching on that of state organs of power.[13] According to Truong Chinh, the final section of Article 4 in the draft Constitution, which stated that Party organizations "operate within the framework of the constitution," represented an effort to respond to these objections. This, he said, will safeguard Vietnamese society against arbitrary and despotic behavior by Party cadres and members.

But Truong Chinh insisted that it was necessary to establish clearly the Party's central role in order "to determine the class character of the state." This, he said, is the most fundamental question in the Constitution. The function of the proletarian dictatorship is "not only to suppress counter-revolutionary acts but also, and chiefly, in building socialism, a new society, a new economy, a new culture, a new people, a well-developed people, with high cultural standards, scientific and technical knowledge, labor skills and socialist virtues." As the experience of the Vietnamese revolution and other proletarian dictatorships elsewhere in the world has shown, this historic mission can only be accomplished under the leadership of a working class party which firmly grasps and applies Marxism-Leninism.[15]

In setting forth the leading role of the Communist Party in the 1980 Constitution, the Hanoi regime was following the model of the 1977 Constitution of the USSR, which stated that "the leading and guiding force in Soviet society and the nucleus of its political system, of all state organizations and public organizations, is the Communist Party of the Soviet Union. The CPSU exists for the people and serves the people."[16] Yet there is evidence that Vietnamese leaders had their own reasons for underlining the importance of the Party's role in the SRV. Beset by external enemies and rising internal dissent, many Party leaders had become increasingly sensitive over matters of security and the Leninist "struggle between two lines." The regime may have seen the constitutional provisions emphasizing the proletarian dictatorship as a crucial means of arming the state against its adversaries within and without.

The SRV departed from the Soviet model on proletarian dictatorship in one respect. Unlike the case in the Soviet Union, the Vietnamese Communist Party is not the only legal political party in the country. Two other minor parties, the Democratic Party and the Socialist Party (representing the interests of the national bourgeoisie and progressive intellectuals, respectively) had been granted a legal existence since the establishment of the DRV in 1945. But the two parties, which were formed under Party leadership to flesh out its united front strategy against the French colonial regime, were not mentioned in the new Constitution and serve only in a figurehead role while consistently following the general line set by the VCP.

The Issue of Collective Mastery

Throughout the remainder of the chapter on the political system, the majority of changes from the 1959 Constitution were in form rather than in substance, but one issue worthy of mention is the degree to which the concept of "collective mastery" (in Vietnamese, *lam chu tap the*) pervades the entire document. In Article 2, for example, it is stated that the historic mission of the SRV is "to establish the collective mastery of the working people." Article 3 declares that:

> In the Socialist Republic of Vietnam, the collective masters are the working people, with the worker-peasant alliance, led by the working class, as the core. The state ensures the continuous perfection and consolidation of the working people's collective mastery in the political, economic, cultural and social fields; collective mastery in the whole country and in each unit; collective mastery over society, over nature, and over oneself.

What is collective mastery, and how was it to be applied in the SRV? The concept appears to have no direct equivalent in the Constitutions of the USSR and the countries of Eastern Europe, but derives from the writings of Marx, Engels and Lenin, who had described socialism as a system of political, economic, cultural and social relations in which the laboring people are the collective masters of the homeland. The term was not mentioned in the 1959 Constitution, but Party General Secretary Le Duan evidently used the term on a number of occasions during the late 1960s and 1970s to describe the relationship between the working masses and the state in the DRV.[17]

At the Fourth Party Congress in December 1976, Le Duan referred to collective mastery in his Political Report, describing it as a system in which "the true and supreme masters are the social community, the organized collectivity of working people, with the worker-peasant alliance as the core."[18] In 1980, the concept was incorporated as one of the signature phrases of the new Constitution and was described by Le Duan in his report to the Central Committee plenum in September as the "quintessence" of the new Constitution.[19]

How was collective mastery to be exercised in Vietnamese society? Unfortunately, the new Constitution had little to say about the issue, merely repeating in Article 6 the phraseology of the 1959 Constitution: in the SRV, "all power belongs to the people." That power, it adds, is exercised through the government organs at all levels which are elected by and accountable to the people. In his report to the Central Committee in September, Le Duan elaborated slightly, pointing out that collective mastery would operate at several levels, through the central and local governments, the popular organizations, in relations between the individual and state, and among individuals themselves.[20]

The Central Government

According to Politburo member Truong Chinh, the primary vehicle for expressing collective mastery in the 1980 Constitution will be through the organs of the state. The supreme governmental body in the SRV is the National Assembly (*Quoc Hoi*). Originally established after the August Revolution in 1945, the National Assembly is described in Article 82 of the 1980 Constitution as "the highest representative body of the people, the highest state authority in the Socialist Republic of Vietnam." As described in the Constitution, its powers are broad. It is the only body vested with constitutional and legislative authority; it decides on basic internal and foreign policies, on tasks and targets of economic and cultural development, and on the main principles regarding the organization and operation of the state apparatus. In fact, it supervises the entire activity of the state.

As in all Marxist-Leninist societies, however, the National Assembly was substantially less influential in fact than it appeared to be on paper, and functioned essentially as a rubberstamp for decisions taken previously by the highest organs of the Party. Party control was established at the start, through the electoral process. While deputies to the National Assembly--like all other candidates for public office in the SRV--were elected on the basis of universal suffrage, with voting equal, direct and secret, in practice the elections were controlled by the Party. Candidates were nominated by the mass organizations at the local level, and few of the seats were contested. At the election held after the promulgation of the 1959 Constitution, for example, there were only 458 candidates for 362 seats. Top Party leaders were elected in their own constituencies by an average of 98 to 99 percent of the total vote.[21]

The 1980 Constitution introduced relatively few changes in the organization and function of the Assembly. As in the past, and as in other Communist societies, actual power is vested in the executive organs of government. The National Assembly meets regularly twice a year, at the convocation of the Council of State (the new collective presidency of the SRV). Its term of office was extended in the new Constitution from four to five years. According to Article 84, the National Assembly "is empowered to prolong its term of office under special circumstances," and extraordinary sessions can be convened by its own decision or at the request of the Council of State or the Council of Ministers. Bills and resolutions are enacted into law by a vote of the majority of all deputies, except for constitutional amendments which, according to Article 147, require a vote of two-thirds of all deputies.

Under the 1959 Constitution, the leading executive body of the National Assembly was the Standing Committee (*Uy Ban Thuong Vu*). Elected by and from among deputies to the National Assembly and headed by a chairman, the Standing Committee served as a permanent executive committee for the National Assembly and had strong executive powers to operate in the intervals between sessions of the Assembly.[22] Under the new Constitution, the Standing Committee has been abolished and replaced by a Council of State, which retains many of the functions of its predecessor and will be discussed below. The office of Chairman of the National Assembly has been retained, however. The Chairman presides over sessions of the Assembly and coordinates its various activities.

The National Assembly elects a number of individual standing committees and two special councils, the National Defense Council and the Nationalities Council, to assist it in its duties. The Standing Committees and the Nationalities Council are empowered to examine draft laws and regulations submitted to them by the National Assembly and to submit suggestions or draft laws and regulations to the Assembly for consideration.[23] The National Defense Council "is empowered to mobilize all forces and potentials of the country to defend the homeland" and may be vested with special duties and powers in case of war.[24]

The Council of State

In terms of the organization of central government, the main departure from the 1959 Constitution is the Council of State (*Hoi Dong Nha Nuoc*). According to Article 98, the Council of State is "the highest continuously functioning body of the National Assembly, and is the collective presidency of the Socialist Republic of Vietnam."

The Council of State replaces the office of the President which had been established under the Constitution of 1959. Its duties are varied, and combine the roles of the Presidency and the old Standing Committee in one body. The Council convenes sessions of the National Assembly, promulgates laws and issues decrees, interprets the Constitution, and supervises the work of the Council of Ministers and local government organs on behalf of the National

Assembly when the latter is not in session. Through its chairman, who serves as the ceremonial President of the SRV, it receives representatives of foreign countries. The Chairman also commands the armed forces and is the Chairman of National Defense Council. Its members, who are elected by the National Assembly, include a chairman, a vice chairman, a secretary-general, and an unspecified number of ordinary members. The term of office is five years, corresponding to that of the National Assembly.

While spokesmen for the regime did not offer detailed reasons for the change in the Office of the Presidency (Truong Chinh remarked only that it would "streamline the machinery of the central administration"), it seems clear that the powerful Office of the Presidency in the 1959 Constitution had been created to accommodate the influential and symbolic figure of Ho Chi Minh, founder of the Vietnamese Communist movement and President of the DRV since its establishment in September 1945.[25] When Ho died in 1969, the Presidency declined into a purely ceremonial office. The new Council of State is apparently an effort to strengthen the tradition of collective leadership which has long been practiced within the Vietnamese Communist Party and can be traced back to Lenin's Testament in 1922.

The Council of Ministers

The highest executive and administrative state body in the SRV is the Council of Ministers (*Hoi Dong Bo Truong*). Composed of a chairman, several vice chairmen, and heads of various ministries and state committees, the Council of Ministers is elected by and accountable to the National Assembly. Like the Council of State, its term of office corresponds to that of the National Assembly. According to a law passed in July 1981, most members of the Council should simultaneously be deputies of the National Assembly.[26] The duties of the Council of Ministers remain essentially unchanged under the new Constitution, although Articles 107 and 112 elaborate slightly on its functions.

Local Government

Since the adoption of the first Constitution in 1946, socialist Vietnam has been essentially a unitary state, with predominant powers vested in the central government.[27] Like many other Communist states, however, the Vietnamese regime felt the need to placate the sensitivities of racial minorities by including constitutional provisions to protect the right of such minorities to preserve and develop their own customs, languages and cultures. This was particularly necessary in the case of Vietnam, where some national minorities (such as the tribal peoples in the Sino-Vietnamese border area) played a significant part in the Vietnamese revolution. Party leaders took considerable care to reassure such groups that they would not be rapidly assimilated into the dominant Vietnamese culture. Following Chinese practice, the 1959 Constitution had declared in Article 3 that, although the DRV was "a single multinational state,"

> all the nationalities living on Vietnamese territory are equal in rights and duties. The state has the duty to maintain and develop the solidarity between the various nationalities. All acts of discrimination against, or oppression of, any nationality, all actions which undermine the unity of the nationalities are strictly prohibited.
>
> All nationalities have the right to preserve or reform their own customs and habits, to use their spoken and written languages, and to develop their own national cultures.
>
> Autonomous zones may be established in areas where people of national minorities live in compact communities. Such autonomous zones are inalienable parts of the Democratic Republic of Vietnam.
>
> The state strives to help the national minorities to make rapid progress and to keep pace with the general economic and cultural advance.

In a gesture to provide concrete form to such promises, the Hanoi regime established special autonomous zones in the provinces north and northwest of the Red River Delta.[28] Yet such commitments clearly conflicted with the overall objective of the Party to lead the entire country to socialism, and in practice the regime attempted cautiously but inexorably to absorb the minority peoples into the mainstream culture of the DRV. Clearly, the operative phrase in Article 3 was "to help the national minorities to ... keep pace with the general economic and cultural advance."

Recent developments suggest that the regime intends to intensify its efforts to assimilate the national minorities into the socialist culture of the SRV: Shortly after the end of the Vietnam War, the autonomous zones in the Sino-Vietnamese border region were abolished. In the 1980 Constitution, most of the references to the national minorities have been eliminated, and are replaced by the simple statement that all national minorities have the right to use their own languages and scripts and "to preserve and promote their fine customs, habits, traditions, and cultures." The state, for its part, "accepts the responsibility to take corrective measures to gradually eliminate inequalities in the levels of economic and cultural development between the different nationalities.[29]

In all other respects, the SRV is a purely unitary state. In the 1980 Constitution, as under its two predecessors, the power of the central government and its laws reigns supreme throughout the entire country. Below the central level, the country is divided into provinces (*tinh*), districts (*huyen*), villages (*land*) and townships (*thi tran*), as well as three large municipalities (Hanoi, Haiphong, and Ho Chi Minh City) directly subordinate to the central government. At each level, government consists of an elected people's Council (*Uy Ban Nhan Dan*), which is elected by the members of the people's council to serve as the executive and administrative body at that echelon.[30] The entire system operates according to the Leninist principle of democratic centralism. People's councils are not only responsible to the local population but also to the people's council at the next higher level. People's committees are accountable to the people's council that elected it and to the people's committee at the next higher echelon. All are ultimately responsible in their activities to the National Assembly and the Council of State in Hanoi. People's councils at all levels have the authority to dissolve their counterparts at the next lowest level "when the latter do serious harm to the interests of the people." Similarly, people's councils have the right to rescind "inappropriate decisions" of organizations under their jurisdiction, and of people's councils and people's committees at the next lower level.[31]

In fact, most of the power in local government resides with the people's committee (and of course the Party committee at that level), rather than with the popularly elected people's council. The largely ritualistic nature of people's council activities, as well as the tendency for the people's committee to intervene in council affairs, occasioned some grumbling during the public discussions held on the draft Constitution.[32] In an effort to meet such criticisms, the drafting committee attempted to clarify and strengthen the role of the people's councils as the local organs of state power. Further measures were introduced in the Law on Local Government passed on June 30, 1983. There is room for skepticism, however, that the new regulations will, in the words of one Vietnamese source, "ensure unified administration by the center while promoting local initiative," so long as the concept of democratic centralism reigns supreme as an operative principle of administration.[34]

Organs of local authority, however, are not the only vehicle for soliciting popular participation in the political process in contemporary Vietnam. Another means of encouraging public involvement lies with the so-called mass associations, representing various functional, ethnic and religious groups like farmers, workers, students, overseas Chinese, and Buddhists, and operating under the umbrella of the Fatherland Front (*Mat Tran To Quoc*). The concept of the united front can be traced back in Party history to the period of its foundation in 1930, but it did not develop into a crucial component of ICP strategy until the 1940s, when so-called "national salvation associations" (*cuu quoc hoi*) under the rubric of the Vietminh Front became a major factor in the recruitment of Vietnamese peasants, workers, women, and ethnic and religious minorities into the revolutionary movement.[34] The concept of the united front assumed considerable importance as a form of sub-governmental linkage between the Party and the masses during the 1950s, when the influence of the Chinese "Maoist" model reached the zenith of its influence in the DRV. But the Vietnamese never applied the "mass line" technique in the peculiarly populist fashion that had been adopted in China, where in the late 1950s and 1960s it was used by radical elements around Mao Zedong as a weapon to mobilize popular support against the entrenched forces of the Party and government bureaucracy. The Vietnamese used their own united front, called the Fatherland Front after 1955, as a means of mobilizing popular support for the Party's internal and external objectives.[35]

After the end of the Vietnam War, the regime's united front activities appeared to languish into a purely formalistic affair, leading some to criticize the activities of the mass organizations as nothing but a ritual. The drafting commission attempted to rectify the problem and revitalize the mass organizations by introducing a specific reference to the role of the Fatherland Front in the new Constitution. In Article 9, the Front was described as the "firm prop" of the state. The Front, it continued,

> promotes the tradition of national unity, strengthens political and moral unity among the people, takes part in building and consolidating the people's power, educates and motivates the people to raise their sense of collective mastery, and to emulate one another in building socialism and defending the country.

The Rights and Duties of Citizens

At the heart of any Constitution lies the issue of the relationship between the individual and the state. In Communist societies, the balance between rights and the needs of the community has always been a sensitive one. According to Marxist doctrine, of course, under Communism the individual will possess perfect freedom, while the state, as an instrument of class oppression, will gradually "wither away." But in the complex transition process to the final Communist utopia, the Party, as sole possessor of sacred scripture, arrogates to itself the full power of the state as an instrument of proletarian dictatorship to oppress reactionary elements and build the foundations of the new society. In this struggle, individuals within society must subordinate their private interests to the overall needs of the community and the state.

The issue was not explicitly addressed in the 1946 Constitution, written at a time when the nation, in Marxist-Leninist terms, was just beginning the national democratic revolution. The charter adopted in 1946 guaranteed all the standard democratic liberties such as freedom of the press, speech, assembly, religion, and travel, and equal rights before the law regardless of creed, color or sex. Duties were limited to military service and observance of the law and the Constitution.[36]

The dichotomy of rights and duties of citizens was more explicitly set forth in the 1959 Constitution. While the standard freedoms were protected in Article 22 through Article 28, Article 38 declared that "the state forbids any person to use democratic freedoms to the detriment of the interests of the state and of the people." Article 39 added that "citizens of the Democratic Republic of Vietnam must abide by the Constitution and the law, uphold discipline at work, keep public order, and respect social ethics."

Paucity of information and wartime conditions make it difficult to assess the DRV performance in the realm of human rights prior to the fall of Saigon in 1975. Political dissent was clearly not tolerated, but the regime appeared to be reasonably scrupulous in observing the freedom of religion, sexual equality, and the rights of minorities to preserve their own way of life.[37] Since the end of the war, however, there have been widespread reports of official transgressions of civil rights, particularly in South Vietnam, where Hanoi's efforts to stamp out the remnants of Western influence have resulted in the alienation of a substantial proportion of the population. Freedom of movement has been severely restricted, while suspected opponents of the regime have been held without trial and often sent to reeducation camps. Freedom of religion, while technically still observed, has been curtailed by government regulations limiting church activities among Buddhists, Catholics, and sects.[38]

Such official abuses of human rights were apparently exposed to widespread criticism during the public discussion of the draft Constitution during the late 1970s. Often such criticism took the form of charges that Party and government officials were guilty of arbitrary and despotic behavior, leading spokesmen for the regime to promise that such behavior would be severely punished. But although the Party did embark on what it described as a thoroughgoing rectification campaign to weed out incompetent, corrupt, and arrogant elements from its ranks, the central point--the primacy of the needs of the state over those of the individual--was not tampered with in the 1980 Constitution. According to Article 54:

> The rights and obligations of citizens reflect the system of collective mastery of the working people, the harmonious combination of the requirements of social life and legitimate individual freedoms, and a guarantee of the identity of the interests between the state, the collective and the individual, on the principle: each for all, all for each.
>
> The rights of citizens are inseparable from their obligations. The state guarantees the rights of citizens; and citizens must fulfill their obligations towards the state and society.

In his report to the National Assembly, Truong Chinh reported on this passage as follows:

> The essence of this relationship is that the citizens' rights are inseparable from their duties. As the citizens have their rights, they must perform their duties. In return as they perform their duties, they are entitled to the rights ensured by the state.

In his own report to the Central Committee plenum in September, Le Duan took the same tack. The organic combination of rights and duties, he said, is a basic element in the concept of collective mastery.[39]

The new Constitution repeats the litany of standard freedoms contained in its two predecessors. As before, however, such rights are qualified. According to Article 67,

> Citizens enjoy freedom of speech, freedom of the press, freedom of assembly, freedom of association and freedom to demonstrate if in accordance with the interests of socialism and of the people.
>
> The state shall create the necessary material conditions for the exercise of these rights.
>
> No one may misuse democratic freedoms to violate the interests of the state and the people.

This stipulation is necessary, said Truong Chinh, "to prevent disruptive elements from fomenting trouble and sabotaging national independence and socialism and the people's genuine interests.[41] Similar restrictions apply to the freedom of religion. According to Article 68: "Citizens enjoy freedom of worship, and may practice a religion. No one may misuse religions to violate state laws or policies."

Other rights are for the first time also stated as obligations. According to Article 58, "work is the primary right, obligation and privilege of citizens. Citizens have the right to work. People fit for work must work as provided by law." In Article 60, education is described as "a right and obligation of all citizens."

The issue of civil rights apparently provoked considerable discussion during the public debate on the draft Constitution. Some participants pointed out that the inclusion of phrases such as "according to law" or "in conformity with the interests of socialism and the people" in stipulations on citizens' rights such as the freedom of movement and residence may give the impression that the Constitution puts limitations on citizens' rights and "gives out with one hand but takes back with the other." In his report to the National Assembly, Truong Chinh took issue with such complaints, pointing out that such phrases were aimed at "preventing enemies and bad elements from making use of these rights to harm the interests of socialism and the legitimate interests of the people. It is completely reasonable and necessary, and to the benefit of the people and socialist revolution in our country."[41]

In fact, some top Party leaders argue that basic rights such as education, housing, and freedom from exploitation are more important than the vaunted "human rights" emphasized by the Western bourgeois democracies. The 1980 Constitution stipulated rights to employment, education, old age assistance, residence and movement that were incorporated in the 1959 charter, and added others such as health care, housing, and equal pay for equal work regardless of sex. Official spokesmen concede that some of these rights cannot be guaranteed at present because of current economic difficulties or, in the case of freedom of movement and residence, because of the continuing conflict with China.[42] Such rights are nonetheless included in the Constitution because they are, in Truong Chinh's words, "fundamental rights of the people" that "must and can be exercised, even if on a limited scale" until they can be fully realized."[43]

The Judicial System

In Western democracies, the judicial branch plays a crucial role in the political system, providing a balance between the executive and legislative authority, interpreting the Constitution, and protecting the citizen against arbitrary action by the state. Its role in Communist societies is less significant. Far from being an independent force within the political system, the courts serve primarily as an instrument of the state in its effort to transform society in a Marxist image. Because of the importance of Marxist-Leninist ideology in the affairs of state, it is the Party, not the courts, that interprets law as well as doctrine.

The judicial system in the DRV developed after the Geneva Conference of 1954 and, as formalized in the 1959 Constitution, was modeled after the system used in the USSR. It was based on the establishment of so-called people's courts at each administrative level and culminating in a Supreme People's Court in Hanoi. Each court was composed of a judge and a number of "people's assessors" (who apparently serve a role roughly similar to that of a jury in the Anglo-American system) elected by and accountable to the people's council at each echelon. In addition to these people's courts, two other types of juridical bodies were military tribunals and "special tribunals" that might be set up "in certain cases" by the National Assembly.

According to the provisions of the 1959 Constitution, the proceedings of the local courts and the military tribunals were made subject to the supervision of the Supreme People's Court, which itself was elected by and accountable to the National Assembly. The Supreme People's Court was also empowered to supervise the proceedings of the special courts, unless the National Assembly decided otherwise at the time they were created.[44]

Also included in the section on the judicial system in the 1959 Constitution were the so-called people's organs of control, the prosecuting offices of the DRV. According to Article 105, people's organs of control were set up at all administrative levels and culminated in a Supreme People's Organ of Control headed by a Procurator General in Hanoi. It was the duty of the people's organs of control to supervise the observance of the law by all central and local organs of state, all government officials, and all citizens. As in the case of the people's courts, the people's organs of control at each level were accountable to the legislative body at that level, and worked under the leadership of higher control organs and the unified leadership of the Supreme People's Organ of Control.

There were few safeguards provided in the 1959 Constitution to protect the rights of defendants. Article 101 stated that cases in the people's courts were to be heard in public "unless otherwise provided for by law," while "the right to a defense is guaranteed the accused." How much such constitutional guarantees served to protect the rights of individual Vietnamese became open to serious doubt after the seizure of the southern provinces in 1975. In its effort to eradicate opposition to the state, the regime bypassed normal legal proceedings. During the roundup of suspected opponents of the revolution in the South, many were sent to reeducation camps and detained for months and even years without trial. According to widespread reports, conditions in the camps were often brutal, and many prisoners were exposed to beating and torture.[45]

Spokesmen for the regime conceded that the judicial system was inadequate and badly needed reform. Law was often made by sublegal government and Party directives. Enforcement of the law was arbitrary, and enforcement officers were not always law abiding. Laws were often not publicized and legal officers were not provided with guidance for enforcement. There was, in fact, a serious lack of people trained in the law. As Truong Chinh pointed out, the Hanoi Law School was not opened until 34 years after the revolution--in his words, a "disastrous delay."[46]

Reform of the judicial branch was therefore high on the agenda for the members of the Constitution Drafting Committee. While the administrative structure provided by the 1959 Constitution was left substantially intact, the new charter elaborated on a number of points left vague in the previous document. One area that was strengthened was the section dealing with the overall purpose of the courts. According to Article 127:

> The People's Courts and People's Organs of Control in the Socialist Republic of Vietnam are, within their competence, obliged to protect the socialist legal system, the socialist system, the working people's right to collective mastery, and socialist property, and to ensure respect for the lives, property, freedom, honour and dignity of citizens.
> Any act encroaching upon the interests of the state or the collective or the legitimate interests of citizens must be dealt with in accordance with law.

The 1980 Constitution also provided for the establishment of appropriate "people's organizations" at the grassroots level to deal with "minor breaches of law and disputes." Traditionally, disputes between families or individuals at the local level were handled informally within the village rather than being referred to the courts. Under Party rule, such cases were in theory to be dealt with under the jurisdiction of the new people's courts set up under the 1959 Constitution, although in practice many were still probably handled at the village or urban precinct level. It is not yet clear how the system has operated, but it is apparent that the regime has returned to the traditional model in order to strengthen the adjudication of disputes at the local level and to encourage citizens to become more involved in managing society and ensuring the enforcement of law. If effective, such organizations should relieve the pressure on the people's courts, and on the legal system itself, which under Party rule has been seriously deficient in providing a formula for resolving civil disputes.[47]

The Economic System

Chapter 2 of the 1980 Constitution deals with the economic system. This section is one of the most important in the entire document, for it is here, above all, that the state assesses progress toward the final stage of classless Communism and sets forth goals for the future. The 1946 Constitution had little to say about economics. On the issue of property ownership, Article 12 said simply that "the rights of possession of Vietnamese citizens are guaranteed." The 1959 Constitution, written shortly after the DRV had just emerged from the first stage of socialist transformation in both urban and rural areas, was more specific about the economic objectives of the state. Article 9 stated that the DRV was "advancing step by step from people's democracy to socialism." The issue of ownership was qualified: the rights of citizens to possess and inherit property were recognized, but capitalists were warned that they would be guided along the path of socialist transformation.

The 1980 Constitution was written at a time of growing tension within the Party over economic policy. The uneasy bargain that had been reached at the Fourth Party Congress to place the demands of ideology and economic growth on an equal footing was now threatened by the economic and social crisis at the end of the decade, and in 1979 the regime had been forced to slow down the advance toward socialism in order to stimulate the productive forces in the economy. The section on the economic system in the 1980 Constitution suggested that the strategy announced at the Fourth Party Congress remained substantially intact. Article 16 stated simply that the state would continue to "combine the development of the productive forces with the institution and perfection of socialist relations of production." There are ample indications throughout the section, however, that advocates of rapid socialist transformation remained influential within the Party leadership. Article 18 stated the general proposition:

> The state conducts a revolution in the relations of production, guides, utilizes and transforms non-socialist sectors of the economy, institutes and consolidates the system of socialist ownership of the means of production, with the aim of building a national economy with two essential components--the state sector under the ownership of the entire people, and the collective economic sector under the collective ownership of the working people.

The state sector plays the leading role in the national economy, and is given priority for development.[48]

Other Articles elaborated on the means of transformation, and on the effects such action would have on individual citizens. The property of feudal landlords and comprador capitalists (in Marxist parlance, those within the manufacturing and commercial sector whose fortunes were linked with foreign imperialist interests) was nationalized without compensation. For the time being, the right of ownership of "lawfully earned incomes, savings, housing, other personal possessions and the means of engaging in authorized private work" was protected by the state, but Article 26 promised that "the private capitalist economy in both urban and rural areas" would eventually undergo socialist transformation by "suitable forms." Moreover, according to Article 28, "the state may, when it deems really necessary to the public interests, purchase or requisition with or without compensation, the property of individuals or of collectives."[49]

In the context of the time, such statements represented more a vision of the future than objective reality. A substantial proportion of the industrial and commercial sector and the majority of cultivable lands in the southern provinces remained in private hands, and the plan announced at the Fourth Party Congress to complete the transformation to socialism by 1980 had been set back by the Central Committee plenum in 1979.

It was probably with that in mind that the 1980 Constitution incorporated a new provision in Article 19 that all land, natural resources, industrial and commercial enterprises, banks, utilities, and means of transportation and communication were ultimately "under the ownership of the entire people." To reassure private farmers or collectivized peasants with private plots, Article 20 added that "collectives and individuals who have the use of the land are allowed to continue to do so and to enjoy the fruits of their labor according to law."

Why had the regime undertaken such a far-reaching measure to extend the authority of the state over the economic resources of the nation? By comparison, Article 12 of the 1959 Constitution had said only that "all mineral resources and water, and all forests, undeveloped land, and other resources defined by law as belonging to the state are the property of the whole people." Drafting Committee Chairman Truong Chinh, conceding that there had been some debate over this provision, justified the measure by stating that nationalization would end the "mismanagement of land through purchase, sale, resale, dispute, or usurpation which is harmful to the unified management of the land by the state" and was "consistent with the interests of the whole society as well as the basic and long-term interests of every citizen." In fact, Article 19 represented a tacit admission that the final transition to full socialism might be delayed for several years in the South. In the meantime, the new provision provided the state with constitutional authority to take necessary measures to control and restrict the activities of private farmers and capitalists.

Culture and Education

To Vietnamese leaders, a key aspect in the creation of a socialist society was the elimination of feudalist and capitalist ideology in the minds of the Vietnamese people and the creation of a new culture based on the emergence of the "new man." The importance of this objective had been recognized in a programmatic sense at the Fourth Party Congress in 1976, which had set forth the goal of realizing the "three revolutions:" in production relations, ideology and culture, and science and technology.[50]

Efforts to create a socialist culture had been underway in the North since 1954 with the adoption of a new educational system and the transformation of art and literature based on the norms of socialist realism. After 1975, the regime faced a similar task in transforming what it viewed as the decadent capitalist culture in the South. As Party leaders soon discovered, this turned out to be a much more formidable challenge, since Western capitalist values and attitudes had been deeply rooted in the southern provinces since the French colonial period. In the months following the seizure of Saigon in April 1975, intensive efforts were undertaken by the new revolutionary regime to eliminate the "poisonous weeds" of bourgeois culture and create the basis for a new socialist culture. The educational system previously in use in the South--based essentially on the U.S. model--was immediately abolished and replaced by a new system patterned after, and integrated with, that in use in the North. In August, the Ministry of Information and Culture of the "Republic of South Vietnam" issued a circular banning the circulation of "politically reactionary and pornographic materials."

The ultimate goal had been set forth by Le Duan at the Fourth Party Congress:

> Our socialist literature and art should endeavor to create beautiful and varied artistic types concerning our new society and man, about the working class, collective peasantry, socialist intellectuals, officers and men of the people's army who reflect our people's revolutionary patriotism and other noble qualities. It must firmly assert the new system, the new way

of life, the new morality and develop the fine national traditions and revolutionary traditions of our people.[51]

By the regime's admission, the attempt had only modest success. The cultural and ideological remodeling of the South turned out to be a complex and difficult task. Western art, literature and music remained popular among southerners, particularly the youth, who continued to display what Party leaders described as decadent attitudes of bourgeois individualism, romanticism, and social alienation. Even more dangerous, such attitudes soon began to affect the behavior of Party members and government officials stationed in the South. Despite official warnings, the regime faced a rising problem of corruption among cadres tempted by the "temporarily shining qualities" of westernized culture in the South.

The importance that Party leaders attached to the issue was clearly demonstrated in the 1980 Constitution. While the 1959 Constitution had made no mention of Marxism-Leninism and had restricted itself to a vague reference in the Preamble to "the constant improvement of the material and cultural life of the people," the new charter devoted an entire chapter to "Culture, Education, Science and Technology." Article 37 set the tone, declaring that the SRV "promotes the ideological and cultural revolution, develops a new culture with a socialist content and a national, party and people's character." The following article stated specifically that "Marxism-Leninism is the ideological system guiding the development of Vietnamese society." The state, it continued,

broadly disseminates Marxism-Leninism, the line and policies of the Communist Party of Vietnam. It preserves and develops the cultural and spiritual values of the nation, absorbs the best of world culture, combats feudal and bourgeois ideologies and the influences of imperialist and colonialist culture; criticizes petty-bourgeois ideology; builds a socialist way of life, and combats backward life-styles and superstitions.

Viewed in its entirety, the 1980 Constitution undoubtedly represented a significant step forward in the eyes of the Party from its predecessor. Whereas the 1959 version was written to accommodate the needs of a country still divided and at an early stage of socialist transition, the new charter reflected the views of a regime determined to complete national reunification by tightening the bonds between the Party and the people and building the foundations of an advanced socialist society throughout the entire country. To strengthen its hand, the regime incorporated statements regarding the leading role of the Party and of Marxism-Leninism in the body of the document. Although the new Constitution was promulgated at a troubled period in the Vietnamese revolution, its provisions echoed a sense of confidence that the ultimate goals of the revolution would surely be achieved without long delay.

The 1980 Constitution in Operation

In the years following the promulgation of the new Constitution in December 1980, the regime presented to the National Assembly additional legislation clarifying the role of the central and local governmental organization.[52] The Party also launched a rectification campaign to weed out corrupt and incompetent Party members and create a streamlined new organization worthy of its leading role in Vietnamese society.

But such organizational changes would not in themselves resolve some of the deeper problems afflicting the country. Much of the concern was related to the economy. During the early 1980s, the policy debate within the Party leadership continued. The regime continued to tolerate the existence of a small capitalist sector to encourage production increases while at the same time maintaining persistent pressure to increase the state share of the economy. The results were mixed. Although industrial and agricultural production began to recover from the crisis years of the late 1970s, the overall performance of the economy remained sluggish, while the realization of an advanced socialist society seemed as far away as ever.

Beyond the nation's economic difficulties, there was also continuing public discontent over the overall performance of the Party and the government. The tone was set by the prestigious Vietnamese intellectual Nguyen Khac Vien. A longtime spokesman for the Hanoi regime, Nguyen Khac Vien issued a public letter to the National Assembly in April 1981 which declared, in effect, that the vaunted concept of "collective mastery" was a fraud. Many of his criticisms were familiar. The mass organizations, he complained, were nothing but a facade, the government apparatus was ineffective, and the Party interfered in the political process. If this continued, he warned, it would become increasingly difficult to mobilize public support to resolve the nation's problems.[53]

Moreover, the regime continued to rely primarily on force to suppress its critics. Throughout the early 1980s, there were persistent reports in the official press of the arrest of dissident elements, many of them members of religious organizations. Critics charged that violations of civil rights continued, particularly in the reeducation camps, where foreign sources reported that thousands of prisoners were held without a formal trial, many of them priests, teachers, civil servants, and journalists. Regime spokesmen conceded that the camps were still in operation, but asserted that ninety percent of those incarcerated were guilty of "capital offenses" and that the government was therefore demonstrating mercy by not putting them on trial.[54]

To many Vietnamese, the source of the regime's problems lay at the top, in a handful of veteran Party leaders who had led the Vietnamese revolution for a generation against France and the United States, but have been unable to meet the new challenges of the postwar era. By early in 1986, it was generally anticipated that the ailing General Secretary Le Duan and other elderly veterans like Truong Chinh and Prime Minister Pham Van Dong would be replaced in their posts at the Sixth Party Congress scheduled to take place at the end of the year. But when Le Duan died of illness in June, he was replaced by 79-year-old Truong Chinh, suggesting that the policy debate within the Party leadership had not yet been resolved.

At the Party Congress held in December, however, Truong Chinh, along with other veteran Party figures, was dropped from the Politburo, and a relative unknown, Nguyen Van Linh, was named Party General Secretary. Linh had earned a reputation for economic pragmatism as chief of the Party's municipal organization in Ho Chi Minh City after the end of the Vietnam War. In the months after his appointment, Nguyen Van Linh quickly put his stamp on the Vietnamese scene. Following Gorbachev's example, the new general secretary called for a new sense of openness (*cong Khai*) in Vietnamese society, and at a writers' conference held in early 1987, he called on intellectuals to speak out against abuses in the system even at the risk of their careers. As a sign that Vietnamese *glasnost* was more than simply a slogan, the regime offered a greater choice of candidates in the elections for the new National Assembly held in April, the first to be held since 1981. It also began to circulate major proposals under consideration by the party leadership for public scrutiny and comment prior to their implementation.[55]

The Congress also announced that the economic reforms first introduced at the beginning of the decade would be continued and even enhanced. Party leaders conceded that in the past they had been too impatient to perfect socialist relations in Vietnamese society, and indicated that in the future they would proceed with greater caution, making liberal use of private sector activities and delaying the collectivization of land in the southern provinces until conditions were favorable. The Congress also called for enhanced efforts to dismantle the Stalinist system of centralized planning and a shift to cost accounting methods to increase the efficiency of the state run enterprises.[56]

modest improvement, although Vietnam is still among the poorest countries
in Asia. In December 1990, a new draft program for the decade was released
for public discussion and consideration. The program indicated that the
current economic reform program would continue, and that the march to a
fully socialist society would not be resumed until after two or three additional
five-year plans. But there was persuasive evidence that the party leadership
was still guided by the norms of Marxist-Leninist orthodoxy. The market
mechanism would continue to be run by the state, and state enterprises would
continue to play the leading role in the industrial sectorof the economy.[57]

The regime showed even greater caution in the realm of political reform.
Although most of the remaining political prisoners held in the re-education
centers had been released, dissidents continued to be persecuted and the
regime made it clear that political reforms on the lines of those adopted in
the Soviet Union would not be adopted. Undoubtedly unnerved by recent
events in China and Eastern Europe, party leaders stated tahat political
stability is the necessary prerequisite for economic progress. The decision was
reaffirmed in the draft program published in December 1990. Socialist
democracy, it asserts is the Vietnamese way. Every individual has the right
and duty to take part in the construction of a better society. The party and
the government will solicit the views of the people prior to implementing
policy, but they will resist all tendencies toward what they term "extreme
democracy" or "bourgeois democracy." The Communist Party remains the
leading force in society, guiding the Vietnamese people toward the final goal
of socialism.[58]

As these lines were written, the party was preparing to convene its
Seventh National Congress in the summer of 1991. That Congress will
undoubtedly be asked to approve the draft program announced the previous
winter. So far, public reaction to the program has been mixed. Many
observers in Vietnam were quick to say that the program was too cautious,
and too vauge to be useful at the local level. Criticism of the emphasis on
political stability and party leadership was quick to appear. The noted
Vietnamese historian Nguyen Khac Vien, who had earlier described "collective
mastery: as a fraud, labelled the current program inadequate and claimed that
unless "a set of broad-based rules for democracy are drawn up and
implemented," Vietnam would never be able to compete with other countries
in the region.[59]

Legacies

What conclusions can be drawn from the above evidence? First and foremost, it seems clear that the driving force behind the 1980 Constitution was Leninist orthodoxy. The references to democratic centralism, the proletarian dictatorship, and Marxist-Leninist ideology all serve as signposts that the Party took its vision of future development from the words and deeds of Vladimir I. Lenin. It is also readily apparent that Hanoi had found a constitutional model in the Soviet Union. Many of the provisions of the 1980 Constitution, and even some of the phraseology, were directly appropriated from the 1977 charter of the USSR. While Vietnamese sources sometimes insisted that the SRV was seeking its own path of development and not simply following the example of Moscow, it is nonetheless clear that Vietnamese leaders, for their own reasons, found much to emulate in the Soviet experience.[60]

This is not to say that local conditions were totally ignored in the new Constitution. As noted above, a number of provisions in the new charter were specifically designed to conform with the particular circumstances of Vietnamese society. Vietnamese leaders would undoubtedly insist that the underlying spirit of the new Constitution is strongly Vietnamese. If the stamp of Lenin can be seen in the dominant role of the Party and the uncompromising emphasis on ideology, that of Ho Chi Minh, though less obtrusive, can be seen in the concept of collective mastery, which attempts to draw upon the historically intimate linkage between the Communist Party and working masses in the Vietnamese revolution. In its emphasis on the importance of popular involvement in the political process, collective mastery is reminiscent of the populist element in Maoism which flourished in China during the late 1950s and 1960s. In Vietnam, however, its direct legacy can be traced back to the early efforts of the Party to build a united front of all progressive and patriotic Vietnamese against the French colonial regime. Moreover, as has been stated above, unlike Mao Zedong, who used the concept of the "mass line" as a tool to mobilize the masses against the Party and government apparatus, the Hanoi regime has firmly subordinated the people's collective mastery to the Party through the concept of democratic centralism and the proletarian dictatorship.

This organic combination of Party rule and mass participation has long been a distinguishing feature of the Vietnamese revolution. Yet there is room for suspicion that there is more Lenin than Ho Chi Minh, more proletarian dictatorship, in the 1980 Constitution. Whether Ho Chi Minh would have approved of the strongly paternalistic character of the present system is beside the point here. The fact is, the gap between the Party and the masses has clearly widened since the end of the Vietnam War. As Nguyen Khac Vien pointed out, in its insistence on a rapid transition to socialism at the expense of economic growth, in its tendency to dominate virtually all aspects of life in contemporary Vietnam, the Party had indeed damaged its image as a servant of the Vietnamese people.

The Sixth Pary Congress took a number of steps to rectify such problems, and there are some promising signs that the regime reconizes the need to adopt new policies and a new work style to achieve an improvement in the relationship between the leadership and the general populace. But if the 1990 draft program is an idication of current thinking, it is doubtful that the essentially Leninist charcter of the state will be transformed in the near future. Although disillusionment with current conditions among many lower and middle level cadres appears to beon the rise, the Party leadership remains deeply imbued with Leninist principles and convinced that it is (in the phraseology of the 1980 Constitution) "the main factor determining all success of the Vietnamese revolution." Recent events in other communist societies have undoubtedly strengthened the conviction in Hanoi that the guiding hand of the the Party will be necessary to navigate the ship of state through the dangerous shoals of the coming decade.

Behind such attitudes lies a long historical tradition of political authoritarianism and Confucian elitism that remains deeply imbeded in the Vietnamese political culture. Official sources in Hanoi are well aware of this problem and frequently criticizes the residual influence of feudal and reactionary attitudes and behavior among Party and government officials and members of the population at large. But the influence of the past can also be seen in the paternalistic character of the current regime and the lack of an alternative in the Vietnamese society to the overwhelming power of the state. Like most societies in Southeast Asia, Vietnam lacks a tradition of individualism and separation of powers that in the West led to the rise of bourgeois democracy. the isolation of the regime from the West during the last thirty years has served to accentuate that difference. It would therefore be premature to assume that Vietnam will ultimately evolve into a more pluralistic system based on a Western model. For the foreseeable future, the SRV will remain under the control of a Communist Party dedicated to its own agenda of socialist transformation, central planning, and the mobilization of the population to achieve the goals of the state. What is perhaps more likely is that the current and future leadership will be more responsive to the needs and aspirations of the Vietnamese people, and less rigid in pursuing the Party's ultimate ideological objectives. Such a policy would be more in line with the long-term interests of the Party and nation as a whole. As Le Duan himself pointed out, any system that underestimates the importance of economics and prefers "the use of authority" to measures that respond to people's needs and produce more wealth for society is contrary to the spirit of collective mastery.[61]

NOTES

1. The USSR, for example, has had four Constitutions in its seventy-year history. The first was approved shortly after the 1917 Revolution, and the second during the period of the New Economic Policy in 1924. The so-called "Stalinist Constitution" of 1936 announced the first successes of the process of socialist transformation. The most recent, promulgated in 1977, describes a society now in the state of "developed socialism." For a discussion of the 1977 Constitution, see Robert Sharlet, "The New Society Constitution," *Problems of Communism*, September-October, 1977, 1-24.

2. This, of course, does not include the two Constitutions promulgated in non-Communist South Vietnam between 1954 and 1975.

3. The 1946 Constitution was never officially promulgated, although it was approved by the National Assembly in 1946. For an English translation of the origins, see Bernard B. Fall, *The Viet-Minh Regime*, Ithaca, Cornell University Southeast Asia Program, 1956.

4. An English-language version of the 1959 Constitution can be found in Bernard B. Fall, *The Two Viet-Nams: A Political and Military Analysis*, New York, Praeger, 1963.

5. In this respect, the 1959 Constitution of the DRV resembled the "Stalinist Constitution" of 1936. For an English-language version of the latter, see Frederick L. Shuman, *Russia Since 1917*, New York, Knopf, 1957.

6. Le Duan's speech is translated in *Foreign Broadcast Information Service (FBIS)*, Volume IV (June 29, 1976), K1-K28.

7. In this decision, Hanoi departed from socialist precedent. Both the Soviet Union and the People's Republic of China went through a relatively extended period of economic moderation before the launching of the socialist transformation process. For a more detailed presentation of the program, see "Material on Fourth Vietnam Workers Party Congress," *FBIS*, Volume IV (Supplement), December-January, 1976.

8. In organizing public discussion of the draft Constitution, the SRV followed Soviet precedent. *See* Sharlet, at 1.

9. For his report to the National Assembly, given on December 12, 1980, see *FBIS*, Volume IV, December 15, 1980, K1-K28.

10. *Id.* K3.

11. *Id.* K6.

12. The term "people's democratic state" appears to have been borrowed from the "people's democracies" set up after World War II in Eastern Europe and refers to a state ruled by a Communist party but still in an early transitional stage to socialism.

13. Truong Chinh report, K20.

14. A similar phrase is found in the 1977 Constitution of the USSR. *See* Article 6.

15. Truong Chinh report, K7.

16. Article 6, Constitution of the USSR. The 1977 Constitution, no longer used the phrase "dictatorship of the proletariat" to describe the nature of the Party rule. The USSR is not described as "a socialist state of the whole people." *See* Article 1.

17. For the reference to the use of the concept in the nineteenth century, see Le Duan's speech at the September 1980 VCP plenum, translated in *FBIS*, Volume IV (January 13, 1981), K7. I am grateful to Professor Moto Furata of Tokyo University for pointing out to me that Le Duan had referred to the term in the 1960s. For a collection of his writings on the subject, see Le Duan, *On the Right to Collective Mastery*, Hanoi, Foreign Languages Publishing House, 1980.

18. Le Duan's political report to the 1976 Congress, *op. cit.*

19. Le Duan, speech at the September 1980 plenum, K3.

20. *Id.* K9.

21. *See* Bernard B. Fall, "North Viet-Nam's New Constitution and Government," *Pacific Affairs*, Volume XXXIII, Number 3, September 1960, 282-283.

22. *See* Article 53 of the 1959 Constitution.

23. Currently there are six committees dealing with the judiciary: economy, planning, and budget; culture and education; technology and science; public health and social welfare; youth, teenagers and children; and foreign relations.

24. Article 90. The importance of the National Defense Council was indicated by the fact that all members were also members of the Party Politburo.

25. *See* Fall, 151.

26. Law on the Organization of the Council of Ministers, printed in *Nhan Dan*, July 17, 1981.

27. Both the 1959 and the 1980 Constitutions included this statement in the introductory section on the Political System. The 1946 Constitution made no specific reference to the issue, but the chapter on local government made it clear that decisions at the local level "must not conflict with orders issued by higher authorities." *See* Article 59.

28. The Tay Bac Autonomous Region (formerly called the Tay Meo Autonomous Region was composed of three provinces in the far northwest. The Viet Bac Autonomous Region consisted of five provinces directly north of the Red River Delta. In both regions, local tribal groups played an active role in administration of the area.

29. Article 5.

30. *See* the Law on the Organization of People's Councils and Committees, broadcast on Hanoi home service July 13-15, 1983.

31. Articles 115 and 124.

32. One suggestion, was to create a standing committee for the people's councils to provide it with a stronger leadership. The suggestion was rejected on grounds that such an organization would duplicate the functions of the administrative committee. *See* Truong Chinh's report, K23.

33. *See* "The Law on the Organization of People's Councils and People's Committees," *Vietnam Courier*, August, 1983, 7.

34. For an analysis of the role of the united front in the Vietnamese revolutionary movement, see my "Building the United Front: The Rise of Communism in Vietnam, 1925-1954," in MacAlister Brown and Joseph J. Zasloff, eds., *Communism in Indochina: New Perspectives*, Lexington, D.C. Heath, 1975.

35. For an analysis of the development of the DRV's institutional structure, see David W.P. Elliott, "Institutionalizing the Revolution: Vietnam's Search for a Model of Development," in William S. Turley, ed., *Vietnamese Communism in Comparative Perspective*, Boulder, Westview Press, 1980.

36. For the list of rights guaranteed Vietnamese citizens under the 1946 Constitution, see Chapter II, Articles 4 through 16.

37. Ethnic minorities, for example, were not required to serve in the Armed Forces during the Vietnam War, although they were certainly encouraged to do so. As another example, members of the overseas Chinese community were not required to take Vietnamese citizenship and were permitted to retain their own schools.

38. For one source documenting this charge, see the January-February 1983 issue of *Indochina Journal* entitled "Religion in Vietnam Today." For a thoughtful article on church-state relations in the SRV, see David G. Marr, "Church and State in Vietnam," *Indochina Issues*, Number 74, April, 1987.

39. Le Duan's speech to the 1980 plenum, 5; Truong Chinh report, K15.

40. Truong Chinh report, K15.

41. *Id.* K.22.

42. For a discussion of the restrictions on movement and residence in the SRV, see Nguyen Long (with Harry H. Kendall), *After Saigon Fell: Daily Life Under the Vietnamese Communists*, Berkeley, Institute of East Asian Studies, 1981, esp. Chapters II and III.

43. Truong Chinh report, K22.

44. Article 104.

45. For charges that up to 65,000 may have died in the camps, see *Asiaweek*, June 7, 1985, 22.

46. Truong Chinh report, K25.

47. *See* Article 128.

48. According to Truong Chinh, there were suggestions during the discussion of the draft Constitution that the private and semi-private sectors of the economy be specifically mentioned in the new charter. The idea was rejected, he said, because "the constitution is the fundamental law of the whole country which must stipulate common provisions valid for the whole country over a rather long period." *See* K22.

49. This statement had been incorporated into the 1959 Constitution, but had provided "appropriate compensation."

50. For a discussion of the "three revolutions," see the Materials on the Fourth Party Congress, *FBIS*, Volume IV, December 27, 1976.

51. *See* Le Duan's speech in *id.*, Volume II, 56.

52. Laws on the judiciary system, the National Assembly, and the Council of Ministers were passed in July 1981. A new law on local government was promulgated in July 1983.

53. The letter appears in a French translation in Georges Boudarel *et al.* (eds.), *La Bureaucratie au Vietnam*, Paris, l'Harmattan, 1983, 115-119.

54. *See* Frederick Moritz in the *Christian Science Monitor*, June 2, 1982.

Nguyen Van Linh encouraged such changes in an anonymous column signed simply "N.V.L. in the official party newspaper *Nhan Dan*. See the *New York Times*, August 10, 1987 and September 9, 1987. According to Nguyen Van Linh himself, the letters N.V.L. stand for "speak and act" (*noi va lam*).

56. *Sixth National Congress of the Communist Party of Vietnam: Documents*, Hanoi, Foreign Languages Publishing House, 1987, Political Report.

57. The draft program was printed in *Nhan Dan*, December 1-3, 1990.

58. *Ibid.*

59. For Nguyen Khac Vien's comments, see the *International Herald Tribune,* March 6, 1991.

60. For a brief comment by a Vietnamese source suggesting that Hanoi is following the Soviet road of development, see the article by Basrbara Crossette, the *New York Times*, August 10, 1987.

61. Le Duan, report to the September 1980 plenum, 4.

SOUTHERN ASIA

THE KINGDOM OF BRUNEI

Constitution and Monarchy in Brunei

Ahmad Ibrahim

Valentine S. Winslow

Introduction and Early Constitutional History

Brunei is today a small independent and sovereign State of 5,765 square kilometers in area (2,226 square miles), occupying two small enclaves in the Malaysian state of Sarawak, with a population (in 1980) of about 225,000. Its economy is sustained, however, largely by considerable oil revenues and its people have the highest GNP in Southeast Asia and yet pay no income tax and benefit from extensive state welfare. it is also the newest member of the Association of Southeast Asian Nations (ASEAN), having joined in 1986.

Brunei once had sovereignty over the whole of Borneo as well as many islands in the Malay Archipelago. By the beginning of the 19th century, however, Brunei's dominion included only what are now the states of Sarawak and Sabah. In 1841 the Sultan of Brunei ceded Sarawak to James Brooks,[1] in 1846 the island of Labuan was ceded to Great Britain, and in 1877 the entire Northern portion of Borneo (what is now Sabah)[2] was ceded to the British North Borneo Company. Under an Agreement dated September 17, 1888, Brunei was placed under the protection of Great Britain[3] and in 1906 by Supplementary Agreement the Sultan agreed to accept a British Resident as the representative of the British Government.[4]

In 1959, the 1906 agreement was replaced by a new Agreement[5] under which Great Britain continued to be responsible for Brunei's defense and foreign relations. In 1959 also, a written Constitution was promulgated.[6] It provided for a Privy Council, a Council of Ministers and a Legislative Council. The Privy Council, presided over by the Sultan, served as an advisory body on constitutional matters. Executive authority was vested in the Sultan, assisted by the *Menteri Besar*,[7] who presided over the Council of Ministers. The Legislative Council was presided over by a Speaker and consisted[8] of eight ex-officio members, six "official" members, three nominated members and sixteen elected members (who were to be appointed by the Sultan at first, but--it was planned--would from 1961, be elected instead).

The Constitution also provided for a Supreme Court, consisting of the High Court and the Court of Appeal. Indirect elections were held in September 1962 to choose representatives to the District Councils and Legislative Council. The result, however, proved abortive. Although the party known as Partai Rakyat Brunei (PRB) won all the seats, the Legislative Council was never allowed to convene. Its leader meanwhile fomented an unsuccessful rebellion leading to the outlawing of the PRB, the suspension of the Constitution, and emergency rule. Another election in 1970 won by a new opposition party also proved abortive, as the executive dissolved the Legislative Council and political activity was discouraged for the time being.

A new treaty of friendship and cooperation was entered into between Brunei and Great Britain on January 7, 1979 under the terms of which Brunei would assume full responsibility as a sovereign and independent State at the end of 1983. On January 1, 1984, a proclamation was made by the Sultan and Yang Di Pertuan. This proclamation referred to the Constitution of 1959 "in accordance with which this Kingdom is regulated and is the supreme law thereof." Thus the revised Constitution of 1959 has applied.

The Constitutional Framework

Religion and Language

The Constitution provides that the religion of the State shall be the Muslim religion, which is defined as the Muslim religion according to the Shafeite sect of that religion.[9] The Sultan is the head of the religion of the State.[10] All other religions may be practiced in peace and harmony by the persons professing them in any part of the State.[11]

The Malay language is the official language of the State.[12]

Executive Authority

The supreme executive authority of the State is vested in the Sultan[13] and is exercisable directly by the Sultan or by the Council of Ministers (Majlis Mesyuarat Menteri Menteri)or any Minister authorized by the Council of Ministers. The Constitution provides for the appointment of a Prime Minister who shall be responsible for the exercise in the State of all executive authority.[14] There shall be such other Ministers as the Sultan may appoint.[15]

The Prime Minister must be a Brunei Malay professing the Muslim religion and belonging to the Shafeite sect of that religion.[16] All the Ministers (including the Prime Minister) are appointed by the Sultan and are responsible to him, holding office during his pleasure.[17]

Privy Council

There is a Privy Council (Ajlis Mesyuarat Di-Raja) consisting of the Regents[18] (if a Council of Regency has been appointed), ex-officio members and appointed members. The ex-officio members include the Prime Minister and the members of the Council of Ministers. The main function of the Privy Council is to advise the Sultan in relation to the exercise of the prerogative of mercy[19] and in relation to the amendment or revocation of any of the provisions of the Constitution.

Council of Ministers

The Council of Ministers is presided over by the Sultan and consists of the Ministers appointed by the Sultan. Every member of the Council of Ministers holds his seat during the pleasure of the Sultan. The Sultan is generally required to consult with the Council in the exercise of his powers and the performance of his duties.[20] The Sultan may act in opposition to the advice given him by the majority of the Council of Ministers, should he in any case consider it right to do so; but he is required to record his reasons for his decision.[21]

Legislative Council

The provisions relating to the Legislative Council have been temporarily suspended.[22] The Constitution, however, makes provision for a Legislative Council (Majlis Mesyuarat Negeri) consisting of six ex-officio members, five official members and ten nominated members. Under reserved powers, the Sultan is authorized to declare a Bill on motion to be passed or carried, if the Council should fail to pass the Bill on motion within a specified time.

Miscellaneous Provisions

The Attorney General

Provision is made for the appointment by the Sultan of the Attorney General. The Attorney General advises on all legal matters connected with the affairs of Brunei referred to him by the Sultan or the Government and has power to institute, conduct or discontinue criminal proceedings before the ordinary courts.[24]

State of Emergency

A state of emergency may be declared where public danger exists whereby the security or economic life of the State is threatened, whether by war or external aggression or internal disturbance, actual or threatened.[25] The proclamation of emergency shall remain in force for not more than two years, but a new proclamation may be issued at or before the end of that period. During the period of emergency, the Sultan may make any orders he considers desirable in the public interest.

Amendment and Interpretation of the Constitution

The power to amend or revoke any of the provisions of the Constitution by proclamation is given to the Sultan. The Sultan must consult the Privy Council in relation to the exercise of this power but is not obliged to act in accordance with the advice of the Council.[26] The Sultan may also refer any question involving the meaning, interpretation, construction or effect of any of the provisions of the Constitution to an Interpretation Tribunal, whose decisions shall be in writing, published in the *Government Gazette*, and binding and conclusive and shall not be called in question in any court.[27] The Interpretation Tribunal consists of a Chairman, who is to be a person who holds or has held high judicial office in, or has for at least ten years been engaged in legal practice in, any part of the Commonwealth, and two other members. The Chairman and members are appointed by the Sultan.

The Sultan's Unique Position

The Sultan, as may be seen from his exclusive power to amend the Constitution, to appoint the Prime Minister and other Ministers to hold office during his pleasure, and to act in opposition to the advice of the Council of Ministers or the Privy Council, is not a mere constitutional monarch. He is a Head of State in every sense of the word, with wide discretionary powers. The Constitution too, it may be noted, is not supreme as there are no limitations on the power of amendment and no powers in any constitutional body other than to advise the Sultan, which advice is not binding on him. If any institution is "supreme" in Brunei, it is neither the Constitution nor the Legislature, but indeed, the Sultan himself, as he has always traditionally been.

However, although he is in theory an absolute monarch, his traditional respect for his advisers and the institutions of the State (including his Privy Council and the Courts) and traditional sense of duty towards his subjects, make him invariably a responsible Head of State in the modern world.

The Courts and Application of Laws

No special provision is made in the Constitution itself for the courts of law. However, the Supreme Court Act[28] provides for the establishment of a Supreme Court in and for Brunei, and for the hearing of appeals from such court to the Judicial Committee of the Privy Council in the United Kingdom. The Supreme Court (first constituted in 1963) consists of the High Court, which comprises the Chief Justice and such number of judges as may be prescribed from time to time by the Sultan; and the Court of Appeal, which comprises the President (of the Supreme Court) and two judges.[29] Judges hold office until the age of 65 and may not be removed except for inability to perform their functions or misbehavior, and even then, only if the question of removal has been referred to the Judicial Committee of the Privy Council and that body has advised removal on such ground.[30] The Sultan also has power to appoint on terms and for a specified period, persons qualified to be judges of the Supreme Court, as Commissioners of the Supreme Court, who will have the same powers, privileges and immunities as a judge.[31]

To be qualified for appointment, a judge must be, or have been, a judge of an equivalent court in some part of the British Commonwealth, or must have been entitled to practice as an advocate or solicitor for not less than seven years.[32] At present, the judges come primarily from among Her Majesty the Queen's Judges in the colony of Hong Kong, and travel to Brunei to hear cases every other month. The arrangement has apparently proved satisfactory so far, and is generally viewed as contributory to confidence in the independence of the judiciary and the administration of justice in the State.

The sources of the law administered in the civil and criminal courts are Brunei and England. By the Application of Laws Act, it is provided that save insofar as other provision has been or may hereafter be made by any written law in Brunei, the common law of England and the doctrines of equity, together with statutes of general application, as administered or in force in England at the commencement of that Act shall be in force in Brunei.[33] However, it is also provided[34] that the said English law shall be in force in Brunei subject to the circumstances of Brunei and its inhabitants and to such qualifications as local circumstances and customs render necessary.

Fundamental Liberties

The Constitution contains no "fundamental liberties" as such apart from the freedom of religion in section 3. However, a large number of common law and statutory rights (as under the Criminal Procedure Code[35]) apply as they might in England; that is, they are not entrenched in a written Constitution and are thus not part of any "supreme" law. Such rights or liberties particularly pertain to rights of accused persons, such as the right to a fair trial, to make an unsworn statement from the dock, legal representation, the rule against "double jeopardy" and the privilege against self-incrimination. In sum, the Sultan is in many respects supreme in the government and law of Brunei, but British legal practice is joined with local traditions.

NOTES

1. An Englishman who assisted in the suppression of a revolt in 1839 against the sultanate of Brunei.

2. Sabah is at present a state in the Federation of Malaysia, as is Sarawak.

3. Brunei became, as did North Borneo and Sarawak, a British Protected State.

4. The Resident's advice had to be accepted on all matters other than those affecting the Muslim religion or local custom.

5. Agreement between Her Majesty the Queen of the United Kingdom of Great Britain and Northern Ireland and His Highness the Sultan of Brunei ("The Brunei Agreement"), 29 September 1959, Notification No. S.109, State of Brunei Supplement Extraordinary to the Government Gazette 1959, Part II, No. 32, 310. Clause 9 revoked the earlier Agreements of 3 December 1905 and 2 January 1906 between the U.K. Government and the Sultan.

6. Constitution of the State of Brunei, 1959, Notification No. S.97, State of Brunei Supplement Extraordinary to the Government Gazette 1959, Part II, No. 30, 153. By Gazette 1959, Part II, No. 30, 153. By Gazette Notification No. S.109 of 1959, made under s.1(2) of the Constitution, the Sultan appointed 29 September as the date for the coming into force of Parts I, II, III, X, XI, and XII of the Constitution. other parts were brought into force by Notification No. S.120 (1959) on 18 October 1959.

Hickling states: "This constitution, which was promulgated by the Sultan with the advice and consent of his "traditional advisors," whose signatures appear at its end, follows to a large extent the 1948 constitutions of the Malay States of what is now the Federation of Malaya ... although certain features are derived from the more common features of colonial government." (R.H. Hickling, Ch. 5, "The Borneo Territories," 120, in Stevens, ed., *Malaya and Singapore: The Borneo Territories*, 1961, L.A. Sheridan).

7. Malay for "Chief Minister." In Malay States, it was possible to have more than one Chief Minister.

8. Constitution of the State of Brunei, 1959, section 24.

9. The Constitution of Brunei Darussalam (Const. I, Laws of Brunei, revised ed. 1984), section 3(1).

10. *Id.*, Section 3(2).

11. *Id.*, proviso to Section 3(1).

12. *Id.*, Section 82.

13. The full title of Brunei's Head of State is: "His Majesty the Sultan and Yang Di-Pertuan of Negara Brunei Darussalam." The abbreviated title used in the Constitution is "His Majesty the Sultan and Yang Di-Pertuan." In this chapter, he is referred to as "the Sultan," for convenience only.

14. The Constitution, *op cit.*, Section 4(3). The Sultan has in fact appointed himself as Prime Minister as well; there appears to be no reason why this cannot be done.

15. The Constitution, Section 4(3).

16. *Id.*, Section 4(5).

17. *Id.*, Section 4(6).

18. The Succession and Regency Act (Const. II, Laws of Brunei), Section 13 provides for the qualifications and appointments of Regents.

19. The Constitution, Section 9, grants to the Sultan discretionary powers of pardon and reprieve of criminal offenders.

20. The Constitution, *op cit.*, Section 18.

21. *Id.*, Section 19.

22. Parts VI and VII of the Constitution were temporarily suspended by the Emergency (Constitution) (Amendment and Suspension) Order 1984 (S.8/84), on Brunei's obtaining independence. In August 1985, a new all-Malay political party, the Brunei National Democratic Party, was formed and registered, with a view to attaining gradual democratization and constitutional reform. However, the party was dissolved by the Registrar of Societies in January 1988 for infringing the Societies Act.

23. *Id.*, Section 4(7).

24. *Id.*, Section 81.

25. *Id.*, Section 83.

26. *Id.*, Section 85.

27. *Id.*, Section 86.

28. Laws of Brunei, Chapter 5.

29. *Id.*, Section 6.

30. *Id.*, Section 8.

31. *Id.*, Section 11.

32. *Id.*, Section 7.

33. Laws of Brunei, Chapter 2, section 2. The date of commencement of the Act was April 25, 1951.

34. *Id.*, proviso to Section 2.

35. Chapter 7, Laws of Brunei.2

9

REPUBLIC OF INDIA

The Constitution as the Situs of Struggle:
India's Constitution Forty Years On*

Rajeev Dhavan

Formal Appearance and Divergent Reality

To an insufficiently informed but otherwise objective observer, the view that the Indian Constitution forms the "cornerstone of [the] ... nation"[1] sits uneasily with the facts. One of the longest Constitutions of the world, it has invited extensive rewriting in the form of innumerable constitutional amendments.[2] For a crucial period of India's contemporary history, its federal structure was unscrupulously subverted by the center imposing its own direct "rule" in preference to stabilizing elected governments in various constituent States.[3] It set up a system of parliamentary government which was continuously threatened by legislators changing their loyalties, crossing the floor and toppling existing governments.[4] Its constitutionally enshrined system of collective responsibility has now been replaced by a massive concentration of power in the hands of the Prime Minister and his extra-constitutional advisors.[5] After much deliberation, the members of the Constituent Assembly disarmed the judiciary so that it would be a mild contrapuntal presence in the apparatus of power. Middle class and rich lawyers and litigants have ruthlessly used and abused court processes to both build up the judicial power[6] and, simultaneously, enmeshed virtually all government processes in labyrinthine litigation that serves private gain without, overall, enriching public processes.[7] The Constitution exuded secular ideals which were later explicitly written into the Preamble.[8] But the authenticity of these ideals continues to be tested, particularly most recently in campaigns for fair treatment for divorced Muslim wives and Hindu widows exhorted into *suttee* (widow burning), and the campaign to replace a Muslim mosque with a Hindu temple.[9] The architect of the Constitution proudly declared that he had made the "individual" and not the group the basic unit of the structure.[10] But, it is various forms of group life that have forged religious, social and political alliances, dominated policy concerns, created linguistic provinces and are, at present, pressing home religious, political and other demands to dismember the nation and rewrite its political map. India proclaims its socialist objectives, but presides over widening differentials

373

between the advantaged and disadvantaged to flimsily cloak atrocities against the latter.[11]

The temptation to dismiss this list of inversions as partial revelations of a much securer and more integrated development is subsumed by concerns over the extent of the disparity between the Constitution and its observance. The more specific concerns concede that a hiatus between constitutional declaration and prevalent practice is not unusual, but dwell on how these disparities reflect on India's salience as a state and affect the state's relationship with civil society which is alleged to have "privatized" the state to dissolve the distinction between "private" and "public" power in any sense other than the continuing possibility of the formal identification of the latter.[12] These specific concerns expand into wider inquiries about how, and with what effect, the Constitution manifests sociopolitical reality.

Political Versus Juridical Constitutionalism

India's Constitution resulted from an elaborate three-year-long process of deliberation. The final product was an unmanageable, but cosmopolitan, mix of borrowings which combined rhetorical goal-setting alongside projected liberal institutions which would not necessarily direct themselves to achieve pre-set teleological aims.   Optimistic accounts present this process of Constitution making as contentious, but, in the end, not problematic.[13] In doing so, such analysis has been influenced by the rhetoric that the Constitution was designed to serve the people but misses the cynical--perhaps, over-cynical--truism that it was intended to constitute and enable elite power struggles.[14] In this depiction, the people (who allegedly gave this Constitution unto themselves and for whose benefit it is dedicated) are presented as manipulable voters and grateful beneficiaries. Once mentioned, their future is mortgaged to elite power politics.[15] As the Constitution evolved through various committees and internal discussions, many members protested its non-participatory nature, and the abandonment of Gandhian ideals.[16]   Others attacked its liberal pedigree, lamenting that nothing had been borrowed from the Soviets.[17]

Dictatorial forms of government having been rejected, two insufficiently separated theoretical forms of constitutionalism seemed to contend for attention. A predominantly British *political constitutionalism* gave a near total leeway to elected institutions to fashion political, public and social life as they pleased, subject--in some versions--to some independent, judicial review of abuses of power.[18] By contrast, demands from various quarters pleaded the case for a *juridical constitutionalism* which specifically earmarked certain values for preferred attention.[19] It was understood, but not sufficiently appreciated, that both these forms of constitutionalism could only be operated and held together by conventional rules of political and institutional morality which would provide stability, ensure elite domination of the theoretically open-ended rules of participation, and preserve the status quo by controlling accretions to the elite themselves.[20]

Juridical and political constitutionalism are two ideal types. The former presents the Constitution as an ideological testament encapsulating certain preferred values which structure public discourse about state power, justice and citizenship. Juridical constitutionalism is necessarily problematic and invites a struggle over ideology and institutional interpretation. Political constitutionalism requires adherence to designated processes and respect for institutional structure but does not foreclose the continuous determination and redetermination of the permanent values underlying the constitutional agenda of the nation. Accordingly the Constitution constitutes politics which has a free hand in defining "law." The separation of "law" from politics and morality is characteristic of English analytical jurisprudence[21] and is supported alike by utilitarians and latter day socialists who wish to endow political law-making institutions with unrestrained powers to achieve utilitarian and socialist objectives, subject, in Diceyian variations of this approach, to a minimal rule of law empowering the ordinary courts of the land to some independent review of manifestly or potentially arbitrary exercises of power.[22]

Until recently, political constitutionalism was regarded as progressive since it allowed socialist rulers to unleash promethean reforms without being bound by a conservative liberalism susceptible to appropriation by the rich and advantaged.[23] However, in recent years, radicals have come to fear the Leviathan power of the state and argue for various versions of juridical constitutionalism.[24] Conversely, conservatives, hitherto full-fledged votaries of juridical constitutionalism, have retreated to a sophisticated version of political constitutionalism which agrees to preserve the process values of democratic participation while strongly refusing to read substantive notions of distributive justice into constitutional dogma.[25] The shifting support for different versions of constitutionalism *might* militate against the intrinsic superiority of any one version and point to a more pragmatic and relativistic choice of alternatives depending on the existing praxical situation.

The following diagram delineates an incomplete typology of constitutional alternatives, which would include combinations of figure 4:[see p.422]

I.   *DICTATORIAL CONSTITUTIONALISM*

    i.   Absolute (D3)
    ii   Restrained/Rule of Law (C3)
    iii.   Socialist (A3)

II. *JURIDICAL CONSTITUTIONALISM*

    i.   *Dictatorial*

        a)   Socialist (A3)
        b)   Liberal (B3)

    ii.   *Democratic*

        a)   Socialist (A2)
        b)   Liberal (B2)

    iii.   *Participatory*

        a)   Socialist (A1)
        b)   Liberal (B1)

III. *POLITICAL CONSTITUTIONALISM*

    i.   *Dictatorial*

        a)   Rule of Law (C3)
        b)   Relativist (D3)

    ii.   *Democratic*

        a)   Rule of Law (C2)
        b)   Relativist (D2)

    iii.   *Participatory*

        a)   Rule of Law (C1)
        b)   Relativist (D1)

Since politics and public life resist being squeezed into neat categories of heuristic explanation, there must be a considerable fusion of a variety of declared ends and styles of governance, which many regimes adopt, avowing commitments deferential to a participatory (redistributive) socialism (A1); or, as they resist, the charge of an uncommitted absolute dictatorship (D3). Equally, many may proudly proclaim fidelity to points of reference on either axis but pay only lip service to them. This typology does not foreclose the possibility of non-elected or dubiously elected governments, nevertheless agreeing to a *constitutional* commitment to some semblance of the rule of law (C3) or an even more elaborate juridical compact (A3/B3).[26] Participatory regimes are distinguished from democratic and other regimes in that the former are not just concerned with creating elected governments but with encouraging and enabling a wide range of participation in public affairs to display more positive portrayals of good citizenship (A1/B1, and--perhaps--C1) even though some may be relativistic in the overall definition of what constitutes a good society (D1). It is also possible to have dictatorial constitutions with no elections but participatory frameworks.[27] That possibility needs to be mentioned because it is not presented in this diagrammatic elaboration of typologies, but such claims are often made and not necessarily implausible. In the main, full-fledged participatory constitutionalism usually evolves within electoral structures. The categories of the rule of law could range from low level commitments to prevent abuses of power to a much more expanded (participatory?) due process. While no premium is necessarily set on any one particular mode of controlling abuse of power, the archetypal instance of locating the review power in an independent body (i.e., the judiciary) may represent a strong version of such institutional arrangements. Overall, these typologies do not seek to portray the sociopolitical ends and styles of governance in any society, but refer to the constitutional commitments which are (usually) explicitly stated or strongly implied in constitutional understandings, declarations and discourse. Thus relativist or rule of law democratic regimes (D2/C2) could develop a strong adherence towards, for example, a redistributive socialism without enshrining this bias as constitutional declaration or formally agreed ideology.[28]

Indian elites are engaged in a bitter struggle for mastery over the ideological meanings and institutional arrangements of the Constitution. Present in the deliberations of the Constitution makers, this struggle has subsumed and transformed the original Constitution. The received experience of the last days of the Raj was consultative but not representative government, and respect for the law but without enabling the judiciary to challenge governmental action (D3).[29] One solution to the problems of

Constitution-making was a full-blown version of the Government of India Act, 1935: elected parliaments at Union and State level, and judiciaries with powers of judicial review of executive and administrative action and a limited interpretative role to resolve intra-federal conflict.[30] This form of *political constitutionalism* (C2) was convenient, familiar, a successful transplant to the white dominions and fitted the mood of the Congress not to be hamstrung by constitutionally consecrated commitments. But a spiral of demands from religious communities, "Untouchables" and other minorities--along with a weak, but identifiable tradition of demands for a Bill of Rights--unravelled a case for some species of *juridical constitutionalism*. These were eloquently articulated in the first set of personal agendas of the chosen few who careered their way into Constitution-making.[31] If Clement Atlee's democratic socialist Britain was the model for *political constitutionalism*, Franklin Roosevelt's America explicated both the problems and possibilities of *juridical constitutionalism*. Reflecting on their then recent constitutional crisis, America's constitutional pundits warned their Indian counterparts that *juridical constitutionalism* would over-empower the judiciary in ways that would strengthen the hands of the advantaged (especially property owners) and hinder socialist objectives to redistribute power, status and wealth.[32]

Real controversies centered around how the various communities were to be represented in elected bodies and the extent to which the guarantee of fundamental rights would impede social reform. Communal representation was rejected but special representation agreed to for certain groups.[33] However, the tumultuous events of partition and the "extraordinary stress and strain ... [and the] tragic happenings of some twelve or fourteen months"[34] meant that central concerns about liberty and "fundamental rights" were "soft pedalled." An influential member of the "inner group" spoke for virtually the entire Assembly when he said:

> The recent happenings in different parts of India have convinced me, more than ever, that all the fundamental rights guaranteed under the Constitution must be subject to public order, security and safety though such a provision, may to some extent, neutralize the effect of the fundamental rights guaranteed under the Constitution.[35]

The most important casualty was the "due process" clause which was converted into an "any process" clause.[36] Alongside, preventive detention by decree of parliament was introduced without--it was thought--too much judicial review.[37] The second was an expansion of the circumstances in which parliament could simply pass laws to curtail religious freedoms.[38] It was in the third area--property rights--that the fiercest of battles was fought.[39] Given declared policies and pending legislation, *political constitutionalists* wanted to symbolically assert their power over a hitherto powerful, but now redundant, landed aristocracy, while ushering in and forging new alliances with the new kulaks who would replace the earlier landlords. But the landlords fought back. The final compromise was untidy. Some features of *juridical constitutionalism* remained (*i.e.*, features of the doctrine of eminent domain: property cannot be expropriated except for public purpose and on payment of compensation),[40] hedged in by massive powers in present and future legislatures to do exactly what they wanted in some situations.

While it appeared that the political constitutionalists had won the day, they had grossly underestimated the potential uses (and, indeed, abuses) of the judiciary. They felt that judges appointed under the Constitution, like the judges of the Raj, would be upright but assimilated to the purposes of the executive.[41] They overlooked the fact that pre-1950 judges, although carefully chosen to work closely with the rest of the government establishment, had never been trusted by the Raj with powers of judicial review of governmental action, except in a very limited way in the Presidency towns and, more generally, in *habeas corpus* cases.[42] They also overlooked the overcrowding of cases in the courts which suggested that, given the opportunity, Indian society would be quite fertile in drawing the courts into constitutional struggles.[43] India's Constitution makers displayed a laid-back lack of concern about the judiciary as a potentially powerful fulcrum around which constitutional thinking and decision-making could revolve. Asked to define a good judge, Nehru could only point to service in some High Court as a qualification.[44] This was a serious miscalculation. By analyzing courts only in terms of judges, not enough attention was paid to the probability that powerful lawyers and litigants would use the courts to appropriate the judicial review, and, indeed, juridical features of the Constitution to advantage.

And this is exactly what happened. Expropriated landlords--in one case hiring the services of the Untouchable leader, B.R. Ambedkar, who was the chief draughtsman of the Constitution--used the courts and appealed to juridical constitutionalism to unsettle agrarian reform legislation or obtain better compensation.[45] They were joined by politicians protesting their detention,[46] journalists complaining of censorship[47] and, in the course of time, by a chorus of others questioning governmental regulation of a myriad of activities while challenging various levels of executive and legislative decision making elaborated in India's ambitious five-year plans. Indian judges reacted to this confused situation confusedly. They were not even practiced in the art of judicial review, let alone the subtleties of juridical constitutionalism. Faced to this confused situation confusedly. They were not even practiced in the art of judicial review, let alone the subtleties of juridical constitutionalism. Faced with constitutional amendments which overturned the relief they gave to expropriated landlords and censored journalists, they retreated from earlier stances.[48] As part of this retreat, they were publicly contrite,[49] promised restraint, sanctioned a vast array of powers to the executive,[50] agreed to an "any process" clause,[51] promised not to interfere in agrarian reform and handed over to Congress majorities in the Union and State legislatures the power to amend the Constitution whenever they wished.[52] Moving away from a full-fledged American juridical constitutionalism (B2), they seemed to have agreed to concentrate on a British rule of law approach (C2) with the judges using the high prerogative writs to control administrative action. But this was an inherently unstable compromise. Lawyers and litigants could mount further attacks on the legality and constitutionality of all varieties of governmental initiatives and actions. Already drawn into the arena of politics, judges emerged as custodians and exponents of new forms of constitutional discourse. Lawyers, like Palkhivala, supported by corporate interests, and judges, like Subha Rao matured nascent constitutional doctrines borrowed from America and elsewhere, found loopholes in existing legislation and, finally, successfully constrained the government's hitherto unrestricted power to amend the Constitution by making amendments subject to the very laws which they sought to amend.[53] Their victory was finally complete when due process elements were read into the "any process" clause[54] and the Supreme Court, ignoring the Congress regime's amendments to retain elements of political constitutionalism, ruled in the *Fundamental Rights Case* that even the constituent power to amend the Constitution was subject to the implied limitation that the *basic structures* of the Constitution could not be altered.[55]

By 1975 these efforts--not always thought through or presented to the courts in a systematic way--had secured certain identifiable patterns. In the *first* place, the relatively low-key rule of law (anti-arbitrariness)-oriented judicial review of administrative action was firmly established along British lines.[56] However, Indian judges granted interlocutory relief more liberally to stultify government action until the final disposal of the case (often) years later.[57] *Secondly*, the Fundamental Rights and other provisions of the Constitution were used to gather together the juristic and ideological framework within which India's version of a liberal juridical constitutionalism (B2/C2) would be developed.[58] *Thirdly*, successive governments tried to reduce constitutional questions to matters of political interpretation (in the hands of the legislature and executive), rather than be controlled by lawyers, judges and jurists, a nascent juridical tradition had made some headway stay and began to replace British-style political constitutionalism as the basic paradigm underlying the Constitution. However, the exact contours of this constitutionalism remained undetermined (A1 or A2, B1 or B2). So, whether this constitutionalism was going to protect certain liberties or seek to engage in a redefinition of substantive justice enshrined in the Preamble and Directive Principles of State Policy was uncertain. *Fourthly*, these three emerging interconnected strands of judicial review (vis-a-vis (i) review of administrative action; (ii) Fundamental Rights and the socialist features of the Constitution; and (iii) the basic structure doctrine) had, by and large, been appropriated by the advantaged (usually the corporate sector, the rich, the salaried middle classes, some organized trade unions and others) rather than the disadvantaged. This had as much to do with the expense of litigation as the jurisprudential pattern emancipating from the emerging juridical constitutionalism.

In 1975, Mrs. Indira Gandhi declared a National Emergency, ostensibly because internal disturbances allegedly threatened the security of India but, in fact, to prevent her being unseated as Prime Minister: At at the end of four years of her five-year parliamentary term the Allahabad High Court-- found her technically guilty of relatively unimportant election malpractices. The "case that shook India" was politically motivated but directly called into question the fragile foundations of the rule of law.[59] Mrs. Gandhi responded by amending the Constitution to make her election unassailable. In an unconvincing Marshallian move, the Supreme Court used the basic structure doctrine to deny that its judicial powers of review could be taken away, but validated the election.[60] However, the Emergency created fresh problems. It called for a tough judiciary to break the back of a wide ranging ouster-of-jurisdiction clause accompanied by a massive rewriting of the Constitution in the name of secular socialism.[61] Judges who resisted the constitutional ouster or tinkered with the new amendments were unceremoniously transferred from the High Court of their home State to other High Courts in far off places.[62] At first, aspects of judicial review over the conditions of detention remained.[63] But not for long. In deciding the *Habeas Corpus* case (1976)[64] which made preventive detention immune from judicial review, the Supreme Court forfeited its leadership role. A reconvocation of pre-1975 juridical constitutionalism was possible only after Mrs. Gandhi's defeat at the polls, following the lifting of the Emergency in 1977.

The Emergency polarized the ruling party. The party distrusted the appropriation of juridical constitutionalism by various vested interests, in many cases, covertly, the same as those that supported the government.[65] This process of appropriation was very wide ranging. The middle classes flocked to the courts to challenge virtually anything and everything.[66] Judges supported these unruly and unsystematic fratricidal middle-class conflicts by granting interlocutory relief against the government, partly because the administrative system was rife with lawlessness and partly because they knew that the judiciary eventually drew support not just from the government, but from the sometimes contrary pressures emanating from the constituency of lawyers and litigants.

Indian constitutionalism--like its law--is caught up in middle-class power struggles. In the long run, constitutionalism cannot acquire wide ranging support if the courts are clogged with the affairs of the advantaged and fails to portray a convincing commitment to India's vast millions who belong to what I have called the "exploited" and "genocide" sectors of the Indian political economy.[67] In India, beyond the "exploited" sector lies a vast number of people who by virtue of being economically redundant are totally vulnerable to social and political excesses. Quite apart from the ultimate pragmatic need to obtain constitutional legitimacy from a wider range of people than the rich and the middle class, a constitutionalism for India which cannot extend the possibility of egalitarian, or for that matter any kind of credible, justice to the millions of India's poor whom the Constitution ostensibly seeks to serve (and who have voting rights) is, inevitably, problematic. The Constitution makers had articulated some non-justicable Directive Principles of State Policy which, described variously as a "veritable dustbin of sentiment" and the soul of the Constitution, include a commitment to provide universal education and redistribute the ownership of power and wealth.[68] The judges, as we shall see later, had been slow to react to the importance of the Directive Principles and were constantly pilloried by politicans for the narrowness of their concerns.[69] Consistent--at least theoretically so--with socialist versions of political constitutionalism, the Congress in a series on constitutional amendments demanded the unrestricted power to fulfill these objectives without being encumbered by Fundamental Rights and other constitutional limitations. And, the judges --even in the *Fundamental Rights* case--had no choice, until recently, but to accede to this demand.[70] Their own constitutional jurisprudence was wanting.

Recognizing this chink in their armor, the judges slowly began to declare their fidelity to the Directive Principles. But this was not enough. For in acceding to the legislature's and the executive's request to have the uncontrolled power to fulfill the Directive Principles, the judges had thrown out the baby with the bath water. They needed to develop a juristic epistemology which would, somehow, consciously articulate the Constitution and the law's fundamental concern for a substantive justice for the vast majority of India's millions who were poor, disadvantaged and voters.

Already embarrassed by the charge that it had been pusillanimous during the Emergency and spurred on by an inchoate alliance of social activists, lawyers, journalists and academics, some judges of the Supreme Court sought to rethink the fundamental concerns of the Constitution and the responsibility of the judges to effectuate these concerns. The result of these efforts has been referred to as India's "Public Interest Law Movement."[71] Although these initiatives have been connected with varieties of social action, the movement as a whole has been a middle class affair.[72] Not having been systematically thought through, its aims are becoming clearer as it gathers momentum. While the implications of these developments are discussed more fully later, a prefatory summary is necessary. Soon after the Emergency, the judges of the Supreme Court developed a credible doctrine of due process, fought anti-arbitrariness through more sophisticated administrative law concepts, revised rules of *locus standi*, and devised more elaborate remedies so that the Court did not just strike down unconstitutional and illegal action but approved remedial administrative and social schemes. In a dramatic gesture, they created a new "epistolary" jurisdiction, whereby a letter by someone genuinely socially concerned to a judge would be converted into a petition, and help would be provided to argue the case this enabled a wide range of people to petition the Court about alleged atrocities and injustices.[73] The Supreme Court--and later, various High Courts--were flooded with complaints about police atrocity, violation of due process, and a wide range of questions which raised issues of social justice. The Supreme Court entered into a partnership with the new self-declared "trustees" of socialism.

But if public interest law provided remedies where none existed before, it also sought, as we shall see later, to alter the basis of India's juridical constitutionalism. Judges, lawyers, and academics prognosticated that their efforts went to the heart and soul of the Constitution which was concerned not just with anti-arbitrariness and liberal human rights, but with a substantive socioeconomic justice which would redistribute power, wealth and status on an egalitarian basis (a shift from B2 to, at least, A2, if not A1).[74] Thus, it was not just a question of arming the executive and the judiciary with the unencumbered power to achieve the Directive Principles, but purporting to define the nation's goals in clearly thought through non-relativistic terms. The judges were making a bid to establish an independent legitimacy by proactively redefining their own role and relationship with a much wider catchment of people than the privileged few who had hitherto determined the agenda of constitutionalism through litigation on an atomistic case-by-case basis.

These developments, as we shall see later, were critically and cautiously received, and cannot just be viewed in terms of their social origins or consequentialist achievements. Many of India's disadvantaged, poor and exploited would need more convincing. After all, they had been promised socialism by politicians like Nehru and through the aegis of many five-year plans. They had also seen these plans diverted away from them to benefit the advantaged themselves. Now, the lawyers and judges were making promises. The cynical would surely ask: where will the next one come from? Public interest law explicates contradictions between society and its declared objectives lest--as a distinguished Indian scholar would have it--Indian society "regress" below to intolerable levels of social justice.[75] It also created a new hermeneutic tradition to project a dramatically different constitutionalism than had been envisaged earlier. In just over thirty years, Indian constitutionalism had swung from the relativistic, "rule of law"-oriented political constitutionalism preferred by its makers to a new juridical constitutionalism which, though vaguely elaborated in the original text, was directed not just at politicians but at every aspect of constitutional authority. The future of this development and how it will be appropriated by civil society cannot be easily predicted. At present, it is fragile. Much depends on who will appropriate the new constitutionalism, and whether a strong alliance of activist support, toughened by the development of institutional skills and countervailing power to use the system will sustain its impetus. Much depends, too, on whether India's rulers will allow it to grow. To that extent, this new struggle over constitutional ideology, and the institutions and processes through which it is articulated, may be passed over and marginalized.

Extra-Constitutionalism: The Privatization of the Indian State

Has the Indian state been privatized by forces in civil and political society to collapse the distinction between public and private power? Arguably, if its public power cannot be separately identified and respected for its integrity but is merely the external expression of private power, the constitutional and legal system may well be a sham.

It is possible to identify several overlapping developments which threaten the salience of the Indian state as the repository of public authority and public law. The irrepressible, even if predictable, rise of *extra-constitutional* activity and authority has manifested itself in ways that undermine the status, authority and efficiency of constitutional institutions and processes to fulfill their designated functions. The effect of the extra-constitutional compenetration of forces in civil society, political society and the constitutional order is reflected in levels of *corruption* which are not just *ad hoc* and casual but can be causally traced to powerful extra-constitutional determinants in civil and political society. It is also reflected in the rise of *state lawlessness*, so that public authorities ignore the constitutionally imposed restraints on the extent and exercise of their power. There is an increase in *inefficiency*. Accompanying this has been a *failure* to develop an *institutional morality*, with the result that there is a hiatus between the purposes underlying the Constitution and its pathological use. These five tendencies--the challenge to authority and extra-constitutionalism, corruption, state lawlessness, endemic inefficiency, and a failure of institutional morality--go some way in supporting the serious indictment that the Constitution is much too pliable to serve as a solid basis for citizenship and public life in India.

The Challenge to Authority

Extra-constitutionalism grows out of a necessarily problematic relationship between civil society, political society and the constitutional order. If the ultimate triumph of the constitutional order is its capacity to settle notions of citizenship and discipline a predictable institutional morality to guide the use of constitutional processes, its failure signifies the refusal of civil or political society (or both) to conform to the normative strictures of the constitutional order. Civil society may seek to corrupt the constitutional order, depriving it of a capacity of independent assessment and decision-making. Caught in between, political society[76] may reflect more easily the stresses and strains generated in civil society, rather than rise to the virtues demanded of it by the constitutional order. Equally, political society may generate its own struggles in the configuration of forces as an independent variable.

Although Indian constitutionalism was predicated on a consensus model, with groups in civil society influencing political parties which, in turn mobilize constitutional institutions and processes, such a system never evolved with any clarity.[77] A democracy based on elections superimposed on a rapidly transforming economy produced new political power brokers and elevated the importance of the party as an extra-constitutional authority. It also unleashed a chaos of opportunities for conflicts among new and old land owners, echelons of the business class, and sections of the bureaucracy--all interested in their own benefit, even if at the expense of orderly social, economic and constitutional development.[78] Alongside this chaos of opportunities was a simultaneous chaos of frustrations which enlarged the number and intensity of those in the "exploited" and "genocide" sectors of the political economy, and who have to contend for life and survival not just with the elements, but with a range of avaricious governmental and non-governmental predators.

The direct challenge to constitutional authority is reflected in the Hobbesian manifestation of the general increase in crime and the breakdown of law and order. Although "reported" crime is an insufficient criterion--more so, in a society where citizens are afraid to report crime lest they themselves be harassed by the police--the government's own estimate indicates a continuing increase from 1960 to 1982, in cognizable offenses (223.3%), including such offenses as murder (213.9%), theft (163%), dacoity, robbery and house breaking (142.2%), cheating (163.9%), and kidnapping and abduction (221.5%).[79] In particular, there is a marked increase in riots and rioters (396.1%).[80] There is some evidence of a more distinct upward slope since 1975. The significance of this gross data can be deflated by reference to demographic increases. Yet the quantum of increase in reported crime has to be contextualized by the informed intuitions of everyday experience which speak of increasing personal and possessional insecurity and a steady increase of police and policing. All this suggests a frightening slippage into a "law and order" society.[81] The Supreme Court's brave attempt to distinguish "public order" from "law and order" is only right in that it curtails the extension of preventive powers in respect of the latter.[82] But the distinction between the two begins to wear thin as more people "help" themselves to what they want without reference to the legal and constitutional system. Some of this increase in disorder can be traced back to legitimate social discontent.[83] However, both the phenomenon and this causal explanation corrodes "rule of law" constitutionalism, even if such disorder is accorded the social legitimacy of being born out of the righteous claims of the disadvantaged and oppressed.

In addition to the increase of individual crime, an increase in wide scale disturbances was graphically portrayed in the horror of riots, looting and murder in the aftermath of Mrs. Gandhi's assassination in 1984.[84] Traced back to entrenched communal and religious differences in Indian society, these events are often stage-managed, fanned by the very politicians who are entrusted with the successful working of the constitutional order. They give rise to death and destruction and result in atrocities against the disadvantaged.[85] Commissions of inquiry offer social explanations, hesitate to reveal the real mischief makers, advise remedial programs, and recommend a more intensely policed society.[86] These collective expressions of violence can be traced back to a tradition of protest in India's independence movement. Civil disobedience strengthened attitudes subversive of the constitutional order despite Gandhi's protestation of loyalty.[87] However, it can be more significantly traced to continuing class conflicts--especially in peasant rebellions and among the urban proletariat--which were ruthlessly suppressed and set the tone, texture and style in which conflict would both be expressed and suppressed.[88]

Independent India has seen challenges to authority not just as episodic interludes but as planned subversive campaigns. Beginning with the challenge of the Naxalities (1948-53, 1967-72)[89] to the supremacy of the government, there have also been regional demands for secession by the Sikhs, Nagas, Gorkhas and others. A bloody battle, resourced locally and internationally, is presently being fought in the Punjab for an independent State of Khalistan for the Sikhs.[90] Pakistan adds to the strain by fighting an undeclared war in Kashmir.

All this has immense implications for Indian constitutionalism. First, Indian constitutionalism has structurally not been able to accommodate and reconcile competing demands. Secondly, individual and collective challenges are often explained and justified as arising for just social reasons, thus legitimizing such conduct and simultaneously delegitimating the constitutional order. Thirdly, a continuing stream of unconstitutional social and political activity takes place without reference to and antithetical to the state and the constitutional order. Finally, such activity provokes a strong reaction from the state which claims emergency regulatory and detention powers over people, the media, public business, and private life to affirm, in effect, a precipitous movement away from constitutional democracy to a "law and order" society. It also results in covert political violence by the state and often brutal handling not just of adversaries, but as part of a casual exercise of power.

But apart from this *external* assault on the constitutional structure, which simultaneously creates "lawlessness" and intensifies an extraordinary concentration of state power, there has also been an *internal* relocation of decision-making away from designated constitutional processes and authority. Civil society uses political society to *influence* decision-making, in order to obtain favorable structures, results and advantages. But contemporary India is witness to the creation of alternative power structures which deprive public decision-making of its independent decision making capacity by reducing it to become no more an expression of private power. Elections have created a machinery of "power brokers" within political parties who tyrannically control rather than merely influence local, State and Union administration. This alters fundamentally the constitutional scheme of vertical administrative responsibility to Ministers who are collectively responsible to parliament.[91] But analysis must look further to the relationship between these political "power brokers" and various caste and other traditional group formations in civil society. It is in this sense that foreign observers have talked of India being run by "factions," congealing symbiotic alliances between traditional groups and the new breed of "power brokers."[92] Undoubtedly, powerful local forces sporting traditional colors manipulate the system; but such an explanation of the phenomenon needs to be placed within a wider and more incisive understanding of the emerging structure of the political economy. Apart from local "factions," there is a much more extensive privatization of public power by emerging classes and groups of people.[93] Unfortunately, even this privatization is characterized by a "free for all" world of deals and eludes the rationality required for even systematic capitalist development. The effect of this privatization is not just to destroy the central importance of designated constitutional processes and institutions in the life of the nation, but to destroy the very essence of constitutionalism which abjures the surrender of public discussion, policy, or decision to the converse world of private reasons for private deals.

The above portrayal captures dangers confronted by the constitutional order while exaggerating them in order to draw a more vivid picture. While parts of the constitutional system--especially at the local level[94]--have been privatized, other parts have not been directly corrupted, but appropriated to systemic manipulation by a mastery of the constitutional processes.[95] There are other parts of the state, including parts of the judiciary and bureaucracy, that retain their capacity for an independent assessment of issues. To that extent, on balance, significant parts of the state remain salient and viable, sensitive to, but independent of, the forces that seek to influence and subvert them. Yet the frequency of ignoring and corrupting the constitutional order is sufficient to pose a serious threat to the constitutional order. This pattern will surely continue as the political economy generates unbridled opportunism and unfulfilled oppressions and frustrations. Forces in civil and political society have still to learn the value of the constitutional order as an instrument through which power in its widest sense is consolidated and exercised.[96]

Corruption

Stories about corruption in India are legendary. Petty corruption is justified on the basis of low wages and penury, with "greasing the palm" augmenting absurd salaries in the face of continuing inflation. But this argument fails to attract to much sympathy because a large part of petty corruption affects the worse off. A great deal of it does not concern the low-wage earner, but fuels the greed of the better off for a consumerism which has been gradually unleashed in India to keep India's lower-middle, middle and rich classes happy. Corruption does not just consist of a small bribe to procure a petty license, to do a job quickly, to avoid going to a police station, to obtain a false certificate or to obtain a small favor from a tax inspector.[97] But corruption extends beyond getting jobs,[98] interfering with examination results,[99] and obtaining favors to take over the running of government itself. As the regime of corruption expands, it becomes a permanent parasitical companion to the working of the welfare and regulatory state and the management of its fiscal arrangements.[100] Some of it can be traced to the texture of India's over-regulated economy, but that cannot justify the levels and forms that corruption has taken and its role and function in the constitutional order. It is in this sense that a High Court judge rejected defenses of corruption as a necessary evil.

> Corruption is the deadliest enemy of every free, civilized society, more so in an egalitarian, welfare, democratic set up like our own. Not only does corruption in the official and non-official sphere hit the economically and socially lower strata of society harder than comparatively better placed citizens, but it also tends to breed dislike for, and want of faith in, the set up which tolerates corruption. And the longer corruption is tolerated in a political set up, the wider and deeper its tentacles spread, with the result that even the agency to root out corruption may have to be closely watched in its activities.[101]

Far from being a problem of unconnected individual transactions, the magnitude and nature of corruption and their impact upon constitutional decision-making have altered greatly over the years. Concerned at first with the magnitude of corruption, the Union government appointed an investigative committee which reported that between 1956-1962 there was a large increase in complaints (4,676 to 20,461) and "vigilance" cases (656 to 19,277).[102] For approximately the same period, penalties were imposed on 5,585 government servants (including 154 senior officers).[103] Yet even this startling sample of reported cases was just the tip of the iceberg. Among other things, the Committee recommended, and the government created, a Central Vigilance Commission which from 1964 reports a steady --but not increasing--stream of "anonymous or pseudonymous" complaints (1964-65: 2,032; 1986: 2122) and "vigilance" cases (1964: 575; 1986: 3,146).[104] An estimate of 1984 reveals that for the previous four years, seven leading departments concerned with revenue earning, contracting and other major expenditure and receipt earning functions (vis-a-vis, Customs and Excise, Income Tax, Defense, Banks, Post and Telegraphs and Works and Housing) contributed 57.5% of the cases.[105] For the period 1964-1984, a sample of 113,608 cases were identified including some connected with abuse of power (4,614), showing favors (2,532), making false receipts (1,903), misappropriating public property (951), civil servants having disproportionate assets (494), and so on.[106] Yet in this sample, there have been a few prosecutions (256) or major (2,119) or minor (2,066) internal administrative penalties imposed. Corruption is not just the "petty corruption" of petty officials but extends to serious allegations against very senior cadres.[107] The Report of 1986 almost proudly declares the ability of the Commission to catch and punish "big fry":

> Of the above officers (49 dismissed, 22 removed and 23 compulsorily retired) the pension of an Ambassador to Bahrain was reduced, a Joint Director in the Oil and Natural Gas Commission was dismissed from service; and a Deputy Engineer in Hindustan Fertilizer Corporation was removed from service. Apart (from)...that prosecution was launched against an Ex.CMD of a nationlised Bank.[108]

Even this declaratory list does not do justice to those too clever to be caught or those too influential to be subjected to scrutiny, reprimand and punishment.

Significantly, corruption does not just involve bureaucracy. The *first* shock in this regard was tracing mismanagement and favors to the table of a Union Minister. Nehru immediately set up an investigation committee into the Mundhra financial scandal (in which government funds were made available for private investment), to confirm India's worst fears.[109] The *second* shock began with allegations of corruption in the office of the Chief Minister of the various States. The *cause celebre* was allegations against Sardar Pratap Singh Kairon, the powerful Chief Minister of the Punjab.[110] His resignation followed a powerful indictment in the report of a Supreme Court judge who investigated the matter. Chief Ministerial corruption continues to plague provincial capitals and has been the subject of innumerable reports.[111] In some examples, instanced during the Emergency (1975-1977) and after, some Chief Ministers seem to have been spared investigation. The more recent case involving Chief Minister Antulay showed how difficult it is to prosecute a Chief Minister for corruption. Legal wrangles, appealed all the way to the Supreme Court, revealed the difficulty in resolving the dilemma of finding the right balance between protecting public servants from frivolous accusations and taking steps to deal with their corruption.[112] Even more recently, a Congress-inspired litigation directed against the flamboyant Chief Minister of Andhra Pradesh--N.T. Rama Rao--shows how fighting corruption is itself not immune from politics. Political witch hunts are legitimated as complaints. Conversely truth and falsity intermingle inelegantly to trivialize exposure of corruption as a *tamasha* (spectacle), inspired by political opportunism rather than serious concern for the constitutional order.[113] The *third* shock has come in the wake of the Bofors scandal, which established that there *were* "kick-backs" in a large defense deal, and which alleged that the beneficiaries were possibly Prime Minister Gandhi and those associated with him.[114] The coffers of the ruling party have often been fed by "kick-backs" from deals and government contracts for the purpose of fighting increasingly expensive elections which, in turn, are charged with the atmosphere of directly bribing the electorate. But the Bofors crisis alleges personal rather than party political corruption in ways and for purposes which reflect on the incapacity of the Prime Minister's office to make defensible public--as opposed to secret and private--decisions.

The persistence of this multi-level corruption challenges the constitutional system. First, it is becoming increasingly difficult to realize the premium that the Constitution places on accountability. Since private purposes infiltrate the system, and the reality behind public decision-making eclipses much from public scrutiny, no proper system of accountability can be set up. Parliamentarians air suspicions and grope powerlessly for facts as their committees demonstrate their limited resources, restricted powers, and inability for rigorous investigation. Instead, a tradition--traceable to the Raj-- has developed of using a Commission of Inquiry (manned by sitting or retired judges) for examining a major crisis concerning ministerial inefficiency and corruption.[115] Consistent with this trend, bureaucratic corruption is dealt with by an in-house Central Vigilance Commission and other internal investigative bodies. In order to offset this tradition, there have been demands for setting up independent statutory ombudsmen (called *Lokpals* in the Union and *Lokayuttas* in the States). The attempt to create such a Lokpal for the Union government failed on four successive attempts;[116] but Lokayuttas have been set up for various States.[117] It is not easy to assimilate these new ombudsmen into the constitutional order. On the one hand, there is a danger of the ombudsmen (which in some legislation also covers ministers) themselves becoming pivotal institutions of accountability to the exclusion of all other constitutional mechanisms. On the other hand, there is a contrary tendency to control, in various subtle ways, the operation of these various ombudsmen so that they do not constitute a serious threat to the further perpetuation of corruption.[118] The simultaneous bureaucratization and regime manipulation of new methods of accountability have impacted greatly on the overall system of collective ministerial responsibility[119] to parliament and the examination of the abuse of power by courts. Existing constitutional mechanisms have been side-stepped as the new structures struggle for independence, style and credibility.

The *second* important constitutional impact concerns the position of civil servants. While they hold office during the pleasure of the President, the Constitution accords them certain processual privileges against attempts to dismiss or remove them from office or reduce their rank.[120] These guarantees were given in order to ensure their independence; but they help to protect the corrupt public servant with as much tenacity as an honest one. While the Supreme Court has been confused about the extent to which civil servants hold office during the pleasure of the President, constitutional amendments have whittled down these guarantees.[121] Even so, a vast number of service cases make their way to courts; and are now being dealt with by a Central Service Tribunal before they make their way to the Supreme Court.[122] The image of a proudly independent civil service, responsible to parliament through their Minister, has given way to one which uses constitutional guarantees to strengthen its independence and invulnerability in order to be corrupt with impunity.[123]

While the incident of corruption has been exaggerated here to portray a more vivid image, it does permeate the system in ways which subvert the public nature of decision-making to further privatize the State. It has generated a parallel economy which has contributed to inflation increased the greed of those in power and their "clients" and given rise to extra-constitutional remedial mechanisms which are in the process of eclipsing the *apparati* which the Constitution designates to ensure efficiency and accountability.[124]

State Lawlessness and Inefficiency

The idea of "state lawlessness" captures both common sense understandings of the arbitrariness of state agencies and the constitutional imbroglio created when such agencies either openly flout or ignore the conditions imposes the law upon their own decision making.

First, there is "direct state lawlessness" when a government agency simply refuses to take decisions or carry out instructions entrusted to it. In innumerable cases, the administration has simply defied court orders. Courts have been obliged to issue notices of contempt in order to secure compliance, not always with success.[125] And if the court's unequivocal orders meet with defiance, the tendency not to carry out instructions within the administration is even more marked. As the system becomes more unreliable and unpredictable, it accelerates the capacity to generate paper work so that every decision calls for an elaborate authentication before anyone will ever act upon it. To obtain an agreed entitlement is as much a problem as securing that entitlement in the first place. This phenomenon is different from the "privatizing" effect of corruption and extra constitutionality, in that the latter processes seek to appropriate public decision-making so as to objectify a personal demand as a legitimate public claim. "Direct state lawlessness" takes place after a legitimate public claim has been made, but is dishonored for reasons of ineptitude, intransigence or corruption.

Second, state lawlessness concerns the "brutalization" of public power. Here, the administration not only acts illegally but does so in a manner which is patently unconscionable. This is particularly marked in relation to the police. It came as a shock to the Supreme Court to discover the kinds of practices that take place in India's prisons.[126] This includes not just the continuance of archaic practices like shackling and continuous solitary confinement, but brutality towards prisoners.[127] A national campaign was fought on women being raped while in custody.[128] Although the Supreme Court refused to take cognizance of an appeal to review an acquittal in such a case, the campaign succeeded in obtaining a change in the law of custodial rape.[129] It was shown that in the State of Bihar under-trials were being held in custody for terms far in excess of the ultimate punishment to be meted out to them for the crime.[13] There was also the hapless spectacle of a Supreme Court case, of boys who had spent their childhood awaiting trial in custody.[131] The conscience of the nation was numbed by the atrocity of police officers blinding accused persons awaiting trial.[132] This shock was compounded further by demonstrations supporting the action of the police in the belief that the blinded victims were accused of heinous crimes (untrue, in a large number of cases, as it happens) which would go unpunished by the processes of the law.[133] The "brutalization" of state power to violate the rule of law and perpetrate atrocities by the state extends beyond the confines of extracted confessions and beatings up in custody to a much more wide-ranging use of the state machinery to perpetuate political and bureaucratic violence. Police kill people in "encounters" and, generally, harass disadvantaged communities. Atrocities are inflicted upon them at the instance of "private" forces using public power. At times Indian governance far from being able to produce good, seems to regress rather than develop civil and political society.[134]

Third, there has also been a lack of rationality about the quality of administrative decision-making. This connotes both the situations portrayed by Fuller where it is impossible for the citizen to respond to what is expected of him[135], as well as lack of rationality in the discretionary exercise of powers.[136] This situation can be traced in part to constitutional amendments which have immunized certain categories of state action from judicial scrutiny.[137] It is also due to interpretations of the equality clause which have allowed state authorities to make widely differentiated classifications of people, situations, and entitlements, but without a rigorous theory of anti-arbitrariness.[138] Relying much more on conservative doctrines of judicial review drawn from English law, courts have been circumspect in their willingness and capacity to review the exercise of wide discretionary authority.[139] A more challenging due process has only been developed in recent years with Justice Bhagwati's celebrated judgment in the *International Airports Authority* case attempts to summarize important principles while demanding greater rationality in government decision-making.[140] What is missing is not just the practice of rational decision-making but also the ideological discipline which asserts that such decision-making is a worthwhile constitutional entitlement and expectation.

Fourth, there has developed the endemic inefficiency of a sprawling "over-developed" state,[141] which spawns bureaucracies which have no direct interest in, or ideological inspiration to, efficiency. There is little room at the top, a general non-recognition of talent and good performance, and promotions through patronage rather than on merit. The system sprawls unevenly in every direction, having swelled, especially in its lower cadres, to enormous proportions. In the course of time, the administration has become an independent variable, protecting its own interest and possessing the power to do so.[142]

Finally, we have already pointed to corruption which erodes public authority and contributes to perpetuating state lawlessness.   All these factors--direct state lawlessness, the brutalization of public power, arbitrariness and a lack of rationality in decision-making, inefficiency, and the lack of incentives for efficiency and corruption--taken together, go beyond marginal lapses from the "rule of law" to constitute a serious drift away from constitutionalism and into lawlessness.

Failure to Develop an Institutional Morality

Discussions of modern constitutionalism have been markedly unsuccessful in identifying its constituent elements. There is little dispute in "rigid" constitutions about identifying a *written core*[143] element. But controversy surrounds the unwritten conventions, institutions, and processes through wich Constitutional power is articulated and disciplined terms. Some constitutional imperatives are formulated in controversial ways or regarded as non-justiciable and or marginal importance be.[144] Ruling elites retain an ambiguity in conventional rules, because they do not wish to be hamstrung by consensus formulations of their own making. Nevertheless, these conventions remain fundamental to governance because they formulate the structure within which elite power games are to be constituted. However, the separation of the *written core* from *conventional* elements is artificial and prevents a proper assessment of the purposes behind any constitution, whom it empowers and for what purposes. There is constant need to take a comprehensive and critical view of constitutional arrangements and the ideological perspectives which hold them together.[145]

The framework of the Indian Constitution favored "elite management" of the powerful representative institutions created by it. Far from making the individual central, the Constitution visualized the creation of new kinds of group life in the form of political parties.[146] In their relationship *inter se*, political parties were expected to respect the *conventional* rules inherited by British constitutionalism and to ensure that those endowed with constitutional power would not deviate from their ascribed function. This was in the interests of providing stability to the framework as a whole and to inveigle others into believing that these arrangements were as sacrosanct to the rulers as they were expected to be to others. Thus, the system envisaged the country being run by a small political elite, itself drawn up by a highly centralized and daunting system of party patronage and politically competitive selection. There were several assumptions on which the success of this constitutional enterprise depended. In the first place, much depended on the existence of an identifiable elite who would develop strong integrated political parties which would create a political society responsive to, but distinct from, civil society. It also hinged on the sacrosanctity with which the conventional rules of behavior would be treated. It was important that the various institutions of the Constitution would not be sent on collision courses against each other, but would be forbearing in working out a system of restraints which would give priority to representative institutions without undermining watch-dog institutions like the judiciary. It was equally important to enable a relatively stable horizontal sharing of power within the federal system.

Unfortunately, none of these assumptions squared with the facts of Indian constitutional life. The identifiable elite was too diverse and disorganized, leaving it to any usurper to arbitrarily claim membership.[147] The sheer number and diversity of aspirants for office introduced a "free for all" rush for power by any means, fair or foul. The system acquired speed but not stability. Political parties failed to acquire salience. At one level, they were dissolved by forces in civil society. At another level, they fell prey to the centralized will of those at the helm at the time.[148] Conventional rules were violated if they were found to be inconvenient. Polarization between cooperating constitutional institutions increased as respective users employed one against the other to further their ends.[149]

The first serious threat came in the form of legislators crossing--or being made to cross--the floor of various legislatures with the result that duly elected political parties were toppled from power.[150] A constitutional amendment now renders such defections more difficult and also silences the back-bench conscientious objector within parties.[151] This was an attempt to make those with majorities almost invulnerably powerful within parliament. Even this has not worked as defections brought down the V.P. Singh government in 1990 forcing premature elections. The failure to develop an institutional morality can also be seen in the excessive and unprincipled use of the "emergency" provisions of the Constitution. These allow the Union to take over the government of a State and place it under the President's rule if the Union feels that the State is not being governed in a constitutional manner.[152] Between 1967 and 1991, these provisions were extensively used against opposition regimes in ways that virtually pronounced the death of federalism.[153] Ironically, in the course of time, India seems to continue to elect opposition governments in important States while returning a Congress government at the Union level. The latter continues to try and undermine the former by discrediting them, imposing financial restraints, and threatening the imposition of President's rule. Inter-institutional skirmishes and confrontations continue between the President and Prime Minister,[154] the Union and the States, and the judiciary and parliament.[155] These are not marginal disagreements in an otherwise fluent structure, but often an opportunistic inter-position of checks without balances.[156]

While the elite system of conventions borrowed from the United Kingdom is being altered under the pressure of increasing competitiveness and political autocracy,[157] the exact contours of this transformation cannot be identified independent of the opportunism that gave rise to it and, could in turn, destroy its initiatives. This furthers the chances of unpredictable and unsystematic use of the system, leaving open wide possibilities for the further privatization of the state.

The Basic Units Of The Constitution: Individuals, Groups, And States

In 1947, India had very difficult choices to make about the basic units in civil and political society which would be expressly or implicitly recognized by the Constitution and entrusted with rights and obligations. The advent of partition had already created the two political units of India and Pakistan.[158] Who and what demands would be accommodated by the new Constitution were questions of fundamental importance. If Pakistan was to be founded on Islamic principles, would India take the hazardous step of establishing a Hindu *ram-raj* (kingdom of god)? And if it did, how would the demands of various minorities be treated? As it happens, India chose to be a secular republic. But this by itself did not resolve the insistent demands of contending groups.

Groups

Even before representative and responsible government was instituted, the British followed a policy of plural representation. Several large religious and cultural minorities were allowed separate consultative, electoral and political representation. Indeed, the creators of Pakistan wedged home their support as an enlargement of this policy. The various "untouchable" groups led by B.R. Ambedkar--later, the architect of the Constitution--challenged Gandhi and the Congress' right to represent them. In a celebrated showdown, Ambedkar was forced to accept a lesser form of representation without abandoning the general principle of separate recognition.[159] The demands of the "untouchables" were accompanied in the Constituent Assembly by the demands of the Muslims, Christians, Buddhists, Jains, Sikhs, Anglo-Indians and a host of others. Even if India was to be a secular democracy, the basis on which group life was to be accommodated was important.[160]

Ambedkar's statement, alluded to earlier, that the individual rather than the group was the basis of the Constitution was a general reply to these extensive claims, as well as a refusal to accept the Gandhian notion of the "village" as the appraopriate basic unit for a future India.[161] As a highly sensitive "untouchable" who had often been badly treated,[162] Ambedkar treated the "village" as a "den of localism" which concealed unbearable social and economic oppression.[163]

During the process of Constitution making, important issues revolved around the British policy of plural representations which continued to inspire many adherents. In the end, various concessions had to be made to group life. The *first* and most important concession was made in respect of group representation itself. Rejecting a general theory of plural representation, a specific concession was made to certain groups. The case of the "untouchables" (by this time renamed "Scheduled Castes" because they were identified by inclusion in a designated schedule) and some tribals (called "Scheduled Tribes" for similar reasons) seemed incontrovertible, no less because the architect of their struggle for separate representation was also the architect of the Constitution.[164] Along with them was tagged on the case for Anglo-Indians.[165] Both were for a transitional period, but have been extended decennially party as an act of faith and partly because such an arrangement helped those in power in an electorally significant way. Controversy continues on whether these reservations have been beneficial or whether they have entrenched identities to provide opportunities to those amongst the disadvantaged who are already privileged.[166]

Second, the cause of the Scheduled Castes, Scheduled Tribes, and groups nebulously described as "backward classes" was also recognized, as the potential recipients of preferential discrimination by the state, especially in matters of state employment and admission to state educational institutions.[167]

Third, while collective recognition was not given to religious and cultural groups, the beliefs, rights and practices of such groups were given protection against interference by the state.[168] But how were these groups to be defined? In an omnibus definition, Sikhs, Jains and Buddhists were characterized as belonging to the Hindu faith.[169] The religious freedom provisions are inherently problematic. They create the potential for groups asserting and laying claim to enclaves of autonomous social and economic power which can resist the egalitarian, secular, socialist objectives declared by the Constitution. Care was taken to prioritize the power of social reform over these protections.[170] Later, the Supreme Court sucessfully claimed the crucial constitutional power to define which religious practices were "essential" to the faith and therefore--on the basis of such judicial recognition entitled to constitutional protection. It then, asserted the reformist power of the judiciary in full measure to determine which practices were "essential" to any faith.[171] In this way, the judiciary was able to extend very greatly the regulatory power of the state over the powerful conurbations of religious power and authority.[172] Conflicts between the state and religious groups occupy center stage in contemporary conflicts, as evidenced by the demands of Sikhs for a separate state and by controversies over the need to change Muslim personal law or abolish "the obligation" of Hindu widows to commit *sati* or replace a Muslim mosque with a Hindu temple. *Fourth*, the Constitution recognized the right of individuals to form associations, the setting up and operation of which could be reasonably restrained in the public interest.[173] Freedom of association, probably intended to create new "modern" groups based on voluntarism and rationality,[174] could thus, be used to provide protection for traditional group orderings, including, perforce, the family and personal laws of those beloning to innumerable faiths.[175] Through generous derogation clauses, the state could also restrict both traditional and family and personal laws of those beloning to innumerable faiths.[175] Through generous derogation clauses, the state could also restrict both traditional and modern group associations which it felt were inimical to "the public interest."[176] The range of groups that could be restricted in this way extended from fanatical orthodox types, to victims of anti-communist witch hunts to trade unions or others found to be threatening or inconvenient.[177] *Fifth*, the Constitution implied--as has been asserted earlier--that a central pivotal role would be occupied by political parties who would constitute political society and control the operation of legislative and executive institutions and processes. This implicit understanding was made explicit in the Fifty-Second "anti-defection" Amendment to the Constitution in 1985.[178]

It is impossible to deny the importance of groups and group life in India. It is also possible nor desirable to eliminate notions of collective togetherness from people's lives. Such collective enterprises define, strengthen and enliven human life, though some groups overwhelm, debilitate and degrade. India has struggled to establish the basis on which various kinds of group life could function as part of civil and political life and to determine their place in the constitutional order. The case for traditional groups continues to be argued as they are displayed as immutable variables in Indian life.[179] The power and strength of such groups and their insidious effect were powerfully demonstrated in the fight of Muslim orthodoxy to deny Muslim wives a favorable and secular right to maintenance;[180] and, more brutally, in the attempt of Rajput Hindu fundamentalists to consecrate *sati* (the burning of widows in their husbands' funeral pyres). Recently the V.P. Singh fell in 1990 as he sought to protect a Muslim mosque from politically motivated Hindus who claimed that it stood on the spot where the Lord Ram was born .[181] It has been powerfully argued that such continuing vestiges of group life are corrosive to the egalitarian secular socialist basis of the Constitution,[182] and that the previous practice--of either allowing various groups to reform their ideology and practices from within[183] or the Supreme Court's attempts to influence such reform by initiating a process of redefining religion[184]--should be abandoned to give way to a stronger constitutional regime which refuses to compromise social change and reform at the expense of religion.[185] The middle ground is held by those who believe that it is possible to hold on to the rich diversity of India's group life while eliminating those exploitative and oppressive elements which are anathema to the new constitutional dispensation.[186] Unfortunately, efforts at reform are counterbalanced by the realities of Indian elections which recreate, further entrench, and feed upon traditional caste, communal and other traditional group life. The argument for preserving tradition and the plea for cautious reform are enmeshed in

Independent India has done much to regulate the power of religious endowments[187] and influential denominational schools,[188] but it has hesitated to enter into a strong confrontation between entrenched traditionalism and a zealous social reform which might alter the very basis of traditional associational life. It has hesitated to uncompromisingly declare that the plethora of entrenched holistic traditions cannot be disaggregated into harmless and endearing elements, on the one hand, and detachable, exploitative elements on the other. It may well be the case that these issues cannot and should not be fudged indefinitely.[189] Though many issues remain unresolved, India's experiment with group life remains insightful, imaginative, resourceful and genuine, and one from which many lessons are to be learned by other jurisdictions faced with the power asymmetries of existing and emerging group life. Yet it portends dangerous decades ahead.

Individuals

Influenced greatly by Western liberalism and, in part, by the needs of an expanding capitalism, the Constitution has deconstructed India's complex group life and seems to make a cutting-the-Gordian-knot style gesture to focus on the individual as the basic unit of the Constitution.[190] While India's innumerable traditions had recognized individuality as a key variable of human existence--and this was marvelously displayed in its philosophical, artistic, musical and other traditions--it had, in its broadest sense, rightly refused to make the individual person its exclusive concern.[191] It is a moot question as to whether the social reform inaugurated by the Raj was an ethnocentric reaction to Indian social morals[192] or a conscious stimulus to the untidy growth of Western individualism.[193] In any event, it is tolerably clear that the legal reform undertaken by the British through the codification of Indian laws sought to constitute Indian society as consisting of individuals exercising their freedom of contract in an infinite variety of disaggregated transactions.[194]

Liberal constitutionalists who dominated the early stages of the movement for independence asserted the need for a Bill of Rights.[195] Largely stimulated by a liberal ideology borrowed from the West, this demand also protested the manner in which the Raj treated individuals as subjects of the Empire. Like most ideological movements, the demands for a Bill of Rights got appropriated by powerful constituencies. A discerning reading of the discussions in the various committees and on the floor of the Constituent Assembly reveals that minorities felt that a strong Bill of Rights would assure them protection.[196] The notion of a Bill of Rights was shamelessly, if not conclusively, taken over by spokespersons of the propertied classes,[197], among whom some landowners had been threatened with the expropriation of their property at reduced or illusory levels of compensation.[198] Significantly, but perhaps understandably, few espoused the cause of the individual as part of a broad theory of human rights.[199] As pointed out earlier, this may be due to a concerted attempt by the leading cabal of Constitution makers to safeguard the rights of the state against excessive individualism, while pointing to the turmoil in post-independent India as a justificatory reason.[200] In any case, fundamental rights were watered down by the simultaneous increase of the power of the state to make inroads into these rights by ordinary legislative action.

Individuals and Elections

The most important and immediate impact of the pivotal position given to the individual was in the area of elections. All of a sudden, the individual became endowed with a significant bargaining power which he or she had never possessed before. Nothing has altered the fabric of India's political life and constitutional priorities more than this significant development. This was not the gradual extension of the franchise starting with a small elite, but a universal empowerment of every adult.[201] After almost four decades of elections, it is necessary to dispel the image of the ignorant manipulated Indian voter who pliantly follows a blend of tradition and charisma. Near contemporary history shows Mrs. Gandhi's massive defeat at the polls and an equally remarkable return to power in 1980. At the same time, the same voter who elected her and her successor to power chose Opposition parties to leadership in various States. Undoubtedly, a great range of traditional and modern ideological motifs and an even more elaborate marshalling of incentives and inducements have been overtly, covertly and subtly brought to bear, and influenced the choice exercised by the electors even though making religious appeals is illegal and could result in the election being invalidated.[202] This has generated the political and electoral articulation of ideological packages drawn from the Western political traditions of liberalism, conservatism and capitalism. It has also given rise to more sinister uses of traditional fundamentalist ideology in ways that have bred violence, intimidation, despair, and social regression. But, inevitably, much of this electoral politics is hard-edged and has resulted in a complex machinery of party politics which not only organizes inducements during elections, but also sets up a continuous and complex operation by which favors are meted out to the often changing alliances of the faithful and feckless.[203] Alongside these networks in political society, elaborate networks in civil society receive and dictate the manner in which the patronage of the state--including its welfare schemes--is to be distributed, thereby effectuating a virtually unarrestable continuance of the privatization of public power. The new groups born out of the *real politik* of elections are not traditional orderings but an untidy, yet effective, emerging alliance of dominant propertied classes. These possess wealth but are also crucial extra-constitutional determinants in the exercise of state power. However, there are enough indeterminacies in the unscrupulous power of these new oligarchies to make it possible for the system to yield more egalitarian or rational results. For using the power of the individual and reaggregating it in new organization forms and ideological understandings could, even against such conspiratorial odds, yield more satisfying results.[204]

Individuals as Possessors of Fundamental Rights

India's Constitution makers, as has been already noted, bargained away only nominal concessions to individual human rights. Treating the individual as a unit of concern rather than a vehicle of entitlement and anxious to assert a parliament dominated political constitutionalism, they constructed a chapter on Fundamental Rights, which *explicates a theory of state control as much as it grounds individual rights as a central feature of the Constitution.* Seeking to protect the individual from state action and defining the state and law in the very widest terms, the Constitution guaranteed equality,[205] seven freedoms[206] (*i.e.,* of speech and expression, to assemble peaceably without arms, to form associations and unions, to move freely throughout the territory of India, to reside and settle in any part of India, to own, hold, and dispose of property [now abolished], and to practice any profession or carry out any occupation, trade or business), certain specific rights in respect of arrest, preventive detention and trial,[207] freedom from exploitation,[208] religious freedom,[209] cultural and educational rights,[210] and rights to go to the higher judiciary to petition the justiciability of these rights.[211] Into this powerful ensemble were written restrictions to ensure equally powerful intrusions by the state. The equality article--unless rigorously interpreted--would allow the state to make wide ranging classifications to treat special classes of people unequally, even though such classifications could not be made on grounds of religion, race, caste, sex, descent, place of birth or residence.[212] The state through parliamentary and executive action could promote preferential discrimination for certain classses of people. The seven enumerated freedoms could be reasonably restrained in the public interest.[213] An "any process" clause displaced a proper due process clause.[214] Social reform was prioritized over religious freedom,[215] the right to property was vulnerable to various specified and general land reforms.[216] While recognizing the rights of individuals to certain freedoms, the Constitution makers ensured that these freedoms were defined by state action, rather than seen as based on any preexisting theory of individualism and individual entitlement.

But this array of restricted freedoms is sufficiently open-textured to make it possible for protagonists in civil and political society, including litigants, publicists and the legal profession, to use the courts to argue through a credible case for a much more expanded theory of liberalism and human rights. Unfortunately, the nature of this struggle has not been sensitively portrayed because of an over-concentration of attention on the institutional struggle between the judiciary and successive governments over land reform.[217] The land reform cases involved expropriated landlords using the right-to-property provisions against the onslaught of a powerful "socialist" program to expropriate them but which, in hindsight, resulted in passing on land to a newly emerging, politically created, middle class peasantry.[218] A conflict between a greedy "has-been" landed class and a government in shining armor produced the rhetoric of outrage and consolidated political constitutionalism at a speed that did not give the legal profession and their clients a chance to ground their opposition in a well worked out theory of liberalism. Rather, the judiciary virtually apologized for their unthinking intransigence, with the result that the cause of a human rights Liberalism retarded into retreat for decades.[219]

The land reform struggle made explicit the heresy already implanted in the Fundamental Rights chapter[220] that, by and large, fundamental rights flowed from legislative and government action and were not really antecedent to it. This pessimistic reconstruction of the Fundamental Rights chapter was comfortably ensconced in the constitutional imagination. In the 1950s, India witnessed neither the liberal theory of individual rights nor expanded liberal conceptions of anti-arbitrariness. A disconcerted attempt to build doctrines of fairness and anti-arbitrariness--which is explicated in the judgments of Justices Fazl Ali, Vivan Bose and Subha Rao--of the Supreme Court did not succeed. The government was conceded vast delegated legislative and executive powers to underpin an over-developed, powerful regulatory state.[221] If the judiciary challenged an extension of the police power of the state--as in the *Newspaper* cases of 1950--the Constitution was immediately amended, and the judiciary succumbed and publicly acknowledged its erroneous interpretation.[222] Fazl Ali J's attempt to establish a due process clause did not succeed.[223] The mantle of Fazl Ali seemed to fall on Justice Subha Rao (1958-1967) who has wrongly been described as the "defender of civil liberties."[224] Subha Rao J. did not articulate a coherent theory of rights. He

(1958-1967) who has wrongly been described as the "defender of civil liberties."[224] Subha Rao J. did not articulate a coherent theory of rights. He concentrated on developing a theory of judicial review, expanding judicial review to cover more aspects of legislative and administrative activity,[225] and making a plea for--but not developing--a theory of anti-arbitrariness.[226] His incomplete achievement was offset greatly by Justice Gajendragadkar who reconciled conflicting demands in an over-rated pragmatic compromise jurisprudence,[227] which expanded state regulation of labor processes[228] and religious endowments,[229] sanctioned a broad state patronage of schemes of preferential discrimination,[230] read limited process rights into detention laws,[231] some (but not too much) procedural fairness into administrative process,[232] and all but succeeded in preserving the legislature's unreserved power to amend the Constitution at will.[233] From 1967 to 1973 an untidy institutional struggle ensued between the judiciary and the legislature.[234] But this was a power struggle between lawyers and judges in an attemnpt to strengthen their enclave of power. At an ideological level, it was less about human rights and more about articulating a limited liberalism protesting the wide discretionary powers of the legislature and executive, to champion an expanded judicial review by the courts.

This is not to suggest that human rights issues did not reach preventive detention, not by expanding notions of liberty but by calling for an observance opf the process rights decreed in the Constitution.[235] It protected news papers from pricing and page control[236] and governmental control of newsprint, [237] but on the basis of a weak theory of the freedom of the press and an incomplete understanding of the press's institutuional needs and its role in India's libeeral democracy.[238] The regulatory state was subjected to judicial review on the basis of Gajendragadkar's legacy theat the state needs to be disciplined if it is to have legitimacy rather than on the basis of well-worked theory of rights.[239] This untidy *apolologia*--labelled "sociologiacal jurisprudence"--limped into prominence, and later into disrepute during the Emergency(1975-1977), occasioning open suspicion after Justice Beg's tenure as Chief Justice ended in 1978.[240]

An attempt to develop a theory of rights arose as a response to, and in the aftermath of, the Emergency. Pro-establishment judges felt the need for a more coherent theory about the exercise of state power as well as about human rights. A coalition of the middle class, drawn from various quarters and widely different perspectives, has attempted to draw various threads together.[241] But it remains fair to agree with the incisive assessment of a leading lawyer that "[t]he constitutional jurisprudence in the hands of the current Court ... seems to lack a theme."[242]

From "Abuse of Power" to a Theory of Rights

After the emergency, the first task of the Supreme Court was to move away from limited judicial review, concerned only with monitoring the "abuse of power" to a rights-based due process, asserting the need for due process wherever liberties were involved. One strand of this development has been concerned with demanding greater rationality from the regulatory state[243] in administrative matters. Another strand has developed in the area of criminal procedure.[244] The Court was confronted with cases from prisoners who had been shackled or kept in solitary confinement. Their rights were not only discussed in the context of existing laws and prison regulations but their fundamental rights.[245] Criminal due process was expanded by the Supreme Court, which, faced with the predicament of accused awaiting trial for intolerable periods of time, issued instructions for the disposition of these cases.[246] If the government was not able to explain the whereabouts of a person last seen being taken into custody, the Court awarded sums in compensation.[247]

Despite this development, one may not yet rely on the constitutionally established right to due process in respect of pre-trial and trial procedures; for this, one continues to depend on statutes.[248] What has developed is an imperfect anti-atrocity due process which will not allow the human being to be degraded and will cure outrageous violations which make a mockery of criminal procedure. Consistent with this, the court has expended its concerns to protect the individual from a wider range of degradations. Thus, it has intervened to prevent continued exploitation of those who have bonded as slave labor[249] or been paid less than the minimum wages.[250] It has also called for an investigation into and an end of the *rickshaw wallah* system, whereby humans tricycle other humans for a paltry sum of money.[251] In a more expanded version, they have investigated the industrial exploitation of those placed in undesirable labor.[252] It has struck a rich chord by wielding this amorphous, but readily identifiable, anti-atrocity and anti-degradation humanitarian jurisprudence which throws its mantle to protect an as yet indefinable categories of the ill-treated, oppressed and degraded.

A concurrent development has been the effort to create a more elaborate theory of egalitarian social justice.[253] The contours of that development have already been discussed in the context of the rise of juridical constitutionalism and will be examined in greater detail later. For our present purposes, it will suffice to point to new developments which, though not free from problems, elaborate new insights into the social obligations of individuals against the backdrop of a much wider constitutional commitment.

It is not being asserted that the case for the libertarian tradition portrayed in the "fundamental rights" chapter was not wholly honestly argued for in the Constituent Assembly.[254] These well-meant declarations were welcomed by the legal community.[255] Judges in both their judicial and extra-judicial pronouncements declared their adherence to maintaining these rights and liberties, and sought to analyze their significance and the role of the judiciary, as part of the democratic tradition.[256] Although the guarantee of "personal liberty" was initially narrowly interpreted by the courts and the courts permitted vast regulatory control including limited pre-censorship of the press, the rhetoric of liberty was articulated as part of the hermeneutic tradition of judges. Even though it was not *fully* reflected in the decision-making of the courts or the *ratio decidendi* of their decisions, the strength of that tradition was kept alive in decisions on preventive detention and in interpreting the extent of administrative and legislative action.[257] It is prominently visible in Justice Khanna's celebrated dissent in the *Habeas Corpus* case in which the majority refused to review detention orders during the Emergency.[258] It was an important consideration in the subsequent, more expanded interpretation of "personal liberty" in the 1960s,[259] and had an important role to play in the development of the humanitarian anti-atrocity jurisprudence identified earlier. In particular, the Supreme Court sought to protect the freedom of the press from excessive regulation of the conditions of employment of working journalists,[260] the fixing of the price and number of pages of newspapers,[261] or the control of newsprint supply.[262] Recent decisions give journalists access to prisoners in jail,[263] a decision from Bombay argues that the press should not be subject to any regulatory control,[264] and a forceful statement was made by the Supreme Court about the role of the press in Indian democracy.[265] Yet, it has been argued that the court has not evolved a coherent theory about the institutional needs of the press in contemporary Indian democracy.[266]

There has been concern for those incarcerated without trial[267] and about patently indefensible action by the government against the press.[268] Yet a full-fledged theory of human rights has been slow to counteract the pro-state biases that had been written into the Constitution, elevated into importance by Nehru's "planned" socialism, and conceptualized in innumerable judgments by the higher judiciary. Human rights figure in the great decisions challenging parliament's power to amend the Constitution[269] and are undoubtedly part of the as yet insufficiently defined "basic structure" of the Constitution which is immune from the otherwise plenary power to amend the Constitution.[270] But an appropriate human rights theory has been developed in an *ad hoc* manner, as the litigation has given the courts opportunity.   Starting with a constitutional conception with a weak theory of human rights, Indian constitutionalism has begun to articulate the minimum standards of how people are to be treated. But it still has a long way to go before these concerns are more boldly and clearly placed within a more complete analysis of Indian democracy and its capacity for social justice. As initiatives in public life for human rights gather momentum, powerful forces in the political economy will both support and resist their being imbricated with the inner workings of the administration and the constitutional system.[271]

States

Besides recognizing individuals and groups, the Constitution superimposed upon the political map of India a division of constitutional power and responsibility between the Union and the States. The background to this development was untidy. The Transfer of Power transferred the territories of the Raj to India and Pakistan, respectively, but left it to the various princely States to determine their fate independently.[272] Regarding that story, it will suffice to be conscious of the complexity of working out constitutional arrangements which would accommodate the multiple demands of these very diverse people, speaking an immense range of languages in different scripts and in innumerable dialects, and possessing religious, cultural, artistic, literary and occupational traditions that stretched back into forgotten centuries. The initial scheme of creating three kinds of States was transitional and, in 1956,[273] gave way to a more clearly identifiable federation consisting of the Centre (the Union), various provinces (the States) and, in the course of time, various territories (the Union territories, which had a full-fledged apparatus of responsible government but which, by virtue of not being full-fledged States, were the administrative responsibility of the Union).[274]

While each State had its own elected legislature, cabinet government and judiciary, the division of power between the Union and the States was heavily weighted to the Centre which had a longer and more important list of exclusive legislative powers ("Union list"). The Union had priority over items in the "Concurrent list," but no powers on matters on the "State list,"[275] a reserve power to legislate for the States under certain conditions prescribed by the Constitution,[276] the capacity to impose administrative directions on the States,[277] the overriding say in most matters concerning taxation, funds and allocative planning,[278] and most important of all, a loosely defined, and therefore dangerous power to impose a State of Emergency on any State when a Governor appointed by the Union government felt the government

of the State "cannot be carried on in accordance with the provisions of [the] ...
Constitution."[279]

Without venturing into any great detail on Union-State relations, it is
necessary to examine the principles on which federal relations have been
constructed, and, in particular, to look at the notion of Statehood in the
Indian Constitution, the Union's power to unsettle institutional arrangements
in the State and, finally, questions concerning the financial autonomy of the
States.

The Notion of Statehood

Many federal questions concerning the States had not been resolved when
the Constitution was promulgated. The Constitution contained very flexible
provisions concerning the territorial integrity of the States. In a wide ranging
provision, the Union Parliament was given the right to form new States out
of the territories of old ones, increase or diminish the area of any State, and
alter their boundaries and name. And while these portentous decisions were
being made, the only procedural concession was the duty to consult the
legislature of the State involved.[280] While controversy abounds on whether
the allocation of powers is too heavily weighted in the Union's favor for India
to be described as a true federation,[281] the real Achilles heel of Indian
federalism is this provision.[282] Capable of great mischief, it has in fact been
used to resurrect and entrench old and new identities.

Why were the States there? Were they created simply because India was
too large and unwieldy? Were the divisions arbitrary, mindlessly following
preexisting arrangements informally established by the British? Were they
designed to promote old and new identities, so that the Union did not just
consist of administrative units but geographic territories possessing the distinct
traditions of distinctly identifiable people? On the one hand, it was felt that
the promotion of fissiparous regional identities would provoke undesirable and
unmanageable centrifugal trends which would endanger a country recently
torn by partition and with a long history of dissensions. On the other hand,
the force of events could give new meaning to the State as a basic unit of the
Constitution.

The new trend began with Nehru conceding to the Telugu-speaking
people a right to their own State of Andhra Pradesh. Malayali-speaking
people were conceded the right to the beautiful coastal State of Kerala. The
State of Bombay was bifurcated into Marathi-speaking Maharashtra and
Gujerati-speaking Gujerat. The demand for a Punjabi speaking province
divided the erstwhile large State of Punjab into the new States of Hindi-

speaking Haryana and Punjabi-speaking Punjab. The Tamils identified with the newly named Tamil Nadu; and Mysore was renamed Karnataka and associated with those speaking Kannada. These joined the already existing linguistically defined Rajasthan (Rajasthani), Uttar Pradesh (Hindi/Urdu), Madhya Pradesh (Hindi), Bihar (Bihari), West Bengal (Bengali), Orissa (Oriya), and a collection of separately identified hill States, in addition to Kashmir which had its own traditions and was also the subject of an international dispute.[283] Clearly, as a result of political practice, States have come to be identified as units possessed with linguistic, regional and cultural traditions. They have been clothed with a persona.

Treating States as more than mere administrative units has great constitutional significance. Since 1945, retreating imperialism redrew the map of the world clumsily and badly. Some of the awesome consequences and absurdities of this malassessment created terrifying wars and perpetuated conflicts which defy resolution. There are considerable demands to redraw the map of the world and of various countries. These demands have not been any less strongly felt in India than elsewhere. To carve more nations out of an already over-burdened political geography seems difficult and runs in the face of a world being made smaller by the global economy. Necessary in some cases, it may create--as it appears to be doing--blood baths in others. Indian constitutionalism, albeit imperfectly, suggests a focus on federalism and creating units of self-government within states as a solution worthy of further investigation.[284]

It is intuitions underlying Indian federalism rather than its actual working that have exemplary possibilities. India parades an impressive example of several non-Congress ruling parties in various States. But its politics also reveals consistent attempts by the Congress regime to dethrone and disable these governments. Indeed, some of the problems behind the Sikh demand of a separate Khalistan carved out of the State of Punjab can be traced to unsavory constitutional and party political attempts to stifle the Sikh rise to democratic power.[285] The opposition administration in the State is now fighting back to give more effective political and constitutional significance to the idea of "statehood."[286] Ostensibly a regressive idea conceding victories to traditionalism, it contains the potential for thinking further about engendering a more responsive local democracy while dealing with the most challenging problem that seems to plague many nations and threatens India.[287] But the intuition of exploring federalism rests on more than a pragmatic problem-solving desire to accommodate dissidence. It implants a creative reassessment of the further possibilities for representative democracy.[288]

The Union's Power to Unsettle the Institutional Arrangements of the State

The Union has been given a considerable say in respect of the constitutional institutions of the State. The Congress party has virtually created a tradition whereby Congress minorities in the State seem responsible to party bosses in Delhi, rather than to their respective legislatures. Non-Congress Ministries are influenced by different constitutionally permitted, but indubitably improper methods. The Governor of a State is appointed by the President. While the Constitution gives him a five-year term of office, it also declares that he hold office during the pleasure of the President. This has been taken to mean that the President can remove him from office. Given their vulnerability,[289] it is not surprising that Governors are seen as agents of the Centre. In most cases, they are bound to follow the advice of their Councils of Ministers.[290] They seem to have an independent right to refuse to accede to Bills passed by the legislature by reserving them for consideration by the President.[291] But their most important power is the role they play in the selection of the Chief Minister. Governors interfere greatly in this process. The most blatant example was Governor Dharma Vira sacking an anti-Congress ministry in West Bengal because the Chief Minister refused to seek a motion of confidence within the excessively tight time schedule imposed by the Governor.[292] The partisan conduct of Governors in selecting Chief Ministers was celebrated by Sampurananand, in Rajasthan in 1967, and by Governor Reddy in Uttar Pradesh in 1970.[293] This practice persists. In 1988, Governor Khurana virtually appointed himself returning office of a non-Congress party in power in Tamil Nadu, by preempting the choice of the party to resolve a succession dispute through its own electoral process unlike govenor Bamala in the same State in 1991 who chose to resign rather than accept the imposition of emergency rule against his advice.[294]

Gubernatorial interference takes a much more menacing stance when the Union through the Governor imposes an emergency President's rule on a State. This power has been used on over eighty occasions.[295] At first it was used to resolve relatively minor constitutional imgroglios. But the imposition of President's rule in Kerala in 1959, on the pretext of a breakdown of law and order in order to dismiss a duly elected Communist government, opened the possibility for an arbitrary use of those provisions.[296] From 1967 to 1977, the Congress government at the Centre used these provisions ruthlessly, and in a wholly unprincipled way, in order to dismiss non-Congress governments. In 1977, the Janata government dismissed the Congress ministries of nine States on the unconvincing constitutional ground that the latter must, perforce, have lost the confidence of the people which had voted the Janata government into power in a massive landslide victory.[297] In 1980 Mrs. Gandhi did exactly the same thing when she returned to power. While this has happened, the courts have stood by declaring that such issues are not justiciable unless actual *malafide* can be proved.[298] Even today President's rule has been imposed in Punjab after the sacking of an elected Ministry government in order to sustain a continuing police State. This power continues to be ruthlessly used except for that brief interlude when V.P. Singh was Prime Minister.

The Union's control over the institutions of State government is not limited to the extraordinary position of the Governor. The Union also possesses vast powers to transfer the judges of one High Court to another court.[299] This makes it possible for the Union to put pressure on High Court judges. Before 1975 such transfers were made with the consent of the judge being transferred. This salutary practice was abandoned during the Emergency (1975-1977).[300] Mrs. Gandhi's return to power inaugurated a regular policy of non-consensual transfers, artfully arguing an unconvincing case that such a national circulation of judges was conducive to national integration.[301] Despite strong dissents led by Justice Bhagwati, the Supreme Court has blessed this policy of transfers, thus giving way to the Union's control of one of the most important units of State government: its High Court.[302] The control of the judiciary adds to the already existing power of the Union to give a range of administrative directions to the State.

Threats to the Financial Viability of the States

The Constitution demarcates a complex financial regime. The Union has considerable powers of taxation. It has powers to levy and collect taxes which it must share with the States and to levy and collect taxes which are collected and appropriated by the States. The States have limited powers to raise their own taxes and money.[303] A Union-appointed Finance Commission determines how the shared taxes are to be allocated.[304] The Union also allocates vast planning resources through the Planning Commission.[305] State Governments discover considerable short falls of money in their budget, which is balanced by a complicated system of loan raising, involving in the main further dependence on the Union. Since independence, State indebtedness has increased from Rs. 449 crores in 1952, to Rs. 2,739 crores in 1961 to a massive Rs. 16,263 crores in 1978. A constitutional commentator on this process computes that during this period "the States' debts have increased by 34 times and the loans from the Union increased by 47 times."[306] Using

financial pressures on constituent units has expanded in many jurisdictions
from a tactic into a full-fledged political strategy. This is apparent in Mrs.
Thatcher's abolition of the Greater London Council in the United Kingdom
and imposition of "rate capping" whereby councils who overspend will be
denied central funds.[307] In 1987-1988, the Congress government of the Union
warned the States about the implications of their budget deficits. There was
every fear that, after years of misuse of the President's rule provisions, the
Union perhaps had found a fresh method of imposing its will on the States
and might use it with consequences which would intrude into the latter's
autonomy.

In the original constitutional dispensation, the framers knew that the
Union would have to be broken into smaller and more manageable units. To
this end, a strong Centre could alter State boundaries and impose its political,
administrative, programmatic and financial will on these units. As the
Constitution has evolved, Indian federalism has clothed the States with their
own identities. The political hiatus of having different regimes in the Union
and the States has thrown up important challenges. This need not occasion
concern. Rajiv Gandhi's short-tempered statement in late 1987 that he would
not hesitate to dismiss anti-national ministries was misplaced, because the
patriotism of these ministries is not in question. Indian federalism is in a
fascinating position to find fresh and stimulating answers to demands for the
right of diverse people for greater self-determination and to encourage greater
participatory democracy within a new cooperative federalism. The State
seems to have acquired character as a basic unit of the Constitution.

To sum up, the structure underlying the Indian Constitution cannot be
reduced to simply determining the relationship between the individual and the
state. A much more complex vision is needed to accommodate the vast
number of demands and social groups, class, and economic movements. For
those aspiring to a classless, non-exploitative society, which aggregates
individuals on the basis of new collectivities based on rational estimate of their
own and India's predicament, a critical evaluation of underlying structure is
long overdue. But first we must fully appreciate the forces that struggle for
mastery and which the Constitution has selectively reconstituted and
unleashed.

The Goal of Social Justice

Replete with borrowings and brought together in an extraordinarily short
time, the Indian Constitution left many issues of fundamental importance
unresolved. One such issue concerned the purposes underlying the

Constitution. Did the Constitution have a goal, seeking to make far reaching changes in Indian society? Or was it simply concerned with providing a framework of institutions and processes through which power would be exercised, with some constitutional limitations, whether in the form of fundamental rights or otherwise? The Constitution makers were in doubt about the need for social reform. The case for extensive restrictions had been argued only partly on the basis of the need to preserve law and order. Greater legitimacy attached to the demand for restrictions because of the more specific commitment to use preferential discrimination schemes to provide greater educational and employment advantages to the disadvantaged; and the campaign to expropriate and redistribute traditional lands to the poor. It was not entirely clear whether the purpose behind these aims was simply to *empower* successive governments or actually to charge them with a duty. It is this issue of *state empowerment* which was heavily underscored in the discussions to create a powerful union government capable of integrating India with planned development. The need for a radical social and economic transformation was accepted, but the Constitution manifested this goal in a much more circumspect way.

The Directive Principles of State Policy declare a range of goals. These goals were in the main socioeconomic in nature, stressing the need to use India's resources for the common good, with particular care to serve the cause of weaker and disadvantaged sections of the community.[308] The Directive Principles were not worked out systematically, and also mention protecting monuments, and places and objects of national interest,[309] separating the judiciary from the executive,[310] and promoting international peace and security.[311] In 1976, various changes were made in the Directive Principles stressing the need to minimize inequalities, provide equal justice and legal aid, and protect forests and wild life.[312] A new part entitled "Fundamental Duties" was added, listing ten duties of every citizen in India. All this was in addition to the Preamble of the Constitution which offered justice (social, economic and judicial), liberty, equality and fraternity in a sovereign democratic, and since 1976, socialist, secular republic.

But what exactly was the status of these Principles? Were they crucial? Or were they simply something which the state and citizen had to bear in mind? The Constitution made it clear that they "shall not be enforceable in any court, but the principles ... laid down are nevertheless fundamental in the governance of the country and it shall be the duty of the state to apply these principles in making laws."[313] The first reaction of the courts was to ignore these principles, virtually refusing to take them into account even in order to structure their preferred interpretation.[314] It was only after the Supreme

Court was accused of total insensitivity to the cause of the poor, while vigorously supporting the rich, that Directive Principles were deemed a significant part of the emerging hermeneutic constitution tradition.[315]   A pioneering judgment of Justice Dhavan of the Allahabad High Court in 1967 suggested a wide ranging use of the Directive Principles for statutory and constitutional interpretation.[316]   Their role as not just an aid to, but an important part of, interpretation was consecrated in the *Fundamental Rights* case[317] which treated these principles as a part of the "basic structure" of the Constitution. Since then, there has been an attractive and imaginative use of these principles as part of constitutional interpretation.[318]   Although these developments had come after a considerable struggle, the incorporation of the Directive Principles into constitutional interpretation was not a quantum leap and did not wholly settle the issue as to teleological aims of the Constitution itself. So far, all that was achieved was arguing that if issues requiring an examination of the Directive Principles arose, the Principles would be defended by a favorable interpretation.

In 1971, Mrs. Gandhi's government--already locked in a losing battle with the Supreme Court over the range of the legislature's power to amend the Constitution--gave a new twist to the debate.   In 1951 and 1954, the Constitution had been amended to immunize legislation connected with land reform and to give virtually total protection from "fundamental rights" challenges to legislation listed in the Ninth Schedule of the Constitution.[319] Faced with a possible challenge to these amendments, in 1971 parliament went further to suggest that anything done in furtherance of *some* Directive Principles was immune from constitutional challenge based on alleged violation of certain fundamental rights.[320]   In 1976, this was extended to cover *all* Directive Principles.[321]   *The fundamental issue underlying the 1951-1954 amendments, made explicit in the 1971 and 1976 amendments, was to reduce the overall Constitution significance of the Directive Principles by treating them as germane only to the issue of the empowerment of the legislature and immunizing certain categories of legislation from a review based on Fundamental Rights.*   In other words, the purpose behind the Directive Principles was not to establish a general constitutional goal, but to further empower the legislature in ways that would immunize it from judicial review. It was a broad based ouster-of-jurisdiction clause. If the legislature decided to lie dormant and do nothing, no issue of Directive Principles would arise. The Supreme Court which had validated the 1951-1954 amendments[322] validated the 1971 amendments in the *Fundamental Rights* case (1973), arguing, however, against any ouster of their power to review each case individually.[323]   By 1979, in *Minerva Mills*,[324] a much more confident Supreme

Court refused to validate the 1976 extension without any rational justification as to why an extension refusing to discriminate between particular Directive Principles was even less acceptable than an arbitrary delineation giving higher priority to some broadly phrased principles than to others.[325] Later, some judges supported the minority view that the immunity of the legislature should extend to all the Principles, treating the 1979 judgment as *obiter dicta*.[326] The 1971-76 "empowerment/immunisation" approach to Directive Principles places the judges in an uncomfortable bind. Confronted by an appeal to lofty ideals, they find themselves carried away to concede absolute powers to the government in the name of socialism and to abnegate their own judicial role. This interpretation of the Directive Principles simply calls upon citizens and judges to trust an absolutist state absolutely. *Minerva Mills* did not settle the issue. The Supreme Court--charged with a sense of history and in quest for a new legitimacy--wanted to create a much more radical Constitution than one which simply empowered successive regimes with blanket immunities for what they did in the name of Directive Principles. They argued that the Constitution did not just have a basic structure, but a distinct socioeconomic goal of ameliorating poverty and achieving an egalitarian distributive justice.[327] In 1976, a forthright argument proclaimed that preferential discrimination in favor of the disadvantaged was part of the equality principle and not an exception to it.[328]

A handful of activists, lawyers, publicists and judges campaigned for a much more exacting and wide ranging constitutional commitment. The initiative has come to be described as the "public interest law" movement.[329] The social justice goals are not treated as merely ancillary to interpretation or empowering and immunizing State action, but as constituting the dominant purpose of the Constitution. To begin with, a landmark judgment liberalized *locus standi* provisions so that issues of social justice could be, and soon were, directly taken to court by a wide range of people.[330] The Court's "epistolary" jurisdiction has already been mentioned. Consistent with the new constitutional mandate, the court became an active participant, investigating facts by setting up commissions of inquiry,[331] and then monitoring schemes of action to ensure compliance.[332] This was more than a creative interpretation of constitutional provisions, although the extension of certain fundamental rights to cover non-state action and the interpretation of corporate, labor, and welfare legislation were inventive.[333]

First, by extending *locus standi*, the Court seemed to urge citizens to fulfill their duty to raise socioeconomic issues. In one judgment, the Court talked of the duty to fund activist centers which were concerned with achieving social and economic goals of the Constitution.[334] In another case, the Court held that it was the (enforceable?) duty of the citizen to respect the national anthem and, presumably, to fulfill other duties written into the Directive Principles.[335] Secondly, by assuming an activist stance, the courts declared it part of their constitutional duty to fulfill these objectives. Thirdly, in passing orders and claiming a partnership with government, they pronounced that it was the duty of the rest of the government to ensure that the goals of the Constitution were not neglected by default.[336] It seemed to be arguing that these duties could not be deferred or left to the legislature. They had to be dealt with immediately. Of course, they had to be grounded in some guaranteed constitutional or statutory right. But an underlying sense of purpose was derived not from these *entitlements*, but from the *goals* of the Constitution.

Legalistic constitutional lawyers might be tempted to be more reductionist and to argue that all that has been achieved was imaginative interpretation coupled with a further empowerment of the legislature. But the judges have done more than concur with the government's favorable-to-itself view of the Directive Principles. They have declared a strong constitutional commitment to what they claim to be the primary purpose of the Constitution, enlarged the role of activist citizens, and become the mediator of both the values and processes by which this purpose can be achieved. Whether this is a desirable trend is another matter. It remains a significant shift in the attitude and beliefs of the major ideologists responsible for giving meaning to the Constitution. Why did these developments take place,[337] whom have they and will they benefit,[338] can they be sustained over time, what direction will they take, and how important are they within a democracy?[339] A cynical examination of these developments may well stress that it is a middle class movement which is part of a struggle to control certain constitutional institutes and process.[340] Yet, the exact contours of relationships between the new "power brokers" have still to be determined. Until that happens, we cannot really call it a "social action" movement.[341]

The future direction of the movement is a matter of concern. Judges within the Supreme Court have protested its haphazard growth, unsure whether the judiciary was not indulging a dangerous usurpation of government beyond its capabilities and constitutionally defined role.[342] Others have found it overtly ambitious and inconsistent.[343] Contextualized in its middle class origins, it has been seen as a "false consciousness" created by people whose quest for status and self-importance have made them "predators on the rest of society."[344] Developed with *ad hoc* spontaneity, there is concern that the Court may be over used by a never-ending spiral of people claiming to act in the public interest.

There is also concern about the process by which these complex issues will be investigated by courts. Will courts abdicate their fact-finding functions to commission of inquiry? And, if the commission's investigation is taken as authoritative and decisive, what will be the procedural safeguards against abuse?[345] The most deeply felt anxiety concerned whether the court was taking on too much, ordering mandatory schemes placing it at loggerheads with government by taking on monitoring and other tasks for which it is ill equipped.[346] Finally, this judicial usurpation of an extremely complex and important pro-active responsibility is subversive of democracy by reposing far reaching functions in the hands of a few professionals with the institutional skills and resources to use the court system effectively.[347]

Yet many of these arguments--both technical and general--accompany the development of any court-centered "public interest law" movement. The significance of the developments in India are both political and constitutional. Politically, the future of this struggle remains indeterminate. Miscalculations might result in fatal reactions; yet, these developments might become an important new feature of the constitutional landscape of India. Constitutionally, there has been an attempt to alter the very basis of the Constitution, to make it goal-based and to put the pursuit of certain egalitarian goals above all others as a continuing necessity reposed in all citizens and agencies of state.

Are Constitutions Made to Measure?

A distinguished constitutional lawyer, who had fought long and hard to curb the abuse of power to amend the Constitution, passed the exasperated verdict that recent changes had degraded the Constitution to one which was "made to measure."[348] This remonstrance has been adjudged part of a narrow polemic between the party in power and a trenchant critic and adversary. It was an attack on the integrity of the government and challenged these changes as serving regime interests, transparently cloaked by an appeal to the Constitution's socialist goals. But this controversy should also make us pause to ask about the nature of a Constitution which is "not made to measure." For the argument is not just about the alacrity with which India's--or any-- Constitution can be amended. Until swept away by an external *tour de force* causing a change in *groundnorm*,[349] the Constitution is alleged to be circumscribed by an original conception crucial to its evaluation. In *law*, Indian judges seemed to have underlined the original conception as its "basic structure," whether to test the validity of doubtful amendments or to identify immutable values intended to inform every aspect of the Constitution's working is not clear.[350]

These issues--which are also part of an important contemporary debate in America[351]--have both a political and a religious flavor. Politically, they attempt to stagnate creative interpretation so that it stays within the bounds of an original conception, but they also seem to indulge a theology of constitutional orthodoxy. It is reminiscent of an argument in Hindu jurisprudence about the meaning of *dharma* ("law" or righteous conduct). To avoid the heresy that *dharma* could itself change, the alternative was to underscore the eminence of *dharma* while permitting different interpretations for different epochs.[352] Yet even this compromise has more than a whisper of heresy in it for those people who believe that *dharma*--like its modern analog, the Constitution--has an essential core meaning which cannot be belittled by hermementic attempts to appropriate it for narrow self-interest.

However, the Indian Constitution was the product of innumerable compromises which makes it difficult either to discern unequivocal original meanings or--once discerned--to defend such meanings as deserving unswerving support in different future settings. Any defensible construction would rest less easily on the dominant intention of the framers of the Constituion than some other basis. And who is entitled to undertake such a construction, for what purpose and with what effect?

This is not to issue a general invitation to relativism by asserting that it is impossible to theorize about justice or to develop an epistemology of law other than the crude analytical theory that law is a species of institutonalized expression of power. Nor is it to assert that constitutional theories should simply be concerned with due process and questions of participatory representation, leaving substantive priorities to flow from the elected democratic institutions. Arguments about justice are necessary and proper.[353]

These arguments do not take place in a vacuum, but in a preexisting historical framework in which the struggle for constitutional meaning and supremacy will take place. To mystify this preexisting framework with an unassailable imminence is surely a *trahison des clercs*. Conversely, the preexisting framework cannot be regarded as totally malleable, prey to every gust of wind trying to give it meaning. An over-simplistic relativism obscures our understanding of the Constitution at any given point in time, trivializes its contemporary significance, and fails to understand the complex social, economic and political processes that hold any constitutional system in place.

Earmarking the Constitution as the situs of struggle does not obviate the need for understanding the complex nature of the struggle, and its manner and form. Inviting versions of liberal constitutionalism conjure nice images of fair and user-friendly constitutional institutions and processes. But constitutions encapsulate systematically encoded power. Capitalist societies develop various methods of control including direct confrontation, brutal putting down in the name of law and order, the co-optation of those who threaten the system, and an effective control of various institutions and processes which are theoretically open-ended and susceptible to universal use. The strength of any existing or emerging *status quo* depends on the strength of the forces that sustain it. Often these forces are themselves non-cohesive and badly assimilated. This may well be the case with Indian capitalism where an acquisitive society has unleashed an unregulated "free for all" to threaten the salience of the Constitution and collapse the distinction between civil society, political society and the constitutional order. Those who have power have to clothe their advantage by creating social legitimacy for themselves and what they are doing. This is necessarily a complex process involving appeals, *inter alia*, to democracy and justice.

India's experiments with the Emergency (1975-1977) showed that the important components for obtaining legitimacy in India consist of holding elections, protecting the independent review of governmental action by courts, not gagging the press and providing social justice.[354] It is futile to look for some sacred original conception underlying the Indian Constitution. But *this is not to deny that, at a given point in time, those using the Constitution operate in an interpreted world.* In looking at constitutional developments, we inevitably profile the judges for prominence, to portray the entirely misleading picture that the fate of the Constitution rests uncomfortably on interactions between a small peer group. But judges are part of an essentially reactive structure whose strategy is determined by lawyers and litigants who plan its use. Other influences also mold this structure and affect its operation, and induce the system to yield, to suffer or to resist change. In the struggle over the Constitution, various arenas of public power are structured for use by some groups and classes in preference by others. This may be achieved by the provisions themselves, the personnel in charge, a structuring of the institutional morality, the price and inaccessibility of the skills and wherewithal required, the use of extra-constitutional mechanisms and so on. Radicals who plead the cause of opening the Constitution out to a wider range of people may find that, once in power, they too feel the need to manage the system far more rigidly in order to offset challenges to their power.[355] India's rulers, often shortsightedly, have tried to strongly control certain arenas of power and to prevent their use by opponents. The use of the President's rule provisions to subvert Indian federalism, the constant defection of legislators to destabilize governments, the attempt to pressurize the judiciary and the administration, the insidious way in which activists have been harassed and deprived of funds, the refusal to tolerate the press, and the use of political violence by state agencies, all illustrate ways the very essence of constitutionalism has been eroded for short-term gains. Public constitutional power must be recognized and respected. A distinguished and discerning observer of Indian law has made a much sharper indictment:

> What has handicapped Indian development has been dishonesty and a want of true belief in the rule of law amongst the public at large. There is no sense of public spirit except at a xenophobic level. Honesty in this sense operates only inside groups not across them. This is the negative side of the achievement of India, peaceful co-existence. The profitability of honesty across groups is still being discovered and who knows how long it will take to become a virtue.[356]

This incisive over-statement grounds the lack of a rigorous "public sense" in the tangled skeins of traditional loyalties that allegedly characterize and plague Indian life. But the quest for this "public sense" is not entirely missing from traditional notions of authority.

The struggle over the Constitution has so far been a struggle between dominant propertied classes, aspiring business, ambitious professionals, frustrated intelligentsia, the civil service, and opportunistic new power brokers.[357] Whether the Constitution can be pried open for more extensive use by the poor and disadvantaged bulk of India's population, victims who are of a haphazardly expanding capitalism, remains the unanswered question and a challenge. So far, the disadvantaged have benefited from the untidy developments.[358] But a more structured dominant capitalism might make a concerted bid to run

> India's political economy ... [to] develop [various notions] of rationality and use the State to maintain its rationality in the market economy as well as the body politic. Without this the stable development of capitalism [cannot] ... be assured. As it happens, the acquisitive forces of Indian capitalism have not been able to give rational substance to India's liberal democracy. Civil society has followed the *irrationality* of its competitiveness and the State has sprawled with civil society and been dissolved by it.[359]

In the long run Indian capitalism threatens to reassert itself, not as a collection of unsavory deals, but triumphantly as the expression of necessity,[360] but hopefully without the bonapartist structure of dictatorship which plagues much of the region and other parts of the world and exists in electorial incarnations in India. It is corrupted forms of such bonaparicism that have dissolved the polity into corruption and drift.

But, so far, India's constitutional processes have been trivialized by opportunism and its institutions undermined by the privatization of the State, collapsing the distinction between public and private power. The Constitution portrayed a very complex vision of individual and group life in civil society, which, in many instances has troubled if not plagued its authors and their successors. *But such a frank analysis of what is happening must, perforce, be seen as one-sided, if we recognize that,* unlike the wholly fragile constitutional structures of so many nations, *India's Constitution has conjured a relative stability.* It has enabled a concentration of power while opening up the possibilities of struggle in a range of arenas. At the end of this process, the judiciary, the press and activism have been strengthened as arenas of resistance, while parliamentary majorities service the elective autocracy of Prime Ministerial power. Above all, the Constitution has instituted a constitutional discourse which continues as an important feature in people's lives and struggles. The Constitution is not a self-fulfilling prophecy; arenas of struggle have to be carved out of it. And if this provokes discontent by unsettling comfortable images of what constitutions are and what they are supposed to do, so much the better.

Figure 4

AN INCOMPLETE TYPOLOGY OF CONSTITUTIONALISM

L E V E L S O F D E M O C R A T I C P A R T I C I P A T I O N

	D none	C Rule of Law	Constitutional Ends	B Preferred Human Rights	A Egalitarian Social Justice	
		Species of Dictatorial Constitutionalism				
3 None						
	Absolutism	Restrained	P O L I T I C A L	Liberal	Socialist	J U D I C I A L
			C O N S T I T U T I O N A L I S M			
2 Elections						
	Relativist	Rule of Law		Liberal	Socialist	
1 Participation						
		Participatory Constitutionalism				

(Right vertical label: CONSTITUTIONALISM)

*For explanatary analysis, see pp.375-384

NOTES

*I must thank Shammy Batra and Michael Anderson for helpful comments; and Parmodh Singh for research help and assistance. I am grateful to the Ford Foundation for a research grant used in the writing of this chapter.

1. G. Austin, *The Indian Constitution: Cornerstone of a Nation*, Delhi, 1971.
2. On the process of amendment see K.C. Markandam, *Amending Process and Constitutional Amendments in the Indian Constitution*, Delhi, 1972; H. Chand, *The Amending Process in the Indian Cosntitution*, Delhi, 1972; P. Diwan, *Indian Constitutional Amendments*, Delhi, 1984; Chaturvedi and Chaturvedi, *Amendments to the Constitution*, Delhi, 1985. R. Dhavan, *The Amendment: Conspiracy or Revolution*, Allahabad, 1978, at 1-29 reviews the amendments until the Forty-Second Amendment Act 1976. After the Emergency, the Constitution (Forty-Third Amendment) Act 1978 sought to repeal and alter some provisions of the 1976 Amendment (*see* R. Dhavan, *Amending the Amendment*, Allahabad, 1978. Since then, the more significant amendments have been: the Constitution (Forty-Seventh Amendment) Act 1984, which added to the Ninth Schedule immunizing more statutes from certain forms of judicial review; the Constitution (Fifty-Second Amendment) Act 1985 which entrenches the political party as part of the constitutional structure and seeks to prevent the legislature from toppling governments by crossing the floor; and the Constitution (Fifty-Ninth Amendment) Act 1988 which allows an internal emergency (prohibited since 1978) to be imposed on the State of Punjab. In the celebrated decision of *Kesavananda v. State of Kerala*, A.I.R. 1973 S.C. 1461, the Supreme Court ruled that amendments to the Constitution would be void to the extent to which they violated the "basic structure" of the Constitution.
3. *Infra* notes 151-2.
4. *Infra* note 150.
5. *Infra* note 154.
6. *See* R. Dhavan, *Litigation Explosion in India*, Bombay, 1986, 165-79 on the statistical data analyzed earlier.
7. The problem is serious. Several Committees have investigated the problem (S.R. Das) *Committee on Arrears in High Courts*, Delhi, 1948; (Shah) *Report of the High Court Arrears Committee*, Delhi, 1972; and several reports of the Law Commission, including Fourteenth Report, *The Reform in Judicial Administration*, Delhi, 1958; Forty-Fourth Report, *On the Appellate Jurisdiction of the Supreme Court in Civil Matters*, Delhi, 1971; Forty-Fifth Report, *Civil Appeals in the Supreme Court on a Certificate of Fitness*, Delhi, 1971; Fifty-Eighth Report, *The Structure and Jurisdiction of the Higher Judiciary*, Delhi, 1978; Seventy-Seventh Report, *Delay and Arrears in Trial Courts*, Delhi, 1979; Seventy-Ninth Report, *Delay and Arrears in High Courts and Other Appellate Courts*, Delhi, 1979. The Law Commission is currently looking at the problem again. On the issue of litigation against the government, the Constitution (Forty-Second Amendment) Act 1976 sought to limit the granting of

interlocutory relief and created procedural restrictions on how the validity of legislation could be questioned. These restrictions were removed by the Constitution (Forty-Fourth Amendment) Act 1978. The Law Commission specifically looked at the problem of anti-government litigation in its Hundreth Report, *Litigation By and Against the Government*, Delhi, 1982. *See* R. Dhavan, *supra* note 6.

8. The Preamble was altered by the Constitution (Forty-Second Amendment) Act 1976 to include a reference to "socialism" and "secularism" in addition to the original characterization of a "sovereign democratic republic." While the Constitution (Forty-Fourth Amendment) Act 1978 restored much of what was changed by the 1976 amendment, these changes in the Preamble remained unscratched. In one sense, the change is purely symbolic. But the Preamble is important as an aid to interpretation, to resolve ambiguities and support nationalization and other measures. *See Excel Wear v. Union of India*, A.I.R. 1979 S.C. 25. The Preamble was deemed to be a source of interpretive intuitions as well as constitutional limitation in *Kesavananda*, *supra* note 2.

9. *Infra* note 181.

10. B.R. Ambedkar, Speech in the Constituent Assembly (1948) VII *Constituent Assembly Debates* hereinafter C.A.D. 38-9 (4 November 1948).

11. For the vast differentials and poverty levels, see V.M. Dandekar and N. Rath, *Poverty in India*, Pune, 1971; M.S. Ahulwalia, "Rural Poverty and Agricultural Performance in Indian," *Journal of Development Studies* 298-323 (April, 1978); P. Bardhan and T.N. Srinivasan eds., *Poverty and Income | Distribution in India,* Calcutta, 1974; P. Bardhan, *Land, Labour and Rural Poverty: Essays in Development*, New York, 1984.

12. On the "private" nature of parts of the Indian State, see A. Shourie, *Institutions in the Janta Phase*, Delhi, 1980.

13. The most celebrated account is Austin, *supra* note 1. B. Shiva Rao, *The Framing of India's Constitution*, Delhi, 1966. *A Study* volume with four volumes of Documents hereinafter *Shiva Rao*: A Study or *Shiva Rao* preceded by volume number is a painstaking collection of data and incisive commentary on the discussion. Mansergh ed., *Transfer of Power*, London, 1970-85, in 12 Volumes; sets the background to the discussions. Apart from suggestions by the Assembly Members themselves, earlier suggestions include K.G. Mashruwala, *Some Particular Suggestions for the Constitution of Free India*, Bombay, 1945; M.N. Roy, *Draft Constitution for Free India*, Delhi, 1945; S.N. Agarwal, *Gandhian Constitution for Free India*, Allahabad, 1946; D.R. Gadgil, *Some Observations on the Draft Constitution*, Poona, 1948.

Other comments on the process of Constitution-making include B.N. Rao, *India's Constitution in the Making*, Calcutta 1960, and H.R. Khanna, *Making of India's Constitution*, Delhi, 1981. On the Constituent Assembly, see A.C. Banerjee, *The Constituent Assembly of India*, Calcutta, 1947; Chanakya, *Indian Constituent Assembly*, Bombay, 1947. For scathing reactions to the newly made Constitution, see L.I. Jennings, *Some Characteristics of the Indian Constitution*, Madras, 1953; K.C. Wheare: "India's New Constitution Analysed" (1950) 52 *Bombay L.R. Jnl.* 25-7; S.N. Shukla,

India's New Constitution, Allahabad, 1951. For a view that such historical processes should be interpreted in the light of present predicaments and teleological aims, see U. Baxi, "The Little Done, the Vast Undone: Reflections on Reading Granville Austin's 'The Indian Constitution,'" (1967) 9 *J.I.L.I.* 323-420, an euphoric yet guarded exhortation. A rigorous account critically evaluating this process of constitutional history has yet to be written.

14. The Constitution, as originally drafted, allowed people's participation through periodic elections, and little else. In English administrative law participatory due process had not been developed (*see*, e.g., *Nakudda Ali v. Jayaratne* (1966) A.C. 66) and few avenues for complaint--other than through parliamentary questions or newspapers--existed, even though provision was made for an Auditor General (Articles 148-51, *Constitution of India*).

15. *See infra* note 203, generally.

16. For what a Gandhian Constitution might include, see S.N. Agarwal, *supra* note 13, and *The Gandhian Plan for the Economic Development of India*, Bombay, 1944; B.B. Majumdar ed., *Gandhian Concept of State*, Calcutta, 1957 for contemporary reactions. The extensive literature on Gandhi's political thought continues to grow. In the Constituent Assembly, Ambedkar vehemently attacked the idea of making the village the basic unit of the Constitution; *see* (1948) VII *C.A.D.* 38-9 (4 November 1947) of D.S. Seth (1948) VII *C.A.D.* 212.

17. A point made by Maulana Hasrat Mohini (1948) VII *C.A.D.* 45; also, D.D. Seth at 212; S. Nagappa at 217-8; B.S. Mann at 226; M. Ismail Sahib at 274. For parallels between Soviet and Indian approaches, see S.S. Dhavan and R. Dhavan, *The New Soviet Constitution: An Indian Introduction*, Delhi, 1978; mimeo.

18. The classic statement is A.V. Dicey, *Introduction to the Law of the Constitution*, London, 1885, tenth edition, 1962. Its significance in modern times is explicated in controversies surrounding whether Britain should have a Bill of Rights (see M. Zander, *A Bill of Rights*, London, 1986). For a critique of Dicey's position in the commonwealth contest, see R. Heuston, *Studies in Constitutional Law*, London, 1961, Chapter 1.

19. Juridical constitutionalism may be concerned solely with process rather than with substantive issues. *See* J. Ely, *Democracy and Distrust: A Theory of Judicial Review*, New York, 1981; L. Tribe, "The Puzzling Persistence of Process-Based Constitutional Theories" (1980), 89 *Yale L.J.* 1063; M. Tushnet, "Darkness in the Edge of Town: The Contribution of John Ely to Constitutional Theory" (1980), 89 *Yale L.J.* 1037. For background, see E.S. Corwin, "The Higher Law Background to American Constitutional Law," (1928) 42 *Harvard L. Rev.* 149, and "The Ideal Element in American Judicial Decision" (1931), 45 *Harvard L. Rev.* 136. As to whether Constitutions have an original meaning or are transformed by interpretation over time, *see infra* note 351.

20. On constitutional morality, note B.R. Ambedkar's somber warning at (1948) VII *C.A.D.* 38). The Draft Constitution had an Instrument of Instructions which articulated this institutional morality. These were, however, dropped from the final

and approved text of 1950. A detailed analysis of "conventions" will reveal how they enable an elite to obtain and retain power. The metaphor of conventions both disciplines and conceals an elite power game. Such motifs of modern constitutional law need to be deconstructed, demystified and put into their empirical context.

21. On the connection betwen the separation of law from morals and the doctrine of parliamentary sovereignty, see R. Dhavan, "Juristic Ethnology of Kesavananda's Case" (1977), *19 J.I.L.I. 489*, and "The Basic Structure Doctrine: A Footnote Comment," in R. Dhavan and A. Jacob eds., *The Indian Constitution: Trends and Issues*, Bombay, 1978 160-78.

22. Dicey's Whiggish distrust of State power is latent in his *Introduction (supra* note 18) and finds overt expression in his *Law and Public Opinion in England*, London, 1905. For recent reassessments of Dicey, see M. McAuslan and J.E. McEldowney, eds., *Law Legitimacy and the Constitution: Essays Marking the Centenary of Dicey's Law of the Constitution*, London, 1985; G. Zellick, "Dicey and the Constitution," (1985), *Public Law* 564-723.

23. See J.A. Griffiths, "The Political Constitution" (1979), 42 *Modern L.R.* 1; T.R.S. Allan, "Legislative Supremacy and the Rule of Law: Democracy and Constitutionalism" (1985), 44 *Cambridge L.J.* 111.

24. See E.P. Thompson, *Whigs and Hunters*, London, 1975; Campbell, *The Left and Rights*, London, 1981; R. Johnson, "Thompson, Genovese and Socialist Human History" (1978), 6 *History Workshop* 79.

25. This is manifest in American constitutional controversies in two distinct ways: the quest for process-based juridical constitutionalism (*see* J. Ely, *supra* note 19); and the insistence on an original meaning which cannot be transformed over time (*infra* note 351). A third alternative would argue that constitutional and legal interpretation is not concerned with policy imperatives, but a universal theory about rights; *see* R. Dworkin, *Taking Rights Seriously*, London, 1977; *A Matter of Principle*, London, 1985; and *Law's Empire*, London, 1986.

26. A claim made by the constitutions of Communist nations, note L. Brezhnev's Speech to the Supreme Soviet Introducing the Constitution of the U.S.S.R. on 4 October 1977.

27. Lenin seemed to suggest that this was possible when responding to Comrade Myasnikev's suggestion for a free press; *see* Lenin, *Collected Works* 32, 504.

28. This has been the basis of Fabian and Labour Party Socialism in England.

29. *See* R. Dhavan, "On the Future of Western Law and Justice in India: Reflections on the Predicament of the Post-Emergency Supreme Court" (1981), *J.B.C.I.* 61-86. Indian High Courts, other than those of the Presidency towns of Calcutta, Bombay and Madras, did not have a prerogative writ jurisdiction (other than *habeas corpus*) and could not, therefore, investigate governmental action before 1950. The prerogative orders jurisdiction of the High Court of the Presidency towns was limited to the town area and did not extend to the province in question as a whole. *See Hamid Hussain v. Banwari Lal Roy, A.I.R. 1947 P.C. 90.*
See H.M. Seevai, "Constitutional Law of India" (1962) 78 *L.Q.R.* 388.

31. *See* B.M.N. Rau, "Notes on Fundamental Rights," 2 September 1946 (II *Shiva Rao* 21-36); K.T. Shah, "A Note on Fundamental Rights," 23 December 1948 (II *Shiva Rao* 36-55); A.K. Ayyar, "A Note on Fundamental Rights," 17 March 1947 (II *Shiva Rao* 67-9); K.M. Munshi, "Note and Draft Articles on Fundamental Rights," 17 March 1947 (II *Shiva Rao* 69-80); Harnam Singh, "Draft on Fundamental Rights," 18 March 1947 (II *Shiva Rao* 81-4); and B.R. Ambedkar's "Memorandum and Draft Articles on the Rights of States and Minorities," 24 March 1947 (II *Shiva Rao* 84-114); *see generally* the documents in II *Shiva Rao* 21-307.

32. *See* C.H. Alexanderwicz, "American Influence on Constitutional Interpretation in India" (1956), *A.J.C.L.* 98; M.K. Nambiyar, "American Borrowings in the Indian Constitution" (1954), *S.C.J.J.* note 1, 151. The importance of this borrowing is celebrated in W. Douglas, *We the Judges*, New York, 1956 an American Supreme Court Judge's diplomatic overstatement. P.K. Tripathi: "Perspectives of the American Constitutional Influence on the Constitution of India," in L. Beer ed., *Constitutionalism in Asia*, California, 1981. The American influence during the process of Constitution-making was routed through B.N. Rau, *supra* note 13. On the modality of the continuing of the American influence on Indian public law, see R. Dhavan, "Borrowed Ideas: On the Impact of American Scholarship on Indian Law" (1985), 33 *A.J.C.L.* 505-26.

33. *See* Austin, *supra* note 1, 149; *Shiva Rao: Study*, 741 ff, especially 754. At first (21 July 1947), the Minority Committee was sympathic to the idea of representation but not separate electorates. But then a policy decision on communal representation was arrived at (*see* II *Shiva Rao* 396-8, 403-10; IV *Shiva Rao* 589 ff). The preliminary discussion in the Constituent Assembly was on 27-28 April, 1947 (V *C.A.D.* 197-291). Ambedkar explained the philosophy on this issue when introducing the Draft Constitution (*see* VII *C.A.D.* 39; 4 November 1948) and it was discussed on 25 May 1949 (VII *C.A.D.* 269-333). Further discussion on the representations of Scheduled Castes and Scheduled Tribes took place on 23-24 August 1949 (IX *C.A.D.* 633-59).

34. *See* K.T. Shah, "Speech to the Constituent Assembly" (1948), VII *C.A.D.* 726.

35. A.K. Ayyar at II *Shiva Rao* 143 in a letter dated 4 April 1947 while discussing the freedom of religion clause.

36. Although a due process clause was introduced as Article 16 of an earlier Draft of the Constitution (*see* II *Shiva Rao* 122, 240-4, 284-6; III *C.A.D.* 468; B.N. Rau at II *Shiva Rao* 22-3; A.K. Ayyar at II *Shiva Rao* 143-4), it was abandoned after a short debate (*see* VII *C.A.D.* 842-57 (6 December 1948); 999-1001 (13 December 1948).

37. Constitutional provisions [Article 22(4) to (7)] allow administrative preventive detention with no review or appeal except to Advisory Boards. Earlier, the Advisory Board procedure could be dispensed with when it was thought necessary (*see* IX *C.A.D.* 1496-1570). The Supreme Court, while accepting this broad philosophy (*see* Gopalan v. State of Madras, *A.I.R. 1950 S.C. 27*), wedged in an overall judicial review for the High Courts and Supreme Courts on grounds these courts had the power to inquire whether the reasons for detention (supplied in order to enable the detainee

to make a representation) matched the need for permissible detention and in the case before the Court (*see Atma Ram v. State of Bombay A.I.R. 1951 S.C. 157; Shibban Lal Saxena v. State of U.P.A.I.R. 1954 S.C. 179; Sodhi Shemshe v. State of Pepsu A.I.R. 1954 S.C.* 476), after which a far-ranging review on this basis was firmly established and continues.

38.   A.K. Ayyar's letter to B.N. Rau on 4 April 1947 (II *Shiva Rao* 143-6), the concern of the Advisory Committee (II *Shiva Rao* 264-7; and further III *C.A.D.* 475-77; VII *C.A.D.* 822-849, 859-90).   K.T. Shah's attempts to deprive religious institutions of all privileges, exemptions and immunities failed (*see* VII *C.A.D.* 888-91, 7 December 1948).

39.   The main discussion is at IX *C.A.D.* 1191-1311 (by far the most vigorous exchange on any matter).   For an earlier discussion on *zamindari* abolition, see VIII *C.A.D.* 508-18; G. Austin, *supra* note 1; H.C.L. Merrillat, *Land and the Constitution*, Bombay, 1970, 51-78; H.M. Jain, *Right to Property*, Allahabad, 1968, 24-56.

40.   Article 31(2) of the Constitution.   The principles of the doctrine of eminent domain were deemed applicable in certain agrarian reforms cases (*see Rameshwar Singh v. State of Bihar A.I.R. 1952 S.C.* 252.   On their interpretation, see *State of W.B. v. Subodh Gopal*, A.I.R. 1954 S.C. 92; *Dwarkadass v. Sholapur Spg. & Mfg. Co.*, A.I.R. 1954 S.C. 119; *Bella Banerjee v. State of W.B.*, A.I.R. 1954 S.C. 170.   These led to the Constitution (Fourth Amendment Act) 1954.   When the Court insisted that the compensation provision, even if not adequate, could not be illusory (*see Vajravelu v. Sp. Dty. Collector*, A.I.R. 1970 S.C. 1017; *R.C. Cooper v. Union of India*, A.I.R. 1970 S.C. 564), further restrictions were imposed by the Constitution (Twenty-Fifth Amendment) Act 1971.   The constitutionally protected right to property was abolished by the Constitution (Forty-Fourth Amendment) Act, 1978.

41.   Little is written about the Judges of the British Raj.   For a preliminary investigation, see R. Dhavan, "Judge and Jurist in India," Notes towards Understanding of Legal Elites in India" (Conference paper, Comparative Judicial Group, International Political Science Association, Bellagio 1985).   On the discussion of the judiciary in the Constituent Assembly, see R. Dhavan, *Justice on Trial: The Supreme Court Today*, Allahabad, 1980, 11-25, 31-9.

42.   On the innovative nature of the empowerment of the Judiciary by the Constitution of India, *see* R. Dhavan, *supra* note 29.   The British had refrained from making the executive accountable to the judiciary.

43.   This is in spite of the *(Rankin) Report of the Civil Justices Committee*, Delhi 1925, which drew an alarming picture of the increase in the arrears of cases.

44.   Speech reported in the Constituent Assembly (1948) VII *C.A.D.* 247 (24 May 1949).

45.   B.R. Ambedkar was one of the lawyers involved in the *Kameshwar Case* (*supra* note 40); I am grateful to R. Sudarshan for drawing my attention to this.

46.   E.g., *Gopalan's* case, *supra* note 37.

47.   *Ramesh Thappar v. State of Madras A.I.R.*, 1950 *S.C.* 124; *Brij Bhushan v. State A.I.R. 1950 S.C.* 127.   The Constitution (First Amendment) Act 1951 made it

possible to restrict free speech on grounds of "public order" and *inter alia*, the security to state.

48. Mahajan C.J. in the *State of Bihar v. Shaibala Devi A.I.R. 1952 S.C.* 329 at pr. 4 p. 330, on matters of preventive detention. On property matters, see R. Dhavan, *The Supreme Court of India: A Socio-legal Analysis of its Juristic Techniques*, Bombay, 1977, 128-205. Certainly Das and Shastri JJ began to show a greater understanding of the government's socialilsm and the need for the government possessing an increased power of regulation and acquisition; see H.C.L. Merillat, "Chief Justice S.R. Das, A Decade of Decisions on the Right to Property" (1960), 2 *J.I.L.I.* 183.

49. E.g., Chief Justice Shastri's speech to the Madras Lawyers' Conference, *A.I.R. 1955 Journal* 25.

50. Thus, the Constitution granted vast powers of delegated legislation (*See In Re Delhi Laws* in re *A.I.R. 1951 S.C.* 332; in *Raj Narain v. Chairman Patna Administration*, A.I.R. 1954 S.C. 569). Extended powers were permitted to regulate "essential supplies" in *H.S. Bagla A.I.R. 1954 S.C.* 465 or for special criminal procedures in some classes of cases (*see Kathi Ranning v. State of Saurashtra, A.I.R. 1952 S.C.* 1237; *State of W.B. v. Anwar Ali Sarkar, A.I.R. 1952 S.C.* 75).

51. *Gopalan's* case, *supra* note 37.

52. *Shankari Prasad v. Union of India, A.I.R. 1951 S.C.* 458.

53. *Golak Nath v. Union of India, A.I.R. 1967 S.C.* 1643.

54. The development of a proper "due process" is traced through *Kochunni v. State of Madraa, A.I.R. 1960 S.C.* 1080 and *R.C. Cooper, supra* note 40, until it finally surfaced in *Maneka Gandhi v. Union of India, A.I.R. 1978 S.C.* 597. Bhagwat J's. judgment in *Maneka* only established the connection between the equality (anti-arbitrariness) articles, substantive reasonableness provisions (Article 19(2) to (6)), and the "any process" provision (Article 21). It was Krishna Iyer J. who transcended previous precedent to appeal for and create the foundation for a wider due process. (*See* R. Dhavan, *Due Process in India: A Preliminary Exploration*, Delhi, Indian Law Institute, 1981 (Mimeo). Other decisions followed through: *Sunil Batra A.I.R. 1978 S.C.* 1487 and 1675; *Charles Sobhraj v. Supdt. Tilhar Jail a.i.r. 1978 s.c.* 1514); *Prem Shanker Shukla v. Delhi Administration W.P. No. 1679* of 1979 (decided 29 April 1980); *Rakesh Kaushik v. B.L. Vig. Supdt. Central Jil W.P. 393* and 549 of 1980 (30 April 1980); *Hussainara Khatoon v. State of Bihar, A.I.R. 1979 S.C.* 1360, 1369, 1377, 1879; *M.H. Hoskot v. State of Maharashtra, A.I.R. 1978 S.C.* 1648). These decisions secured the case for due process in criminal justice, but not in every aspect of criminal procedure. A much less secure administrative due process has been developed. This is ironic in that *Maneka's* case, from which these breakthroughs derived sustenance, concerned the administration.

55. *Keshavananda's case, supra* note 2.

56. *See generally* Jain and Jain, *Principles of Administrative Law*, Bombay, 1971, 1973, 1979 and 1986 edns.; M.A. Fazal, *Judicial Review of Administrative Action in India and Pakistan*, Oxford, 1967; S.P. Sathe, *Administrative Law*, Bombay, 1984; I.P. Massey,

Administrative Law, Lucknow, 1985; M.P. Jain, *Changing Face of Administrative Law*, Bombay, 1985.

The Supreme Court and High Courts acquired the power of judicial review under the Constitution and naturally followed English decisions, deriving, until recently, more inspiration from English decisions than from their own sense of ingenuity and innovation. The impact of *Ridge v. Baldwin* (1965) *A.C.* 40 (applying natural justice and participatory obligations in the administration) was immediately felt in India (*see Sri Bhagwan v. Ramchand A.I.R. 1965 S.C.* 1767; *Associated Cement Companies, A.I.R. 1965 S.C.* 1595; *P.L. Lakhanpal v. Union of India, A.I.R. 1967 S.C.* 1567; *A.K. Kraipak v. Union of India, A.I.R. 1970 S.C.* 150). Principles established in *In the Delhi Laws* and other cases (*supra* note 50) were enlarged (e.g., *Gwalior Rayon Co. v. Assistant Commissioner Sales Tax, A.I.R. 1974 S.C.* 1660; *N.K. Papiah v. Excise Commissioner, A.I.R. 1975 S.C.* 1007. But note the dissent (*Vasan Lal v. State of Bombay, A.I.R. 1961 S.C.* 4) and its ultimate success in *Devi Dassan v. State of Punjam, A.I.R. 1967 S.C.* 1895. Principles of review of administrative discretion have been established (*Barim Chemicals v. Company Law Board, A.I.R. 1967 S.C.* 295; *Rehtas Industries v. S.D. Agarwal A.I.R. 1969 S.C.* 707; *Narayan Dass v. State of M.P. A.I.R. 1972 S.C.* 2086), though they need to be fleshed out. The Court is developing more exacting principles to root out arbitrariness (*see R.D. Shetty v. International Airports Authority, A.I.R. 1979 S.C.* 1628) and the doctrine of promissory estoppel against the government (*Motilal Padampat Sugar Mills v. State of J.P. A.I.R. 1979 S.C.* 621).

57. Much litigation against the government by way of prerogative writs and appeal is filed to obtain interlocuatory relief. The Supreme Court's attempt to distribute its work load to the High Courts in certain classes of cases (*P.N. Kumar v. Municipal Corporation of Delhi* decided 2 November 1987) provoked an angry response from the Bar. The extent to which interlocutory relief is granted can be seen from R. Dhavan, *The Supreme Court Under Strain: The Challenge of Arrears*, Bombay 1979, and *Litigation Explosion*, *supra* note 6. Apart from a rule of thumb based on an intuitive understanding of the real facts, there has been an insufficient exploration of the principles on which interlocutory relief ought to be granted (*see Assistant Collector C.E. Chandan Nagar v. Dunlop (India) Ltd. A.I.R. 1985 S.C.* 330). The position in some High Courts has reached absurd proportions (*see M/s Samarias Trading Co. v. S. Samuel, A.I.R. 1985 S.C.* 61).

58. India's Constitution was intended to be juridical rather than political. In the earlier controversies (*see* R. Dhavan, *The Supreme Court and Parliamentary Sovereignty*, Delhi, 1976) neither side denied the importance of the constitutional framework and purpose. Nehru's government stressed political constitutionalism, but it was never argued until Mrs. Gandhi's day that this was an open-ended invitation to any regime to try and do whatever they like. These issues were often fudged both by the "regime left" (e.g., P.B. Gajendragadhar, *Law, Liberty and Justice*, Delhi, 1965 and *Constitution of India*, Delhi, 1970, as well as the ingenious right (*see* K.S. Hegde, "Directive Principles of State Policy" (1971) *S.C.J. Jnl.* 50 ff) so that even the "basic structure" doctrine formulated in *Kesavananda* (*supra* note 2) has been explored

properly. More recently, Indian jurists have sought to ground juridical constitutionalism in principles of distributive justice (*see* P.N. Bhagwati, "Judicial activism and public interest litigation" (1985), 23 *Columbia Journal of International Transactions* 561-77; *Bandhua Mukti Morcha v. Union of India, A.I.R. 1984 S.C.* 802).

59. The title of Prashant Bhushan's incisive *The Case That Shook India* (Delhi 1977), which gives a blow-by-blow account of how the petitioner and his lawyer, Raj Narain and Shanti Bhushan, respectively, planned their strategies to unseat Mrs. Gandhi.

60. *Indira Nehru Gandhi v. Raj Narain* (A.I.R. 1975 S.C. 1950).

61. *See generally* the Constitution (Forty-Second Amendment) Act 1976 which in turn was amended by the Constitution (Forty-Fourth Amendment) Act 1978; *and see* R. Dhavan, *The Amendment ... and Amending the Amendment, supra* note 2.

62. *Union of India v. S.H. Sheth, A.I.R. 1977 S.C.* 2328, which admitted the possibility of punitive transfers (pr. 15 p. 2339) but permitted such a policy in the public interest. Note Bhagwati J.'s dissent especially at pr. 47 P. 2850-1 and the judgment of the Gujerat High Court (1977), 17 *Gujerat L.R. (F.B.)* from which this was an appeal.

63. *Union of India v. Bhanu Das, A.I.R. 1976 S.C.* 1207.

64. *A.D.M. Jabalpur v. Shiv Kant Shukla, A.I.R. 1976 S.C.* 1207.

65. *Infra* note 240. Since the Emergency, Congress Governments have inaugurated a policy of compulsory transfers of High Court Judges (in particular, at this stage, Chief Justices) in the name of national integration. This policy has been approved by the Supreme Court in *S.P. Gupta v. Union of India, A.I.R. 1983 S.C.* 149.

66. *See* R. Dhavan, *supra* note 6.

67. *See* R. Dhavan, "Managing Legal Activism: Reflections on India's Legal Aid Programme" (1986), 15 *Anglo American Law Review* 281-309.

68. On the directive principles, *see generally* K. Markanadam, *Directive Principles of State Policy*, Delhi, 1966; N.V. Paranjpe, *The Role of Directive Principles Under the Indian Constitution*, Allahabad, 1975. Discussion on these can be found in *Shiva Rao: A Study* 319-34. The description of these provisions as a "veritable dustbin of sentiment" comes from T.T. Krishnamachari in the Constituent Assembly (1948) *VII C.A.D.* 583 (24 November 1984). The attempt to extract a "Directive Principles Jurisprudence" (*see* P. Diwan and V. Kumar, eds., *Directive Principles Jurisprudence*, Delhi, 1982), has produced electric results. Influential analysis of the Directive Principles includes P.K. Tripathi, "Directive Principles of State Policy" (1954), *S.C. Jnl.* 7-46; U. Baxi, "Directive Principles of State Policy" (1969), 11 *J.I.L.* 245-69; K.S. Hegde, "Directive Principles," *supra* note 58).

69. The pre-1973 interpretation of Directive Principles is summarized in R. Dhavan, *supra* notes 48, 87-95. The first imaginative use of these principles was made by Dhavan, J. in *Balwant Raj v. Union of India A.I.R. 1968* All. 14. In *Kesavananda's* case, *supra* note 2; the Directive Principles have acquired a more secure role in interpreting constitutional amendments, and the Constitution and Statutes generally.

70. Unfortunately, much of the discussion has been on whether the court's jurisdiction has been ousted from examining legislative action to achieve the aims of

some (*see* Constitution Twenty-Fifth Amendment Act 1971) or all (Constitution Forty-Second Amendment Act 1976) of the Directive Principles. *Kesavananda's* case (*supra* note 2); *Minerva Mills v. Union of India, A.I.R. 1980 S.C.* 1789; *Waman Rao v. Union of India, A.I.R. 1981 S.C.* 271, which seemed to countenance an ouster of the court's jurisdiction in respect of only some of the Directive Principles mentioned in the 1971 amendments, allowing review in all other cases from 24 April 1973 (the date of the *Keshavananda* ruling). For the view that statutes to achieve the Directive Principles are immune from review, see *Sanjeev Coke Mfg. Co. v. Bharat Cooking Coal Ltd., A.I.R. 1983 S.C.* 239. These controversies continue (*see Minerva Mills Co. v. Union of India, A.I.R. 1986 S.C.* 2030; *Panipat Woolen and General Mills Col. v. Union of A.I.R. 1986 S.C.* 2081; *see generally* Seervai, *Constitutional Law of India*, Bombay, 1985 II, 1680-82; *Supplement Volume*, Bombay, 1988, 298-9. *Query*: What is the rationale behind giving some Directive Principles priority over others?

71. *Infra* note 329.

72. *Infra* note 340. Perhaps this is inevitable in that a great number of activist movements are the work of elites, while many others remain, in Olson's phrase, "free riders" (*see* M. Olson, *The Logic of Collective Action*, Cambridge, Mass., 1965.

73. On the growth of the letter--petitioner--or "epistolary jurisdiction" as Upendra Baxi calls it, see U. Baxi, "Taking Suffering Seriously: Social Action Litigation in the Supreme Court of India," in R. Dhavan *et al.*, eds., *Judges and the Judicial Power*, Bombay, 1985, 289-315; *Sunil Batra v. Union of India, Prem Shanker and Rakesh Kaushik, supra* note 54); *Kadra Pahadiya v. State of Bihar, A.I.R. 1981 S.C.* 1167; *Munna v. State of U.P., A.I.R. 1982 S.C.* 806; *Sant Bir v. State of Bihar, A.I.R. 1982 S.C.* 1470; *Shrinivas v. State of Bihar, A.I.R. 1982 S.C.* 1391; *People's Union of Democratic Rights v. Union of India, A.I.R. 1983 S.C.* 150; *Veena Sethi v. State of Bihar, A.I.R. 1983 S.C.* 339; *Sheela Barse v. State of Maharashtra, A.I.R. 1983 S.C.* 378; *Sanjit Roy v. State of Rajashthan A.I.R. 1983 S.C.* 328; *Bandhua Mukti Morcha* (*supra* note 58; note Pathak J. pleads for systematic rules in this area); *Salal Hydro Electric Project v. State of J.K., A.I.R. 1984 S.C.* 177; *Ram Kumar Mishra v. State of Bihar, A.I.R. 1984 S.C.* 547; *Laxmi Kant Pandey v. Union of India, A.I.R. 1984 S.C.* 1855; *Mukesh Advani v. State of N.P., A.I.R. 1985 S.C.* 1368; *State of H.P. v. A Parent of a Student in a Medical College* (holding that a letter petititon cannot conceal the identity of the writer and containing important rules about such petitions); *State of W.B. v. Sampat Lal, A.I.R. 1985 S.C.* 195 (letter petition cannot normally by pass normal process and remedies); *Rural Litigation and Entitlement Kendra Dehradun v. State of U.P., A.I.R. 1985 S.C.* 652; *State of H.P. Umedram* (1986), 2 *S.C.C.* 68; *Dhirendra Chamoliv. State of U.P.* (1986), 1 *S.C.C.* 37; *Banwasi Ashram v. State of U.P.* (1986), 5 *S.C.C.* 753.

74. *See* P.N. Bhagwati (*supra* note 58) and *Law, Freedom and Social Change*, Bangalore University, Janmabhoomi Trust, 1979. The breakthrough in these matters was made by Justice V.R. Krishna Iyer, on whom see H. Swaroop, *For the Law is Made*, 1984; K.M. Sharma, "The Judicial Universe of Mr. Justice Krishna Iyer," in Dhavan *et al.* (*supra* note 73).

75. U. Baxi, *Crisis in the Indian Legal System*, Delhi, 1980, 355-8.
76. The distinction between "civil" and "political" society in India defies exact delineation. We can visualize several concentric circles. The inner circle encompasses the activity of constitutionally designated institutions. The second circle includes those who formally run political parties. The third circle consists of those who control or influence the party at any level of its operation. In one sense, Gandhi was in the third circle. But post-Independence India has produced less salutary examples. Although those in the fourth circle who influence and corrupt those in the first three circles strictly belong to "civil society," their work has come to merge with what is done in political society. As the normative significance of the Constitution weakens, these neat concentric arrangements become blurred.
77. *See* R. Kothari, *Politics in India*, Boston, 1970; and *Democratic Policy and Social Change in India*, Delhi, 1977. More generally, see W.H. Morris-Jones, *Government and Politics in India*, London, 1971; R.L. Hardgrave, *India: Government and Politics in a Developing Nation*, New York, 1986 edn.; and Pye, *Asian Power and Politics: The Cultural Dimensions of Authority*, Cambridge, 1985.
78. For an analysis of the compenetration of forces in civil and political society, see the delightful P. Bardhan, *The Political Economy Development in India*, Oxford, 1980; P.S. Jha, *A Political Economy of Stagnation*, Bombay, 1980. For more benign, yet alarming analysis of this phenomenon as virtually inevitable from a commitment to growth *and* democracy, see F. Frankel, *India's Political Economy 1947-77: The Gradual Revolution*, Princeton, 1978.
79. Calculated from *Crime in India*, Annual Reports, from 1960-62.
80. *Id.*
81. S. Hall, *Drifting into a Law and Order Society*, London, NCCL Lecture, 1978.
82. *See Romesh Thappar* and *Brij Bhusan* (*supra* note 47), and *Shaibala* (*supra* note 48). On the distinction between "law and order" and "public order," see *Supdt. Central Jail v. R.M. Lohia, A.I.R. 1960 S.C.* 633, at pr. 12 pp. 639-40; and especially Hidayatuallh C.J., *Arun Ghosh v. State of West Bengal, A.I.R. 1970 S.C.* 1228 at pr. 3, 1229-30.
83. *See* especially P.R. Rajgopal, *Social Change and Violence: The Indian Experience*, Delhi, 1987; and *Communal Violence in India*, Delhi, 1987.
84. Mrs. Gandhi's assassination led to riots in Delhi. For victim accounts, see U. Chakravarti and N. Haksar, *The Delhi Riots: Three Days in the Life of the Nation*, Delhi, Lancer International, 1987; *Report of the Citizen's Commission: Delhi 31 October to 10 November 1984*, Delhi, 1984; P.U.D.R. and P.U.C.L., *Who are the guilty: Report of a Joint Inquiry into the Causes and Impact of the Riots in Delhi from 31 October to 10 November*, Delhi, 1984; Citizens for Democracy, *Truth about Delhi Violence*, Delhi, 1984; S. Gupta, S. Shourie, R. Nedi, and P. Roy, *The Assassination and After*, Delhi, 1985. Justice Thakkar's inquiry into the murder is still not available and remains confidential (*Times of India* 6-8 August 1986). Justice Mishra's Inquiry (*Report of the Justice Rangunatha Miohra Committee inquiry*, Delhi, 1985) is sufficiently ambivalent to require further inquiries; and reports from Justice Kapur

and from Justice Banerjee and Justice Jain. Justice Kapur's report is confidential and the other inquiry was frustrated by court orders (*see Indian Express* 15 Dec. 1987).

85. *See generally* P.R. Rajgopal, *Communal Violence in India*, Delhi, 1987, especially *Table* at 196-7; G. Krishna, "Communal Violence in India" (1985), *E.P.W.* (12 January) 61-79.

86. *See Reports of the Commission of Inquiry into Communal Disturbances: Mallegaeon*, Delhi, 1967 Chairperson: Raghubar Dayal; *Report of the Commission of Inquiry into Communal Disturbances: Ranchi-Hatia* (Delhi, 1967, 1968, Chairperson: Raghubar Dayal); *Report of the Commission of Inquiry into Communal Disturbances: Jainpur, Suchetpur, District Gorakhpur,* U.P. Delhi, 1967; 1969; Chairperson: Raghubar Dayal; *Report-Inquiry into The Communal Disturbances at Abamhabad and Other Places in Gujarah on or after 18th September 1969* (Chairperson: Jagmahan Reddy); *Report of the Commission of Inquiry into Communal Disturbances at Bhiwana, Jalgoon and Mahad in May 1970* (Chairperson Madon); *Report of the Commission of Inquiry: Shahdara Disturbances of August 19-22,* (Delhi 1973; Chairperson: V. D. Krishna; *Report of the Three Member Commission of Inquiry to inquire into the Communal Disturbances that took place in April 1979 in and around Jamshedpur* (Chairperson: Jitendra Narayan).

87. The protestation of loyalty is undoubtedly ingenious. Gandhi played his hand well, declaring his cause, inviting further punishment and publicity, and bringing the system into disrepute without alleging it. *See* F. Watson, *The Trial of Gandhi,* London, 1969; and more generally, J. Brown, *Civil Disobedience: The Mahatma in Indian Politics*, Cambridge, 1974, and *Gandhi's Rise to Power*, Cambridge, 1972. The exact extent of each campaign needs to be analyzed (e.g., S. Henningham, "The Social Setting of the Champaran Satyagraha" (1976), *13 I.E.S.H.R.* 59-73, D. Hardiman, *Peasant Nationalist of Gujarat: Kheda District* 1917-34 Delhi, 1981.

88. The extensive literature on this is summed up in S. Sen, *Peasant Movements in India Mid-Nineteenth and Twentieth Century,* Delhi, 1982; and generally M.S.A. Rao ed., *Social Movements in India*, Delhi, 1984 edn.

89. For a well-known account, see S. Banerjee, *In the Wake of Nalbari: A History of the Naxalite Movement in India*, Calcutta, 1980.

90. On the Punjab crisis, see especially M. Tully and S. Jacob, *Amritsar: Mrs. Gandhi's Last Battle*, Calcutta, 1983; P. Kumar, M. Sharma, A. Sood, and A. Handa, *Punjab Crisis: Context and Trends*, Chandigarh, 1984; K. Singh and K. Nayar, *Tragedy of Punjab: Operation Bluestar*, Delhi, 1984. The Government's own explanation is in *White Paper on the Punjab Agitation 10 July 1984*, Delhi, 1984.

On the historical antecedents, see R. Kapur, *Sikh Separatism: The Politics of Faith,* London, 1986, and more generally K. Singh, *History of the Sikhs*, Princeton, 1966; G. Singh, *A History of the Sikh People*, Delhi, 1979.

91. The Punjab crisis (*supra* note 90) is an important test for both Indian federalism and Indian secularism.

92. For example, P. Brass, *Factional Politics in an Indian State: The Party in Uttar Pradesh*, California, 1965. This thesis is rightly criticized as myopic and providing only partial insights that obscure our understanding of contemporary India. For an account of the intellectual pedigree of this approach, see D. Hardiman, "The Indian 'Faction': A Political Theory Examined," in R. Guha, ed. *Subaltern Studies: Writing on South Asian History and Society*, Delhi I, 1982, at 198-231.

93. *Infra* note 123.

94. This often results in both manipulation and brutalization of power at the local level (*see* D. Bayley, "Police and Political Order in India" (1983), 23 *Asian Survey*; R. Dhavan's official report (*Public Interest Litigation in India: An Investigative Report*, Delhi, 1981) recommends that local arrangements should take into account the collapse of the local state.

95. Within a broad analysis of power *see* S. Lukes, *Power*, London, 1974, the system is clearly tilted heavily in favor of the rich and powerful. But even relatively open-ended processes have been manipulated by the advantaged. It has been suggested that the disadvantaged, too, can use constitutional process effectively by combining political mobilization with institutional skills; *see* S. Scheingold, *The Politics of Rights: Lawyers, Public Policy and Political Change*, New Haven, 1974. Theoretically, such systemic manipulation is inevitable but could be treated as an exercise in the "privatization of the State" if comprehensively and consistently applied over a part of the State or its processes over a period of time. At this juncture, democracy is helpless to prevent the asymmetries of civil society from perpetuating inequitable use of supposedly egalitarian institutions and processes.

96. *See* R. Dhavan, *supra* note 6, at 169-79, surmising that the more advantaged sectors would now prefer a system which they can manipulate over one in which "private deals" determine all outcomes. In this sense, "rationality" is also seen as an ideological motif. It serves as a vehicle for a particular class to order the political economy for class domination.

97. E.g., *C.R. Bansi v. State of Maharashtra, A.I.R. 1971 S.C.* 78. Sometimes it is important to introduce speed into the system (*Gian Singh v. State of Punjab, A.I.R. 1974 S.C.* 1024; *Shantilal v. State of Rajasthan, A.I.R. 1976 S.C.* 739; *Deonath Dudhnath v. State, A.I.R. 1967 Bombay* 1), or to obtain a certification (*e.g., M.C. Sulkunte v. State of Mysore, A.I.R. 1976 S.C.* 2462; *Mansingh v. State of Haryna, A.I.R. 1973 S.C.* 910, *A.I.R. 1968 S.C.* 1292).

98. *Narsinghan v. State, A.I.R. 1969 A.P.* 271; *Kesho Prashad v. State A.I.R. 1967 S.C.* 511.

99. *Manshankar v. State of Gujarat, A.I.R. 1970 Gujarat* 97; *State of Gujarat v. M.P. Dwivedi, A.I.R. 1973 S.C.* 330.

100. E.g., people claiming to be ticket examiners or with State authority (*see N.G. Mitra v. State of Bihar, A.I.R. 1970 S.C.* 1636; *Bajrang Lal v. State of Rajasthan, A.I.R. 1976 S.C.* 1008); to avoid going to a police station (*Ram Swarup v. State, A.I.R. 1967 Delhi* 26) or connected with bail (*Deep Chand v. State A.I.R. 1966 Punjab* 392), to trade without a license (*Munilal v. Delhi Administration, A.I.R. 1971 S.C.* 525; *R.J.*

Singh v. State of Delhi, A.I.R. 1971 S.C. 1552; *Mangesh v. State, A.I.R. 1969 Goa* 106), or to get a better contract (*B.C. Goswami v. Delhi Administration, A.I.R. 1973 S.C.* 1457), or to be allowed an adoption (*Shiv Raj v. Delhi Administration, A.I.R. 1968 S.C.* 141), or to obtain a tender (*Manwal Bhutoria v. State of West Bengel, A.I.R. 1970 Calcutta* 253) or an airline seat (*Somnath v. State of Rajasthan, A.I.R. 1972 S.C.* 1490) or sanction to dig a well (*Ram Charan v. State, A.I.R. 1967* All 321), or to get an electrical connection (*R.P. Arora v. State of Punjam, A.I.R. 1973 S.C.* 498). These are cases representative of the very small proportion of cases in which people are caught and prosecuted.

101. *Kesho Prasad v. State, A.I.R. 1967 Delhi* 51, at pr. 6, 53.

102. *Report of the Committee on the Prevention of Corruption*, Delhi, 1964; Chairperson: Santhanam).

103. *Id.* 15. Note other statistical data in this section of the report at 14-27.

104. *Central Viligance Commission: Annual Report 1964-5* and *1986* (at 8.1). Officials may be prosecuted under Chapter IX of the Indian Penal Code (Sections 161-171: "Of Offences by or relating to Public Servants), the Prevention of Corruption Act 1947, and other Union of State Statutes.

105. Central Vigilance Commission, *Annual Report 1984* at pr. 4.2, 18.

106. *Id.* pr. 4, 21.

107. *Id.* 4.6, 22.

108. Central Vigilance Commission, *Annual Report 1986*, pr. 2, 3, and 9, 15.

109. *Report of the Commission of Inquiry into the Affairs of the Life Insurance Corporation of India*, Delhi, 1958, Chairperson: M.C. Chagla. The most celebrated inquiry into the Central Government was the *Shah Commission of Inquiry, Interim Reports* Volumes I, II and III, and *Final Reports*, Delhi, 1978. See more recently, reports into the Fairfax Affair (about the employment of a foreign company to investigate the financial dealing of Indian Nationals abroad (*see Report of the Thakkar-Natrajan Commission of Inquiry*, Delhi, 1987.

The country was denied a full-fledged inquiry into the possibility of the Prime Minister's involvement into the "Kickbacks" from an arms deal; but a parliamentary inquiry is looking into the matter (*infra* note 114); *see also*, however, the *Report of the Railway Inquiry Committee* 1954-5 Delhi, 1956 Chairman: J.B. Kriplani; *Report of the Committee of Inquiry (Steel Transaction) Department of Iron and Steel*, Delhi, 1968.

110. *Report of the Commission of Inquiry*, Delhi, 1964 Chairperson: S.R. Das.

111. *See* A.G. Noorani, *Minister's Misconduct*, Delhi, 1973. On ministerial misconduct in the State Government, see Government of Orissa, *Report of the Commission of Inquiry* (1969: H.R. Khanna's Report on Patnaik and others); Government of Jammu and Kashmir, *Report of a Commission of Inquiry* (1967, N. Rajgopala Ayyangar Report on Bakshi Ghulam Mohammed); Government of Orissa, *Report of Justice J.R. Mudholkar, Special Judge for Inquires* (1968), concerning H.K. Mahtab), and *Report of the Orissa Inquiry Commissioner* 1971-2; 1972, Report of

Sarjoo Prasad on Dr. H.K. Mahtab); Government of Kerala, *Report of the Commission of Inquiry* (1971, Report of S. Velu Pillai on K.R. Gouri, Imbichi Bawa).
112. On whether Chief Minister Antulay of the Government of Maharashtra could be charged for offenses under the Indian Penal Code, see *State of Maharashtra v. R.S. Nayak, A.I.R. 1982 S.C.* 1249; *R. S. Nayak v. A.R. Antulay, A.I.R. 1984 S.C.* 684; *A.R. Antulay v. R.S. Nayak, A.I.R. 1984, S.C.* 718. For a reversal of these cases see the *Antulay* judgment pronounced on 29 April 1988; see further U. Baxi: *Liberty and Corruption*, Lucknow, 1990.
113. For a curious use of the High Court to clear the pitch for an inquiry into the conduct of Chief Minister Rama Rao of Andhra Pradesh by the Central Government, see *India Today*, 15 January 1988, 40; 31 January 1988, 34. The courts are often called upon to intervene in Commissions of Inquiry (e.g., *State of J. & K. v. Bakshi Ghulam Mohammad, A.I.R. 1967 S.C.* 122), or preliminary investigations leading to an inquiry (e.g., *Harekrishna Mahtab v. Chief Minister, Orissa, A.I.R. 1971 Orissa* 175). Strictures from the courts on the conduct of Ministers can lead to resignations (*see* Jain and Jain, *supra* note 56, 960 note 4).
114. The Bofors Crisis was nearly responsible for toppling the Gandhi government in 1987. A Joint Committee of both Houses of Parliament inquired into the matter (*see Report of the Joint Committee to Inquire into Bofors Contract*, Delhi, 1988; Chairperson: Shankaranand. For a speculative review see P. Bhushan: *Bofors: The Selling of a Nation*, Delhi, 1990.
115. These are formal inquiries using judges, under the Commission of Inquiries Act, 1952. However, after the Thakkar Commission Inquiry into the murder of Mrs. Gandhi (*supra* note 84), Justice Mishra's inquiry into the Delhi riots (*supra* note 74), and the Thakkar-Natrajan inquiry into the Fairfax Affair (*supra* note 109), such inquiries seem to have lost credibility. A distinguished scholar questions the desirability of using judges for such purposes (U. Baxi, "The Larger Issues" (1986), *The Law Magazine* (January) 30.
116. E.g., Administrative Reforms Commission, *Interim Report on the Problem of the Redress of Citizen's Grievances*, Delhi, 1966; M.P. Jain, *Lokpal Ombudsman in India*, Delhi, 1969; Jaganadhan and Mukhija, *Citizens' Administration and Lokpal Ombudsman in India*, Delhi, 1969; S.K. Agrawala, *The Proposed Indian Ombudsman*, Delhi, 1971; S.P. Sathe, "Lokpal and Lokayukta: The Indian Ombudsman" (1969), 38 *Journal of University of Bombay* 265; D.C. Rowat, "The Proposed Ombudsman for India" (1971), 5 *J.C.P.S.* 284; R. Dhavan, "Engrafting the Ombudsman Idea on a Parliamentary Democracy: A Comment on the Lokpal Bill 1977" (1977), 19 *J.I.L.I.* 257; S.L. Verma, "Lokpal Bureaucracy and the Common Man (1978), 24 *I.J.P.A.* 1130-58; Jain and Jain, *supra* note 56, 936-49, K.S. Shuklar and S.S. Singh, *Institution of Lokayukta in India*, Delhi, 11 PA, 1985 mimeo.
117. *See* these statutes of Lokayuktas in various States: Orissa Lokpal and Lokayukta Act, 1970; Maharashtra Lokayukta and Upa-Lokayukta Act, 1971; Rajasthan Lokayukta and Upa-Lokayukta Act, 1973; Bihar Lokayukta Act, 1973; Uttar Pradesh Lokayukta and Upa-Lokayukta Act, 1975; Madhya Pradesh Lokayukta

and Upa-Lokayukta Act, 1981; Gujarat Lokpal and Lokayukta Act, 1975; Andhra Pradesh Lokayukta and Upa-Lokayukta Act, 1983; Karnataka Lokayukta Act, 1984.
118. Note the retaliatory actions by Ministers found guilty of corruption, in Jain and Jain, *supra* note 56, 948. They also report on the instance of a writ petition that the Lokpal was not to be trusted and should therefore be removed. *Quis Custodet Ipsos Custodes?*
119. *See* R. Dhavan, *supra* note 116.
120. Article 311 of the Constitution. Judges discuss much the extent to which these provisions fetter the common law doctrine that civil servants hold office during the pleasure of the sovereign (in this case, the President). *See P.L. Dhingra v. Union of India, A.I.R. 1958 S.C.* 36; *State of U.P. v. Babu Ram Upadhayaya, A.I.R. 1961 S.C.* 751; *Moti Rama v. N.E. Frontier Railway, A.I.R. 1964 S.C.* 600; and *Union of India v. Tulsi Ram, A.I.R. 1985 S.C.* 1416.
121. Constitution (Fifteenth Amendment) Act, 1963; and Constitution (Forty-Second Amendment) Act, 1976.
122. The Administrative Tribunals Act (No. 13 of) 1985, as amended by the Administrative Tribunals (Amendment) Act, 1986. The constitutionality of these provisions was unsuccessfully challenged in *S.P. Sampath Kumar v. Union of India, A.I.R. 1987 S.C.* 386.
123. On the growth of a self-serving white collar and bureaucratic sector of the political economy, see P.S. Jha (*supra* note 78) 111-33; P. Bardhan (*supra* note 78) 51-2. For contributions and bibliographic accounts of the dilemmas faced by the administration, see R.B. Taub, *Bureaucracy under Stress*, Calcutta, 1969, a somewhat idiosyncratic collection of interviews, especially 139 ff.; S.K. Roy, *Bureaucracy at the Crossroads*, Delhi, 1979, and material cited there.
124. For a general review of problems, see the *Reports of the Administrative Reforms Commissions*, Delhi, 1966-9; for more specific problems of accountability in the Indian context, see T.N. Chaturvedi ed., *Administrative Accountability*, Delhi, 1984; more generally, see Smith and Hague, *The Dilemma of Accountability in Modern Government*, London, 1971.
125. On the refusal of the government to follow the orders of the courts, see R. Dhavan, *Contempt of Court and the Press*, Bombay, 1980, 93-6. More recently, Bhagwati C.J. gave expression to his frustration that district judges do not carry out orders of the Supreme Court, in *Sheela Barse v. Union of India* (1986), 3 *S.C.C.* 596 at 598.
126. On prisons, *see* U. Baxi, *supra* note 75, at 121-243. Largely as a result of efforts of Justice Krishna Iyer, the rights of prisoners have been given more considered attention by the Supreme Court; *see* cases cited *infra* note 127, from *Sunil Batra* onwards.
127. Earlier cases established prisoners' right to free speech (*State of Maharashtra v. Prabhakar, A.I.R. 1966 S.C.* 424); decent conditions of incarceration (*D.B.M. Patnaik v. State of A.P., A.I.R. 1974 S.C.* 2092); and rights of journalists to visit prisoners condemned to death (*Prabha Dutt v. Union of India, A.I.R. 1982 S.C.* 6).

But the real breakthrough came in *Sunil Batra* (*supra* note 54), which held solitary confinement not necessary unjust ; *see* also *Charles Sobhrai, supra* note 54, on conditions of imprisonment; *Kishore Singh v. State of Rajasthan, A.I.R. 1981 S.C.* 625 (shackling and solitary confinement); *Prem Shankar Shukla, supra* note 54; *Rakesh Kaushik, supra* note 54.

128. *See* U. Baxi *et al.*, "An Open Letter to the Chief Justice" (1980), *1 S.C.C. Jnl.* 17.

129. The Criminal Law (Amendment) Act, 1983, inserting Sections 228A (on the identity of the victim), 376A (rape by separated husband), 376B (rape in custody, remand home or hospital), and substituting Section 376 of the Indian Penal Code; *see also* Eighty-Fourth Report, *Rape and Allied Offences: Some Questions of Substantive Law, Procedure and Evidence*, Delhi, 1980.

130. *See Hussainanara Khatoon* (*supra* note 54). In *Kamladevi v. State of Punjab, A.I.R. 1984 S.C.* 1895, a plea was made to release those who had been held after "Operation Bluestar" (the army operation into the Golden Temple of the Sikhs). Where there are illegal detentions (*see Bhim Singh v. State, A.I.R. 1986 S.C.* 1086; *Sebastian v. Hongray, A.I.R. 1984 S.C.* 571), compensatory sums have been awarded. *See also People's Union for Democratic Rights v. State of Bihar, A.I.R. 1987 S.C.* 355.

131. *Kadra Pahadia* (*supra* note 73). There are later cases on the sexual exploitation of juveniles (e.g., *Munna, supra* note 73); the detention of alleged lunatics for excessive periods of time (*Sant Bir, supra* note 73); *Veena Sethi, supra* note 73); custodial violence towards female prisoners (*Sheela Barse, supra* note 73); extent of detention for petty offenses (*Ahmed Hussain Khan v. State of A.P., A.I.R. 1984 S.C.* 1855); and exploitation and moral degradation of children (*Sheela Barse v. Union of India* (1986) 3 *S.C.C.* 596.

132. For an account, *see* U. Baxi (*supra* note 75) 348-56; also *Anil Yadav v. State of Bihar, A.I.R. 1982 S.C.* 1008 (suspended superintendant allegedly responsible denied relief by the court). There is no limit to police atrocities. Consider *State of U.P. v. Ram Sagar Yadav, A.I.R. 1985 S.C.* 416, where a falsely accused victim was brutally murdered because he registered a further request for a bribe; see further *Amnesty International Handout ASA/20/02 86*, dated 29 January 1986.

133. *See* Gobind Das, *The Supreme Court in Quest for Itself*, Lucknow, 1987.

134. U. Baxi (*supra* note 75) 356-8.

135. *See* Fuller, *The Morality of Law*, London, 1964, 33-8.

136. Thus, "wide discretionary authority" or a total lack of predictability is corrosive of law's function. In response to this, more structured decision making has been suggested in K.C. Davis, *Discretionary Justice*, New York, 1969; and R. Baldwin and K. Hawkins, "Discretionary Justice: Davis Reconsidered" (1984) *P.L.* 570.

137. This has been a recurring feature of constitutional amendments. In addition to reversing court decisions, a blanket ouster of jurisdiction was affected by the Constitution (First Amendment) Act 1951, which created a Ninth Schedule to the Constitution giving total immunity to statutes listed in it. Their constitutional validity could not be challenged as violative of the important fundamental rights.

Additions to this list were made by the Constitution (Fourth Amendment) Act, 1954; Constitution (Seventeenth Amendment) Act, 1964; Constitution (Twenty-Fifth Amendment) Act, 1972; Constitution (Thirty-Fourth Amendment) Act, 1974; Constitution (Thirty-Ninth Amendment) Act, 1975 (some of the items in the 1975 amendments were removed by the Constitution (Forty-Fourth Amendment) Act, 1978; Constitution (Forty-Second Amendment) Act, 1976; Constitution (Forty-Seventh Amendment) Act, 1984.   In addition, the Constitution (Twenty-Fifth Amendment) Act, 1971 and the Constitution (Forty-Second Amendment) Act, 1976 gave immunity to statutes which sought to fulfill the purposes of some (1971 amendments) or all (1976 amendments) Directive Principles of State Policy; see further *Minerva Mills* and other cases (*supra* note 70).

138. Note Justice Subha Rao's protest against using a much too wide doctrine of classification in interpreting Article 14 (equality) of the Constitution in *Lachman Das v. State of Punjab, A.I.R. 1963 S.C.* 222 at pr. 50 240.

139. This is especially true of the earlier cases on delegated legislation (*see In re Delhi Laws* and subsequent cases cited *supra* note 50, culminating in Mathew J.'s view in *Gwalior Rayon* and *N.K. Papia, supra* note 56; *Cf. Registrar for Co-operative Societies v. Kunjabmu, A.I.R. 1980 S.C.* 350.

140. R.D. Shetty, *supra* note 56.

141. A phrase from H. Alavi, "The State in Post-Colonial Societies: Pakistan and Bangladesh," in K. Gough and H.P. Sharma eds. *Imperialism and Revolution in South Asia*, New York, 1973, 145-73.

142. *Supra* note 123, especially P.S. Jha (*supra* note 78); P. Bardhan (*supra* note 78).

143.   This can be traced back to Dicey (*supra* note 18) 127-8; for different terminology, see Lord Birkenhead L.C., in *McCawley v. King* (1920) 691 at 703-4. Written "core" elements which are constitutionally and institutionally significant can also be identified in "flexible" constitutions even though such elements are *constitutionally* indistinguishable from other legislation because they do not require a special procedure to alter or amend them.

144.   The subject of constitutional conventions has generated a great deal of controversy (*see* Dicey, *supra* note 18) Chapters 14 and 15; Jennings, *Law and the Constitution*, London, 1953, Chapter 3; deSmith, *Constitutional and Administrative Law*, London, 1972, 47-66; O. Hood-Phillips, *Constitutional and Administrative Law*, London, 1973, 27-8, 77-91; Marshall and Moodie, *Some Problems of the Constitution*, London, 1967, 25-40.   But the *ex-cathedra*--even if not legally enforceable-- significance of these conventions requires historical deconstruction. Clearly, Dicey borrowed these formulations from his contemporaries (*see* O. Hood-Phillips, "Constitutional Conventions: Dicey's Predecessors" (1969), 29 *Modern L.R.* 137; H.W. Arndt, "The Origin of Dicey's Concept of the 'Rule of Law'" (1957), 31 *Australian L. J.* 117). Conventions represent rules which the elites have invented for themselves, and constitute exclusive power games for particular power elites.

145. In this sense, it seems pointless to talk of the triumph of the "written" over the "unwritten" Constitution (*e.g.*, U. Baxi, *Courage, Craft and Contention: The Indian*

Supreme Court in the Eighties, Bombay, 1985, except that it implies we ought to trust legalism because we cannot trust ourselves. It also raises fundamental epistemological questions about the nature of the written Constitution (for the American discussion, *see infra* note 351) and the relationship betwen written rule and its appropriation by civil and political society.

146. This is implicit in the Council of Ministers being collectively responsible to the lower house of the legislature (Articles 75(3) and 164(3) of the Constitution). Indeed, there was an assumption that political parties would retain some collective integrity. But they did not. It is the failure of this collective integrity and its consequences that led to the Constitution (Fifty-Second Amendment) Act, 1985 which gave specific recognition to "political parties" and sought to prevent parliamentary parties from splitting unless they could muster a significant one-third support.

147. *See*, e.g., P. Brass, "National Power and Local Politics" (1984), 18 *Modern Asian Studies* 89-118.

148. Centralized control characterized Mrs. Gandhi's advent into politics and plagued the government of her son, Rajiv Gandhi. It has perpetuated Machiavellian politics, which serves no purpose other than political survival and the acculturation of power for its own sake.

149. Such institutional polarity can be seen in the use of courts against the government for decisional, symbolic and ideological gains (*infra* note 156), and in the persistent popularity of State governments. They are run by political parties other than Congress (I) which is in power at the Centre. In turn, the Centre uses unscrupulous measures against the States (*supra* note 155). The other major arena of opposition against the government is the press (*see* R. Dhavan, *Only the Good News: On the Law of the Press*, Delhi, 1987).

150. *See* S.C. Kashyap, *The Politics of Power: Defections and State Politics*, Delhi, 1974; P. Diwan, "*Aaya Ram, Gaya Ram: The Politics of Defection*" (1979), 21 *J.I.L.I.*, 291-312; on the toppling of the Janata government at the Centre, see M.V. Pylee, *Crisis, Conscience and the Nation*, Delhi, 1982.

151. The Constitution (Fifty-Second Amendment) Act, 1985 introduced the Tenth Schedule to the Constituiton. For an energetic even if sprawling analysis, see Masodkar, *Law Relating to Electoral Disqualification*, Bombay, 1986. Since then V.P. Singh's government fell as a result of defections and the Supreme Court is examining the constitutional validity of the anti-defection amendment.

152. *See generally* Article 356 as amended by the Constitution (Forty-Second Amendment) Act, 1976; the Constitution (Forty-Fourth Amendment) Act, 1978; the Constitution (Fifty-Eighth Amendment) Act, 1976; and the Constitution (Fifty-Ninth Amendment) Act, 1988. The 1976 amendments enabled the imposition of an Emergency in a geographic area smaller than a State (*Query*: A domestic house?). That power remains. The 1978 amendments forbade President's rule where there was an "internal emergency." This was permitted for Punjab by the 1988 and 1990 amendments.

153. The formal details on the use of these provisions are in Lok Sabha Secretariat, *President's Rule in the States*, Delhi, 1988; *see generally*, R. Dhavan, *President's Rule in the States*, Bombay, 1978; S. Maheshwari, *President's Rule in India*, Delhi, 1977; B. Dua, *President's Rule in India*, Delhi, 1984.

154. Legally, the President is bound by the advice of the Prime Minister (*see Shamsher Singh v. Union of India, A.I.R. 1974 S.C.* 2192, which also took judicial notice of the tensions between the Prime Minister and the President over the Hindu Code Bill); *see* M.C. Setalvad, *My Life: Law and Other Things*, Bombay, 1971, 171-3; K.M. Munshi, *Pilgrimage to Freedom*, Bombay, 1967, I, 508-600. During the Janata regime, President Reddy's role in selecting the Prime Minister led to the downfall of the Janata Party (*see* Pylee, *supra* note 150). There were also conflicts between President Zail Singh and Prime Minister Rajiv Gandhi over the President's power to dismiss the Prime Minister, his right to refer Bills passed by the legislature back, and his granting permission to prosecute the Prime Minister (*see* H.M. Seervai (*supra* note 70), *Supplement* (1987) 549-69; *India Today*, 15 April 1988, 72-80 for the machinations surrounding the last days of Zail Singh's days in office). *See generally* R.V. Pal, *The Office of Prime Minister in India*, Delhi, 1983; L.N. Sharma, *The Indian Prime Minister: Office and Powers*, Delhi, 1976.

155. For early signs of this conflict, see Government of Tamil Nadu, *Report of the Centre: State Relations Inquiry* (1971); West Bengal, *Document on Centre, State Relations* (reported in 1977) 23 *I.J.P.A.* 1117-26). The early policy of political interference (*see* R. Dhavan, *supra* note 153) has now been replaced by the imposition of financial constraints. *See* M.P. Singh, "Indian Federalism: Structure and Issues," in P. Leelakrishnan and Sadasivan Nair, eds., *New Horizons of Law*, Cochin, 1971, 33-61, and the material cited there.

156. On this conflict, see R. Dhavan (*supra* note 58); L. Rudolph and S. Rudolph, "Judicial Versus Parliamentary Sovereignty: The Struggle over 'Stateness' in India" (1981), 19 *Journal of Commonwealth and Comparative Politics* (November).

157. It is ironic that although the Constitution and the Supreme Court have become central to an understanding of modern Indian politics, there is simultaneously a confusion created by the chaos of opportunities generated by the asymmetries perpetuated by development; on the political dimensions of growth, see H. Hart, "The Indian Constitution: Political Development and Decay" (1980), 20 *Asian Survey* 429; W. Morris-Jones, "The Politics of the Indian Constitution" in V. Bogdanor, ed., *Constitutions in Democratic Politics*, London, 1987, 128-55.

158. The publication of documents about partition (*see* Mansergh, ed., *Transfer of Power*, London, 1970-83, in 12 volumes); P. Ziegler, *Mountbatten: The Official Biography*, London, 1985; and further journalistic investigations (e.g., L. Collins and D. Lapierre, *Freedom at Midnight* (1975). A. Shourie, *Religion in Politics*, Delhi, 1987 has created fresh controversy about the creation of Pakistan. In particular, Ayesha Jalal's *The Sole Spokesman Jinnah, the Muslim League and the Demand for Pakistan*, Cambridge, 1985 claims that partition came as a result of the stance of the Congress rather than Jinnah. This view seems to have gathered support from Seervai (*supra*

note 70, Supplement (1987)) 1-168. But historical analysis cannot just concern itself with official documents; it must deconstruct these documents to portray the existing sociopolitical situation and the full implications of the Muslim League's parity (not partition) demand. The starting point in the causation of events cannot be chosen arbitrarily.

159. See B.R. Ambedkar, *What Congress and Mr. Gandhi Have Done to the Untouchables*, Bombay, 1936 and *Mr. Gandhi and the Emancipation of Untouchables*, Bombay, 1943. For a view sympathetic to Ambedkar's stand, see R. Dhavan, *Fighting for Rights: A Study of B.R. Ambedkar*, London, 1976, mimeo.

160. See generally M. Galanter, *Competing Equalities: Law and the Backward Classes in India*, California, 1984, 7-18, 188-221, 282-360. On the inclusion of groups as "latent" constitutional entitites, see R. Dhavan, "Religious Freedom in India" (1986), 35 *A.J.C.L.* 209.

161. Second-hand intuitions about what a Gandhian Constitution would have contained can be seen in S.N. Agarawala, *supra* note 13. Article 40 of the Constitution did, however, impose a duty on the State to organize village *panchayats*. For official views of how this can be done, see Balwant Rai Mehta, *Report of the Team for the Study of the Community Projects and National Extension Service*, Delhi, 1958; Ashok Mehta, *Report of the Committee on Panchayat Raj Institutes*, Delhi, 1978.

162. See D. Keer, *Dr. Ambedkar--Life and Mission*, Bombay, 1971; E. Zelliot, *Dr. Ambedkar and the Mahar Movement* (University of Pennsylvania Ph.D., 1969); W. Kuber, *Dr. Ambedkar: A Critical Study*, Delhi, 1973.

163. Ambedkar speech in Constituent Assembly (1918), VII *C.A.D.* 38-95 (N 4).

164. Articles 330, 332 and 335 extended for ten-year periods by the Constitution (Eighth Amendment) Act, 1959; Constitution (Twenty-Third Amendment) Act, 1969; Constitution (Forty-Fifth Amendment) Act, 1980. On how the provisions have worked, see L. Dushkin, "Scheduled Caste Politics" in M. Mahar, ed., *Untouchables in Contemporary India*, University of Arizona, 1972; M. Galanter, "Compensatory Discrimination in Political Representation: A Preliminary Assessment of India's Thirty-Year Experience with Reserved Seats in Legislatures" (1979), 14 *E.P.W.* 437-54; G. Narayana, "Social Background of Scheduled Caste M.P.'s: A Socio-Economic Profile 1962-71" (1978), *E.P.W.* 1603-8; C. Parvathamma and R.T. Jangam, "India's Scheduled Caste M.P.s: A Socio-Economic Profile" (1969), 5 *Journal of Karnataka Social Sciences* 153; O. Mendelsohn, "A Harijan Elite: The Lives of Some Untouchable Politicians" (1986), 21 *E.P.W.* 501.

165. Articles 331, 333 and 334 of the Constitution. Note that special quotas for Anglo-Indians in the services and by way of grants to their educational institutions were also allowed in the first ten years by Articles 336 and 337 of the Constitution.

166. Note the framework for discussion provided by M. Galanter (*supra* note 160) 105-117 identifying various factors that can be taken into account. At one level, it has been generally argued that discrimination is violative of principles of equality (*see* J. Edwards, *Positive Discrimination,* London, 1937). This is rejected by the Supreme Court of India in *State of Kerala v. N.M. Thomas, A.I.R. 1976 S.C.* 490 and *Vasanth*

v. State of Karnataka, A.I.R. 1985 S.C. 1495. Equally, it is difficult to deny that such programs affect some mobility--even if among the cream of the disadvantaged (*see* O. Mendlesohn (*supra* note 163)). Despite some marginal effect and the fact that any such program entrenches identities (*see* Surendra Kumar and R. Dhavan, "An Act of Will: A Report on Compensatory Discrimination in India" in S. Kumar, ed., *Affirmative Action in England and India,* London, Report to the Commission for Racial Equality, 1988, mimeo), the overall effect has been beneficial. Yet, even if more complex by economic and traditional criteria being used to identify disadvantage (as suggested by the Mandal Report of the Backward Classes Commission for Racial Equality, 1989.) The overall effect has been benificial. The implementation of the Mardal Report in 1991 led to savage riots in India. V.P. Singh's government fell. The policy of reservations has become a crucial political issue.

167. Articles 15(4) and 16(4) of the Constitution. For a full review of how these provisions have worked, *see* Galanter (*supra* note 160), especially 119-360 on the identification of beneficiaries of the "Other Backward Classes," other than those nominated for recognition in Constitutional Schedules (*id.* 154-87).

168. Article 25 giving the right to practice, profess and propagate one's religion; Article 26 on the right to manage religious affairs; Article 27 on freedom from payment of taxes for the promotion of any religion; and Article 28 on freedom as to attendance for religious instruction or religious worship in certain educational institutions; *see* further R. Dhaven (*supra* note 160) generally.

169. Explanation I and II to Article 25 of the Constitution.

170. Article 25(1) subjects freedom of religion to "public order, morality and health" and to the other provisions of the Part (i.e., the Chapter on Fundamental Rights). Article 25(2) allows the State to (1) regulate or restrict any economic, financial, political or other secular activity which may be associated with religious practice, and (b) provide for social welfare or reform, or throw open public Hindu institutions to all classes and sections of Hindus. Curiously, the courts have used these derogation provisions less than outlawing many religious practices as not "essential" to the religion. In this way they have insisted that certain sects (like the Swami Narayans) belong to a particular religion even when the latter proclaim that they do not (*see Yagnapurushdasji v. Muldas, A.I.R. 1966 S.C.* 1119) and have told the followers of certain sects that they do not constitute a religion (*see S.P. Mittal v. Union of India, A.I.R. 1983 S.C.* 1, on the followers of Aurobindo).

171. This test was propounded by Mukerjee J. in *Commr. H.R.E. v. Swamiar, A.I.R. 1954 S.C.* 282, at pr. 19 290. On the career and manipulation of the "essentiality" test, *see* R. Dhavan (*supra* note 160) 220-A. Judges seem to have added the requirement of rationality (*see Durgah Committee v. Hussain Ali, A.I.R. 1962 S.C.* 1403; *Yagnapurushdasji, supra* note 170) and seem to have become less thorough in their examination of questions of essentiality (*see Bijoe Emmanuel v. State of Kerala* (1986), 3 *S.C.C.* 615).

172. Since the middle of the nineteenth century, controls on religious endowments have increased. *See* R. Dhavan, "The Supreme Court and Hindu Religious Endowments 1950-75" (1978), 20 *J.I.L.I.* 52-102 and the material cited there.

173. Article 19(1) read with Article 19(4) of the Constitution.

174. Freedom of association has been dealt with in an all-encompassing way (*see State of Madras v. V.G. Row, A.I.R. 1952 S.C.* 196), and in particular to protect trade unionism (*Raja Kulkarni v. State of Bombay, A.I.R. 1954 S.C.* 73) and the associational freedoms of civil servants (*P. Balakotiah v. Union of India, A.I.R. 1958 S.C.* 232); *Kameshwar Prashad v. State of Bihar, A.I.R. 1962 S.C.* 1166). However, there is nothing to suggest that traditional associations cannot obtain the benefit of these provisions (*see Damyanti v. Union of India, A.I.R. 1971 S.C.* 966; *D.A.V. College, Jullundur v. State of Punjab, A.I.R. 1971 S.C.* 1737), which allows the State massive powers of general regulation (*Raghubar Dayal v. Union of India, A.I.R. 1962 S.C.* 263), including a denial of the fundamental right to strike (*Radhey Shyam v. P.M.G. Nagpur, A.I.R. 1965 S.C.* 311).

175. Although Article 44 of the Constitution declared the achievement of a uniform civil code as an objective, the "family" as defined by personal laws remains an important protected institution. While Hindu law has been codified, some of its major institutions including the joint family have remained unscathed (*see* R. Dhavan, *supra* note 48, 278-379, and the cases and materials cited there). In particular, controversy surrounds the codification of Muslim personal law; *see generally* M. Imam, ed., *Minorities and the Law*, Bombay, 1972; T. Mahmood, ed., *Islamic Law in Modern India*, Bombay, 1972, *Family Law Reform in the Modern World*, Bombay, 1972, and *An Indian Civil Code and Islamic Law*, Bombay, 1976.

176. This phrase used in Article 19(2) to (6) was given a wide interpretation in *V.G. Row's* case (*supra* note 174) at 200.

177. It is precisely witch hunts against Communists and trade unions that were at the root of *Balakotiah* and *Kaeshwar* (*supra* note 174). Besides pressures on public servants, there have been attempts to force people to join organizations set up by the State (*see Tika Ramji v. State of U.P., A.I.R. 1956 S.C.* 676; *All India Bank Employees Association v. National Insurance Tribunal, A.I.R. 1962 S.C.* 171), or to celebrate the national character (*see Bijee Emmanuel, supra* note 171).

178.*Supra* note 151.

179. Such groups are depicted as lively and innovative and crucial to India's image. For an earlier historical and social survey, see Rudolph and Rudolph, *The Modernity of Tradition*, Chicago, 1967).

180. These long-standing controversies (e.g., *Itwari v. Asghari, A.I.R. 1960 ALL* 680) gradually made their way to the Supreme Court. *See Zohara Khatoon v. Muhammad Ibrahim, A.I.R. 1981 S.C.* 1243; *Bai Tahira v. Ali Hussain, A.I.R. 1979 S.C.* 362; *Fuzlumbi v. K. Khader, A.I.R. 1980 S.C.* 1730). They erupt in *Mohd, Ahmad Khan v. Shah Bano, A.I.R. 1985 S.C.* 945, and the judgment resulted in a national controversy (*see India Today*, 31 March 1986, at 30-7; 31 March 1986, at 90-105; *The Week*, 24

May 1986) and led to the enactment of the *Muslim (Protection of Rights) Divorce Act 1986. See* Justice V.R. Krishna Iyer's *Commentary*, Lucknow, 1986.

181. On attempts to deal with *sati* under British rule, see E. Thompson, *Suttee*, London, 1928; V.N. Datta, *Sati*, Delhi, 1987. On the persistence of *Sati* in post-independence India, see K. Sangari and S. Vaid, "*Sati* in Modern India: A Report" (1981), *E.P.W.* 1284-88. The issue surfaced again in September 1987 with Roop Kanwar's alleged *sati* in a village in Rajasthan. The ensuing public outcry led to the *Sati* (Prevention) Act, 1987 (*see* M. Daruwala, "Overkill of the *Sati* Bill," *Statesman*, 21 November 1987; K.Mahajan, "*Sati* Bill Loopholes," *Hindustan Times*, 22 December 1987; *see also* (1987) *E.P.W.* 1834, 1891, 1919 and 1946), and the Rajasthan Sati (Prevention) Act 1987 (*see Indian Express*, 4 December 1987).

182. For a comprehensive bibliography, see R. Dhavan (*supra* note 160) at note 5; especially M. Ghouse, *Secularism, Society and the Law*, Delhi, 1973. This view was espoused strongly by Nehru who wanted a secular society in which group life was based on voluntary rational associations (*see* Nehru, *An Autobiography*, Delhi, 1982, 507-08). Note the generous derogation provisions to balance out constitutionally guaranteed freedoms (*supra* 168-70).

183. The case for reform from within the ideology of the religions themselves can be seen from the contributions of Justice Beg, "Islamic Jurisprudence and Secularism" (139-52) and Justice Dhavan, "Secularism in Indian Jurisprudence" (102-38), in G.S. Sharma, ed., *Secularism: Its Implications for Law and Life*), Bombay, 1966. Justice Dhavan showed how this could be done in *Itwari* (*supra* note 180). A less careful handling of such reform in *Shah Bano* (*supra* note 180) erupted in national controversy.

184. On the Supreme Court's reformism, see Gajendragadkar J.'s judgments in *Durgah Committee* and *Yagnapurushdasji* (*supra* note 170) and *Tilkayat v. State of Rajashthan, A.I.R. 1963 S.C.* 1638. On the problems of defining a Hindu in *Yagnapurushdasji*, see Derrett, "Hindu--A Definition Wanted for the Purpose of Applying Hindu Law" (1968), 70 *Z.V.R.* 110; M. Galanter, *infra* note 186; more generally, see P.K. Tripathi, "Secularism, Constitutional Provision and Judicial Review" (1966), 8 *J.I.L.I.* For more recent decisions, see *Jagdishwaranand v. Police Commr. Calcutta, A.I.R. 1984 CAL.* 51; S.P. Mittal (*supra* note 170) and *Bijoe Emmanuel* (*supra* note 171).

185. E.g., A. Shourie, *Religion in Politics*, Delhi, 1987, especially "Secularism--Real and Counterfeit" 287-334; note also the attitude of Raj Kumari Amrit Kumar when India's Constitution was being drafted (II *Shiva Rao* 212-3).

186. E.g., M. Galanter, "Hinduism, Secularism and the Indian Judiciary" (1971), 21 *Philosophy East and West* 457-87.

187. R. Dhavan, *supra* note 172.

188. For a review of the case law and the drift into total regulation, *see* R. Dhavan, *supra* note 160, at 239-41; *A.P. Christians Medical Educational Society v. State of A.P., A.I.R. 1986 S.C.* 1890; *Frank Anthony Public School Employees Association v. State* (1986), 4 *S.C.C.* 707.

189. This is my personal reaction to the *sati* incident of September 1987 (*supra* note 181) and to a lesser extent to the *Shah Bano* decision (*supra* note 179). Murder, cruelty and exploitation cannot be tolerated in a civilized society. Communities-- both majority and minority--cannot be left to devise their own "reformist" solutions on the basis of a gradualism where by a vast number of people are driven to death and destitution in the name of religious advancement.

190. Note Ambedkar's celebrated claim in the Constituent Assembly (*supra* note 10). This is reflected in the chapter on fundamental rights which individuates group rights by reposing them in individuals).

191. However, it is quite clear that India has refused to make the individual its sole concern. This is manifest in two ways. In the first place, the Constitution specifically recognized certain forms of group life which were guaranteed fundamental freedoms while others were given electoral and other benefits. Secondly, matters of collective concern were expressed in the Directive Principles of State Policy (*supra* notes 68-70) and by the insertion of "secularism" and "socialism" in the Preamble of the Constitution (*supra* note 8).

192. *See generally* C.H. Heimsath, *Indian Nationalism and Hindu Social Reform*, Princeton, 1964.

193. For the influence of utilitarianism, see E. Stokes, *The English Utilitarians and India*, Cambridge, 1959. More recently, Keith Smith has written an intellectual biography of Sir Fitzjames Stephen, with a chapter on his work as a legislator in India, forthcoming, Cambridge. More incisive explanations are needed of specific normative changes (e.g., R. Kumar, *Western India in the Nineteenth Century*, London, 1968, 74-83, 153-60, 209-228) and in the use of law in the political economy as a whole (e.g., D.A. Washbrook), "Law, State and Society in Colonial India" (1981), 15 *Modern Asian Studies* 649-721.

194. On codification, see Whitley Stokes, *The Anglo-Indian Codes*, Oxford, 1887 in two volumes; B.K. Acharya, *Codification in British India*, Calcutta, 1914; C. Ilbert, "Indian Codification" (1889), 5 *L.Q.R.* 352-69; and, "Sir James Fitzjames Stephen as a Legislator" (1984), 10 *L.Q.R.* 352-69; D.S. Desika Char, *Centralised Legislation: A History of the Legislative System in British India from 1834 to 1861*, London, 1963, 167-225 (on the Law Commission), 270-321 (on the legislation). It has been argued that all this did was to entrench the "black letter" law tradition (*see* J.D.M. Derrett, "Legal Science During the Last Century," in M. Rotondi, ed., *Inchieste di dirrito Comparato*, Padua, Cedam, 1976, 413-35; R.C. Majumdar and K. Datta, "Legislation and Justice," in R.C. Majumdar *et al.*, eds., *The History and Culture of the Indian People (Volume 9): British Paramountcy and the Indian Renaissance*, Bombay, 1963, 339-53. The exact intent behind, and impact and appropriation of the Codes needs more rigorous assessment.

195. The original Constitution of India Bill 1895 (I. *Shiva Rao* 5-15) contained no provision for a Bill of Rights. This is equally true of the Congress League Scheme 1916 (*id.* 25-30), the Congress Resolution for Self Determination 1918 (*id.* 31-42),

the National Demand (*id.* 39). Rights are mentioned in the Commonwealth of India Bill 1925 (*id.* 43-44) and the *Nehru Report* (*id.* 58 at 59-60).

196. Note the discussions of the Sub-Committee on Minorities in II *Shiva Rao* 199-209.

197. For the constitutional discussions (*see supra* note 39). Apart from dominating discussion in the Assembly, it has also, until recently, dominated constitutional litigation (*see* R. Dhavan, *supra* note 58, 192-214).

198. Undoubtedly, the traditional landlords were threatened with expropriation with Bills pending in the Assemblies of Uttar Pradesh, Bihar and Madras. These were specifically protected by the insertion of Articles 31(3) to (6) of the Constitution, but needed further protection by the insertion of Articles 31A and B, by the Constitution (First Amendment) Act 1951; *see* further, *supra* note 137.

199. Unfortunately, various accounts of Constitution-making (including Austin, *supra* note 1); *Shiva Rao: A Study, supra* note 13; S.K. Chaube, *Constituent Assembly of India: A Springboard of Revolution*, Delhi, 1973; and others, *see supra* note 13 do not contextualize and deconstruct discussion in terms of the political economy. Austin does portray some of the sociopolitical interactions.

200. This is particularly marked in the changing attitude of A.K. Ayyar (*supra* notes 34-5) which was supported by Ambedkar and others. Later, Ambedkar recounted the need for discipline of the Drafting Committee (*see* XI *C.A.D.* 975 (25 November 1949). As a result, the due process clause was made an "any process" clause (*supra* note 36) and extensive restraints were placed on the religious freedom clause (*supra* note 38); *see* more *generally* R.H. Retzlaff, *Constituent Assembly of India and Problems of Indian Unity*, Cornell, Ph.D., 1960.

201. Articles 326 (adult suffrage), 325 (non-discrimination), 327-8 (parliament and State legislatures to make enabling laws), 329 (extent of judicial review), and 324 (supervision of Election Commission).

202. Section 123(2) of the Representation of Peoples Act, 1951 prohibits undue influence which involves social ostracism, excommunication, expulsion from caste or community, invoking divine displeasure or spiritual censure. Section 123(3) is concerned with appeals to religion, race, caste, community, language which would affect voting choices or (*vide* 3A) provokes enmity between classes. These provisions have provoked considerable case law; *see* R. Dial and A. Dial, *Election Law*, Delhi, 1977, 476-86, *Supplement* 158-64; A.N. Ayyar, *The Law of Elections*, Madras, 1966, 169-88; M.K. Nair, *The Law of Elections*, Cochin, 147 ff., especially 154-8.

203. On elections, see M. Weiner *et al.*, eds., *Studies in Electoral Politics in Indian States, Volume I: The Communist Parties of West Bengal*, Delhi, 1974; *Volume II: Three Disadvantaged Sectors*, Delhi, 1975; *Volume III: The Impact of Modernisation*, Delhi, 1977; *Volume IV: Party Systems and Cleavages*, Delhi, 1978. Also M. Weiner and R. Kothari, eds., *Indian Voting Behavior: Studies in the 1972 General Election*, Calcutta, 1977; R. Kothari, ed., *Context of General Election in 1967*, Bombay, 1969; N.D. Palmer, *Elections and Political Development*, Delhi, 1975.

204. To the misfortune of Indian political science, it has adopted "western" analysis of the caste and communal basis of Indian political life and paid insufficient attention to new organizational forms and ideological motivations, alleging the latter are of cosmetic and rhetorical importance.

205. Article 14 of the Constitution.

206. Articles 19 and 31 of the Constitution.

207. Article 20-1 of the Constitution.

208. Article 23-4 of the Constitution.

209. Article 25-8 of the Constitution.

210. Article 29-30 of the Constitution.

211. Article 32 of the Constitution.

212. Articles 15(3), (4), 16(3) and (4) of the Constitution.

213. Article 19 of the Constitution.

214. Article 21 of the Constitution.

215. *Supra* note 170.

216. *See* Articles 31(1) and (2) which were qualified by Articles 31(3) to (6) and later Articles 31A, B and C of the Constitution.

217. *Supra* note 197.

218. There are several official reports on the impact of land reforms see P.C. Josh, *Law Reforms in India*, Delhi 1976.

219. Since issues of liberalism and human rights were tied to the discussion about agrarian reform and socialism, it was not until after the Emergency (1975-77) that a coherent theory of human rights developed. Although preventive detention was monitored by judicial review (*see* R. Dhavan, *supra* note 48, Chapter 4) and press rights were protected (*see* R. Dhavan, *supra* note 149), there was little systematic thinking about human rights issues.

220. Articles 12-36 of the Constitution.

221. *Supra* note 50.

222. *Supra* notes 47 and 48.

223. Fazl Ali J. in *Gopalan, supra* note 37.

224. A title conferred by V.D. Mahajan, *Chief Justice Subha Rao: Defender of Civil Liberties*, Delhi, 1967.

225. Subha Rao J's position on civil liberties must, perforce, remain enigmatic in his most famous cases. He seemed content to assert the power of judicial review (*see M.S.N. Sharma v. S.N. Sinha, A.I.R. 1959 S.C.* 395; dropping his points of dissent when a broad power of review was accepted (*In re: Article 143, A.I.R. 1965 S.C.* 745); *Deep Chand v. State of U.P., A.I.R. 1959 S.C.* 648; *Vajravelu* (*supra* note 40) attacking the compensation on the grounds that it violated the equality article; *Golak Nath* (*supra* note 53) where he asserted the power of review over constitutional amendments but did not use it; *Kharak Singh v. State of Punjab, A.I.R. 1963 S.C.* 1295, where review was asserted on the narrow grounds that the regulation in question was not "law," rather than on the basis of liberty. His victories were limited, as, indeed, the objectives that inspired them.

226. Note his attack on the doctrine of classification (*supra* note 138), but without a systematic exposition of the principles underlying the judicial review of administrative action of T.S. Rama Rao, "Justice Subha Rao and Property Rights" (1967), 9 *J.I.L.I.* 568 at 575-9.

227. Gajendragadkar's approach can be discerned from his extra-judicial writing (*supra* note 58) and biographical material; *see* V. D. Mahajan, *Chief Justice Gajendragadkar*, Delhi, 1956, and Gajendragadkar, *To the Best of My Memory*, Bombay, 1983.

228. For a review, *see* S.N. Dyanai, "Justice Gajendragadkar and Labour Law" (1967), 7 *Jaipur L.J.* 69.

229. *See* P.K. Tripathi, "Mr. Justice Gajendragadkar and Constitutional Interpretation" (1966), 8 *J.I.L.I.* 479, and "Secularism ...." (*supra* note 184); and his various judgments (*infra* notes 230-34).

230. Gajendragadkar J's somewhat eclectic criteria for identifying "backwardness" in *Balaji v. state of Mysore, A.I.R. 1963 S.C.* 649, simultaneously provided a framework and permitted various governments to do what they pleased. The quest for a manageable criterion continues; *see Vasanth* (*supra* note 166), which despite its self-assured style is far from being the last word on the subject.

231. e.g., *Sadanandan v. State of Kerala, A.I.R. 1966 S.C.* 1925.

232. Note especially *Sri Bhagwan and Ramchand A.I.R. 1965 S.C.* where the rules of natural justice were expounded. But he preserved a balance between administrative autonomy and process considerations.

233. *Sajjan Singh v. State of Rajasthan, A.I.R. 1965 S.C.* 845. He elaborated his views on the subject in *Indian Parliament and Fundamental Rights*, Bombay, 1972.

234. From *Sajjan Singh* (*supra* note 233) through *Golak Nath* (*supra* note 53) to *Kesavandanda* (*supra* note 2) represents a constant tussle between the legislature which made constitutional amendments (*see supra* note 2) and the judiciary which claimed a power of review over the changes.

235. For its record until the Emergency, *see* R. Dhavan (*supra* note 48) 206-78; on the predilections of judges during emergency, *see* J.D.M. Derrett, "Emergency and Preventive Detention in India" in P. Robb and D. Taylor, eds., *Rule, Protest and Identity*, London, 1978, 83.

236. *Sakal Newspapers v. Union of India, A.I.R. 1973 S.C.* 106; *I.E. Newspapers Ltd. v. Union of India, A.I.R. 1986 S.C.* 515.

237. *Bennet Coleman v. Union of India, A.I.R. 1973 S.C.* 106; *I.E. Newspapers Ltd. v. Union of India, A.I.R. 1986 S.C.* 515.

238. This refers to the needs of the press insofar as they affect its viability and the discharge of its functions in a democracy, including its needs for finance and resources, communication networks, access to governmental and other information, confidentiality of sources, immunity from prosecution on certain matters, and so on. Indian law states the traditional common law view that the rights of the press are no greater than those of the individual; *see Arnold v. King* (1947), 41 *I.A.* 149 at 167 quoted with approval in *M.S.N. Sharma* (*supra* note 225) at pr. 13, at

402; Seervai (*supra* note 170; I, 346-7). For the view that the institutional needs of the press have not been given due recognition, *see* R. Dhavan (*supra* note 149), and "Freedom of the Press" in *Leelakrishnan* and *Sadasivan Nair*, eds. (*supra* note 155) 1-32.

239. In all this, Justice Gajendragadkar emerges as a somewhat enigmatic character, respected for his judicial independence and statesmanship and capacity for jurisprudence, yet as someone translucently giving broad leeway to the demands of Nehru's Socialism. In one sense he was the ideal, independent-thinking, regime judge.

240. Gajendragadkar's sociological jurisprudence (*supra* notes 227-33 and 239) did not create but influenced the demand for a regime jurisprudence from "committed" judges. This led to a controversy about the kind of judges who could be trusted with the office of the Chief Justice of India; *see* M. Kumaramangalam, *Judicial Appointments*, Delhi, 1973; V.A. Seyid Muhammad, *The Constitution: For Haves and Have Nots*, Delhi, 1973; A.R. Antulay, *Appointment of a Chief Justice*, Bombay, 1973; N.A. Palkhivala, *A Judiciary Made to Measure*, Bombay, 1973; K. Nayar, ed., *Supersession of Judges*, Delhi, 1973; K.S. Hegde, *Crisis in the Judiciary*, Delhi, 1973. For Nehru's views on the judiciary, see A. Jacobi, "Nehru and the Judiciary" (1977), 19 *J.I.L.I.* 169-81. Mrs. Gandhi claimed to have confidence in all but a few political judges (*see* (1976) *R.S.D.* 216-7) but seemed deeply distrustful of the institution of the judiciary even before her famous election case (*supra* notes 58-59).

241. *Supra* 219.

242. Govind Das (*supra* note 133) 139.

243. *E. Royappa v. State of Tamil Nadu, A.I.R. 1974 S.C. 555; Maneka Gandhi* (*supra* note 54); *R.D. Shetty* (*supra* note 56); *Ajay Hasia v. Khalid Mujib, A.I.R. 1981 S.C. 487*. While these cases have imported a new vigor (*Seervai, supra* note 70,272-9), India has still to develop a full-fledged administrative and criminal due process.

244. *Infra* notes 246-8.

245. *Supra* notes 126-7.

246. See *Hussainana Khatoon* (*supra* note 54); *Veena Sethi* (*supra* note 73).

247. *Rudul Shah, Sebastian M. Hongray, Bhim Singh* and *People's Union of Democratic Rights* (*supra* note 130); *cf. Sampat Lal* (*supra* note 73).

248. *Hussainana Khatoon* (*supra* note 54); *Ahmad Hussain Khan v. State of A.P., A.I.R. 1984 S.C. 1855*.

249. *Bandhua Mukti Morcha* (*supra* note 54); *Mukesh Advani* (*supra* note 73); *Neerja Chowdhry v. State of M.P., A.I.R. 1984 S.C. 1099*.

250. *Sanjit Roy, People's Union of Democratic Rights: Ram Kumar Mishra* (*supra* note 73); also in *Re: Matter of P.R.E. of Wages of Prisoners, A.I.R. 1983 Kerala 261*.

251. *Azad Rickshaw Pullers' Union v. State of Punjab, A.I.R. 1981 S.C. 14*.

252. *FCI Workers Union v. F.C.I., A.I.R. 1985 S.C. 488* (contract workers); *B.H.E.L. Workers' Association v. Union of India, A.I.R. 1985 S.C. 652* (contract workers); *Labourers Working on Salal Project v. State of J.K., A.I.R. 1984 S.C. 177*. For

decisions gradually to expand the rights of labor, even to participate in winding up petitions, see *D.C. & C.M. Co. Ltd. v. Union of India, A.I.R. 1983 S.C.* 937.
For important decisions on equal pay for equal work, see *Randhir Singh v. Union of India, A.I.R. 1982 S.C.* 879. But the Court seems to be backing off from its earlier more interventionist stance.

Public interest litigation has extended from environmental issues (*see Rural Litigation and Entitlement Kendra, supra* note 73; *M.C. Mehat (I) v. Union of India* 1986), 2 *S.C.C.* 176; *M.C. Mehta (II) v. Union of India* (1986), 2 *S.C.C.* 325) to a host of other matters concerning public amenities (*Janki v. Sardar Nagar Municipality, A.I.R. 1986 Bombay* 186), land rights of adhivasis (*Banwasi Sewa Ashram, supra* note 73). Its limits have not been delineated carefully.

253. This has been developed in two distinct ways. Before the Emergency (1975-77), it was part of the government's repertoire against the courts (*supra* note 240). Since the Emergency, it has developed by Justices Krishna Iyer, Bhagwati and D.A. Desari as a rigorous tool to define constitutional objectives and devise a new tradition in constitutional interpretation (*supra* note 74).

254. This is an assumption which calls for further research (*supra* note 199).

255. For the reception of these provisions by the legal community, *see* R. Dhavan (*supra* note 48) 6-19, summarizing and commenting on the literature.

256. E.g., M. Hidayatullah, *Democracy and Judicial Process in India*, Delhi, 1968; P.B. Gajendragadkar, *Law, Liberty and Social Justice* (*supra* note 58).

257. The importance of personal liberty is mentioned in most decisions on preventive detention since *Gopalan* (*supra* note 37). Their importance is recognized by the majority even in the famous Emergency detention case (*A.D.M. Jabalpur v. S. Shukla, A.I.R. 1976 S.C.* 1207 (e.g., Beg J. at pr. 200 at 1293, and especially prs. 350-73, at 1309-14 citing earlier case law; Bhagwati J. at pr. 526-33, at 1364-8).

258. Khanna J. in *A.D.M. Jabalpur* (*supra* note 257), especially pr. 130, at 1242 (on freedom), pr. 150-1, at 1252-3 (on due process), pr. 154-6, at 1254-6 (on personal liberty); *cf.* Beg J. at pr. 276, at 1290-2.

259. *See* Kharak Singh (*supra* note 225); *Govind v. State of M.P.* (1975), 2 *S.C.R.* 946; *Maneka Gandhi* (*supra* note 54). There has also been an expansion of the meaning of "life" in Article 21 (*Olga Tellis v. Bombay Municipal Corporation* (1985), 3 *S.C.C.* 545.

260. *Express Newspapers Ltd. v. Union of India, A.I.R. 1958 S.C.* 578.

261. *Sakal Newspapers* (*supra* note 236).

262. *Bennett Coleman* (*supra* note 237).

263. *Prabha Dutt* (*supra* note 127); *Sheela Barse's* case, *Times of India*, 18 September 1987.

264. Pendse, J. in *Bennett Coleman v. Union of India, A.I.R. 1986 Bombay* 321.

265. Justice Vekantaramiah in *I.E. Newspapers* (*supra* note 237). He has also elaborated his views in a pamphlet, "A Free and Balanced Press", New Delhi, TRF Institute, 1986) 9-40; *see Express Newspapers Pvt. Ltd. v. Union of India, A.I.R. 1986 S.C.* 908.

266. *See* R. Dhavan, "Freedom of the Press" (*supra* note 238), and *Only the Good News* (*supra* note 149).

267. *Supra* note 130.

268. *Express Newspapers* (*supra* note 265). Such harassment continues as, for example, when the *Indian Express'* offices were raided in August, 1987 in the aftermath of the newspaper's revelations of high level involvement in the corruption in the Bofors deals.

269. *See Golak Nath* (*supra* note 53) and *Keshavananda* (*supra* note 2); and R. Dhavan (*supra* note 58), Chapters 3 and 5.

270. The basic structure doctrine appears to have been developed only to restrain constitutional amendments from ousting judicial review. This limited functional use--to counteract ouster clauses--has not been transcended to effectuate a more incisive constitutional jurisprudence about the teleological goals of the Constitution, the principles of its functioning, interpretative approaches or the principles of justice which form objectives and inform decision-making. Because its more imaginative use poses both intellectual and political problems, the "basic structure" doctrine has reinforced rather than supplanted political constitutionalism.

271. For an optimistic view of the rise of the written Constitution, see U. Baxi (*supra* note 145). No doubt the Constitution will begin to structure discussion about public affairs and play some role in influencing decision-making. Yet its place in the life of the nation is indeterminate, as the pathology of its use often ignores its presence. *Cf.* Hart and Morris-Jones (*supra* note 157).

On the enormity of this problem, see S.S. Dhavan, *What are the Princely States?* Allahabad, 1939. The problems of absorbing these States in India can be seen from V.P. Menon, *The Transfer of Power in India*, Calcutta, 1957, and *Story of the Integration of the Indian States*, Bombay, 1956. For a sketch, see *Madhav Rao Scindhia v. Union of India, A.I.R. 1971 S.C.* 530 (on the constitutionality and implications of the Constitution (Twenty-Sixth Amendment) Act, 1971 taking away the Privy Purses of the erstwhile princely rulers).

273. *See* Constitution (Seventh Amendment) Act, 1956.

274. Articles 239-43 of the Constitution.

275. Articles 254 and 255 of the Constitution.

276. Articles 249, 250 and 252 of the Constitution.

277. Articles 256-63 of the Constitution, especially Articles 256-60.

278. Articles 265-290A, 293 of the Constitution.

279. Article 356 of the Constitution.

280. Article 3 of the Constitution. For a somewhat lax interpretation of the procedural requirements, see *B. Cabulal v. State of Bombay, A.I.R. 1960 S.C.* 51; *Mangal Singh v. State of Punjab, A.I.R. 1967 S.C.* 944.

281. Seervai (*supra* note 70) 146-64; *cf.* K.C. Wheare, *Federal Government*, London, 1963, 27, calling it quasi-federal; P.K. Tripathi, "Federalism--the Reality and the Myth" (1974), 3 *J.C.B.I.* 251-77, and the note in rejoinder by A. Prasad, "Nature of Indian Polity--A Rejoinder" (1977), 6 *J.C.B.I.* 68. The Supreme Court also appears

to have entered into the controversy in *State of West Bengal v. Union of India, A.I.R. 1963 S.C.* 1241; *State of Karnataka v. Union of India, A.I.R. 1978 S.C.* 68. The real test is not the imbalance in the distribution of power but the existence of viable and relatively invulnerable geographic units.

282. This means that the States are vulnerable in respect of their territorial integrity; *see* R. Dhavan, "Is India a Federal State?" (1966), 1 *Allahabad University Law Journal* 62-7.

283. Consideration to these matters was prioritized fairly early (*see* B.R. Ambedkar, *States and Minorities: What are Their Rights and How to Secure Them in the Constitution of Free India?* Delhi, 1955. Linguistic States are a *fait accompli*, even though questions about language as a medium of instruction and controversies about the national language are not resolved.

284. There is vast literature on Indian federalism. Some concerns the political relationship between the Centre and the State (*supra* notes 152-3), some with financial aspects (*infra* note 306). The States have expressed their concern (*infra* note 286) and the Centre is examining the problem (*see* the Administrative Reforms Commission's *Report on Centre-State Relations* (Delhi, 1969) and the *Report of the Commission on Centre-State Relations*, Delhi, 1988 (Chairperson R.S. Sarkaria) is awaited. For general anthologies evaluating India's experience, see S. N. Jain *et al.*, eds., *The Union and the States*, Delhi, 1972; R. Dhavan and A. Jacob, eds., *The Indian Constitution* (*supra* note 21) 357-87; A. Prashad, *Centre-State Powers Under Indian Federalism*, Delhi, 1981; K.M. Kurian and P.N. Verghese, *Centre-State Relations*, Delhi, 1981. What has eluded India is a cooperative federalism in which the Centre is tolerant to the existence of opposition ministries in the States, and to the development of fair institutional mechanisms to resolve problems of administrative cooperation and resource transfers and distribution.

285. *Supra* note 90.

286. The Opposition's demands are reflected in the Rajmannar Report and the West Bengal Memorandum (*supra* note 155). More recently (1985-7), various States submitted responses and proposals to the Sarkaria Commission (*supra* note 284).

287. For a range of problems arising from the existence of ethnic and other identities in various countries, see J. Stone, *Racial Conflict in Contemporary Society*, London, 1985, and material cited there.

288. It is precisely because the partition of nations since 1945 has been badly done that problems of self-determination have erupted in military confict in Asia, Africa, the Middle East, Ireland and America. Equally, fresh problems have arisen about the rights of tribals and aboriginals in a more fundamental way than the simple demand for fairness and non-discrimination. Federalism and decentralization remain important possible solutions unless the map of the world is to be continually redrawn to accommodate opportunism and justice.

289. It is a moot question whether the Governor holds office during the pleasure of the President (Article 156(1)) or can do so for the prescribed term of five years (Article 156(3)). Sri Bhagwan Sahay, who chaired the *Report of the Committee of*

Governors, Delhi, 1972, told me that he regretted not making a positive recommendation about security of tenure for Governors, who had lost a sense of identity with the State they were supposed to serve and had become functionaries of the government at the Centre.

290. Article 163 of the Constitution enjoins the Council of Ministers to advise the Governor. This advice is binding except in certain matters (*see Shamsher Singh*, *supra* note 154). Real problems have arisen about the Governor swearing in Chief Ministers with no absolute majorities (*see* R. Dhavan, *supra* note 153). Governors have also been privy to promulgating ordinances and timing matters so that they have usurped the function of the legislatures (*see D.C. Wadhwa v. Union of India*, *A.I.R. 1987 S.C.* 579--a petition based on D.C. Wadhwa's *Re-Promulgation of Ordinances: A Fraud on the Constitution of India*, Puna, 1983.

291. Article 200 of the Constitution: *see* A. Jacob, "Presidential Assent to State Bills--A Case Study" (1970), 12 *J.I.L.I.* 151-9; J.R. Siwach, *The Office of the Governor*, Delhi, 1978, 221-53.

292. The crisis began when Governor Dharam Vira sacked his Chief Minister because the latter refused to call the Assembly three weeks earlier than when the Governor wanted him to (*see Mahabir v. Prafulla Chandra, A.I.R. 1968 Calcutta* 198).

293. On the Sampuranand proclamation, see (1967) *L.S.D.* cols. 109, 130-238 (18 March 1967); (1967) *R.S.D.* cols. 1937-2020 (3 April 1967); 2107-2120 (4 April 1967). The proclamation in Uttar Pradesh was also transparently political because it was revoked within 18 days (without a parliamentary discussion) to allow for a new Ministry to be formed.

294. On the death of the popular Chief Minister M.G. Ramachandran, there was a competition for the leadership of the party in power. Governor Khurana did not allow the party in power to select its own leader. He acted as the *de facto* Returning Office of a crisis and imposed President's rule (*see India Today*, 31 January 1988).

295. *See generally* R. Dhavan (*supra* note 153).

296. President's rule was imposed in Kerala because of internal disturbance (*see K.A. Aboo v. Union of India, A.I.R. 1965 Kerala* 229 on such impositions); note the debates (1959), *L.S.D.*, cols. 2814-2926 (17 August 1959); 3046-3206 (19 August 1959); 3327-3424 (20 August 1959); (1959) *R.S.D.* cols. 1542-1698 (24 August 1959); 1759-1861 (25 August 1959).

297. *State of Rajasthan v. Union of India, A.I.R. 1977 S.C.* 1631; *see* R. Dhavan and A. Jacob, "The Dissolution Case--Politics at the Bar of the Supreme Court" (1977), 19 *J.I.L.I.* 257-82.

298. On 17 February 1980, Mrs. Gandhi, having returned to power, dissolved the Ministries of various State legislatures and imposed President's rule. This was for the same reason as the Janata dissolutions in 1977; namely, that a massive victory at the polls by a party in power in Delhi meant that opposition parties in power in various States had lost the confidence of the electorate, whose support they must win again in a general election. For the debates, see (1980) *L.S.D.* cols. 196-306 (25 March 1980); 321-410 (26 March 1980); (1980) *R.S.D.* cols. 196-392 (27 March 1980).

299. S.P. Gupta (*supra* note 65). Note the earlier decision in S.H. Seth (*supra* note 62). This latter 3:2 verdict gave validity to the transfer of judges during the Emergency (1975-77) and opened up the possibility for the further manipulation of the judiciary, see the acerbic but incisive views of Seervai (*supra* note 70) 2265-2454; J.B.C.I., *Special Number on the Higher Judiciary* (1982) 9(2) *J.B.C.I.* 203-451, especially N.A. Palkhivala (203-17); S. Sahay (218-31), U. Baxi (231-40); S. Khurshid (344-55).
300. For the unsuccessful challenge to these transfers during the Emergency (1975-77), *supra* note 62. There were 16 transfers made while an intimidating list of 56 proposed transfers posed as pressure and threat (*see* Seervai, *supra* note 70) 2265-6.
301. The post-Emergency policy was upheld in S.P. Gupta (*supra* note 65). The circular in question is quoted in full by Seervai (*supra* note 70) 2275; *see also* (1981) *L.S.D.* 221-79, 16 April 1981). The policy has been badly and inconsistently interpreted in the compulsory transfer of Chief Justices.
302. Note Bhagwati's dissent in S.H. Sheth (*supra* note 62), which he sustained in S.P. Gupta (*supra* note 65).
303. Articles 268-79 of the Constitution.
304. Articles 280-1 of the Constitution.
305. *See generally* S.P. Marathe, *Regulation and Development: India's Policy Experience of Controls over Industry* Delhi, 1986.
306. P. Diwan, *Union-States Fiscal Relations*, Delhi, 1981, 144; H. Patel, "Growing Indebtedness of States: A Case Against Statutory Debt Limit on State's Debt" (1977), 11 *J.C.P.S.* 70-85; D.T. Lakadwala, "Eight Finance Commission Recommendations" (1984), 19 *E.P.W.* 1529-24. Onb problems of finance, *see also* D.D. Panigrah, *Centre-State Financial Relations in India*, Delhi, 1985.
307. *See* M. Loughlin, *Local Government in the Modern State*, London, 1986, analyzing some of the restraints Mrs. Thatcher's government has imposed on local authorities.
308. Articles 38-9, 40-3, 45-8 of the Constitution.
309. Article 49 of the Constitution.
310. Article 50 of the Constitution. Note the plea for a uniform civil code in Article 44.
31.. Article 51 of the Constitution.
312. The Constitution (Forty-Second Amendment) Act, 1976 added Articles 39A (legal aid), 43A (participation of workers), 48A (protection of environment), and 51A (providing for Fundamental Duties).
313. Article 37 of the Constitution.
314. *State of Madras v. Champakam Doraijan, A.I.R. 1951 S.C.* 226; and *supra* notes 68-9.
315. *Kesavananda, supra* note 2 and R. Dhavan, *supra* note 58; on the Supreme Court and what was expected of it, *see supra* note 240.
316. S.S. Dhavan J. in *Balwant Raj* (*supra* note 69).
317. *Kesavanandan, supra* note 2.
318. *Supra* notes 68-70.

319. Constitution (First Amendment) Act, 1951 and Constitution (Fourth Amendment) Act, 1954; and R. Dhavan (*supra* note 58), Chapters 2 and 3.

320. The Constitution (Twenty-Fourth Amendment) Act, 1971; Constitution (Twenty-Fifth Amendment) Act, 1971; R. Dhavan (*supra* note 58), Chapter 3.

321. Constitution (Forty-Second Amendment) Act, 1976.

322. See *Shankari Prashad* (*supra* note 52); *cf. Golak Nath* (*supra* note 53).

323. *Kesavanandan* (*supra* note 2).

324. See *Minerva Mills* and other cases (*supra* note 70).

325. Bhagwati J. correctly refused to distinguish between two classes of Directive Principles on the basis that one class was a preferred objective; Seervai (*supra* note 70) 1623, seems to have missed the point.

326. *Sanjeev Coke* (*supra* note 70).

327. *Supra* note 58.

328. See *N.M. Thomas* (*supra* note 166), *Vasanth* (*supra* note 166); and note the warnings of the consequences of an over-generous positive discrimination policy in *Akhil Bharati Soshit Karmchari v. Union of India, A.I.R. 1981 S.C.* 298.

329. On the growth of the public interest law movement, see R. Dhavan, *Public Interest Litigation in India: An Investigative Report*, Delhi, 1981; *Report for the Committee for the Implementation of Legal Aid Schemes* (CILAS). The early literature is collected in R. Dhavan, ed., *Public Interest Litigation: Some Introductory Readings*, Delhi, CILAS, mimeo, 1982. The initial flush of Supreme Court cases have been examined by U. Baxi (*supra* note 73) 289-315. The subsequent case law can be found in Massey (*supra* note 56) 273-310; A. Prakash, "Public Interest Litigation" (1984) *A.S.I.L.* 324-332; P. Singh, "Public Interest Litigation" (1985) *A.S.I.L.* 160; "Public Interest Litigation" (1986) *A.S.I.L.* 483.

A critical response is a document in a series of articles by P. Singh, "Access to Justice: Public Interest Litigation and the Supreme Court of India" (1981-82) 10-11 *Delhi Law Review* 156, "Vindicating Public Interest Through the Judicial Process: Trends and Issues" (1983), 10 *Indian B.R.* 228; "Thinking About the Judicial Vindication of the Public Interest" (1985), *S.C.C. Jn. 11*; "Bandhua *Mukhti Morcha*: Social Action and the Indian Supreme Court" (1985), 12 *Indian B.R.* 228; and "Judicial Socialism and Promise of Liberation: Myth and Truth" (1986), 28 *J.I.L.I.* 336.

For the reaction of judges, see P.N. Bhagwati, *Judicial Activism and Public Interest Litigation*, Dharwar, 1985, and *Social Action Litigation: The Indian Experience*, Colombo, I.C.E.S., 1985, mimeo; and also *supra* note 58; O. Chineppa Ceddy, "Socialism, Constitutionalism and Legal Aid Movements in India," *A.I.R. 1986 Journal* 1-8; G.M. Lodha, "Home Delivery System of Justice," *A.I.R. 1983 Journal* 73-9.

Activists and lawyers have responded to the movement with enthusiasm; *see* I. Jaisingh, "Evaluating Social Action Litigation" (1986), 1 *Lawyer* 2 and "Social Engineering through SAL" (1986), 1 *Lawyer* 4-7; G. Mukhoty, "Public Interest Litigation: A Silent Revolution?" (1985), 1 *S.C.C. Journal* 1-11. Criticial evaluations appear in journal literature; *see* A.G. Noorani, "Public Interest Litigation" (1984),

E.P.W. 1568; N. Gupta, "Public Interest Litigation" (1984), *K.L.T. Jnl.* 23-7; M.K. Prasad, "Public Interest Litigation: A New Horizon," *A.I.R. 1984 Journal* 1-4; S. Patel, "Contract Labour and PIL," *E.P.W.* 2153; (1983) Comment "Jail Now--Trial Later" (1983), 2 *S.C.D. Jnl.* 42-4; P. Leelakrishnan, "Access to Legal Service and Justice" (1984), *C.U.L.R.* 473-83; N.R. Madhava Menon, "Public Interest Litigation: A Major Breakthrough in Our Delivery of Social Justice" (1982), 9 *J.B.C.I.I.* 150-65; Editorial (1984-5) 89 *C.W.N.* 125-8, 148-52; N. Rajgopalan, "Constitutional Issues in Public Interest Litigation in India" (1984), 8 *C.U.L.R.* 16-22; M. Krishnan Nair, "Public Interest Litigation" (1984), 8 *C.U.L.R.* 484-92; K.N. Chandrasekharan Pillai, "Role of Teachers and Students of Law in Public Interest LItigation" (1984), 8 *C.U.L.R.* 503-7; Comment, "Public Interest Law in India" (1984), 21 *L.Q.* 1-6; Y.R. Reddy and Y.P. Reddy, "Personal Liberty and Public Interest LItigation--A Perspective" (1986), *S.C.J. Jnl.* 13-20; D.C. Jain, "The phantom of public interest" (1986), 3 *S.C.C. Jnl.* 30-7, and *A.I.R. 1986 Journal* 85; M. Krishna Prashad, "Public Interest Litigation: A New Horizon," *A.I.R. 1986 Journal* 1; A.K. Dixit, "Public Interest Law and Legal Aid" (1986), 2 *Kan. L.J.* 50-5; K. Adhakrishnan, "Public Interest Litigation and Bonded Labour" (1986), *Andh. L.T.* 8-12; R. Dhavan (*supra* note 67).

330. S.P. Gupta V. Union of India, *supra* note 65. On epistolary jurisdiction and the extent of its use, *see supra* note 73. Wide rules of *locus standi* were developed by Krishna Iyer, J. in *Fertiliser Corporation Kamgar Union v. Union of India, A.I.R. 1981 S.C.* 344, and settled in S.P. Gupta (*supra* note 65); *see* A. Shourie, "Why the Hon'ble Could Should Hear Us" (1981), 4 *S.C.C. jnl.* 1-30; M.N. Chaturvedi, "Liberalising the Requirement of Standing in Public Interest Litigation" (1984), 26 *J.I.L.I.* 42-54; S.P. Sathe, "Public Participation in the Judicial Process: New Trends in Law of *Locus Standi* with Particular References to Administrative Law" (1984), 26 *J.I.L.I.* 1-12.

331. The idea of Commissions of Inquiry by courts can be seen in a number of cases; *see Bandhua Mukti Morcha* (*supra* note 73); *Baxi v. State of U.P.* (1986), 4 *S.C.C.* 106; *Mukesh Advani Rural Litigation and Entitlement Kendra, Salal Hydroelectric Ram Kumar Mishra, Banwasi Sewa Ashram* (*supra* note 73). The status of the findings of these Commissions of Inquiry raises important questions about the delegation of judicial power and due process generally. *Bandhua Mukti Morcha* (*supra* note 73) does not really resolve these issues satisfactorily.

332. *Azad Rickshaw Pullers* (*supra* note 251); *Shiv Shankar Daval Mills v. State of Haryana, A.I.R. 1980 S.C.* 1037; *Indermal Jain v. Union of India, A.I.R. 1984 S.C.* 415; "Kamani Tubes Case," *Times of India,* 29 January 1988.

333. *See* cases cited, *supra* notes 249-52.

334. *Centre for Legal Research v. State of Kerala, A.I.R. 1986 S.C.* 2195.

335. *Bijoe Emmanuel* (*supra* note 171).

336. *See* R. Dhavan (*supra* note 67). For an incomplete but interesting explanation, *see* U. Baxi, *The Supreme Court and Politics,* Lucknow, 1980.

337. For a preliminary exploration, see R. Dhavan (*supra* n. 67).

338. R. Dhavan, "For Whom? And for What?" (Paper for an International Conference for Social Action Groups, Ahmedabad, 1981. These problems will, no doubt, surface as such litigation moves on from assisting identifiable beneficiaries to servicing the wider public interest (e.g., in consumer or environmental matters or regarding procedural fairness). Note, *Bihar Legal Support Society v. Chief Justice of India* (1986), 4 *S.C.C.* 767, asked the Supreme Court to be clear in its mind about whom it wishes to service in matters of public interest law.

339. At present, a great deal depends not just on the capacity of the courts to deal with such matters, but also on the extent to which social activists can build a legal capability from public funds, relatively independent of the prohibitively expensive private market economy of lawyering. *See* R. Dhavan, *Public Interest Litigation* ... (1981), (*supra* note 329). Two further important dimensions: the courts could become primary institutions of complaint, accountability and relief; and, it would create another layer of power brokers. Both these developments could have important implications for Indian democracy.

340. More research is needed on the class and group nature of the movement. This will reveal a great deal more about its real relationship with activism, its capacity for self sustenance, its salience as a distinct social process, and whether it is essentially parasitic in nature or not; see R. Dhavan, "Where Will the Next One Come From--Reflections on India's Legal Aid Programme" (Paper to South Asia Seminar, Austin, Texas, 1985.

341. Baxi's insistence on calling it "social action litigation" (*supra* note 73) assumes a strong and integrated relationship between activists--no less lawyers than any other. For a typology of varieties of social activism, see R. Dhavan and M. Partington, "Co-optation or Independent Strategy, "The Role of Social Action Groups" in J. Cooper and R. Dhavan, eds., *Public Interest Law*, Oxford, 1986, 235-60.

342. Apart from Pathak J's judgments in *Bandhua Mukti Morcha* and *Umedram* (*supra* note 73) on the limits of public interest law, there is concern that such litigation may seek to circumvent normal legal and administrative processes (*Sampat Lal, supra* note 73). The overall anxiety of the Court can be seen from a list of questions referred to a Constitution Bench in *Sudipto Muzumdar* (1983), 2 *S.C.C.* 258 which do not ever appear to have been answered.

343. S.K. Agarwala, *Public Interest Litigation in India,* Bombay, 1985; D.C. Jain (*supra* note 329).

344. A comment made by C. Alvarez, "Marginal Men" (1983), VIII *Book Review* (No. 3) 143-6.

345. *Supra* note 331.

346. S.K. Agarwala (*supra* notes 320 and 343). The judges are aware of the problems in this area.

347. This is one inescapable conclusion to be drawn from the institutionalization of public interest law; *see* Dhavan, *Public Interest Law* (1981), *supra* note 329 and M. Galanter, "New Patterns of Legal Services in India" in his *Law and Society in India*, Delhi, 1990 with a critical introduction by R. Dhavan.

348. A phrase adapted from N. Palkhivala (*supra* note 240).

349. The *groundnorm* doctrine is not free from politics, as was discovered by Pakistani judges in *State v. Dosso, P.L.D. 1958 S.C.* 533, and more acutely in *Asma Jilani v. Government of Punjab, P.L.D. 1972 S.C.* 139 (*see* T.K.K. Iyer, "Constitutional Law in Pakistan", 21 *A.J.C.L.* (1973) 759). For the antics of African courts, see *Laknami v. Western State* (1970), note 20 *I.C.L.Q.* 177); *Sallah v. Attorney General* (1970, note 20 *I.C.L.Q.* 315). The *cause celebre*, following the declaration of independence by Ian Smith in Rhodesia, was *Madzimbamuto v. Larner Burke* (1969) *A.C.* 645. The literature on this case is critically evaluated in J.W. Harris, "When and Why Does the Groundnorm Change?" (1971), *C.I.J.* 103, who takes the ingenious view that the groundnorm is an analytical tool in the hands of jurists rather than judges and political actors who must make evaluative decisions.

350. On its actual use and potential, *see supra* notes 70 and 270.

351. For a symposium on the subject, *see Perspectives on the Authoritativeness of Supreme Court Decisions* (1987), *Tulane L. Rev.* 977-1098, especially contributions from Edwin Meese, III (179-90), M. Tushnet (1917-26), S. Levinson (1071-8), John Stick (1979-92).

352. *See generally* R. Lingat, *Classical Law of India*, California, 1979.

353. These comments should not be taken to equate the indeterminacy of questions of substantive justice with the impossibility of their resolution. India's rulers and rules cannot assume legitimacy for what they do unless they can tackle these questions as an act of necessity. Apart from these pragmatic considerations, constitutional lists must also ponder over these questions as an act of faith.

354. Many queries need to be resolved here. Mrs. Gandhi sought legitimacy precisely on the grounds that the "greatest good of the largest number" required "socialism", a twenty-point program to eliminate povery, reduce social and economic differentials, and provide a streamlined administration unhampered by legal niceties by which lawyers invoked judicial review. These instruments of legitimacy were rejected for the rule of law, press freedom, judicial review, democracy, and a controlled interference with the rights and privacies of the individual even in a country where the major problem is to achieve social and economic equality lest the people rise against the inequity of difference. A great deal of research needs to be done on how and why certain instruments of legitimacy were so decisively invoked during, and in the aftermath of, the Emergency (1975-1977).

355. Thus, many major programs relating to compensatory discrimination, relaxation of official secrecy, media liberalization, and anti-corruption measures lie fallow. This article was written in 1988.

356. J.D.M. Derrett, "A Post-Weberian Approach to Indian Social Organisation and the Reform of Law in Present-Day India" in O. Botto, ed., *Max Weber L' India*, Torino, 1986, at 91.

357. *Supra* note 123.

358. To this extent, public interest law as a movement is potential, though party politics has not caught up with it as yet. At present, it is a maturing response to the

embarrassment felt by the middle class when faced with the absurd levels of degradations of the weak and the equally absurd high handedness of those in power.

359. R. Dhavan, *supra* note 6.

360. This point is made in order to try and understand the demand for rationality rather than evaluate the remedial steps that would be taken to create a "rational" society. In a sense, any emotive use of language can create an a-contexual false consciousness. As Milan Kundera puts it in his *Unbearable Lightness of Being*, London, 1984, 11, "[M]etaphors are not to be trifled with. A single metaphor can give birth to love."

REPUBLIC OF INDONESIA

*Democracy in Indonesia: Pancasila Democracy**

Padmo Wahjono

Indonesia's Constitutions and Democracy

On August 18, 1945, one day after the Republic of Indonesia proclaimed its independence, the Indonesian Constitution[1] was ratified and *Pancasila*,[2] given expression in the Preamble to the Constitution, was established as the nation's guiding philosophy. Two committees worked on the document: the *Badan Penyelidik Usaha Persiapan Kermerdekaan Indonesia* (Investigatory Committee for the Preparation of Indonesian Independence), and the *Panitia Persiapan Kemerdekaan Indonesia* (Committee for the Preparation of Indonesian Independence), or PPKI.[3] The Investigatory Committee drafted the initial version of the Constitution and the PPKI put the document into final form and ratified it. In these two committees then, "the founding fathers"[4] composed the Constitution, thereby establishing the basis for democracy in Indonesia.

Nearly all of the composers of the Constitution had been educated in Western Europe, or had attended schools which were based on the Dutch version of the Western European educational system. Accordingly, when constructing the theoretical foundation for the Indonesian state, their point of departure was the body of theory which had developed in Western Europe up to that time. These Western theories were then adapted to the Indonesian context in order that they be in line with the fundamental convictions of the Indonesian people.

The first line of the Preamble to the Constitution reads as if the composers were in strict agreement with "the Super Powers" as the end of World War II approached:

"Whereas independence is the right of every nation ..."[5] Despite this receptability to Western ideas however, the composers of the Constitution did not blindly follow Western theory, but first studied the shortcomings arising from the application of the theory in Europe and elsewhere. They then tried to find a way around the shortcomings, seeking a more appropriate formulation based on the fundamental convictions of the Indonesian people: this was found in *Pancasila*. Accordingly, democracy in Indonesia is based on *Pancasila* and is called *Pancasila* democracy.

The first step following the establishment of *Pancasila* as the state's guiding philosophy in the Preamble to the Constitution was the elaboration of the main points contained in that Preamble. There were four essential points:

. Indonesia should be a unified state;
. the state should strive for social justice;
. the state should be based on the Sovereignty of the People; and
. the state should be based on Belief in the One Supreme God
according to a just and civilized humanitarianism.[6]

As reflected in number 1 above, unity was a central concern of the composers of the Constitution. In developing a working definition of "unified state," they examined the three existing streams of thought concerning statehood:

a) The perspective based on the theory of individualism, like that taught by Thomas Hobbes and John Locke (17th century), Jean Jacques Rousseau (18th century), Herbert Spencer (19th century), and H.J. Laski (20th century).

b) The perspective based on the theory of class conflict, like that taught by Marx, Engels, and Lenin.

c) The perspective based on the theory of integralism, like that taught by Spinoza, Adam Muller, and Hegel (18th and 19th centuries).

The integralist approach was felt to be most appropriate to the Indonesian context. According to this theory, the state should be an integral arrangement of the society, where every region, every group, and every member of society is interrelated with all of the others in an organic whole.[7]

The overall well-being of the people is the highest priority of a state founded on the integralist way of thinking. The integralist state does not side with the strongest or most numerous group, does not consider one individual as its center, but, rather, is a state which guarantees well-being for all its people in one indivisible whole.

In Western Europe, however, this organic theory had been used to support a totalitarian nationalism (i.e., in Germany, *"ein totaler Fuhrerstaat"*), and so the composers of the Constitution modified the theory, producing an Indonesian adaptation based on the principle of family-togetherness (*gotong royong*[8]).

Indonesian integralism thus provides a foundation for the state which is different from and, in fact, established in opposition to foundations based on individualism or totalitarianism.[9] In the Unified State (*Negara Persatuan*), the interests of the state are above any group or individual interest, but all individuals and all groups are encompassed and protected by the state. Indonesia seeks the unity of all its people in a single integrated whole.[10]

Another of the essential points from the Preamble which is particularly relevant to the formation of the Indonesian state is number 4 above: "The state is based upon Belief in the One Supreme God according to a just and civilized humanitarianism." This principle was formulated more forcefully in Article 29, Paragraph 1 of the Constitution:

The State is based upon Belief in the One Supreme God. This principle expresses the religiosity of the Indonesian people,[11] a religiosity which was to become the first of *Pancasila's* five principles. Accordingly, the state which is based on *Pancasila* cannot conceivably be a secular state.

On the other hand, the composers of the Constitution emphasized that the Republic of Indonesia was not to be a "religious state." A religious state, as the term is generally understood, implies that both the leadership as well as the prevailing body of law of such a state are based on a single religion: that is not the case in Indonesia.

Chapter XXIX, Article 2 of the Constitution reads: "The state guarantees the freedom of every inhabitant to embrace their own religion and to worship according to their own religion and beliefs."

This formulation clearly indicates that the state as defined by the Indonesian people does not give precedence to one religion, enabling that religion to become the basis for the state, but, equally clearly, it indicates that the state is not to be characterized as secular. The state must guarantee the freedom of every inhabitant (and not only every citizen) to embrace their own religion and to worship according to their own religion.[12] Indonesian integralism based on family-togetherness thus does away with the secular-state-versus-religious-state dilemma.

The Indonesian perspective on statehood, as detailed in the Preamble to the Constitution, is thus based on unity and religiosity, not on individualism. In the latter, the basis for the state is the abstract concept of a "social contract" (*vertraq*) among free individuals, a mutual agreement between those in power and those who submit to power, between those who give orders and those who follow orders. In the Indonesian conception, what is given priority is the common goal (*Gesammtakte*), based on "Belief in the One Supreme God." The state according to the Indonesian people is established: "with the blessing of God Almighty and [is] impelled by the noble ideal of a free national life."[13] Furthermore, a people is said to form a state if they meet the following qualifications: "free, unified, sovereign, just, and prosperous."[14]

With this background understanding of how the Indonesian people conceive of statehood, our analysis of democracy in Indonesia, a large portion of which will concern the organization and operation of the government, will proceed as follows:

In the first section, I will discuss the theoretical-constitutional foundation of *Pancasila* democracy. This foundation will be subdivided into ten sections:

The organizational structure of the state;
The highest organ of state authority;
The institution for the representation of the people;
The presidency (the mandatary system[15]);
human rights;
The legal basis for the state;
The constitutional basis for government;
The institutional organs of the state and their interrelations;
The goals of democracy in Indonesia; and
The "safeguarding"[16] of *Pancasila* democracy.

These ten aspects of the constitutional foundation of government will be called the "mechanism for *Pancasila* democracy."

In part 2, the exercise of democracy in Indonesia will be analyzed from its beginnings in the early history of Indonesia up to the establishment of the five-year government cycles (the government calendar).[17] Section A will consider the following:

The formation of the highest organ of state authority (the institution for representation) the determination of the guidelines for state policy;
The election of the president as mandatary of the representatives of the people;
The formation of the government; and
The formation of the other organs of state.

These five elements of the exercise of *Pancasila* Democracy can be called "the formation of a dynamic yet stable government."

Section B of that section will consider the remaining aspects of the government calendar:

The composition of legal statutes;

The determination of a budget for national income and expenditure;
The supervision of the course of government;
The annual report of the president; and
The president's end-of-term accounting.

These five elements of the exercise of *Pancasila* Democracy will be called "the effort to organize state operations on the basis of coordination, harmony, and balance, reflecting family-togetherness in government" (checks and balances).

Together, these ten aspects of the exercise of *Pancasila* Democracy constitute the government calendar and have their source in the Indonesian Constitution or "Fundamental Written Law" (governmental "convention"). Both the "Fundamental Written Law" and the "Fundamental Unwritten Law" are governed by the principles and ideals contained in the Preamble to the Constitution, the essence of which is *Pancasila*.[18]

In the final two sections of part two, we will take a brief look at two more aspects of the exercise of democracy in Indonesia which were established by the composers of the Constitution: the organization of government and the advancement of social welfare.[19] Fulfillment of the former will be analyzed under the heading "The Safeguarding of *Pancasila*," and the fulfillment of the latter under the heading "The Implementation of *Pancasila*."

The Theoretical-Constitutional Foundation of Pancasila Democracy

The Organizational Structure of the State

The first fundamental issue to be resolved by the composers of the Constitution was the determination of the organizational structure of the state. A variety of forms of state organization were suggested at the meetings of the *Badan Penyelidik Usaha Persiapan Kemerdekaan Indonesia* (Investigatory Committee for the Preparation of Indonesian Independence) and discussions deal with the following questions: Should Indonesia be a federal state or a unitary state? Should Indonesia be a monarchy, a feudal state, or a republic?

The composers eventually chose the unitary state because it fit better with the idea of a unified state. The history of the nationalist movement in Indonesia during the colonial period also led Indonesian nationalists to conclude that a federation would have made it easier for the colonists, who were seeking to reassert their authority, to split the nation with their policy of "*divide et impera*."

In choosing between a monarchy and a republic, most of those present felt that Indonesia should have an elected head of state, not a king or queen who rules for life and is succeeded by a blood relative. Fifty-five members of the *Panitia Persiapan Kermedekaan Indonesia of PPKI* (The Committee for the Preparation of Indonesian Independence) voted for a republic and six voted for a kingdom.[20]

The organizational structure of the state was thus determined in a democratic fashion[21] and later given definitive form in Chapter I, Article 1, Paragraph 1 of the Constitution: The State of Indonesia is a Unitary State and in form a Republic.

A second, and related, fundamental issue concerned the territorial boundaries of the Republic of Indonesia. Many of those present felt that this issue could be resolved by following the boundaries established by the great Indonesian kingdoms of the past: the kingdoms of Majapahit and Sriwijaya flourished in Indonesia during the ninth and thirteenth centuries, respectively, and both produced a geopolitical orientation or awareness among the peoples of the Archipelago.[22] Other members of the PPKI, however, sought a more practical definition: the territorial boundaries set by Dutch colonialism.[23]

Another voice pointed out that the issue of territorial boundaries was difficult to determine given that the war in Asia had only just ended. Precise boundaries were seen as difficult to determine because the question of boundaries was tied up with questions of international law.[24]

From the results of a polling of those present, it was clear that the majority wanted a territory which exceeded the territory of the former Dutch colony. H.A. Salim,[25] realizing the difficulty of obtaining that territory outright, suggested a way to get the desired territory. He suggested that initially the boundaries follow the boundaries of the Dutch colony, but that the people of other areas who desired to join the Republic of Indonesia be allowed to do so.[26] Thus in the Preamble to the Constitution, the state is seen as encompassing: "Everywhere that Indonesian blood flows."[27]

This principle was later to be followed concerning the territories of West Irian and East Timor, both of which, through a process of self-determination, chose to join the Republic.[28]

Although the constitutional formulation was thus very broad, in one of its meetings, the PPKI defined precisely the territorial divisions for the Republic of Indonesia. Initially, there were eight provinces: Sumatra, West Java, Central Java, East Java, the Lesser Sundas, the Maluccas, Sulawesi and Kalimantan.[29] The number of provinces (also known as Level 1 Regions) has since grown to 27, a development not unlike the substantial growth in the number of states in a federated nation like the United States of America.

The Highest Organ of State Authority

A democratic government draws its power from the power of the people. In Indonesia, following Western terminology, this concept is referred to as *Kedaulatan Rakyat* (the Sovereignty of the People). The highest authority of the people, however, can take one of several different shapes, depending on what perspective is taken concerning who is to be considered "the people." In the West, it is thought that "the people," as represented in the institutions of state, and by those who hold the positions of highest authority, should be "men of principle" (the learned few) or "men of property." This perspective leads to a government of the elite (*"Menschen von Besitz und Bildung"*), and thus was felt to be inappropriate to the Indonesian context.

Conversely, if "the people" are identified with the have-nots and the ignorant (the proletariat), the result is often an absolutist democracy, where the leader names himself the leader of the people only to exploit the very people he claims to represent.

Therefore, in determining the structure for the highest authority of the people, certain qualifications were established which reflected the fundamental convictions of the Indonesian people. Specifically, the Sovereignty of the People was to be based on the five principles of *Pancasila*:

.   Belief in the One Supreme God;
.   a just and civilized humanitarianism;
.   the unity of Indonesia;
.   a democracy guided by the wisdom arising from consultation and representation;
.   social justice for all Indonesian people.[30]

Pancasila is thus the source of the highest organ of state authority and thereby provides the foundation for the Indonesian state.

This principle was enshrined in the Constitution in Chapter I, Article 1, Paragraph 2: "Sovereignty is vested in the people and exercised fully by the *Majelis Permusjawaratan Rakjat* or MPR (the People's Consultative Assembly)."

According to this formulation, the highest organ of state authority remains in the hands of the people and is not passed off to or usurped by any other institution. As we shall see below, the Constitution also provides stipulations for referenda to be held under certain circumstances. But since sovereignty is already exercised fully by the MPR in the name of the people, the holding of a referendum constitutes an "ultra-democratic device."[31] In Indonesia, the highest organ of state authority remains with and cannot be alienated from the people.

The Institution for the Representation of the People

The existence of an institution for representatives in the governmental structure of the democratic state has taken on a mythos which cannot be ignored. But both historically and empirically, it is difficult to prove the truth of the assertion that such an institution is necessary for the operation of a state whose highest authority is the people. The Indonesian nation, however, was unable to free itself from this myth and it uses a system of representation as well.

In Indonesian integralist thinking, the institution of representation is necessary in order that the highest authority of the people play its role in the organization and operation of government. In other words, the highest institution of representation exists to execute sovereignty.[32]

In the liberalist conception, majority rule ("*volunte generale*") is made the foundation for the operation of the state via the representative system. In order to make a decision, one must either have consensus, a majority of the votes, or some variation, like two-thirds of the votes. This majority can be obtained through the formation of a coalition, or by the victory of a single party in a two-party election system. Neither of these concepts (neither a coalition with opposition, nor the two-party system with opposition) is used in Indonesia's integralist system.

In the Indonesian conception, the execution of representation must be consistent with the idea of national unity and thus is not based on the will of the largest or most powerful group. It is the state interest which must override all group interests. The highest organ of representation must therefore pay attention to all aspects of a given problem and examine the problem from every perspective before a decision is made.[33] This method is called "*bermusyawarah*" (group consultation) and the highest organ of state authority is called the *Majelis Permusyawaratan Rakjat* or MPR (People's Consultative Assembly). Clearly, it is difficult to find an equivalent or translation for this institution in any other system of government.[34]

To understand the powers of the MPR, we must therefore look at its function. The MPR executes the people's sovereignty by:

a) upholding the Constitution;

b) upholding the *Garis Besar Huluan Negara* or GBHN (Guidelines for State Policy); and

c) electing the President.

The decision-making process is the same as in Western representative systems: if all are in agreement, there is consensus (*mufakat*), and this is attempted first; only if dissent persists will majority rule decide the issue.[35] In addition, there are cases in which a particular number of votes is needed, i.e., changing the Constitution requires a two-thirds majority.[36] But whether by consensus, majority rule, or some variation thereof, the approach must always be based on consultation.

The MPR consists of the members of the *Dewan Perwakilan Raykat* of DPR (Council of Representatives) along with appointed regional delegates and certain non-party groups.[37] Thus the DPR, or parliament as it is known in Western theory, is only part of the MPR.

The DPR consists of members of sociopolitical organizations (the political parties) and together with the President has the authority to make laws and establish the budget for income and expenditure. In addition to this legislative and budgetary authority, the DPR has the authority to oversee the President in his organization of the government, although the President is not accountable to the DPR.[38]

The Indonesian conception of representation is crystalized in the fourth pillar of *Pancasila* which calls for: A democracy guided by the wisdom arising from consultation and representation.

According to the Indonesian formulation then, democracy is to be based on wisdom and reason, carried out by means of consultation, and applied in the institution of representation. This is true of the regional governments as well as of the Indonesian national government.[39]

The Presidency

In the Indonesian system of government, the President is known as the *Mandataris* (Mandatary) of the MPR. As Mandatary, the President is obliged to carry out the program of government known as the *Garis Besar Huluan Negara* or GBHN (Guidelines for State Policy)[40] established by the MPR.

The power and responsibility for running the government are in the hands of the President. The President must nonetheless submit to the authority of the MPR, and must carry out the decisions of the MPR. The President is not "*neben*" (equal) but "*untergeordnet*" (subordinate) to the MPR.[41] On the other hand, the President is not responsible to the DPR: the DPR stands not above but at the side of the President. The President must seek the accord of the DPR in shaping laws and in determining the state budget for income and expenditure. The President must work together with the representatives of the people, but the President's position does not depend upon the DPR.

The President is also the head of the executive arm of government[42] and is responsible for seeing to it that the laws of the nation are implemented. In this capacity, the President controls the government as dictated by the Constitution. But this control is not absolute; there is no dictator in Indonesia.

The President must carefully heed the voice of the DPR because the DPR can always oversee the actions of the President. If the DPR believes that the President has truly violated state principles as given form in the Constitution or established by the MPR, the DPR can then invite the MPR for a special session in order to seek an accounting from the President.[43]

The Constitution dictates that the President is to be assisted by a Vice-President and a Cabinet of Ministers. The Ministers are appointed and removed by the President, and they lead the various departments of government. Although the Ministers are dependent on the President, they are not merely high-ranking officials: it is the Ministers who are responsible for carrying out much of the day-to-day business of the executive arm of government ("*pouvoir executief*").

As the heads of specific departments, each of the Ministers has access to expertise in a given area. As a result, Ministers have a great influence on the President. In determining government policy and coordinating government operations, the Ministers work together under the leadership of the President.[44]

The Republic of Indonesia's system of government is not based on the parliamentary model but is, more precisely, a presidential system. Thus the Ministers are not responsible to the DPR, although they are required to explain their policy decisions before the DPR in order that the DPR carry out its function of overseeing the course of government.

One final aspect of the Presidency in Indonesia is the role of the President as Head of State.[45] In this capacity, the President:

a) holds supreme authority over the Army, Navy and Air Force;

b) appoints diplomatic representatives, consults and receives the diplomatic representatives of other nations;

c) with the approval of the DPR: declares war against other states; makes peace with other states; concludes treaties with other states;

d) is empowered to proclaim martial law according to the conditions and with the consequences prescribed by law;

e) with the advice of the *Mahkamah Agung* (Supreme Court), grants pardon, amnesty, abolition and rehabilitation;

f) bestows titles, decorations for merit and other marks of honors, as well as letters of promotion for state officials and other civil servants.

Finally, in addition to receiving assistance from the Vice-President and Ministers, the President is assisted by a staff of advisors known as the *Dewan Pertimbangan Agung* (Supreme Advisory Council). This body provides answers to questions posed by the President and has the right to put forward recommendations to the government.[46]

Human Rights

In accordance with the Indonesian integralist perspective, the rights and responsibilities of an individual are determined by his or her relations with others. There are no human rights which are independent of these interrelations. There are two different categories of human rights in Indonesia: the society-wide category encompasses all inhabitants, and the more limited state category encompasses all citizens.[47] Inhabitants rights and citizens rights are not identical.

The rights of citizens include the following: equality before the law and the obligation to obey the law; equal status in government, and the oblgiation to support the government; the right to work and to a reasonable standard of living; the right and obligation to participate in the defense of the state; the right to national education; the rights enjoyed by inhabitants. In addition, the Constitution dictates that all citizens must, without exception, show respect for the law and government.

The rights of inhabitants include the following: the freedom of assembly; the freedom of association; the right to express both spoken and written opinion; the freedom for each to embrace their own religion and worship according to their own religion; the poor and orphaned shall be cared for by the state.

This formulation is different from that characteristic of the liberalist state based on "life, liberty and property." In the liberalist state, there are said to be political, economic, and sociocultural rights. If human rights in Indonesia are put into that framework, we find the following:

Political Rights: the freedom of assembly; the freedom of association; the right to express both spoken and written opinion; equality before the law and the obligation to uphold the law; equal status in government and the obligation, without exception, to respect the government.

Economic Rights: the right to work; the right to a reasonable standard of living.

Sociocultural Rights: the right to education; guarantees for the poor; the freedom for each to embrace their own religion; the right and opportunity to defend the state.

All of the above are protected by the Constitution and have been given further formulation in statutes insofar as has been necessary to keep pace with developments in society.

Legal policy concerning human rights has been guided by the following interpretation of the Constitution: "All articles, those concerning only citizens as well as those concerning all inhabitants, carry with them the right of the Indonesian people to build a democratic state which promotes social justice and humanitarianism."[48]

The Legal Basis for the State

The idea of the rule of law is unique to Western European theories of statehood, and a state based on such theory is usually referred to as a "*Rechtsstaat.*" As a nation which puts high priority on written law as well as a variety of customary legal systems ("*adat*" law), the Republic of Indonesia adheres to the rule of law. But whereas in the liberalist systems of government, the concept of the rule of law is used to protect basic rights, in the Indonesian system, it is used to prevent the creation of a state which is based solely on power ("*Machtstaat*").[49]

Because Indonesia's highest authority remains faithful to the principle of the sovereignty of the people, that authority will be realized in the process of formulating written law. It is even emphasized in the Constitution that the implementation of the principles set forth therein are to be left to statutes which are easier to formulate, revise, and repeal as compared with the Constitution.[50]

The rule of law in Indonesia also has the following consequences:

a) The source of both the "Fundamental Written Law" (the Constitution) as well as the "Fundamental Unwritten Law" (governmental convention) are the ideals of law. These ideals are given definite form in the principles contained in the Preamble, in the five pillars of *Pancasila*. In brief then, one can say that *Pancasila* is the source of the highest law;[51]

b) The makers of the law are the President (the mandatary) and the DPR, and they are accountable for their actions to the MPR which is the implementor of the sovereignty of the people. The MPR can determine which laws are to be formulated as well as order a legislative review of the existing regulations for the composition of law;[52]

c) All persons have the same status before the law and are obligated, without exception, to respect the law;[53]

d) The judiciary is independent of the other organs of the government;

e) The function of law in Indonesia is to serve as protector: it must be democratic, and promote social justice and humanitarianism;

f) The right to revise legislation (other than constitutional legislation) is in the hands of the Supreme Court insofar as there is damage arising from the old statutes: the Supreme Court is responsible for "Judicative-Review." Revision of the Constitution (and related legislation) is in the hands of the MPR: the MPR is responsible for "legislative review."[54]

The Constitutional Basis for Government

The government is headed by the President as Mandatary of the MPR. The MPR, however, is still responsible for implementing sovereignty in the name of the people, and does not delegate all of its authority to the President: the power of the head of state is not absolute.

These limitations have their basis in the stipulation that the government is to be based on a constitutional system, not on absolutism.[55] The constitutional formulation is as follows: "The President of the Republic of Indonesia is vested with the power of Government in accordance with the Constitution."[56] This formulation is different than that usually associated with the liberal "*Rechtsstaat*" wherein government is based on fundamental statutes ("*wetmatigheid van bestuur*") which are then developed in legal codes ("*rechtmatigheid van bestuur*") as appropriate ("*doelmatig*") to the needs of the society (as reflected in the term "Social Service State": "*verzorgingsstaat*").

Indonesian constitutionalism has developed directly from and is consistent with *Pancasila* and the Constitution of 1945. Indonesian constitutionalism is a strict interpretation of the Indonesian *Pancasila*-ist, integralist perspective; and Indonesian constitutionalism has grown out of the fundamental concepts and principles of the Constitution. These concepts and principles constitute the "basic ideas" which have given shape to *Pancasila* Ideology. Indonesian constitutionalism is thus consistent with *Pancasila* Ideology, and both work to promote a democratic national life.

Today, the effort to create a society-wide understanding of *Pancasila* Ideology has become one of the programs of the Cabinet: *Pancasila* Ideology is being disseminated in order to develop a national life based unambiguously on *Pancasila* Democracy, thus strengthening national unity.[57]

The Institutional Organs of State and Their Interrelations

This issue is known in Western theory as the structure of government ("*regeeringsvorm*"), and it concerns the division of labor among the organs of the state apparatus in organizing and determining the activities of government. The theory best known for this is the "*trias politica*" of Montesquieu. The composers of the Constitution, however, felt that this "*trias politica*" theory was no longer consistently applied even in Western Europe and thus "the founding fathers" sought another scheme for organizing the institutional organs of the state.[58] They determined that the government be structured as follows:

a) There is a single highest organ of state authority which holds sovereignty in the name of the people (the MPR):[59]

b) One part of this institution (the DPR) together with the executive arm of government shapes laws and the state budget for income and expenditure;

c) The government is headed by the President as Mandatary of the MPR;

d) In order to expedite presidential duties, the President is assisted by a body of advisors known as the *Dewan Pertimbangan Agung* (Supreme Advisory Council);[60]

e) The Supreme Advisory Council, in turn, is advised by a body known as the *Badan Pemeriksa Keuangan* (Financial Auditing Office) which serves to upgrade the Council's ability to cope with budgetary matters;[61]

f) The *Mahkamah Agung* (Supreme Court) is the head of the judiciary and is independent of the other organs of government.[62]

The institutions of the state in Indonesia thus include, on the one hand, the highest organ of the state--the MPR; and on the other hand, the Presidency, the DPR, the Supreme Court, the Supreme Advisory Council, and the Financial Auditing Office. This institutional set-up was given permanent form in an MPR Resolution in 1978 and is based on the Constitution, not directly on the "*trias politica*" theory.

In the Indonesian theory of statehood, the regional governments are also often considered institutions of the state. Since Indonesia is a unitary state, Indonesia will never have sub-regions within its boundaries which constitute states unto themselves. The regions of Indonesia are divided into provinces (or Level 1 Regions), and the provinces are further divided into smaller regions (or Level 2 Regions). Each of these regions has certain autonomous features,[63] and is governed by regional representative councils which, as with the national DPR and MPR, are based on consultation.

The Goals of Democracy in Indonesia

As is true in the West, democracy in Indonesia is not a goal in and of itself. If in the West freedom and equality are the goals of democracy, in Indonesia the primary goal of democracy is the creation of just and prosperous society based on the fundamental convictions of the people as expressed in *Pancasila*. Democracy in Indonesia also has as its goal the fulfillment of human potential for virtue and dignity. The goals of democracy in Indonesia are thus the development of Indonesian society and the full realization of the human potential of the Indonesian people.[65]

This effort to develop Indonesia's potential was given formulation in the *Elucidation of the Constitution*.[66] The Constitution contains only the fundamental guidelines which are to instruct the central government and other state institutions concerning the organization and operation of the state and the advancement of social welfare.[67] The organization and operation of the state can be seen as the political aspect of government, and the advancement of social welfare can be seen as the social aspect. Using *Pancasila* as a tool, Indonesia seeks to develop both aspects of the life of its people.

A just and prosperous society based on *Pancasila* will:
protect the people everywhere that Indonesian blood flows;
promote the general welfare; improve the standard of living; and participate in establishing a world order founded upon freedom, eternal peace, and social justice.[68]

In the Constitution, it was also made clear that the most essential prerequisite for government officials is the integralist (family) "spirit." That spirit, reflected in the behavior of the officials, must be alive and dynamic in order that the ideas contained in the Constitution be upheld. To ensure that this spirit be continually renewed, a resolution of the MPR in 1978 established guidelines known as *Pedoman Penghayatan dan Pengamalan Pancasila* (The Compass for the Internalization and Realization of Pancasila). With these guidelines, it is hoped that the virtue and "human dignity" of the people, all supporters of the idea of *Pancasila* democracy, will be cultivated.

The Safeguarding of Pancasila Democracy

The survival of a state is dependent on the fundamental convictions of its people. Thus, the safeguarding of the Republic of Indonesia is dependent on the effort to safeguard *Pancasila*. Accordingly, the composers of the Constitution established several protective measures.

The first measure, typical of other constitutions as well, was to make the procedure for changing the Constitution especially difficult. To ratify a proposed change, two-thirds of the MPR must be present, and two-thirds of those present must be in agreement with the proposed change.[69] If, however, the desired change is a technicality, a question of terminology for instance, then there is no need for any special procedure, as outlined in the "*Verfassungs-wandlung*" theory, changing the accepted meaning of a given term without actually replacing that term can be approved on the basis of "Fundamental Unwritten Law" (governmental convention).

A more significant change, a change in the interpretation of *Pancasila* itself, would threaten the very basis of the Indonesian state. To protect against this, a second measure was taken by the composers of the Constitution. Since *Pancasila* is considered to be uniquely and specifically Indonesian, the Constitution requires that the President of the Republic of Indonesia be a native-born Indonesian.[70] When the Constitution was first drafted, the President was also required to be Muslim, but this further qualification was removed for the sake of national unity just before the ratification of the Constitution.

It has also been pointed out that *Pancasila* was formulated within the Preamble to the Constitution, and not as one of the articles in the "body of the Constitution." Therefore, *Pancasila* is immune even to Article 37 which provides for the revision of the constitutional statutes: *Pancasila* is a "*Staatsfundamental norm*."

The Exercise of Pancasila Democracy

The Struggle to Achieve a Stable Yet Dynamic Government

The Formation of the Highest Organs of the State

The first step in the formation of the organs of state was the formation of the highest representative authority which would determine the Constitution, formulate the guidelines for state-policy, and elect the head of state. Immediately following the proclamation of independence on August 17, 1945, the *Panitia Persiapan Kemerdekaan Indonesia* or PPKI (Committee for the Preparation of Indonesian Independence) functioned as the highest authority.[71] The PPKI ratified the Constitution on 18 August 1945. Since the MPR, DPR, and the Supreme Advisory Council, stipulated by the Constitution, were not yet formed at that time, all state power was exercised by the President with the aid of a *Komite Nasional Indonesia* or KNI (Indonesian National Committee).[72]

The KNI included representatives from all territories, some elected by the people, and some who were appointed, the latter appointed only after consideration of the make-up of the people in the areas which they were to represent.[73] Thus, initially, the highest authority was the President assisted by a KNI.

This government structure was only intended to last six months, but because of the independence war against the [Dutch] colonialists, who sought to reestablish control over Indonesia with the aid of other powerful nations who had won World War II, it was maintained for a longer period of time.

The KNI was elected on August 23, 1945 and inaugurated on August 29, 1945, but did not actually exercise authority until October 16, 1945 when Vice Presidential Resolution No. X,[74] gave the Committee legislative power. Soon thereafter, day-to-day operations were delegated to a Working Subcommittee. The KNI thus performed the duties of the MPR and the Working Subcommittee performed the duties of the DPR.

On November 3, 1945, a government declaration called for the formation of political parties, and soon ten such parties were established. A cabinet based on the parliamentary model was then established on November 14.[75] The Dutch government was also busy at that time, forming states in the regions which it had reoccupied with the aim of forming a federal nation (1946-1950) where the highest authority would rest with the Dutch Colonial Government. Ultimately, with the Dutch recognition of Indonesian independence on 27 December 1949, a compromise was reached whereby a federal government was established, still based on *Pancasila*, but with the name "The United States of the Republic of Indonesia."

This forced arrangement endured for only six months. On August 15, 1950, an agreement was reached to establish a Unitary State as had been proclaimed on 17 August 1945. This Unitary State, however, was still to be based on the parliamentary system which had been used since the formation of the first parliamentary cabinet on November 14, 1945. Thus in place of the Constitution of 1945, a Provisional Constitution was established in 1950, wherein the highest authority was exercised by the President along with the DPR.[77]

On September 29, 1955, the first nationwide elections were held. Nineteen political parties and various other groups participated in electing representatives to served in the DPR. Following that September election, a second election was held on December 15, 1955 to elect the Constituent Assembly, which was to be responsible for drafting a new Constitution.[78]

The Constituent Assembly, however, did not succeed in establishing a new Constitution, and, with the Decree of the President on July 15, 1959, the Constitution of 1945 was reinstated. The highest authority rested once again with the President in a system known as "Guided Democracy." Then, with a presidential decree in 1959, the Interim MPR was established, and it held its first session in November of 1960 in Bandung. A decade later, following the elections of 1971 in which ten political parties participated, the Interim MPR was transformed into the "Highest Organ of State Authority" in compliance with the dictates of the Constitution.

Although the members of the Indonesian Armed Forces were not entitled to participate in the 1971 election, representatives of the Armed Forces were appointed to seats in the MPR. The rationale behind the appointments was the decisive role that the Armed Forces had played in the formation of the Republic of Indonesia as well as Indonesian electoral experience, which had demonstrated that the electoral impact of the Indonesian Armed Forces was splintered by the influence of the political parties. The performance of a sociopolitical function as well as its usual professional function led to the *dwi-fungsi* (dual function) conception of the Indonesian Armed Forces.

In 1977, the political party system was streamlined: only two parties and one organization of functional groups (*golong karya*[79]) were allowed to put forward candidates for the elections. Members of the Indonesian Armed Forces were still appointed as before, serving to stabilize and dynamize the government. The procedures adopted in 1977 have been followed up to the present.

The Determination of the Garis Besar Haluan Negara (Guidelines for State Policy)

Whereas in the liberal systems of government, the winning party or coalition determines the program of government, in the Indonesian political system, the program of government is determined by the MPR once every five years. The program is the dynamic concretization of the goals of the state, given form in a development plan known as the *Garis Besar Haluan Negara* or GBHN (Guidelines for State Policy). In accordance with the principle of the sovereignty of the people, government planning is determined by the representatives of the people, and is implemented by the President as Mandatary. Thus, the informal criterion for choosing a President is his ability to implement the program of government established in the GBHN.

In the early years of the Republic of Indonesia, the GBHN had not yet been formally determined, although decisions concerning territorial boundaries and which governmental departments would be needed had been made.[80] Following the formal adoption of a parliamentary system in 1950, wherein the Cabinet was headed by a Prime Minister, the government program was determined by coalition among the members of that Cabinet.

Only in 1960, after the return to the Constitution of 1945 with Interim MPR Resolution No. 1 1960, was the first GBHN established. These guidelines were the systemization of the presidential speech entitled "Rediscovering Our Revolution" or "The Political Manifesto of the Republic of Indonesia." The essential elements of this State Speech reflected the Constitution of 1945: "Indonesian Socialism," "Guided Democracy," "Guided Economy," and the "Unique Character of Indonesia."[81] Later, an effort was made to have the Interim MPR itself formulate the GBHN, but sessions of the MPR in the early years of the New Order (1966-1968) were still not able to complete the process due to time constraints.

Since the formal establishment of the MPR after the election of 1971, the following system has been used: the Mandatary prepares material for the GBHN in advance, thereby giving the MPR sufficient time to discuss and finalize the Guidelines. The Mandatary has called on the *Badan Perancang Pembangunan Nasional* or BPPN (The National Development Planning Council) to organize the materials necessary for the formation of the Guidelines. Information is also supplied by the *Dewan Pertahanan Keamanan Nasional* (National Security ICouncil), and by the *Panitia Sebelas* (Committee of the Eleventh[82]).

Guidelines for the state can be implemented in the Resolutions of the MPR as well as in the GBHN.[83] In 1985, the MPR approved a resolution whereby the leader of the MPR himself must take the initiative in gathering together the materials for formulation of the GBHN.[84] The efforts of the leader of the MPR thus complement the Mandatary's preparation of materials.

The Election of the President

The President is elected by the MPR and, as we have seen, is the Mandatary of the MPR. The President must be capable of implementing the GBHN which is determined by the MPR, and the general guidelines for the state dictated by the Constitution. This capacity, along with the provision that the President is required to be a native Indonesian are the chief prerequisites for the President.[85] The Constitution dictates that the President is to serve a term of five years.[86]

In Indonesian history, the individual selected to be President has always been an individual whose service to the nation has been quite evident. The first President[87] was the leader of the nationalist movement during the colonial era, and he succeeded in "nation and character building" to the point where the Indonesian people were able to proclaim their independence. As we have seen, his State Speech of 1959 formed the basis for the first GBHN: at that time, the Interim MPR even recommended that he be made President for life, a decision which contradicted the Constitution. The first President's demise in 1966 reflected his inability to fulfill the aspirations of the people, particularly with respect to the Indonesian Communist Party which had directly attempted to undermine *Pancasila* with its coup d'etat of September 1965.[88]

With the MPR repudiation of his mandate, the first President's term of office had ended, and the New Order[89] began. The government programs of the Old Order were abandoned and the chief criterion for any succeeding President became the ability to move the country toward development. Today, the President's capacity to effectively set the nation on the course of development is more important than that he can be reelected several times.[90] And since the MPR has shown itself willing to revoke the President's mandate (as experienced by the first President), the President's end-of-term accounting has become more important.

The Formation of the Government

The Indonesian system of government is a presidential system and it is the President who actively directs the Cabinet. This was not always the case. Although the first Cabinet following the Declaration of Independence in 1945 was formed in this way,[91] on November 11, 1945 before even three months had passed, the Working Subcommittee of the KNI (*Komite Nasional Indonesia*: Indonesian National Committee) recommended that Ministers be accountable to the Working Subcommittee rather than to the President. Shortly thereafter, on November 14, 1945, a liberalist system was implemented with the formation of a cabinet whose prime ministers were appointed from among the political parties which were in coalition.

This parliamentary system continued until July 25, 1966, when the government returned to the presidential system with the ascension of the New Order. In reality, the President had already been reinstalled as head of the Cabinet beginning with the 1959 Proclamation of Guided Democracy and the return to the Constitution of 1945. Up until 1966, however, the title "Prime Minister" was still used. Beginning in 1966, the President was given the title

"Supreme Commander of the Indonesian Armed Forces" in addition to the previously held title "Great Leader of the Revolution." The situation in Indonesia at that time[92] led to a new theory of executive power which called for enhancing the power of the President.

From November 11, 1945 until July 25, 1966, a period of roughly 21 years, there had been 24 cabinets. One can imagine the instability of the government during that period. There was no time to implement government policies, no way for the government program to be executed appropriately, and thus no sustained government. The Indonesian people tried using the parliamentary system and it failed. Since the return to the presidential system in 1966, the executive arm of government has consisted of the President and his Ministers; they are not responsible to the DPR and do not represent political parties. Indonesia has returned to the system of government based on *Pancasila* and the Constitution of 1945.[93]

The Formation of the Other Organs of State

In addition to the MPR, DPR and the executive arm of government (the President and Ministers), the Constitution calls for a Supreme Court, Supreme Advisory Council, and Financial Auditing Office, and the Bank of Indonesia serves as the central bank.[94]

The Supreme Court is the highest organ of the judiciary, and holds authority independent of the other organs of government. The Supreme Court was given shape according to the dictates of the Constitution as elaborated in legal codes. This highest organ of the judiciary is governed by two codes of law: *Undang Undang tentang Kekuasaan Pokok Kehakiman* ("Laws Concerning the Essential Powers of the Judiciary") and *Undang Undang tentang Mahkamah Agung* ("Laws Concerning the Supreme Court").[95] The former establishes four systems of justice in Indonesia: Public Law (civil and criminal); Religious Law; Military Law; and Administrative Law. Each system has its own courts at both the first level and the appellate level, but the final court of recourse for all four is the Supreme Court.

The Supreme Advisory Council is appointed for a five-year term and serves as the advisor to the President.[96]

The members of the Financial Auditing Office are also appointed to a five-year term.[97] This office is not subordinate to government authority, nor is it above the government, although it oversees state finance. The Financial Auditing Office forwards the results of its audits to the DPR, thereby improving DPR capability to process the budget; it serves as an advisor to the DRP.

These organs of government, although not staffed by elected officials, nonetheless have been established in a manner consistent with the Constitution and they operate according to law. Similarly, legal codes govern the operation of governmental institutions at the regional level.[98]

The five aspects of the formation of the Indonesian government discussed above demonstrate the historical movement toward a government which is stable yet dynamic. The government promotes the development of the people according to the people's own dictates as established by their representatives in the MPR.

This struggle has continued for over forty years since Indonesia gained its independence, despite various disturbances, both domestic and foreign. Concerning international relations, diplomacy has played and continues to play a major role in the development of the Republic of Indonesia. Paragraph 4 of the Preamble to the Constitution of 1945 reads: "(Indonesia shall) participate in establishing a world order founded upon freedom, eternal peace, and social justice. These principles guide Indonesian Diplomacy."

Coordination, Harmony, and Balance in the Organization of the State ("Checks and Balances")

The Composition of Legal Statutes

In consonance with liberal thought, individual freedoms are protected in the Indonesian system of government in the form of laws which are made by the executive arm of government together with the representatives of the people. These laws, reflecting agreement between the representatives of the people and the organizers of the state, embody the aspirations of the people. According to the Constitution itself, constitutional dictates are to be given detailed formulation in written law.[99] Making law is thus a crucial aspect of government, and must reflect the existence of coordination, harmony and balance within the organization of the state and between the Mandatary (the President) and the representatives of the people in the DPR.

Among the constitutional dictates are the following every law proposed by the executive arm of government requires the agreement of the DPR;[100] the DPR also has the right to propose laws;[101] the approval of the DPR is required for the President to declare war, make peace, and conclude treaties with other states.[102]

Constitutionally, agreement between the executive arm of government and the DPR is a prerequisite for the formation of new statutes. The Constitution dictates that two kinds of law be established: statutes regulating the organization of government, and statutes regulating the advancement of social welfare.

The former concern the organization of the state, i.e., political matters, whereas the latter concern the fulfillment of the needs of the people in general.

The Determination of the State Budget for Expenditure and Income

Although the President is not accountable to the DPR, he must still obtain the approval of the DPR in order to establish the state budget.[103] The budget is established every year by law. Should the DPR not approve the budget submitted by the executive arm of government, the government is required by constitutional decree to implement the budget from the preceding year. This procedure demonstrates the power of the DPR. Since the President and Ministers are not accountable to the DPR however, should the DPR reject the budget, the preceding year's budget is implemented and the matter ends there. Once again we see the pattern of coordination, harmony and balance in the organization of the state.

As established by law, at the beginning of each budget cycle the President hands over responsibility for the budget to the DPR.[104] Thus one can understand the rationale underlying Article 23, Paragraph 5, of the Constitution which states: "To examine all matters pertaining to public finance, a Financial Auditing Office shall be established by law. The results of its audits shall be presented to the DPR."[105]

On March 5, 1960, the President dissolved the DPR because it had rejected the budget submitted by the executive arm of government. This presidential decision violated the principles enshrined in the Constitution: in budgetary matters, the DPR has greater authority than the executive arm of government.[106] At present, an agreement has been reached whereby the executive arm of government must submit a plan for the budget early enough so that the DPR has sufficient time to discuss it and finalize it before the beginning of the fiscal year in April.

The Supervision of the Course of Government

All members of the DPR also become members of the MPR when the MPR holds its session once every five years, and thus the DPR can at all times oversee the actions of the President. If the DPR truly believes that the President has transgressed one of the fundamental principles established by the Constitution or by a resolution of the MPR, the DPR can invite the MPR for a special session to seek an accounting from the President. The nadir in coordination, harmony, and balance in the organization of the state would be reached if the President's mandate were to be withdrawn by the MPR. This happened to the first President in March of 1967.

A second form of constitutionally dictated supervision of government is the overseeing of state finances by the Financial Auditing Office. As has already been explained, this institution serves to strengthen the DPR's ability to review the budget submitted by the executive arm of government.[107]

The third form of supervision is by the Supreme Court[108], the pinnacle of the judiciary. Even the system for administrative justice culminates in the Supreme Court, different from the Western European systems, where the highest organ of administrative justice is a state advisory board (in France, "*Counseil d'Etat*"). In Indonesia, the institution for administrative justice has the authority to resolve disputes between the executive arm of government and the people which arise in the process of the administration of the state. This institution was only created in 1978 by a resolution of the MPR, and it is thus still in the process of formation.[109]

There are also internal mechanisms for supervision held by the executive arm of government which can be made use of by society. The awareness and understanding of these mechanisms is currently in the process of being spread to the society at large, and their effectiveness is on the increase. Internal supervision is carried out by the following: the Financial and Development Auditing Office; the Inspector General for Development; the Ministry for the Regulation of the State Apparatus; *Komando Operasi Pemulihan Keamanan dan Ketertiban* or *KOPKAMTIB* (Operational Command for the Restoration of Security and Order) with its *Operasi Tertib* or *OPSTIB* (Operation to Establish Order);[110] the Inspector General of each Department; and the Territorial Inspectors in the regions. All of the above are coordinated by the Vice-President.

One final mechanism of supervision is the Supreme Court's authority to make legal rulings concerning the other organs of the state.[111] If the rulings are preventative in nature and concern the organization of the government, they serve as a kind of "pre-judicial" review; if they concern proposed bills or other legal statutes, they serve as a kind of "pre-legislative" review. In addition, the legal system as a whole has a Commissioner who oversees the implementation of the decisions of the courts.

All of these supervisory mechanisms are instruments for the achievement of coordination, harmony and balance in the organization of the state. And as is appropriate in any system of government, the police provide a mechanism for general supervision of citizens, indirectly influencing the organization and operation of the government.

The Annual Report of the President

This convention has its origins in the State Speech which was traditionally given every August 17 on the occasion of the anniversary of independence. The first such State Speech to be considered an Annual Report was the President's speech of August 17, 1959 which was later declared the "Political Manifesto of the Republic of Indonesia" by the Interim MPR. Since that year, the State Speech has contained information concerning state policy, and with the beginning of the New Order in 1965, the State Speech has been given before the DPR. The date has also been changed to August 16 from August 17 in order that the anniversary itself be devoted entirely to commemorations of independence.

The State Speech provides information concerning the policies that have been implemented and those proposed for the year to come in the GBHN. The State Speech is divided into two parts: the first part is read aloud before the DPR and is political in nature; the second part is an appendix to the first part, and is technical in nature.

With the material provided in this State Speech, the DPR has concrete data, enabling it to claim its supervisory rights, like the right to question, enquete, interpellate, and so on.[112] This state custom is another mechanism for coordination, harmony and balance in the organization of the state.

The President's End-of-Term Accounting

Presidential accounting before the MPR at the end of each term has also become a norm during the New Order. This practice was approved by the MPR and given permanent formulation as part of the MPR's *Peraturan Tata Tertib* (Regulations for Order).[113] The MPR must evaluate the presidential accounting and present their evalution in the form of a resolution. This presidential account has its source in the Constitution, although it is not explicitly outlined in the Articles.[114]

The President submits the end-of-term accounting to the newly elected MPR (after the general elections). This procedure has given rise to debate concerning whether the accounting ought not to be submitted to the outgoing MPR. However, since a report on the general elections to select the representatives is to be included in the accounting, the accounting can only conceivably be submitted after the election and the formation of the new

MPR. Constitutionally, the end-of-term accounting must be submitted to the MPR which is legally functioning at the time the accounting is given, so the procedure outlined above has continued up to the present.

In addition to the submission of end-of-term accounting, the President must also, for the sake of the continuity of the government, pass on materials to the MPR to be used in the formation of the GBHN.

The ten aspects of government which have been grouped together, both those reflecting "the formation of a stable yet dynamic government," and those reflecting "the effort to organize and operate the state on the basis of coordination, harmony, and balance," constitute the five-year cycle of the Indonesian government.

These aspects of government are rooted in the constitutional mechanism for *Pancasila* Democracy (the "Fundamental Written Law"); they are the manifestation of *Pancasila* Democracy "in action" ("Fundamental Unwritten Law"). The Constitution implicitly makes an allowance for unwritten law. The *Elucidation of the Constitution* defines such constitutionally approved unwritten statutes as "regulations which arise and are observed in the practice of organizing the state, even if not written."[115] This interpretation provides the basis in administrative law for the activities which comprise the government calendar, what Indonesian politicians refer to as the "Five-year Mechanism for National Leadership." It is this mechanism which has now become the norm and it can thus be called the essence of Indonesian political culture. This organizational scheme for the operation of government is democratic and is based on *Pancasila*; it has grown and will continue to grow even more democratic, faithful to and consistent with *Pancasila* and the Constitution.

Having described *Pancasila* Democracy "in action," we now turn to a consideration of how the procedures for government have been implemented. The Constitution contains specifications for the organization and operation of government, and the advancement of social welfare. The former concerns the active functioning of government. The operation of government cannot be divorced from *Pancasila*, which is an absolute prerequisite for the proper functioning of the Republic of Indonesia. The continuity of *Pancasila* must be guaranteed, and effort to ensure such continuity will be examined, below.

The advancement of social welfare represents the effort of the government to achieve a just and prosperous society based on *Pancasila*, the compass and "yardstick" for national development. National development encompasses the entire Indonesian society and all Indonesian people. Thus, the implementation of *Pancasila* required both the development of society and the development of the people (both "nation and character building").[116] At the heart of the advancement of social welfare is the implementation of *Pancasila* for national development, examined later.

The Safeguarding of Pancasila

The safeguarding of *Pancasila* is the *sine quo non* for the maintainance of the Republic of Indonesia. Constitutionally, *Pancasila* is safeguarded by the provision which requires that, for a proposed change in the Constitution to become law, at least two-thirds of the members of the MPR be present at the vote and two-thirds of those present vote in favor of the change.[117]

Another constitutional safeguard for *Pancasila* is the provision that the President must be an indigenous Indonesian in order that s/he be able to comprehend the Indonesian people's concept of government.[118] An early draft of the Constitution further required that the President be Muslim, clearly another effort to safeguard the guiding philosophy which was to become the foundation for the nation.

Historically, even in the period when the liberal parliamentary system was used, in the Constitution of the United States of Indonesia as well as in the Interim Constitution of 1950, *Pancasila* was the foundation for the state. And academic theory has strengthened the position of *Panacsila*: since *Pancasila* was placed in the Preamble to the Constitution, it is not bound by the articles in "the body of the Constitution." *Pancasila* comprises a fundamental norm for the state ("*staatsfundamental norm*").[119] To alter the "*Staatsfundamental norm*" would be equivalent to altering the state which was proclaimed on 17 August 1945.

In the twelve years from 1946 to 1958, however, there were no less than twelve revolts which threatened *Pancasila*, including revolts based on religion revolts based on territorial disputes ("*separatisme*"). These rebellions were put down, but they made clear the necessity for more strongly safeguarding *Pancasila* with political measures.

The first President attempted to protect the nation from rebellion and other forms of instability through what was known as the "Conception of the President, 1959." The first President felt that stability and the defense of *Pancasila* could only be achieved with the support of the four main political parties. Thus he sought to work together with all four: the nationalist party, the religious party, the socialist party, and the communist party.

This presidential strategy eventually took shape around three central components: Nationalism, Religion, and Communism (the Indonesian equivalents are *Nasional*, *Agama* and *Komunis* and thus this presidential ideology was known as *Nasakom*). *Nasakom* was based on guided-democracy where the leader of the nation was to be titled "The Great Leader of the Revolution." *Nasakom* was believed to be capable of protecting the state, the people, and their fundamental convictions, but with the Communist coup d'etat on 30 September 1965,[120] *Nasakom* was proven incapable of safeguarding *Pancasila*.

After the Communist rebellion was put down by the Indonesian Armed Forces, a national consensus was reached whereby the Indonesian Armed Forces, who had an oath of fidelity to *Pancasila*, would have to safeguard *Pancasila*.[121] The Indonesian Armed Forces were not allowed to participate in the general elections, but rather were appointed to one-third of the seats in the MPR, to ensure that there would be no changes in either the Constitution or in *Pancasila*.[122]

The process of democratization continued apace, and in 1983, the MPR called for the codification of the procedure for appointment of the members of the Indonesian Armed Forces. The MPR Resolution stipulated that a law be drafted which would require that a referendum be held concerning any proposed change in the Constitution. Today, then, the MPR must seek public approval of any proposed change in the Constitution, particularly of any proposed change in *Pancasila*.

The history of political parties in Indonesia reveals that allowing ideologies other than *Pancasila* to be the basis for political activity constitutes an ongoing threat to *Pancasila*. The Communist rebellion and the extent to which the parties clung to their own separate ideologies in past elections has led the MPR to determine that *Pancasila* must be the sole foundation for all Indonesian organizations. A recent MPR resolution called for the updating of the *Undang Undang Kepartaian* (Laws on Political Parties) and for the establishment of new laws concerning mass organizations in general.[123] Both of the above serve to fulfill the dictates of Article 28 of the Constitution, whereby it is stated that the freedom of assembly will be protected by law. It is hoped that these infrastructural improvements will further guarantee the safeguarding of *Pancasila*.

Indonesia's experience with the Indonesian Communist Party, which had direct affiliations with various non-political organizations, led to the formulation of regulations banning such mass parties. According to the new regulations for party structure, the political parties are to consist of only active members with the great majority of the Indonesian public serving as an apolitical "floating mass."[124] The sociopolitical entities which are allowed to become contestants in the elections are limited to two parties and one organization of functional groups (*Golkar*), all three of which are to have *Pancasila* as their sole foundation.

Other social organizations based on religion, profession, or common interest are not allowed to have any organizational connection with the sociopolitical entities. All of these organizations, however, must have *Pancasila* as their sole foundation. The two political parties and the organization of functional groups compete with one another, each offering its own particular program for government, and the different ideas resulting from this process are then integrated into the GBHN. All three contestants have the same right to participate in the formulation of the GBHN. The ideas which most accommodate the aspirations of the people will, of course, gain the greatest support of the people.

Just as the Declaration of Independence comprises the sole foundation for all political parties in America, *Pancasila* comprised the sole foundation for all political parties in Indonesia.

The Implementation of Pancasila

If, in the organization and operation of government, the safeguarding of *Pancasila* is given highest priority, and is based on a "security approach," then in the advancement of social welfare, the implementation of *Pancasila* in national development is given highest priority, and is based on a "prosperity approach."

The operation of the Indonesian government, as has already been discussed, is based on "state policy" or *Haluan Negara*. *Haluan Negara* represents a dynamic, concrete application of national goals to the program of government. The essence of *Haluan Negara* is determined by the MPR and is given form in the GBHN which organizes the five-year plans (the *Repelita*). Since the advancement of social welfare requires "planning" which is in line with national priorities, it is formulated directly in the GBHN. State planning must follow the dictates of the Constitution and thus follow the fundamental ideas which spring from *Pancasila*.

In the years immediately following the 1945 Proclamation of Independence, the struggle to defend the Republic from both internal and foreign threats left no time for activities which would bring development to the nation and advance the social welfare. The instability of the government and the great number of rebellions during the parliamentary era meant that the programs for national improvement formulated by the political parties were never effectively implemented.

With the formation of the Interim MPR in 1960, the guidelines of national development planning were established for the first time.[125] These guidelines were to cover the years 1961-69 and were later augmented by the

Deklarasi Ekonomi, or *Dekon* (Economic Declaration) of 1963, which dealt directly with the problems of the national economy. From the beginning of the effort to advance social welfare, economic concerns have constituted a principle focus of government planners.

Since 1973, the following formulation has been in used: "The *Garis Besar Haluan Negara* (Guidelines for State Policy) is the statement of national priorities, and thus the realization of the will of the people, and represents, in essence, the plan for national development."[126]

The plan for national development encompasses the following areas: economy, religion and culture, politics, the apparatus of state, law, the press and foreign relations, and national security.

In the process of implementing *Pancasila*, economic concerns are given precedence. Economic growth provides the means to achieve social welfare and thus there is an economic aspect to *Pancasila* Democracy.[127]

At this juncture, we need to have an "economic interpretation of the Constitution." The economic system which was to underlie development was given the following general formulation in Article 33 of the Constitution:

1) The economy shall be organized as a cooperative endeavor based on the principle of family life;

2) The State shall control those means of production which are important for the state and which dominate the economic life of the people;

3) The land, the water, and the natural resources contained therein shall be controlled by the state and exploited for the greatest prosperity of the people.

In striving to fulfill these fundamental economic objectives, there are still many obstacles to be faced. Many liberalist ideas are still followed but they do not fit in with the spirit of the Constitution (Article 33 above) and its further elaboration in the GBHN. In Indonesian economic democracy, the following must be avoided:

a) The system of "free-flight liberalism" which has led to the exploitation of humanity and nations, and which has given rise to and maintained Indonesia's structurally weak position in the world economy;

b) the system of statism (*"etatisme"*) whereby the state and its accompanying economic apparatus is dominant, thus pressuring and killing the potential creative strength of the units of the economy outside the state sector;

c) the socially damaging monopolization of economic strength by one group.[128]

As compared with the safeguarding of *Pancasila*, economically, socially and culturally, Indonesia is still struggling to defend its principles, just as politically Indonesia had to struggle with a parliamentary system from 1946 to 1959, but then was able to reinstate the Constitution of 1945. There is still a long struggle ahead in the implementation of *Pancasila* for national development.[129]

NOTES

*Translated from Indonesian by Joseph H. Saunders. Throughout the chapter, translator's notes are indicated by "(trans.)" at the end of the note or the portion of a note he contributed. Any views expressed therein are those of the translator, and not necessarily those of the author.

1. In the Indonesian Language, the term used for the Constitution is "*Undang-Undang Dasar 1945.*" The inclusion of the year is important because Indonesia has had two other constitutions: the 1949 Constitution of the Republic of the United States of Indonesia (which was implemented upon transfer of sovereignty from the Dutch), and the 1950 Provisional Constitution (which was implemented following the breakdown of the federal system and the reestablishment of the Republic of Indonesia). Since this chapter will concern almost exclusively the Constitution of 1945, which was reinstated in 1959 and has been used ever since, I have elected to drop the "of 1945" from my references to it (trans.).

2. *Pancasila* means literally "five principles," and, as will be discussed at length below, it is now considered the immutable foundation of the Indonesian state (trans.). [*Editor's Note.* On the meaning and application of Pancasila, the author recommends, in English, the following publications of the Board to Promote Education Implementing the Guidance to the Perception and Practice of Pancasila: *Pancasila: The State Foundation and Ideology of the Republic of Indonesia* (1990); *Decree of the People's Consultative Assembly of the Republic of Indonesia No. II/MPR/1988 on the Guidelines of State Policy* (1991); and *Nugroho Notosusanto, Dwi Fungsi Abri: The Dual Function of the Indonesian Armed Forces, Especially since 1966*(1991). The Board's address is J1. Taman Pejambon 2, Jakarta, Indonesia.]

3. For a better understanding of these two committees and the circumstances under which they came into existence, *see* Benedict R. Anderson,*Java in a Time of Revolution*, Ithaca, Cornell University Press, 1972, 52, 62-72 (trans.).

4. All expressions enclosed by quotation marks were in English (or another non-Indonesian language) in the original (trans.).

5. A full translation of the Indonesian Constitution of 1945 appears at the end of this Chapter. That translation and all references to the Constitution here are from Daniel Lev, *The Transition to Guided Democracy*, Ithaca, Cornell University, Department of Asian Studies Monograph Series, 1966 (trans.).

6. Adapted from *Penjelasan Undang Undang Dasar 1945* (Elucidation of the Constitution of 1945), Umum, No. II, as explained in Notonagoro, *Pembukaan Undang Undang Dasar 1945*, 1959. [The Elucidation of the Constitution of 1945 (hereafter Elucidation) was published simultaneously with the official publication of the text of the Constitution on February 15, 1946, and contains principles to govern the interpretation of the Constitution. Since I have found no English translation of the Elucidation, all references will be to the Indonesian version (trans.).]

7. Adapted from remarks made by Soepomo: Minutes of the*Badan Persiapan Usaha Kemerdekaan Indonesia*. Material on file at the Indonesian National Secretariat, Jakarta. [Since there are a large number of general references to the Minutes of both the *Badan Persiapan Usaha Kemerdekaan Indonesia* (hereafter*Badan Persiapan*) and the *Panitia Persiapan Kemerdekaan Indonesia* (hereafter PPKI), and since all of those minutes are only available in the Indonesian National Secretariat files, hereafter the Committee names will be abbreviated as above, and the reference to the National Secretariat will not be repeated (trans.).]

8.*Gotong Royong*, given in parentheses in the original, is the Javanese concept of cooperative community endeavor (trans.).

9. Adapted from remarks made by Soepomo: Minutes of the *Badan Persiapan*.

10. Adapted from*Penjelasan Undang Undang 1945* [hereafter *Penjelasan*]. *See* note 6, Umum, No. II.

11. Adapted from *Penjelasan,mengenai pasal 29, ayat 1*.

12. Since the formation of the third Indonesian Cabinet in October 1946, Indonesia has had a Department of Religion to safeguard this principle.

13. Excerpted from paragraph 3 of the Preamble to the Constitution. [The original reads "*Atlas berkat rakhmat Allah Yang Maha Kuasa dan dengan didorongkan oleh keinginan luhur sapaya berkehidupan kebangsaan yang bebas*" (trans.).]

14. Excerpted from paragraph 2 of the Preamble to the Constitution.

15. As will be explained below in section 4 of Part I, in technical terms, the Indonesian head of state receives his mandate from the*Majelis Permusyawaratan Rakyat* or MPR (the People's Consultative Assembly) and he is termed the Mandatary (*Mandataris*) of the MPR (trans.).

16. The Indonesian reads *Pelestarian demokrasi Pancasila*." *Pelestarian* literally means "to make eternal"; the connotation of the original is thus stronger than that conveyed by the English "safeguarding" (trans.).

17.*See also* Padmo Wahjono,*Penerapan Pancasila dalam Demokrasi di Indonesian*, Balai Pustaka, 1983.

18. Adapted from *Penjelasan*, Umum No. III; and Padmo Wahjono,*Sistem Hukum Nasional dalam Negara Hukum Pancasila*, 1983.

19. *See* also Mohammad Koesnardi, *Susunan Pembagian Kekuasaan menurut Undang Undang Dasar 1945*.

20. Adapted from the Minutes of the*Badan Persiapan, Panitia Dasaad*, 10 July 1945.

21. Benedict R. Anderson,*op cit.*, discusses the role of the occupying authority--the Japanese--and questions the democratic nature of the selection of members for the committees (trans.).

22. Adapted from the Minutes of the*Badan Persiapan, Panitia Otto Iskandardinata*, 11 July 1945.

23. Adapted from remarks made by Mohammad Hatta: Minutes of the*Badan Persiapan*, 11 July 1945.

24. Adapted from remarks made by Maramis: Minutes of the *Badan Persiapan*, 11 July 1945.

25. Haji Agus Salim was a well-known figure in the prewar nationalist movement (trans.).

26. Adapted from remarks made by Haji Agus Salim: Minutes of the *Badan Persiapan*, 11 July 1945.

27. Excerpted from the fourth paragraph of the Preamble to the Constitution. [The Indonesian reads: "*Seluruh Tumpah Darah Indonesian.*" This is a particularly difficult phrase to translate. *Tumpah darah* literally means bloodshed, but idiomatically, can refer to birth; so the translation could also read: "Every place where Indonesians are born" (trans.).

28. For documentation to the contrary, *see* Julie Southwood and Patrick Flanagan, *Indonesia: Law, Propaganda, and Terror*, London, Zed Press, 1983 (trans.).

29. Adapted from the Minutes of the *Panitia Persiapan Kemerdekaan Indonesia* (PPKI), 19 August 1945.

30. Adapted from paragraph 4 of the Preamble to the Constitution.

31. Adapted from MPR Resolution No. IV/MPR/1983.

32. Adapted from the Constitution, Article 1, Paragraph 1.

33. Adapted from *Penjelasan, mengenai pasal 3*.

34. The Constitution's stipulations for the MPR are in Articles 2 and 3.

35. *See* Chapter XI, *Tata Tertib Majelis Permusyawaratan Rakyat*, MPR Resolution No. I/MPR/1983.

36. *See* the Constitution, Article 37.

37. *See* the Constitution, Article 2.

38. Adapted from *Penjelasan, Umum, Kedudukan Dewan Perwakilan Rakyat Adalah Kuat*.

39. *See* the Constitution, Article 18. *See also* Solly Lubis, *Perkembangan Garis Politik dan Perundang-undangan Mengenai Pemerintahan Daerah di Indonesia*.

40. For a better understanding of GBHN, *see* below section II, 2, "The Determination of the *Garis Besar Haluan Negara*" (trans.).

41. Adapted from *Penjelasan*, Umum No. II and III, *Sistem Pemerintahan Hegara*.

42. I have translated the title "*Kepala Kuasaan Executif*" as "head of the executive arm of government" (trans.).

43. Adapted from *Penjelasan*, Umum No. V, VI, dan VII, *Sistem Pemerintahan Negara*.

44. Adapted from *Penjelasan*, Umum, *Menteri Negara bukan Pegawai Tinggi Biasa*.

45. Adapted from *Penjelasan*, mengenai pasal 10, 11, 12, 13, 14 and 15.

46. Adapted from *Penjelasan*, mengenai pasal 16. *See also Undang Undang* No. 4 (National Law No. 4) 1978.

47. Adapted from *Penjelasan*, mengenai pasal 27; *see also* Kuntjoro Poebopranoto, *Hak-hak Azasi Manusia dan Pancasila*, 1975.

48. Excerpted from *Penjelasan*, mengenai pasal 28; *see also* Hazairin, *Demokrasi Pancasila*, 1973.

49. Adapted from *Penjelasan*, Umum, *Sistem Penerintahan Negara*.

50. Adapted from *Penjelasan*, Umum, No. IV, *Undang Undang Bersifat Singkat*.

51. Adapted from *Penjelasan*, Umum No. III, *Undang Undang Dasar Menciptakan Pokok-pokok Pikiran yang Terkandung di dalam Pembukaan dalam Pasal-pasalnya*.

52. *See* Interim MPR Resolution No. XIX/MPR/1966.

53. *See* the Constitution, Article 27.

54. *See* Sri Soemanti, *Hak Menguji Materiil di Indonesia*, 1972.

55. Adapted from *Penjelasan* Umum No. II, *Sistem Pemerrintahan Negara*; *see also* Padmo Wahjono, *Indonesia Negara Berdasar Atlas Hukum*, 1982.

56. Excerpted from the Constitution, Article 4.

57. *See* Part III (*Krida ke III*) of the *Program of the Fourth Development Cabinet, 1983-1988*.

58. Adapted from remarks made by Soepomo: Minutes of the *Badan Persiapan*, 15 July 1945 and 19 August 1945.

59. National Law, *Undang Undang tentang Susan dan Kedudukan* MPR, DPR, and DPR Daerah 1985; *see also* Djokosoetono, *Mengenai Perwakilan Golongan Fungsional dalam Guru Pinandito*, 1984.

60. *See Undang Undang* No. 4 (National Law No. 4), 1978.

61. *See Undang Undang* No. 5 (National Law No. 5), 1973.

62. *See Undang Undang* No. 14 (National Law No. 14), 1985.

63. The original reads "*Di daerah-daerah yang bersifat autonom tersebut*" (trans.).

64. Adapted from *Penjelasan*, mengenai pasal 18.

65. *See* MPR Resolution No. II/MPR/1983, *Arah Pembanguan Jangka Panjang*.

66. For a brief discussion of the *Elucidation*, *see* note 6 (trans.).

67. Adapted from *Penjelasan*, Umum, *Sistem Undang Undang Dasar*.

68. Adapted from the Preamble to the Constitution, Paragraph 4.

69. *See* the Constitution, Article 37.

70. *See* the Constitution, Article 6.

71. *See* the Constitution, Transitional Provision No. 1.

72. *See* the Constitution, Transitional Provision No. 4.

73. Adapted from remarks made by Mohammad Hatta: Minutes of the PPKI, 19 August 1945. [For documentation supporting a contrary view, *see* Benedict R. Anderson, *op cit.*, at 62-65. The KNI was a direct successor of the PPKI and the members of the PPKI had been chosen by the Japanese authorities (trans.).]

74. For an English translation and analysis of this Resolution, *see* Benedict R. Anderson, id., 172-173 (trans.).

75. For a detailed account of the decision to adopt a parliamentary system, *see* Benedict R. Anderson, id., Chapters 9 and 10, 190-231 (trans.).

76. *See Piagam Persetujuan Penandatanganan Konstitusi republik Indonesia Serikat*, 14 December 1949.

77. *See Undang Undang Dasar Sementara 1950* (the Provisional Constitution of 1950); *see also* Harun Al Rasyid, *Proklamasi, Konstitusi dan Dekrit Presiden*, 1968.

78. *See Undang Undang Dasar Sementara 1950*, Article 134; *see also* Pranarka, *Sejarah Penikiran tentang Pancasila*, 1985, and Soediman Kartohadiprodjo, *Beberapa Pemikiran tentang Pancasila*, 1978.

79. *Golkar* was originally formed in 1964 by the Army to coordinate its allies against what it saw as the rising influence of the Indonesian Communist Party. In the late 1960s and early 1970s, it was turned into a large-scale political-bureaucratic machine for winning elections, and all government employees are pressured to join it. *Golkar* won a large majority in the elections of 1971 and 1977. *See* M.C. Ricklefs, *A History of Modern Indonesia*, London, Macmillan Asian Histories Series, London, 1981, 272-279 (trans.). [*Editor's Note.* On the question of succession to President Soeharto's very long-lasting leadership and the much-anticipated legislative (1992) and presidential (1993) elections, see Donald K. Emmerson, "Indonesia in 1990: A foreshadow Play," *Asian Survey*, February, 1991, 179-187.]

80. *See* the Minutes of the PPKI, 19 August 1945.

81. The original reads: "Intisarinya ialah *U*ndang Undang Dasrar 1945: *S*ocialism Indonesia, *D*emocracy Indonesia, dan *K*epribadian Indonesia (USDEK)" [trans.).

82. The name of this committee reflects the date on which the formal transfer of authority from President Sukarno to President Suharto took place: March 11, 1967 (trans.).

83. From 1973 to 1985, the MPR produced on the average eight to ten Resolutions per year.

84. *See Keputusan Pimpinan Majelis Permusyawaratan rakyat*, 1985.

85. *See* the Constitution, Article 6, Paragraph 1.

86. *See* the Constitution, Articles 4 and 7.

87. The first President of Indonesia was Sukarno, who officially held that title from 1945 to 1967 (trans.).

88. *See* Interim MPR Resolution No. XXXiii/MPRS/1967. [It remains in question whether the coup of 30 September-1 October 1965 was in fact Communist-inspired. *See* Benedict R. Anderson and Ruth McVey, *A Preliminary Analysis of the October 1, 1965, Coup in Indonesia*, Ithaca, NY, Cornell Modern Indonesia Project, Interim Reports Series, 1971 (trans.).]

89. "New Order" is the title the Suharto regime has chosen for itself. "Old Order" has been used in retrospect to refer to the Sukarno regime (trans.).

90. *See* MPR Resolutions No. V/MPR/1083 and No. VI/MPR/1983.

91. The first Cabinet consisted of 12 Ministers who headed departments, and five *Menteri Negara* ("Ministers of State").

92. Here the author is referring to the abortive coup of October 1, 1965 and the ensuing months of massacre. Estimates on the death toll in late 1965 and early 1966 range from 100,000 to one million. *See also* note 88 (trans.).

93. For an analysis of Indonesia's current leadership, *see* David Jenkins, *Suharto and his Generals*, Ithaca, NY, Cornell Modern Indonesia Project, Monograph Series, 1984 (trans.).

94. Adapted from *Penjelasan*, mengenai pasal 23.

95. *Undang Undang* No. 14, 1985.

96. *Undang Undang* No. 4, 1978.

97. *Undang Undang* No. 5, 1973.

98. *Undang Undang* No. 5, 1974 and *Undang Undang* No. 5, 1979.

99. Adapted from *Penjelasan*, Umum, *Sistem Undang Undang Dasrar menurut Undang Undang Dasrar 1945.*

100. *See* the Constitution, Article 20.

101. *See* the Constitution, Article 21.

102. *See* the Constitution, Article 11.

103. *See* the Constitution, Article 23.

104. *See* Arifin Soeria Atmadja, *Mekanisme Pertanggung-jawaban Keuangan Negara,* 1986.

105. Excerpted from *Penjelasan*, mengenai pasal 23, ayat 5.

106. Adapted from *Penjelasan*, mengenai pasal 23.

107. *See* the Constitution, Article 23. Paragraph 5.

108. *See Penjelasanw*, mengenai pasal 24 and 25.

109. *See* MPR Resolution No. IV/MPR/1978; *see also* Syachran Basah, *Eksistensi dan Tolok Ukur Atribusi Badan Peradilan Administrasi di Indonesia,* 1984.

110. *KOPKAMTIB* was established on a temporary basis in 1965. Southwood and Flanagan are critical of its present role: "Today it is more powerful than ever, with powers to arrest and detain, to issue decrees, influence policy, stifle political activity ... and control the press. Essentially the existence of *KOPKAMTIB* means that Indonesia is a military-security state, under *de facto* martial law." From Julie Southwood and Patrick Flanagan, *Indonesia: Law, Propaganda and Terror*, London, Zed Press, 1983, 57 (*see also* 83-96), (trans.).

111. *See* MPR Resolution No. III/MPR/1078, Article 11.

112. *See Tata Tertib DPR Republik Indonesia.*

113. MPR Resolution No. I/MPR/1083, Article 4.

114. *See Penjelasan*, Umum No. 3, *System Pemerintahan Negara.*

115. Excerpted from *Penjelasan*, Umum No. 1, *Undang Undang Dasar Sebagian dari Hukum Dasar.*

116. *See* MPR Resolution No. II/MPR/1983, *Tujuan Penbangunan; see also* Padmo Wahjono, *Bahan-bahan Penataan Pedoman Penghayatan dan Penjamalan Pancasila,* 1979.

117. *See* the Constitution, Article 37; *see also* MPR Resolution No. I/MPR/1983.

118. *See* the Constitution, Article 6.

119. *See* Notonagoro, *Pancasila Darar Filsafat Negara Republik Indonesia,* 1951.

120. For information on the coup, *see supra* note 92 (trans.).

121. *See Konsensus Nasional 1966* and *Undang Undang* (National Law) *tentang Sussunan Kedudukan*, MPR, DPR, dan DPRD, 1969.

122. The author is referring here to Article 37 which requires a two-thirds majority of the MPR to approve a change in the Constitution (trans.).

123. *See Undang Undang mengenai Organisasi Kemasyarakatan.*

124. The "floating mass" concept has been used to narrowly define what campaign activities will be allowed and when; the people of the society are to work in unison with minimal politicization (trans.).

125. *See* Interim MPR Resolution No. II/MPR/1960. In 1947, the *Panitia Pemikir Siasat Ekonomi* (Committee to Consider Economic Goals) drafted a plan for the organization of the Indonesian economy (*see* the Committee's "*Dasar Pokok daripada Plan Mengatur Ekonomi Indonesia*").

126. Excerpted from MPR Resolution No. I/MPR/1083, *Pengertian Garis Besar Haluan Negara*.

127. *See* Edi Swasono, *Sistem Ekonomi dan Demokrasi Ekonomi*, 1985; and Mubiyarto, *Moral Ekonomi Pancasila*, 1981.

128. Adapted from MPR Resolution No. I/MPR/1983, *Arah Pembangunan Jangka Panjang*.

129. *Editor's Note*. For assessments, see Emmerson, *supra* mpte 79; Hans Thoolen, ed., *Indonesia and the Rule of Law: Twenty Years of "New Order" Government*, London, Frances Pinter, 1987; and Ulf Sundhausen, "Indonesia: Past and Present Encounters with Democracy," in Daimond *et al.*, eds., *Democracy in Developing Countries: Asia*, Boulder, Lynne Rienner, 1989, at 423.

APPENDIX

THE INDONESIAN CONSTITUTION OF 1945*

Preamble

Whereas independence is the right of every nation, therefore colonialism must be abolished from the face of the earth as it is contrary to the dictates of human nature and justice.

And the struggle for Indonesian independence has now reached that glorious moment, having led the Indonesian people safely to the threshold of independence for an Indonesian State which is free, united, sovereign, just, and prosperous.

With the blessing of God Almighty and impelled by the noble ideal of a free national life, the Indonesian people do hereby declare their independence.

Further, in order to establish a government of the State of Indonesia which shall protect the entire Indonesian people and the whole of the land of Indonesia, and in order to promote the general welfare, to improve the standard of living, and to participate in establishing a world order founded upon freedom, eternal peace, and social justice; therefore the Independence of the Indonesian People is embodied in a Constitution of the State of Indonesia, which Constitution shall establish a Republic of the State of Indonesia in which the people are sovereign and which is based upon: Belief in the One Supreme God, a just and civilized humanitarianism, the unity of Indonesia, and a democracy guided by the wisdom arising from consultation and representation, which democracy shall ensure social justice for the whole Indonesian people.

CHAPTER 1
Form and Sovereignty
Article 1

1. The State of Indonesia is a unitary state and in form a Republic.
2. Sovereignty is vested in the people and exercised fully by the People's Consultative Assembly (*Madjelis Permusjawaratan Rakjat*).

---

*[Courtesty of the translator] This translation by Daniel S. Lev was first published as an Appendix to The Transition To Guided Democracy: Indonesian Politics, 1957-1959, Ithaca, MONOGRAPH SERIES, Modern Indonesia Project, Southeast Asia Program, Cornell University, 1966. Based on several other translations which have appeared since 1945, including two published by the Ministry of Information in Djakarta.

CHAPTER II
The People's Consultative Assembly
(*Madjellis Permusjawaratan Rakjat*)
Article 2

1. The People's Consultative Assembly consists of the members of the Council of Representatives (*Dewan Perwakilan Rakjat*, Parliament) and delegates of the regions and other groups in accordance with rules prescribed by law.
2. The People's Consultative Assembly shall assemble in the capital at least once every five years.
3. All decisions of the People's Consultative Assembly shall be taken by majority vote.

Article 3

The People's Consultative Assembly shall decide upon the Constitution and determine the basic outlines of state policy.

CHAPTER III
The Executive
Article 4

1. The President of the Republic of Indonesia is vested with the power of Government in accordance with the Constitution.
2. In exercising his responsibilities, the President is assisted by a Vice-President.

Article 5

1. The President, acting with the consent of the Council of Representatives, exercises legislative powers.
2. The President shall enact such government regulations (*peraturan pemerintah*) as are necessary for the proper execution of the laws.

Article 6

1. The President shall be a native-born Indonesian.
2. The President and the Vice-President shall be elected by the People's Consultative Assembly by majority vote.

Article 7

The President and Vice-President hold office for a term of five years, and thereafter are eligible for re-election.

Article 8

In event of the President's death, resignation, removal from office, or inability to exercise his duties during the term of his office, he is succeeded by the Vice-President until that term is expired.

Article 9

Before assuming their offices, the President and Vice-President shall, by religious oath or affirmation, solemnly declare before the People's Consultative Assembly or the Council of Representatives as follows:

Oath of the President (Vice-President): "I swear before God, that to the best of my ability I shall faithfully and conscientiously fulfill the duties of the President of the Republic of Indonesia, maintain the Constitution and faithfully execute all laws and regulations, and dedicate myself to the service of State and Nation."

Affirmation of the President (Vice-President): "I do solemnly affirm, that to the best of my ability I shall faithfully and conscientiously fulfill the duties of the President of the Republic of Indonesia, maintain the Constitution and faithfully execute all laws and regulations, and dedicate myself to the service of State and Nation."

Article 10
The President holds the highest authority over the Army, Navy, and Air Force.

Article 11
The President, with the consent of the Council of Representatives, declares War, makes peace, and concludes treaties with other states.

Article 12
The President is empowered to proclaim martial law. The conditions governing a proclamation of martial law, and the consequences thereof, shall be prescribed by law.

Article 13
1. The President appoints diplomatic representatives and Consuls.
2. The President receives the diplomatic representatives of foreign states.

Article 14
The President has authority to grant pardon, amnesty, abolition, and rehabilitation.

Article 15
The President has authority to bestow titles, decorations for merit, and other marks of honor.

CHAPTER IV
The Supreme Advisory Council
(*Dewan Pertimbangan Agung*)
Article 16

1. The composition of the Supreme Advisory Council shall be determined by law.
2. The Supreme Advisory Council is responsible for giving advice on matters submitted to it by the President, and has the right to submit proposals to the Government.

CHAPTER V
The Ministries
Article 17

1. The President is assisted by Ministers of the State.

2. Ministers are appointed and discharged by the President.

3. The Ministers direct Departments of the Government.

CHAPTER VI
Local Government
Article 18

The division of the territory of Indonesia into large and small units and the composition of their government shall be prescribed by law, with due regard for and observance of the principle of consultation and the traditional rights of areas with extraordinary status.

CHAPTER VII
The Council of Representatives
Article 19

1. The composition of the Council of Representatives shall be prescribed by law.

2. The Council of Representatives shall assemble at least once every year.

Article 20.

1. Every statute requires the consent of the Council of Representatives.

2. In the event that a bill is rejected by the Council of Representatives, that bill may not be submitted for a second time during the same session of the Council of Representatives.

Article 21

1. Members of the Council of Representatives have the right to initiate bills.

2. In the event that such a bill is approved by the Council of Representatives but rejected by the President, that bill may not be submitted for a second time during the same session of the Council of Representatives.

Article 22

1. In cases of emergency, the President has the authority to enact government regulations in place of statutes.

2. Government regulations thus enacted shall be submitted to the next session of the Council of Representatives for ratification.

3. In the event that such government regulations are not ratified, they are revoked.

CHAPTER VIII
Finance
Article 23

1. A budget of receipts and expenditures shall be determined each year by the Council of Representatives. In the event that the Council of Representatives does not approve the budget proposed by the Government, then the budget for the preceding year remains in force.

2. Every tax imposed for the purpose of government revenues shall be based upon a statute.

3. The form and denominations of currency shall be determined by law.

4. Other matters concerning public finance shall be prescribed by law.

5. To examine all matters pertaining to public finance, a Financial Auditing Office (*Badan Pemeriksa Keuangan*) shall be established by law. The results of its audits shall be presented to the Council of Representatives.

CHAPTER IX
The Judiciary
Article 24

1. Judicial authority is vested in a Supreme Court and such other judicial bodies as are established by law.

2. The organization and competence of the courts shall be determined by law.

Article 25

The conditions of appointment and removal from office of judges shall be prescribed by law.

CHAPTER X
Citizenship
Article 26

1. Native born Indonesians and other naturalized according to law are citizens.

2. The conditions affecting citizenship shall be prescribed by law.

Article 27

1. All citizens have the same status in law and in government and shall, without exception, respect the law and the government.

2. Every citizen has the right to work and to a reasonable standard of living.

Article 28

The freedom of assembly and association, of expression of spoken and written opinion, and similar freedoms shall be provided for by law.

CHAPTER XI
Religion
Article 29

1. The state is based upon Belief in the One Supreme God.

2. The state guarantees the freedom of every inhabitant to embrace his own religion and to worship according to his religion and his beliefs.

CHAPTER XII
National Defense
Article 30

1. Every citizen has the right and the responsibility to participate in the defense of the state.
2. Matters concerning defense shall be provided for by law.

CHAPTER XIII
Education
Article 31

1. Every citizen has the right to an education.
2. The Government shall provide and manage a system of education, which shall be provided for by law.

Article 32
The Government shall promote and develop the national culture of Indonesia.

CHAPTER XIV
Social Welfare
Article 33

1. The economy shall be organized as a cooperative endeavor based on the principle of family life.
2. The State shall control those means of production which are important for the state and which dominate the economic life of the people.
3. The land, the water, and the natural resources contained therein shall be controlled by the state and exploited for the greatest prosperity of the people.

Article 34
The poor and the orphaned shall be cared for by the State.

CHAPTER XV
The National Flag and Language
Article 35

The Indonesian National Flag is the Honored Red and White.

Article 36
The national language of Indonesia is Indonesian.

CHAPTER XVI
Amendment of the Constitution
Article 37

1. In order to amend the Constitution, a quorum of two-thirds the membership of the People's Consultative Assembly is required.
2. Decisions shall be taken by a two-thirds majority of those attending.

Transitional Provisions

Article I

The Preparatory Committee for Indonesian Independence shall prepare and arrange the transfer of administration to the Government of Indonesia.

Article II

All existing state institutions and laws shall remain in force so long as new ones have not been created in accordance with this Constitution.

Article III

The President and Vice-President shall be elected initially by the Preparatory Committee for Indonesian Independence.

Article IV

Before the formation according to this Constitution of the People's Consultative Assembly, the Council of Representatives, and the Supreme Advisory Council, their authority shall be exercised by the President with the assistance of the National Committee.

11

MALAYSIA

The Constitution of Malaysia and
The American Constitutional Influence

Ahmad Ibrahim

M.P. Jain

A. The Malaysian Constitutional System (Ahmad Ibrahim)

The influence of the American Constitution on the Malaysian Constitution is at best indirect and not direct. This is because of the historical background to the emergence of the Federation of Malaya and later of Malaysia as a sovereign nation, and in particular to the circumstances under which the Federal Constitution was drafted and enacted. Unlike the Constitution of the United States or even that of India, the Constitution of Malaysia was not drafted by the people or a Constituent Assembly of Malaysia. The Constitution was the fruit of joint Anglo-Malayan efforts and indeed, even the Malayan Parliament had no hand in its drafting.

Origins of the Malaysian Constitution

As a result of a constitutional conference held in London from January 18 to February 6, 1956, attended by a delegation from the Federation of Malaya consisting of four representatives of Their Highnesses the Rulers, the Chief Minister and three other Ministers, and also by His Excellency the High Commissioner and certain of his advisers, proposals were made for the appointment of an independent Commission to make recommendations for a Constitution for a fully self-governing and independent Federation of Malaya within the British Commonwealth. These proposals were approved by Her Majesty the Queen and Their Highnesses the Rulers and in consequence a Constitutional Commission was appointed. This consisted of the Rt. Hon. Lord Reid, a Lord of Appeal in Ordinary, as Chairman and members from the United Kingdom, Australia, India and Pakistan. A representative from Canada was also appointed but he was unable to serve. The terms of reference of the Constitutional Commission were as follows:[1]

to examine the present constitutional arrangements throughout the Federation of Malaya, taking into account the position and dignities of Her Majesty the Queen and of their Highnesses the Rulers; and

to make recommendations for a federal form of Constitution for the whole country as a single, independent, self-governing unit within the Commonwealth based on Parliamentary democracy with a bicameral legislature which would include provision for:

a) the establishment of a strong central government with the States and settlements enjoying a measure of autonomy (the question of residual legislative power to be examined and to be the subject of recommendations by the Commission) and with machinery for consultation between the Central Government and the States and settlements on certain financial matters to be specified in the Constitution;

b) the safeguarding of the position and prestige of Their Highnesses as Constitutional Rulers of their respective States:

c) a constitutional *Yang di Pertuan Besar* for the Federation to be chosen from among Their Highnesses the Rulers;

d) a common nationality for the whole of the Federation;

e) the safeguarding of the special position of the Malays and the legitimate interests of other communities.

The Commission duly submitted its report; the report together with three draft Constitutions for the Federation, Malacca and Penang were published on February 21, 1957. A working party was then appointed by the British Government, the Conference of Rulers, and the Government of the Federation to make a detailed examination of the Report and to submit recommendations thereon. Upon the basis of these recommendations, the new Federal Constitution, together with the Constitution of Malacca and Penang were promulgated upon Merdeka Day, August 31, 1957. The Federation of Malaya consisted of the Malay States--the Federated Malay States of Selangor, Negeri Sembilan, Perak and Pahang; and the Unfederated Malay States of Johore, Kedah, Perlis, Kelantan and Trengganu--and the Colonies of Penang and Malacca. The Malay States were, in theory at least, independent Malay Kingdoms. After the reoccupation of the country from the Japanese in 1946, the British Government tried to make the whole of the country into a colony under the style of the Malayan Union; but this was opposed by the Malays through their political organization, the United Malays National Organization or UMNO. As a result, new agreements were negotiated between His Majesty the King and the Rulers of each of the Malay States and the Federation of Malaya was set up in 1948.

The Preamble to the Federation of Malaya Agreement, 1948, had expressed the desire of the United Kingdom Government and Their Highnesses the Rulers that "progress should be made towards eventual self-government." To this end, elections for 52 seats on the Federal Legislative Council were held in July 1955; and when the legislature with an elected majority was constituted, consideration was then given to the next step towards independence. This led to the holding of the Constitutional Conference in 1956 and the proposal to set up the Constitutional Commission. Thus was independence achieved by the transfer of power and jurisdiction of Her Majesty the Queen. As stated in the Federation of Malaya Agreement, 1957,

> As from the 31st day of August 1957, the Malay States and the settlements shall be formed into a new Federation of States by the name of the Federation of Malaya; and thereupon the said settlements shall cease to form part of Her Majesty's dominions and Her Majesty shall cease to exercise any sovereignty over them and all power and jurisdiction of Her Majesty or of the Parliament of the United Kingdom in or in respect of the Settlements or the Malay States or the Federation as a whole shall come to an end.[2]

When subsequently in 1963, Sabah and Sarawak (and, until 1965, Singapore) joined the Federation, Her Majesty again relinquished her jurisdiction in Sarawak and Sabah (and Singapore), which were then British colonies. The Federation then came to be called Malaysia.

Another historical fact to remember is that the Constitution is the result of compromises reached between the major races in the Federation of Malaya -- the Malays, the Chinese, the Indians.[2A] Political power was originally in the hands of the Malay Rulers and the Malays, but it was agreed that citizenship rights should be granted to all races who regarded Malaya as their permanent home. In return, certain measures were agreed upon to safeguard the special position of the Malays, especially in education, trade and commerce. Under the British rule, the rural areas where the Malays predominated had been neglected in favor of the urban areas where the Chinese and Indians predominated; the safeguards were needed in order to improve the conditions in the rural areas and to bring up the educational and economic level of the Malays to be able to compete equally with the other races. Safeguards were also agreed on for the religion of the Malays, Islam, and for the Malay Language as the national language of the Federation.

When Sabah and Sarawak joined the Federation, safeguards were also provided for the natives of Sabah and Sarawak.

The Malaysian Constitution and the United States Constitution

There are many similarities between the American Constitution and the Malaysian Constitution but even within the similarities there are differences. And apart from that there are important differences between the two Constitutions.

Written Constitution

Like the American Constitution, the Malaysian Constitution is written. Although the bulk of the Civil Law in Malaysia is based on the English model, in the matter of the Constitution the Malaysian Constitution does not follow England in having an unwritten Constitution. The Malaysian Constitution exists as a separate written document and this shows the indirect influence of the American Constitution. The American Constitution is the model of a written Constitution and when the British Commonwealth countries began to draft their written Constitutions, it was to the American Constitution that they looked for guidance and inspiration. Thus we had the Constitutions of Australia, Canada and later India. The Malaysian Constitution itself is to a large extent modeled on the Indian Constitution. The American Constitution is a short one, containing only seven articles in the original text with twenty-six additional articles inserted by amendments. It includes only essential and fundamental provisions which are stated in general terms, leaving other provisions to be dealt with by legislation. The Malaysian Constitution, on the other hand (like the Indian Constitution), is more elaborate and detailed. The Malaysian Constitution has 181 Articles, but many amendments have been introduced and the new Articles are numbered, for example, 15A, 16A, 43A, 43B, 43C and 161A, 161B and so on. There are also 13 Schedules.

Supremacy of the Constitution

The Malaysian Constitution states in its Article 4 that the Constitution is the Supreme Law of the Federation. The effect of this is that any law passed after Merdeka Day (that is, 31st August 1957) which is inconsistent with the Constitution shall to the extent of the inconsistency be void. In regard to existing law, that is laws made before Merdeka Day, Article 162 of the Constitution provides that they shall continue to be in force, unless repealed or modified; but in applying the provision of any such law, the Court may apply it with such modifications as may be necessary to bring it into accord with the provisions of the Constitution.

As the Malaysian Constitution is the Supreme Law of the land, the Malaysian Government is a limited Government and has to work within the Constitution. Though the *Yang di Pertuan Agong* enjoys legal authority as the Sovereign, he has sworn to uphold the Constitution; if any official act is unconstitutional or unlawful, the Minister when he acts may be called to account in the courts.[3]

Similarly, the power of the Government or a Minister or public official is limited by the Constitution. The legislative bodies, Parliament and the State Legislative Assemblies, may make law only on subjects specified in the Constitution and provided it is not contrary to the Constitution.

The American Constitution states: "This Constitution and the Laws of the United States which shall be made in pursuance thereof shall be the supreme law of the land; and judges in every state shall be bound thereby, anything in the Constitution or the laws of any state to the contrary notwithstanding." There is thus no express provision stating that laws which conflict with the Constitution are invalid and the basic principle had to be established by the courts.

Judicial Review

In order to adjudicate on the unconstitutionality or invalidity of the acts of the executive and of the legislature, the Malaysian Constitution establishes an independent judiciary whose members may not before the retiring age of 65 be removed from office, except on the recommendation of a committee of not less than five judges; and whose salaries and condition of service cannot be altered to their disadvantage, and who are entitled to a pension.[4]

This power of judicial review again is alien to English Law, under which Parliament is supreme; and again, this power may be said to be derived indirectly from the American Constitution.

The power of judicial review is limited by the Constitution itself in Malaysia. Article 4(3) of the Malaysian Constitution provides:

> The validity of any law made by Parliament or the legislature of any State shall not be questioned on the ground that it makes provision with respect to any matter with respect to which Parliament or, as the case may be, the legislature of the State has no power to make laws, except in proceedings for a declaration that the law is invalid on that ground or:

a) if the law was made by Parliament, in proceedings between the Federation and one or more States;

b) if the law was made by the legislature of a State, in proceedings between the Federation and that State. Article 4(4) of the Malaysian Constitution also provides: "Proceedings for a declaration that a law is invalid on the ground mentioned in Clause (3)... shall not be commenced without the leave of a judge of the Federal Court; and the Federation shall be entitled to be a party to any such proceedings and so shall any State that would or might be a party to proceedings brought for the same purpose under paragraph (a) or (b) of the Clause.

On the other hand, proceedings to declare an act of the executive or a law passed by the legislature to be invalid because it is contrary to the Constitution, as for example, if it contravenes any of the provisions relating to fundamental liberties, may be brought in any Court. However, even here restrictions are placed in Article (4)2 of the Malaysian Constitution which provides in effect that the validity of any law shall not be questioned on the ground that:

a) it imposes on the right of freedom of movement but does not relate to the matters mentioned therein, that is the security of the Federation or any part of it, public order, public health or the punishment of offenders;
b) that it imposes such restrictions as are mentioned in Article 10(2) but these restrictions were not deemed necessary or expedient by Parliament for the purposes mentioned in that article.

The United States Constitution, by contrast, does not itself restrict judicial review; any restrictions are those imposed by the courts themselves, for example, by the doctrine of *locus standi*.

Fundamental Liberties

The United States Constitution enshrines fundamental liberties in general terms, and the scope and limits of these rights have been worked out in the courts. The Malaysian Constitution on the other hand expressly provides that certain fundamental liberties are qualified and may be diminished.

Thus, Article 9(2) of the Malaysian Constitution provides that every citizen has the right to move freely throughout the Federation and to reside in any part thereof, but this is subject, *inter alia*, to any law relating to the security of the Federation or any part thereof, public order, public health or the punishment of offenders.

Article 10(2) of the Malaysian Constitution, again, provides in effect that Parliament may impose:

a) on the rights to freedom of speech and expression such restrictions as it deems necessary or expedient in the interest of the security of the Federation or any part thereof, friendly relations with other countries, public order or morality and restrictions designed to protect the privileges of Parliament or of any legislative Assembly or to provide against contempt of court, defamation or incitement to any offense;
b) on the right to assemble peaceably and without arms, such restrictions as it deems necessary or expedient in the interest of the security of the Federation or any part thereof or public order;
c) on the right to form associations, such restrictions as it deems necessary or expedient in the interest of the security of the Federation or any part thereof, public order or morality.

Equal Protection

In the American Constitution the concept of equal protection is not elaborated and the courts have to determine the extent and limits of that right. In the Malaysian Constitution on the other hand certain types of discrimination are prohibited, but exceptions are allowed. Article 9(1) declares that all persons are equal before the law and entitled to the equal protection of the law. Article 8(2) on the other hand provides:

Except as expressly authorized by this Constitution, there shall be no discrimination against citizens on the ground only of religion, race, descent or place of birth in any law or in the appointment to any office or employment under a public authority or in the administration of any law relating to the acquisition, holding or disposition of property or the establishing or carrying out of any trade, business, profession, vocation or employment.

This right is then clearly subject to the exceptions authorized by the Constitution. Among them, for example, is Clause (5) of Article 8 itself, which provides that the Article does not invalidate or prohibit, among other things, any provision regulating personal law or any provision or practice restricting office or employment connected with the affairs of any religion or of an institution managed by a group professing any religion, to persons professing that religion. Article 153 of the Constitution provides that it shall be the responsibility of the *Yang de Peruan Agong* to safeguard the special position of the Malays and natives of any of the States of Sabah and Sarawak and the legitimate interests of other communities in accordance with the provisions of the Article. It expressly provides for reservation of quotas in respect of services, permits and education for the Malays and natives of Sabah and Sarawak.

Due Process of Law

The American Constitution contains the "due process" concept whereby no person shall be deprived of his life, liberty or property without due process of law. This concept has been interpreted by the American courts in such a way that the law must not be arbitrary or capricious and the law itself may have to conform to the rules of natural justice.

In the Malaysian Constitution, Article 5(1) provides that no person shall be deprived of his life or personal liberty "save in accordance with law," and Article 13 provides that no person shall be deprived of property "save in accordance with law." Until recently, the Malaysian courts have interpreted "law" in these provisions to mean only enacted law;[5] but this view has been held to be wrong and the position in Malaysia may be said to approximate the American position, although the term "due process" itself is not used. This has been the result of two Privy Council decisions on appeals from Singapore, which have been accepted in Malaysia. In *Ong Ah Chuan v. Public Prosecutor*,[6] Lord Diplock said:

> In a constitution founded on the Westminster model, and particularly in that part of it which purports to assure to all individual citizens the continued enjoyment of fundamental liberties of rights, references to "law" in such contexts as "in accordance with law," "equality before the law," "protection of the law" and the like in their Lordship's view refer to a system of law which incorporates those fundamental rules of natural justice that had formed part and parcel of the common law that was in operation in Singapore at the commencement of the Constitution. It would have been taken for granted by the makers of the Constitution that the "law" to which the citizens could have recourse for the protection of fundamental liberties assured to them by the Constitution would be a system of law that did not flout these fundamental rules. If it were otherwise it would be misuse of language to speak of law as something which affords "protection" for the individual in the enjoyment of his

fundamental liberties and the purported entrenchment (by Article 5) of Articles 9(1) and 12(1) would be little better than a mockery.

The decision of the Privy Council in *Ong Ah Chuan's* case has been reaffirmed by the Privy Council in *Haw Tua Tan. Public Prosecutor,*[7] and both these cases have been accepted as authoritative in Malaysia. Thus, in the Federal Court case of *Che Ani bin Itam v. Public Prosecutor*, Raja Azlan Shah L.P. said, relying on *Ong Ah Chuan's* case:[8]

> It is now firmly established that "law" in the context of such constitutional provisions as Articles 5, 8 and 13 of the Constitution refers to a system of law which incorporates those fundamental rules of natural justice that had formed part and parcel of the common law of England that was in operation at the commencement of the Constitution.

We might note that in coming to the decision in *Ong Ah Chuan's* case, Lord Diplock denied any reliance on the American Constitution or even on the Indian Constitution:[9]

> Their Lordships are of opinion that decisions of Indian Courts on Part III of the Indian Constitution should be approached with caution as guides in the interpretation of individual articles in Part IV of the Singapore Constitution, and that decisions of the Supreme Court of the United States on that country's Bill of Rights, whose phraseology is now nearly two hundred years old, are of little help in construing the provisions of the Constitution of Singapore or other modern Commonwealth Constitutions which follow the Westminster model.

Right to Counsel

The Malaysian Constitution in Article 5(3) provides that: "Where a person has been arrested he shall be informed as soon as may be of the grounds of his arrest and shall be allowed to consult and be defended by a legal practitioner of his choice." This provision has been interpreted by the courts in Malaysia to mean that although the right to counsel commences from arrest, the right cannot be exercised immediately, as a balance has to be struck between that right on the one hand and on the other the right of the police to protect the public from wrongdoers by apprehending them and collecting whatever evidence exists against them.

In the American Constitution on the other hand the Sixth Amendment provides, *inter alia*: "In all criminal prosecutions the accused shall enjoy the right ... to have the assistance of Counsel for his defense." This provision has been interpreted by the American courts to mean that the right to counsel commences from the moment of arrest and that the accused is entitled to counsel from that moment.

Federal Principle

The Constitution of the United States establishes an association of States so organized that the powers are divided between a general government which in certain matters--for example, the making of treaties and the coining of money--is independent of the governments of the associated States, and on the other hand State governments in certain matters are in their turn independent of the central government. This involves that General and regional governments both operate directly upon the people; each citizen is subject to two governments. As the Tenth Amendment made clear in 1791, "the powers not delegated to the United States by the Constitution nor prohibited by it to the states, are reserved to the states respectively or to the people."

The Malaysian Constitution, like the Indian Constitution, provides for a federal list, a state list, and a concurrent list which spell out in great detail federal subjects, state subjects and concurrent subjects with respect to which the Federation, he states, and both the Federation and the States have legislative and executive power. As we have seen, the terms of reference for the Constitutional Commission which drafted the Constitution were to establish a strong central government; and this is why we find that most of the important powers, including those of finance, are given to the Federation. Although Article 77 provides that the residual power of legislation shall be with the States, the scope of this power is very limited.

The Senate and the House of Representatives

Both the United States and Malaysia have bicameral legislatures but the Senate (*Dewan Negara*)in Malaysia is more like the House of Lords in England than the Senate in the United States. In the United States the members of the Senate are elected directly by the people of the different States. Although there is power[11] in Malaysia for Parliament to provide that the members of the Senate to be elected in each State shall be elected by the direct vote of the electors of that State, this has not been implemented.

Instead, members of the Senate for the State are elected by the Legislative Assembly of the States. Moreover, the appointed members of the Senate at present exceed the numbers elected by the States--43 members are appointed and 26 are elected.

The Senate in Malaysia has less power than the lower house, the House of Representatives(*Dewan Rakyat*), and can at best delay legislation (except for constitutional amendments).[12] In contrast, the Senate in the United States appears to be powerful and its approval essential.

Unlike their position in the United States, the civil courts in Malaysia are Federal Courts. The only State Courts are the *Sariah* (Islamic law) Courts and the Native Customary Courts.

Besides those already noted there are other significant differences between the Constitutions of the United States and of Malaysia.

The Malaysian System of Government

Constitutional Monarchy and Parliamentarism

Malaysia does not follow the American presidential system and instead follows the Parliamentary Cabinet System on the Westminster model. The head of State is the *Yang di Pertuan Agong* [Paramount Ruler, King], who is a constitutional monarch, much like the British Queen, who normally acts on the advice of the Cabinet or a Minister. In Malaysia the *Yang di Pertuan Agong* is elected by the Malay Rulers from among themselves and holds office for five years. The *Yang di Pertuan Agong* is an important component of Parliament; he summons, prorogues, and dissolves Parliament, he addresses Parliament on important occasions (as on the opening of the Parliamentary sessions), and bills passed by the House of Representatives and the Senate only become law when assented to by him.[124] Executive authority is vested in him. He appoints the Prime Minister *Perdana Mentri* and the other members of the Cabinet. Civil Servants, though appointed by an independent Public Service Commission, hold office, subject to certain constitutional safeguards, during the pleasure of the *Yang di Pertuan Agong*. The *Yang di Pertuan Agong* also appoints Ambassadors and many principal officers such as the Chairmen and members of the various Service Commissions established by the Constitution, and the Attorney-General and Auditor General. As regards the armed forces, he is Commander-in-Chief and officers hold commissions from him, although he cannot issue orders to them.

As regards the Judiciary, until recently the *Yang di Pertuan Agong* was the final court of appeal, appeals being referred for advice to the Privy Council in England, but appeals to the *Yang di Pertuan Agong* have now been abolished. The *Yang di Pertuan Agong* appoints the Lord President of the Supreme Court, the Chief Justices and the Judges; writs issue from the High Court in his name and he has the power to grant pardons, reprieves and respites in regard to the Federal Territory and in certain emergency cases.

Although the *Yang di Pertuan Agong* appears to be invested with a lot of power, he normally acts on advice. Article 40(1) of the Malaysian Constitution provides that in the exercise of his functions under the Constitution or Federal Law, the *Yang di Pertuan Agong* shall act in accordance with the advice of the Cabinet or a Minister acting under the general authority of the Cabinet, except as otherwise provided under the Constitution. Article 40(2) then provides that the *Yang di Pertuan Agong* may act in his discretion in the performance of the following functions: the appointment of a Prime Minister; the withholding of consent to a request for the dissolution of Parliament; the requisition of a meeting of the Conference of Rulers concerned solely with the proceedings, positions, honors and dignities of the Malay Rulers; and in any other case mentioned in the Constitution.

The Conference of Rulers *Majlis Raja Raja* is a body established by the Constitution consisting of the nine Rulers and the four *Yang di Pertuan Negeri* (of Penang, Malacca, Sabah and Sarawak). It has no direct legislative, executive or financial power, but it is the most prestigious body in the country. Its main function is to exchange views with the Federal Government on matters of national importance.

In the Conference the *Yang di Pertuan Agong* acts on the advice of the Prime Minister, and each Ruler and *Yang di Pertuan Agong* acts on the advice of the Chief Minister. The Conference of Rulers has an important advisory function in the appointment of certain officials like the Judges, the Chairman of the Public Services Commission, and the Auditor-General. Some amendments to the Constitution, especially those relating to sensitive issues and the Conference of Rulers itself require the consent of the Conference of Rulers.

The Head of Government in Malaysia is the Prime Minister. The Malaysian Constitution provides that the *Yang di Pertuan Agong* shall appoint as Prime Minister to preside over the Cabinet a member of the House of Representatives who in his judgment is likely to command the confidence of the majority of the members of that House. Other Ministers and Deputy Ministers are appointed by the *Yang di Pertuan Agong* from among the members of either House of Parliament on the advice of the Prime Minister. Thus, the Prime Minister must be a member of the House of Representatives and the Ministers must be members of either House; the choice of the Prime Minister is therefore more limited. Unless a person has been elected as a Member of the House of Representatives, he must be appointed as Senator before he can be a Minister or Deputy Minister. The Prime Minister's party or coalition of parties must have a majority in the House of Representatives; they are responsible to the people not directly but through their elected representatives. If the Prime Minister's party or coalition of parties loses the confidence of the majority in the legislature, they have to give up office, unless the Prime Minister is able to persuade the *Yang di Pertuan Agong* to dissolve Parliament. If there is a fresh election, then the party in power will only continue to hold power if it succeeds in obtaining a majority of seats in the House of Representatives. Thus, unlike the United States, there is no separation of powers between the Executive and the Legislature. The members of the Executive are also members of the Legislature and they can only continue to hold office if they command the confidence of the Legislature. As the Executive has a majority of votes in the Legislature, it can to a certain extent control the proceedings of the Legislature. There is mutual cooperation rather than separation of powers.

Parliament, unless sooner dissolved, shall continue for five years from the date of its first meeting and shall then stand dissolved.[13] Elections will then be held to decide which party or parties will secure a majority in the House of Representatives and therefore will be invited to constitute the Government.

The Malay Rulers and the State Constitutions

Royalty has survived in Malaysia and there are nine Malay Rulers whose sovereignty, prerogatives, powers and jurisdiction are safeguarded by the Constitution. The Rulers are constitutional monarchs and generally act on the advice of the State Executive Council or a member thereof, except where the State Constitution provides that the Ruler may act at his discretion. Each State has its Constitution and these have to follow the essential provisions set out in the Eighth Schedule to the Federal Constitution.

The States which do not have Rulers have *Yang di Pertuan Negeri* who are appointed by the *Yang di Pertuan Agong* in accordance with the State Constitution. The *Yang di Pertuan Negeri* also generally acts on the advice of the Executive Council or a member thereof, except where the State Constitution provides that he may act in his discretion. Each of the States has a unicameral Legislative Assembly and the system of Government follows the Parliamentary-Cabinet system. The *Menteri Besar* or Chief Minister is appointed by the Ruler or *Yang di Pertuan Negeri* as he commands the confidence of the Assembly, and he and the members of the Executive Council will only continue to hold office so long as he commands the confidence of the Assembly.

The Legislative Assembly, like Parliament, unless sooner dissolved, shall continue for five years from the date of its first sitting and shall then stand dissolved.

Malays and Natives of Sabah and Sarawak

Owing to the neglect of the rural areas during the British occupation, the majority of races in Malaysia--the Malays and the Natives of Sabah and Sarawak--have been left behind in education, commerce and industry. In order to redress the balance and make the Malays and Native peoples better able to compete with the immigrant races who live mainly in the urban areas, special provision is made in the Malaysian Constitution for the reservation of quotas in respect of services, permits, the public service, and education for the Malays and Natives of Sabah and Sarawak. Article 153 of the Constitution makes it the responsibility of the *Yang di Pertuan Agong* to safeguard the special position of the Malays and the Natives of Sabah and Sarawak and at the same time to safeguard the legitimate interests of the other communities in Malaysia. In exercising his functions under the Constitution and Federal Law, in accordance with Article 153, the *Yang di Pertuan Agong* shall not deprive any person of any public office held by him or the continuance of any scholarship, exhibition or other educational or training privileges or special facilities enjoyed by him.

Thus, the Constitution tries to achieve not only equality before the law but also economic and social equality. The Government in Malaysia has therefore striven to achieve social justice for all and under the New Economic Policy, the Government is determined to eradicate poverty in the urban and rural areas and to restructure society so as to achieve economic equality and social justice.

National Language

The Malaysian Constitution provides that Malay (*Bahasa Malaysia*) shall be the national language and so the Malay language has to be used for all official purposes.[14] However, no person is prohibited or prevented from using (otherwise than for official purposes) any other language or from teaching or learning any other language. Although Malay is the national language,

English is still extensively used and in fact efforts have been made to improve the standard of English, which has declined somewhat since independence.

Islam

The Malaysian Constitution provides that Islam is the religion of the Federation; but other religions may be practiced in peace and harmony in any part of the Federation.[15]

In his oath of office, the *Yang di Pertuan Agong* declares that he shall at all times protect the religion of Islam and uphold the rules of law and order in the country. In each of the Malay States which has a Ruler, the Ruler is the Head of the Islamic Religion in his State. In the Federal Territory, Penang, Malacca, Sabah and Sarawak, the *Yang di Pertuan Agong* is the head of the Islamic Religion. Freedom of religion is also guaranteed in the Constitution; every person has the right to profess and practice his religion, and subject to limitations which may be imposed on propagation of any religious doctrine or belief among Muslims, to propagate it.[16] This power has in fact been used largely to control deviant teachings in Islamic theory and practice.

Citizenship

The Malaysian Constitution provides for four categories of citizenship: by operation of law; by registration, by naturalization; and by incorporation of territory. A person born in Malaysia is a citizen only: a) if he was born on or after Merdeka Day (August 31, 1957) and before October 1962; b) if he was born after September 1962 but before September 16, 1963, if one of his parents was at the time of his birth either a citizen or a permanent resident or he was not born in any other country; and c) if he was born on or after September 16, 1963 if one of his parents was at the time of the birth either a citizen or a permanent resident.[17]

The United States Constitution, on the other hand, provides that "all persons born or naturalized in the United States and subject to the jurisdictions thereof, are citizens of the United States and of the State where they reside."

Emergency Powers

In order to meet the dangers of subversion and Communist insurrection, power is given under the Malaysian Constitution for Parliament and the

Government to act against subversion and emergency situations.[18] Legislation against subversion has been enacted in the form of the Internal Security Act, which enables orders of preventive detention to be made. Moreover, if *Yang di Pertuan Agong* is satisfied that a grave emergency exists whereby the security or economic life of the Federation or any part of it is threatened, he may issue a Proclamation of Emergency. If a Proclamation of Emergency is issued when Parliament is not sitting, the *Yang di Pertuan Agong* shall summon Parliament as soon as may be practicable. Until both Houses of Parliament are sitting, the *Yang di Pertuan Agong* may promulgate ordinances that have the force of law, if satisfied that immediate action is required. A Proclamation of Emergency and any ordinance promulgated under it must be laid before both Houses of Parliament and, if not sooner revoked, shall cease to have effect if resolutions are passed by both Houses of Parliament annulling such proclamation or ordinance. A resolution annulling a proclamation or ordinance does not affect the legality of anything done by virtue thereof, nor does it affect the power of the *Yang di Pertuan Agong* to issue a new Proclamation or to promulgate an ordinance under the new proclamation.[19]

While a Proclamation of Emergency is in force, the executive authority of the Federation shall, notwithstanding the Constitution, extend to any matter within the legislative authority of a State. It also extends to the giving of directives to a State Government or to any of its officers or authorities. While a Proclamation of Emergency is in force, Parliament may, notwithstanding anything in the Constitution, make laws in regard to any matter, if it appears to Parliament that the law is required by reason of the emergency. Article 79 (relating to the exercise of concurrent legislative powers) does not apply to such a law, so that the State Government does not have to be consulted. Nor shall any provision of the Constitution apply which requires any consent or concurrence to the passing of a law, or any consultation with respect thereto, or which restricts the coming into force of a law after it is passed or the presentation of a Bill to the *Yang di Pertuan Agong* for his assent. Parliament has, however, no power under the clause to pass any law relating to any matter of Islamic law or with respect to any matter of Native law and custom in Sabah and Sarawak. No provision of any Ordinance promulgated under the Article and no provision of any Act of Parliament, which is passed while a Proclamation of Emergency is in force and which declares that the law appears to Parliament to be required by reason of the emergency shall be invalid on the ground of inconsistency with any provision of the Constitution; but this provision does not validate any provision inconsistent with the provisions of the Constitution relating to any matter of Islamic Law, or with respect to any matter of Native law or custom in the States of Sabah or Sarawak, or relating to citizenship or language.[20]

At the expiration of a period of six months beginning with the date on which a Proclamation of Emergency ceases to be in force, any ordinance promulgated in pursuance of the proclamation and to the extent that it could not have been validly made but for Article 150 (relating to the Proclamation of Emergency), any law made while the proclamation was in force, ceases to be effective, except as to things done or omitted to be done before the expiration of that period.[21]

Proclamations of Emergency have been promulgated in Malaysia, in May 1969 after the outbreak of communal riots in Kuala Lumpur, and to deal with constitutional crises in the State of Sarawak in 1966 and Kelatan in 1977. The Emergency promulgated in 1969 has not yet been lifted and Malaysia is therefore still in a State of Emergency, mainly because of the persistence of Communist insurgency in the country.

Even during the Emergency, there are restrictions on preventive detention. The person detained has to be told of the grounds of his detention, and no citizen shall continue to be detained unless an advisory board has considered any representations made by him and has made recommendations to the *Yang di Pertuan Agong* within three months of receiving such representations or within such longer period as the *Yang di Pertuan Agong* may allow.[22]

Sensitive Issues

One result of the communal riots in 1969 is that restrictions have been placed on the questioning of certain sensitive issues. In imposing restrictions, in the interest of security of the Federation or any part of it or public order, on the freedom of speech and expression, the right to assemble and the right to form associations under Article 10 of the Malaysian Constitution, Parliament may pass any law prohibiting the questioning of any matter, right, status, position, privilege, sovereignty or prerogative established or protected by the provisions of Part III (relating to citizenship), Article 152 (National Language), Article 153 (special position of Malays and Natives of Sabah and Sarawak and the legitimate interest of other communities), or Article 1818 (saving of the sovereignty of the Rulers), otherwise than in relation to the implementation thereof as may be specified in such law.[23] The restrictions apply even to members of Parliament and members of the Legislative Assemblies; the immunity of members of Parliament and of members of the Legislative Assembly from proceedings in court shall not apply to any person charged with an offense under the law passed by Parliament under Article 10(4) or with an offense under the Sedition Ordinance, which makes it an offense to question any of the sensitive issues.[24]

Moreover, it is provided that a law making an amendment to Clause 4 of Article 10 and any law passed thereunder, the provisions of Part III (citizenship), Article 38 (the Conference of Rulers), Article 63(4) (restriction of immunity of members of Parliament), Article 70 (Precedence of Rulers), Article 71(1) (Federal Guarantee of State Constitutions), Article 72(4) (restriction of immunity of members of Legislative Assembly), Article 152 (National Language) and Article 153 (special privileges of Malays and Natives of Sabah and Sarawak and the legitimate interests of other communities) can only be passed with the consent of the Conference of Rulers.[25]

Constitution Interpretation and Change

Amendment of the Constitution

Unlike the American Constitution, the Malaysian Constitution has been amended a good number of times. It is generally amendable by Parliament if two-thirds of the total members of each House of Parliament approve. No ratification by the States is necessary. The need for amendment has arisen because the Malaysian Constitution is long and detailed, and contains many matters which could have been left to ordinary legislation.

As the National Front--[*Barisan Nasional*] composed of parties representing the various races in Malaysia--which has been in power since Merdeka Day, has been able to command a two-thirds majority in Parliament, there have been a large number of amendments to the Malaysian Constitution, the general effect of which seems to be to strengthen the central government.

Interpreting the Constitution

In interpreting the Constitution the Courts in Malaysia have tended to refer to English decisions and, to a lesser extent, to Indian decisions. Counsel have sometimes argued on general principles and referred to such doctrines as due process, the basic structure of the Constitution, and the rule of harmonious construction; but the Judges have preferred to take a practical view and have looked to the terms of the Constitution itself. In the case of *Loh Kooi Choon v. Public Prosecutor*,[26] Raja Azlan Shah F.J. referred to Thomas Paine and Frankfurter J.:

A Constitution has to work not only in the environment in which it was drafted but also centuries later. "The vanity and presumption of governing beyond the grave is the most ridiculous and insolent of all tyrannies. Man has no property in man; neither has any generation any property in the generations which are to follow.... It is the living and not the dead that are to be accommodated" (Thomas Paine, *Rights of Man*).

Later in his judgment he quotes Frankfurter J.: "The ultimate touchstone of any constitutionality is the Constitution itself and not any general principle outside it." His conclusion was:

Whatever may be said of other Constitutions, they are ultimately of little assistance to us because our Constitution now stands in its own right, and it is in the end the working of the Constitution itself that has to be interpreted and applied and this wording "can never be overridden by the extraneous principles of other Constitutions" -- see *Adegbenro v. Akintola & Anor* (1963) 3 *all E.R.* J44, 551. each country forms its Constitution according to its genius and for the good of its society. We look at other Constitutions to learn from their experiences and from a desire to see how their progress and well-being is enured by their fundamental law.[27]

Court Reference to U.S. Constitutional Analysis

In recent years, especially with the establishment of the Supreme Court as the successor to the Federal Court, judges in Malaysia have been more ready to accept citations from American courts. A 1987 example offers fit conclusion for this overview of Malaysian constitutionalism, illustrating how different threads are woven together in judicial disposition of cases.

In *Malaysian Bar v. Government of Malaysia*[28] the question at issue was the constitutionality of subsection (1)(a) of Section 46A of the Legal Profession Act, 1976, which restricts membership of the Bar Council, State Bar Committee, and any Committee of the Bar Council or Bar Committee to advocates and solicitors of not less than seven years' standing. The appellants argued that the requirement violates the equal protection clause of Article 8 of the Federal Constitution. Mohammed Azmi S.C.J., in giving the majority judgment of the Supreme Court that the provision did not violate the equal protection clause, as it was based on reasonable and permissible criteria, said:

The concept of equal protection is not universal. At one end of the spectrum are countries like Australia which have no equal protection clause in their Constitutions (see *Australian Federal System* by Lane, Second Edition, page 856). At the other end is the United States of America which by its Fourteenth Amendment provides that "No State shall ..., nor deny to any person within its jurisdiction the equal protection of the laws." Although judicial determination employed the due process clause of the Fifth Amendment to achieve the same result, if the Federal Government classifies individuals in a way which would violate the equal protection clause. It should be noted that the Fifth Amendment contains no equal protection clause, but it does forbid discrimination that is so unjustifiable as to be violative of due process (see *Shapiro v. Thompson*[29] and *Boiling v. Sharpe*).[30] The courts also set the same standards for validity under the Fifth Amendment due process and the Fourteenth Amendment equal protection clauses, which are both jointly referred to as the equal protection guarantee. To be valid under either clause, the United States Supreme Court has used a stricter standard of review in the area of fundamental rights or suspect classification than in the area of economics or social welfare. In particular, a legislative classification must not be based upon impermissible criteria or used arbitrarily to burden a group of individuals. To attain constitutional validity, the courts must be satisfied that the State has a legitimate governmental interest as opposed to mere governmental purpose in creating the burden or restriction when dealing with fundamental rights guaranteed by the Constitution. (See *Handbook on Constitution Law* by Nowak, Rotunda, and Young at pages 517-535.) In this country, the equal protection guarantee can be found in Article 8 of the Federal Constitution, [especially] ... "8(1). All persons are equal before the law and entitled to the equal protection of the law. 8(2). Except as expressly authorized by this Constitution, there shall be no discrimination against citizens on the ground only of religion, race, descent or place of birth in any law" ....

Following the principle laid down in *Lindsley v. National Carbonic Gas Co.*[31] and *Datuk Haji Harun bin Haji Idris v. Public Prosecutor*,[32] if the basis of the difference has a reasonable connection with the object of the impugned legislation, the difference and therefore the law which contains such provisions are constitutional and valid. In his argument, Raja Abdul Aziz, counsel for the appellants, has referred extensively to two American essays, one published in 1949 in the *California Law Review* entitled "The Equal Protection of the Laws"[37 *Cal. L. Rev.* 341] and the other published in 1969 in the *Harvard Law Review* On "Developments: Equal Protection;" [82 *Harv. L. Rev.* 1067, 1170.] I have considered the two essays in the light of current development of the law on equal protection in the United States, including the U.S. Supreme Court decision in *In re Griffiths* ...[33]

The durational experience requirement only delays the opportunity of new lawyers to become candidates or be appointed to the governing bodies, and as such it is valid provided the length of the delay is not patently unreasonable. In the United States, although the constitutionality of a durational residency requirement in elections is still an open question, the U.S. Supreme Court affirmed ... in *Chimento v. Stark*[34] ... that the State has a legitimate interest in creating a seven-year durational residency requirement in an election for governorship, and the delayed opportunity to become a candidate was also held to be valid in terms of the equal protection guarantee.... In the same way, the seven-year requirement helps to ensure that lawyers would have sufficient professional experience and would also familiarize themselves with the various problems of the Bar before they serve in the governing bodies of the legal profession. The seven-year period ... has not been shown to be patently unreasonable in terms of professional experience. I am therefore of the opinion that the classification in sub-section (1)(a) of section 46A is based on reasonable and permissible criteria.... No fundamental rights guaranteed by the Federal Constitution have been violated by the impugned subsection, and on the basis of suspect classification, it has passed the "intelligible differentia and nexus" test. Indeed, (it) ... satisfied even the "legitimate or compelling State or governmental interest" test, required in the United States.

In his dissent, Alleh Abas L.P., analyzing the history of equality jurisprudence in Malaysia, the United States and India, held that the impugned subsection:

embodies a classification without any reasonable basis and which is purely arbitrary and discriminatory with no sufficient nexus with the objective and purpose sought to be achieved by its enactment. If a person admitted as an advocate and solicitor of the High Court is entitled to practice immediately upon his admission, there appears to be no plausible justification for providing for such person as a class or group to be without representation in respect of that class or group on their professional governing and other related bodies until and unless he has attained the status of an advocate and solicitor of not less than seven years" standing.

Whether American constitutionalism will be similarly pivotal in future judicial debates, and if so how, is not clear. Malaysian constitutional law will evolve within the system described here and in the interplay of the courts with the Executive and Parliament discussed in the remainder of this chapter.

B. *Fundamental Rights in Malaysia* (M.P. Jain)

The United States Constitution has been operative for over 200 years, and has exerted a powerful impact on constitutional development in many countries. Here, an assessment is offered of the influence of the American Bill of Rights on the Fundamental Rights guaranteed by the Federal Constitution of Malaysia. The guaranteed fundamental rights of the people, the concept of judicial review, and federalism--these are the concepts of the U.S. Constitution most influential on other constitutions.[35] The most famous clause known abroad is the "due process" clause as contained in the Fifth and Fourteenth Amendments.[36]

Undoubtedly, the basic idea that a written constitution should guarantee some rights of the people is of American origin and has been adopted in Malaysia from the U.S.A. The institution of judicial review to safeguard and protect these rights has also been borrowed from the U.S. Constitution. In general, the idea regarding what basic rights of the people ought to be guaranteed has also been borrowed from the U.S.A., as most of the rights guaranteed in the U.S. would seem to be guaranteed in Malaysia as well.

But there the similarities end; the contrasts between U.S. and Malaysian schemes of fundamental rights are many. The wordings of constitutional provisions in Malaysia guaranteeing fundamental liberties differ too much from the phraseology of the relevant clause in the U.S. Constitution. The language used in Articles 5 to 13 of the Malaysian Constitution to define fundamental rights is not as broad as in the U.S. Constitution. Then, unlike the American Constitution, the Malaysian Constitution itself imposes drastic restrictions on each of these rights. The overall result is that the fundamental rights clauses in the Malaysian Constitution do not constitute much of an effective restraint on the legislative power of Parliament to curtail any of these rights. During the thirty years the Constitution has been in force, no single legislative enactment so far has been held to be void for being unconstitutional. Also, over these years, several amendments of the Constitution have been undertaken with a view to curtail some of these rights. These constitutional amendments reveal the following trends: 1) the powers of the executive have been broadened; 2) the scope of judicial review has been curtailed; 3) the Emergency provisions have been strengthened; and 4) the fundamental rights have been diluted to some extent.

Over and above this, the courts have adopted a narrow literalistic approach to these constitutional provisions. While interpreting these provisions, Malaysian Courts do not depend much on American case law. To mention one typical example of such judicial approach, while interpreting Article 8 of the Malaysian Constitution (which is the equality clause equivalent to the U.S. Constitution[37]) in the first and foremost case, *Datuk Haji Harun bin Haji Idris v. Public Prosecutor,*[38] the Federal Court in its judgment did not cite even a single American case, although a number of Indian cases on the parallel provision in the Indian Constitution (Article 14)[39] were cited. The courts have assiduously discouraged all attempts at invoking any help from the U.S. Constitution (or even the Indian Constitution) in interpreting these clauses. The standard answer of the courts to these attempts has been that the Malaysian Constitution ought to be interpreted on its own terms without importing foreign influence.[40]

As noted in the earlier section, the Privy Council said in *Ong Ah Chuan*[41] that these Articles differ considerably in their language from and are much less compendious and detailed than those in the Indian Constitution under the heading "Fundamental Rights." They differ even more widely from the Bill of Rights in the U.S. Constitution. In fact, the U.S. Constitution has exerted minimal direct influence on the emergence of fundamental rights in Malaysia. The efficacy of the fundamental rights is further reduced in Malaysia because of the presence of Articles 149 and 150 in the Constitution, referred to above.[42]

Personal Liberty

While the notion of personal liberty being a guaranteed right may have been borrowed from the U.S., the constitutional provision in Malaysia guaranteeing personal liberty bears a closer resemblance to the parallel provision in the Indian Constitution than to that in the U.S. Constitution. The Fifth Amendment which says: "No person can be deprived of his life, liberty or property without *due* process of law." The Fourteenth Amendment also says: "... nor shall any State deprive any person of life, liberty, or property without due process of law."

The U.S. Supreme Court has laid emphasis on the word "*due*" as meaning "just," proper" or "reasonable" according to the judicial view. Therefore, the courts can pronounce whether a law affecting a person's life, liberty or property is reasonable or not. The term "law" has also been interpreted more broadly than statutory law. Under the due process doctrine, the U.S. Supreme Court has endeavored to secure fair criminal trials.[43] Infliction of cruel and unusual punishment has also been invalidated by the Supreme Court.[44] But the due process clause is not limited to personal liberty only. The term "liberty" has been broadly interpreted to comprise economic rights and right of contract. Currently, the U.S. Supreme Court is endeavoring to derive from the word "liberty," a constitutional protection for privacy, personal autonomy and some family relationships. The broad ambit of "liberty" becomes clear from what the Supreme Court said in *Meyer v. Nebraska:*.[45]

> [The liberty protected by due process] denotes not merely freedom from bodily restraint, but also the right of the individual to contract, to engage in any of the common occupations of life, to acquire useful knowledge, to marry, establish a home and bring up children, to worship God according to the dictates of his own conscience, and, generally, to enjoy those privileges long recognized at common law as essential to the orderly pursuit of happiness by free men.

A law forbidding use of contraceptives has been invalidated as invading the right of privacy--a penumbral right emanating from the V and XIV Amendments.[46] It has also been ruled that a pregnant woman has a right to abort within the first trimester:[47] "The right of privacy ... is broad enough to encompass a woman's decision whether or not to terminate her pregnancy."

The Constitution of India has Article 21 guaranteeing personal liberty: "No person shall be deprived of his life of personal liberty without procedure established by *law*." What does the expression "law" mean?

The question was raised in *Gopalan*[48] in 1950 in which the validity of the Preventive Detention Act, 1950 (PDA) was challenged. The Supreme Court was invited to assess the reasonableness of both the substantive and the procedural provisions of the Act. It was argued on behalf of *Gopalan, inter alia*, that: i) the term "law" in Article 21 should include "natural justice," and so the PDA to be valid must include principles of natural justice; ii) the expression "procedure established by law" incorporates the American concept of procedural due process, and so the Court could test the reasonableness of the procedure laid down in the PDA.

The Court rejected these arguments and held that the concept of natural justice was vague and so could not be applied. The term "law" in Article 21, the Court ruled, meant only "enacted law." The Court also rejected the argument based on the "due process" clause of the U.S. Constitution. Article 21 was held not to incorporate the American doctrine of due process. Thus, the PDA could not be tested on the ground of reasonableness. The word "law" in Article 21 was held to mean only statutory law and nothing more. Whatever procedure such a law laid down would be valid. The function of the Court was only to see that the requirements of the law were faithfully observed, nothing more. The Court thus exhibited an extremely literal and "positivist" attitude.

Gopalan thus meant that a person could be deprived of his personal liberty under a statutory provision only. The Court sought to ensure that the procedure laid down in the law, authorizing deprivation of personal liberty of a person was observed to the letter of the law. No deviation therefrom was permitted. The reasonableness of the law or the procedure laid down therein could not be gone into by the Court.

But then the Supreme Court changed its earlier opinion and gave a new orientation to Article 21 in *Maneka Gandhi v. Union of India*,[49] a landmark constitutional case; in these words:

> "The attempt of the court should be to expand the reach and ambit of the fundamental rights rather than attenuate their meaning and content by a process of judicial construction. Article 21 and "procedure established by law," the Court has now repudiated the mechanical *Gopalan* approach and ruled that reasonableness must be projected in the procedure contemplated by Article 21: "The procedure must be right and just and fair and not arbitrary, fanciful or oppressive; otherwise, it would be no procedure at all and the requirement of Article 21 would not be satisfied."

The procedure laid down in a law has to be "reasonable," thus bringing the concept of procedural due process into Article 21.

The Court has greatly emphasized procedural safeguards in the area of personal liberty: "The history of personal liberty is largely the history of insistence on observance of procedure. And observance of procedure has been the bastion against wanton assaults on personal liberty over the years." The Supreme Court played an activist role in *Maneka Gandhi* in order to give protection to the life and personal liberty of individuals. The *Gopalan* approach left personal liberty vulnerable, with no security against harsh legislation. *Gopalan* only fortified "personal liberty" against executive action insofar as it must be according to procedure established by law.

Since the *Maneka* decision, the courts have come to lay greater emphasis on the right of personal liberty, the procedure in a law restricting personal liberty must be reasonable; many significant changes have been introduced by the Supreme Court in the administration of criminal justice. For example:

1) The court has criticized long delays in criminal trials, particularly of those who are accused of petty crimes and have to remain in prisons for long periods pending their trial. Procedure which keeps so many people behind

bars without trial cannot be "reasonable, just or fair.[50] The court has ordered release of such under trials as have remained in prisons longer than even the maximum punishment which could be imposed on them under the law for their offense.

2 The court has suggested that provisions regarding bail be changed so that poor accused persons will be released on their personal bonds. Bail must not always be of financial security. The poor cannot furnish the same and so perforce they must remain in prison pending trial.[51]

3) States should provide legal aid to the poor accused persons who face the jeopardy of a prison sentence.[52]

Many other changes, besides the above, have been effectuated by the Court in the administration of criminal justice.[53]

The term "personal liberty" used in Article 21 has a narrower compass than the expression "liberty" used in the due process clauses in the U.S. Constitution. Still, the Indian Supreme Court has not confined the term "personal liberty" merely to its narrow, literal meaning of "freedom of the person from restraint" but has given it a broader meaning. For example, in *Maneka Gandhi*, the Court has ruled that the right to travel abroad is a part of "personal liberty" guaranteed by Article 21. The Court has ruled that the expression "personal liberty", in Article 21, is of the widest amplitude and "it covers a variety of rights which go to constitute the personal liberty of man." Thus, the Supreme Court has held that the telephonic conversation of an innocent citizen would be protected by courts against wrongful or high-handed interference by police tapping. The protection is not for the guilty against the efforts of the police to vindicate the law.[54] In 1986, the Supreme Court ruled that the word "life" in Article 21 includes "the right to livelihood," as the right to life conferred is wide and far-reaching. Article 21 provides protection against arbitrarily taking away life; equally important, "no person can live without the means of living, that is, the means of livelihood."[55] The Court quoted with approval Field J. in *Munn v. Illinois*:[56] "Life means something more than mere animal existence and the inhibition against the deprivation of life extends to all those limits and faculties by which life is enjoyed." With this background, we can now discuss the Malaysian guarantees to life and personal liberty under Art. 5(1): "No person shall be deprived of his life or personal liberty save in accordance with law." Art. 5(1) appears to owe its origin to Art. 21 of the Indian Constitution, but there is one difference in phraseology: Art. 5(1) does not contain, while Art. 21 contains, the word "procedure.

On the whole, the Malaysian apex Court has consistently interpreted Article 5(1) narrowly. The attitude of the Court has been extremely literal and has been very much in contrast with the attitude displayed by the Indian Supreme Court, especially after *Maneka*. In Malaysia, the Court has restricted the scope of freedom of personal liberty by narrowly interpreting the expression "personal liberty" in Article 5(i), and by ruling that Article 5(1) does not insist on any procedural safeguards in the matter of deprivation of "personal liberty."

An example of the restrictive interpretation of "personal liberty" is furnished by the *Government of Malaysia v. Loh Wai Kong*, where the Federal Court excluded the right to travel to a foreign country from the scope of Article 5(1).[57] The Federal Court confined Article 5(1) to guaranteeing a person, citizen or otherwise, except an enemy alien, freedom from being unlawfully detained. The Court pointed out that Article 5(1) speaks of "personal liberty," "not of liberty *simpliciter*," and is limited to the right of the person or the body of the individual. Thus, "a citizen has no fundamental right to leave the country and travel abroad," and the "issue of a passport" is "only a privilege which can be exercised with the concurrence of the executive; it is not a right." The Executive has discretion whether or not to issue a passport.[58] However, the Court added a rider: "Though the citizen does not have a right under our Constitution and our law to a passport, the Government should act fairly and *bona fide* when considering application for a new passport or for the renewal of a passport and should, ... rarely refuse to grant them." The Executive is expected to behave in the same way as when exercising its other discretionary powers. The Government "must act *bona fide*, fairly, honestly and honourably." "If it is established that Government has acted *mala fide*, or has in other ways abused this discretionary power, the court may ... review Government's action and make the appropriate order." The Court will then apply well-established principles of Administrative Law to review Government's exercise of discretionary power.

An important implication of the Court ruling in *Loh Wai Kong* is that no law is required in Malaysia to regulate the issue, denial or cancellation of a passport. The Executive can perform these tasks under its administrative powers. A basic question arises: if a person has *no* right to a passport, will he have standing in a court to challenge improper denial of a passport?

In the same case, the High Court had adopted a different view, and had ruled that "personal liberty" includes liberty of a person not only from being incarcerated or restricted to live in any part of the country, but would also include the right to cross the frontiers in order to enter or leave the country when one so desires. Thus, the right to travel abroad was recognized by the High Court. Refusal or delay in granting a passport to a person was tantamount to preventing him from leaving the country and would amount to a restraint on his person.[59] Obviously, the Federal Court did not agree with the High Court's liberal approach and advocated a narrow and restrictive view of Article 5(1).

In *Karam Singh v. Menteri Hal Ehwal Dalam Negeri, Malaysia*,[60] Tun Suffian, F.J., comparing Article 5 of the Malaysian Constitution with Article 21 of the Indian Constitution, said that while the word "procedure" was to be found in Article 21, the same was missing from Article 5. According to him, this difference made the Indian cases irrelevant to the interpretation of Article 5(1).

The structure of Article 5(1) is such that it authorizes deprivation of life and personal liberty in "accordance with law." This means that Parliament can make a law restricting personal liberty. The view expressed in *Karam Singh*, as mentioned above, means that a law restricting personal liberty need not lay down any procedure for the purpose. Thus, if a law depriving a person of his life or personal liberty provides for no procedure, nothing can be done. If a law lays down no procedure, the Court will not imply any procedural safeguards therein by invoking the concept of natural justice.

Even if a procedure is laid down in the concerned law, it need not be complied with strictly, and the Court can ignore deviance from the prescribed procedure. Procedural lapses in cases of deprivation of personal liberty can be ignored. This view makes protection of personal liberty very weak indeed; for in many cases of deprivation of personal liberty, only procedural safeguards may help. Such a view completely excludes the American concept of "due process"--substantive or procedural --from Article 5(1). There is no substantive or procedural restriction on the legislature and whatever law it makes affecting "life" or "personal liberty" is constitutionally valid. The Malaysian position on Article 5(1) thus seems to be very different from the Indian position on Article 21, especially after *Maneka*.[61]

This extremely positivistic view received a jolt with the Privy Council pronouncement in *Ong Ah Chuan v. Public Prosecutor*,[62] a case from Singapore where a similar constitutional provision prevails. The question raised in the case was regarding the validity of some provisions of the Misuse of Drugs Act (1973). Section 15 of the Drugs Act says that proof of possession of controlled drugs in excess of the minimum quantities stated in the section would give rise to a rebuttable presumption that such possession is for the purpose of "trafficking." Section 15 was challenged as unconstitutional. Further, Section 29, which imposes a mandatory death penalty for "trafficking" in controlled drugs in excess of the higher minimum quantities stated in the Second Schedule, was likewise challenged as inconsistent with the Constitution.

The Public Prosecutor took recourse to the ultimate positivistic argument on behalf of the Government that if deprivation of life or personal liberty takes place under an Act passed by Parliament, the constitutional requirement of Article 5(1) would be satisfied, however arbitrary or contrary to fundamental rules of natural justice the provision of such Act may be. The Privy Council rejected the argument in such a "startlingly broad form." The Privy Council pointed out that the argument involved "the logical fallacy of *petitio principii*." The Court is not relieved of the duty to determine whether the provisions of an Act of Parliament relied upon to justify depriving a person of his life or liberty are inconsistent with the Constitution. The word "law" in Article 5(1) could not mean statutory law only; it should be interpreted as referring to "a system of law which incorporates those fundamental rules of natural justice...in the common law of England that was in operation in Singapore at the commencement of the Constitution."[63]

The Privy Council pointed out that one of the fundamental rules of natural justice in criminal law is that a person should not be punished for an offense unless it has been established to the satisfaction of an independent and unbiased tribunal that he committed it. What fundamental rules of natural justice do require is that there should be material before the Court that is logically probative of facts sufficient to constitute the offense with which the accused is charged. However, the Privy Council held Section 15 of the Drugs Act constitutionally valid: "Presumptions of this kind are a common feature of modern legislation concerning the possession and use of things that present danger to society like addictive drugs, explosives, arms and ammunition." There was no conflict with any fundamental rule of natural justice and so no constitutional objection to a statutory presumption (provided that it was rebuttable by the accused), that his possession of controlled drugs in any measurable quantity, without regard to specified minima, was for the purpose of trafficking in them. The Privy Council also upheld the mandatory death sentence as not being unconstitutional: "There is nothing unusual in a capital sentence being mandatory." Clarifying its position in *Haw Tuan Tan v. Public Prosecutor,*[64] the Privy Council said that what it had said in *Ong Ah Chuan* only meant that criminal procedure should not offend "some fundamental rule of natural justice." The Privy Council refused to draw "a comprehensive list of what constitutes fundamental rules of natural justice applicable to procedure for determining the guilt of a person charged with a criminal offense." The Privy Council also clarified that the rules of criminal procedure or of evidence as they existed in Singapore (or in Malaysia) when the Constitution came into force have not been perpetuated. The Legislature remains free "to enact whatever laws it thinks appropriate to regulate the procedure to be followed in the trial of criminal offenses; subject only to the limitation that such procedure does not offend against some fundamental rule of natural justice." The Supreme Court in Malaysia has accepted the position as laid down by the Privy Council in *Ong Ah Chuan*, and applied it in *Che Ani binti Itam*.[65] The significance of the expression "fundamental rules of natural justice" is not easy to comprehend. It can be interpreted to mean that the view expressed in *Karam Singh* and other cases that Article 5(1) does not refer to procedure is not correct and that a law depriving "life" or "personal liberty" must lay down a procedure for the purpose. Also, that any procedure laid down in any such Act may not be accepted as valid; the courts can scrutinize the procedure to ascertain if it departs from, or is in accordance with, the fundamental rules of natural justice. Or, it can mean that the criminal procedure should not violate some rule of natural justice. It can also be interpreted to mean that if a law is silent as to procedure, natural justice can be implied. But Article 5(1) does not incorporate any substantive restriction of legislation to interfere with personal liberty. In effect, the judicial pronouncements since *Ong Ah Chuan* do not reveal any significant change in the judicial approach to Article 5(1).

Even after *Ong Ah Chuan*, the Supreme Court has expressed the same old, narrow, literalistic approach to the scope and content of Article 5(1). In *Public Prosecutor v. Lau Kee Hoo*,[66] the Federal Court ruled that the mandatory death sentence for possession of ammunition in a security area, provided under Section 57(1) of the Internal Security Act, 1960 is not *ultra vires*, and does not violate, Article 5(1). Article 5(1) itself envisages the possibility of Parliament providing for the death penalty. In this connection, reference was made to an Indian case, *Maru Ram v. India*,[67] but the Federal Court refused to follow the same. Tun Suffian L.P. stated in this connection: "[W]e should decide cases before us in the light of our own constitution, our own laws and the conditions in our own country which are not necessarily the same as conditions in other countries." The Lord President also cited what Ong, C.J., had said in *Karam Singh* about the Indian Judges being "indefatigable idealists."

In *Att. Gen. Malaysia v. Chiow Thiam Guan*,[68] the High Court, while holding Section 57(1) ISA valid, had observed:

> As regards Article 5(1) of the Constitution the law is that if Parliament deems it necessary that the death penalty should be mandatory it is not within the province of the court to adjudicate upon the wisdom of such a law. The law may be harsh but the role of the court is only to administer the law as it stands.

The matter was brought again before the Federal Court in *Lau Kee Hoo v. Public Prosecutor*[69] in the wake of another decision of the Supreme Court of India in *Mithu v. State of Punjab.*[70] The Court reiterated its earlier decision on the matter.[71] Raja Azlan Shah, F.J., delivering the decision of the Court, reiterated that the death penalty was constitutional and that the Parliament enjoyed plenary powers to enact the law in question:

> There is a continuing debate as to the wisdom and effectiveness of capital punishment in particular under section 57(1) of the Internal Security Act, 1960 but we think the matter has never been in doubt. Parliament has the plenary powers to enact it.

As regards *Mithu*, the Judge observed: "What may be an appropriate course of reasoning in a case involving capital punishment in India is not to be literally or even analogically applied to a case under section 57(1) of the Internal Security Act, 1960."

Ordinarily a life sentence means imprisonment for 20 years. But an amendment to the Firearms (Increased Penalties) Act, 1971, provides for life imprisonment being equated to the duration of natural life of the person sentenced. This was challenged as being violative of Article 5(1).[72] The argument against the validity of the statutory provision in question was based on *Maneka Gandhi v. Union of India*. But the Malaysian Supreme Court upheld the same in *Che Ani bin Itam v. Public Prosecutor.*[73] In *Maneka*, the Indian Supreme Court introduced elements of procedural due process in Article 21. The Supreme Court of Malaysia has consistently refused to accept these liberal Indian authorities as persuasive in interpreting Article 5(1). As stated above, the Federal Court accepted the Privy Council ruling in *Ong Ah Chuan.*[74] But even then, the Court maintained: "we can see nothing in the statutory provision sought to be impugned before us to infringe the proposition enunciated. There is nothing arbitrary, fanciful or oppressive in the legislatively defined sentence...." In this case, the Supreme Court supported its view by referring to the U.S. Supreme Court decision in *Carmona v. Ward*[75] where a writ of *certiorari* was denied to challenge the constitutionality of a mandatory life sentence imposed under a State law for possession of an ounce of cocaine. Reference was also made to *Rummel v. Estelle,*[76] where, by a majority, the U.S. Supreme Court upheld a statute authorizing a mandatory sentence of life imprisonment on a third conviction of a felony less than a capital felony. "The principles underlying these decisions apply equally in the case before us in relation to the mandatory nature of the maximum term of the sentence imposable by a specific statutory definition for a specific offence." The Lord President [Chief Justice] said further: "The legislature in doing so no doubt had in mind the object and purpose to be achieved by such a provision and it cannot accordingly be arbitrary in any sense of the word."

A glimmer of liberal interpretation became visible in 1986 in *Cheow Siong Chin v. Timbalan Menteri Hal Ehwal Dalam Negeri, Malaysia*,[77] where the High Court held that a person detained under Section 2(i) of the Restrictive Residence Enactment is entitled to an inquiry before an order is made against him under Section 2(ii), even though there may be no specific provision to that effect. There are basically three steps in making orders under the Enactment. The first step is *prior* to arrest and detention. Under Section 2(i), the Minister makes an order for arrest and detention of the person concerned after making such inquiry as he may deem necessary. There is no right to be heard at this stage. The second stage is the making of the order of restricted residency under Section 2(ii) after detention. There is provision for the Minister to make such further inquiry as he may deem necessary. At this stage, the concerned person should be given a right to be heard. The Court derived this right by reading Article 5(1) into the Enactment:

> The Constitution (by clauses (1) and (3) of Art. 5)[78] clearly upholds the principle of *audi alteram partem*.
>
> [T]he absence of a specific provision for an inquiry under the Enactment does not mean that an enquiry should not be held. This is because the Constitution must be read into the Enactment.

Clause (1) of Article 5 provides that no person shall be deprived of his personal liberty save in accordance with law. "Law" is defined in Article 160 of the Constitution to include "the common law insofar as it is in operation in the Federation." The Court therefore said: "The right to be heard is a principle of common law. Further, Clause (3) of Article 5 of the Constitution will be meaningful if a person is given the constitutional right to be defended but deprived of the forum to exercise that right." But whether the Supreme Court of Malaysia will accept the High Court view remains doubtful.

Preventive Detention

Prevention detention, i.e., detention without trial, is a constitutionally recognized institution in Malaysia. However, the Constitution prescribes a few safeguards for a person so detained.[79] The authority passing the detention order has to inform the concerned person of the grounds for this detention and the allegations of fact on which the order is based. A detainee has a right to make representation against his detention. No one can be held in detention for longer than three months (or within such longer period as the *Yang di Pertuan Agong* may allow) unless an advisory board has considered his representation. The advisory board is to consist of three persons appointed by the *Yang di Pertuan Agong.* The chairman must have the qualifications of a High Court Judge. And the two other members are appointed by the *Agong* after consultation with the Lord President of the Supreme Court. The Government is not obligated to follow the recommendations of the advisory board. Thus, beyond these minimal procedural safeguards, there is no restriction on its power to make law providing for preventive detention. The Parliament can itself provide for better safeguards than what are stipulated in the Constitution.

There exist several laws in Malaysia providing for *preventive detention*.[80] Preventive detention exists in India as well, but Article 22 of the Indian Constitution seeks to provide somewhat better safeguards to a detainee than does Article 151 of the Malaysian Constitution. Additionally, there exists an attitudinal difference between the apex courts in the two countries. The Supreme Court of India has claimed a fairly broad judicial review power in the area of preventive detention, arguing that preventive detention infringes upon the right to personal liberty guaranteed by Article 21. The Supreme Court has therefore applied principles of administrative law to control administrative discretion to order preventive detention, and has also insisted on a scrupulous observance of procedural safeguards as contained in Article 22, the Preventive Detention Law, and safeguards implied by the Court from these provisions.[81] On the other hand, the Malaysian apex court has shown disinclination to exercise such a review power. The Court has invoked the wartime English cases like *Liversidge v. Anderson*[82] in its support to deny judicial review and also interpreted Article 5 (1) narrowly as said above. To exemplify the judicial attitude, reference may be made to *Karam Singh v. Menteri Hal Ehwal Dalam Negeri*,[83] wherein the appellant challenged an order of preventive detention passed by the Minister of Home Affairs under the Internal Security Act on several grounds: it was made *mala fide*; the Minister had not applied his mind, and had passed the order in a casual and cavalier manner; the facts supplied to the appellant were vague, insufficient and irrelevant and thus hampered the appellant in the exercise of his right to make representations, consequently invalidating the original order of detention. A number of cases from India were cited in support of the appellant's contentions. The fact remains that, in India, several orders of preventive detention have been quashed by the courts on the several grounds mentioned above.[84] But the Malaysian Supreme Court dismissed the case saying: 1) the order was made by the Minister in exercise of a valid legal power; 2) the onus lay on the appellant to show that the power had been exercised *mala fide* or improperly and that he had not been able to discharge the onus; 3) defects in the form of the order did not show that the Executive had not adequately applied its mind to the desirability of detaining the appellant and, therefore, the order was not invalidated; 4) the question where there was reasonable cause to detain the appellant was a matter of opinion and policy and such a decision could only be taken by the executive; 5) the vagueness, insufficiency or irrelevance of the facts supplied to the appellant did not make the order bad; if the appellant thought the allegations to be vague, insufficient or irrelevant, he could have asked for more particulars.

The power to order preventive detention was placed on a high pedestal by all the Judges, making it practically unchallengeable. This is borne out by the following, from the Judgment of Tun Suffian, F.J.:

> [I]t is not for a court of law to pronounce on the sufficiency, relevancy or otherwise of the allegations of fact furnished to him. Whether or not the facts on which the order of detention is to be based are sufficient or relevant, is a matter to be decided solely by the executive. In making their decision, they have complete discretion and it is not for a court of law to question the sufficiency or relevance of these allegations of fact.

Four notable points emerging from the several judgments in *Karam Singh* may be mentioned here. One, there is hardly any discussion in the various decisions on the content and scope of Article 5. No attempt was made by the appellant to bring in the American concept of "due process of law" in Article 5. No reference was made to any American case on personal liberty. The only reference to Article 5 one finds in *Karam Singh* is in the judgment of Tun Suffian F.J. where, comparing Article 5 with Article 21 in the Indian Constitution, he said that while the word "procedure" was to be found in Article 21, it was missing in Article 5, which, as noted earlier made the Indian cases on preventive detention irrelevant to Malaysia.

Two, the challenge to the order of detention was not based on procedural grounds really, though the Court thought so. The challenge, in effect, was based on grounds on which, in administrative law, an administrative discretion can be challenged. In effect, the challenge was on substantive and not procedural grounds. Three, there was no doubt that the views expressed by the Malaysian Judges were at variance with those of the Indian Judges on similar points. But the Malaysian Judges refused to accept the views of the Indian Judges by calling them "indefatigable idealists"--whatever the implications of this statement may be. In the words of Ong C.J.:

Perusing both English and Indian authorities has been no small task, but at the end of it all I would sum up by saying that, in my humble opinion, English courts take a more realistic view of things, while Indian judges, for whom I have the highest respect, impress me as indefatigable idealists seeking valiantly to reconcile the irreconcilable whenever good conscience is pricked by an abuse of executive powers.[85]

Four, the above statement, comparing the judicial attitudes of British and Indian Judges, seems to be based on a misconception. In England, there is no written Constitution and there are no constitutionally entrenched fundamental rights. The task of the English Judges is to interpret and apply statutory law. On the other hand, the Indian Judges have a much more onerous task to discharge. They have to defend and protect fundamental rights guaranteed by a written Constitution; their approach has to be more liberal and less literalistic as regards the interpretation of the Constitution. Since personal liberty is protected by Article 21, any law which deprives a person of his personal liberty has to be interpreted strictly and any exercise of administrative power seeking to deprive a person of his personal liberty has to be kept strictly within the confines of the law.

Later cases in Malaysia show that judicial review of preventive detention may be available on a few grounds. One, *mala fides* of the detaining authority. But, in practice, it is well nigh impossible to prove the ground of *mala fides* since what is required to prove *mala fides* is "proof of improper or bad motive ... and not mere suspicion," and what needs to be made out is not lack of *bona fides* of the police but the want of *bona fides* of the detaining authority "as well as the non-application of mind on the part of the detaining authority which for this purpose must be taken to be different from the police."[86] It is extremely difficult to establish *mala fides* as the court has itself said that the onus of proving *mala fides* "is normally extremely difficult to discharge...." Two, judicial review of preventive detention is possible on the basis that the grounds of detention are not within the scope of, or relevant to the objects stated in the enabling statute.[87] Three, an order of preventive detention can be quashed if any fundamental condition is not fulfilled. Thus, in *Re Tan Boon Liat*[88] (the only case in which an order of preventive detention has ever been quashed), the Federal Court held by a majority that detention beyond three months was invalid. In this case, the advisory board had failed to report within three months, as was then required by Article 151, but the detention was continued. This was challenged. Tun Suffian L.P. took the view that the condition of the advisory board's recommendation within three months (as required by Article 151 at that time) was a "fundamental condition" or a "condition precedent" for further detention. If this condition precedent was not satisfied, then the continued detention would become unlawful as it would not be "in accordance with law" as required by Article 5(1). He thus put the matter on substantive grounds or "condition precedent," he indirectly confirmed the view expressed by him in *Karam Singh* that Article 5(1) does not cover the procedural part of the law authorizing detention.[89]

The Government had contended against any judicial review in this case by invoking the clause in the Ordinance saying that the *Yang di Pertuan Agong*'s decision was "final and shall not be called into question in any court." Tun Suffican L.P. overruled this contention saying that the exclusionary clause in question applied only to "real decisions and not to *ultra vires* decisions."

The present-day judicial interpretation of Article 5(1) makes it extremely weak. The primary purpose of Article 5(1) is to protect life or personal liberty of a person against administrative action but not against legislative action. If the administration does not follow the law (substantive provisions, not procedural) in depriving a person of his liberty, it can be challenged under Article 5(1) as not being in accordance with law. But it is doubtful if any law made by the legislature can be challenged as unconstitutional if it deprives a person of his liberty. According to the present-day judicial view of Article 5(1), the responsibility for protection and preservation of personal liberty of individuals is thrown by and large on Parliament rather than on the courts. There are no substantive restrictions on the power of Parliament to enact legislation interfering with personal liberty. Such a law does not have to fulfill any procedural requirements. The courts have only to ensure that the Executive obeys the substantive provisions of the law; the courts exercise no veto over legislation. Jayakumar pleaded in a 1967 article[90] that Article 5(1) should be interpreted as being broader and not narrower than Article 21 of the Indian Constitution. He had pleaded that Article 5(1) should cover both substantive and procedural due process and not be taken in the sense of *Gopalan*. But as things have turned out, Article 5(1) has proved to be much weaker than its Indian counterpart. In the U.S.A., the institution of preventive detention does not exist as a peacetime measure. Under the Internal Security Act, 1950, preventive detention is provided for during war, invasion or insurrection. A detainee has a right to consult a lawyer. He has a right to a preliminary hearing before a hearing officer appointed by the President and he can introduce evidence in his defense and cross-examine witnesses testifying against him. The detainee can take an appeal from the hearing officer to the Board of Detention, he can then go to the Court of Appeals and finally to the Supreme Court.[91] On comparison, the American law has a very restrictive range of operation, and contains much better safeguards for a detainee than does the Malaysian law which has a much wider range of operation.

Protection Against Ex Post Facto Laws and Double Jeopardy

According to Article 7(1), no person can be punished for an act or omission which was not punishable by law at the time it was done or made. No person can be made to suffer greater punishment for an offense than was prescribed by law at the time it was committed. The protection against *ex post facto* laws has been held not applicable to retrospective criminal laws of a procedural nature.[92] But reference may be made in this connection to *P.P. v. Mohd. Ismail*.[93] The defendant was found guilty on April 15, 1983 of trafficking in a dangerous drug in violation of section 39B(1) of the Dangerous Drug Act. On the same date, an amendment of section 39B(1) took effect eliminating the court's discretion to sentence a defendant to either life imprisonment or death. The amendment of section 39B(2) made the death penalty mandatory. The Court ruled that the amendment was enacted after the commission of the offense in the instant case, and, therefore, because of Article 7(1), it could not apply to offenses committed prior to the effective date of the amendment. Consequently, in the instant case, the Court retained discretion to sentence the defendant either to life imprisonment or death. According to Article 7(2), a person acquitted or convicted of an offense shall not be tried again for the same offense.

Right to Counsel

According to Article 5(3), when a person is arrested, he has a right to consult a counsel of his choice and also to be informed as soon as may be of the ground of his arrest. But the right to consult a lawyer has been weakened somewhat by the Federal Court's decision in *Ooi Ah Phua v. Officer in Charge, Criminal Investigation, Kedah/Perlis*:[94] "The right of an arrested person to consult his lawyer begins from the moment of arrest, but ... the right cannot be exercised immediately after arrest." In this case, the appellant was arrested on a charge of gang robbery on December 26, 1974, but he was not allowed to see his lawyer until January 5 when the matter was brought before the Court on an application for *habeas corpus*; the Court dismissed the action, emphasizing that "a balance has to be struck between the right of the arrested person to consult his lawyer...and...the duty of the police to protect the public from wrongdoing by apprehending them and collecting whatever evidence exists against them." The Court also ruled that *habeas corpus* was not the right remedy for the applicant's complaint that he had been denied access to a lawyer. The Federal Court made no reference to any corresponding U.S. decision, such as *Miranda v. Arizona*.[95] In the High Court, when counsel for the applicant urged the Court to compare the right with the equivalent right under the U.S. Constitution, the Judge replied as follows (Hashim Yeop A Sani J.):

> In my view it is futile to compare any of the rights protected in Part II of our Constitution to their equivalents under the Constitution of the U.S. for the simple reason that almost all rights under the Constitution of the U.S. are in absolute terms whereas under our Constitution most if not all ... are in qualified terms.[96]

The matter was reconsidered by the Federal Court in *Hashim bin Saud v. Yahaya bin Hashim.*[97] The appellant was arrested on suspicion of being involved in the theft of an electrical generator, and detained in police custody. He was not allowed to see a lawyer for more than ten days. He was told that he could see his lawyer only after the completion of police investigation. During the course of its judgment in this case, the Federal Court referred to the U.S. cases of *Miranda* and *Massiah v. United States.*[98] The Court referred to the U.S. position as follows: "In the United States an accused person shall have the assistance of counsel and if he asks for counsel police investigation must stop until the counsel is available and that he must be informed of his right...."[99] But the Federal Court ruled that in Malaysia: "The pre-trial right of an arrested person to be allowed to consult a lawyer is merely one particular manifestation of the general right to be allowed to consult and be defended by a legal practitioner of his choice (Art. 5(3)." In Malaysia, the right to consult a lawyer starts right from the day of arrest, but it cannot be exercised immediately after arrest if it impedes police investigation or the administration of justice.

Right to Equality

The concept of equality, found in the Fourteenth Amendment of the U.S. Constitution, has played a commendable role in the promotion and preservation of human freedom. *Brown v. Board of Education*[100] is well known, in which the Supreme Court condemned segregation on the ground that it is perverse, inherently objectionable and unequal. Classification on the basis of "race" has been held to impinge on the guarantee of equal protection, and "race" has been held as not "rational *indicia*" to classify. "Separate educational facilities are inherently unequal," the Supreme Court has declared. In *Reed v. Reed,*[101] distinction based on sex or gender has been held to be unconstitutional. The Court has declared that classification cannot be made on the basis of criteria wholly unrelated to the objective of the statute. A classification must be reasonable, not arbitrary, and must rest upon some ground of difference having a fair and substantial relation to the object of the legislation, so that all persons similarly circumstanced shall be treated alike. Then there is the case of *Yick Wo v. Hopkins*[102] laying down the principle that the right to equality strikes at administrative discrimination.

The right to equality is guaranteed in India by Article 14. The courts have used this provision in a number of ways, to control legislative power as well as administrative discretion, and pervasively to maintain certain basic human values. A legislature is entitled to make reasonable classification for purposes of legislation and to treat all in one class on an equal footing. According to the Supreme Court, "Article 14 of the Constitution ensures equality among equals; its aim is to protect persons similarly placed against discriminatory treatment." It does not, however, operate against rational classification. Any classification to be reasonable should fulfill the following two tests: 1) It should not be arbitrary, artificial or evasive. It should be based on an intelligible *differentia*; and 2) the *differentia* adopted as the basis of classification must have a reasonable relationship to the object sought to be achieved in question. By applying these tests, the courts have held a number of laws unconstitutional since the inauguration of the Constitution in 1950.[103] In the area of administrative discretion, Article 14 is used in two ways: uncontrolled discretion cannot be conferred on the administration; arbitrary or discriminatory action by the administration in the exercise of discretionary power is constitutionally invalid. There is massive case law in India in this area.[104] Since 1986, the Supreme Court has been insisting that any governmental action which is unreasonable is bad, as unreasonableness negates equality. For example, the Supreme Court of India held a clause in a contract between an employee and a Government undertaking, empowering it to terminate his service at three months' notice, to be unconscionable and violative of Article 14.[105] The Court has evolved three basic principles in this connection: a clause in a contract if unfair and unreasonable, entered into between parties not having equal bargaining power, is bad; the State cannot take any arbitrary or discriminatory action; natural justice is a part of the constitutional guarantee of Article 14.

In Malaysia, the right to equality has been guaranteed. According to Article 8(1), all persons are equal before the law and entitled to equal protection of the law. Discrimination on the ground only of religion, race, descent or place of birth has been outlawed.[106] Discrimination has also been prohibited against any citizen on the grounds only of religion, race, descent or place of birth in the administration of any educational institution maintained by a public authority.[107]

The scope and content of the equality clause in Malaysia remain vague, as there has not been much case law so far around the right to equality. It does not seem to have served much of a useful purpose and has not so far played any significant role in the constitutional process in Malaysia. The full potentialities of the equality clause as yet remain to be fully explored in Malaysia, but the courts can do so only if they shed their positivistic approach to the Constitution.

The first significant case on the equality clause was *Datuk Haji Harun bin Haji Idris v. Public Prosecutor.*[108] The question involved the constitutional validity of Section 418A of the Criminal Procedure Code which authorizes the Public Prosecutor to transfer any criminal case from a lower court to the High Court for trial. This provision was challenged under Article 8(1). The argument was that Section 418A confers unrestricted power on the Public Prosecutor to pick and choose any criminal case and transfer the same to the High Court for trial, thus subjecting the accused to several disabilities: several procedural disabilities; for certain offenses, the High Court could award him a stiffer sentence than the lower court; he was deprived of one appeal stage. Section 418A lays down no guidelines to regulate the discretion of the Public Prosecutor. Abdoolcader, J. in the High Court ruled in *Public Prosecutor v. Datuk Harun*[109] that Section 418A was unconstitutional. He laid down the general proposition that a law conferring power to classify is void, if it does not lay down any clear policy and leaves it to the unfettered and unregulated discretion of the Executive. The Court ruled that *ex facie*, Section 418A purports to give unrestrained power of selection to the Public Prosecutor without any guide, object or apparent policy in the section itself or anywhere else in the code. Transfer of the case of the accused for trial from a lower court to the High Court subjected him to hostile discrimination, i.e., the sessions court could award him a sentence of five years' imprisonment and fine up to $20,000, but there was no limit on the power of the High Court to impose sentences of fine and imprisonment. The Court also ruled that Article 145(3) of the Constitution should be read subject to Article 8(1). On appeal, the Federal Court reversed the High Court and held Section 418A constitutionally valid under Article 8(1).[110] It ruled that Article 8(1) was subject to Article 145(3).[111] The Court accepted the principle of reasonable classification and also that it was for the Court and not the legislature to decide whether a classification was reasonable or not. But, held the Court, there was classification in Section 418A insofar as the Public Prosecutor was expected to transfer to the High Court only cases of "unusual difficulty" or of "unusual importance." The Court then went on to observe:

> The Attorney General, however, even before the trial, had sources of information and he had information not available to the court and if

armed with this information he decided to act under section 418A, the court should not on that account alone, strike down the section.

Thus, in effect, the Federal Court rationalized the conferment of practically uncontrolled discretionary power on the Public Prosecutor.

In several later cases, similar broad discretionary powers conferred on the Attorney General under various other laws have been upheld. For example, unlawful possession of a fire-arm is an offense that can be tried under three separate laws with three different punishments: under the Arms Act, seven years' imprisonment; under the Firearms Increased Penalties Act, 14 years; under Section 57 of the Internal Security Act, a mandatory sentence of death. It is for the Public Prosecutor to charge a person under any of these legal provisions. For the same offense, different persons could be charged by the Public Prosecutor under different legal provisions. The law under which a person is charged determines his ultimate fate, whether he gets a death sentence or a mere sentence of imprisonment.

But even such a broad power vested in the Public Prosecutor without any guidelines has been held to be constitutionally valid vis-a-vis Article 8 in *Johnson Tan Seng v. Public Prosecutor.*[112] The Court said that the Attorney General may discriminate without contravening Article 8. "The choice is entirely the Attorney General's." The proposition was reiterated that Article 8 should be read subject to Article 145(3). There really seems to be no reason why Article 8 should be subjected to Article 1453). Article 145(3) does not say so. On the other hand, Article 8 is a fundamental liberty, and if this title has any real significance, the provisions therein ought to prevail over other parts of the Constitution. In 1986 for the first time, the courts in Malaysia in two cases held parts of laws made by Parliament void under Article 8(1). In *Malaysian Bar v. Government of Malaysia,*[113] a provision in the Bar Act saying that a lawyer of less than seven years' standing is disqualified to be a member of the Bar Council, Bar Committee or "of any committee of the Bar Council/Committee" was challenged under Article 8. The Court justified the seven years' standing rule on the ground that the affairs of the Bar ought to be managed by professionally independent lawyers so as to achieve an independent Bar. The Court ruled that "a law is bad if it is discriminatory, unreasonable and if there is no *nexus* between the law and objects of the statute in question."

In 1987, the High Court rendered a significant pronouncement on Article 8.[114] The object of the Pensions Adjustment Act is to provide additional benefits to pensioners and to extend those benefits to their dependents. But the benefits under the Act are not made available to non-resident pensioners.

This was challenged as discriminatory under Article 8 by a non-resident pensioner who had served in Malaysia for nearly 28 years and was living in India after retirement. The High Court ruled invalid the provision excluding the non-resident pensioners from the benefits under the Act, saying that the non-resident pensioners should not be excluded from the benefits under the Act. The Court ordered that the pension of the non-resident pensioners should not be excluded from the benefits under the Act. The Court also ordered that the pension of the non-resident applicant be adjusted in accordance with the provisions of the Act in question and that arrears together with eight percent interest be paid to him. The Court said:

> Pensioners are a diminishing race. They have given the best years of their lives in the service of the country. And now in their twilight years we are depriving the pensioners who left the country of the additional benefits that we are giving to those who are resident in Malaysia.

The important principle laid down by the Court is: "Pensioners are a class by themselves and no part of them can be treated differently from the other pensioners merely because of their place of abode." The Court observed that "there is no evidence to show how and why the non-resident pensioners were excluded from the Act. There appears to be no basis for their exclusion. The classification here is clearly discriminatory and arbitrary."

The Court observed further: "Pension rights are vested rights and by virtue of Article 8(1) no law can be passed to exclude a class of pensioners from the benefits of any later law on the ground that they do not reside in Malaysia."

> [Such a restriction] is arbitrary and discriminatory and is against the fundamental right of a person to be equal before the law and entitled to the equal protection of the law. This article extends to all persons whether they are Malaysian citizens or not.

The inspiration for the above judicial pronouncement seems to have come from a parallel Indian case, *D.S. Nakara v. Union of India.*[115] The Government of India announced a liberalized pension scheme for retired government servants but made it applicable to those who had retired after March 31, 1979. The Supreme Court ruled that this was discriminatory and violated Article 14. The scheme must apply to all pensioners as one class for the purpose of revision of pension. Division of pensioners into two classes on the basis of the date of retirement was not rational and, therefore, was arbitrary and unprincipled.

Freedom of Speech

In a democratic country, freedom of speech and freedom of the press are crucial. Freedom of speech and expression is the life-blood or the core of democracy. Democracy depends and thrives on consent and persuasion. For this, it is extremely necessary that people are given freedom to express and communicate their views. Without adequate freedom of speech, political parties cannot function. Newspapers are an integral part of a democratic society as they play a very important role in dissemination of news and views to the people. It is the function of the newspapers to inform the public of the policies and operations of the Government. It is their obligation to bring to light the reasons why the Government has acted in a particular manner and also to discuss the pros and cons of a government action. It is only when the public is duly informed that proper views and opinions can be formed and expressed. But, as no freedom can be *absolute*, so the freedom of speech also cannot be absolute. This right, as any other right, has to be subject to proper restrictions. If a public interest is served by keeping speech and expression free, there may also be a public interest in imposing some restrictions on it for certain purposes. But the drawing of this balance between two conflicting interests is an extremely difficult task.

In America, the freedoms of speech and the press are separately guaranteed by the First Amendment: "The Congress shall make no law ... abridging the freedom of speech or of the press." The same restriction is read into the State Constitutions by virtue of the Fourteenth Amendment. On its face, the provision is absolute, but the courts have read certain restrictions into it. The core issue in free speech is the extent to which a person will be allowed to criticize the government. For this purpose, the U.S. Supreme Court has evolved such tests as "clear and present danger,"[116] and has increasingly promoted *robust, uninhibited* and *wide open* debate of public issues.

The historic *Pentagon Papers* case illustrates this commitment. President Richard Nixon's government sought a permanent injunction to prohibit publication by the *New York Times* of a government-written history of the U.S. role in Indo-China. No Act prohibited publication of the material in question. The President claimed as Commander-in-Chief that the security of the country was at stake and so invoked the court's equity jurisdiction to issue an injunction. But the Supreme Court, on a six-to-three vote, vacated the injunction in deference to freedom of the press.[117] Justice Hugo Black stated: "I believe that every moment's continuance of the injunctions against these newspapers amounts to a flagrant, indefensible, and continuing violation of the First Amendment.... [The words of the Amendment] *support the view* that the press must be free to publish news, *whatever the source*, without censorship, injunctions, or prior restraints...."

Justice William Douglas said:

> The disclosure may have a serious impact. But that is no basis for sanctioning a previous restraint of the press. Any prior restraint on expression comes to this court with a "heavy presumption" against its constitutional validity.

The Court pointed to the line between secrecy and openness in governmental affairs: "The autonomous press may publish what it knows and may seek to learn what it can." The press is free to do battle against secrecy and deception in government.

In India, freedom of speech and expression is guaranteed by Article 19(1)(a), but under Article 19(2), a legislature can impose *reasonable* restrictions on this right in the interest of the sovereignty and integrity of India, the security of the State, friendly relations with foreign States, public order, decency or morality, or in relation to contempt of court, defamation or incitement to an offense. By interpreting Article 19(1)(a) liberally and making use of the word "reasonable" before "restriction" in Article 19(2), the courts have been able to provide a good deal of protection to the freedom of speech and expression and the freedom of the press. Several legislative and administrative regulations on this freedom have been voided by the courts. Imposition of pre-censorship on a newspaper,[118] prohibiting a newspaper from publishing its own views on matters of topical interest,[119] regulation of the number of pages in a newspaper according to the price charged,[120] allotment of newsprint with a view to control circulation of big newspapers,[121] all have been vetoed by the courts as infringing Article 19(1)(a). The offense of "sedition" has now been redefined--exciting bad feelings towards the Government is not enough; it is also necessary to show that the activities in question have a tendency to create disorder.[122] The expression "reasonable restriction" has been interpreted to mean that a restriction should be reasonable both from substantive and procedural aspects, and it is ultimately for the courts to adjudge whether a restriction is reasonable or not. Further, a restriction should have a rational nexus with the objects mentioned in Article 19(2) for which restrictions can be imposed on the freedom of speech.[123]

But the constitutional provisions in Malaysia guaranteeing freedom of speech are conceived very differently from the U.S., so much so that there is no parallelism between the two countries in this area. Although the model used for drafting the Malaysian provisions is the relevant model in India

(Article 19(1)(a) read with Article 19(5)), there are significant differences between the two, the Malaysian provision being the weaker of the two. A reading of the provisions of Article 10 indicates that this is the least "entrenched fundamental liberty" in Malaysia. Article 10(1) provides: "Every citizen has the right to freedom of speech and expression;" but Article 10(2)(a) adds limitations: Parliament may by law impose on the freedom of speech "*such restrictions as it deems necessary or expedient*" in the interest of: The security of the Federation or any part thereof; friendly relations with other countries; public order and morality; restrictions designed to protect the privileges of Parliament or of any legislative Assembly; or to provide against contempt of court, defamation; or incitement to any offence. The scope of Article 10(1)(a) is further narrowed, and that of Article 10(2)(a) further broadened by Article 4(2)(b). According to this, the validity of any law cannot be questioned on the ground that it imposes *such* restrictions as are mentioned in Article 10(2), but those restrictions were "not deemed necessary or expedient by Parliament for the purposes mentioned in that Article."

Restrictions can be imposed on the freedom of speech "in the interest" of the purposes mentioned in Article 20(2)(a). The words "such restrictions as Parliament *deems necessary or expedient*" "in the interest of ..." appear to mean that what restriction is to be imposed is a matter for Parliament to decide. It is for the legislature to assess whether a particular restriction on freedom of speech is "necessary" or "expedient" for the objects mentioned therein. If these words were not there, then the courts could have gone into the question whether a particular restriction is "necessary" or "expedient," say, for security of the Federation or not; whether the restriction is excessive or justified "in the interest of." But as it is, the legislative judgment becomes final. This idea is reinforced by Article 4(2)(b) that the courts cannot go into the question whether any restriction is "necessary" or "expedient" or not in the interest of a stated objective. Article 4(2)(b) reduces the scope of challenge to legislation restricting the freedom of speech; for whether or not Parliament deems its restriction necessary or expedient is not a justiciable issue. But this still leaves the question that a restriction should have *some*," "nexus," some relationship or connection with an objective stated in Article 10(2)(a). It therefore means that if a restriction has "absolutely" no "nexus" or "relationship" with a stated purpose, then the same cannot be sustained under Article 10(1)(a) read with Article 10(2)(a) and Article 4(2)(b). To take another view will make Article 10(1)(a) completely redundant and otiose. No constitutional provision is to be interpreted in such a manner as to make it redundant.

In many constitutions in the Commonwealth, one can find the word "reasonable" before restrictions, i.e., Malta, Jamaica, and India. But in Malaysia, the word "reasonable" before "restriction" is not to be found in Article 10(2)(a) and, instead, one finds the words "necessary" and "expedient." The words "necessary" and "expedient" are the antithesis of the word "reasonable." The underlying idea is to make Parliament the final judge of "what restrictions" to impose. The "extent," "nature" or "scope" of the restriction is for Parliament and not for the Court to decide. If it is a "reasonable" restriction, then the Court can assess the reasonableness of the restriction; the Court can ensure that the restriction should not be "excessive" or "arbitrary"; it should be such as may *strike a proper balance* between the freedom of speech and "*social control*," so that the rights guaranteed to the people might be limited only to the extent necessary to protect and preserve society. In a country requiring a "reasonable restriction" "in the interests of," a double safeguard is available, that of *nexus*. The question however, is how far Article 4(2)(b) restricts the power of the Judiciary to assess the relationship of a restriction with the objective. The effect of Article 4(2)(b) does not seem clear. Some of the questions which arise are: Does it mean that any restriction is beyond judicial scrutiny on any ground whatsoever, even when the restriction has no *nexus* with any of the purposes mentioned in Article 10? Or, does it mean that the only ground on which a restriction cannot be challenged is that it was not deemed "necessary or expedient" by Parliament?

If the second view is adopted, then the question whether a restriction is "in the interests of" a purpose stated in Article 10 may still be open to judicial scrutiny. But if the first view is adopted, then Article 10(2)(a) will impose no restriction on the legislature which can impose any restriction it likes for any purpose it likes, and interpreted like this, Article 10(2)(a) will cease to be a fundamental right in the traditional sense. To give some worthwhile meaning to Article 10(2)(a) as a fundamental right, it seems necessary to read the words "in the interests of" as somewhat controlling, and to say that the restriction must have some rational nexus with one of the objectives stated in Article 10(2)(a). In Malaysia, the courts are not empowered to declare a restriction "inexpedient" or "unnecessary" because it is excessive and declare the law bad on that basis. But the test of "nexus" ought to be applied still and the courts ought to make use of it in a creative manner.

On the whole, judicial protection to these rights appears to be minimal. The protection of the freedom of speech in Malaysia is by and large the responsibility of Parliament rather than of the courts. A reading of the constitutional provisions guaranteeing freedom of speech indicates that while the right is protected against executive interference without law, Parliament's power to restrict this right by ordinary legislation is without any significant restriction.

Article 10(4) further curtails the freedom of speech. Parliament may restrict freedom of speech by enacting a law to prohibit the questioning of any matter, right, status, position, privilege, sovereignty or prerogative established or protected by the provisions of Part III, Articles 152, 153 or 181 otherwise than in relation to the implementation thereof as may be specified in such law.

In Malaysia, there is no separate provision in the Constitution to guarantee freedom of the press. Therefore, freedom of the press has to be spelled out of the general constitutional provision guaranteeing freedom of speech and expression. Thus, the press has no special status or rights which are not available to any other citizen. The editor and the manager of a paper are, while writing in the press, merely exercising their right to speech and expression like any other citizen.

Significant restrictions are imposed in Malaysia on the freedom of speech and press through several statutory provisions. A few of the more important may be briefly noted. The most important is the Sedition Act, 1948, which defines Sedition as "an act, speech, words, publication or other thing which has a 'seditious tendency.'" Seditious tendency is defined as a tendency:

a) to bring into hatred or contempt or excite disaffection against any Ruler or against any Government;

b) to excite the subject of any Ruler or the inhabitants of any territory governed by any Government to attempt to procure in the territory of the Ruler or governed by the Government the alteration, otherwise than by lawful means, of any matter as by law established;

c) to bring into hatred or contempt or to excite disaffection against the administration of justice in Malaysia or in any State;

d) to raise discontent or disaffection amongst the subjects of the *Yang di Pertuan Agong* or of the Ruler of any State or amongst the inhabitants of Malaysia or of any State; or

e) to promote feelings of ill-will and hostility between different races or classes of the population of Malaysia; or

f) to question any matter, right, status, position, privilege, sovereignty or prerogative established or protected by the provision of Part III of the Federal Constitution or Art. 152, 153, or 181 of the Federal Constitution.

Under Section 3(3), the intention of the person charged with the offense of sedition is irrelevant, if in fact the act had, or would, if done, have had a seditious tendency. Thus, the concept of sedition is very broad in Malaysia. The law says that certain things cannot be criticized. For example, stirring up hatred or contempt against the government is sedition. There is no need to show that the speech has a tendency to create disorder. This is clarified by the Court in *Public Prosecutor v. Oh Keng Seng.*[124] By Section 2, a speech is seditious if it has a "seditious tendency" which is defined in Section 3(1). In the instant case, the speech was held seditious with the observation: "Whatever his intention might have been respondent has ... gone beyond the limit of freedom of speech...." The Court observed further:

> Again whilst ... the prosecution is not obliged to prove that anything said in the speech was true or false, evidence to show that the allegations made were false whether wilfully or inadvertently so, would increase the likelihood that such utterances would have a seditious tendency.

The important point to note is that according to the English law, in order to constitute sedition, the words complained of have to be of such a nature as "*to be likely to incite violence, tumult or public disorder.*" But under the Sedition Act in Malaysia, no such intention is necessary. The statutory definition of sedition is to be applied as given in the Act. Common law principles cannot be imported to interpret the statutory definition.

The Law of Sedition is somewhat different in India. In India the Sedition Law is contained in Section 124A, I.P.C. which punishes any person who by words, spoken or written, brings or attempts to bring into hatred or contempt, or excites disaffection towards the government established by law. In the pre-Independence era, this section had been interpreted very broadly, and mere exciting or attempting to incite bad feelings towards the government was held punishable whether it resulted in public disorder or disturbance or not.[125]

After Independence, under the new Constitution, in *Kedar Nath v. Bihar,*[126] the Supreme Court interpreted the provision restrictively. Only such utterances would be penal as "are intended, or have a tendency, to create disorder or disturbance of public peace by resort to violence." Thus, the Indian law has been brought at par with the English common law. Mere strong criticism of government is not penal in India until it has the tendency or intention of creating public disorder.

But, in Malaysia, the Indian position has not been accepted. Here, there is no need to show that the words have a tendency to create disorder to become seditious. In *Public Prosecutor v. Ooi Kee Saik,*[127] Raja Azlan Shah, J. observed as follows:

> The dividing line between lawful criticism of Government and Sedition is this--if upon reading the impugned speech as a whole the court finds that it was intended to be a criticism of government policy or administration with a view to obtain its change or reform, the speech is

safe. But if the court comes to the conclusion that the speech used naturally, clearly and indubitably, has the tendency of stirring up hatred, contempt or disaffection against the government, then it is caught within the ban of paragraph (a) of Sect. 3(1) of the Act...

[I]n the context of the Sedition Act it (disaffection) means more than political criticism; it means the absence of affection, disloyalty, enmity and hostility. To "excite disaffection" in relation to a Government refers to the implanting or arousing or stimulating in the minds of people a feeling of antagonism, enmity and disloyalty tending to make government insecure. If the natural consequence of the impugned speech is apt to produce conflict and discord amongst the people or to create race hatred, the speech transgresses paragraphs (d) and (e) of S.3(1). Again paragraph (f) of S.33(1) comes into play if the impugned speech has reference to question any of the four sensitive issues--citizenship, national language, special rights of the Malays, and the sovereignty of the Rulers.

This view has been reiterated in *Public Prosecutor v. Fan Yew Teng*.[128] Thus, the principle is that a speech is seditious under Section 3(1) if "read as a whole, used naturally, clearly, and indubitably, [It] has the tendency of stirring up hatred, or contempt against the Government." Once it is proved that the words complained of were spoken, the author "will be conclusively presumed to have intended the natural consequences stated in Section 3(1) of the Act. It is immaterial whether or not the words complained of could have the effect of producing, or did in fact produce, any of the consequences enumerated in the section. It is also immaterial whether the impugned words were true or false. It is not open for the author "to say that he did not intend his words to have the meaning which they naturally bear."

In *Fan Yew Teng v. P.P.*[129] the question was whether a published article was seditious or not. The main points emerging from the Federal Court decision are as follows:

1) The test to be applied is whether or not the article complained of has in fact a seditious tendency. In other words, the law is such that it is immaterial whether the words complained of are true or not.

2) Thus, acts, speeches, words or publications constitute sedition if they have a seditious tendency as defined in S.3 of the Act.

3) Mere criticism is "not sufficient to constitute sedition." In a parliamentary democracy, government always welcomes constructive criticism. The speech should not be expressive of a seditious tendency.

4) Malaysia is a plural society. Within diversity, unity is sought to be built here. Anything which disturbs that unity cannot be taken lightly (an issue which smacks of racialism in trying to score a political advantage).

Freedom of speech can also be restricted under Section 27(2) of the Police Act. No meeting can be held without a police license. A license can be issued by the officer-in-charge of the concerned police district if he is satisfied that the meeting is not likely to be prejudicial to the interest of the security of the Federation or to excite a disturbance of the peace. The officer can impose conditions subject to which the meeting is to be held.

In *Madhavan Nair v. Public Prosecutor*,[130] the respondent was granted a license for holding a political rally. One of the conditions of the license was that the licensee must ensure that speeches at the rally should not touch on matters relating to the M.C.E.[131] results and on the status of Bahasa Malaysia as the national language as laid down in the Constitution. The list of speakers at the rally was also authorized. One of the authorized speakers contravened the condition, and was punished. In the instant case, the organizer of the meeting was also held guilty. The Court pointed out in relation to the organizer that he as a licensee assumed responsibility for the entire conduct of the rally and its component members. He could not now repudiate his responsibility by saying that violation of the license condition took place without his consent or even without his knowledge or in his absence. The magistrate trying Nair had referred the matter to the High Court on the point whether the condition took place without his consent or even without his knowledge or in his absence. The magistrate trying Nair had referred the matter to the High Court on the point whether the condition in question was constitutional. It was argued that the condition contravened Article 10. Could Parliament have made such a condition? The Court said: "CL.2(a) speaks of restrictions deemed 'necessary or expedient in the interest of the security of the Federation'" and restrictions "designed to provide against incitement to any offence. Where such entirely subjective words have been used, it is not within the competency of the courts to question the necessity or expediency of the legislative provision." Section 3(1)(f) of the Sedition Act spells out the same issues as are mentioned in Article 10(4). To talk on the language issue is seditious. The Court also ruled that the police officer in question was authorized to impose such a condition.

In *Chai Choon Hon v. Ketua Polis Daerah Kampar*,[132] a condition in the police license issued under Section 27(2) of the Police Act restricted the number of speakers at the assembly. The license was issued to a political party holding a dinner and lion dance between 5 P.M. and 11:30 P.M. Seven conditions were imposed by the police officer. Some of these conditions were now challenged as unconstitutional under Article 10(1) of the Constitution. One of these conditions restricted the number of speakers to seven only and speeches on political issues were forbidden. The High Court had ruled the last condition (prohibiting speeches on political issues) to be an unreasonable restriction violating the right of the freedom of speech, but held valid the condition restricting the number of speakers. The Supreme Court, on appeal from the High Court, held that the condition restricting the number of speakers to seven was "unreasonable." The Court said that the question related not to the "constitutionality" but rather to "reasonableness." There was no valid reason for the restriction imposed on the number of speakers within the time limit granted in the license. The particular condition was held unreasonable "in the circumstances as the police had the means to deal with any infringement of the time frame specified in the license under the provisions of S.27 of the Act."

In *P. Patto v. Chief Police Officer, Perak,*[133] an application for license by a political party under Section 27(2) of the Police Act to hold a dinner and lion dance was rejected by the Chief Police Officer. On the day of the event, half an hour before the scheduled time, the rejection of the application was communicated to the applicant. The Supreme Court ruled that the refusal was wrong for two reasons: 1) the power to grant the license vested in the officer-in-charge, police district, and not in the Chief Police Officer who was only an appellate authority. 2) Refusal was intimated only half an hour before the scheduled time which rendered the right of the applicant to appeal to the higher authority entirely nugatory.

The Printing Presses and Publications Act[134] has been enacted to regulate the use of printing presses and the printing, importation, production, reproduction, publishing and distribution of publications. No person can keep a printing press for use, or use the same, without a license. The licensing power is vested in the Minister in the following words: he may "in his absolute discretion" grant such a license or may at any time revoke or suspend such a license for any period he considers desirable. An unlicensed press can be forfeited by the Court. A permit is also needed to print, import, publish, sell, circulate or distribute, any newspaper printed in Malaysia or Singapore. Again the Minister may grant, revoke or suspend such a permit in his "absolute discretion". The Minister may in his "absolute discretion", by order published in the *Gazette*, prohibit the printing, importation, production, publishing, sale, issue, circulation, distribution or possession of any publication containing any material which is in any manner prejudicial or likely to be prejudicial to public order, morality, security, the relationship with any foreign government, or which is contrary to law or is prejudicial to public interest or national interest.

In the above Act, the expression "absolute discretion" has been used several times. What exactly is the significance of this expression? Obviously, what this expression seeks to convey is that the discretionary decision taken by the Minister is beyond judicial review. But should a discretionary decision be free from all judicial review and control? The courts in the common law countries do not subscribe to the theory that a discretion can be completely beyond judicial review.[135] In this connection it may be noted what Raja Azlan Shah, Ag. C.J. said in *Pengarah Tanah dan Galian Wilayah Persekutuan v. Sri Lempah Enterprises*[136] about authority having unfettered discretion:

> I cannot subscribe to this proposition for a moment. Unfettered discretion is a contradiction in terms .... It does not seem to be realized that this argument is fallacious. every legal power must have legal limits, otherwise there is dictatorship...In particular, it is a stringent requirement that a discretion should be exercised for a proper purpose, and that it should not be exercised unreasonably. In other words, every discretion cannot be free from legal restraint, ... where it is wrongly exercised, it becomes the duty of the courts to intervene. The courts are the only defence of the liberty of the subject against departmental aggression. In these days when government departments and public authorities have such great powers and influence, this is a most important safeguard for the ordinary citizens; so that the courts can see that these great powers and influence are exercised in accordance with law. I would once again emphasize ... that "public bodies must be compelled to observe the law and it is essential that bureaucracy should be kept in its place."[137]

Freedom of Religion

Though Islam has been declared to be the religion of the Federation,[138] there is religious freedom guaranteed to others. Every person has the right to profess and practice his religion,[139] subject to any law relating to public order, public health or morality. Every religious group has freedom to maintain its own religious affairs, establish and maintain institutions for religious and charitable purposes, and so on.[140] A person has a right to propagate his religion subject to any restrictions which a State law may impose on propagation of any religious doctrine or beliefs among the Muslims.[141] The religion of a person under the age of 18 years is to be decided by his parent or guardian.[142] Article 12(3) states that "no person shall be required to receive instruction in or to take part in any ceremony or act or worship of a religion other than his own."

In *In re Susie Teoh*,[143] the High Court explained the significance of these constitutional provisions. In this case, the plaintiff came to know that his 17-year-old daughter had been converted to Islam without his knowledge and consent. The father sought a declaration from the Court that he had the right to decide the religion of his minor daughter and invoked Article 12(4) for this purpose. The Court refused to give the declaration. The Court argued that under Article 11(1), the girl of 17 years and 8 months of age "was surely a person who could decide for herself in the exercise of her constitutional right to profess and practice her chosen religion." Further, "the infant has that right (to choose her own religion) where she does it on her own free will in view of Articles 11 and 12 of the Federal Constitution." The Court has laid emphasis on the words "shall be required" in Article 12(3). This means that a person may do either or all these things on his own free will. Article 12(3) applies only if he does not do it (i.e., receive instruction in any ceremony or act of worship in a religion other than his own) voluntarily. In that case, only Article 12(4) will apply. The Court has thus ruled that Articles 12(3) and (4) would not apply to the specific case as there was no element of force or compulsion. In India, freedom of religion is guaranteed by Articles 25 to 28. These provisions are broadly worded and have been interpreted broadly by the Supreme Court. Moreover, as the preamble says, India is a "secular" country having no official religion.[144] The provisions in the Malaysian Constitution are, to some extent, based on the Indian Constitution.

In the U.S., religious freedom is guaranteed by the First Amendment which says, *inter alia*: "Congress shall make no law respecting an establishment of religion, or prohibiting the free exercise thereof ..." There is no official religion in the U.S. It is forbidden to establish a State church. As the U.S. Supreme Court observed in *Everson v. Board of Education*:[145] "Neither a State nor the Federal Government can set up a church. Neither can pass laws which aid one religion, aid all religions, or prefer one religion over another ..." From the court decisions, a three-part test has emerged regarding the interpretation of the Establishment Clause: "In order to pass muster, a statute must have a secular legislative purpose, must have a principal or primary effect that neither advances nor inhibits religion, and must not foster an excessive government entanglement with religion."[146]

As there is a paucity of case law in Malaysia interpreting Article 12, it is difficult to say how far the concepts developed in the U.S. and India will be taken into account in Malaysia as regards the concept of freedom of religion.

In the mid-1980s Section 29SA was added to the Penal Code of Malaysia; *inter alia*, it makes it a penal offense for any person to cause disharmony, disunity or feelings of enmity, hatred or ill will, on grounds of religion, between persons or groups of persons professing the same or different religions. The offense is punishable with imprisonment up to three years. If the offense is committed in the proximity of any place of worship or in any assembly engaged in the performance of religious worship or ceremony, the imprisonment may extend to five years. The word "religion" in this provision is intended to cover all religions including Islam. The constitutional validity of this provision has been challenged.[147]

Right to Property

The right to property is very well protected in the U.S. through the Fifth Amendment which says, *inter alia*: "nor be deprived of life, liberty, or property, without process of law; nor shall private property be taken for public use, without just compensation." The State can thus take property for public use, without the owner's consent, upon making just compensation to him.[148] An important point is that in the U.S. compensation is payable for "taking" property which is a broader concept than vesting of possession or ownership of property in the government. If regulation of the property right goes too far, it may be regarded as "taking" of property, and compensation may become payable. "When regulation goes too far it will be recognized as a taking."[149] The question of compensation is justiciable as it is a question of a constitutional right. "The problem of according the just compensation directed to be paid upon a taking for a public use presents great difficulties."[150]

Protection is granted to property by the Malaysian Constitution. Article 13(1) declares: "No person shall be deprived of property without adequate compensation." These provisions do not have much similarity with the Fifth Amendment of the U.S. Constitution, mentioned above. In Article 13(1), the words "due process of law" are not to be found; instead, one finds the words "authority of law." In Article 13(2), the word "taking" is missing which will permit a good deal of economic regulation without the need of compensating the affected person.

The Malaysian provisions are based on Articles 31(1) and 31(2) of the Indian Constitution as they existed in 1957. The Indian Supreme Court was giving a broad interpretation to these Articles which the Government did not relish. For all practical purposes, through a series of pronouncements,[151] the Supreme Court incorporated the concept of "taking" in the word "deprivation." This led to constitutional amendments diluting property rights. The development of property rights in India subsequent to 1957 is not important, but the Indian Judicial pronouncements prior to 1957 are relevant to Malaysia.

The most important case on the constitutional provision in Malaysia is *Selangor Pilot Association v. Government of Malaysia.*[152] The appellant association was providing pilotage service at the port of Swettenham. Under a law, pilotage service was taken over by the Port Authority. The Authority also took over the physical assets of the appellants, launches, and so on, and paid compensation for the same, but refused to pay to the Association compensation for the loss of good will and for loss of future profits. The Federal Court found that the appellant association had been providing pilotage service since 1946, and it had tangible assets as well as good will. The Court also ruled that the good will did constitute property and that the word "property" in Article 13(1) should be construed broadly so as to include both corporeal and incorporeal rights. Even though the good will had not been acquired, the appellant association ought to be given compensation as it had been deprived of the same. On this point, the Court said:[153]

> In Malaysia too a person may be deprived of his property or his property may be acquired by or on behalf of the State by a mere negative or restrictive provision interfering with his enjoyment of property, even if there has been no transfer of the ownership or right to possession of that property to the State.

The association had been legislated out of business; they had been deprived of the business of supplying pilotage service through a negative or restrictive provision interfering with the enjoyment of its property and therefore it was entitled to compensation.

The above-mentioned view of the Federal Court was based on such Indian cases on the then-existing Articles 31(1) and 31(2) as *Saghir Ahmad v. State of Uttar Pradesh,*[154] *State of West Bengal v. Subodh Gopal Bose,*[155] and *Dwarkadas Shrinivas v. Shoalapur Spinning and Weaving Co. Ltd.*[156] In India, in the course of time, the property right has been diluted, as stated above.[157]

On appeal from the Federal Court to the Privy Council, by a majority, the Federal Court decision was overturned. The Privy Council distinguished between "deprivation" and "acquisition." No compensation was payable for the former. As the good will was not acquired by the Port, no compensation was payable.

In all this discussion, however, one thing stands out--there is no reference to the American Constitution at all or to any American case pertaining to property right, by either the Federal Court or the Privy Council.

An interesting question was raised in *Kulasingham.*[158] Under the Land Acquisition Act, 1960, private property may be acquired by the Government for certain purposes on payment of compensation. The Act makes no provision for giving an opportunity to raise objections against the proposed acquisition. It was argued, *inter alia*, that Article 13(1) should be so interpreted as to provide a right to pre-acquisition hearing to one whose property was sought. But the Federal Court refused to concede this point.

However, since Article 13(2) insists on "adequate compensation" for property acquired, the courts have ruled that a long time gap between the acquisition order and the assessment of compensation is not valid, for, by the lapse of time, prices of the property do go up and assessment of compensation with reference to property value on an anterior date cannot be regarded as "adequate compensation." In *Oriental Rubber & Palm Oil Sdn. Bhd. v. Pemungut Hasil Tanah, Kuantan,*[159] there was a delay of about three and a half years between the notification acquiring land and the making of the award. The Court held that the delay was unreasonable and an injustice to the landowner, because the compensation award given in 1983 was based on the market value of the land in 1979. Such a delay was tantamount to an abuse of power rendering the inquiry and all subsequent proceedings null and void. In another case, *Re Application of Tan Oon,*[160] there was a delay of eight years between the notification and the award and, consequently, the Court quashed the award. The Court argued that delay was inconsistent with the scheme of the Land Acquisition Act. "Any other interpretation of the scheme of the Act would make the Act to be in contravention of Article 13 of the Constitution and as such invalid."

Concluding Remarks

The concept of human rights represents an attempt to protect the individual from injustice and oppression. The pedigree of the idea can be traced back, historically, to the doctrine of Natural Law. But in its modern garb, the idea of justiciable, enforceable human rights, is the gift of the U.S. Constitution to the modern world.

The purpose of entrenching fundamental rights in the Constitution is to insulate these rights from being undermined by a transient majority. A government in a parliamentary system having a majority in the popular chamber (even though elected on a minority vote in the country) can play with the rights of man according to political expediency. The majority in Parliament may be swayed momentarily by an emotional reaction to some particular situation. Only when the fundamental rights are entrenched in the Constitution in such a manner that they cannot be changed by the ordinary legislative procedure, but can only be changed by the more elaborate process of constitutional amendment, can the fundamental rights of the people be protected to some extent. Along with this, there should be a vigilant judiciary always on guard to protect the fundamental rights against any undue encroachment by the Government. But all these constitutional safeguards will fail to work unless and until there is an alert public opinion conscious of its rights. After all, as is well said: the price of liberty is constant vigilance.

The sum and substance of the above discussion of the constitutional provisions of the Malaysian Constitution concerning fundamental liberties seem to indicate that the scope of such liberties is very restrictive. The fundamental liberties enshrined in the Malaysian Constitution do not effectively control the powers of Parliament to affect the rights of the people. The provisions have been so drafted as to impose only nominal restraints on Parliament in the matter of fundamental liberties. The scope for judicial review is minimal. Moreover, the courts themselves, by adopting the positivistic and literal approach to the Constitution, have deprived themselves of the opportunity of playing any creative role in expanding the scope of fundamental liberties. The courts have given a restrictive, rather than an expansive, interpretation to these provisions. The courts have assiduously eschewed liberal judicial views from other constitutions such as that of the U.S., in the matter of interpretation of fundamental liberties provisions in the Malaysian Constitution. Thus, the fundamental rights in the U.S. Constitution do not seem to have exerted any direct influence on the fundamental liberties in the Malaysian Constitution.

The use of the term "fundamental liberties" in the Constitution, instead of the expression "fundamental rights" is itself very suggestive. It indicates that the scope of people's guaranteed liberties is the residue of freedom allowed by law, the remnant left over when all restrictions imposed by statutory law have been subtracted. Many provisions guaranteeing fundamental liberties are so framed as to leave the freedoms with very little substance or content, insofar as Parliament remains free to impose any restriction it likes on those freedoms. No wonder that within the last thirty years for which the Constitution has been in force, only a very few laws passed by Parliament or a State Legislature have come to be held unconstitutional by the judiciary.[161] In fact, there have been only a very few challenges to parliamentary laws on the ground of infringement of any fundamental liberty. The main responsibility therefore to preserve and maintain the rights of the people, in Malaysia, falls on Parliament itself. It is Parliament's own good sense and auto-limitations arising out of the people's traditions, mores and opinions, which may discourage Parliament, on the one hand, from enacting legislation curtailing fundamental rights and, on the other hand, encourage it to preserve the same. While in normal times, Parliament has broad powers to restrict some of the fundamental liberties, during the period of emergency, Parliament's power, and consequently its responsibilities, increase a great deal. Parliament, and the executive in its own right, secure unlimited power of legislation. Therefore, in the Malaysian constitutional and political processes, the role of Parliament becomes crucial in the matter of preservation of the people's rights against undue curtailment by the executive during the Emergency.

In the area of human rights in Malaysia, since the commencement of the Constitution, on the whole, several trends become discernible. One, the scope of certain "fundamental liberties" has been narrowed down by the process of constitutional amendment, and, thus, greater legislative competence has come to be conferred on Parliament to enact legislation imposing restrictions. Two, Parliament has enacted several laws restricting certain basic human rights like freedom of speech, personal liberty, and so on. Thirdly, because of the Emergency, the Executive has made certain regulations which affect these rights.[162]

The Malaysian Parliament, like Parliaments elsewhere, is subject to Government leadership, for the majority in Parliament supports the Government and Government through the party system controls the majority. Parliament has power to express no-confidence in the Cabinet and the Cabinet can seek dissolution of Parliament. The opposition in Malaysia is weak. The central Government is formed by the *Barisan Nasional*--an alliance of three main political parties representing the three races--the United Malay National Organization, the Malaysian Chinese Association and the Malaysian Indian Congress--and several other small political parties.[163] The Government command the bulk of votes in *Dewan Rakyat*. Above all, there is the constant fear of Communist insurgency in the country which has resulted in the continuation of the Emergency for a long time and there is, thus, a psychological atmosphere in favor of restraints on rights and liberties of the people.

NOTES

1. *See Malayan Constitutional Documents*, vol. 1 (2d ed.), 1962, Preface, xii.

2. Federation of Malaya Agreement, 1957, Clause 3.

2A. [*Editor's Note*: Malaysia is ruled by a political coalition (*Barisan Nasional,* National Front) representing the Malayan *bumiputra* (55% of the population) in the UMNO, the Chinese-Malaysians (36%) in the Malaysian Chinese Association (MCA), and Indian-Malaysians (8%) in the Malaysian Indian Congress (MIC). Communal tensions among these and other ethnic groupings run high at times, as in 1987, and the bloody ethnic riots of 1969 are still well remembered. A major goal remains maintenance of a reasonable degree of pluralist harmony and rights protection with a Malay-dominated political framework. On 1987, see Deane K. Mauzy, "Malaysia in 1987: Decline of 'The Malay Way,'" *Asian Survey*, Vol. 28, No. 2, February, 1988, 213; and "Malaysia," *Asia 1988 Yearbook* (Hong Kong: Far Eastern Economic Review, 1988), p. 179. On later developments, see Fred R. von der Mehden, "Malaysia in 1990: Another Electorial Victory, "*Asian Survey*, Feb., 1991, 164-171. Since a 1988 split in the UMNO, the new UMNO (UMNO Baru) has been the strongest part of the 11-party front.]

3. *See*, e.g., *Merdeka University v. Government of Malaysia* (1982), 2 *Malayan Law Journal* [hereafter *M.L.J.*].

4. *Federal Constitution*, Article 125.

5. *See Karam Singh v. Menteri Hal Ehwal Dalam Negeri* (1969) 2 *M.L.J.* 129.

6. *Ong Ah Chuan v. Public Prosecutor* (1981) 1 *M.L.J.* 64 at 71. [*Editor's Note*, For facts and argument in this case, *see text infra* at note 62, and text of chapter 13 *infra* at note 54.]

7. (1981) 2 *M.L.J.* 49.

8. *Che Ani bin Itam v. Public Prosecutor* (1984) 1 *M.L.J.* 113, at 115.

9. *Ong Ah Chuan v. Public Prosecutor* (1981) 1 *M.L.J.* 64 at 71.

10. *Doi Ah Phua v. Officer-in-Charge of Criminal Investigations Kedah/Perlis* (1975) 2*M.L.J.* 198.

11. *Federal Constitution*, Article 45(4).

12. *Id.* Article 68.

12A. [*Editor's Note*, Prior to a severe constitutional controversy in 1983, the *Yang de Pertuan Agong* had the power to veto legislation. The real power resides in the Prime Minister.]

13. *Id.* Article 55(3). [*Editor's Note*, On the 1990 elections, *see* von der Mehden, *supra* note 2A.]

14. *Id.* Article 152. *See Merdeka University v. Government of Malaysia* (1982) 2 *M.L.J.* 243.

15. *Id.* Article 3.

16. *Id.* Article 11.

17. *Id.* Part III and Second Schedule.

18. *Id.* Part Xi.

19. *Id.* Article 150.
20. *Id.* Articles 150(4)-(6A).
21. *Id.* Article 150(7).
22. *Id.* Article 151.
23. *Id.* Article 10(4).
24. *Id.* Articles 63(4) and 72(4). *See Mark Koding v. Public Prosecutor* (1982) 2 *M.L.J.* 120.
25. *Id.* Article 159(5).
26. *Loh Kooi Choon v. Public Prosecutor* (1977) 2 *M.L.J.* 187, at 188-189.
27. *Id.*
28. (1987) 2 *M.L.J.* 165.
29. (1954) 394 *U.S.* 618, 638.
30. (1954) 347 *U.S.* 497.
31. (1977) 2 *M.L.J.* 155, 165-166.
32. (1977) 2 *M.L.J.* 158.
33. (1911) 220 *U.S.* 61, 76-79; 55 *L.Ed.* 369.
34. Among the cases cited were: (1973) 413 *U.S.* 717; 37 *L.Ed. 2d* 910; (1973) 353 *F. Supp.* 1211; (1973) 414 U.S. 802; 83 U.S. (1873) 16 *WALL* 36; 21 *L.Ed.* 220; (1886) 118 *U.S.* 356; 30 *L.Ed.* 220; A.I.R. 1951 *S.C.* 318, 326; (1943) 320 *U.S.* 81, 100; 87 *L.Ed.* 1774; (1981) 430 *U.S.* 365; 29 *L.Ed. 2d* 534.
35. Grant, "The Natural Law Background of Due Process," 31 *Col. L. Rev.* 56; Corwin, "The 'Higher Law' Background of American Constitutional Law," 42 *Harv. L. Rev.* 149. Raoul Berger, *Government by Judiciary* 1977; Abraham, *The Judiciary: The Supreme Court in the Government Process* 1977.
36. *Infra* Section V.
37. *Infra* Section VIII.
38. (1977) 2 *M.L.J.* 158.
39. *Infra* Section VIII.
40. *Infra* notes 66 and 70.
41. (1981) 1 *M.L.J.* 64.
42. *See supra* Section A, IV, and *infra* Section II for details.
43. *Mapp v. Ohio*, 367 *U.S.* 643 (1961); *Miranda v. Arizona*, 384 *U.S.* 436 (1966); *Argersinger v. Hamlin*, 407 *U.S.* 25 (1972).
44. *Robinson v. California*, 370 *U.S.* 660; *Furman v. Georgia*, 408 *U.S.* 238 (1972).
45. 262 *U.S.* 390 (1932).
46. *Griswold v. Connecticut*, 381 *U.S.* 479 (1965).
47. *Roe v. Wade*, 410 *U.S.* 113 (1973).
48. *A.K. Gopalan v. State of Madras, A.I.R. 1950 S.C.* 27.
49. *A.I.R. 1978 S.C.* 597.
50. *Hussainara Khatoon v. Bihar, A.I.R. 1979 S.C.* 1360, 1369.
51. *Id.*
52. *M.H. Hoskot v. State of Maharashtra, A.I.R. 1978 S.C.* 1548.
53. For details, *see* Jain, *Indian Constitutional Law*, §§ 589 *et seq.*
54. *R.M. Malkani v. State of Maharashtra, A.I.R. 1973 S.C.* 157.
55. *Olga Tellis v. Bombay Municipal Corporation, A.I.R. 1986 S.C.* 180.

56. 94 *U.S.* 113 (1877).

57. (1979) 2 *M.L.J.* 33.

58. *Id.* 36.

59. *Loh Wai King v. Government of Malaysia* (1978) 2 *M.L.J.* 175.

60. (1969) *M.L.J.* 129.

61. *See also* M.P. Jain, "Constitutional Remedies," in Trindade & Lee, eds., *The Constitution of Malaysia*, 1984, 165.

62. *Supra* note 41 and text at note 6.

63. *Id.*

64. (1981) 2 *M.L.J.* 49.

65. *Che Ani bin Itam v. Public Prosecutor* (1984) 1 *M.L.J.* 113. [*Editor's Note*, For a quotation from this holding, see *supra* text at note 8.]

66. (1983) 1 *M.L.J.* 157.

67. *A.I.R. 1980 S.C.* 2147. Section 433A, Cr. P.C. obligates actual detention in prison for a full 14 years as a mandatory minimum in two classes of cases: (i) where the Court could have punished the offender with death but did not; or (ii) where the Court did punish the culprit with death but the sentence was commuted to life imprisonment. The Supreme Court of India ruled in *Maru Ram v. Union of India*, that this was not an arbitrary provision and was not invalid. Deterrence is a valid punitive component and even for reformation a long hospitalization in prison is necessary.

68. (1983) 1 *M.L.J.* 51.

69. (1984) 1 *M.L.J.* 110.

70. *A.I.R. 1983 S.C.* 473. Section 303, I.P.C., prescribes that if a person under sentence of life imprisonment commits murder, he must be punished with death. The Supreme Court ruled in *Mithu* that the provision was wholly unreasonable and arbitrary and violated Article 21. The Court emphasized that the last word on the question of justice and fairness does not rest with the legislature; it is for the courts to decide whether the procedure prescribed by a law for depriving a person of his life or liberty is fair, just and reasonable.

71. *Public Prosecutor v. Lau Kee Hoo* (1983) 1 *M.L.J.* 157.

72. *A.I.R. 1978 S.C.* 597.

73. (1984) 1 *M.L.J.* 113.

74. *Supra* note 41.

75. (1979) 99 S.Ct. 874.

76. (1980) 100 S. Ct. 1133.

77. (1986) 2 *M.L.J.* 235.

78. *Infra.*

79. Article 151.

80. The Internal Security Act; The Emergency (Public Order and Prevention of Crime) Ordinance, 1969.

81. Jain, *Indian Constitutional Law*, 1987, 605-630; Jain, "Judicial Creativity and Preventive Detention in India" *J.M.C.L.* 261 (1975).

82. (1942) *A.C.* 206.

83. (1969) 2 *M.L.J.* 129.

84. *Id.*

85. *But See* Abdoolcader, J., in *Yeap Hock Seng*, who has suggested that "where there is a dearth of local authority, the Indian decisions are entitled to the greatest respect and will normally be followed ..." because "our Constitution and laws providing for preventive detention have been primarily drawn from Indian sources...."

86. *Yeap Hock Seng @ Ah Seng v. Minister of Home Affairs, Malaysia* (1975) 2 *M.L.J.* 279.

87. *Yeap Hock Seng, supra*; *Re Tan BOon Liat* (1975) 2 *M.L.J.* 83, upheld by the Federal Court in 1977, 2 *M.L.J.* 18.

88. (1977) 2 *M.L.J.* 108.

89. (1969) *M.L.J.* 129.

90. Jayakumar, "Constitution Limitations on Legislative Power in Malaysia," 9 *M.L.R.* 101 (1967). He had cautioned that reliance on *Gopalan* to interpret Article 5(1) would be unwise. *See also* Jayakumar, "Emergency Powers in Malaysia," in Tun Suffian ed., *The Constitution of Malaysia*, 1978, 328, 356.

91. Emerson & Haber, *Political Thought and Civil Rights in the U.S.A.*, 1967, 1, 168.

92. *Lim Sing Hiaw v. P.P.* (1965) 1 *M.L.J.* 85.

93. (1984) 2 *M.L.J.* 219.

94. (1975) 2 *M.L.J.* 198.

95. 86 *S. Ct.* 1602 (1966).

96. (1975) 1 *M.L.J.* 93-94.

97. (1977) 2 *M.L.J.* 116.

98. 377 *U.S.* 201 (1964).

99. (1977) 2 *M.L.J.* 116-17.

100. 347 *U.S.* 483 (1954) overruling *Plessey v. Ferguson*, 163 *U.S.* 537, which had accepted segregation between blacks and whites in the field of education as valid so long as facilities provided for both were equal even though separate. *See also Swann v. Charlotte Mecklenburg Board of Education*, 402 *U.S.* 1 (1971).

101. 404 *U.S.* 71 (1971). *See also Frontiero v. Richardson*, 411 *U.S.* 677 (1973) holding discrimination based on sex invalid.

102. 118 *U.S.* 356.

103. M.P. Jain, *Indian Constitutional Law* 471-82.

104. *Id.* 483-97. *See also* M.P. Jain, *The Evolving Indian Administrative Law* (1953).

105. *Central Inland Water Transport Corp. Ltd. v. Brojo Nath, A.I.R. 1986 S.C.* 1571.

106. Article 8(2).

107. Article 12(1).

108. (1977) 2 *M.L.J.* 158.

109. (1976) 2 *M.L.J.* 116.

110. *Supra* note 75.

111. Article 145(3) runs as follows: "The Attorney General shall have power exercisable at his discretion to institute, conduct or discontinue any proceedings for an offense, other than proceedings before a *Shariah* court, a native court or a court martial."

112. (1977) 2 *M.L.J.* 70.

113. (1986) 2 *M.L.J.* 225. [*Editor's Note*, For more extended discussion and quotations from this decision, see *supra* text at note 28.]

114. *The Straits Times*, February 21, 1987.

115. *A.I.R. 1983 S.C.* 130. *See also* M.P. Jain, *Indian Constitutional Law*, 1987, 475.

116. Three major decisions in the historical development of U.S. free speech doctrine are: *Schenck v. United States*, 294 *U.S.* 47 (1919); *Dennis v. United States*, 341 *U.S.* 494 (1951); *New York Times v. Sullivan*, 375 *U.S.* 254 (1964).

117. *New York Times Co. v. United States*, 403 *U.S.* 713.

118. *Brij Bhushan v. State of Delhi*, *A.I.R. 1950 S.C.* 129.

119. *Virendra v. State of Punjab*, *A.I.R. 1957 S.C.* 896.

120. *Sakal Papers v. Union of India*, *A.I.R. 1962 S.C.* 305.

121. *Bennett Coleman & Co. v. Union of India*, *A.I.R. 1973 S.C.* 106.

122. *Kedar Nath v. State of Bihar*, *A.I.R. 1962 SD.C.* 955. *See also infra* note 95.

123. Jain, *Indian Constitutional Law*, 1987, 526-39.

124. (1977) 2 *M.L.J.* 206.

125. *Queen Empress v. Bal Gangadhar Tilak*, 251 *A.* 1.

126. *A.I.R. 1962 S.C.* 955.

127. (1971) 2 *M.L.J.* 108, 111.

128. (1975) 1 *M.L.J.* 176.

129. (1975) 2 *M.L.J.* 235.

130. (1975) 2 *M.L.J.* 264.

131. Malaysian Certificate of Education.

132. (1986) 2 *M.L.J.* 203.

133. (1986) 2 *M.L.J.* 204.

134. Act 304.

135. M.P. Jain, *Administrative Law of Malaysia & Singapore*, 271 *et seq.*

136. (1979) 1 *M.L.J.* 135. *See also* (1979) *Survey of Malaysian Law* (hereinafter *SML*) 52 for comments on the case by the author; *Padfield v. Minister of Agriculture and Fisheries* (1968) 1 *All ER* 694.

137. (1979) 1 *M.L.J.* 135, at 148.

138. Art. 3(1).

139. Arts. 11(1) and 11(5).

140. Art. 11(3).

141. Art. 11(4).

142. Art. 12(4).

143. (1986) 2 *M.L.J.* 228.

144. On these provisions, *see* M.P. Jain, *Indian Constitutional Law*, 1987, 635-46.

145. 330 *U.S.* 1.

146. *Woleman v. Walter*, 433 *U.S.* 229.

147. *Mamat bin Daud v. Govt. of Malaysia* (1986) 2 *C.L.J.* 118.

148. *U.S. ex rel. T.V.A. v. Welch*, 327 *U.S.* 546, 554; *Kohl v. U.S.* 91 *U.S.* 367.

149. *Pennsylvania Coal Co. v. Mahon*, 260 *U.S.* 393. *See also Penn Central Transportation Co. v. City of New York*, 438 *U.S.* 104.

150. Biuret & Cohen, *Constitutional Law* 577 (1985).

151. *State of West Bengal v. Subodh Gopal Bose*, *A.I.R. 1954 S.C.* 92; *Saghir Ahmad v. State of Uttar Pradesh*, *A.I.R. 1954 S.C.* 728; *Deep Chand v. State of Uttar Pradesh*, *A.I.R. 1959 S.C.* 648. For a full discussion on the Fundamental Right of Property in India, *see* Jain, *Indian Constitutional Law*, 1987, 662-702.

152. (1975) 2 *M.L.J.* 66.

153. *Id.* 69.

154. *Supra* note 150.

155. *Supra* note 150.

156. *A.I.R. 1954 S.C.* 119.

157. *Supra* text with note 119.

158. *S. Kulasingham v. Commissioner of Lands, Federal Territory* (1982) 1 *M.L.J.* 204. For detailed comment by the author, *see* (1982) *Survey of Malaysian Law*.

159. (1985) *M.L.J.* 257.

160. (1985) 2 *M.L.J.* 67.

161. In the *Bar Council* case, *supra* note 113, a part of the law was held invalid under Article 8. In a 1987 case, *supra* note 114 (unreported), the Pensions Adjustments Act denying enhanced pensions to non-resident, ex-government employees was invalidated, again under Article 8.

162. [*Editor's Note*: In 1986 and 1987 a series of Court decisions went against the Government of Datuk Seri Dr. Mahathir bin Mohamad, Prime Minister since 1981. High Court Justice Harun presided in a number of cases: upholding a challenge to a Home Ministry expulsion order against a foreign journalist (1986); granting a writ of *habeas corpus* to one detained under the Internal Security Act (February, 1987) with the Supreme Court later concurring (November, 1987), the first such writ action for an ISA detainee; and ruling against a Home Ministry decision on a citizenship application (July, 1987). *Far Eastern Economic Review*, March 5, 1987, 53; *Straits Times*, November 4, 1987; Mauzy, *op cit.* 216.]

163. Although the Front retained its two-thirds majority in the 1990 parliamentary elections (127 of 180 seats), their share of the popular vote dropped 3.2% to 54.2%, and the number of opposition seats in Parliament (53) and the State legislatures rose substantially over 1986 election results. See von der Mehden, *supra* note 2A, at 167-169.

12

REPUBLIC OF THE PHILIPPINES

The 1987 Constitution of the Philippines:
The Impact of American Constitutionalism Revisited*

Enrique M. Fernando

Emma Quisumbing-Fernando

The Bicentennial Year of the Constitution of the United States marked the birth of the 1987 Constitution of the Republic of the Philippines. The Filipino people voiced their approval of a draft Constitution submitted by an appointive Constitutional Commission in a plebiscite held on February 2, 1987. As of that date then, in accordance with the Article on Transitory Provisions, the 1987 Constitution came into being, with its explicit mandate that it "shall take effect immediately upon its ratification and shall supersede all previous Constitutions."[1] It is this new charter of government and of liberty of the Filipino people that will be commented on, primarily from the standpoint of the impact thereon of American constitutionalism.

What is readily apparent even from a cursory perusal of the rather lengthy 1987 Philippine Constitution is much less reliance on American doctrines and precedents. It is true, of course, that there is adherence to the separation of powers principle. There is an affirmation anew, in well-nigh identical language, of the traditional civil and political rights. The difference in phrasing reflects favorably on the commitments of its framers to such civil liberties. There was, however, a marked effort on their part to embody such further changes as will be more in consonance with the ideals of a people accustomed to accept Western legal ideas, but with greater appreciation of its distinctively Oriental heritage and culture. Philippine constitutionalism is on the ascendant. It is well that it is so.

Introductory: The Constitutions of 1935 and 1973

It is of course true, as observed by Justice Holmes, that continuity with the past is not a duty but only a necessity. It does not follow, however, that there be complete acceptance of what has been. There is always room for what is perceived to be desirable changes. A great deal of what has been the settled law may continue to be so, but with conditions far from static, innovations are not to be ruled out. In the oft-quoted aphorism of Dean Pound, law may be stable, yet it cannot stand still.

The 1935 Constitution

Thus it was that in both the 1935 and the 1973 Philippine Constitutions, new approaches were evident. As to the former, the well-known Filipino jurist, Jose P. Laurel, a leading delegate to the 1934-1935 Constitutional Convention and later a Justice of the Philippine Supreme Court, could affirm: "The separation of powers is a fundamental principle in our system of government."[2] Nonetheless, the Executive was given a dominant position. The same jurist could speak of the President of the Philippines as being "endowed with broad and extraordinary powers and expected to govern with a firm and steady hand without vexatious or embarrassing interference and much less dictation from any source...."[3]

The original provision in the 1935 Constitution was for a unicameral legislative body, the National Assembly. It was not until the 1940 amendments that a bicameral legislature came into being, composed of a Senate and a House of Representatives. As to the judiciary, while the courts can exercise the power of judicial review, the 1935 Constitution required a two-thirds vote to annul a legislative act or a treaty. In addition, there were independent constitutional bodies, the Office of the Auditor-General and the Commission on Elections, which were created by the 1940 amendments.

A more significant innovation was the adoption of an Article entitled Declaration of Principles.[4] It has five sections providing for: 1) the Philippines being a republican State with sovereignty residing in the people; 2) the defense of the State being a prime duty of government with citizens called upon to render personal, military or civil service; 3) the renunciation of war as an instrument of national policy; 4) the natural right and duty of parents in the rearing of the youth for civic efficiency, receiving the aid and support of the government; and 5) the promotion of social justice to ensure the well-being and economic security of all the people being the concern of the State. It is this last principle that laid the basis for a number of economic, social, and cultural rights. It is a matter of pride for the Philippines that its fundamental law antedated by thirteen years the equivalent provisions in the Universal Declaration of Human Rights. Then, as well as now, the cognate provision on protection to labor is considered of equal significance in the state effort to assure the well-being and economic security of all the Filipino people.[5]

Even so, the time came when the 1935 Constitution was looked upon as a remnant of colonialism, the Philippines being an unincorporated territory of the United States from 1899 to 1946. Necessarily, its constitutional law was pretty much the same as that of the sovereign power. Moreover, there was a great deal of truth to the charge that the working of the 1935 Constitution, especially its Bill of Rights, owed much to the first Ten Amendments of the American Constitution--its Bill of Rights--as well as to the Thirteenth Amendment prohibiting slavery and the Fourteenth Amendment enshrining the principal guarantees of due process and equal protection.

Much is made of the fact that the leaders of the 1934-1935 Constitutional Convention, except for its President Claro M. Recto, also a highly-respected jurist, were products of the College of Law, University of the Philippines. In that premier institution, American Constitutional law was taught by Dean George A. Malcolm, later as a Justice of the Supreme Court, the foremost exponent of American constitutionalism. Two of the eminent leaders of the Convention, the aforesaid Jose P. Laurel and Manual A. Roxas, later the first President of the Republic of the Philippines, were among his brightest students. A more sober and realistic view of the lack of validity of such a charge came from the late Chief Justice Concepcion in these words:

> With due respect to those who entertain such a view, I am unable to find a colonial tinge in our supreme law except the time of its making and the limitations imposed therefor by the United States. But these limitations were embodied in an ordinance appended to the Constitution, in order that such ordinance may automatically cease, as it automatically ceased to be effective on July 11, 1946. The body of the Constitution appears on its face to be intended for the Republic of the Philippines, subject to the limitations contained in said ordinance, but only during the regime. Hence, the colonial provisions of the Constitution are not part thereof since the establishment of our Republic.[6]

Nor were those people of the conviction that the 1935 Constitution was flawed by its colonial character the only proponents of change. "There was the group of militant youth, including in its ranks bright young men and women, for whom Marxism whether of the Moscow or the Peking brand, supplied the remedy for the Malady that afflicted Philippine society.... They were not reconciled to minor modifications."[7] There was still another group in this clamor for change.

With less vehemence but with equal seriousness, political leaders of stature, mostly in Congress, educators of note, professionals, primarily lawyers, journalists, and civic-minded citizens spoke to the same effect. There was this significant difference though: there were only a few among them who would go so far as to tinker unduly with the property relationship. Their dissatisfaction did not go that far. The amendments proposed by them deal on the whole with the governmental structure, the adoption of the parliamentary system being the first in their agenda.[8]

The 1973 Constitution

It was this group that prevailed in the 1971-1972 Constitutional Convention, created under a legislative act approved in 1967. The election for delegates was held in November 1970, with the body being convened in June of 1971. The Convention adopted a modified parliamentary system. It adhered to the tradition of a strong executive, the Prime Minister having all the powers of the Philippine President under the 1935 Constitution. Its other main accomplishment was the emphasis on social, cultural, and economic rights.

The 1981 amendments to the 1973 Constitution restored the powers of the Executive to the President, although retaining the position of the Prime Minister. Yet purportedly there was no change in the form of government. This notwithstanding, the Philippine Supreme Court in a 1981 decision ruled that with such amendments, the presidential system was once again operative.[9]

The adoption of certain aspects of a parliamentary system in the amended Constitution does not alter its essentially presidential character. Article VII on the presidency starts with this provision: "The President shall be the head of state and chief executive of the Republic of the Philippines." Its last section is an even more emphatic affirmation that it is a presidential system that obtains in our government. Thus: "All powers vested in the President of the Philippines under the 1935 Constitution and the laws of the land which are not herein provided for or conferred upon any official shall be deemed and are hereby vested in the President unless the *Batasang Pambansa* provides otherwise." There is a provision, of course, on the Prime Minister, but the Constitution is explicit that while he shall be the head of the Cabinet, it is the President who nominates him from among the members of the *Batasang Pambansa*, thereafter being elected by a majority of all the members thereof. He is primarily, therefore, a Presidential choice. He need not even come from its elected members. He is responsible, along with the Cabinet, to the *Batasang Pambansa* for the program of government but as approved by the President. His term of office as Prime Minister shall commence from the date of his election by the *Batasang Pambansa* and shall end on the date that the nomination of his successor is submitted by the President to the *Batasang Pambansa*. Any other member of Cabinet or the Executive Committee may be removed at the discretion of the President. Even the duration of his term then depends on the Presidential pleasure, not on legislative approval or lack of it. During his incumbency, he exercises supervision over all ministries, a recognition of the important role he plays in the implementation of the policy of the government, the legislation duly enacted in pursuance thereof, and the decrees and orders of the President. To the Prime Minister can thus be delegated the performance of the administrative functions of the President, who can then devote more time and energy in the fulfillment of his exacting role as the national leader. As the only one whose constituency is national it is the President who, by virtue of his election by the entire electorate, has an indisputable claim to speak for the country as a whole. Moreover, it is he who is explicitly granted the greater power of control of such ministries. He continues to be the Executive, the amplitude and scope of the functions entrusted to him in the formulation of policy and its execution leading to the pat observation by Laski that there is not one aspect of which that does not affect the lives of all. The Prime Minister can be of valuable assistance indeed to the President in the discharge of his awesome responsibility, but it is the latter who is vested with powers, aptly characterized by Justice Laurel in *Planas v. Gil*, as "broad and extraordinary being expected to govern with a firm and steady hand without vexatious or embarrassing interference and much less dictation from any source." It may be said that Justice Laurel was referring to his powers under the 1935 Constitution. It suffices to refer anew to the last section of the Article of the present Constitution on the presidency to the effect that all powers vested in the President of the Philippines under the 1935 Constitution remain with him. It cannot be emphasized too strongly that under the 1935 Constitution "The Executive power shall be vested in the President of the Philippines."[10]

Now as to the Bill of Rights under the 1935 Constitution, it was retained essentially as worded. The objection in some quarters that it was couched in the language of Anglo-American fundamental rights and was therefore no longer responsive to modern times fell on deaf ears. Nor was there any acceptance of the view that such terminology did not sufficiently take into account Philippine conditions. Indeed, for most delegates in the 1971-1972 Constitutional Convention, it was desirable to let well enough alone. For them, the working of the specific guarantees of technical precision and perspicuous brevity, to quote Madison, proved to be a source of strength. At the same time, there could be discerned in the language used an element of flexibility assuring adaptability to meet changing conditions. What is more, there is likewise a distinct advantage in retaining the tried and tested phraseology in that there is an affirmance of the views expressed in leading decisions, both Philippine and American. The danger of erroneous construction is thus minimized. Only two new rights were added. One is the express recognition of the right of the people to have access to official records, documents, and papers pertaining to official acts, transactions or decisions subject to such limitations as may be provided by law.[11] The other new right added requires the speedy disposition of cases before all judicial, quasi-judicial, or administrative bodies.[12] Of the rights found in the 1935 Constitution, two were strengthened with the provision that any evidence obtained in violation of the search and seizure clause becomes inadmissible, and the provision adopting the *Miranda* ruling concerning the right to remain silent during custodial interrogation.[13]

As for social, cultural, and economic rights, the distinctively Philippine element in its fundamental law, the 1973 Constitution expanded their scope and made them more concrete and specific. In the 1935 Constitution, it is declared: "The promotion of social justice to insure the well-being and economic security of all the people should be the concern of the State."[14] In the 1973 Constitution, such a principle is set forth in two sections of the Article on Declaration of Principles and State Policies. According to the first of such sections: "The State shall promote social justice to ensure the dignity, welfare, and security of all the people. Towards this end, the State shall regulate the acquisition, ownership, use, enjoyment and disposition of private property, and equitably diffuse property ownership and profits."[15] According to the other section: "The State shall establish, maintain, and ensure adequate social services in the field of education, health, housing, employment, welfare, and social security to guarantee the enjoyment by the people of a decent standard of living."[16] Protection to labor, according to this Article, was made more precise in this wise:

> The State shall afford protection to labor, promote full employment and equality in employment, ensure equal work opportunities regardless of sex, race, or creed, and regulate the relations between workers and

employers. The State shall assure the rights of workers to self-organization, collective bargaining, security of tenure, and just and humane conditions of work. The State may provide for compulsory arbitration.[17]

The 1973 Constitution likewise was much more emphatic than its 1935 equivalent in its concern for agricultural workers: "The State shall formulate and implement an agrarian reform program aimed at emancipating the tenant from the bondage of the soil and achieving the goals enunciated in this Constitution."[18]

As to the right to education, the 1973 Constitution as did the 1935 Charter, imposed on the State the duty to "establish and maintain a complete [and] adequate" system of education but added that it be "integrated" as well as "relevant to the goals of national development."[19] It must be "a system of free public elementary education and, in areas where finances permit, ... free public education at least up to the secondary level."[20] Lastly: "The State shall provide citizenship and vocational training to adult citizens and out-of-school youth, and create and maintain scholarships for poor and deserving students."21

A brief historical note is not amiss. The 1973 Constitution was in force and effect during times of emergency, from 1973 to 1986. For the first eight years, the Philippines was under a regime of martial law, which was not lifted until January 17, 1981. As to crimes involving national security, the privilege of the writ of *habeas corpus* continued to be suspended. That was necessary in view of the continuing insurgency in certain areas of the country.

Under such circumstances, strict adherence to constitutional ways was not always easy. There was, nonetheless, a determined effort to follow the rule of law. The announced policy of the then administration was to abide by what the fundamental law and the applicable statutes decreed. As could be expected under such a troubled period and conditions of stress, performance did not always match profession. At times, excess of zeal was the cause. Also, the struggle against communism was so intense that on a number of occasions it led to abuse on the part of the military and the police. At no time, during such years, was appeal to the judiciary fruitless. As will be apparent in the discussion of the function of judicial review, the Supreme Court of the Philippines, when appealed to for redress, displayed an attitude of judicial activism.

With the foregoing as background, the rest of this work is devoted to a brief and admittedly inconclusive appraisal of the latest Philippine experiment in constitutionalism in terms of the lesser impact of American constitutional law and the correspondingly greater influence of the lessons learned from the immediate past, the present needs, and the hopes of the future. Necessarily, the nationalistic aspect is on the ascendant. As noted at the outset, it is well that it is so. This is by no means to imply that there is a lesser recognition of the debt owed the great American jurists in the growth and development of Philippine constitutional law.

Before proceeding to such a survey, a few pages will be devoted to the events that led to the framing of the 1987 Constitution.

The Framing of the 1987 Constitution

The 1987 Constitution is the product of a revolutionary regime. That it possesses such a character is expressly admitted in Proclamation No. 3 of the Corazon Aquino administration, issued on March 25, 1986. It provided for a Provisional Constitution. The first paragraph of its "Whereas" clauses speaks of "the new government [being] installed through a direct exercise of the power of the Filipino people assisted by units of the New Armed Forces of the [Republic of the Philippines]."[22] There was likewise an admission of such revolutionary character of the present regime when in the second paragraph there was the explicit admission that "the heroic action of the people was done in defiance of the provisions of the 1973 Constitution,"[23] the fundamental law then in force when the revolt took place.

Such a characterization received confirmation from a Philippine Supreme Court resolution promulgated on December 11, 1986:

> Finally, petitioner's reply to comment concedes that the events which took place and culminated in the assumption of power of the Aquino government on February 25, 1986 were political acts. As such, they were done outside of, and in disregard of the existing legal and constitutional framework. Indeed, the second "whereas" clause of Proclamation No. 3 declared: "the heroic action of the people was done in defiance of the provisions of the 1973 Constitution, as amended."[24]

Such a Provisional Constitution, issued as Proclamation No. 3 on March 25, 1986, was not the product of a constitutional convention or a constitutional commission. Nor was it submitted to the people for ratification. It was issued on the sole authority of Mrs. Corazon C. Aquino, the losing candidate for the Presidency in the February 1986 election. So it was declared by the *Batasang Pambansa*, the legislative body under the 1973 Constitution, which had the power to canvass the election returns and proclaim the winner.   After conducting such a canvass, it proclaimed Ferdinand E. Marcos as the duly-elected President on February 5, 1986. Instead of filing a protest, Corazon C. Aquino assumed the Presidency as a result of the revolt in February 22-25 of that month. She had no choice but to admit in her Proclamation that her power to do so arose from what she asserted to be the "sovereign mandate of the people."[25]

This clear rejection of the then fundamental law notwithstanding, the first Article 26 of the Provisional Constitution is entitled "Adoption of Certain Provisions of the 1973 Constitution as Amended."   There were three categories: 1) certain Articles, the most notable being Article IV in the Bill of Rights, were adopted *in toto*; 2) some other Articles, retained "insofar as they are not inconsistent with the provisions of the Provisional Constitution"; and 3) the remaining Articles dealing with the *Batasang Pambansa*, the legislative body;[27] the Prime Minister and Cabinet;[28] the Amending Process[29] and the Transitory Provisions,[30] superceded.

With the abolition of the *Batasang Pambansa*, necessarily she assumed legislative power, thus confirming that under the revolutionary regime, President Aquino had the prerogative of issuing decrees.[31] It was by virtue of such legislative power that she created a Constitutional Commission to be composed of members appointed by her to frame a new Constitution. In a statement that accompanied Proclamation No. 3 on the Provisional Constitution of the Revolutionary Government, she declared: "To hasten the restoration of full normal constitutional government, [she] shall appoint, within 60 days, men and women of probity and patriotism to a Constitutional Commission which will draft a constitution that will be submitted to the people in a national plebiscite."[32] With "a new permanent Constitution and a duly elected parliament, [there is a] return to a fully-pledged representative government."[33] The time frame was within one year from such Proclamation.

Thereafter, on April 23, 1986, she issued Proclamation No. 8, the Law Governing the Constitutional Commission of 1986, providing for such a body to be "composed of not more than fifty (50) national, regional, and sectoral representatives who shall be appointed by the President."[34] The national representatives were to be "men or women of national standing, experienced in government or with recognized competence in their respective fields."[35]

Regional representatives were to be chosen from persons "who have held elective offices ... to be apportioned among the thirteen (13) regions as nearly as may be according to the number of their inhabitants on the basis of the latest census."[36] Sectoral representatives were chosen, among others, from farmers, fishermen, workers, students, professionals, business, military, academic, ethnic, and other similar groups.[37] To be qualified, a member of the Commission must be "a natural born citizen of the Philippines, a qualified voter, of recognized probity, independence, nationalism, and patriotism."[38]

Its opening session was scheduled for June 2, 1986, at the Session Hall of the former *Batasang Pambansa*.[39] Vice-President Salvador H. Laurel was to preside at its opening session until a presiding officer was elected from among its members.[40] The Commission was granted the powers of a deliberative body such as the determination of its rules, the discipline of its members for disorderly behavior, included in which was the power to expel by a two-thirds vote, the holding of sessions in any place in the Philippines.[41] A Member was entitled to the usual parliamentary immunities of freedom of speech and freedom from arrest.[42]

It would have been more democratic if the members had been elected rather than appointed. When the appointments were announced, however, the Filipino people had no cause for dissatisfaction. The national representatives were eminently qualified. Included among them were the now-deceased former Chief Justice Roberto Concepcion, a distinguished constitutionalist; former Speaker Jose P. Laurel; and former Senators Lorenzo Sumulong and Francisco Rodrigo, skilled parliamentarians. A retired Justice of the Supreme Court, Cecilia Munoz Palma, was elected President, with the Vice-President being former Senator Ambrosio B. Padilla. A delegate to the 1971 Constitutional Convention, Napolion Y. Rama was chosen Floor Leader, his assistants being a fellow delegate in such convention, Jose D. Calderon and a former Senator, Ahmad Domacao Alonto, who is one of the two Muslim leaders appointed. The other was former Ambassador Yusuf P. Abubakar. As in the two former Constitutional Conventions, of 1934-1935 and 1971-1972, most of the members were lawyers. Academe, religious, youth, agriculture, and labor were duly represented.

The draft of the 1987 Constitution was approved on October 12, 1986, and signed on October 15. Two of the forty-seven members of the Commission did not sign the document. As noted at the outset, it was ratified on February 2, 1987, and became effective on that day.

The 1987 Constitution: Lesser Impact of American Constitutional Law

During the period of American sovereignty in the Philippines, dating from 1899, American constitutional law had a binding force. It was authoritative in character. This was so even after the Philippines adopted its 1935 Constitution. After July 4, 1946, however, with its independence gained and the Republic of the Philippines established, American constitutional law lost its binding force in this jurisdiction. It was at the most persuasive. It was no longer for Philippine courts a matter of deference but of reference. They possessed freedom of choice. Still, the practice of citing American precedents was not abandoned. It was not just a manifestation of what Justice Cardozo so felicitously referred to as the judicial inclination for a parsimony of effort. It seems quite fitting when Philippine law is couched in language borrowed from the American Charter. Such an approach becomes even more difficult to resist when the American Supreme Court decision relied upon would be most appropriate in resolving the constitutional issue raised. At times, it suffices to refer to American decisions for comparative law purposes.

It is easily understandable then why the impact of American Constitutional Law was easily discernible when the Philippines was under the 1935 Constitution. Even then, however, and as it should be, Philippine courts saw to it that due weight was given to local conditions so as to avoid the peril of what American legal realists so aptly termed the slot-machine theory of jurisprudence. With the 1973 Constitution, as originally framed and as amended in 1981, embodying concepts more attuned to Philippine needs and Philippine ways, the case for such a judicial attitude became even more formidable.

The 1987 Constitution of the Philippines with its many novel provisions finding no counterpart either in the Federal or State Constitutions of the United States, and in light of the conditions and circumstances that led to its adoption, appears to be even less likely to be interpreted or construed with the aid of foreign law. Moreover, the juristic climate of opinion is not favorable to reliance on rulings and precedents that come from abroad. Accordingly, the impact of American constitutional law on the Philippine legal system has been further minimized. In three areas, however, American constitutional law still furnishes a reservoir of doctrines and precepts to be weighed and considered in the adjudication of cases: the separation of powers as the basic concept in the structure and organization as well as the interrelationship of the three main departments of government; the Bill of Rights as the embodiment of the traditional freedoms, political and civil in nature; and judicial review as the vehicle to assure the supremacy of a constitution. As to those provisions in the 1987 Constitution on social and economic rights, the impact of American constitutional law is at most minimal, except where labor legislation is concerned.

Separation of Powers: The Three Departments of Government and Their Interrelationship

"The separation of powers," as noted a few pages back, citing a leading Supreme Court decision less than a year after the effectivity of the 1935 Constitution, "is a fundamental principle in our system of government."[43] The next sentence stated: "It obtains not through express provision but by actual division."[44] Thus, as to the legislative department: "The Legislative power shall be vested in a National Assembly."[45] As to the executive department: "The Executive power shall be vested in a President of the Philippines."[46] Then, as to the Judicial department: "The Judicial power shall be vested in one Supreme Court and in such inferior courts as may be established by law."[47] The opinion next set forth the essentials of the American constitutional law concept of the separation of powers: "Each department of the government has exclusive cognizance of matters within its own jurisdiction, and is supreme within its own sphere. But it does not follow from the fact that the three powers are to be kept separate and distinct that the Constitution intended them to be absolutely unrestrained and independent of each other."[48]

The latter point was given an even more emphatic affirmation in another noteworthy decision promulgated three years later in these words:

The classical separation of governmental powers, whether viewed in the light of the political philosophy of Aristotle, Locke, or Montesquieu, or of the postulations of Mabini, Madison, or Jefferson, is a relative theory of government. There is more truism and actuality in interdependence than in independence and separation of powers, for as observed by Justice Holmes in a case of Philippine origin, we cannot "lay down with mathematical precision and divide the branches into watertight compartments" not only "because the great ordinances of the Constitution do not establish and divide fields of black and white" but also because, even the more specific of them are found to terminate in a penumbra shading gradually from one extreme to the other. (*Springer v. Government* [1928] 277 *U.S.* 189; 72 *Law ed.* 845, 852).[49]

Up to the time that the 1971-1972 Constitutional Convention met, the Philippines never followed an inflexible and rigid concept. According to a 1970 decision of the Philippine Supreme Court, "the principle of separation of powers is a relative theory of government not to be enforced with pedantic rigor. As a principle of statemanship, the practical demands of statecraft would argue against its theoretical application."[50] Clearly then, it is well-nigh impossible to assign certain powers to one department to the total exclusion of either of the other two. The overlapping of governmental functions is recognized as unavoidable and inherent in the principle itself. In American constitutional law, the system of checks and balances constitutes one of its elements.

The Executive can act as a check on the legislative department by his veto power. There is, however, a check on its exercise, as an act may still become a law should the necessary votes to override such veto be obtained. There is, likewise, the further participation of the Executive in the legislative process by his power to call the lawmaking body into special session, whenever he so chooses. His appointing power, on the other hand, is subject to the check supplied by the need for confirmation on the part of either the legislature or one of its committees as may be provided by the Constitution. The judiciary in turn is subject to the check coming from the legislature, which can create courts, define their jurisdiction except the minimum jurisdiction of the Supreme Court, the sole constitutional court. Lastly, the courts, with the Supreme Court having the final say, can check the two other departments in the exercise of the function of judicial review.[51]

The reality of interdependence of the executive and legislative departments was even more apparent under the 1973 Constitution, both in its original version and as amended in 1981. In the original version, a modified parliamentary system was adopted,[52] a prime ministerial government. The post of the Presidency was retained, but it was made explicit: "The President shall be the symbolic head of state."[53] It was "the Prime Minister,[who could exercise the executive power] with the assistance of the Cabinet,"[54] and designate "the head of the Government."[55] He had control of all the ministries; was commander-in-chief of all the armed forces with power to suspend the privilege of the writ of *corpus* or place the Philippines or any part thereof under martial law; could appoint the high officials of the government, both civilian and military; could exercise the pardoning power; could contract and guarantee foreign and domestic loans; and was vested with all the powers of the President under the 1935 Constitution.[60] That the government established by the 1973 Constitution was more prime ministerial than parliamentary was made self-evident by the grant of the veto power to the Prime Minister, in theory an agent of the legislative body.[61] An even more conclusive proof that such indeed was the case and that the tradition of a dominant executive was not only adhered to but also strengthened was the grant to the Prime Minister in the 1976 amendments to the 1973 Constitution of the power "to meet the exigency" arising from "a grave emergency or a threat of imminence thereof" or from the failure of the legislative body or inability "to act adequately in any matter for any reason that in his judgment requires immediate action ... *to* issue the necessary decrees, orders, or letters of instruction, which shall form part of the law of the land."[62]

In the original version, then, of the 1973 Constitution, there was a clear departure from the theory of separation of powers as known to American constitutional law. With the primacy of the Executive established and placed beyond doubt, it was felt that during the times of stress during which the 1973 Constitution was intended to operate, the Executive, whether in the person of the Prime Minister and subsequently the President after the 1981 amendments, would be able to cope with the serious problems of state, the most pressing of which was the threat to national security. After the approval of the amendments on April 7, 1981, and the assumption once again by the President of the powers granted to the Executive by the 1935 Constitution, the government reverted to the presidential system. Such amendments, however, provided likewise that there be a Prime Minister, who was to be "the head of the Cabinet," nominated by the President but "elected by a majority of all the members" of the *Batasang Pambansa*.[63] The Prime Minister was vested with the power of "supervision" of the ministries or cabinet members, but it was the President who had the "control."[64] The Supreme Court could then conclude in a decision already referred to: "The adoption of certain aspects of a parliamentary system in the amended Constitution [1973] does not alter its essentially presidential character."[65]

The 1987 Constitution continues the form followed in the 1935 Constitution of "actual division". First, "The legislative power shall be vested in the Congress of the Philippines, which shall consist of a Senate and a House of Representatives, except to the extent reserved to the people by the provision on initiative and referendum."[66] Then as to the executive department, "The executive power shall be vested in the President of the Philippines."[67] Lastly, "The judicial power shall be vested in one Supreme Court and in such lower courts as may be established by law."[68]

It is the judiciary that is not affected by the adoption of later Constitutions. The legislative department now shares the law-making power with the people.

> The Congress shall, as early as possible, provide for a system of initiative and referendum, and the exceptions therefrom, whereby the people can directly propose and enact laws or approve or reject any act or law or part thereof passed by the Congress or local legislative body after the registration of a petition therefor signed by at least ten per

centum of the total number of registered voters, of which every legislative district must be represented by at least three per centum of the registered voters thereof.

Thus, Congress no longer possesses the totality of legislative power. This is one of the more meaningful innovations of the 1987 Constitution.[69]

The Presidency retains the whole of the executive power, but its exercise in times of emergency is subject to significant checks from both Congress and the Supreme Court.

The President shall be the Commander-in-Chief of all the armed forces of the Philippines and whenever it becomes necessary, he may call out such armed forces to prevent or suppress lawless violence, invasion or rebellion. In case of invasion or rebellion, when the public safety requires it, he may, for a period not exceeding sixty days, suspend the privilege of the writ of *habeas corpus* or place the Philippines or any part thereof under martial law.[70]

It must be noted that under both the 1935 and 1973 Constitutions, such power could be exercised not only when there was an invasion or rebellion, but also when there was imminent danger thereof. Also, there was no such time limitation.

The rest of this Section specifies the checks that may be interposed by either the Congress or the Supreme Court. As to the former:

Within forty-eight hours from the proclamation of martial law or the suspension of the privilege of the writ of *habeas corpus*, the President shall submit a report in person or by writing to the Congress. The Congress, voting jointly, by a vote of at least a majority of all its Members in regular or special session, may revoke such proclamation or suspension, which revocation shall not be set aside by the President. Upon the initiative of the President, the Congress may, in the same manner, extend such proclamation or suspension for a period to be determined by the Congress, if the invasion or rebellion shall persist and public safety requires it. The Congress, if not in session, shall, within twenty-four hours following such proclamation or suspension, convene in accordance with its rules without need of a call.[71]

Now as to the Supreme Court:

The Supreme Court may review, in an appropriate proceeding filed by any citizen, the sufficiency of the factual basis of the proclamation of martial law or the suspension of the privilege of the writ or the extension thereof and must promulgate its decision thereon within thirty days from its filing.[72]

A specific power, that of contracting and guaranteeing foreign loans, limited under the 1973 Constitution by a law that could be enacted in the future now has to be shared with the Central Bank:

> The President may contract or guarantee foreign loans on behalf of the Republic of the Philippines with the prior concurrence of the Monetary Board, and subject to such limitations as may be provided by law. The Monetary Board shall, within thirty days from the end of every quarter of the calendar year, submit to the Congress a complete report of its decisions on applications for loans to be contracted or guaranteed by the Government or government-owned and controlled corporations which would have the effect of increasing the foreign debt, and containing other matters as may be provided by law.[73]

Like the 1935 and 1973 Constitutions, the 1987 Constitution expressly mentions such other specific executive powers as the control over all departments, bureaus, and offices;[74] pardons,[75] appointments,[76] and the submission of a budget of expenditures and sources of financing.[77] While the first and the last of the above powers were retained from the previous Constitutions, the President, as was the case in the 1935 Constitution, can exercise the pardoning power only after conviction by final judgment, and the appointing power only with the consent of a Commission on Appointments, except as to members of the judiciary.

Clearly, Congress has it in its power to become an even more effective check on presidential leadership. Such a trend is equally evident in the case of the judiciary, more specifically the Supreme Court. Now, instead of the President having the discretion he previously enjoyed in the choice of justices and judges to be appointed, he is limited to a choice "from a list of at least three nominees prepared by the Judicial and Bar Council for every vacancy."[78] The Judicial and Bar Council is a constitutional body "under the supervision of the Supreme Court composed of the Chief Justice as *ex officio* Chairman, the Secretary of Justice, and a representative of the Congress as *ex officio* Members, a representative of the Integrated Bar, a professor of law, a retired Member of the Supreme Court, and a representative of the private sector."[79] Nor is his discretion limited only on whom he can appoint, but also as to when he should appoint: "For the lower courts, the President shall issue the appointment within ninety days from the submission of the list."[80]

The regular members of the Council shall be appointed by the President for a term of four years with the consent of the Commission on Appointments. Of the Members first appointed, the representative of the Integrated Bar shall serve for four years, the professor of law for three years, the retired justice for two years, and the representative of the private sector for one year.[81]

Of even more significance is the explicit grant of authority to the Supreme Court to inquire into the validity of the suspension of the privilege of the writ of *habeas corpus* or the proclamation of martial law.[82] In either of such cases as above noted, the Court, "in an appropriate proceeding filed by any citizen, the sufficiency of *its* factual basis" may be reviewed.[83]

Such a ruling, but limited only to the suspension of the privilege of the writ, was promulgated in a case decided under the 1935 Constitution, when then President Ferdinand E. Marcos in August of 1971 issued such a decree. In a landmark opinion, the first of its kind in a common law jurisdiction, according to a Nigerian legal scholar, it was held that the Supreme Court was "unanimous in the conviction that it has the authority to inquire into the existence of said factual cases in order to determine the constitutional sufficiency thereof."[84] The opinion laid equal stress on this point: "In the exercise of such authority, the function of the Court is merely to check--not to supplant--the executive, or to ascertain merely whether he has gone beyond the constitutional limits of his jurisdiction, not to exercise the powers vested in him, or to determine the wisdom of his act."[85]

Nor is it the Presidency alone that has lost some of its powers vis-a-vis the Judiciary. So has the Congress of the Philippines. Witness this provision: "No law shall be passed reorganizing the Judiciary when it undermines the security of tenure of its members."[86] As under the 1935 and 1973 Constitutions, the Congress has the power to enact a reorganization measure, affecting all courts inferior to the Supreme Court, the only constitutional tribunal. The lower courts were and are legislatively-created courts. The language in the 1987 Constitution is well-nigh identical to the preceding Charters: "The judicial power shall be vested in one Supreme Court and in such lower courts as may be established by law."[87] The power to create or establish carries with it the power to abolish. There is an explicit recognition of such competence in the lawmaking body as long as such abolition is in good faith[88] and does not undermine "the security of tenure."

The independence of the judiciary is further assured by this limitation on the power of Congress over public funds and the power of the President over the release of amounts appropriated: "The Judiciary shall enjoy fiscal autonomy.   Appropriations for the Judiciary may not be reduced by the legislature below the amount appropriated for the previous year and, after approval, shall be automatically released."[89]   Then there is this categorical recognition of the judicial power "to determine whether or not there has been a grave abuse of discretion amounting to lack or excess of jurisdiction on the part of any branch or instrumentality of the Government."[90]   Even if the full discretionary authority is vested either in the President or Congress or any official in either department, an abuse thereof is subject to judicial correction.

In the light of the above, the once dominant position enjoyed by the Executive is now a thing of the past.   The principle of separation of powers as known to Philippine law has undergone major modification.   Moreover, in the interrelationships of the three departments, it is the Supreme Court that has improved its position as against the other two.

The rest of this discussion on the structure of government briefly summarizes the provisions of the 1987 Constitution on the three departments and the three independent Constitutional Commissions.

The Legislative Department: The Congress of the Philippines

The Congress of the Philippines shall consist of a Senate and a House of Representatives.   The Senate shall be composed of twenty-four Senators who shall be elected at large by the qualified voters of the Philippines.[91]   A Senator must be a natural-born citizen, at least thirty-five years of age on the day of election, able to read and write, a registered voter, and a resident of the Philippines for not less than two years immediately preceding the day of election.[92]   His term of office shall be six years, and he cannot serve for more than two consecutive terms.[93]

The House of Representatives is composed of not more than 250 members, unless otherwise fixed by law.   Members are generally elected from legislative districts apportioned among the provinces, the cities, and the Metropolitan Manila area in accordance with the number of their respective inhabitants, and on the basis of a uniform and progressive ratio.   As provided by law, others are elected through a party-list system of registered national, regional, and sectoral parties or organizations.[94]   The party-list representatives constitute twenty per centum of the total number of representatives including those under the party list.[95]

A Member of the House of Representatives must be a natural-born citizen, at least twenty-five years of age on the day of election, able to read and write, and, except the party-list representatives, a registered voter in the district in which he shall be elected, and a resident thereof for not less than one year immediately preceding the day of election.[96] He is elected for a term of three years, and may not serve for more than three consecutive terms.[97]

A Senator or Member of the House of Representatives enjoys the privilege to be free from arrest in all offenses punishable by not more than six years' imprisonment while Congress is in session. Nor shall he be questioned or held liable in any other place for any speech or debate in Congress or in any committee thereof.[98]

The Congress convenes once every year for its regular session and continues for such number of days as it may determine until thirty days before the opening of its next regular session. It may be called in special session at any time by the President.[99] The Senate shall elect its President, and the House of Representatives its Speaker, by a majority vote of all its respective members.[100]

There shall be a Commission on Appointments consisting of the President of the Senate, as *ex officio* Chairman, twelve Senators and twelve Members of the House of Representatives, elected by each House on the basis of proportional representation from the political parties and parties or organizations registered under the party-list system represented therein.[101]

The Congress, by a vote of two-thirds of both Houses in joint session assembled, voting separately, shall have the sole power to declare the existence of a state of war.[102] In times of war or other national emergency, the Congress may, by law, authorize the President, for a limited period and subject to such restrictions as it may prescribe, to exercise powers necessary and proper to carry out a declared national policy. Unless sooner withdrawn by resolution of Congress, such powers shall cease upon the next adjournment thereof.[103]

All appropriation, revenue or tariff bills, bills authorizing the increase of the public debt, bills of local application, and private bills shall originate exclusively in the House of Representatives, but the Senate may propose or concur with amendments.[104] The veto power of the President may be overridden by a two-thirds vote of all the Members of both Houses.[105] No money shall be paid out of the Treasury except in pursuance of an appropriation made by law.[106] No law shall be passed increasing the appellate jurisdiction of the Supreme Court as provided in the Constitution without its advice and concurrence.[107]

The Executive Department: The Presidency

The executive power shall be vested in the President of the Philippines.[108] No person may be elected President unless he or she is a natural-born citizen, a registered voter, able to read and write, at least forty years of age on the day of the election, and a resident of the Philippines for at least ten years immediately preceding such election.[109] The Vice-President shall have the same qualifications and term of office as the President. He may be appointed as a member of the Cabinet, without the requirement of confirmation.[110]

The President and the Vice-President shall be elected by direct vote of the people for a term of six years. The President shall not be eligible for any reelection. The Vice-President cannot serve for more than two terms. Voluntary renunciation of the office for any length of time shall not be considered as an interruption in the continuity of the service for the full term for which he was elected.[111] The returns of every election for President and Vice-President, duly certified by the board of canvassers of each province or city, shall be transmitted to the Congress, directed to the President of the Senate, who shall then open all the certificates in the presence of the Senate and the House of Representatives in joint public session. The Congress, upon determination of the authenticity and due execution thereof in the manner provided by law, shall canvass the votes. The Supreme Court sitting *en banc* shall be the sole judge of all contests relating to the election, returns, and qualifications of the President or Vice-President, and may promulgate its rules for the purpose.[112]

The President shall have an official residence. The salaries of the President and Vice-President shall be determined by law and shall not be decreased during their terms. No increase in said compensation shall take effect until after the expiration of the term of the incumbent during which such increase was approved. They shall not receive during their tenure any other emolument from the government or any other source.[113] The functions of the Presidency may be gleaned from the previous discussion on the powers vested in such office.

The Judicial Department: The Supreme Court and Lower Courts

As provided in Article VIII, the judicial power is vested in one Supreme Court and in such lower courts as may be established by law.[114] The Supreme Court shall be composed of a Chief Justice and fourteen Associate Justices. It may sit *en banc* or in its discretion, in divisions of three, five or seven members. All cases involving the constitutionality of a treaty, international or executive agreement, or law and all other cases which under the Rules of Court are required to be heard *en banc*, including those involving the constitutionality, application, or operation of presidential decrees, proclamations, orders, instructions, ordinances, and other regulations, are decided with the concurrence of a majority of the members who actually took part in the deliberations on the issues in the case and voted thereon. Cases or matters heard by a division are decided or resolved with the concurrence of a majority of the members who actually took part in the deliberations on the issues in the cases and voted thereon, and in no case, without the concurrence of at least three of such Members.[115]

The powers of the Supreme Court are enumerated, which include original jurisdiction over cases affecting ambassadors, other public ministers and consuls, and over petitions for *certiorari*, prohibition, *mandamus, quo warranto*, and *habeas corpus* and appellate or *certiorari* jurisdiction. It may revise, reverse, modify or affirm on appeal or *certiorari* final judgments and orders of lower courts in all cases in which the constitutionality or validity of any treaty, international or executive agreement, law, presidential decree, proclamation, order, instruction, ordinance or regulation is in question; all cases involving the legality of any tax, import, assessment, or toll, or any penalty imposed in relation thereto; all cases in which the jurisdiction of any lower court is in issue; all criminal cases in which the penalty imposed is *reclusion perpetua* or higher; and all cases in which only an error or question of law is involved.[116] Among its enumerated powers are the promulgation of rules concerning the protection and enforcement of constitutional rights, pleading, practice and procedure in all courts, the admission to the practice of law, the Integrated Bar, and legal assistance to the underprivileged. Such rules shall be uniform for all courts of the same grade and shall not diminish, increase, or modify substantive rights.[117] The Supreme Court is likewise vested with the power of administrative supervision over all courts and the personnel thereof.[118]

The qualifications of a Member of the Supreme Court or any lower collegiate court are: he must be a natural-born citizen, at least forty years of age, and must have been for fifteen years or more a judge of a lower court or engaged in the practice of law in the Philippines. While Congress may prescribe the qualifications of judges of lower courts, no person may be appointed judge thereof unless he is a citizen and a member of the Philippine Bar. A Member of the judiciary must be a person of proven competence, integrity, probity and independence.[119]

The salaries of Justices and judges are fixed by law and during their continuance in office shall not be decreased.[120] They hold office during good behavior until they reach the age of seventy years or become incapacitated to discharge the duties of their office.[121]   The Supreme Court *en banc* has the power to discipline judges of lower courts or order their dismissal by a vote of a majority of the members who actually took part in the deliberations on the issues in the case and voted thereon.[122]

The Members of the Supreme Court and of other courts may not be designated to any agency performing quasi-judicial or administrative functions.[123]   The conclusions of the Supreme Court in any case are reached in consultation before the case is assigned to a Member for the writing of the opinion of the Court.   Any Member who took no part, or dissented, or abstained from a decision or resolution must state the reason therefor.   The same requirements are observed by all lower collegiate courts.[124]   No decision may be rendered by any court without clearly explaining the facts and the law on which it is based.   No petition for review or motion for reconsideration may be refused due course or denied without stating the legal basis.[125]

The Constitutional Commissions: The Civil Service Commission, the Commission on Elections, the Commission on Audit

The Constitution provides for three independent Constitutional Commissions, namely, the Civil Service Commission, the Commission on Elections, and the Commission on Audit.[126]

The Civil Service Commission, as the central personnel agency of the Government, maintains a career service and adopts measures to promote morale, efficiency, integrity, responsiveness, progressiveness, and courtesy in the civil service.[127]   The Civil Service Commission is composed of a Chairman and two Commissioners who shall be natural-born citizens of the Philippines and, at the time of their appointment, at least thirty-five years of age, with proven capacity for public administration, and must not have been candidates for any elective position in the elections immediately preceding their appointment.   The Chairman and the Commissioners are appointed by the President with the consent of the Commission on Appointments for a term of seven years, without reappointment.[128]

The Commission on Elections enforces and administers all laws and regulations relative to the conduct of an election, plebiscite, initiative, referendum, or recall.   The Chairman and six Commissioners are appointed by the President with the consent of the Commission on Appointments for a term of seven years without reappointment.[129]   Commissioners must be natural-born citizens of the Philippines and, at the time of their appointment, at least thirty-five years of age, holders of a college degree, and must not have been candidates for any elective position in the immediately preceding elections. A majority, including the Chairman, must be members of the Philippine Bar with at least ten years of law practice.[130]

The Commission on Audit has the power, authority, and duty to examine, audit, and settle all accounts pertaining to the revenue and receipts of, and expenditures or uses of funds and property, owned or held in trust by, or pertaining to, the Government or any of its subdivisions, agencies, or instrumentalities, including government-owned and controlled corporations, with original charters, and on a post-audit basis: a) constitutional bodies, commissions and offices that have been granted fiscal autonomy under this Constitution; b) autonomous state colleges and universities; c) other government-owned or controlled corporations with original charters and their subsidiaries; and d) such non-governmental entities receiving subsidy or equity, directly or indirectly, from or through the government, which are required by law of the granting institution to submit such audit as a condition of subsidy or equity.[131]

It is composed of a Chairman and two Commissioners, who must be natural-born citizens of the Philippines and, at the time of their appointment, at least thirty-five years of age, certified public accountants with not less than ten years of auditing experience, or members of the Philippine Bar who have been engaged in the practice of law for at least ten years, and must not have been candidates for any elective position in the elections immediately preceding their appointment. At no time shall all Members of the Commission belong to the same profession. The Chairman and the Commissioners shall be appointed by the President with the consent of the Commission on Appointments for a term of seven years without reappointment.[132]

Constitutional Rights: Civil and Political

It bears repeating that the framers of the 1935 Constitution were fully aware that the traditional civil and political rights, which found expression in the 1899 Malolos Constitution of the first Philippine Republic, and in the organic acts under American sovereignty, would not suffice to solve the problem of mass poverty, then as well as now of the utmost gravity. That explains the inclusion of the emerging social, cultural, and economic rights. The 1973 Constitution, in both its original and amended versions, not only continued but also expanded this welcome trend. Moreover, while in the 1935 Constitution there was adherence to the creed of free enterprise, the *laissez faire* doctrine was rejected, as so clearly made manifest in a leading Supreme Court decision: "It (the 1935 Constitution) entrusted to our government the responsibility of coping with social and economic problems with the commensurate power of control over economic affairs. Thereby it could live up to its commitment to promote the general welfare through state action."[133] The 1987 Constitution, as noted, is even more committed to such rights, quite essential in the realization of a life of dignity for all.

Considering that the language on civil and political rights used in both the 1935 and 1973 Constitutions came from the equivalent provisions of the United States Constitution as found in its First Amendment and the so-called Civil War Amendments, the impact of American constitutional law decisions was quite marked. In the 1987 Constitution, however, what is readily noticeable is that in the area of physical freedom, especially the rights of an accused person, there are a number of novel provisions.

The civil and political rights in the 1987 Constitution include: 1) basic rights to life, liberty, equality, and property as safeguarded by due process and equal protection; 2) specific rights of liberty of religion, speech, press, assembly, and association; 3) specific rights of physical liberty including the guarantees to an accused. The latter two classes of civil rights are necessary for the political right of suffrage to be meaningful.

The Basic Rights to Life, Liberty, Equality, and Property as Safeguarded by Due Process and Equal Protection

So central are the basic rights provisions to the Constitution and to its similarities to and differences from the United States Constitution that we here take the liberty of quoting from them at length:

"No person shall be deprived of life, liberty, or property without due process of law, nor shall any person be denied the equal protection of the laws."[134]

"Free access to the courts and quasi-judicial bodies and adequate legal assistance shall not be denied to any person by reason of poverty."[135]

"Private property shall not be taken for public use without just compensation."[136]

"No law impairing the obligation of contracts shall be passed."[137]

"All persons shall have the right to a speedy disposition of their cases before all judicial, quasi-judicial or administrative bodies."[138]

Civil Rights: Freedoms of Religion, of Speech, Press, and Association

"No law shall be made respecting an establishment of religion, or prohibiting the free exercise thereof. The free exercise and enjoyment of religious profession and worship, without discrimination or preference, shall forever be allowed. No religious test shall be required for the exercise of civil and political rights."[139]

"No law shall be passed abridging the freedom of speech, of expression, or of the press, or the right of the people peaceably to assemble and petition the government for redress of grievances."[140]

"The right of the people to information on matters of public concern shall be recognized. Access to official records, and to documents and papers pertaining to official acts, transactions, or decisions, as well as to government research data used as basis for policy development, shall be afforded the citizen, subject to such limitations as may be provided by law."[141]

"The right of the people, including those employed in the public and private sectors, to form unions, associations, or societies for purposes not contrary to law shall not be abridged."[142]

Civil Rights: Physical Freedom Including Rights of an Accused

"The right of the people to be secure in their persons, houses, papers, and effects against unreasonable searches and seizures of whatever nature and for any purpose shall be inviolable, and no search warrant or warrant of arrest shall issue except upon probable cause to be determined personally by the judge after examination under oath or affirmation of the complainant and the witnesses he may produce, and particularly describing the place to be searched and the persons or things to be seized."[143]

"The privacy of communication and correspondence shall be inviolable except upon lawful order of the court, or when public safety or order requires otherwise as prescribed by law."[144] "Any evidence obtained in violation of this or the preceding section shall be inadmissible for any purpose in any proceeding."[145]

"The liberty of abode and of changing the same within the limits prescribed by law shall not be impaired except upon lawful order of the court. Neither shall the right to travel be impaired except in the interest of national security, public safety, or public health, as may be provided by law."[146]

"Any person under investigation for the commission of an offense shall have the right to be informed of his right to remain silent and to have competent and independent counsel preferably of his own choice. If the person cannot afford the services of counsel, he must be provided with one. These rights cannot be waived except in writing and in the presence of counsel.

"No torture, force, violence, threat, intimidation, or any other means which vitiate the free will shall be used against him. Secret detention places, solitary, incommunicado, or other similar forms of detention are prohibited.

"Any confession or admission obtained in violation of this or (Section 17) hereof shall be inadmissible in evidence against him.

"The law shall provide for penal and civil sanctions for violations of this section as well as compensation to and rehabilitation of victims of torture or similar practices, and their families."[147]

"All persons, except those charged with offenses punishable by *reclusion perpetua* when evidence of guilt is strong, shall, before conviction, be bailable by sufficient sureties, or be released on recognizance as may be provided by law. The right to bail shall not be impaired even when the privilege of the writ of *habeas corpus* is suspended. Excessive bail shall not be required."[148] "In all criminal prosecutions, the accused shall be presumed innocent until the contrary is proved, and shall enjoy the right to be heard by himself and counsel, to be informed of the nature and cause of the accusation against him, to have a speedy, impartial, and public trial, to meet the witnesses face to face, and to have compulsory process to secure the attendance of witnesses and the production of evidence in his behalf.[149] "The privilege of the writ of *habeas corpus* shall not be suspended except in cases of invasion or rebellion when the public safety required it."[150] "No person shall be compelled to be a witness against himself."[151]

"No involuntary servitude in any form shall exist except as punishment for a crime whereof the party shall have been duly convicted."[152] "Excessive fines shall not be imposed, nor cruel, degrading or inhuman punishment inflicted. Neither shall death penalty be imposed, unless, for compelling reasons involving heinous crimes, the Congress hereafter provides for it. Any death penalty already imposed shall be reduced to *reclusion perpetua*. The employment of physical, psychological, or degrading punishment against any prisoner or detainee or the use of substandard or inadequate penal facilities under subhuman conditions shall be dealt with by law."[153]

"No person shall be imprisoned for debt or non-payment of a poll tax."[154] "No person shall be twice put in jeopardy of punishment for the same offense. If an act is punished by a law and an ordinance, conviction or acquittal under either shall constitute a bar to another prosecution for the same act."[155] "No ex post facto law or bill of attainder shall be enacted."[156]

The Concept of a Bill of Rights

Article III of the Bill of Rights and Article V on Suffrage adhere closely to the formulation followed in the 1935 Constitution, namely, that the rights safeguarded are those of the traditional kind--civil and political. The former separately and collectively leaves an individual free from any restraint on or interference with his person, thus the better to enjoy the comfort and amenities of life consistent with like freedom by others. The latter assures a citizen's participation in government consistent with the principle that sovereignty resides with the people. The distinction should not be overlooked. Civil rights ordinarily are enjoyed by the inhabitants of a state, whether citizen or alien. Political rights, on the other hand, may be exercised only by the citizens.

Civil and political rights may likewise be viewed in their negative aspect as freedom from. The citizen is not to be restricted or limited in his freedom to think or to act, except that in the latter case where the community welfare requires some limits on what he may lawfully do. This is unavoidable as he is a member of society composed of human beings, who like him have their own needs to satisfy and desires to gratify. On the whole, however, civil and political rights result in what has come to be known as a negative or limited state.

Social, cultural, and economic rights are claims that must be attended to by government to promote the individual's health and well-being, both physical and intellectual. They are necessary for the realization of one's potentialities. In cases where an individual suffers from deficiency in either or both physical and intellectual endowments, the duty of government to work for a life of dignity for all remains undiminished. It may as a matter of fact be called upon to do more. Hence these rights result in an affirmative or positive state.

There is also a growing body of scholarship that considers the question from the standpoint of rights as entitlements. One whose civil or political rights are violated can go to court for redress. The state is under a duty to respect his liberty. Thus in the exercise of the intellectual freedom of either speech or press, he cannot be subject to previous restraint or subsequent liability. It would be a gross disservice to constitutionalism if the choice of one's religion or the observance of its ritual would be visited by a deprivation or a penalty. These rights, however, are not absolute. There are restraints that living in society impose. So likewise would it be an aberration if one unfortunate enough to be prosecuted would be denied a fair trial. Such a conclusion may not be warranted if for instance one's claim is based on the rights to work, one of the most valuable social and economic rights. As of this stage, especially in developing countries, it would be unrealistic to impose on their government such an inescapable duty.

The Impact of American Constitutional Law Doctrines on Civil Rights Likely to Lessen

In the 1935 and 1973 Constitutions, the Bill of Rights provisions adopted the language of the previous Philippine organic acts. In a leading case[157] involving freedom of speech and the press decided during the period of American sovereignty, there was this historical reference:

> The Filipino patriots in Spain, through the columns of *La Solidaridad* and by other means invariably in exposing the wants of the Filipino people demanded "liberty of the press, of cults, and of associations...." The Malolos Constitution, the work of the Revolutionary Congress, in its Bill of Rights, zealously guarded freedom of speech and press and assembly and petition.[158]

The opinion went on to state:

> Next comes the period of American-Filipino cooperative effort. The Constitution of the United States and the State constitutions guarantee the right of freedom of speech and press and the right of assembly and petition.... The Philippine Bill, the Act of Congress of July 1, 1902, and the Jones Law, the Act of Congress of August 29, 1916, continued this guaranty. The words quoted [First Amendment] are not unfamiliar to students of Constitutional Law, for they are counterpart of the First Amendment to the Constitution of the United States, which the American people demanded before giving their approval to the Constitution.[159]

After this came a highly significant statement: "These paragraphs found in the Philippine Bill of Rights are not threadbare verbiage. The language carries with it all the applicable jurisprudence of great English and American Constitutional Cases."[160]

To the extent that the language of the 1987 Constitution, as in the two previous Charters, remains identical, then the relevance--but not the compelling force--of the above dictum is apparent. It must be stated anew that from July 4, 1946, when the Philippines obtained its independence, the influence of "great American Constitutional cases" has perceptively waned.[161]

Such a result was unavoidable with the introduction of the social justice principle in the 1935 Constitution. Thus, to cite a specific instance, the scope of the due process protection to property under American law, was, in the Philippines, certainly less. The scope was even more constricted under the 1973 Constitution when it was explicitly provided that to attain social justice, "the State shall regulate the acquisition, ownership, use, enjoyment, and disposition of property, and equitably diffuse property ownership and profits."[162]

In some respects the 1987 Constitution goes even further:

> The use of property bears a social function, and all economic agent shall contribute to the common good. Individuals and private groups, including corporations, cooperatives, and similar collective organizations shall have the right to own, establish, and operate economic enterprises, subject to the duty of the State to promote distributive justice and to intervene when the common good so demands."[163]

The continuing impact of American constitutional law even under the 1987 Constitution is most evident in cases involving the intellectual freedoms. It suffices to cite this excerpt from a recent unanimous decision:

> Free speech, like free press, may be identified with the liberty to discuss publicly and truthfully any matter of public concern without censorship or punishment.   There is to be then no previous restraint on the communication of views or subsequent liability whether in libel suits, prosecution for sedition, or action for damages or contempt proceedings unless there be a "clear and present danger that [the State] has a right to prevent." Freedom of assembly connotes the right of the people to meet peaceably for consultation and discussion of matters of public concern. It is entitled to be accorded the utmost deference and respect. It is not to be limited, much less denied, except on a showing, as is the case with freedom of expression, of a clear and present danger of a substantive evil that the state has a right to prevent.[164]

As is obvious, it is the clear and present danger test, not the balancing of interest approach that the Philippines has adopted.   Since Philippines' documents have explicitly recognized freedom of association as far back as the Malolos Constitution of 1899, while the First Amendment recognizes it only by implication, the influence of American precedents has not been substantial.

As to physical freedom, including the rights of an accused, the changes introduced by the 1987 Constitution will necessarily lessen the impact of American constitutional law. To the extent, however, that such modifications would not be relevant in a pending case, then reference to what may be considered in point is likely to continue. If so, the American Supreme Court decisions considered to have a high persuasive value might well derive from the Warren Court. During the sixteen years that Earl Warren was Chief Justice, from 1953 to 1969, the Philippine Supreme Court, then construing applicable provisions of the 1935 Constitution couched in similar language of their counterparts in the American Charter looked with favor on precedents issuing from that Court. In the 1973 Constitution, the exclusion of illegally seized evidence and the ban on custodial interrogation came from two leading American Supreme Court decisions.[165]

The Slight Impact of American Constitutional Law on Social, Cultural, and Economic Rights

A constitution to be worthy of its high estate should mirror the ideals and aspirations of the people. There are goals to be reached, objectives to be attained, principles to be observed. A constitution then should set the direction of where the nation is headed and indicate in general terms the policies to be followed so that it arrives at its destination. Necessarily there must be a realistic appraisal of present conditions. For there are problems to be solved, some of extreme urgency. There are then priorities to meet. Nor should thought be given solely to the present. There should be a judicious anticipation of the future. For it is ever the hope that a constitution, in the language of Story, may "endure through a long lapse of ages, the events of which *are* locked up in the inscrutable purposes of Providence."[166] A constitution then, to borrow from Cardozo, "states or ought to state not rules for the passing hour, but principles for an expanding future."[167]

With the Philippines faced with the problem of widespread poverty--an affliction from which the country suffers even now--it becomes understandable why the 1934-1935 Constitution Convention took the bold step of including social justice and protection-to-labor provisions in the 1935 Constitution. The 1973 Constitution expanded and vitalized such principles. The 1987 Constitution attests to the flowering of these vital components of social, cultural, and economic rights. The belief that without them, the hope of a life of dignity would prove to be illusory has been enhanced by the passing of the years.

Focus on Social Justice and Protection for Labor

As in the 1935 and 1973 Constitutions, the focus in the present Charter is on social justice and the cognate principle of protection to labor. Unlike the relatively brief previous formulations of such rights, the 1987 Constitution devotes several sections in Article II to a "Declaration of Principles and State Policies"[168] and a comprehensive Article on Social Justice and Human Rights.[169]

Some Article II Provisions:

"The State shall promote a just and dynamic social order that will ensure the prosperity and independence of the nation and free the people from poverty through policies that provide adequate social services, promote full employment, a rising standard of living, and an improved quality of life for all."[170]

"The State shall promote social justice in all phases of national development."[171]

"The State affirms labor as a primary social economic force. It shall protect the rights of workers and promote their welfare."[172]

"The State shall promote comprehensive rural development and agrarian reform."[173]

Article XIII deals extensively with Social Justice and Human Rights:

Sec. 1. "The Congress shall give highest priority to the enactment of measures that protect and enhance the right of all the people to human dignity, reduce social, economic, and political inequalities, and remove cultural inequities by equitably diffusing wealth and political power for the common good.

"To this end, the States shall regulate the acquisition, ownership, use, and disposition of property and its increments."

Sec. 2. "The promotion of social justice shall include the commitment to create economic opportunities based on freedom of initiative and self-reliance.

Labor

Sec. 3. "The State shall afford full protection to labor, local and overseas, organized and unorganized, and promote full employment and equality of employment opportunities for all.

"It shall guarantee the rights of all workers to self-organization, collective bargaining and negotiations, and peaceful concerted activities, including the right to strike in accordance with law. They shall be entitled to security of tenure, humane conditions of work, and a living wage. They shall also participate in policy and decision-making processes affecting their rights and benefits as may be provided by law.

"The State shall promote the principle of shared responsibility between workers and employers and the preferential use of voluntary modes in settling disputes including conciliation, and shall enforce their mutual compliance therewith to foster industrial peace.

"The State shall regulate the relations between workers and employers, recognizing the right of labor to its just share in the fruits of production and the right of enterprises to reasonable returns on investments, and to expansion and growth."[176]

Agrarian and Natural Resources Reform

Sec. 4. "The State shall, by law, undertake an agrarian reform program founded on the right of farmers and regular farm workers, who are landless, to own directly or collectively the lands they till or, in the case of other farm workers, to receive a just share of the fruits thereof. To this end, the State shall encourage and undertake the just distribution of all agricultural lands, subject to such priorities and reasonable retention limits as the Congress may prescribe, taking into account ecological, developmental, or equity considerations, and subject to the payment of just compensation. In determining retention limits, the State shall respect the rights of small landowners. The State shall further provide incentives for voluntary land-sharing."[177]

Sec. 5: "The State shall recognize the right of farmers, farm workers, and landowners, as well as cooperatives, and other independent farmers' organizations to participate in the planning, organization, and management of the program, and shall provide support to agriculture through appropriate technology and research, and adequate financial, production, marketing, and other support services."[178]

Sec. 6: "The State shall apply the principles of agrarian reform or stewardship, whenever applicable in accordance with law, in the disposition or utilization of other natural resources, including lands of the public domain under lease or concession suitable to agriculture, subject to prior rights, homestead rights of small settlers, and the rights of indigenous communities to their ancestral lands.

"The State may resettle landless farmers and farm workers in its own agricultural estates which shall be distributed to them in the manner provided by law."[179]

Sec. 7: "The State shall protect the rights of subsistence fishermen, especially of local communities, to the preferential use of the communal marine and fishing resources, both inland and offshore. It shall provide support to such fishermen through appropriate technology and research, adequate financial, production, and marketing assistance, and other services. The State shall also protect, develop, and conserve such resources. The protection shall extend to offshore fishing grounds of subsistence fishermen against foreign intrusion. Fish workers shall receive a just share from their labor in the utilization of marine and fishing resources."[180]

Sec. 8: "The State shall provide incentives to landowners to invest the proceeds of the agrarian reform program to promote industrialization, employment creation, and privatization of public sector enterprises. Financial instruments used as payment for their lands shall be honored as equity in enterprises of their choice."[181]

Urban Land Reform and Housing

Sec. 9: "The State shall, by law, and for the common good, undertake, in cooperation with the private sector, a continuing program of urban land reform and housing which will make available at affordable cost decent housing and basic services to underprivileged and homeless citizens in urban centers and resettlement areas. It shall also promote adequate employment opportunities to such citizens. In the implementation of such program the State shall respect the rights of small property owners."[182]

Sec. 10: "Urban or rural poor dwellers shall not be evicted nor their dwellings demolished, except in accordance with law and in a just and humane manner.

"No resettlement of urban or rural dwellers shall be undertaken without adequate consultation with them and the communities where they are to be relocated."[183]

Sec. 11: "The State shall adopt an integrated and comprehensive approach to health development which shall endeavor to make essential goods, health and other social services available to all the people at affordable cost. There shall be priority for the needs of the underprivileged, sick, elderly, disabled, women, and children. The State shall endeavor to provide free medical care to paupers."[184]

Sec. 12: "The State shall establish and maintain an effective food and drug regulatory system and undertake appropriate health manpower development and research, responsive to the country's health needs and problems."[185]

Sec. 13: "The State shall establish a special agency for disabled persons for their rehabilitation, self-development and self-reliance, and their integration into the mainstream of society."[186]

Women

Sec. 14: "The State shall protect working women by providing safe and healthful working conditions, taking into account their maternal functions, and such facilities and opportunities that will enhance their welfare and enable them to realize their full potential in the service of the nation."[187]

Article XIV on Education, Science and Technology, Arts, Culture, and Sports Education

"The State shall protect and promote the right of all citizens to quality education at all levels and shall take appropriate steps to make such education accessible to all."[188]   The State shall also maintain a system of "education relevant to the needs of the people and society", and compulsory free public education. A "system of scholarship grants, student loan programs, and other incentives shall be available to deserving students in both public and private schools, especially to the underprivileged."

The state will also maintain out-of-school study programs particularly those that respond to community needs; and
Provide adult citizens, the disabled, and out-of-school youth with training in civics, vocational efficiency, and other skills.[189]
All education institutions shall include the study of the Constitution as part of the curricula.
They shall inculcate patriotism and nationalism, foster love of humanity, respect for human rights, appreciation of the role of national heroes in the historical development of the country, teach the rights and duties of citizenship, strengthen ethical and spiritual values, develop moral character and personal discipline, encourage critical and creative thinking, broaden scientific and technological knowledge, and promote vocational efficiency.
At the option expressed in writing by the parents or guardians, religion shall be allowed to be taught to their children or wards in public elementary and high schools within the regular class hours by instructors designated or approved by the religious authorities of the religion to

which the children or wards belong without additional cost to the Government.[190]

Educational institutions, other than those established by religious groups and mission boards, shall be owned solely by citizens of the Philippines or corporations or associations at least sixty per centum of the capital of which is owned by such citizens. The Congress may, however, require increased Filipino equity participation in all educational institutions.

The control and administration of educational institutions shall be vested in citizens of the Philippines.

No educational institution shall be established exclusively for aliens and no group of aliens shall comprise more than one-third of the enrollment in any school. The provisions of this subsection shall not apply to schools established for foreign diplomatic personnel and their dependents and, unless otherwise provided by law, for other foreign temporary residents. Subject to conditions prescribed by law, all grants, endowments, donations, or contributions used actually, directly, and exclusively for educational purposes shall be exempt from tax.[191]

Academic freedom shall be enjoyed in all institutions of higher learning. Every citizen has a right to select a profession or course of study, subject to fair, reasonable, and equitable admission and academic requirements. The State shall assign the highest budgetary priority to education and ensure that teaching will attract and retain its rightful share of the best available talents through adequate remuneration and other means of job satisfaction and fulfillment.[192]

Language

The National Language of the Philippines is Filipino." The government encourages Filipino as a medium of official communication and as language of instruction.[193] "For purposes of communication and instruction, the official languages of the Philippines are Filipino and, until otherwise provided by law, English."

Regional languages are "auxiliary official languages in the regions" and "auxiliary media of instruction" there. "Spanish and Arabic shall be promoted on a voluntary and optional basis."[194] The Constitution was promulgated in Filipino and English and translated into local languages, Arabic, and Spanish.[195] Congress is mandated to set up a national language commission to promote the development of Filipino and other languages.[196]

Science and Technology

"Science and technology are essential for national development and progress.   The State shall give priority to research and development, invention, innovation, and their utilization.

"The Congress may provide for incentives, including tax deductions... Scholarship, grants-in-aid, or other forms of incentives shall be provided to deserving" and able students.[198]

The State encourages "the widest participation of private groups, local governments, and community-based organizations in the generation and utilization of science and technology,"[199] and is charged with securing the rights of scientists, inventors, artists, and other gifted citizens to their intellectual property and creations, particularly when beneficial to the people..."[202]

Arts and Culture

"The State shall foster the preservation, enrichment, and dynamic evolution of a Filipino national culture based on the principle of unity in diversity in a climate of free artistic and intellectual expression,"[203] and shall patronize arts and letters.[204]   Cultural studies and ensure equal access to cultural opportunities through the educational system, community cultural centers, and other means will be promoted.[205]

Sports

Finally the 1987 Constitution encourages physical education, sports programs, and league competitions throughout the country "to foster self-discipline, teamwork, and excellence for the development of a healthy and alert citizenry."[206]

The Minimal Influence of American Constitutional Law Doctrines

These social, cultural, and economic rights attest to the value that the Philippines places on the "dignity of every human person"[207] by supplementing the traditional civil and political rights.   So it has been since the 1935 Constitution.   This time though, the emphasis is even more marked.   It is understandable why.   Countries which do not have severe problems of poverty may feel that their citizens can even do without them.   Through their own individual initiative and effort, they can provide for themselves.   Third World countries--and the Philippines is in that group--do not have such good fortune. It was therefore unavoidable for the framers of the 1987 Constitution to spell out in a more specific manner this cluster of rights. Thereby, there is the hope and the promise that ultimately there will be "a rising standard of living, and an improved quality of life for all."[208]

No purpose would be served then--and perhaps hopes frustrated and expectations unfulfilled--if there be reliance in American precedents. For one thing, the United States is not a signatory to the United Nations Covenant on Economic and Social Rights. During the Lockner[209] era in American constitutional law, Cardozo could affirm: "*Laissez-faire* was not only a counsel of caution which statesmen would do well to heed. It was a categorical imperative which statesmen as well as judges would obey."[210] As was stated in a concurring opinion in a leading Philippine decision:[211] "For a long time, legislation tending to reduce economic inequality foundered on the rock that was the due process clause, enshrining as it did the liberty of contract."[212] Such concurrence did likewise state:

> Nevertheless, the social and economic forces at work in the United States to which the New Deal administration of President Roosevelt was most responsive did occasion, as of 1937, greater receptivity by the Supreme Court to a philosophy less rigid in its obeisance to property rights.[213]

Reference was then made to the judicial acceptance of such a view: "At any rate by 1943, the United States was reconciled to *laissez-faire* having lost its dominance." In the language of Justice Jackson in the leading case of *West Virginia State Board of Education v. Barnette*:

> We must transplant these rights to a soil in which the *laissez-faire* concept or principle of non-interference has withered at least as to economic affairs and social advancements are increasingly sought through closer integration of society and through expanded and strengthened governmental controls.

In the Philippines, the *laissez-faire* doctrine was rejected by the 1935 Constitution. The reason was so well put by the Supreme Court:

> The areas which used to be left to private enterprise and initiative and which the government was called upon to enter optionally and only "because it was better equipped to administer for the public welfare than is any private individual or group of individuals," continue to lose their

well-defined boundaries and to be absorbed within activities that the government must undertake in its sovereign capacity if it is to meet the increasing social challenges of the times. Here, as almost everywhere else the tendency is undoubtedly towards a greater socialization of economic forces. Here of course this development was envisioned, indeed adopted as a national policy by the Constitution itself in its declaration of principle concerning the promotion of social justice.[214]

That was so under the 1935 Constitution, which had only the beginning of social, cultural, and economic rights. Such an approach is much more relevant now under the 1987 Constitution. Hence the inevitability of the conclusion that whatever influence under the due process and equal protection guarantees American constitutional law decisions may exert, it is likely to be minimal.

Judicial Review Under the 1987 Constitution

The 1987 Constitution, like the 1935 and 1973 Charters, assumes the existence of judicial review by regulating its exercise.[215] As cited earlier, "all cases involving the constitutionality of a treaty, international or executive agreement, or law, which shall be heard by the Supreme Court en banc, and all other cases which under the Rules of Court are required to be heard en banc..."[216]

The Supreme Court shall have the following powers:.... (2) Review, revise, reverse, modify, or affirm on appeal or *certiorari* as the law or the Rules of Court may provide, final judgments and orders of lower courts in .... (a) All cases in which the constitutionality or validity of any treaty, international or executive agreement, law, presidential decree, proclamation, order, instruction, ordinance or regulation is in question.[217]

This function exists to assure the supremacy of the Constitution. It follows that there should be no hesitancy or timidity on the part of the judiciary, especially the Supreme Court, when an appropriate case calls for its exercise. That militancy has been termed "judicial activism," an alertness on the part of the courts to detect whether a command of the Constitution has been disregarded or ignored. Thus, while the other two departments are coordinate, the validity of their acts is subject to judicial scrutiny, not as a manifestation of "judicial supremacy" but in fulfillment of its duty to decide a case. When a question of constitutionality is raised and its answer necessary for the task of adjudication, the judiciary has no choice. It must act. Nor does it suffice that it assumes jurisdiction, it must see to it that in the decision rendered there is full fidelity to what the Constitution ordains.[218] "It is peculiarly the duty of the judiciary," as was emphasized in a leading case, "to say what the law is, to enforce the Constitution, and to decide whether the proper constitutional sphere of a department has been transcended. The courts must determine the validity of legislative enactments as well as the legality of all private and official acts."[219]

Nor does judicial activism necessarily lead to the nullification of the assailed legislative or executive acts. Such a result, according to Professor Black, is the checking work of judicial review.[220] He spoke of it as a "negative function," although it "can itself be of high value."[221] There is this other aspect of judicial review, in Professor Black's formulation the "affirmative function," described by him as a "means of validating governmental action against constitutional doubt."[222] That for him is the legitimating work of judicial review.[223]

The Constitution remains paramount. The ruling that the measure challenged has not been shown to be unconstitutional conduces in its acceptance and support in a regime where the rule of law holds sway. This assumption of jurisdiction precisely to settle doubts about the constitutionality of governmental acts is likely to prove more beneficial to developing nations where the government, to solve the problem of mass poverty, is called upon to undertake massive projects and to enact a greater number of regulatory measures. Necessarily, where property rights are adversely affected by the exercise either of the police power or of eminent domain, there could be assertions of unconstitutional deprivation. The Court in the exercise of the power of judicial review could settle such a controversy. Under the 1987 Constitution, more specifically the social justice provisions,[224] all doubts must be resolved against an undue insistence on the claims of property.

Judicial activism is not invariably the norm to follow. At times, the question raised is political, to follow the traditional American constitutional law terminology. It signifies, according to retired Chief Justice Concepcion speaking for the Supreme Court in *Tanada v. Cuenco*,[225] "'questions which under the Constitution are to be decided by the people in their sovereign capacity, or in regard to which full discretionary authority has been delegated to the legislative or executive branch of the Government.' It is concerned with issues dependent upon the wisdom, not legality of a political measure."[226] If so, the principle of judicial self-restraint prevails. There must be respect and deference shown to what was decided in such other forum. It is not for the judiciary to interfere. Such a matter is outside its jurisdiction.

Even on a matter concededly within its competence, the Court may avail itself of the techniques of avoidance, relying on compliance with certain standards to call into play the power of judicial review, thus enabling it to base its decision on a non-constitutional ground.[227] Such an approach is a recognition that the function of judicial review is both delicate and awesome. It is never more so than when the judiciary is called upon to pass on the validity of an act of the President or the Congress in the exercise of power granted to them to cope with an emergency or crisis situation.[228] For in such cases, the courts must be duly mindful of the fact that the President or the Congress did take into consideration the conditions calling for such a measure. When it is considered further that the Constitution does admit that the sphere of individual freedom contracts and the scope of governmental authority expands during times of emergency, it becomes manifest why an even greater degree of caution and circumspection must be exercised by the courts when, on this matter, they are called upon to discharge the function of judicial review. The exceptional character of the situation is thus underscored. Even then, however, the duty to do so remains. The existence of an emergency does not justify any disregard of the applicable constitutional guarantees. If it were otherwise, then it would signify that the Constitution ceases to be operative in times of danger to national safety and security. That should never be the case.[229]

Requisites for the Exercise of the Power of Judicial Review

While thus inherent in judicial power, the courts have adopted certain standards to guide them in the exercise of this function of judicial review. What are the standards? *People v. Vera*[230] enumerates them: 1) the existence of an appropriate case; 2) an interest personal and substantial by the party raising the constitutional question; 3) the plea that the function be exercised at the earliest opportunity; 4) the necessity that the constitutional question be passed upon in order to decide the case.[231]

Test of Validity

The cardinal principle is the supremacy of the Constitution. The judiciary then has the duty to assure that its mandates are respected by all agencies of government. In passing upon the validity of any governmental act, whether executive, legislative or judicial, or whether from the national or local government, the only question is one of power. The courts have to determine whether power has been conferred on the public official and whether such power is not violative of any provision of the Constitution. If it is not, then the action fails. Questions of wisdom or expediency of the act are not for the courts to decide.[232]

Effects of a Declaration of Nullity

Where the assailed legislative or executive act is found by the judiciary to be contrary to the Constitution, it is declared null and void. As the Civil Code of the Philippines puts it: "When the courts declare a law to be inconsistent with the Constitution, the former shall be void and the latter shall govern. Administrative or executive acts, orders and regulations shall be valid only when they are not contrary to the laws of the Constitution."[233] The above provision of the Civil Code reflects the orthodox view that an unconstitutional act, whether legislative or executive, is not a law, confers no rights, imposes no duties, and affords no protection.[234] It should be thus as the Constitution is supreme and provides the measure for the validity of any action taken by either the legislative or the executive branch. For that matter, not even the Supreme Court has the power under the Constitution to disregard its commands. If it should happen thus, what is done is tainted by nullity.[235]

As expressly affirmed in *Serrano de Agbayani v. Philippine National Bank*:[236] "Such a view has support in logic and possesses the merit of simplicity." It has to be qualified though. The above decision makes clear why it should be so:

It may not however be sufficiently realistic. It does not admit of doubt that prior to the declaration of nullity such challenged legislative or executive act must have been in force and had to be complied with. This is as until after the judiciary, in an appropriate case, declares its invalidity, it is entitled to obedience and respect. Parties may have acted under it and may have changed their positions. What could be more fitting than that in a subsequent litigation, regard be had to what had been done while such legislative or executive act was in operation and presumed to be valid in all respects. It is now accepted as a doctrine that prior to its being nullified, its existence as a fact must be reckoned with. This is merely to reflect awareness that precisely because the judiciary is the governmental organ which has the final say on whether or not a legislative or executive measure is valid, a period of time may have elapsed before it can exercise the power of judicial review that may lead to a declaration of nullity. It would be to deprive the law of its quality of fairness and justice then if there be no recognition of what had transpired prior to such adjudication.[237] In the language of an American Supreme Court decision:[238] "The actual existence of a statute, prior to such a determination [of unconstitutionality], is an operative fact and may have consequences which cannot justly be ignored. The past cannot always be erased by a new judicial declaration. The effect of the subsequent ruling as to invalidity may have to be considered in various aspects--with respect to particular relations, individual and corporate, and particular conduct, private and official.[239]

This language has been quoted with approval in *Araneta v. Hill* and in *Manila Motor Co., Inc. v. Flores.* An even more recent instance is the opinion of Justice Zaldivar speaking for the Court in *Fernandez v. Cuerva and Co.*[240]

Partial Invalidity

Where it is shown that only a portion of a treaty or a statute or an executive order or a municipal ordinance is violative of the Constitution, that which is valid, if it could be separated, may be given force and effect. There is the requirement though that it could stand by itself and would likely have been enacted had the legislative body assumed that the objectionable portion was beyond its power to pass. Nor is this all. What remains by itself must have the attribute of completeness, the excision of that void portion not productive of results inconsistent with the legislative purpose. This is so for what is invalid is devoid of any significance, so that the legislative will find expression in that part of the statute not infected with infirmity.[241]

By Way of a Summary

The conclusion that emerges from this survey of the 1987 Constitution is that more--much more--than the two previous Charters, the new fundamental law has a distinctively indigenous cast. It is inspired by the hope that the Government thereby instituted "shall embody [Filipino] ideals and aspirations, promote the common good, conserve and develop [the national] patrimony and make secure to the present and future generations the blessings of independence and democracy under the rule of law and a regime of truth, justice, freedom, love, equality, and peace...."[242]

From the standpoint of constitutionalism, what is most commendable is the explicit reference that such ideals be attained "under a rule of law" and through "a regime of justice" as well as "love,"[243] in addition to the previous attributes found in the two earlier Constitutions.

There can be no more emphatic endorsement of constitutionalism than that. The concept of the rule of law would be meaningless if there be no recognition of the Constitution as the highest law--entitled to deference and respect. There is likewise the recognition that it should be justice through law but administered with compassion. The national creed is then made manifest: The Filipinos strive to build "a just and humane society"[244] through this fundamental law.

It may be noted likewise that the 1987 Constitution sets forth in detail the prescription to attain that kind of society and--as a result--suffers from verbosity. Apparently, there was the fear that unless the legislative body is specifically directed as to what should be done and for whose benefit, the social, economic, and cultural rights would lose part of their significance for the attainment of the good life.

Even as to the separation of powers principle, there are now stronger checks on the Executive. Both Congress and the Supreme Court can have gained in the process. The judiciary appears to be the major beneficiary.

Even now Supreme Court opinions still cite American decisions. There appears to be a trend, however, toward less reference to such sources. That tendency is likely to continue. The impact of American constitutional law will thus be further reduced. It will be constitutionalism triumphant--but Philippine style. That is as it should be.[246]

NOTES

*The senior author of this chapter, then an Associate Justice of the Supreme Court of the Philippines, along with the then Chief Justice Oemar Seno Adji of Indonesia, then Lord President Tun Mohamed Suffian of Malaysia, and the late Professor Nobushige Ukai, was one of the four Asian jurists invited in 1976 to take part in the Bicentennial celebration of the American Declaration of Independence. Thereafter, he contributed Chapter VIII of Lawrence Ward Beer (ed.), *Constitutionalism in Asia: Asian Views of the American Influence* (1979) [hereafter Beer, *Constitutionalism in Asia*]. That chapter bore the title of "The American Constitutional Law Impact on the Philippine Legal System."

1. 1987 Constitution, Article XVII, Sec. 27. The omitted phrase read: "Upon its ratification by a majority of the votes cast in a plebiscite held for that purpose."
2. *Angara v. Electoral Tribunal*, 63 *Phil.* 139, 156 (1963). *"Phil."* stands for *Philippine Reports*.
3. *Planas v. Gil*, 67 *Phil.* 62 (1939).
4. 1935 Constitution, Article II.
5. *Id.* Art. XIV, Sec. 6 provides: "The State shall afford protection to labor, especially to working women and minors, and shall regulate the relations between landowner and tenant, and between labor and capital in industry and agriculture. The State may provide for compulsory arbitration."
6. Concepcion, *Thirty Years of the Philippine Constitution*, 72-73 (1965). The Commonwealth of the Philipines was the government during the transition period from November 15, 1935, to July 4, 1946, when the Philippines declared its independence. While American sovereignty remained, the Philippines enjoyed the utmost autonomy, except as to foreign affairs, defense, imports, exports, currency, coinage and immigration.
7. E.M. Fernando, *The Constitution of the Philippines*, 2d ed., 7 (1977).
8. *Id.*, 8.
9. *Free Telephone Workers Union v. Minister of Labor*, 108 *SCRA* 757 (1981). *"SCRA"* stands for *Supreme Court Reports Annotated*, an unofficial publication of all Philippine Supreme Court opinions.
10. *Id.*, 763-765. Reference is made to the relevant provisions of the 1935 Constitution, Article VII, Secs. 1, 8, 9, and 16 and Article IX, Sec. 1, 2, 4 and 10. *Planas v. Gil* is reported in 67 *Phil.* 62 (1939). The senior author penned the opinion.

11. 1973 Constitution, Article IV, Sec. 6.

12. *Id.*, Article VI, Sec. 16.

13. *Id.*, Article VI, Sec. 4, par. 2 and Sec. 20. The *Miranda* decision is reported in 348 *U.S.* 436 (1966).

14. 1935 Constitution, Article II, Sec. 5.

15. 1973 Constitution, Article II, Sec. 5.

16. *Id.*, Article II, Sec. 7.

17. *Id.*, Article II, Sec. 2. This Article, an innovation in the 1935 Constitution entitled "Declaration of Principles," was designated as "Declaration of Principles and State Policies." In addition to what is found in the former Article II in the 1935 Constitution, the above section on protection to labor was added, as were sections recognizing the vital role of youth in nation-building, with the State called upon to promote their physical, intellectual, and social well-being (Section 5); affirming that civilian authority is at all times supreme over the military (Section 8); and guaranteeing and promoting the autonomy of local government (Section 10).

18. *Id.*, Article XIV, Sec. 12.

19. *Id.*, Article XV, Sec. 8(1).

20. *Id.*, Sec. 8(5).

21. *Id.*, Sec. 9(6). [*Editor's Note.* The constitutional developments described are best considered together with the course of the Ferdinand Marcos era. After a career in the Senate and as an attorney, Ferdinand Marcos was elected President of the Philippines by a landslide in 1965. In 1969, he became the first President elected for a full second four-year term. The Constitution banned a third term. In 1971 and 1972, a constitutional convention debated notable possible changes in the 1935 basic document; but Marcos intervened, declared martial law on September 21, 1972, and in 1973 provided a Constitution tailored to his preferences and enhanced power. (on the 1973 Constitution *see* text *supra* at note 8. Between 1972 and 1986, although praised at times by American Presidents, President Marcos' regime was criticized increasingly at home and abroad for authoritarian disregard of individual rights, large-scale corruption favoring relatives and "cronies," and policies seriously damaging to the Philippine economy.

In January, 1981, Marcos technically ended martial law, but retained extraordinary executive and legislative powers. His authoritarian constitutional system began to unravel after the murder of his long-time principal rival, Benigno Aquino, shot in the head at Manila Airport upon returning from exile in August, 1983, and with the withdrawal of support by Phillipine and international financial circles as foreign debt skyrocketed. Outrage over the Aquino assassination and the failure to bring the guilty to justice emboldened the opposition to challenge Marcos more openly. For example, the press was less rigidly censored in its treatment of the Marcos family. In 1984, moderates formed the National Movement for Free Elections (NAMFREL) to independently monitor the perennially fraudulent elections and the power of the opposition in the National Assembly (*Batasang Pambansa*) rose dramatically in elections.

The Catholic Church became the most outspoken advocate of human rights. Other domestic and foreign voices were raised for economic reform and democratization; but the charismatic center of the "People's Revolution" which followed was the widow of Benigno Aquino, Corazon Aquino. Irked by criticism but still confident, on November 3, 1985 Marcos called for a presidential election to demonstrate his continuing popularity with the voters. On December 3, "Cory" Aquino became the main opposition candidate in her first bid for public office. Before the February 5 "snap election" for President, concerned Marcos supporters unsuccessfully challenged the legality of such an election before the Supreme Court. Enrique Fernando, one of the two authors of this chapter, testified in favor of the election. He had recently retired at seventy, the mandatory age, as Chief Justice of the Supreme Court. *See* David P. Chandler *et al.* eds., *In Search of Southeast Asia: A Modern History* (revised edition), Honolulu, University of Hawaii Press, 1987, 431-442; and the annual surveys of the Philippines in *Asian Survey*, February, 1984-1991.]

22. Proclamation No. 3, first "Whereas" clause.

23. *Id.*, second "Whereas" clause.

24. *G.R.* No. 76449 (*Kilusang Bagong Lipunan v. Commission on Elections and the Budget Minister*).

25. Proclamation No. 3. [*Editor's Note*: The authors' characterization of Mrs. Aquino as "the losing candidate for the Presidency in the February 1986 election" is at variance with the more common view: "Mrs Aquino clearly won the election, but Marcos's machine claimed the victory." (Chandler, *In Search of Southeast Asia*, 441). The *Batasang Pambansa*, Marcos' carefully controlled legislature, did indeed proclaim Marcos elected; but extensive fraud was found by independent election observers. Both Aquino and Marcos claimed victory; mass demonstrations and military defections in favor of Aquino settled the issue. Marcos and his wife Imelda were forced into exile in Hawaii. On March 25, 1986, President Aquino issued Proclamation No. 3, a Provisional Constitution referred to as "the Freedom Constitution," abolishing the *Batasang Pambansa* and most restraints on individual rights, and promising a new Constitution. The Constitution was approved by plebiscite on February 2, 1987, with 76.37% in favor and only 22.65% opposed (Carolina G.

Hernandez, "The Philippines in 1987: Challenges of Redemocratization," *Asian Survey*, February, 1988, 231). The Constitution's Transitory Provisions stated that, with approval of the charter, the incumbent and the vice-president would serve a six-year term ending in 1992; thus, the vote further legitimized the February Revolution and Aquino's mandate to rule.]

26. *Id.*, Article I has three sections.

27. 1973 Constitution, Article VIII.

28. *Id.*, Article IX.

29. *Id.*, Article XVI.

30. *Id.*, Article XVII.

31. Proclamation No. 3, Article II, Sec. 1 provides: Until a legislature is elected and convened under a new Constitution, the President shall continue to exercise legislative power.

32. Proclamation No. 3, Prefatory Statement.

33. *Id.*,

34. Proclamation No. 8, Sec. 2, par. (1).

35. *Id.*, Sec. 2, par. (2).

36. *Id.*, Sec. 2, par. (3).

37. *Id.*, Sec. 2, par. (4).

38. *Id.*, Sec. 4.

39. *Id.*, Sec. 9, par. (2).

40. *Id.*, Sec. 9, par. (3).

41. *Id.*, Sec. 9, pars. (5) and (6).

42. *Id.*, Sec. 11.

43. *Angara v. Electoral Commission*, 63 *Phil.* 139, 156 (1936).

44. *Id.*,

45. 1935 Constitution, Article VI, Sec. 1. The 1940 amendments vested the legislative power "in a Congress of the Philippines, which shall consist of a Senate and a House of Representatives."

46. *Id.*, Article VII, Sec. 1.

47. *Id.*, Article VIII, Sec. 1.

48. *Angara v. Electoral Commission*, 63 *Phil.* 139, 156.

49. *Planas v. Gil*, 67 *Phil.* 62 (1939). This decision was penned by the same Justice Jose P. Laurel who wrote the *Angara* opinion. The citation came from the dissent of Justice Holmes in *Springer*.

50. *Luzon Stevedoring Corp. v. Social Security Commission*, 34 *SCRA* 178 (1970).

51. *Cf. Angara v. Electoral Commission*, 63 *Phil.* 139, 156-157.

52. The modified parliamentary system became operative only on June 12, 1978. It ought to have started on January 17, 1973, the date of effectivity of

the 1973 Constitution. The National Assembly provided for therein was not, however, convened. At that time, the Philippines was already under martial law under a Presidential Proclamation dated September 21, 1972. The then incumbent President Ferdinand E. Marcos continued as such until a new legislative body, the *Batasang Pambansa*, was created under the 1976 amendments to the 1973 Constitution.

53. The 1973 Constitution, original version, Article VII, Sec. 1.

54. *Id.*, Article IX, Sec. 11.

55. *Id.*,

56. *Id.*, Article IX, Sec. 11.

57. *Id.*, Article IX, Sec. 12.

58. *Id.*, Article IX, Sec. 13.

59. *Id.*, Article IX, Sec. 14.

60. *Id.*, Article IX, Sec. 16.

61. *Cf. id.*, Article VIII, Sec. 20(1) "Every bill passed by the National Assembly shall, before it becomes a law, be presented to the Prime Minister. If he approves the same, he shall sign it; otherwise, he shall veto it and return the same with his objections to the National Assembly...."

62. *Cf. id.* 1976 Amendments, par. 6. This provision continued to be in force and effect after the 1981 amendments vested anew the executive power in the President.

63. 1973 Constitution after 1981 amendments, Art. IX, Sect. 1.

64. *Id.*, Article IX, Secs. 9 and 10.

65. *Cf. Free Telephone Workers Union v. Minister of Labor and Employment,* 108 *SCRA* 757, 763 (1981).

66. 1987 Constitution, Article VI, Sec. 1.

67. *Id.*, Article VII, Sec. 1.

68. *Id.*, Article VIII, Sec. 1.

69. *Id.*, Article VI, Sec. 32.

70. *Id.*, Article VII, Sec. 18.

71. *Id.*, Article VII, Sec. 18, par. 1.

72. *Id.*, Article VIII, Sec. 18, par. 3.

73. *Id.*, Article VII, Sec. 20. The corresponding provision in the 1973 Constitution is found in Article VII, Sec. 14.

74. *Id.*, Article VII, Sec. 17.

75. *Id.*, Article VII, Sec. 19.

76. *Id.*, Article VII, Sec. 16.

77. *Id.*, Article VII, Sec. 22. [*Editor's Note*: As a means of dealing with the serious problem, in the Philippines and elsewhere, of family-based corruption,

the 1987 Constitution of the Republic of the Philippines establishes an anti-nepotism provision in Section 13, Article 7:

> The spouse and relatives by consanguinity or affinity within the fourth civil degree of the President shall not during his tenure be appointed as Members of the Constitutional Commissions, or the Office of the Ombudsman, or as Secretaries, Undersecretaries, chairmen or heads of bureaus or offices, including government-owned or controlled corporations and their subsidies.

In the Constitution's spirit of opposing political dynasty, Congress passed a law in 1987 prohibiting election candidacy at the national and local levels to "relatives of high-ranking government officials within the second degree of consanguinity;" but this took effect *after* relatives of powerful politicians had stood for office in the first local elections, January 18, 1988. Hernandez, "The Philippines in 1987," 233. Article 2, Section 26: "The State shall guarantee equal access to opportunities for public service, and prohibit political dynasties as may be defined by law.]

78. *Id.*, Article VIII, Sec. 9.

79. *Id.*, Article VIII, Sec. 8, par. (1).

80. *Id.*, Article VIII, Sec. 9.

81. *Id.*, Article VIII, Sec. 11.

82. *Id.*, Article VIII, Sec. 18, par. (3).

83. *Id.*, Article VII, Sec. 18, par. (4).

84. *Lansang v. Garcia*, 42 *SCRA* 448 (1971). The Court held that there was sufficiency of the "factual bases." It was the same Chief Justice, whose last public service was rendered as Chairman of the Judiciary Committee of the 1986 Constitutional Commission, of which he was the most distinguished member. The academic member was Professor T. Aguda.

85. *Id.*, at 473. There was likewise a *habeas corpus* petition to contest the validity of the proclamation of Martial Law, *Aquino, Jr. v. Ponce Enrile*, 59 *SCRA* 183 (1974). The Court was equally into the sufficiency of the facts justifying such a proclamation. The then Chief Justice Querube Makalintal, who penned the prevailing opinion, expressed his view thus: "The present state of Martial Law in the Philippines is peculiarly Filipino and fits into no traditional pattern or judicial precedents." With the present provision in the Constitution, no doubt may be entertained.

86. *Id.*, Article VIII, Sec. 2.

87. *Id.*, Article VII, Sec. 1. In both the 1935 and the 1973 Constitutions, the term used is "inferior courts." *Cf.* Article VIII, Sec. 1, 1935 Constitution and Article X, Sec. 1, 1935 Constitution as amended.

88. This authoritative doctrine was declared in *De la Llana v. Alba*, 112 *SCRA* 294 (1982), relying on this excerpt from *Cruz v. Primicias Jr.*, 23 *SCRA* 998 (1968): "As well-settled as the rule that the abolition of an office does not amount to an illegal removal of its incumbent is the principle that in order to be valid, the abolition must be made in good faith." (At 1003.)

89. 1987 Constitution, Article VIII, Sec. 1, second paragraph.

90. *Id.*, Sec. 3.

91. *Id.*, Article VI, Sec. 2. [*Editor's Note*: The first elections for both Houses of Congress were held on May 11, 1987. Supporters of Cory Aquino won almost all Senate seats, and most House seats. However, since President Aquino's political base is a coalition of political groups, not a single political party, competing allies sometimes divided her support too widely to win, at both the local and national levels.]

92. *Id.*, Article VI, Sec. 2.

93. *Id.*, Article VI, Sec. 3.

94. *Id.*, Article VI, Sec. 4.

95. *Id.*, Article VI, Sec. 5, par. 1.

96. *Id.*, Article VI, Sec. 5, par. 2G.

97. *Id.*, Article VI, Sec. 7.

98. *Id.*, Article VI, Sec. 11.

99. *Id.*, Article VI, Sec. 15.

100. *Id.*, Article VI, Sec. 16.

101. *Id.*, Article VI, Sec. 16.

102. *Id.*, Article VI, Sec. 23, par. 1.

103. *Id.*, Article VI, Sec. 23, par. 2.

104. *Id.*, Article VI, Sec. 24.

105. *Id.*, Article VI, Sec. 27, par. 1.

106. *Id.*, Article VI, Sec. 29, par. 1.

107. *Id.*, Article VI, Sec. 30.

108. *Id.*, Article VII, Sec. 1.

109. *Id.*, Article VII, Sec. 2.

110. *Id.*, Article VII, Sec. 3.

111. *Id.*, Article VII, Sec. 4, pars. 1 and 2.

112. *Id.*, Article VII, Sec. 4, pars. 3 and 4.

113. *Id.*, Article VII, Sec. 6.

114. *Id.*, Article VIII, Sec. 1.

115. *Id.*, Article VIII, Sec. 4.

116. *Id.*, Article VIII, Sec. 5, pars. 1 and 2.

117. *Id.*, Article VIII, Sec. 5, par. 5.

118. *Id.*, Article VIII, Sec. 6.

119. *Id.*, Article VIII, Sec. 7.

120. *Id.*, Article VIII, Sec. 10.

121. *Id.*, Article VIII, Sec. 11, 1st sentence.

122. *Id.*, Article VIII, Sec. 11, 2d sentence.

123. *Id.*, Article VIII, Sec. 12.

124. *Id.*, Article VIII, Sec. 13.

125. *Id.*, Article VIII, Sec. 14.

126. *Id.*, Article IX, Sec. 1.

127. *Id.*, Article IX, B, Sec. 1.

128. *Id.*, Article IX, C, Sec. 1. Of those first appointed, the Chairman shall hold office for seven years, a Commissioner for five years, and another Commissioner for three years, without reappointment. Appointment to any vacancy shall be only for the unexpired term of the predecessor. In no case is a Member appointed or designated in a temporary or acting capacity.

129. *Id.*, Article IX, C, Sec. 2. Of those first appointed, three Members hold office for seven years, two Members for five years, and last members for three years, without reappointment. Appointment to any vacancy shall be only for the unexpired term of the predecessor. In no case is a Member appointed or designated in a temporary or acting capacity.

130. *Id.*, Article IX, C. Sec. 1.

131. *Id.*, Article IX, D, Sec. 2.

132. *Id.*, Article IX, D, Sec. 1, pars. 1 and 2. Of those first appointed, the Chairman holds office for seven years, one Commissioner for five years, and the other Commissioner for three years, without reappointment. Appointment to any vacancy is only for the unexpired portion of the term of the predecessor. In no case is a Member appointed or designated in a temporary or acting capacity.

133. *Edu v. Ericta*, 35 *SCRA* 481, 491 (1970); *cf. Agricultural Credit and Cooperative Financing Administration v. Confederation of Unions*, 30 *SCRA* 649 (1969).

134. 1987 Constitution, Article III, Sec. 1.

135. *Id.*, Article III, Sec. 2.

136. *Id.*, Article III, Sec. 9.

137. *Id.*, Article III, Sec. 10.

138. *Id.*, Article III, Sec. 16.

139. *Id.*, Article III, Sec. 5.

140. *Id.*, Article III, Sec. 4.

141. *Id.*, Article III, Sec. 5.
142. *Id.*, Article III, Sec. 6.
143. *Id.*, Article III, Sec. 2.
144. *Id.*, Article III, Sec. 3, par. 1.
145. *Id.*, Article III, Sec. 3, par. 2.
146. *Id.*, Article III, Sec. 6.
147. *Id.*, Article III, Sec. 12, pars. 1 to 4.
148. *Id.*, Article III, Sec. 13.
149. *Id.*, Article III, Sec. 14.
150. *Id.*, Article III, Sec. 15.
151. *Id.*, Article III, Sec. 17.
152. *Id.*, Article III, Sec. 18, pars. 1 and 2.
153. *Id.*, Article III, Sec. 19, pars. 1 and 2.
154. *Id.*, Article III, Sec. 20.
155. *Id.*, Article III, Sec. 21.
156. *Id.*, Article III, Sec. 22.
157. *United States v. Bustos*, 37 *Phil.* 731 (1918). The opinion was penned by Justice George A. Malcolm, who as the founder and later Dean, as well as Professor of Constitution Law, taught the foremost leaders of the 1934-1935 Constitutional Convention. It is worth mentioning that this 1918 decision, which imposed the rigid requirement on the judiciary to test libel actions in terms of their effect on press freedom antedated the landmark American Supreme Court opinion of *New York Times Co. v. Sullivan*, 376 U.S. 254, by thirty-six years. It still speaks authoritatively.
158. *Id.*, 739.
159. *Id.*, 740.
160. *Id.*,
161. English "constitutional cases" never did possess a status similar to that exerted by American constitutional doctrines.
162. Constitution, Article XII, Sec. 5.
163. Constitution, Article XII, Sect. 6.
164. *Reyes v. Bagatsing*, 125 *SCRA* 553, 560-561 (1983). The two principal American decisions relied upon are *Thornhill v. Alabama*, 310 *U.S.* 88 (1940) per *Murphy, J. and Schenck v. United States*, 249 *U.S.* 47 (1919) per Holmes, J. The remainder of the above excerpt cited from the opinion in *Thomas v. Collins*, 323 *U.S.* 516 (1945), penned by Justice Rutledge.
165. The two American decisions are *Mapp v. Ohio*, 367 *U.S.* 643 (1961), per *Clark, J. and Miranda v. Arizona*, 348 *U.S.* 436 (1966) per Warren, C.J. The provision on excluding illegally seized evidence is found in Article IV, Sec. 4., par. 2 of the 1973 Constitution, reproduced in Article III, Sec. 3, par. 4 of the

1987 Constitution. The ban on custodial interrogation is found in Article IV, Sec. 20 of the 1973 Constitution and reproduced in Article III, Sec. 12, par. 1 of the 1987 Constitution.
166. *Cf. Martin v. Hunter's Lessee*, 1 *Wheat* 304 (1816).
167. Cardozo, *The Nature of Judicial Process* 83 (1921).
168. 1987 Constitution, Article II.
169. *Id.*, Article XIII.
170. *Id.*, Article II, Sec. 9.
171. *Id.*, Article II, Sec. 10.
172. *Id.*, Article II, Sec. 21.
174. *Id.*, Article XIII, Sec. 1, pars. (1) and (2).
175. *Id.*, Article XIII, Sec. 2.
176. *Id.*, Article XIII, Sec. 3.
177. *Id.*, Article XIII, Sec. 4. [*Editor's Note*: As of 1991, the Government Comprehensive Agrarian Reform Program (CARP) had been successfully obstructed by a conservative Congress. See, for exampole, D. G. Timberman, "The Philippines in 1990: On On Shaky Ground," *Asian Survey*, Feb. 1991, at 157.]
178. *Id.*, Article XIII, Sec. 5.
179. *Id.*, Article XIII, Sec. 6.
180. *Id.*, Article XIII, Sec. 7.
181. *Id.*, Article XIII, Sec. 8.
182. *Id.*, Article XIII, Sec. 9.
183. *Id.*, Article XIII, Sec. 10.
184. *Id.*, Article XIII, Sec. 11.
185. *Id.*, Article XIII, Sec. 12.
186. *Id.*, Article XIII, Sec. 13.
187. *Id.*, Article XIII, Sec. 14.
188. *Id.*, Article XIV, Sec. 1.
189. *Id.*, Article XIV, Sec. 2, pars. (1) to (5).
190. *Id.*, Article XIV, Sec. 3, pars. (1) to (3).
191. *Id.*, Article XIV, Sec. 4, pars. (1) to (4).
192. *Id.*, Article XIV, Sec. 5, pars. (1) to (5).
193. *Id.*, Article XIV, Sec. 6. [*Editor's Note*: Filipino should not be confused with Pilipino which is really Tagalog. Filipino, a *lingua franca*, mixes various local and foreign languages variously in different regions.]
194. *Id.*, Article XIV, Sec. 7.
195. *Id.*, Article XIV, Sec. 8.
196. *Id.*, Article XIV, Sec. 9.
197. *Id.*, Article XIV, Sec. 10.

198. *Id.*, Article XIV, Sec. 11.

199. *Id.*, Article XIV, Sec. 12.

200. *Id.*, Article XIV, Sec. 13.

201. *Id.*, Article XIV, Sec. 10.

202. *Id.*, Article XIV, Sec. 13.

203. *Id.*, Article XIV, Sec. 14.

204. *Id.*, Article XIV, Sec. 15.

205. *Id.*, Article XIV, Sec. 18, pars. (1) and (2).

206. *Id.*, Article XIV, Sec. 19, pars. (1) and (2).

207. 1987 Constitution, Article II, Sec. 2.

208. *Id.*, Article II, Sec. 9.

209. *Lochner v. New York*, 198 *U.S.* 45.

210. Cardozo, *The Nature of Judicial Process* 77 (1921).

211. *Agricultural Credit and Cooperative Financing Administration v. Confederation of Unions*, 30 *SCRA* 649 (1969).

212. *Id.*, 669. The concurring opinion relied likewise on the famous dissent of Justice Holmes in *Lochner*.

213. *Id.*, 671. The West Virginia decision is reported in 319 *U.S.* 624. As late as 1973, the plurality opinion in *San Antonio School District* (411 *U.S.* 1) could affirm that education was not a right afforded explicit or implicit protection under the United States Constitution.

214. *Agricultural Credit and Cooperation Financing Administration v. Confederation of Unions*, 30 *SCRA* 649, 669 (1969).

215. *Cf. Angara v. Electoral Commission*, 63 *Phil.* 139, 156 (1936).

216. 1987 Constitution, Article VIII, Sec. 4, par. (2). The equivalent provisions in the 1935 and 1973 Constitutions are found in Article VIII, Sec. 10 of the former and Article X, Sec. 2, par. (2) of the latter.

217. *Id.*, Article VIII, Sec. 5, par. 2(a). The equivalent provisions in the 1935 and 1973 Constitutions are found in Article VIII, Sec. 20, par. (1) of the former and Article X, Sec. 5, par. 2(a) of the latter.

218. Where lower courts, which under the Constitution include all courts other than the Supreme Court, are concerned, this caveat from Cooley commends itself: "It must be evident to any one that the power to declare a legislative enactment void is one which the judge, conscious of the fallibility of the human judgment, will shrink from exercising in any case where he can conscientiously and with due regard to duty and official oath decline the responsibility." I. Cooley, *Constitutional Limitations*, 8th ed. 332 (1927).

219. *Alejandrin v. Quezon*, 46 *Phil.* 83, 88 (1924). The opinion was Justice Malcolm's.

220. *Cf.*, Black, *The People and the Court* 56-58 (1962) and Murphy, *Elements of Judicial Strategy* 17-18 (1964).

221. *Id.*, 87. *Cf.* Cardozo, *Nature of Judicial Process* 143 (1921): "The great ideals of liberty and equality are preserved against the assaults of opportunism, the expediency of the passing hour, the erosion of small encroachments, the scorn and derision of those who have no patience with general principles by enshrining them in constitutions and consecrating to the task of their protection a body of defenders."

222. Black, *op cit.*, 87.

223. *J.M. Tuason Co., Inc. et al. v. Court of Appeals*, J.B.L. Reyes, J.

224. According to Article II, Sec. 6 of the Constitution: "The State shall promote social justice to ensure the dignity, welfare, and security of all the people. Towards this end, the State shall regulate the acquisition, ownership, use, enjoyment, and disposition of private property and equitably diffuse property ownership and profits."

225. 103 *Phil.* 1051 (1957).

226. *Id.*, 1067.

227. *Cf. Ashwander v. Tennessee Valley Authority*, 297 *U.S.* 298, Brandeis, J., concurring.

228. *Cf.* 1987 Constitution, Article VII, Sec. 18 and Article VI, Sec. 23.

229. *Cf. Ex parte Milligan*, 4 *Wall.* 123 (1866).

230. 65 *Phil.* 56 (1937).

231. *Dumlao v. Comelec*, 95 *SCRA* 429.

232. L-23127, April 29, 1971; 38 *SCRA* 429.

233. Article 7.

234. *See Norton v. Shelby County*, 118 *U.S.* 425 (1886).

235. *Id.*, 434.

236. L-23127, April, 1971, 38 *SCRA* 429.

237. *Id.*, 434.

238. *Williams v. Standard Oil Co.*, 278 *U.S.* 235, 242.

239. *Id.*, 434-435. The cases cited are *Chicot County Drainage District v. Baxter States Bank*, 308 *U.S.* 371, 374 (1940). The Philippine cases cited are reported in 93 *Phil.* 1002, 99 *Phil.* 378 (1956) and L-21114, Nov. 28, 1967, 21 *SCRA* 1095 (1929).

240. *Id.*, 435.

241. *Cf. Barrameda v. Moir*, 25 *Phil.* 44 (1913). *See also Dumlao v. Commission on Elections*, L-52245, January 22, 1980, 95 *SCRA* 392.

242. 1987 Constitution, Preamble. [*Editor's Note*: Besides a Preamble, the Philippine Constitution, in Article 2, contains a "Declaration of Principles (6 in number) and State Policies", and this is followed by the "Bill of Rights"

(Article 3). The document moves by stages from the general to the particular, from philosophical principles underlying the system to technically specific rights.

Among provisions of special note in the "State Policies," besides the earlier mentioned ban on political dynasty are the statements on nuclear weaponry and the right to life:

> Section 8. The Philippines, consistent with the national interest, adopts and pursues a policy of freedom from nuclear weapons in its territory."
> Section 12. The State recognizes the sanctity of family life and shall protect and strengthen the family as a basic autonomous social institution. It shall equally protect the life of the mother and the life of the unborn from conception....

243. *Id.,*
245. *Id.,*
246. For a commentary by a constitutionmal lawyer among the Authors of the 1987 Constitution, *see* Joaquin Bernas, S.J., *The Constitution of the Republic of the Phillipines: An Annotated Text*, Manila, Rex Book Store, 1987. For an assesment, *see* Karl D. Jackson, " The Phillipines: A Sarch for a Suitable Democratic Solution, 1946-1986," in L. Diamond *et al.*, eds, *Democracy in Developing Countries: Asia*, Boulder, Lynne Rienner, 1989, 231-265.

REPUBLIC OF SINGAPORE

The Constitution of the Republic of Singapore

Valentine S. Winslow

When the United States Constitution came into being, it did not create a new independent nation--it was already there, albeit a confederation; indeed its very framers were acknowledged to be a revolutionary body, devoid of legitimacy. Yet the Constitution did establish a national government unique in its structure, and has endured, been enriched by extended and changing interpretations thereof, and served as an inspiration, if not a model, for successive candidates for nationhood. It has not always served others as well as it served the United States, but like the French Declaration of the Rights of Man and the Citizen (1787), and the Universal Declaration of Human Rights (1948), it has been a beacon of light to others. At its inception, it served as a fine example of comprehensive division and control of abuse of power. When, as a less urgent afterthought, the fundamental liberties arrived in the form of the first ten Amendments, the Constitution has served as a symbol of freedom, expressed in the widest possible terms, but possibly less realistically than the French "Declaration."

More importantly, it has brought to framers of subsequent constitutions elsewhere, concepts like "constitutionalism," "constitutional supremacy," "judicial review," and "equal protection." It has itself drawn upon concepts like "due process" from the English and "separation of powers" from Montesquieu, and given life and meaning to them by their concrete expression and implementation.

The "framers" of the Constitution of the Republic of Singapore have not drawn directly from the U.S. Constitution but have drawn greatly from the British (unwritten) Constitution and the Malaysian Constitution,[1] the latter having itself drawn from U.S. concepts and the Indian Constitution. The Indian Constitution, it may be said, is itself a masterpiece in its comprehensiveness, and drew greatly from the U.S. Constitution. Thus there has been influence in Singapore from the U.S. Constitution, but it has been indirect in nature.

The Making of the Constitution

Singapore's history began in 1819 when it was ceded, as an almost unpopulated island, by the Rulers of the state of Johore to the East India Company (who recognized its strategic potential). Its constitutional history may be said to have begun when it was made part of the British Crown Colony known as the "Straits Settlements" in 1867.[2] It had by then gained a motley population of (largely) immigrants of Chinese, Indian and Malay stock, respectively, with an influential European minority. In 1946, after World War II, Singapore was separately administered as a Crown Colony,[3] the rest of the former Straits Settlements forming part of the Malayan Union.

If we understand the term "constitution" to mean an organic instrument under which government powers are both conferred and circumscribed,[4] then Singapore has had several such "constitutions" preceding the single written Constitution it has today. The first was the Singapore Colony Order-in-Council, 1946, whereby Singapore and its dependencies, the Cocos or Keeling Islands and Christmas Island were to be administered as the Colony of Singapore, separate from the Straits Settlements. This created for Singapore its own Governor, Supreme Court and Legislative Council. The second was the "Rendel" Constitution of 1955, being no more than an Order-in-Council[5] promulgated by the United Kingdom Government for the Colony of Singapore as a result of a comprehensive study of the constitutional framework and a report made by a Constitutional Commission appointed by Singapore's Governor and chaired by Sir George Rendel. This introduced a Legislative Assembly and a Council of Ministers. However, the elected Government, with most Assemblymen of other political parties, sought self-government leading to full independence.

Constitutional Conferences between representatives of the Colonial Government and all Singapore political parties led to the promulgation by the United Kingdom Government of another "constitution," namely, The Singapore (Constitution) Order-in-Council 1958.[6] This gave Singapore full internal self-government. The communist threat through subversion prompted desire for some sort of union or "merger" with the Federation of Malaya, which was an independent state that was successor to the Malayan Union. This was achieved by Singapore becoming a new State in the now-renamed Federation of Malaysia on September 16, 1963, after the approval of the plan by the people of Singapore in a referendum. Singapore now had its fourth constitution, a State Constitution[7] based on the 1958 Constitution, as well as a Federal Constitution, the Constitution of Malaysia, which, in cases of conflict with the Singapore Constitution, would prevail. Finally, owing to irreconcilable differences with the Federal Government, Singapore seceded from the Federation on August 9, 1965, by mutual agreement.[8]

On secession, the State Constitution of 1963 provided the constitutional framework for the new independent and sovereign state of Singapore. However, it was obvious that this would not be sufficient. Thus, transitional provisions contained in the Republic of Singapore Independence Act, 1965[9] provided that: i) certain provisions of the Constitution of Malaysia would continue in force; ii) all laws in force in Singapore on August 9, 1965 should continue in force but should be construed with such modifications, adaptations, qualifications and exceptions as might be necessary to bring them into conformity with the Republic of Singapore Independence Act and with the independent status of Singapore; and iii) the President (acting on Cabinet advice) was authorized for the next three years to make modifications by order (delegated legislation) published in the *Government Gazette*, in any "written law," which appeared to be necessary or expedient in consequence of the independence of Singapore upon separation from Malaysia.[10]

The Singapore Government, being wary of drafting a new Constitution too rapidly, and without sufficient thought, allowed Singapore to depend thus on the provisions of another nation's Constitution! However, in 1979, a constitutional amendment was passed, authorizing the Attorney General to print and publish a consolidated "reprint" of the Constitution of Singapore, as amended from time to time, amalgamated with such of the provisions of the Constitution of Malaysia as were applicable, into a single, composite document. The Attorney General has accordingly caused to be printed such a reprint, which is, for all purposes, deemed to be the "authentic" text of the Constitution of Singapore. This reprint, with any subsequent amendments, is for all purposes, then, Singapore's present single-document Constitution.[11] However, to underline the fact that the present Constitution is based on the 1963 State Constitution, Article 156 states that (subject to the transitional provisions) "this Constitution shall come into operation immediately before 16th September 1963."

It will be seen that as Singapore was not already an independent state attempting to place its house in order, when devising a constitution, as the American Confederation was, its approaches to a constitution were very different. Successive "constitutions" were not drafted by meetings of conventions, by workshops, or even by its own legislatures hammering out and refining the draft provisions in Parliamentary committees or debates in the House. As was the case with many other former colonies, Singapore's future governments had to make their requests in constitutional conferences, study the reports of constitutional commissions, and be willing to accept the implementation of many institutions of colonial origin, whether or not they were the most suitable for it; for the alternative was to have independence delayed or postponed. Colonial paternalism inevitably accompanied colonial patronage. And any "constitution" that arrived was the product of legislation by the colonial legislature or order in council of the colonial government. It would be left to the independent nation to make alterations (sometimes, in many former colonies, drastic) to the superstructure more appropriate to its own particular circumstances.

Constitutional Supremacy

Article 3 of the Constitution provides that "Singapore shall be a sovereign republic to be known as the Republic of Singapore."

Article 4 reads:

> This Constitution is the supreme law of the Republic of Singapore and any law enacted by the Legislature after the commencement of this Constitution which is inconsistent with this Constitution shall, to the extent of the inconsistency, be void.

This "supremacy" clause differs from the U.S. Constitution's Article VI (clause 2) in that clause ensures the primacy of federal laws, including the Constitution and treaties, over State law. Singapore's clause declares what is left unsaid in the U.S. Constitution and which needed to be declared as only logical, in the celebrated U.S. Supreme Court decision of *Marbury v. Madison.*[12] There, Chief Justice Marshall had made two (for our purposes) important propositions:

1) The Constitution is the superior paramount law of the nation, unchangeable by ordinary means; and

2) An act of the Legislature repugnant to the Constitution is void, so that the Constitution, and not such act, must govern the case where the two are in conflict.

Obviously, Marshall had read his *Federalist* No. 78 by Alexander Hamilton which encapsulated the probable intention of the framers of the Constitution! The Malaysian Constitution first had such a provision. Singapore modeled its Article 4 on this, and so avoided the necessity for any circuitous judicial interpretation to reach the same conclusion as Marshall.

In addition to this, Singapore's Article 4 contains a third concept, drawn from the doctrine of "severability," which is emphasized in Indian constitutional law. This makes it possible to hold only the offending part of an Act void as unconstitutional, so as to save the rest and allow it to have effect.

Supremacy and the Amending Proces

Finally, it is worth noting that the U.S. Supreme Court, in *Marbury*, also indicated that a Constitution, if it was a superior paramount law, should not be changed by ordinary means, like an ordinary act.   Indeed, supremacy (provided for in Article 4) is supported by Article 5(2), which provides that:

A Bill seeking to amend any provision in this constitution shall not be passed by Parliament unless it has been supported on Second and Third Readings by the votes of not less than two-thirds of the total number of the Members thereof.

By Article 5(1), this procedure is subject to Article 8, whereby a Bill seeking an amendment to Part III of the Constitution must be additionally supported at a national referendum by not less than two-thirds of the total number of registered electors.   Article 6 in Part III (Articles 6-8) basically prohibits the surrender or transfer of Singapore's sovereignty or control over its police force or armed forces without the prior approval of electors at a referendum as specified.

It may be of interest to note that the two-thirds majority requirement in Parliament was not always there.   There was such a requirement in the 1963 Constitution, but on Singapore's secession from Malaysia, that Constitution was amended to provide only that the Constitution could be amended "by a law enacted by the legislature."[13]   This prompted much academic speculation that the Constitution was not supreme, or that it possessed only one quality to distinguish it from an ordinary act: that any amendment would have to be express, not implied.   However, in 1979, the two-thirds majority was restored,[14] and is to be found in the present Constitution.

Judicial Review and the Judicial Power

The necessary corollary to supremacy is the power of judicial review, also claimed and exerted in *Marbury*.   There is no express provision declaring this power, but it must necessarily follow from Article 4.   Further, Article 93 provides that "The judicial power of Singapore shall be vested in a Supreme Court and such subordinate courts as may be provided by any written law for the time being in force."   The Judicial Committee of the Privy Council approved of a definition of the words "judicial power" in a Commonwealth Constitution to mean "the power which every sovereign authority must of necessity have to decide controversies between its subjects, or between itself and its subjects, whether the rights relate to life, liberty or property."[15] The "judicial power" must necessarily include the power to interpret the law, including the Constitution, as part of the process of determining controversies.

In Singapore, the "Supreme Court" consists of the High Court exercising original and appellate jurisdiction, a Court of Appeal for civil appeals from the High Court, and a Court of Criminal Appeal, to entertain criminal appeals from the High Court.[16] The High Court has general supervisory and revisionary jurisdiction over subordinate courts.[17] The High Court also has powers, *inter alia*:

> "to issue to any person or authority directions, orders or writs, including writs of the nature of habeas corpus, mandamus, prohibition, quo *warranto* and certiorari, or any other, for the enforcement of any of the rights conferred by any written law or for any purpose.[18]

It would be fair to say that the power of judicial review to the extent of declaring legislative or executive acts unconstitutional does reside in our courts--at least, the superior courts, in view of the above provision. The High Court has had occasion to pronounce on constitutionality and has in 1985, for example, held an administrative practice to be unconstitutional as contrary to the equal protection clause of the Constitution and even found a U.S. Supreme Court decision helpful in reaching its conclusion.[19]

The term "judicial power" (to be found also in Article 3 of the U.S. Constitution), connotes also an aspect of the separation of powers, namely, that the whole of that power is vested exclusively in the courts.

System of Government and Separation of Powers

In its system of government, Singapore differs markedly from the United States. Singapore has a parliamentary (cabinet) system of government, with a President (since Singapore chose to be a republic) who is a constitutional head of state with few discretionary powers, having generally to act on the advice of the Cabinet or Prime Minister.[20]

Singapore's similarities with the United States in government lie mainly in the broad separation of powers, in that the Constitution clearly defines the Executive, the Legislature and the Judiciary. It states that the "executive authority" of Singapore is vested in the President,[21] and is exercisable by him, by the Cabinet, or any Minister authorized by the Cabinet. The Legislature consists of the President and Parliament.[22] Part VIII provides for the

Judiciary, in whom are vested the judicial power. Security of tenure for members of the superior court Judiciary guarantees their independence.

Singapore differs substantially from the United States in its adherence to many facets of the British "Westminster" system of government: The Cabinet is fully drawn from an elected Parliament, and they are collectively responsible[23] to Parliament. The President appoints from among Members of Parliament a Prime Minister, who in his judgment, is a person likely to command the "confidence" of the majority of Members; he, in turn, then appoints the members of his Cabinet.[24] In addition, the President may appoint Judges on the advice of the Prime Minister, who does not consult Parliament, only the Chief Justice. Judges are permitted to sit on Inquiry Commissions and administrative tribunals, and this will not be regarded as exercising "executive" power, as this would be in accordance with British practice. Further, the Attorney General may sit on the Legal Service Commission, which determines the appointments, promotions, transfers, dismissals and, generally, discipline of members of the "Legal Service," which includes subordinate court judges. This again has precedents in the British Commonwealth, such as Kenya, but not in the United States.

Generally, a partial fusion of executive and legislative powers in the same body or the same persons is not regarded as taboo, but on the contrary, conducive to the smoother working of the machinery of government. It is only in the Judiciary (particularly the superior court judiciary) that separation of powers is considered essential--i.e., to the fair administration of justice, held in high regard in British (as in American) constitutional theory.

"Checks and Balances"

Singapore does not have the checks and balances between the various organs of government that the U.S. system of government possesses. The powers of the Executive and the Legislature are distinct, and each has little power to control the other by obstructing it. The President and Parliament have no "veto" powers over each other. Parliament may not "impeach" the President although Article 17(3) allows Parliament to remove him from office by a resolution supported by at least two-thirds of the total number of its members.[25] Although the Government of Singapore may sue and be sued,[26] the President himself shall not be liable to any proceedings whatsoever in any court.[27] It is unlikely that any claim of "executive privilege" will be easily defeated as it was in *U.S. v. Nixon*,[28] where President Nixon's claim of the privilege of immunity from judicial process was not sustained. In fact, in Singapore, the Executive may be shielded, as the British Executive is, by the protection of the Official Secrets Act, "Crown Privilege" (in Singapore, known as the privilege of "affairs of State"), and many of the "prerogative" powers of the British Crown. Thus, the Executive can declare war, make decisions relating to foreign affairs, and all matters pertinent to defense or national security without reference to Parliament.

The only "control" that Parliament has over the Executive is the accountability of the Executive to Parliament under the doctrine of "ministerial responsibility." Thus, Parliament may query executive decisions by the "Parliamentary Question," have tabled for discussion in "Adjournment Debates," matters of crucial importance; or it can vote on a motion of no confidence to defeat a government of the day, so that it must resign and either seek new leadership or request a dissolution of Parliament for the purpose of seeking a fresh electoral mandate. Also, Ministers may themselves be held in breach of Parliamentary privilege for lying or failing to disclose matters to the House. Thus, Parliament may discipline a Minister as one of their number for breach of privilege, or Ministers may have to answer, as members of Parliament, to their electorate at election time. This is in fact the British approach to politics and government.

The other side of this coin, however, is the very real control the Executive indeed has over the members of Parliament who come from the same party as the ruling party. As Ministers hail from the same party, the government "whip" can insist that members of the party vote in favor of a government motion or Bill and refuse to allow independent voting. This naturally makes much of the "accountability" of the government to backbenchers to be theoretical, if not mythical. Members of the ruling party in Parliament generally do not vote against the government (and rarely abstain from voting), when the "whip" is employed. To do so would be to invite party discipline or to threaten the life of one's own party in government.

Finally, it is worth observing that the Executive, acting in the name of the President, has wide discretionary powers (besides war and foreign affairs). Acting on Cabinet advice, the President may even proclaim a state of emergency, thereby following Acts of Parliament or Executive "ordinances" to be promulgated, notwithstanding their inconsistency with (most) provisions of the Constitution.[29]

The Future of the Parliamentary System and the Presidency

Although Singapore's Parliamentary (Cabinet) system of government had so far worked well, with a strong Prime Minister and a constitutional head of state with few personal discretionary powers (whereas in the U.S., the

President combines both roles), there was no guarantee that this system would remain unaltered. Generally, the government treads warily when altering the Constitution, as it does not favor hasty changes, and is "not in favour of exchanging old lamps for new ones";[30] but it has also always stressed that a draftsman of the Constitution must be cognizant of Singapore's own conditions and the contingencies that may arise.[31] Thus, in early 1985, the Prime Minister intimated that the purely constitutional head of state role might change, and that a scheme was under study to enhance the role of the President to make him a partially executive President, by granting him a discretionary power to block a future government's attempts to spend Singapore's fairly large accumulated foreign reserves.[32] It would apparently take some two to three years to prepare a "White Paper" on the matter.I n July 1988, the long-awaited "White Paper"[33] was presented to Parliament. This argued that the existing constitution was inadequate, as it gave untrammeled power to the Prime Minister and Cabinet, and that it was necessary to introduce a "two-key" mechanism whereby the President, to be elected directly by the people, would serve as a watchdog or custodian in two areas where he would have the discretion to grant or withhold his concurrence to decisions of the Prime Ministers and the Cabinet: i) the spending of the state's accumulated reserves or assets; and ii) key public appointments. Otherwise, it argued, the Parliamentary system of government would not be affected. Thus the President was to have "veto" power in these two areas.

A second, modified White Paper[34] emerged in August 1990, with more concrete proposals, including some additional discretionary powers the elected President was to wield. This was soon afterwards followed by a draft Constitution Amendment Bill which was referred to a Select Committee of Parliament to receive public representations and prepare a Report on a Bill. The Report[35] was presented to Parliament. The Bill, as amended by Select Committee, was passed on January 18, 1991.[36]

The President shall, in future, be elected for a six-year term[37], and a presidential candidate must be a citizen of at least forty-five years of age, and be similarly qualified as candidates for Parliament, such as by being resident in the State for an aggregate of ten years prior to nomination. In addition (and here the qualification is unique), he must for the previous three years, have held a designated office such as Chief Justice, Minister, Attorney-General, Permanent Secretary, a chairman or chief executive officer of certain types of corporation, of held office in any other similar or comparable position of seniority and responsibility in any other organization or department of equivalent size or complexity in the public or private sector "which, in the opinion of the Presidential Elections Committee, has given him such experience and ability in administering and managing financial affairs as to enable him to carry out effectively the functions and duties of the office of President."[38] A council of Presidential Advisors is also provided for, to advise the President in the exercise of his discretionary powers.

In another unique provision,[39] a presidential candidate must not be a member of any political party on the date of his nomination. This was in direct response to many representations which urged candidates' political neutrality to enable a President to exercise his discretion independently of any party political considerations, independently of any party political considerations including those of the party in power, as he would otherwise be ineffective in being a check on the government; or may be an unthinking thorn in the side of the government if he belonged to an opposition party.

As one of the White Papers envisaged, he will not be an "executive" President, unlike the Presidents of France or Sri Lanka.[40] Instead, the proposed new President is a hybrid between a purely constitutional head of state, with limited or no discretion to refuse Cabinet advice, and an executive President. Indeed, he has partial executive powers, in the form of a veto power in certain matters only, but with no power to take the initiative in any action. Also, as President, he will continue to have the executive authority of the State vested in him, and thus the Presidency is not a separate organ of government, but is rather an institution forming part of the executive, and which exercises a check on another part of the executive, namely the Prime Minister and the Cabinet.

Federal or Unitary State?

Singapore had never, on its own, considered being anything other than a unitary state, owing to its small size. Only when Singapore was part of the Federation of Malaysia from September 1963 until August 1965, was it a state within a larger federation. Centralized administration has been favored always, and only regional "Town Councils" are in existence at present, as part of a pilot scheme which may in the near future be implemented on a larger scale throughout the nation.

Unicameralism or Bicameralism

Two previous constitutional commissions in Singapore had rejected unicameralism as a proposed feature of its political system.[41] The "Rendel Commission" of 1954 thought there was no strong case for a second legislative chamber in Singapore and that "it would be a serious mistake to attempt to create one."[42] Reasons given included Singapore's small geographical size (wherein special representation which might evolve would be unnecessary and undesirable), undue complication, and difficulty in finding enough suitable candidates. In 1966, the Wee Chong Jin Constitutional Commission reported that it was unable to accept the proposal of an Upper House in Parliament if its members were to be nominated or elected by specific minority groups.[43] Instead, it proposed that there should be a "Council of State," an advisory body of able, mature and respected citizens, separate from Parliament, to advise on legislation in order to guard against provisions discriminatory of racial, religious or linguistic minorities. The Commission did not state whether this proposal was inspired by any particular country's constitutional set-up, but it seems that there were parallels in Kenya's "Lennox-Boyd Constitution" of 1958, where a Council of State was created; and in the Constitution of the Fifth French Republic, where there was (and is) a Constitutional Council.

The government accepted the proposal of this body, and in 1969, a "Presidential Council" was set up, with the specific function of drawing the attention of Parliament to "differentiating" (or discriminatory) measures in any Bill or subsidiary legislation, and the general function of reporting on such matters affecting persons of any racial or religious community as might be referred to it by Parliament or the government. It was renamed the "Presidential Council for Minority Rights" in 1973. It is required generally that a Bill passed by Parliament must be referred to the Council who may make an adverse report within thirty days, barring which, it will be sent to the President for his assent, whereupon it will become law. In three exceptional cases, a Bill may be presented for assent without being conveyed to the Council, or be presented for assent despite an adverse report, if its presentation is supported by a resolution passed by at least two-thirds of the members of Parliament. So far, it appears that the Council has not yet made an "adverse report."

The Legislature and Legislative Powers

As pointed out earlier, the "Legislature" in Singapore comprises the President and Parliament. Unlike the United States, the Constitution does not contain enumerated legislative powers. Neither is there express power in the Constitution for it to delegate its powers to other bodies, including members of the Executive. There is only a procedural provision: Article 58 provides that (subject to the Presidential Council's intervention), "the power of the Legislature to make laws shall be exercised by Bills passed by Parliament and assented to by the President."

As Singapore has no competing Legislature as federal states have, the Legislature, it is generally accepted, has the same legislative power as the United Kingdom Parliament, as far as subject matter of legislation is concerned. Theoretically, the Legislature may legislate on any matter, subject to any inconsistency with the Constitution itself. Also, the Legislature may amend the Constitution itself, provided it follows the "manner and form" required by the Constitution.[44] Thus, a two-thirds majority of all members of Parliament is normally required, except that a national referendum is additionally required in any surrender of sovereignty or relinquishment of control over its police or armed forces.[45]

There are, nevertheless, instances where specific legislative authority is required--so that the matter is placed beyond the jurisdiction of the Executive. Thus, Article 142 states that: "No tax or rate shall be levied by, or for the purposes, of Singapore, except by or under the authority of law." "Law" is defined in Article 2 to include both written law and common law.

It is also the Legislature that must approve of estimated government expenditure, making provision for it in annual "Supply" Bills.[46] Article 67 empowers the Legislature to make provision by law for the remuneration of Members of Parliament. Article 98 stipulates that Parliament shall by law provide for the remuneration of Judges of the Supreme Court; and empowers it to provide for their terms of office other than remuneration.

Article 63 also stipulates: "It shall be lawful for the Legislature by law to determine and regulate the privileges, immunities or powers of Parliament." Pursuant to this the Legislature has passed an Act to determine and regulate the same.

Parliament has considerable control over its own procedure: It may make, amend or revoke Standing Orders for the regulation and orderly conduct of its own proceedings and dispatch of business;[47] Parliament's decision is final on any question whether a Member of Parliament has vacated his seat;[48] and Parliament may discipline its own members or "strangers" for breach of privilege or contempt of Parliament.[49]

Parliament also has power to elect the Speaker and Deputy Speaker, and, until 1991, to elect the President.

Parliamentary procedures and functions are modeled closely on those of the United Kingdom House of Commons, and the privileges, immunities and powers enjoyed by Members, the Speaker and Committees, shall be the same as those presently enjoyed by the House of Commons and its equivalent personnel, save as expressly provided by the Constitution or the Parliament (Privileges, Immunities and Powers) Act.[50]

The "Bill of Rights"

While Singapore was a Colony, and then an internally self-governing State, it had no "fundamental liberties" in its constitutions. Any "liberties" would have been only those applicable under the common law, and we would have been no different from England in this respect. However, when Singapore became a part of the Federation of Malaysia, it also became subject to the "fundamental liberties" contained in the Federal Constitution, based largely on the 1957 Federation of Malaya Constitution, which had drawn much strength from the Indian Constitution (and which, of course, had been profoundly influenced by the U.S. Constitution).

On Singapore's departure from the Federation, it allowed the liberties provisions (with one major exception) to continue to apply until such time as Singapore was ready with its own new draft Constitution. They continued to so apply until 1980, when Singapore combined the Malaysian provisions, with modifications, with the Singapore Constitution into one composite "Reprint," which is our present Constitution.

Part IV of the Constitution is entitled "Fundamental Liberties" and contains eight important Articles.

Restrictions on Liberties

Unlike the U.S. Constitution, all but two of the liberties are subject to limitations, ordinarily permitting the Legislature to restrict the liberty by law relating to some stated public interest (such as security, public order or morality). The two absolute rights are the prohibition of slavery (Article 10(1)[51] and the prohibition of the banishment or exclusion from Singapore of citizens (Article 13(1)). In this, Singapore has been influenced by the Indian Constitution, which contains power to limit (but not to do away with altogether) fundamental rights in stated circumstances.

"Due Process" and Liberty of the Person

The "due process of the law" concept found in English constitutional law, being first used in a statute of King Edward III in 1354, was readily embraced by the United States. However, Indian draftsmen shied away from this amorphous concept, preferring to allow deprivation of one's life or personal liberty only "according to procedure established by law."[52] Malaysia, and so too, Singapore, preferred to be even narrower in stating their equivalent of the Fifth and Fourteenth (sec. I) Amendments of the United States. Thus, Article 9(1) states: "No person shall be deprived of his life or personal liberty save in accordance with law."

Indian, Burmese and Malaysian cases had long held that the American concept of "due process" (substantive and procedural) was not applicable in the context of their constitutional provisions on personal liberty; and that their constitutions only prohibited limitations other than by means of duly *enacted* law.[53] In Singapore, academic opinion was divided. However, in 1981, the Privy Council heard an appeal from Singapore in the landmark decision of *Ong Ah Chuan v. Public Prosecutor.*

In *Ong*, the appellants had been convicted of drug trafficking. They argued that the statutory presumption in the Misuse of Drugs Act that the accused had a controlled drug in their possession for the purpose of trafficking, was in conflict with the "presumption of innocence" which was imported into the Constitution by Article 9(1) as a fundamental rule of natural justice. The Privy Council said that the Constitution should be given a "generous interpretation": that the word "law" in Article 9(1) included "fundamental rules of natural justice," which included the presumption of innocence. However, they did not feel that the statutory presumption had conflicted with that presumption of innocence, and thought that the presumption was not in conflict with the Constitution.

Lord Diplock said:

> In a constitution founded on the Westminster model, and particularly in that part of it that purports to assure to all individual citizens the continued enjoyment of fundamental liberties or rights, references to "law" ... in their Lordships' view, refer to a system of law which incorporates those fundamental rules of natural justice that had formed part and parcel of the common law of England that was in operation in Singapore at the commencement of the constitution.[54]

It is generally felt by commentators that as these rules are "fundamental," they are both substantive and procedural in nature.[55]

Personal Liberty

The Fifth and Fourteenth Amendments in the U.S Constitution express the right not to be deprived of "liberty" without due process of law;

Singapore's Article 9 uses the term "personal liberty," which is borrowed from India's Article 21. It may be that this term is thus limited to liberty of a physical nature or freedom from bodily restraint only. It is doubtful that it will be open to our courts to take the same wide interpretation the U.S. Supreme Court has taken, to embrace, *inter alia*, the right to make decisions about one's lifestyle and the right to privacy. However, as Indian Supreme Court authorities would be most persuasive where the Indian Constitution or legislation are worded similarly, it is open to us to follow the Indian approach, which is also fairly broad.

In *Maneka Gandhi v. Union of India*,[56] where the right to travel abroad was held to be a part of "personal liberty," Bhagwati J. (as he then was) of the Indian Supreme Court said that "personal liberty" in Article 21 "is of the widest amplitude and covers a variety of rights which go to constitute the personal liberty of man, and some of them have been raised to the status of distinct fundamental rights and given additional protection under Article 19(1)."

"Cruel and Unusual Punishment"

The Eighth Amendment stipulation that cruel and unusual punishments must not be inflicted, has no equivalent in Singapore. In 1966, the Wee Chong Jin Constitutional Commission reported that in its view, it was beneficial to write into the Constitution of Singapore the following "fundamental" right: "No person shall be subjected to torture or to inhuman or degrading punishment or other treatment."[57]

Although this recommendation was among those found "acceptable" by the government, it was never included in any subsequent revision of the Constitution. As sentences of caning are highly regarded as a deterrent for certain types of crime, it may be this factor that has caused reluctance in implementation.

Equal Protection

The equivalent to the Fourteenth Amendment (sec. I) of the American Constitution is to be found in Article 12(1) of Singapore's Constitution. This reads: "All persons are equal before the law and entitled to the equal protection of the law."

This clause in fact contains two concepts, taken directly from the Indian Constitution's Article 14 adaptation of the U.S. provision. It is said that equality before the law (apparently taken from the Irish Constitution) is a "negative" concept which emphasizes that no one is above the law, and corresponds to A.V. Dicey's second aspect of the Rule of Law; and that equal protection is a "positive" concept, postulating the application of the same laws, without discrimination, to all persons similarly situated.[58]

Article 12(2) goes on to spell out prohibited grounds for discrimination (much as the Indian provision does), thus obviating the need for courts to identify "suspect" classifications or "facially invidious discrimination." It prohibits discrimination against citizens on the ground only of religion, race, descent or place of birth, in any law or in the appointment to any public office or employment or in the administration of any law relating to property transactions or the establishing or carrying on of any trade, business, profession, vocation or employment. Article 16 similarly prohibits discrimination on these grounds only in the administration of public educational institutions or the provision of financial aid out of public funds for education or maintenance of students.

Although the interpretation of the equality and equal protection clause calls for the doctrine of "reasonable classification," it is really the Indian courts' approach to the application of the doctrine, with its emphasis on not only reasonableness and rationality, but on rational nexus with the legislative purpose, that has been influential in Malaysian and Singapore courts. The reasonable classification test, as explained by Indian courts, has been accepted in Singapore.[59] U.S. Supreme Court authorities, are, nevertheless, occasionally cited with approval.[60]

It would seem that Article 12 also obviates the need for any "Bills of Attainder" clause such as Article I, sec. 9 in the U.S. Constitution. It may be that there is also no need for an equivalent of the now lapsed Equal Rights Amendment, as this may be encompassed by Article 12(1), unless it is sought to make sex discrimination invidious per se.

Finally, although Singapore is a multi-cultural, multi-racial and multi-lingual nation, with English as the main language of education and business, no present need appears to have arisen for "affirmative action" programs for minorities, supported constitutionally. The government appears to believe that communities falling behind the general average in economic or educational performance need to be helped and encouraged to upgrade themselves (particularly through training or education) so as to enable them to lift themselves up by their own bootstraps, as it were; and that positive discrimination in favor of any group, disregarding merit, may cause resentment in other communities. As the government frequently points out, our history as an independent entity is short, and our social cohesion, "fragile."

Speech and Expression, Assembly and Association

The freedoms of speech, the press, and peaceful assembly in the First Amendment are couched in absolute terms. Yet it has been found necessary for even this most prized of American freedoms, to be limited by constitutional interpretation. Thus the "clear and present danger," "bad tendency," and "fighting words" tests have emerged. So too have the laws of libel and obscenity, police powers and the interests of national security been found necessary bases for limitation. Singapore's Article 14 guarantees the rights of freedom of speech and expression, peaceable assembly and association for all citizens. However, Article 14(2) grants the power to Parliament to impose "such restrictions as it deems necessary" in certain named (State) interests.

Thus, freedom of speech and expression may be restricted in the interest of Singapore's security, friendly relations with other countries, public order or morality, to protect the privileges of Parliament, or to provide against contempt of court, defamation, or incitement to any offense.

The right to assemble peaceably may be restricted in the interest of security or public order; and the right to form associations may be restricted in the interest of security, public order or morality, and by law relating to labor or education.

It is at once necessary to say that there are many laws indeed that do restrict these rights. Censorship of films and publications, press controls and the widespread requirement by statute or delegated legislation of permits or licenses--to hold a procession or a public meeting, to run a printing press or publish a newspaper--means in effect (to use the old aphorism), that "everything is forbidden, save what is expressly permitted." The formidable array of various discretionary powers (usually untested in court) in granting "permission" for acts in exercise of many facets of these civil rights, ensure that the relevant official authorities (whether bureaucrats or police) closely monitor activity outside of election periods that may be of a "public" or "political" nature, for fear of acts or words that may have a tendency to upset the social fabric. Officials, even where they have a clear discretion and may not be under pressure from above, are cautious in exercising it in any way that is less than consistent; for consistency is more likely to produce fairness, and petty bureaucrats prefer rules to the exercise of genuine discretion. This, it is suggested, is not an unfair observation of administrative "culture"; for the feeling is so widespread, and the earnestness of the official in appearing impartial and incorruptible, almost legendary in a developing society.

India, in respect of similar rights, allows for the doctrine of "reasonableness" of restrictions. This doctrine appears unlikely to apply in Singapore. Alternatively, it may be possible to argue that the restrictions cannot reasonably be said to be required for the interest "deemed necessary or expedient," and that Parliament has merely attempted to employ a "colourable device" to evade constitutional limitations, so as to impose restrictions.[61] This argument has yet to be used successfully in Singapore's courts.

Freedom of Religion

Article 15(1) states that "Every person has the right to profess and practice his religion and to propagate it." Unlike the First Amendment, this clause does not prohibit the establishment of religion. Singapore is a secular State, multi-religious in every way, with large minorities of Christians, Buddhists, Muslims and Hindus, with most of the population probably Taoist or agnostic. There is naturally a reluctance to have any State religion, or to excite religious sensitivities by allowing State-run television or radio to run religious services or be used for proselytization. It may be possible, of course, for the Constitution to be amended to establish a religion, but this seems most unlikely--except in the event of Singapore entering into a union with Malaysia again (which had Islam as its State religion when Singapore was part of that Federation and continues to do so). On the other hand, Article 16(2) allows every religious group to establish and maintain institutions for the education of children and to provide religious instruction; and by Article 15(2), every group has the right to establish or maintain institutions for religious or charitable purposes.

Again, unlike the First Amendment, the right to profess and practice one's religion is not stated in absolute terms, for Article 15(4) excepts from the right, "any act contrary to any general law relating to public order, public health or morality." It is possible that conscientious objection may be thus subordinated to the needs of compulsory military service (provided for by the Enlistment Act for all male citizens and permanent residents), or that a blood transfusion to save life would prevail on the grounds of health over Christian Science or other religious objection.

Rights to Property?

There is *no* right in the Constitution to property. On Singapore's departure from the Malaysian Federation, a deliberate decision was made to omit this right, in its application to Singapore, although the rest of the Malaysian "Bill of Rights" continued to apply. Malaysia's Article 13 promises that no person shall be deprived of property save in accordance with law; and that no law shall provide for the compulsory acquisition or use of property without adequate compensation. This has analogies with the Fifth and Fourteenth Amendments.

The Constitution Commission of 1966 recognized that land, being scarce and an increasingly valuable commodity, would be needed for public purposes over the years in Singapore, and so proposed a modified version of the Malaysian provision to reflect a just and fair balance between the public interest and private ownership. They thus proposed that: "No law shall provide for the compulsory acquisition or use of property except for a public purpose or a purpose useful or beneficial to the public and except upon just terms."[62]

The government was quick to disagree with this proposal, precisely because of the need for acquisition for public purposes. It decided that rights to property and of "fair" or "just" compensation should not be included in the Constitution, as it might lead to a flood of litigation and disputes over the quantum of compensation.[63] Since then, land acquisition programs have been extensive, and the pace of urban and rural development, frenetic. Such development is hardly likely to have been possible with a right to property and just compensation. But whose complaints ultimately matter if land is acquired from the few and resold as a slice of public housing to the many at prices not possible if the land had been purchased by public authorities at prevailing fair market prices?

Retrospective Criminal Laws

The U.S. Constitution prohibits *ex post facto* laws in Article I, sections 9 and 10. In Singapore, Article 11(1) prohibits retrospective laws, but spells out more fully the scope of the provision.[64] It would seem that "law" probably refers to legislation only. Further, it appears to protect against retrospective criminal law, and not civil liability. Also, the provision is substantive, not procedural in character: retrospective modifications of procedure or rules of evidence appear not to be caught by the provision. Thus, in one case, the Court of Criminal Appeal ruled that the removal by legislation of the accused's right to make an unsworn statement from the dock after the commission by him of the offense charged, was not the removal of a substantive right, and the new procedure applied to the accused, there being no contravention of the constitutional provision.[65]

Guarantees of a Fair Trial

The Fourth, Fifth and Sixth Amendments contain various provisions which tend to ensure a fair trial and fair treatment for persons who are arrested or searched. In Singapore, these aspects of a fair trial are generally also applicable, but they are provided for partly in Articles 9 and 11, partly by statute, and partly by the common law.

The Fourth Amendment protects against unreasonable searches and seizures, and against "general" warrants. In Singapore, the Criminal Procedure Code sets out in detail the proper procedure for searches and seizures, and issue and service of warrants. Improper procedure will result in illegality. The only difference lies in the effects of illegality. In the U.S., illegal search and seizure will result in the inadmissability of evidence so obtained. In Singapore, the common law, as in Britain, provides for a judicial discretion to exclude illegally obtained evidence--and only where its use will operate unfairly against the accused and prejudice his fair trial.

The Sixth Amendment guarantees a speedy and public trial, an impartial jury, the right to know the nature and cause of the accusation and to be confronted with the witnesses against oneself, and to have the assistance of counsel for one's defense. In Singapore, a public trial is provided for by statute.[66] Instead of jury trial, one is triable in capital cases, by two High Court Judges who are required to be unanimous in a guilty verdict, by the Criminal Procedure Code. Where there is insufficient provision in statute, the common law guarantees a fair hearing, by application of the rules of natural justice.

Article 9(3) stipulates that a person arrested "shall be informed as soon as may be of the grounds of his arrest and shall be allowed to consult and be defended by a legal practitioner of his choice." The courts have reiterated in *Lee Mau Seng v. Minister for Home Affairs, Singapore & Anor.*,[67] that the right to consult counsel is available to a person arrested "within a reasonable time after his arrest" even when one is detained without trial under preventive detention powers, but that refusal of access to legal advice would not necessarily result in the accused's continued detention being held to be unlawful. In this respect, the Court distinguished the American case of *Johnson v. Zerbst*,[68] where *habeas corpus* was held to be applicable because imprisonment after conviction, after denial without effective waiver of the right to counsel, was unlawful.

The Fifth Amendment guarantees a Grand Jury to one accused of a capital or infamous crime, protection from double jeopardy for the same offense, and the privilege against self-incrimination (besides due process). In Singapore, one has a right to a "preliminary inquiry" before a Magistrate under the Criminal Procedure Code, where one is facing trial before the High Court (where more serious offenses are triable, and carry heavier sentences generally than in the lower courts). This gives the accused an opportunity of pre-trial "discovery" of the prosecution case against him and an opportunity also to reserve his defense until the trial itself. The privilege against self-incrimination derives not from the Constitution, but from statute and common law. Under the Criminal Procedure Code, the accused is free to refuse to give evidence or to refuse to answer questions in the witness box, but risks adverse inferences being drawn against him if the court considers this course "proper." A suspect has a common law right to remain silent when speaking to the police. Even a person who is neither a witness nor an accused person has a common law privilege against self-incrimination.

Article 11(2) of the Constitution guarantees protection from double jeopardy for the same offense except in a case of a retrial ordered by a superior court after the earlier conviction or acquittal is quashed by it. At common law, this double jeopardy doctrine is referred to as "*autrefois convict*" or *autrefois acquit*." In a recent case, the Privy Council ruled that the doctrine applied not only to successive criminal trials, but also to successive disciplinary proceedings under a statutory code governing any profession.[69]

The privilege of the writ of *habeas corpus*, which is guaranteed in Article I, section 9 of the U.S. Constitution is in Singapore apparently available to all arrested persons under Article 9(2). Where complaint is made to the High Court that a person is being unlawfully detained, "the Court shall inquire into the complaint and unless satisfied that the detention is lawful, shall order him to be produced before the Court and release him." It would appear, from a Singapore decision,[70] that *habeas corpus* is not an available remedy for a person detained without trial under the Internal Security Act, owing to the words in section 74 of that Act which state: "Any person detained under the powers conferred by this section shall be deemed to be in lawful custody." As the Act was passed under an emergency of subversion provision in the Constitution, Article 149, the Act can in fact derogate from the Constitution for a provision of such a law (or any amendment to it) "is valid notwithstanding that it is inconsistent with any of the provisions of Article 9, 11, 12, 13, or 14 ..."[71]

The U.S. Constitution allows for suspension "when in Cases of Rebellion or Invasion the Public Safety may require it."[72] This provision seems really to allow for the kind of situation already provided for in the Internal Security Act, which certainly is a law passed for the "public safety"; but it arguably goes further than cases of rebellion or invasion, and deals with acts of a more covert nature.

Emergency Powers

There is no express provision for emergency situations in the U.S. Constitution, apart from Article I, section 9 in respect of *habeas corpus*, and it would seem that state police powers are the only other legitimate way to deal with emergencies. However, Singapore has two specific provisions that deal with emergencies. Article 149, as pointed out above, empowers the Legislature to make laws inconsistent with certain provisions of the Constitution. Article 150 allows the President (acting on Cabinet advice) to issue a Proclamation of Emergency. Either the Legislature, by Acts of Parliament thereunder, or the President, by "ordinances," when Parliament is not sitting, may make laws notwithstanding their inconsistency with the provisions of the Constitution--except those relating to religion, citizenship or language. Further, it would seem that the emergency may be any situation threatening "the security or economic life of Singapore." The Privy Council has said that:

> "Although an emergency" to be within that article must be not only grave but such as to threaten the security or economic life ..., the natural meaning of the word is capable of covering a very wide range of situations and occurrences, including such diverse events as wars, famines, earthquakes, floods, epidemics and the collapse of civil government.[73]

It is well-settled that the government is the sole judge of whether the security or economic life of the nation are threatened, and it only has to state that it is "satisfied" that such a threat exists. Only positive proof of bad faith on the part of the government may arguably cause a Proclamation of Emergency to be "justiciable" or open to challenge in a court on the ground that it is *ultra vires*.[74]

Conclusion

It is accepted as a general proposition that constitutions are products of their nations' histories and circumstances. More often than not, their contents are profoundly influenced by the make-up of the people of the nation, and especially, the particular people who debate and draft them. One nation's meat and drink may be another's poison. One nation may embrace the spirit of liberalism; another may be moved by important considerations of pluralism. Singapore is no different in this respect from the U.S., although its own influences have been vastly different. Only in the realm of the fundamental rights or liberties is there an air of some universality.

An important question for most of the young nations of the world is how relevant the U.S. model is for them. Many new nations do not forge a Constitution which is capable of surviving centuries with little change because of the malleability of judicial interpretation according to the times and the circumstances. One of the strengths of the U.S. Constitution is that it could always be viewed with different spectacles, in a continuum of time. Other nations are, not surprisingly, wary of this unpredictability, and dependence on judicial idiosyncrasy. Thus many opt for the detailed provision in a Constitution for all eventualities, couched in language that must receive, more often than not, a predictable literal or legalist interpretation. The spirit of a provision or of the whole Constitution need not then be looked at. The experience of other nations must thus be more limited, less animated (even muted), than Americans have been led to expect from the Supreme Court. Singapore Courts will find it difficult to give the Constitution the generous interpretation that it deserves. This is in part due to the training of most of its Judges, not in the arena of constitutional interpretivism, but in that of the British legal system with its unwritten Constitution, rules of statutory interpretation hardly suitable for constitutions, and only slightly assuaged by the spirit of the common law tradition.

Singapore's Constitution has had only indirect influence from the U.S. Constitution. There have been direct borrowings from the Malaysian Constitution and more influences from the Indian Constitution, with its non-absolute rights and concepts of inbuilt limitations. There is even a "directive of state policy," an Indian concept, in Article 152, which enjoins the Government "constantly to care for the interests of the racial and religious minorities of Singapore," and to safeguard the interests of the Malays (as the indigenous people of Singapore) and the Malay language. Also, the Courts are more readily persuaded by Indian decisions on the doctrine of reasonable classification in the equality provision, personal liberty, emergency powers and preventive detention, to name but a few examples of subject matter. Finally, the influence of British concepts has been all-pervasive. Judges and the legal profession think in terms more of concepts like the Rule of Law than of constitutional supremacy, independence of the judiciary, and of rules of natural justice rather than judicial review. Legal traditions are essentially

British in nature, and Judges closer to the British in their conservatism, than the American in their activism--especially in matters constitutional.

Recent times have seen even the beginnings of a partial retreat from doctrines inherited from colonial masters, because local traditions are different from those the masters led others to believe in. The Parliamentary system of government, and the traditional notion of the Rule of Law, *inter alia*, are undergoing re-evaluation. The institution of constitutional head of state may occasionally be restructured with more discretionary executive powers. In less fortunate societies, inherited democratic systems are frequently under attack, with traditions of opposition politics resented or misunderstood; and the Parliamentary system seen not as a gentleman's game but as a deadly trial by combat. Often, the inherited constitutional concepts are seen to be increasingly irrelevant and sometimes done away with because of the discovery of some supervening unsuitability. More often, however, excessive legalism is seen as an answer preferable to tradition and the liberal spirit. Constitutions are rarely appreciated until considerable time has elapsed since inception. The U.S. Constitution is two centuries old. Other fledgling constitutions, like the Singapore Constitution, need time to mature. A continually evolving constitution is in many ways like the revolution that is not yet over.

NOTES

1. A point earlier made by S. Jayakumar, "The Singapore Constitution and the United States Constitution," in *Constitutionalism in Asia: Asian Views of the American Influence*, L.W. Beer, ed., University of California Press, 1979, 182.

2. The Government of the Straits Settlements Act, 29 and 30 Vic. c. 115, passed on 10 August 1866 by the United Kingdom Parliament. It came into operation on 1 April 1867.

3. The Straits Settlements (Repeal) Act, 1946 (9 and 10 Geo. 6.c.370; and the Singapore Colony Order-in-Council, 1946, sec. 3 [1946 No. 46, *S.R.&O.*, and *S.I.*, Revd. 1948, vol. XXI, 9]. The Straits Settlements ceased to be a single colony on "the appointed day," i.e., 1 April 1946.

4. *See* Bernard Schwartz, *A Commentary on the Constitution of the United States of America* (1963), Vol. I (The Powers of Government), 1.

5. Singapore Colony Order-in-Council 1955 (U.K.) S.I. 1955, No. 187.

6. 2 *S.I.* 1958, No. 1956.

7. The Constitution of the State of Singapore (S.I. 1963, No. 1493), promulgated through the (United Kingdom) Sabah, Sarawak and Singapore (State Constitutions) Order-in-Council: 2 S.I. 1963, 2656.

8. The Independence of Singapore Agreement (*Singapore Govenrment Gazette Extraordinary*, No. 66, 1965, 7 August 1965).

9. Act No. 9 of 1965 (Singapore).

10. *Id.*, secs. 6, 13.

11. The Constitution of the Republic of Singapore, Reprint No. 1 of 1980 (Revised ed. 1985, Statutes of the Republic of Singapore). It is this (present) document which will hereafter be referred to as "the Constitution."

12. 1 *Cranch* 137 (1803).

13. *See* Constitution (Amendment) Act 1965 (Act. No. 8 of 1965), sec. 8.

14. *See* Constitution (Amendment) Act 1979 (Act No. 10 of 1979), sec. 7.

15. *Labour Relations Board of Saskatchewan v. John East Iron Works Ltd.* (1949) A.C. at 149, endorsing the words of Griffiths C.J. in *Huddart Parker Pty. Ltd. v. Moorehead* (1909) 8 *C.L.R.* at 357.

16. Supreme Court of Judicature Act (Chapter 322, Revised ed., 1985, *Singapore Statutes*), sec. 7.

17. *Id.*, sec. 17. *See also* secs. 23-26.

18. *Id.*, sec. 18(2)(a).

19. *Howe Yoon Chong v. The Chief Assessor, Singapore, & Anor.* [1985] 1 *M.L.J.* 182. The Supreme Court decision cited with approval was *Sioux City Bridge Co. v. Dakota County*, 260 U.S. 441 (1922).

20. Article 21.

21. Article 23.

22. Article 38.

23. Article 24(2).

24. Article 25.

25. See below on on the presidency and parliament, where it is pointed out that the Constitution has been amended by Act No. 5 of 1991, which was passed on 18 January 1991. Most of the amendments had not yet been brought into operation at tiem of writing in May 1991 but when they have Article 17(3), *inter alia*, will have been repealed and substituted by an new Articel 22L, whereby the President will be removable by a resolution passed by three-quaters of the total number of Members of Parliament, after a tribunal of at least five Judges has reported to the speaker that he is permantly incapable of discharging his functions by reason of mental or physical infirminty, or that he has been guily of certain other allegations made against him. These other grounds for removal are: intentional violation of the constitution, treason, misconduct or corruption involving the abuse of the powers of his office, or any offense involving fraud, dishonesty or moral turpitude.

26. Article 37(2).

27. Article 17(2). However, for the reasons stated in note 25 above, this provision will also be substituted by a new Article 22k, whereby the President shall not be liable to any legal proceedings whatsoever for acts or omissions in his official capacity, or to any legal proceedings during his term of office, for acts or omissions in his private capacity.

28. 418 U.S. 683 (1974).

29 Article 150.

30. The Prime Minister, Mr. Lee Kuan Yew, speaking at the (then) University of Singapore, *Straits Times*, 3 January 1978.

31. *Id.*

32. Parliamentary Debates, Singapore: Official Report, Vol. 46, No. 3, columns 223-5 (23 July, 1985).

33. *Constitutional Amendments to Safeguard Finacial Assets and the Integrity of the Public Services*, Cmd. 10 of 1988 (29 July 1988).

34. *Safeguarding Finacial Assets and the Integrity of the Public Services*, Cmd. 11 of 1990 (27 August 1990).

35. *Report of the Select Committee on the Constitution of the Repubic of Singapore (Amendment No. 3) Bill* [Bill No. 23/90], Parl.9 of 1990 (December 18, 1990)

36. *Constitution of the Republic of Singapore (Amendment) Act 1991* (Act No.5 of 1991)

37. Constitution, Article 20(1), as amended by clause 4 of the Act (*supra.*)

38. Constitution, Article 19(2), as amended by clause 4, *supra.*

39. Article 19(2) (f), *supra.*

40. Cmd. 10 of 1988, para.20.

41. From 1963-65, however, it must be remembered, Singapore formed a part of the Federation of Malaysia, and thus became, for a short time, part of a State with a bicameral federal legislature, apart from the individual state legislatures.

42. Report of the Constitutional Commission, Singapore (1954), para. 83. *See also* *generally* Section VII entitled "Minority Proposal for a Second Chamber," paras. 76-92.

43. Report of the Constitutional Commission, 1966, Ch. III, para. 49.

44. *See The Bribery Commissioner v. Ranasinghe* (1964) 2 *All E. R.* 785; *A.G. for N.S.W. v. Trethowan* (1942) *A.C.* 526. These cases subscribe to the "new" view of the doctrine of Parliamentary sovereignty or supremacy, whereby legislation is considered reviewable for failure to observe the procedural requirements set out in the Constitution. All countries with written constitutions that are "supreme" necessarily subscribe to this view; it is unclear if it could apply to the United Kingdom or any country without the notion of constitutional supremacy.

45. *See* Articles 4-5 and 6-8 of the Constitution.

46. Articles 144-45.

47. Article 52.

48. Article 48.

49. Parliament (Privileges, Immunities and Powers) Act (Cap. 217, 1985 ed., *Singapore Statutes*).

50. Sec. 3, Parliament (Privileges, Immunities and Powers) Act.

51. This corresponds to the Thirteenth Amendment (sec. I) and Article 4 of the United Nations Universal Declaration of Human Rights (1948).

52. Article 21, Constitution of the Republic of India.

53. *See, e.g., Gopalan v. State of Madras, A.I.R.* (1950) S.C. 27; *Tinsa Maw Naing v. Commissioner of Police, Rangoon,* (1950) *Burma L. R.* 17; *Arumugam Pillai v. Government of Malaysia,* (1957) 2 *M.L.J.* 29.

54. (1981) 1 *M.L.J.* 64, 71.

55. *See* A.J. Harding (1981), 23 *Mal. L.R.* 226; and T.K.K. Iyer, (1981) 23 *Mal. L.R.* 213.

56. *A.I.R.* 1978 *S.C.* 597. *See, especially,* paras. 54-63.

57. Report of the Constitutional Commission, 1966, para. 40.

58. M.P. Jain, *Indian Constitutional Law* (3d ed. 1978), 11. *See also* P.G. Polyviou, *The Equal Protection of the Laws,* (1980) 90-91.

59. *See Lee Keng Guan v. Public Prosecutor,* (1977) 2 *M.L.J.* 95; *Ong Ah Chuan v. Public Prosecutor,* (1981) 1 *M.L.J.* 64.

60. *See Howe Yoon Chong v. The Chief Assessor, Singapore & Anor.,* (1985) 1 *M.L.J.* 182. This case was discussed earlier in this chapter. And *see Hiwe Yiib Chong v. Chief Assessor* (1988) 1 *M.L.J.* 51; and *Howe Yoon Chong v. Chief Assessor* (1990) 1 *M.L.J.* 321.

61. *See* Privy Council decision in *Hinds v. The Queen,* (1977) *A.C.* 195, 224.

62. Report of the Constitutional Commission, 1966, paras. 41-42.

63. Parliamentary Debates, Singapore: Official Report, Vol. 25, No. 14, column 1052; and No. 20, column 1424-25 (Minister for National Development).

64. Article 11(1) reads: "No person shall be punished for an act or omission which was not punishable by law when it was done or made, and no person shall suffer

greater punishment for an offence than was prescribed by law at the time it was committed."

65. *Haw Tua Tau v. Public Prosecutor*, (1980) 1 *M.L.J.* 2.

66. Supreme Court of Judicature Act (Cap. 322, 1985 ed., *Singapore Statutes*), sec. 9. The Subordinate Courts Act (Cap. 321), sec. 7, provides for public hearings in the lower courts.

67. (1971) 2 *M.L.J.* 137.

68. 58 *S. Ct.* 1019.

69. *Harry Lee Wee v. Law Society of Singapore*, (1985) 1 *W.L.R.* 362.

70. *Lee Mau Seng v. Minister for Home Affairs, Singapore & Anor.* (*op. cit.*).

71. Article 149(1), as amended by Act No. 1/1989. A Singapore Court of Appeal decision, *Chung Suan Tze v. The Minister of Home Affairs and Others* (1989) 1 *M.L.J.* 69, had approved of the trend in the common law towards taking an objective, rather than a subjective view of the administrative discretionary powers, so as to widen the scope of judicial review of executive acts, including decisions to detain without trial. However, subsequent legislative amendments have neutralized the affect of the decision. Since January 30, 1989. There can be no judicial review of any decision of the Minister or of the President made under the Internal Security Act save in regard to any question of procedural irregularities in relation to the Act's requirements. See: Article 149(3) of the Constitution (as amended by Act No. 1 of 1989); and sec. 8B of the Internal Security Act (as amended by Act No. 2 of 1989).

72. Article I, Sec. 9(2), Constitution of the United States of America.

73. Lord MacDermott in *Stephen Kalong Ningkan v. Government of Malaysia*, (1968) 2 *M.L.J.* 238.

74. See the several valuable judgments of the Malaysian Federal Court in *Stephen Kalong Kingkan v. Government of Malaysia*, (1968) 1 *M.L.J.* 119.

LIST OF ABBREVIATIONS USED

A.C. Appeal Cases

A.I.R. All India Reporter

All E.R. All England Reports

Cap. Chapter (i.e., Statutes)

The Constitution:--The Constitution of the Republic of Singapore, Reprint 1980 (1985 ed.)

Mal. L.R. Malaya Law Review

M.L.J. Malayan Law Journal

S.I. Statutory Instruments

 (United Kingdom)

S.R.& O, and S.I.--Statutory Rules and Orders and Statutory Instruments (Revised, 1948)

W.L.R. Weekly Law Reports

KINGDOM OF THAILAND[1]

The Development of Constitutionalism in Thailand:

Some Historical Considerations

Preben A.F. Aakesson

Marut Bunnag

Rujira Bunnag

The History of Thai Kingship

The journey of the Thai peoples from nationhood in the distant past through the period of absolutism (the period of "*Chao Chiwit*," the "lords of life"), to the constitutionalism which began with the Revolution of 1932, is long and largely unrecorded. In addition to the lack of early written records, the 1767 sacking of the then capital of the Ayudhya Kingdom by the Burmese resulted in the destruction of a vast amount of records and accounts through deliberate acts of the conquering Burmese. The destruction is estimated by Thai scholars to be as much as ninety percent of all written records. This event also brought about the fall of the Ayudhya Dynasty (1350-1767 A.D.) in Thailand and gave rise to the current and forward-looking Chakri Dynasty of which the present king is the ninth. The early development remains obscure and, as a noted Thai scholar stated, "The history and development of the social structure of the Thais ... causes much perplexity; darker still lie the origin and growth of the law and its administration for evidence is ... scanty in the extreme."[2]

It is nevertheless established, partly through examination of the few extant evidences of early Thai kingship practices, among them the so-called Sukhothai Stone inscription, that early Thai kingship rules were based upon the Hindu Code of Manu, the ancient Hindu jurisprudence, as well as upon influences from the Khmer Empire. But, whether the Manu Code system came to the Thais during the Sukhothai period (1238-1350 A.D.), the following Ayudhya period, or during a period even earlier than Sukhothai, has not and may never be firmly established. Suffice it to say that the Code of Manu was generally adopted by the Thais with their own modifications and additions, and Thai kingship practices were attuned to its generally egalitarian precepts. However, the Code did not come directly to the Thais. It was introduced through the Mon people who translated the Code of Manu from Sanskrit to Pali, and it was from this that the Thai translated and adopted the Code of Manu for their own use. The Mon formed a kingdom in what is now central Thailand where they were dominant during the eighth to the twelfth centuries. Thus, it is possible that the Thais adopted the Code of Manu before the Sukhothai period through early exposure to the Mons governing practices.

While the date of adoption of the Code of Manu cannot be established, it is known that formal Thai government precepts based upon the Code were in existence during the Ayudhya period. With additions and modifications, this system prevailed until the close of the nineteenth century. Through its transformation from Hindu to Mons to Thai, the Code of Manu became the *Dhammasattham*. It became the basis and guiding source of Thai kingship and is now part of the Thai national heritage.

In Thai mythology, the Dhammasattham, like its Hindu model, the Code of Manu, is supposed to have been derived from supernatural sources and to be the basis for divine verity and equity. It was thus a sacred and eternal expression of truth. In the modification of the original Code, the Thais "modernized" its provisions to harmonize with local custom and social philosophy. In doing so, the Thais avoided inclusion of most, if not all, of the purely Hindu religious features and brought it into consonance with Buddhist religious thought and practice, since Buddhism was the state religion of the Thai and had been so for many centuries previously. In its expression, the Dhammasattham was fundamentally an expression of individual freedom and private rights in both civil and criminal matters. It became the cornerstone of the King's Justice. From the early Ayudhya period, Thai kingship was guided by a parallel system of precepts based upon decisions by individual Thai kings. Some of these decisions became precedents upon which later governing rules were based during the Ayudhya period, while others were only used as precedents during the reign of the king who made the change in the first place. Out of the long-lasting decisions grew a set of rules embodied in a digest of royal decisions: The *Rajasattham*. These royal decisions formed the precedents which were blended with the Dhammasattham during the latter part of the Ayudhya period and the Dhammasattham became divided into two parts. The one was the *Mula Attha*, containing the original precepts of the Manu Code while the second, the *Sakha Attha*, was the digest of the Rajasattham and was designed to preserve, modernize and supplement the Mula Attha.

During the middle and latter part of the Ayudhya period, Europeans arrived in Thailand, settling mostly in the royal city of Ayudhya and along the Chao Phraya River which coursed through Ayudhya. It is noteworthy and a testimony to the steadfastness of the Thai people that while the presence of Europeans made some impact on the Thai intellectual culture--even by their mere presence--contemporary European influences were unable to impact importantly upon the direction and development of Thai kingship. While this impact did lead to the development of extra-territoriality which was to bedevil Thai kings and governments until well into the twentieth century and, eventually, to drastic changes in Thai governing practices, it may be said that Thailand remained Thai and Buddhist, and the fairly comprehensive legal system and the practices of kingship in the nation of Thailand remained basically uniform.

Following a long and severe siege, Burmese forces in 1767 overcame the defenses of the capital city, Ayudhya, and laid it waste. The intensity of long enmity between the two countries was such that, in conquering the city, the invaders went to great lengths to destroy the fabric of Thai civilization as represented in Ayudhya. It has been recorded that practically all irreplaceable official records, administrative files, annals, legal documents and literature in force in the Kingdom was saved from the remains of the late capital.

The result was that the Thai capital was moved, first to Thonburi and, soon after that, for additional security, to Krungthep (Bangkok) where it remains. Because of continuing wars and the move from Ayudhya to the new capital of Bangkok, it was not until almost 40 years later that King Rama I (1782-1809), the founder of the present Thai royal dynasty, the Chakri Dynasty, was able to devote time and effort to revise the law governing all aspects of life in Thailand. In 1805, four years before his death, he appointed a Royal Commission to rewrite the law. The Code of 1805, commonly called the Law of the Three Great Seals[3] was more than a restatement of the then present law; it was written to incorporate forward-looking laws in the light of the then current knowledge and learning. The Ayudhya Dhammasattham was augmented by existing royal decrees and edicts. It was so foresighted that it remained in force for some 90 years throughout the Kingdom, although many parts of the law were rewritten and revised during that time.

King Rama IV, commonly called King Mongkut, who reigned from 1851 to 1868, undoubtedly served as the fuse that lit the modernization process of Thailand. He foresaw the upcoming relations among nations of Europe and Thailand (as well as with the rest of South and East Asia) and discerned recurringly the necessity for law changes--in fact, or by simply overlooking existing law provisions where they appeared to be in conflict with present-day conditions or with needs of the community. Nevertheless, despite his acknowledged foresightedness, King Mongkut did nothing to alter the absolute rule prevailing in Thailand. Perhaps his greatest accomplishment was the manner in which he allowed his son, the next king, to be educated and raised to become the wisest king of Thailand until the advent of the present one.

He was King Rama V, commonly known as King Chulalongkorn (1868-1910). Through education and contacts, King Chulalongkorn foresaw the coming era of Western influence on Thai affairs and became determined to prepare this country for this advent and he assuredly sowed the seeds which in 1932 led to constitutional government in Thailand. He appointed Royal Commissions to delve into and reform existing laws through which the kingdom had been ruled.

King Chulalongkorn soon perceived that mere law reform of the existing Code was not enough to accommodate the country in the new, modern era. He was determined to bring about a General Reform.

During his reign, while still remaining an absolute monarch, radical changes were instituted: Upon his formal coronation in 1873, King Chulalongkorn clearly showed evidence that he had been intent upon reform of the government since he was placed upon the throne of Thailand in 1868, at the age of fifteen. He abolished the ancient custom of prostration before the king, royalty and high-ranking officials, deeming it to be a symbol of oppression and a social evil. At the same time, until an attempted coup in 1874, King Chulalongkorn began to plan reformation of the system to benefit the common people and add to their well-being and happiness.

As a result of the so-called Front Palace Incident of December, 1874, King Chulalongkorn ceased work to modernize but his conviction never weakened that, to progress into the modern world, Thailand had to reform its system of government. This reform, nevertheless, was not encouraged, when the question of changes in the structure of the monarchy arose; it was, in fact, also resisted by Ministers and Princes. Despite this strong and clear resistance to changes of the monarchy, King Chulalongkorn was surprisingly lenient to those who advocated a constitutional form of government. This was evidenced by his handling of a petition, written in 1887 by eleven Princes and senior officials, including the king's brothers, Princes Phittayalap, Naret and Sawat. In this petition the authors advocated the establishment of a constitutional, parliamentary government. David M. Engel states:[4]

> The petitition came near the end of a long period of quiet after the young king's initial flurry of reform, and was remarkable for several

reasons. The very fact of its presentation to the king revealed the extent to which ideas of governmental change were current among the elite and tolerated by the monarch himself. The mildness of the king's reply was further evidence of his readiness to listen even to ideas which might challenge the very legitimacy of his rule ...

The petition argued that as Thailand was a small and powerless country when compared to the colonial powers, Thailand should follow others' example and Europeanize the type of government to avoid absorption into a colonial power system. The petitioners also quoted a number of reasons why Thailand was endangered from attacks from beyond its borders and they maintained that Thailand could not depend upon any protection from international law and treaties as, they maintained, such laws would only be respected by the European powers if applied to so-called civilized countries.

In short, the petition proposed that a Constitution be written and that a Parliament be established to perform the legislative function, and that the absolute reign should be replaced by a constitutional one with a Cabinet to make major governmental decisions. Freedom of speech should be guaranteed, providing the right to hold public meetings and to establish a free press.

In his reply to the petitioners, King Chulalongkorn decidedly rejected the propositions put forward but agreed that some of the criticisms were well-founded. He cited a number of factors militating against the institution of a constitutional parliamentary form of government, along them he cited the entrenched groups of officials within the Thai "establishment" who would fiercely oppose change and work to negate any reforms instituted; he also felt that the inefficiency of Thai bureaucracy would work against change, that Thailand lacked sufficient numbers of educated, trained men who could help formulate new laws and that some powerful ministers would certainly resist all serious changes of the system even to the extent of resigning, abruptly creating chaos in government. The king stated that he felt that before other changes were to be instituted, the administrative system first had to be reformed and such initial changes had to succeed in fact.[5]

Early in his reign, King Chulalongkorn established two bodies which might well be regarded as forerunners of a democratic system: an advisory Privy Council and an advisory Council of State. King Chulalongkorn explained that the creation of these two new, foreign-inspired bodies was to help increase the happiness of the people, to nullify old customs and laws which served in the main to oppress the people and, to speed up the development of Thailand. The two new Councils were expected to aid the king with advice and information and serve as focal points for criticism of proposed changes in law and administration. However, following the attempted revolution in December, 1874, the work of these new Councils declined and it was not until early in the 1890s that King Chulalongkorn revived the concept of these supporting bodies.

In 1895, King Chulalongkorn established a Legislative Council (*Rathamontrisapha*) which some scholars see as King Chulalongkorn's way to prepare Thailand for the adoption of a democratic form of government, although this view is discounted by other scholars.[6] Nevertheless, this strengthening of the legislative system went hand in hand with a complete change of Thai bureaucracy setting up a modern form of government with ministries, in the European fashion.

The work of codification of laws and of writing new laws was to fill existing loopholes in the government and thus to ensure that law might be adequate to meet the demands of life and justice. In all of this, King Chulalongkorn, in his wisdom, managed to democratize the manner in which the laws were fashioned--an especially curious fact considering the work was being made in an absolute monarchy. His Majesty caused any law perceived to be needed to be drafted within the Government Department in which the law was needed. He submitted this draft to the scrutiny of a so-called Legislative Council (L.C.) consisting of some forty members, ministers of State and nominees chosen by His Majesty. This body which, in effect, was a legislative body in an absolute monarchy, examined law proposals (made mostly by His Majesty but also by the members of the L.C. after consultation with His Majesty), forwarded the finished legislation to His Majesty for Royal Assent, after which it was made law by Royal Proclamation. One such law, promulgated in 1905, circumscribing severely the practice of slavery in Thailand, must, from a human and humane point of view, be regarded as a major accomplishment in Thailand's history. It remained for King Chulalongkorn's son, King Vajiravudh-Rama VI, to promulgate the law which finally abolished slavery in Thailand, in 1912.

The Legislative Council gradually fell into disuse as the laws required by King Chulalongkorn were finished. In addition, His Majesty then also served notice that he was not contemplating diminution to the absolute monarchy in Thailand when, in 1895, he caused the procedures for succession to be altered so that the first son of a reign, first born in the line of succession, became king as a right subject to selection. Prior to that, Chakri Kings had been elected by an Accession Council which examined various factors relating to accession. King Vajiravudh became the first Chakri Dynasty King to ascend the Throne of Thailand as a natural Heir Apparent.

In 1912, soon after the beginning of the Reign of King Vajiravudh, a plot was uncovered aiming at the institution of a "limited monarchy." This showed that there were growing forces among civilian and military officials who were now seeking more rights within the framework of the monarchy. The plot was uncovered; the plotters were caught and punished.

In 1917, H.R.H. Prince Chakrabongse, but for a non-Thai mother actually next in line of succession to the Throne, proposed to his Royal Brother, King Vajiravudh, that the Legislative Council established by King Chulalongkorn be resurrected.[7] The King voiced his personal feeling that he agreed, being a constitutionalist at heart; however, he stated that his advisors, Thai, British, and American, advised against such a move on the basis that the average Thai citizen was not yet ready for this move, since the bulk of the people were not educated enough to know how to elect their own representatives and, if the representatives were selected by the King, such selectees would be regarded as the King's "yes" men.

King Vajiravudh instituted many reforms which, deliberately or inadvertently, aided in the natural progression of the Kingdom of Thailand from an absolute Monarchy to a modern constitutional one. In 1913, for example, he had the Thai Nationality Act promulgated by which any person born in the Kingdom of Thailand would acquire Thai nationality. In 1916, the King decreed that all Thai families should have surnames and it became a matter of honor for high-ranking Thai families below the Royal House to beseech his Majesty to name the family. In 1924, King Vajiravudh enacted a law requiring compulsory and free primary education for all Thai children.

But at the same time, His Majesty also caused a Law of Royal Succession which established the line of succession declaring that sons of deceased Heir Apparents were to succeed to the Throne before the brother to the Heir. This law also established the precedence among the children of the Queens of King Rama V. Thus, the son of Queen Saowabha took precedence by age over all others, followed by the sons of Queen Sawaeng (Mother of the Mahidol Dynasty). Sons of other Queens of King Rama V followed in rank by age as did other Princes. Nevertheless, King Vajiravudh reserved to himself the right to nominate his successor, if need be. While the law disqualified heirs of Princes who married foreign ladies, the fact that a Prince married a commoner did not disqualify an heir springing from such a marriage.

King Prajadhipok, Rama VII, presided over the abolition of the absolute monarchy and the institution of the constitutional Monarchy by which Thailand is now governed. He ruled from 1925 to 1932 as an absolute monarch and reigned from 1932 to 1935 as a Constitutional Monarch. He then resigned and went to England to remain until his death in 1941. King

Prajadhipok was a king with liberal tendencies and sympathies but, as he said upon his ascent to the Throne, he had only experience as a soldier and did not have any real experience in the art of government. It became his intention to create a so-called Supreme Council (*Abirata Sabha*) to help him in the task of ruling the country. However, this Council was to be composed of royal relatives, uncles and half-brothers, and no commoners were to be included. This Council met weekly and served His Majesty as advisor on both public and family matters.[8]

During the several years preceding 1932, the world financial crisis, the world slump, impacted seriously on Thailand; various measures were put into effect by the King to lessen the blow on the tottering Thai economy but these did not succeed. Among the measures taken by King Projadhipok was a reduction of government expenditures and of the number of officials on the Civil List.

The most serious effect that this measure had was to cause a storm of complaints by the officials made redundant and their families. While the Thai budget was thereby being balanced, the King's action also served to increase nascent discontent. This, in turn, spawned a renewed conviction among the intelligentsia of Thailand that it was now time for the common but educated people to be allowed to share in the government of the country. In the middle of 1932, on June 24, a group of intellectuals, including Pride Panomyong and Kuang Abhaiwongse, working with middle-ranking military officers, such as Colonel Phraya Bahol and Colonel Phraya Song and Captain Luang Pibulsonggram, staged the overthrow of the absolute monarchy in favor of a new democratic and parliamentary constitutional monarchy. After some hesitation, his Majesty, King Prajadhipok, continued as a constitutional king.

Constitutional Monarchy

When the overthrow of the Thai absolute monarchy took place, King Prajadhipok was at his summer residence at Hua Hin, some 150 miles south of Bangkok. When the coup was engineered by the 114 plotters, the so-called "promoters,"[9] various high-ranking Princes were detained to ensure the cooperation of the King and his return to Bangkok. A deterrent to return was an anonymous pamphlet purportedly issued by the "Peoples Revolutionary Party" (which the "promoters" claimed to represent), attacking the whole Chakri family as usurpers of King Taksin's throne in the late 18th Century.[10] Nevertheless, King Prajadhipok decided to return as a constitutional monarch. This was not really contrary to the wishes of the King as he is said to have expressed an interest earlier in establishing a constitutional monarchy but felt that, in 1932, such a move would be premature.

The first (interim) Constitution of Siam Act was promulgated and published in the *Government Gazette* on 27 June 1932.[11] Pridi Panomyong and Kuang Abhaiwongse were said to be, respectively, chief civilian architect of the Constitution and the civilian most active in the coup; the latter because of Kuang's access to the communications system of the nation due to his position in the Thai postal and telephone-telegraph service. Both Pridi and Kuang had been students in France as had the military leader, Captain Luang Pibulsongkram. Pridi imagined the political development of the country in three stages: 1) adoption of the Interim Constitution with a seventy-member Peoples' Assembly and a small Peoples' Committee (Cabinet) selected from among the seventy; 2) within six months, a new, permanent Constitution with an Assembly, one-half of which would be selected by the Peoples' Revolutionary Party and one-half indirectly elected; and 3) within ten years, or when fifty percent of the population had completed primary education, a full-fledged, elected National Assembly.

The Interim Constitution did call for a one-house Peoples' Assembly, and a government body called the Peoples' Commission headed by a Chairman who would be equivalent to a Prime Minister. The first Chairman was one of the so-called "promoters," Phraya Mano, who formerly was president of the Supreme Appeals Court during the Absolute Monarchy. It is worth noting that, in the Interim Constitution, there was no declaration of the rights and duties of the Thai people.

On 10 December 1932, a new permanent Constitution of the Kingdom of Thailand, B.E. 2475,[12] was promulgated in the name of H.M. King Prajadhipok. In this Constitution, an Assembly of the Peoples' Representatives was established based upon indirect election at the village and subdistrict levels (*tambol*), the electors of which were to elect the members of the People's Assembly. Instead of a Peoples' Commission, a Council of Ministers was appointed from among members of the Peoples' Assembly, consisting of a Prime Minister and not less than fourteen and not more than twenty-four Ministers.

The 10 December 1932 Constitution provided in Chapter II for the "Rights and Duties of the Thai People." The first section abolished the privileges previously carried by those with titles, so that all people would be equal before the law. The second section proclaims freedom of religious belief so long as such is not contrary to civic duties, or inconsistent with public order or public morals. The third section stated: "Subject to the provisions of law, every person shall enjoy full liberty of his person, abode, property, speech, writing, association or vocation...." The last section of this chapter proclaimed that every person had the duty to respect the law, defend the country, pay taxes, and adhere in other ways to the conditions and in the manner provided by law. A law on compulsory education was later promulgated and aimed at general primary education.

After several minor coups, an attempted rebellion, and adjustments in the power structure of Thailand over the next five to six years, the Thai military emerged as the dominant power factor in the country. The Thai public did not take any great part in these events except as spectators. After the presentation of his new, radical economic plan, which aimed at the nationalization of land and proposed making land workers and farmers into governmental officials, Pridi Panomyong, the leader of the civil faction of the dominant Peoples' Revolutionary Party (Promoters), was exiled for being pro-communist. Anti-communist laws were subsequently introduced.

At this point, Lt. Col. Luang Pibulsongkram, who successfully put down the attempted rebellion against the new regime in 1933, was ascendant. His Majesty, King Prajadhipok, abdicated on 2 March 1935 and the successor, ten-year-old Prince Ananda Mahidol, ascended the throne as King Ananda, Rama VIII, under a regency of three senior officials.

During these early days, the compulsory primary education scheme was pursued vigorously; it was estimated that from sixty to eighty percent of school-age children attending school in the 1930s were literate. In November, 1937, the first direct elections for the National Assembly took place. Ninety-one out of 182 representatives were elected; the other 91 were appointed. After the September 1938 elections, Luang Pibulsongkram became Prime Minister on 26 December and veered sharply towards nationalistic, rightist policies and ties to Japan. He also instituted a change in local government political units establishing seventy provinces in place of the *monthon* system, thus reducing local government power in national affairs. In addition, in 1939 he changed the name of the country from "Siam" to "Thailand," stating that this would be a sign that the country belong to the Thai, not to the commercially powerful Chinese minority in Thailand. The Prime Minister changed the Thai calendar year from one beginning on 1 April and ending on 31 March to conform with the calendar in general use in the West, 1 January to 31 December.

On 12 December 1941, the Pibulsongkram government concluded a military alliance with Japan, and about six weeks later, this alliance was fortified by a declaration of war against the United States and Great Britain. However, the Thai Minister to the United States, M.R. Seni Pramoj, refused to obey the orders from Bangkok and instead began the Free Thai Movement, supporting the Western democracies. In Great Britain, the leader of the Free Thai was Prince Subha Savasti, while Pridi Panomyong, freed of taint, along with Kuang Abhaiwongse, became leader of activities inside Thailand. After the war, these anti-Japanese activities, with the support by the U.S. government, enabled Thailand to escape having to make serious reparations to Great Britain and France as an alleged collaborator of the Japanese.

After the war, on 10 May, B.E. 1489 (1946), a new Constitution of Thailand was promulgated by its publication in the *Government Gazette*. This replaced the 1932 Constitution, as amended in 1939, 1940 and 1942. Chapter 2, on the Rights and Duties of the Thai People, is similar to that of the 1932 Constitution except that it includes a section entitling every person to "the right to submit petitions under the conditions and in the manner prescribed by law...." This Constitution was superseded by another on 23 March 1949, which included provisions for appointment of a full Senate by the King and substantially increased the power of the monarchy. However, this also did not last long as a coup on 29 November 1951 annulled the 1949 Constitution; the government then reverted to the 1932 (December) Constitution. This latter Constitution remained in force until it was abolished by Field Marshal Sarit Thanarak, in late 1958. A new Provisional Constitution was promulgated and remained in force until 1968 when yet another "permanent" Constitution came into force. But this was done away with in 1971 when a so-called internal, bloodless coup further entrenched the then-existing government of Field Marshal Thanom Kittikachorn. Thanom abolished political parties and dissolved Parliament.[13]

However, his strong man approach to the solution of political problems in Thailand floundered upon a massive opposition by the Thai electorate spearheaded by students, principally from the premier Thammasat University, in the late summer and fall of 1973. The opposition to the Thanom regime began as demonstrations in favor of students expelled for allegedly anti-government publications and activities, for demanding the release of jailed critics of the regime and the promulgation of a new Constitution. The Thanom regime fell on October 14, 1973.

In late 1974, a new Constitution which was very liberal was promulgated during the regime of Prime Minister, Dr. Sanya Dharmasakti. The regime of Dr. Sanya was followed by three governments in quick succession, respectively of M.R. Seni Pramoj, M.R. Kukrit Pramoj, and M.R. Seni Pramoj; each regime was basically liberal in outlook. By October, 1976, the last of these governments had fallen due to very serious student unrest and quick, brutal retaliatory moves by military and right-wing organizations and individuals.

This resulted in the installation as Prime Minister of former Supreme Court (*Dika*) Justice, Thanin Kraivichien. His repressive and authoritarian regime was followed in October, 1977 by that of Army General Kriangsak Chomanand whose moderate government persisted until February, 1980. A broadly based political coalition was then formed by the commander-in-chief of the Thai Army, General Prem Tinsulanond. His government was based upon the collaboration of two major political parties, the Democrat Party and the Social Action Party, and won widespread public acclaim for its even-handed policies and by the appointment of experts in a variety of fields of endeavor.   On December 22, 1978, a new, liberal Constitution was promulgated and it remained in force until 1991. Prem succeeded himself as Prime Minister five times until 1988,[14] when Chatichai Choonhavan took the helm.

The 1978 Constitution was abrogated with a bloodless coup against the elected government of Prime Minister Chatichai Choonhavan on 23 February, 1991, with charges of corruption and disrespect for the military in the air. The coup was led by Arny General Sunthorn Kongsompong, acting for the so-called National Peacekeeping Council(NPKC), comprised mostly of high-ranking military officers. Upon seizing power, the NPKC declared martial law and abolished the sitting Cabinet and Parliament, with the approval of King Bhumibol Adulyadej.   Anand Panyarachun[58], the much respected former Permanent Secretary of the Ministry of Foreign Affairs, was chosen Interim Prime Minister; he in turn selected a 33-member Interim Cabinet of generally well-regarded civilians, civil servants, and military persons.   On March 1 the NPKC issued an Interim Constitution ("Constitution for the Administration of the Kingdom, B.E. 2534 (1991);" Appendix 5) which gives it much say in government until the new "Permanent Constitution" is promulgated, Probably in late 1991; elections are expected not long after.   The Interim Cabinet selected an Interim National Legislative Assembly in which 182 of 292 members are of the Armed Forces, as well as a nineteen-member Constitution-Drafting Committee.[15]

Institutions of Government

The Constitution of 1978,[16] promulgated on December 22 of that year, is a wide-ranging document containing, as Chapter III, twenty-four sections dealing with the "Rights and Liberties of the Thai People" and, as Chapter IV, seven sections regarding the "Duties of the Thai People."   In addition, Chapter V of the 1978 Constitution includes "Directive Principles of State Policies."   This section tends to reinforce the rights of the Thai people through affirmation of policies which are to serve as guidelines for Thai governments. Although the remainder of this chapter deals primarily with constitutional protections of individual rights and freedoms, a few brief comments about the Thai governmental structure under the 1978 Constitution may be helpful to the general reader.

The *King* is head of state and head of the armed forces (Sections 2 and 8). The sovereign power vested in the King is said to derive from the Thai people. The King exercises legislative power through the National Assembly, executive power through the Council of Ministers, and judicial power through the Courts (Section 3). The King is advised by the Privy Council, whose members and President are appointed by the King.

The *National Assembly* is a bicameral legislature. The Senate is appointed by the King, upon recommendation by the Prime Minister. The 268 members of the Senate may not belong to any political party. The House of Representatives consists of 347 members, belonging to Thailand's numerous political parties, and elected directly by the Thai people.

The *Prime Minister* is appointed by the King with the advice of the National Assembly. With the advice of the Prime Minister, the King also appoints the 44-member Council of Ministers. Recent Prime Ministers, from Kriangsak Chomanan to Prem Tinsulanond to Chatichai Choonhavan have had military backgrounds or careers, as have a substantial minority of the members of the Council of Ministers. Indeed, political coalition building in Thailand since 1977 has involved a delicate balancing of interests among contending political parties and military factions.

The *Court System* of Thailand is composed of a three-level judiciary administered by the Ministry of Justice. All judges are appointed by the King upon recommendation of the Judicial Service Commission, a twelve-member group consisting primarily of high-ranking judges and judicial retirees. The Supreme Court (*Sarn Dika*) is a court of final appeal in all civil and criminal matters and in labor, juvenile, and bankruptcy cases. The Court of Appeals (*Sarn Uthorn*) is an intermediate level court, which hears cases appealed from all courts of first instance except the Central Labor Court (whose decisions can be taken directly to the Supreme Court for review). The Courts of First Instance in the Bangkok metropolitan area include: the Civil and Criminal Courts, the Central Juvenile Court, the Central Labor Court, the Bangkok Magistrates' Courts, the Thonburi Civil, Criminal and Magistrates' Courts, and the Minburi Provincial Court. Outside the Bangkok metropolitan area, the Courts of First Instance in the provinces include: 89 Provincial Courts, 17 Magistrates' Courts, and 5 Juvenile Courts.[17]

The Human Rights and Liberties of the Thai People

To a limited degree, the Thai people enjoyed a number of human and civil rights during the era of the absolute monarchy. Properly speaking, these "rights" were privileges instituted, in the main, by benevolent monarchs. These rulers were acting in accordance with the sacred law, the *Thammasattham*, which was derived from the Hindu law restated by Mons legal scholars and then augmented by King-made decisions, the *Rajasattham*.

While these rights prevailed for long periods of time and, generally survived the change from the absolute to the constitutional monarchy, this was not because the people were entitled to them, but rather because of the will of the monarch; they thus lacked constitutional guarantees and permanence. It has been said, for example, that after the reign of the forward-looking and benevolent King Chulalongkorn, the succeeding Kings, Rama VI and Rama VII "made no attempt to nullify the body of law which King Chulalongkorn had created *but* ... they both failed to pursue the logic of the reforms which had been created, to continue the developmental process which their predecessor had set in motion...."[18] The author cites as an example of the dissatisfaction of the leaders of the 1932 revolutionary movement, the special status accorded the Royal Princes under King Prajadhipok. They were regarded as being in a special class above the laws and authority of the judiciary, which status allowed the Princes to escape any legal sanction for their misconduct or impropriety other than as approved by the King.

It may be said that it was the King's uncaring disregard for the growing political decisiveness of the leaders of the people which finally led, in 1932, to the replacement of the absolute monarchy with the constitutional kingship. It is ironical, perhaps, that the Law of Royal Succession, which was one of the causes given for the replacement of the absolute monarchy, was later confirmed (but subject to Assembly approval) and expanded to include female succession in succeeding constitutions.

In contrast to the freedoms and liberties enjoyed by the Thai people during some seven hundred years of absolute monarchy, the Rights of the People given in Chapter II of the Constitution of the Kingdom of Siam B.E. 2475 (amended to "Thailand" in 1939),[19] were meager, indeed. Four sections proclaimed both the "Rights and Duties of the Thai People." The first of these sections simply declared that subject to provisions of the Constitution, all persons are equal before the law and any titles acquired in any way whatsoever do not entitle the holder to any legal privilege.

The following two sections guaranteed religious freedom so long as the religious activities did not contravene the civic duties of a citizen or go against public order or public morals. The Constitution provided that every person has, within the law, rights to liberty, to have property, to free speech, writing, and publication, to education and to participate in public meetings, associations and to choose one's vocation. The last section outlines the duties and responsibilities of Thai persons.

The constitutional rights of the Thai people were expanded by the 1946 (B.E. 2489) Constitution of the Kingdom of Thailand, promulgated on May 10, by the addition of a section which proclaimed the right of a Thai person to submit petitions in accordance with the law.

The rights and liberties of the Thai people grew gradually until, with the enactment of the Constitution of the Kingdom of Thailand, B.E. 2521 (1978),[20] they were outlined in twenty-four sections while the duties of the people were given in a separate Chapter consisting of seven sections. This Constitution remained in continuous force until 1991, and was the longest-lasting of Thailand's "Permanent" Constitutions.[21]

The 1978 Constitution is remarkable in that, under Chapter I headed General Provisions, it proclaims that "The Thai people, irrespective of their birth or religion, shall enjoy equal protection under the Constitution," while under the heading of Rights and Liberties of the Thai People, the Constitution states that "All persons are equal before the law and shall enjoy equal protection under the law." This is virtually a double affirmation of the equality for which the Thai people are still striving.

As stated above, a number of the rights and privileges enjoyed by the Thai people now, like those of the U.S. Constitution's Bill of Rights, are guaranteed by the Constitution. However, many such rights have their roots and beginnings in the days of the early absolute monarchs. For example, the right to petition, the abolition of slavery (as unlawful forced labor), the right to a fair and speedy trial under existing laws, the right to official legal aid for the poor, and the right to be protected against the acts of corrupt public officials are some of the rights enjoyed by the Thai people before the advent of the constitutional monarchy in 1932.

The Right to Petition

While this right was not included in the 1932 Interim Constitution or the 1932 "permanent" Constitution, it did appear in the 1946 document and this right has been included in all subsequent Constitutions. Section 42, Chapter III of the Constitution of the Kingdom of Thailand, 1978, states that "Every person shall have a right to present a petition upon the conditions and in the manner provided by law...."[22]

However, the earliest reference to the right to petition is shown in the so-called Sukhothai Stone Inscription thought to have been authorized by the venerated King Ramkhamhaeng in 1292, a segment of which states:

> He has hung a bell in the opening of the gate over there: if any commoner in the land has a grievance which sickens his belly and grips his heart, and which he wants to make known to his ruler and lord, it is easy; he goes and strikes the bell which the King has hung there: King Ramkhamhaeng, the ruler of the Kingdom, hears the call; he goes and questions the man, examines the case, and decides it justly for him. So the people of this ... *muang* of Sukhothai praise him....[23]

The practice of "ringing the bell" or, eventually, hitting a drum, was continued more or less regularly throughout the centuries of the Sukhothai and the succeeding Ayudhaya dynasties and the practice was continued into the present Chakri Dynasty reign of King Rama III. The next King, Rama IV or Mongkut, felt that this practice was not effective and he instituted the practice of holding weekly meetings to hear complaints or petitions in person.

King Rama V's (Chulalongkorn's) legal and judicial reforms during the period from 1892 to 1908, brought access to redress of grievances through the court system within reach of all Thai citizens. However, as late as 1884, direct access to the King was still granted, as may be discerned from a proclamation which set forth the proper manner in which to form queues at the palace door on designated days to present petitions to the King.

The Abolition of Slavery and Forced Labor

This section of the Constitution views Slavery and Forced Labor as being severely restrictive forms of an individual's freedom of choice in life. The first state of being is regarded as being more severe than the other.

Slavery was long practiced in Thailand and was finally abolished completely by an act of the absolute King Rama VI, Vajiralongkorn, in 1912 which was not subject to any parliamentary decision of the constitutional era. Forced labor, on the other hand, was allowed on the books far along into the twentieth century. The Constitution of Thailand, B.E. 2521 (1978), states in Chapter III, Section 31:

> Forced Labour shall not be imposed except by virtue of law specifically enacted for the purpose of averting imminent public calamity or by virtue of the law which provides for its imposition during that time when the country is in a state of armed conflict or war or when a state of emergency or martial law is declared....

This specification limits severely the danger of forced labor within reasonable legal parameters.

The ending of slavery was a gradual matter beginning in 1874 when King Chulalongkorn decreed that children of slaves could be redeemed to become free and, at any rate, would become free at the age of twenty-one. However, King Rama IV, Mongkut, had issued edicts earlier aimed at easing the lot of slaves and serfs.   After his accession to the throne in 1868, King Chulalongkorn, had that year, B.E. 2411, proclaimed the year of freedom of slavery. At the time of King Chulalongkorn, slaves could assert most of the legal rights of free people. They often chose to sell their independence for various reasons and the terms of those contracts often allowed them to redeem their freedom upon repayment of the original purchase price. King Chulalongkorn had observed how difficult the abrupt abolition of slavery had been in the United States and in Imperial Russia, and may have been attempting to avoid such turmoil in Thailand. For that reason, the process of emancipation of slaves extended over some forty years, into the reign of King Vajiralongkorn, in 1912. King Chulalongkorn asserted as reasons for abolition that as a group, slaves paid far less taxes, got free upkeep from their masters, and held no jobs readily helping the progress of the country. By 1905, King Chulalongkorn decreed that no one would be allowed to sell himself into slavery, that redemption could be made by slaves at less cost than hitherto, and that all children of slaves in non-Muslim areas were to become free.

As noted above, forced labor is dealt with in Section 31 of Chapter III of the 1978 Constitution: forced labor shall not be imposed except by virtue of law enacted to avert some public calamity or to impose forced labor during armed conflict or war or when a state of emergency or martial law is declared.

The corollary to slavery, forced labor, was long used in Thailand during the absolute monarchy. King Chulalongkorn instituted severe restrictions on this practice around the turn of the century by replacing this with a more equitable tax system and by beginning a system of general military service. Neither the institution of the taxation nor the general military draft covered all the people of Thailand, as forced (*corvee*) labor was still used selectively to improve public works, roads and water transportation avenues, as well as to assist authorities in apprehending criminals at large, among other tasks. In the case of military service, all men between eighteen and forty years of age were included in the draft for active service and two years of reserve duty. However, certain categories of men were exempt from the draft, including monks, members of hill tribes, college students, government officials and, curiously, Chinese immigrants and their relations. Exemptions were also made for farmers and people who paid a certain amount of tax, as well as for members of the royalty who were to be commissioned officers in the armed forces.

The elimination of general forced labor and the institution of the general draft essentially brought to the fore a new legal concept--service for the general good of the country for which a certain stipend was to be paid. It brought into being, before the institution of the constitutional monarchy, a new equality among all classes of Thai people relating to obligations owed by the citizen to ensure the well-being of all.

Equal Treatment Before the Law

The 1978 Constitution, like the constitutions before it, specified that all people are equal before the law. However, the 1932 Interim Constitution did not mention this while the Permanent Constitution of that year stated that, subject to the provisions of the Constitution, all persons were equal before the law. The 1946 Constitution was unequivocal in its expression that all persons are equal before the law, and so on. Section 23 of the Chapter on the Rights and Liberties of the Thai People of the 1978 Constitution states that "All persons are equal before the law and shall enjoy equal protection under the law...."

However, long before the constitutional monarchy was instituted, Thai law proclaimed that, with some exceptions, such as for members of royalty who were subject to the Palace Law and for slaves, all Thai people were to be treated equally before the law (albeit within the parameters of an absolute monarchy). David Engels comments on King Chulalongkorn's announcement through his Minister of Justice on January 14, 1906, concerning the supervision of the new military draft:

Apparently the private citizen had gained an enforceable right to fair treatment and to due process in his dealings with at least one administrative agency. Not only were his obligations to the government made less oppressive and distributed more fairly among the population as a whole, but the entire administrative procedure was now described by statute and reviewable in the Courts of the Ministry of Justice.... The demands of the state were to be reasonable and necessary, they were to be distributed in the form of obligations owed equally by nearly all citizens, and they were to be administered with fairness according to detailed rules which the Thai judiciary was empowered to review and enforce....[24]

Freedom of Religion

This freedom has been an integral aspect of every constitution promulgated in Thailand except for the 1932 Interim Constitution. In addition, in the sections dealing with His Majesty the King, every constitution except the above-mentioned 1932 Interim Constitution, proclaims that "The King is a Buddhist and Upholder of Religions." That is, a supporter not just of *a* religion, the Buddhist religion, but of *all* religions extant in Thailand under law.

Section 25, Chapter III of the 1978 Constitution proclaims:

Every person shall enjoy full liberty to profess a religion, a religious sect or creed, and to exercise a form of worship in accordance with his belief, provided that it is not contrary to his civic duties or to public order and good morals.

In exercising the liberty referred to in paragraph one, every person is protected from any act of the State, which is derogatory to his rights or detrimental to his due benefits, on the ground of professing a religion, a religious sect or creed, or of exercising a form of worship in accordance with his belief different from that of others....

However, it is an historical truism that freedom of religious belief has been granted to Thais and foreigners at least since the sixteenth century. Already in 1662, there were French and Portuguese missionaries in Ayudhaya and King Louis XIV of France, was moved, in 1673, to write a letter of thanks to King Narai (1656-88) for the latter's good treatment of French missionaries. During the reign of King Rama II, it was said that there were about 800 Thai Christians in Bangkok, most of Portuguese ancestry. King Rama II also gave complete tolerance to all religions and protected the Christian priests and churches as much as he did those of Islam.[25] The first Protestant missionaries came to Thailand in 1828 during the reign of King

Rama III; American missionaries began continual residence in Thailand in 1833. It was said that their work was almost or altogether fruitless as they baptized mostly their servants, many of whom were not Thai. The Catholics returned to Thailand in 1830 and had a community of a bishop, eight priests and some nuns. In 1835, American missionaries, led by Dr. D.B. Bradley, set up the first printing press in Thailand using Thai alphabet type.

King Mongkut, Rama IV, stated in an edict: "No just ruler restricts the freedom of his people in the choice of their religious belief by which each man hopes to find strength and salvation in his last hour, as well as in the future beyond.... There are many precepts common to all religions...."[26]

It is well known among Thais that both King Mongkut and his son, King Chulalongkorn, Rama V, helped a number of Christian churches during their reigns with monetary and other support. The present location of the Anglican "Christ Church" in Bangkok was a gift of land by the latter King.

Freedom of Speech

The Permanent Constitution of 1932 proclaimed in Chapter II, Section 14, that among other enumerated liberties, and "Subject to the provisions of law, every person shall enjoy full liberty of ... speech...." This freedom was reiterated in the 1946 Constitution and expanded upon in the 1978 basic law. In the latter Constitution in Chapter III, Section 34 provides:

Every person shall enjoy the liberty of speech, writing, printing and publication.

The restriction on such liberty shall not be imposed except by virtue of law specifically enacted for the purpose of maintaining the security of the State or safeguarding the liberties, dignity or reputation of other persons or maintaining public order or good morals or preventing deterioration of the mind or health of the public.

The press owner shall be a Thai national subject to the conditions prescribed by law.

No grant of money or other properties shall be made by the State as subsidy to a private newspaper....

Carefully circumscribed rules relating to freedom of speech existed prior to the constitutional monarchy. King Mongkut, Rama IV, regarded speech criticizing the government of the Thai people as one of the lesser evils. He maintained that criticisms came under two categories: either they are true and there is no reason to voice them, or false and everyone might know or soon would know that they were untrue and therefore unnecessary. If the speaker knows his points are true, then as a good citizen, he should bring the matter before a court, or even before the King himself, to effect correction.

During the time of King Chulalongkorn, about 1874, a Council of State and a Privy Council were set up at the direction of the King. Among the procedures to be followed was a free and equal discussion of legislative matters about to become law. This freedom of discussion (speech) was not, of course, extended to the common people, but carefully circumscribed by dicta laid down by the King.

This restriction on people's ability to speak freely was more carefully stated in an 1899 Royal Ordinance on defamation.[27] The Ordinance explained that while it was good that private citizens gained more freedom to air their views on many subjects, as this permitted honest, well-intentioned expressions of feeling, it was also bad since it gave opportunity for dishonest undertakings and attempts to hinder the progress of the country. For those reasons a new law was to be promulgated, i.e., on defamation.

In fact, there were very specific limits put upon free speech. For example, people were not allowed freely to criticize judges sitting in judgment in a case; this restriction was incorporated in the Chulalongkorn-inspired Civil Procedure Code of 1908.

As mentioned above, restrictions against defamation were incorporated in the Royal Ordinance of 1899. For example, speech injurious to Thailand's relations with foreign countries was forbidden. Such could be punished even if the allegations stated or published were true, according to the 1908 Criminal Code. In addition, criticism of the Thai King, the Royal House or government were forbidden, as such tended to create distrust in the monarch, the monarchy, and/or the existing government. Furthermore, speech tending to change the form of government by force, or seeking to create animosity among the Thai people was also prohibited.

In sum, freedom of speech was considered important by Kings of Thailand before the change to constitutional monarchy took place; King Chulalongkorn desired thereby to encourage Thai citizens to participate, within limits, in the reformation of the Thai nation.

Freedom of Education

Thai constitutions, beginning with the 1932 (permanent) Constitution specified in Chapter II, Section 14 that, subject to provisions of law, every person shall enjoy full liberty of education, as one of ten citizen entitlements. This general provision gradually became more and more refined in succeeding constitutions until, in the 1978 Constitution, a Thai citizen's right to education is given in three separate Chapters. Chapter III, Section 35, states:

> Every person shall enjoy the liberty of education, provided that such education is not contrary to his civic duties under the constitution, and to the law relating to compulsory education and the law relating to the organization of educational establishment....

Chapter IV, Section 52, on the Duties of the Thai People, specifies that every person has the duty to receive an education and training under the conditions and in the manner provided by law. Finally, in Chapter V, Section 60, on the Directive Principles of State Policy, the Constitution requires that the State should promote and support education and professional training to suit the needs of the country; that the State has the exclusive duty to organize and supervise and control the educational establishment; that the State should provide support to indigent persons for their education and occupational training while, generally, compulsory education in the educational centers of the State should be free of charge; and finally, that the State should allow higher educational establishments to manage their own affairs, within the limits provided by law.

As with many other rights and freedoms accorded the Thai people, the freedom of education has its roots in policies established during the absolute monarchy antedating the constitutional era beginning in 1932.

The creation of the first complete Thai alphabet by King Ramkamhaeng in about 1283 A.D. was the initial step in the slow development of a Thai educational system, through the eras of the Sukhothai, Ayudhya and Chakri dynasties. With few changes, this alphabet continues in use today with forty-four consonants, thirty vowels and five tonal signs.[284]

Early education was given mainly to the children of the royal and princely courts. Later, Buddhist monks taught in various temple (*wat*) schools. For example, during his early life, the later King Rama II, Issarasunthorn, was educated at a *wat* school in Thonburi. The teaching of the monks gradually spread to the vicinity of *wats* all over the country.

During his 1871 trip through South East Asia as an eighteen-year-old, Chulalongkorn, visited both Singapore (under British rule) and the Dutch East Indies (under the rule of Holland). His Majesty came back to Thailand impressed by the works done by the European rulers and convinced that education was a major key to progress in a nation. Among his early projects was to establish a model school for Princes and sons of ranking nobles. The school was named Rajkumar College, and the King's brothers, half brothers and later his own sons were sent to classes often taught by foreign teachers brought into Thailand. English was among the key subjects being taught. King Chulalongkorn was so pleased by the success of the Rajkumar College that he also established a school for sons of junior officials and merchants, Rose Garden School. This school became the forerunner of many government secondary schools.[29

When King Chulalongkorn opened the Rose Garden (*Suan Kularb*) School, he declared: "All children from my own to the poorest should have an equal chance of education."[30] He saw in education an opportunity to escape the fate of many neighboring countries, which had become vassals of European powers. Prince Damrong, the half brother of King Chulalongkorn, became Minister of Education (later of Interior) late in the century. He began to establish a modern educational scheme by adapting the old *wat* school buildings to use for primary education purposes. At the time, there was a lack of teachers, so a teachers' college was established. Over time, new state primary schools, Christian religious missionary schools, and Thai private schools were established, greatly encouraged by J.G.D. Campbell, a British subject loaned to Thailand by the British government for two years (1899-1901).

However, the law requiring free and compulsory primary education was promulgated by King Rama VI, Vajiralongkorn, following World War I and prior to the establishment of constitutional monarchy in 1932.

Suits Against Government Officials

Section 43, Chapter III of the 1978 Constitution provides: "The right of a person to sue a Government agency which is a juristic person as liable for an act done by an official is protected...." This section is reinforced specifically by two additional sections: Section 58, Chapter V enjoins the State to "organize the systems of official service and other State affairs for the achievement of efficiency and should take every measure to prevent and suppress corruption...." Section 57 requires the State to enforce the law to assure the people of safety in life, in their persons and property, and to ensure their peace.

As with many of the rights constitutionally protected and enjoyed by the Thai people, the right to seek and obtain redress from acts by government officials evolved from edicts or regulations of the era of absolute monarchy in Thailand. The Three Seals Law Code, promulgated between 1805 and 1808 by King Rama I, the founder of the current Chakri dynasty, and named *Phra Buddha Yod Fa* posthumously, included a number of laws concerning private individuals in relation to officials and regarding the behavior of officials. The aim was to inculcate a high moral standard especially for courtiers and officials. In the Law of Offenses against the Government of the Three Seals Code, it was a punishable offense for any official to threaten to injure or to persecute the people, or to behave in a corrupt manner or dishonestly. In like manner, in the Law of Offenses against the People, officials were required to accept all suits brought to them by the people, and to refrain from punishing or persecuting those who brought complaints; it further stated that no person should be punished or imprisoned without just cause.[31]

During the time that King Chulalongkorn worked to reform Thai government practices and organs, restraints were placed upon the rights of people to sue government officials for malfeasance in office. In 1901, an edict forbade the courts to accept criminal suits brought by citizens against government officials unless some preconditions were fulfilled; for example, enough evidence had to be given the court before any trial to convince the court of the official's guilt; only then would a summons be sent to the official in question. Moreover, only if the official ignored the summons was an arrest warrant to be issued. In 1903, an order by the Minister of Justice stipulated that if an official was appointed by His Majesty, The King, the latter would have to give His permission to institute an action against His appointee. However, no such permission had to be obtained to take action against officials appointed by others.

Regardless of the restraints on rights noted above, it "is significant at least in the development of legal theory, however, that the behavior of government officials was increasingly subjected to rules and restrictions imposed upon them by law and enforceable against them by the public...."[32] While certain limitations on suits against government officials for official misconduct, such as misappropriation of government funds, acceptance of bribes and misuse of official position to injure others, were established, it is certain that government officials during the reign of King Chulalongkorn became subject to greater and more detailed regulation than had previously been the case. As David Engel says, "In the newly restructured judiciary, private citizens could more readily enforce these regulations when official misconduct occurred...."[33]

Conclusions

The rights and liberties of the Thai people established in the 1978 Constitution, some of which are discussed above, are legacies from the past, both from prior constitutions, beginning with the 1932 (permanent) document, and from edicts and laws and regulations having their roots in the country's absolute monarchy period.

Some of the basic constitutional rights accorded the Thai people, such as the political right to vote and to stand for election, have existed since the first Permanent Constitution. Both men and women have enjoyed these rights under general conditions common to all.

Women are not only able to be elected to Parliament, but also to ascend to the highest political offices of the land (given sufficient political support). The country may accept a Princess as the Reigning Queen of Thailand under Chapter II, Section 20, which states: "In the absence of a Prince, the National Assembly may approve the succession of a Princess...."

The 1978 Constitution affirmed that every person shall enjoy equal liberty of person, and that the accused in a criminal case shall be presumed innocent until convicted by a final judgment of an offense; until then such a person must not be treated as a convict. The Constitution also guaranteed that indigent accused persons can seek and obtain legal aid support from the State.

In addition, the Constitution ensured a person the rights to liberty of dwelling, to protection against unlawful entry, to own property, and to assemble peacefully without arms, in accordance with provisions of law.

The development of many elements contained in the 1978 Thai Constitution had roots in the past history of the Thai absolute monarchy. Despite terrible foreign attacks and invasions and bloody internal conflicts among those seeking control of the reins of power, over the centuries since the beginning of a coherent Thai (Siamese) Kingdom, the Thais have managed to evolve a generally good and benevolent governmental system ultimately aiming to serve the interests of the people.

The surprising aspect of this development is that the people at large, in the past, had little if any hand in shaping the destiny of the country. It was almost entirely the ideas and work of benevolent, albeit despotic, rulers. Their often far-reaching policies: a) produced a largely coherent and like-minded citizenry; b) developed ways and methods of promoting freedom of action to the benefit and progress of the nation at large and regulated by those elements of the people who, under the ruler, held sway; c) through abundant harvests of foodstuffs, developed a lively trade with foreign countries, near and far; d) kept the country largely free and independent over long periods of time; and e) persistently avoided the scourge and bane of most Asian principalities: the takeover of the nation by a colonial power, in the name of "progress" or "civilization."

NOTES

1. Please note that, throughout this Chapter, the name "Thailand" is used rather than the ancient "Siam" except where a special reason makes use of Siam preferable.

2. Justice T. Kraivixien, P.C., "Administration of Justice in Thailand," *The Legal System*, Bangkok, Thai Bar Association, 1969.

3. After the seals of the Ministry of Defense, the Ministry of Interior and the Ministry of Finance, which were depicted on the front page.

4. David M. Engle, *Law and Kingship in Thailand during the Reign of King Chulalongkorn*, Ann Arbor, University of Michigan Papers on South and Southeast Asia, No. 9, 1975.

5. *Id.*

6. *Id.*

7. H.R.H. Prince Chula Chakrabongse, *Lords of Life: A History of the Kings of Thailand*, Bangkok: DD Books, 3d ed. 1982.

8. *Id.*

9. *Id.* Chula Chakrabongse only about 70 plotters.

10. *Id.* at 312.

11. *See* Appendix 1, Interim Constitution of Siam Act , B.E. 2475 (June, 1932). "B.E." refers to the Buddhist Era.

12. *See* Appendix 2, Constitution of the Kingdom of Thailand Act, B.E. 2475 (December, 1932).

13. *Editor's Note*. For an annual account of major developments in Thailand, see February issues of *Asian Survey*, 1970 on.

14. *Editor's Note*: Despite two abortive military coup attempts in 1981 and 1985, General Prem's tenure as Prime Minister was for the most part a time of stability and prosperity. In 1987, however, the coalition government showed increasing signs of internal tension, which began to focus on a controversial legislative proposal dealing with copyright protection (thoughtby some to reflect pressure by the United States). In April, 1988, sixteen members of the Democrat Party resigned from the Council of Ministersand Prem promptly called for gereral elections in order to forestall a possible vote of no confidence.

In July 1988 elections resulted in a continuation of the four-party coalition that had supported the previous government (consisting of the Chart Thai, Social Action, Democrat and Rassadorn parties) with the addition of a fifth party (United Democracy). Prem unexpectedly declined an offer to lead this coalition, however, urging the party leaders to select as Prime Minister someone who, unlike himself, had stood for election. The coalition leaders subsequently agreed upon Chatichai Choon havan of the Chart Thai party, which had led in the results of the general elections by winning 87 seats. Chatichai assumed the office of Prime Minister in August 1988.

15. The ostensible reason for the coup was growing dissatisfaction among high-ranking military officers with the nation's progress, and with alleged lack of honesty among politicians and businessmen, who were accused of corruption, vote-buying practices, and acting to denigrate the good name of the Thai Armed Forces. Besides tasks noted in the text, the Interim Cabinet was charged with seeking out corruption in government and locating ill-gotten funds. The Speaker of the Interim Assembly is Dr. Ukrit Mongkolnavin, a former Speaker of the Assembly under the 1978 Constitution. The Constitution-Drafting Committee is headed by Deputy Prime Minister Meechai Ruchupan and assisted by draftsmen from the Office of the Juridical Council. In May, 1991, the Assembly Speaker speculated that elections might be held between the end of 1991 and April, 1992. [*Editor's Note*: For background, see Scott R. Christensen, "Thailand in 1990: Political Tangles, "*Asian Survey*, Feb., 1991, 196-204; and Chai-Anan Samudavanija, "Thailand: A Stable Semi-Democracy," in L. Diamond *et al.*,eds., *Democracy in Developing Countries: Asia*, Boulder, Lynne Rienner, 1989, 305.]

16. *See* Appendix 4, the Constitution of the Kingdom of Thailand, B.E. 2521 (December 22, 1978), Chapters II, III, IV and V.

17. [Editor's Note: Despite two abortive military coup attempts in 1981 and 1985, General Prem's tenure as Prime Minister was for the most part a time of stability and prosperity. In 1987, however, the coalition government showed increasing signs of internal tension, which began to focus on a controversial legislative proposal dealing with copyright protection (thought by some to reflect pressure by the United States). In April, 1988, sixteen members of the Democrat Party resigned from the Council of Ministers and Prem promptly called for general elections in order to forestall a possible vote of no confidence.

The July 1988 elections resulted in a continuation of the four-party coalition that had supported the previous government

See generally Marut Bunnag and Preben A.F. Aakesson, "The Legal System of Thailand," in Kenneth R. Redden, ed., *Modern Legal Systems Encyclopedia, Supplement One* (1987).

18. D.M. Engel, *Law and Kingship*, 121.

19. *See* Appendix 3, an English translation of the Constitution of the Kingdom of Thailand, B.E. 2489 (1946) (as amended, B.E. 2482 (1939)), 4-5.

20. Appendix 4.

21. The 1978 Constitution was in force until 23rd of February, 1991 and was undoubtedly the longest-lasting Constitution since the advent of the constitutional monarchy, in 1932.

22. Appendix 4.

23. Griswold and Prasert, "The Inscription of King Rama Gamben of Sukhodaya (1292 A.D.): Epigraphic and Historical Studies, No. 9," *J.S.S.* 59, pt. 2 (July 1971), 205-06.

24. D.M. Engel, *Law and Kingship*, 99, 100.

25. Chula Chakrabongse, *Lords of Life*, 132.

26. *Id.* at 152.
27. D.M. Engel, *Law and Kingship*, at 111 and 112.
28. H.R.H. Prince Chula Chakrabongse, *Lords of Life*, at 25.
29. *Id.*, at 224.
30. *Id.*
31. D.M. Engel, *Law and Kingship*, at 100.
32. *Id.*, 101.
33. *Id.*, 102.

APPENDIX I

INTERIM CONSTITUTION OF SIAM ACT*

PHRABAT SOMDET PHRA PARAMINTHARAMAHA PRAJADHIPOK

PHRA POK KLAO CHAO YU HUA

is graciously pleased to proclaim that:

Whereas His Majesty has been requested by the People's Revolutionary Party to lower Himself to be under the Constitution of Siam so that the country will be more developing; and Whereas His Majesty accepts the request of the People's Revolutionary Party;

Be it, therefore, enacted by the King, as follows:

CHAPTER I
GENERAL PROVISIONS

Section 1. The sovereign power belongs to the people.

Section 2. The following persons and groups of persons shall exercise the power on behalf of the people as may be hereafter provided in the Constitution:

1. the King;
2. the Assembly of the People's Representatives;
3. the People's Commission;
4. the Court.

CHAPTER II
The King

Section 3. The King is head of the State. Acts, judgments of the Courts, and other matters as may be specifically provided by the law must be made in the name of the King.

Section 4. The King of the State is Phrabat Somdet Phra Paramintharamaha Prajadhipok Phra Pok Klao Chao Yu Hua. The Succession to the Throne shall be in accordance with the Palace Law on Succession B.E. 2467 and with the approval of the Assembly of the People's Representatives.

Section 5. If the King is unable to perform His functions on account of temporary necessity, or is absent from the Kingdom, the People's Commission shall exercise the rights on His behalf.

Section 6. No criminal action shall be brought against the King. It is the duty of the Assembly of the People's Representatives to make a decision thereon.

Section 7. Any action carried out by the King must be countersigned by a People's Commissioner with the approval of the People's Commission, otherwise it is unenforceable.

CHAPTER III
The Assembly of the People's Representatives
Part 1
Power and Duties

Section 8. The Assembly of the People's Representatives has the power to enact all Acts which shall come into force upon their proclamation made by the King.

If the King fails to cause the proclamation of an Act within seven days after the date of His receiving it from the Assembly, and gives the reason for refusing to sign it, He may return it to the Assembly for re-deliberation. If the Assembly resolves to reaffirm its former resolution with which the King does not agree, the Assembly has the power to promulgate such Act.

Section 9. The Assembly of the People's Representatives is vested with the power of control over the administration of the State and the power to remove any People's Commissioner or any Government official from office.

Part 2
The People's Representatives

Section 10. Membership of the Assembly of the People's Representatives shall be in compliance with the following periods:

First Period

As from the date of enforcement of this Constitution until the date the members in the second period assume office, the People's Revolutionary Party by the Military Council as its representative shall appoint seventy temporary members of the Assembly of the People's Representatives.

Second Period

Within six months or until the government organisation is well established, the Assembly is composed of two categories of members to perform any activity jointly:

Members of the first category, who are representatives to be elected by the people, one for each Changwat. A Changwat with more than 100,000 population shall elect an additional representative for every 100,000; any fraction thereof if amounting to one-half of 100,000 shall be counted as 100,000.

Members of the second category, who are members in the first period in such number as equal to the members of the first category. In case of the excessive number, they shall select the ones among themselves who will remain in their membership. In case of a shortage, the existing members shall select other persons to fill the vacancies.

Third Period

As one-half of the population throughout the Kingdom has completed the primary education, and not later than ten years after the date of enforcement of this Constitution, the members of the Assembly of the People's Representatives must all be the persons who are elected by the people, and there shall be no member of the second category any longer.

Section 11. A candidate for representative of the first category shall possess the following qualifications:

1. passing the political examination under such syllabus as may be established by the Assembly;
2. being twenty years of age;
3. not being an incompetent or quasi-incompetent person;
4. not being deprived, by a judgment of the Court, of the right to be a candidate;
5. being of Thai nationality under the law;
6. in respect of the candidate for representative of the first category in the second period, a prior approval of the members in the first period is required for the fact that he is above suspicion of bringing disorder.

Section 12. The election of members of the first and second categories shall be held under the following procedure:

1. people in a village elect the Village representatives who will vote at an election of Tambon representatives;
2. Village representatives elect the Tambon representatives;
3. Tambon representatives elect members of the Assembly of the People's Representatives.

The election of members in the third period shall be held under the law hereafter enacted which shall provide a direct election of members of the Assembly of the People's Representatives.

Section 13. Representatives of the first category shall hold office for a term of four years from the date of assuming office; provided that, when the third period has come, the representatives in the second period must forthwith vacate office as from the date the representatives in the third period assume office notwithstanding their unexpired term of four years.

If the office of a representative becomes vacant for any reason other than the expiration of term, the members shall select other persons to fill the vacancies;

provided that the new representative shall serve for the remainder of term of the outgoing person.

Section 14. A person, irrespective of sex, shall have the right to vote at the election of Village representatives if he possesses the following qualifications:

1. being twenty years of age;
2. not being an incompetent or quasi-incompetent person;
3. not being disenfranchised by a judgment of the Court;
4. being of Thai nationality under the law.

The qualification of Village representatives and Tambon representatives shall be in compliance with section 11.

Section 15. The finality of any election of representatives shall be by a majority of votes. In case of an equality of votes, the second election shall be held. In case of an equality of votes at the second election, a neutral man shall be appointed by the candidates to cast a deciding vote.

Section 16. Apart from the Expiration of term of office, a representative shall vacate office upon lacking any of qualifications under section 11, or death, or resolution of the Assembly removing him from office when the Assembly is of the opinion that he brings detriment to the Assembly.

Section 17. If a criminal charge is brought against any member of the Assembly of the People's Representatives, the Court must first obtain the permission of the Assembly before accdepting the charge.

---

*B.E. 2475 (1932). Published in the *Government Gazette*, Vol. 49, dated 27 June.

APPENDIX 2

CONSTITUTION OF THE KINGDOM OF THAILAND*

SOMDET PHRA PARAMINTHARAMAHA PRAJADHIPOK
MAHANTADEJA NADILOK RAMATHIBODI
PHRA POK KLAO CHAO PANDIN SIAM
General Provisions

Section 1. Thailand is a unified and indivisible Kingdom. The Thai people, irrespective of their birth or religion, shall enjoy equal protection under this Constitution.

Section 2. The sovereign power is derived from the Thai people. The King as Head of the State shall exercise such power under the provisions of this Constitution.

CHAPTER 1
THE KING

Section 3. The King shall be enthroned in a position of revered worship and shall not be violated.

Section 4. The King is a Buddhist and Upholder of religions.

Section 5. The King holds the position of Head of the Thai Armed Forces.

Section 6. The King shall exercise the legislative power by and with the advice and consent of the Assembly of the People's Representatives.

Section 7. The King shall exercise the executive power through the Council of Ministers.

Section 8. The King shall exercise the judicial power through the Courts established by law.

Section 9. The succession to the Throne shall be in accordance with the Palace Law on Succession B.E. 2467 and with the approval of the Assembly of the People's Representatives.

Section 10. Whenever the King is absent from the Kingdom or unable to perform His functions for whatever reason, He will appoint a Regent or a Council of Regency with the approval of the Assembly of the People's Representatives. In the case where the King does not make such appointment or is unable to do so, the Assembly of the People's Representatives shall proceed to make the appointment. Pending such appointment, the Council of Ministers shall temporarily compose the Council of Regency.

Section 11. Members of the Royal Family in the rank of Momchao or upwards whose titles are acquired by birth or bestowal shall not be subject to politics.

CHAPTER 11
RIGHTS AND DUTIES OF THE THAI PEOPLE

Section 12. Subject to the provisions of this Constitution, all persons are equal before the law. Titles acquired by birth, by bestowal or in any other way do not give rise to any privilege whatsoever.

Section 13. Every person shall enjoy full liberty to profess a religion or creed and to exercise a form of worship in accordance with his own belief; provided that it is not contrary to his civic duties and is not inconsistent with public order or public morals.

Section 14. Subject to the provisions of law, every person shall enjoy full liberty of his person, abode, property, speech, writing, publication, education, public meeting, association or vocation.

Section 15. Every person shall have the duty to respect the law, to defend the country and to render assistance to the official service by payment of taxes and in other ways under the conditions and in the manner provided by law.

---

*Published in the *Government Gazette*, Vol. 49, dated 10 December B.E. 2475 (1932). In the original text, the word was "Siam" but replaced by "Thailand" under the Constitution Amendment on the Changing of the Name of the Country, B.E. 2482 (1939).

CONSTITUTION OF THE KINGDOM OF THAILAND*

ANANDA MAHIDOL

Enacted on the 9th Day of May B.E. 2489 [1946];
Being the 13th Year of the Present Reign.

On Thursday the 9th of May in the Year of our Lord 2489 corresponding to the period of the Waxing Moon in the lunar month of Visaka in the Year of the Dog, His Majesty King Ananda Mahidol, appearing at the Ananta Smagom Throne Hall in the midst of the great concourse of members of the Royal Family, representatives of foreign countries, members of the Assembly of the People's Representatives, officials, civil and military, who attend, in order of their rank, on His Majesty, is graciously pleased to proclaim that His Majesty King Prajadipok, Phra Pok Klao, in granting the opportunity to His officials and people to take part and have a voice in leading Thailand to progress in the future, was graciously pleased to grant a Constitution for the administration of the country on the 27th Day of June B.E. 2475, as a temporary measure, so that the Assembly of the People's Representatives and the People's Committee might arrange for and proceed with the policy of administration suitable to the change. Thereafter, his Majesty was graciously pleased to direct the Assembly of the People's Representatives to deliberate and

draft the Constitution of the Kingdom of Thailand in order to make it the permanent basis of the mode of administration in the future. The Assembly of the People's Representatives therefore appointed a sub-committee to draft the Constitution.

When the sub-committee had successfully compiled the permanent Constitution for His Majesty, and submitted it to the Assembly of the People's Representatives which, after deliberation, passed a resolution and submitted it to His Majesty together with the recommendation. After thorough and careful consideration, His Majesty was pleased to have the Constitution of the Kingdom of Thailand enacted and promulgated as and from the 10th Day of December B.E. 2475.

GENERAL PROVISIONS

Section 1. Thailand is one Kingdom and is indivisible. The Thai people of whatever race or religion are all equally entitled to be under the protection of this Constitution.

Section 2. The sovereign power emanates from the Thai people. The King, who is the Head of the Nation, only exercises it in conformity with the provisions of this Constitution.

CHAPTER 1
THE KING

Section 3. The person of the King is sacred and inviolable.

Section 4. The King shall be a Buddhist and is the Upholder of Religions.

Section 5. The King is the Head of the Thai Armed Forces.

Section 6. The King exercises the legislative power through the Congress.

Section 7. The King exercises the executive power through the Council of Ministers.

Section 8. The King exercises the judicial power through the Courts.

Section 9. Subject to the approval of the Congress, succession to the Throne shall be in accordance with the Law on Succession, B.E. 2467.

Section 10. When the King intends to be absent from the Kingdom or, for any reason whatever, should be unable to carry out His functions, He shall appoint a Regent or a Council of Regency with the approval of the Congress. If the King does not make such appointment or is unable to do so, the Congress shall proceed to make the appointment. Pending such appointment, the three oldest members of the Senate shall compose the Council of Regency.

Section 11. In case the Throne becomes vacant and no Regent has been appointed according to section 10, the three oldest members of the Senate shall temporarily compose the Council of Regency.

CHAPTER 2
RIGHTS AND DUTIES OF THE THAI PEOPLE

Section 12. All persons are equal according to law. Titles acquired by birth, by bestowal or in any other way do not give rise to any privilege whatsoever.

Section 13. Every person is entirely free to profess any religion or creed and to exercise the form of worship in accordance with his own belief; provided that it is not contrary to the duties of a citizen and is not inconsistent with public order or public morals.

Section 14. Subject to the provisions of law, every person enjoys full liberty of the person, abode, property, speech, writing, publication, education, public meeting, association or vocation.

Section 15. Every person has the right to submit petitions under the conditions and in the manner prescribed by law.

Section 16. It is the duty of every person to respect the law, to defend the country and to assist the Government by the payment of taxes and in other ways under the conditions and in the manner prescribed by law.

APPENDIX 4

CONSTITUTION OF THE KINGDOM OF THAILAND
SOMDET PHRA PARAMINTHARAMAHA BHUMIBOL ADULYADEJ
SAYAMINTHARATHIRAT BOROMMANATTHABOPHIT

Enacted on the 22nd day of December B.E. 2521 [1978]
Being the 33rd Year of the Present Reign.

May there be virtue. Today is the eighth day of the waning moon in the first month of the year of Goat under the lunar calendar, being Friday, the twenty second day of December under the solar calendar, in the 2521st year of the Buddhist Era.

Phrabat Somdet Phra Paramintharamaha Bhumibol Adjulyadej Mahitalathibet Ramathibodi Chakkri Narubodin Sayamintharathirat Borommanatthabophit is graciously pleased to proclaim that He was advised by the National Legislative Council that since the grant of the Constitution of the Kingdom of Thailand B.E. 2475 by His Majesty King Prajadhipok Phra Pok Klao Chao Yu Hua, His Majesty's Uncle, there had been amendment to the Constitution and promulgation of new Constitutions on several occasions, and sometimes the changes of situation in the country had resulted in the promulgation of an Interim Constitution, pending the drafting of a permanent Constitution. All Constitutions and Interim Constitutions that had been promulgated were in unity with one another in adhering to the democratic regime of government with the King as Head of the State who should exercise the legislative power through the National Assembly, the executive power through the Council of Ministers, and the judicial power through the Courts. The essential differences between them laid in the forms of the National Assembly and in the relationship between the legislative and the executive powers, depending on the changing situation of the country for the time being. This revealed the faithful adherence of the Thai people to the democratic regime of government with the King as Head of the State, which was in accordance with the will of His Majesty's Uncle, King Prajadhipok Phra Pok Klao Chao Yu Hua, in granting the power to administer the State affairs to the Thai people. The adherence to the democratic regime of government with the King as Head of the State had been inherited until the present time. Even the Constitution for the Administration of the Kingdom B.E. 2520 had demonstrated such will and entrusted the task of drafting the Constitution to the National Legislative Council so that a general election should be held within the 2521st year of the Buddhist Era.

The National Legislative Council had appointed a Committee charged with the duty of drafting the Constitution. When the Constitution had been completely drafted, the National Legislative Council considered the Draft Constitution in three readings in accordance with the common will of the Thai people in upholding the independence and security of the Nation, preserving the religion to become everlasting, enthroning the King as Head of the State and in the hearts of the Thai people, adhering to the democratic regime of government with the King as Head of the State as the means of administering the State affairs, upholding and protecting the right and liberties of the Thai people, and uniting to secure justice, prosperity and happiness for all Thai people.

Having carefully determined and revised the Draft Constitution in the light of the situation of the country, the National Legislative Council passed a resolution approving the presentation of the Draft Constitution to the King for His Royal Signature to promulgate it as the Constitution of the Kingdom of Thailand.

Having thoroughly examined the Draft Constitution, the King deemed it expedient to grant His Royal assent in accordance with the resolution of the National Legislative Council.

Be it, therefore, commanded by the King that the Constitution of the Kingdom of Thailand be promulgated to replace, as from the date of its promulgation, the Interim Constitution for the Administration of the Kingdom B.E. 2520 promulgated on 9th November B.E. 2520.

May the Thai people unite in protecting the Constitution of the Kingdom of Thailand in order to maintain the democratic regime of government and the sovereign power of the Thai people in the province of the Kingdom, and to bring about happiness, prosperity and dignity to His Majesty's subjects according to the will of His Majesty in every respect.

Chapter I
General Provisions

Section 1. Thailand is a unified and indivisible Kingdom.

Section 2. Thailand adopts a democratic regime of government with the King as Head of the State.

Section 3. The sovereign power is derived from the Thai people. The King as Head of the State shall exercise such power through the National Assembly, the Council of Ministers and the Courts in accordance with the provision of this Constituiton.

Section 4. The Thai people, irrespective of their birth or religion, shall enjoy equal protection under this Constitution.

Section 5. The provision of any law, which is contrary to or inconsistent with this Constitution, shall be unenforceable.

The King

Section 6. The King shall be enthroned in a position of revered worship and shall not be violated.

No person shall expose the King to any sort of accusation or action.

Section 7. The King is a Buddhist and Upholder of religions.

Section 8. The King holds the position of Head of the Thai Armed Forces.

Section 9. The King has the prerogative power to create titles and confer decorations.

Section 10. The King selects and appoints qualified persons President of the Privy Council and not more than fourteen Privy Councillors to constitute the Privy Council.

The Privy Council has a duty to render such advices to the King on all matters pertaining to His functions as He may consult, and has other duties as provided in this Constitution.

Section 11. The selection and appointment as well as the removal of a Privy Councillor shall depend entirely upon the Royal prerogative.

The President of the National Assembly shall countersign the Royal Command appointing or removing the President of the Privy Council.

The President of the Privy Council shall countersign the Royal Command appointing or removing other Privy Councillors.

Section 12. A Privy Councillor shall not be a senator, member of the House of Representatives, government official holding a permanent position or receiving a salary, official of a State enterprise, or member or official of a political party, and must not manifest loyalty to any political party.

Section 13. Before taking office, a Privy Councillor must make a solemn declaration before the King in the following words:

"I (name of the declarer), do solemnly declare that I will be loyal to the King and will faithfully perform my duties in the interests of the country and of the people. I will also uphold and observe the Constitution of the Kingdom of Thailand in every respect."

Section 14. A Privy Councillor vacates his office upon death, resignation, or removal by a Royal Command.

Section 15. The appointment and the removal of officials of the Royal Household and of the Royal Chief Aide-de-Camp shall depend entirely upon the Royal prerogative.

Section 16. Whenever the King is absent from the Kingdom or unable to perform His functions for whatever reason, He will appoint a person Regent with the approval of the National Assembly, and the President of the National Assembly shall countersign the Royal Command.

Section 17. In the case where the King does not appoint a Regent under section 16, or in the case where the King is unable to appoint a Regent, the Privy Council shall submit the name of a person suitable to hold the office of Regent to the National Assembly for approval. Upon approval by the National Assembly, the President of the National Assembly shall make an announcement in the name of the King, of the appointment of such person as Regent.

Section 18. In the absence of the Regent under section 16 or section 17, the President of the Privy Council shall be Regent pro tempora.

In the case where the Regent appointed under section 16 or section 17 is unable to perform his duties, the President of the Privy Council shall temporarily act as Regent.

While being Regent under paragraph one or acting as Regent under paragraph two, the President of the Privy Council shall not perform his duties as President of the Privy Council. In such case, the Privy Council shall select a Privy Councillor to act temporarily as President of the Privy Council.

Section 19. Before taking office, the Regent appointed under section 16 or section 17 shall make a solemn declaration before the National Assembly in the following words:

"I (name of the declarer), do solemnly declare that I will be loyal to His Majesty King (name of King) and will faithfully perform my duties in the interests of the country and of the people. I will also uphold and observe the Constitution of the Kingdom of Thailand in every respect."

Section 20. The succession to the Throne shall be in accordance with the Palace Law on Succession B.E. 2467 and in accordance with the approval of the National Assembly. In the absence of a Prince, the National Assembly may approve the succession by a Princess.

The amendment of the Palace Law on Succession B.E. 2467 shall be made in the same manner as an amendment of the Constitution.

Section 21. In the case where the Throne becomes vacant, the Privy Council shall, in accordance with section 20, submit the name of the Heir to the Throne to the National Assembly for approval. Upon the approval of the National Assembly, the President of the National Assembly shall invite such Heir to ascend the Throne and proclaim him King.

Pending the proclamation of the name of the Heir to the Throne under paragraph one, the President of the Privy Council shall temporarily be Regent. In the case where the Throne becomes vacant while the Regent has been appointed under section 16 or section 17 or while the President of the Privy Council is acting as Regent under section 18 paragraph one, such Regent, as the case may be, shall continue to be Regent until the proclamation of the name of the Heir to the Throne.

In the case where the Regent who has been appointed and continues to be Regent under paragraph two is unable to perform his duties, the President of the Privy Council shall act temporarily as Regent.

Chapter III

Rights and Liberties of the Thai People

Section 22. All persons shall enjoy rights and liberties subject to the provisions of the Constitution.

Section 23. All persons are equal before the law and shall enjoy equal protection under the law.

Section 24. All persons shall enjoy political rights.

The exercise of political rights shall be in accordance with the provision of law.

Section 25. Every person shall enjoy full liberty to profess a religion, a religious sect or creed, and to exercise a form of worship in accordance with his belief; provided that it is not contrary to his civic duties or to public order or good morals.

In exercising the liberty referred to in paragraph one, every person is protected from any act of the State, which is derogatory to his rights or detrimental to his due benefits, on the ground of professing a religion, a religious sect or creed, or of exercising a form of worship in accordance with his belief different from that of others.

Section 26. No person shall be inflicted with a criminal punishment unless he has committed an act which the law in force at the time of commission provides it to be an offence and imposes a punishment therefor, and the punishment to be inflicted on such person shall not be heavier than that provided by the law in force at the time of commission.

Section 27. An alleged offender or an accused in a criminal case shall be presumed innocent.

Before the passing of a final judgment convicting a person of having committed an offence, such person shall not be treated as a convict.

Section 28. Every person shall enjoy the liberty of his person.

The arrest, detention or search of a person, irrespective of the circumstances, shall not be made except by virtue of law.

Section 29. In the case where the alleged offender or the accused is poor and unable to pay for his own advocate, that person is entitled to obtain legal aid from the State as provided by law.

Section 30. In the case where any person was inflicted with a criminal punishment by a final judgment, if it appears in the judgment of the court reopening the case thereafter that he did not commit the alleged offence, he shall be entitled to compensation and to recover any right he had lost by virtue of the results of the judgment upon the condition and in the manner provided by law.

Section 31. Forced labour shall not be imposed except by virtue of law specifically enacted for the purpose of averting imminent public calamity or by virtue of the law which provides for its imposition during the time when the country is in a state of armed conflict or war, or when a state of emergency or martial law is declared.

Section 32. Every person shall enjoy the liberty of dwelling.

Every person is protected for his peaceful habitation in and for possession of his dwelling. The entry into a dwelling without the consent of its possessor or the search thereof shall not be made except by virtue of law.

Section 33. The property right of a person is protected. The extent and restriction of such right shall be in accordance with the provision of law.

The succession is protected. The right of succession of a person shall be in accordance with the provision of law.

The expropriation of immovable property shall not be made except by virtue of law specifically enacted for the purpose of public utility, national defence, exploitation of national resources, town and country planning, agricultural or industrial development, land reform, or other public interests, and fair compensation shall be paid in due time to the owner thereof as well as to the person having the right thereof, who suffers loss by such expropriation, as to be specified by law.

The amount of compensation under paragraph three shall be assessed with due regard to the mode of acquisition, nature and situation of the immovable property as well as the cause and purposes of the expropriation so as to secure social justice.

The immovable property, acquired by way of expropriation for a certain purpose, if not being used to fulfill that purpose within the period of time prescribed by law, shall be returned to the original owner or his heir unless it is used for other purposes according to paragraph three pursuant to the provision of law.

The return of immovable property to the original owner or his heir under paragraph five and the claim of compensation paid shall be in accordance with the provision of law.

Section 34. Every person shall enjoy the liberty of speech, writing, printing and publication.

The restriction on such liberty shall not be imposed except by virtue of law specifically enacted for the purpose of maintaining the security of State or safeguarding the liberties, dignity or reputation of other persons or maintaining public order or good morals or preventing deterioration of the mind or health of the public.

The press owner shall be a Thai national subject to the conditions prescribed by law.

No grant of money or other properties shall be made by the State as subsidy to a private newspaper.

Section 35. Every person shall enjoy the liberty of education; provided that such education is not contrary to his civic duties under the Constitution, and to the law relating to compulsory education and the law relating to the organization of educational establishments.

Section 36. Every person shall enjoy the liberty to assemble peacefully and without arms.

The restrictions on such liberty shall not be imposed except by virtue of law specifically enacted for the case of public meetings and for securing public conveniences in the use of public places or for maintaining public order during the time when the country is in a state of armed conflict or war, or when a state of emergency or martial law is declared.

Section 37. Every person shall enjoy the liberty to form an association, union, league, co-operative or any other group.

The formation, incorporation, management and dissolution of an association, union, league, co-operative or any other group shall be in accordance with the provision of law.

Section 38. Every person shall enjoy the liberty to form a political party for the purpose of performing political activities through the means of a democratic regime as provided in this Constitution.

The formation, incorporation, management and dissolution of a political party shall be in accordance with the provision of the law on political parties.

A political party shall openly disclose its sources of income and expenditure.

Section 39. Every person shall enjoy the liberty of communication by lawful means.

The censorship, detention or disclosure of communication betwen persons including any other act disclosing a statement in the communication between persons, shall not be effected except by virtue of law specifically enacted for public order or good morals, public safety, or for maintaining the security of the State.

Section 40. Every person shall enjoy the liberty of travelling and the liberty of making the choice of his residence within the Kingdom.

The restriction on such liberties shall not be imposed except by virtue of law specifically enacted for the purpose of maintaining the security of the country, public order, public welfare, town and country planning or welfare of the youth.

No person of Thai nationality shall be deported or prohibited from entering the Kingdom.

Section 41. Family rights are protected.

Section 42. Every person shall have a right to present a petition upon the conditions and in the manner provided by law.

Section 43. The right of a person to sue a Government agency which is a juristic person to be liable for an act done by its official is protected.

Section 44. Persons who are in the armed forces and the police force, government officials, local government officials and employees of State organizations shall enjoy the same rights and liberties under the Constitution as those accorded to the people unless such enjoyment is restricted by law, by-law or regulation issued by virtue of law specifically enacted in so far as it is concerned with politics, efficiency or discipline.

Section 45. No person shall exercise the rights and liberties under the Constitution against the Nation, religion, the King and Constitution.

Chapter IV
Duties of the Thai People

Section 46. Every person shall have a duty to uphold the Nation, religion, the King and the Democratic Regime of Government under this Constitution.

Section 47. Every person shall have a duty to defend the country.

Section 48. Every person shall have a duty to serve in the armed forces as provided by law.

Section 49. Every person shall have a duty to comply with the law.

Section 50. Every person shall have a duty to pay taxes and duties imposed by law.

Section 51. Every person shall have a duty to render assistance to the official service as provided by law.

Section 52. Every person shall have a duty to receive education and training under the conditions and in the manner provided by law.

Chapter V
Directive Principles of State Policies

Section 53. The provision of this Chapter is intended to be used as directive principles for legislating and determining the policies, and shall not give rise to any cause of action against the State.

Section 54. The State shall maintain the institution of kingship, the independence and integrity of its territories.

Section 55. The State should promote friendly relations with other countries and adopt the principle of reciprocity.

Section 56. The State shall arrange for the maintenance of the armed forces for safeguarding its independence, security of the State and national interest.

The armed forces shall be employed in an armed conflict or a war, for the protection of the institution of kingship, for suppressing a rebellion and a riot, for maintaining the security of the State and for national development.

Section 57. The State shall enforce the law and order so that the people may be assured of the safety in their lives, persons and property as well as in their peaceful existence.

Section 58. The State should organize the systems of official service and other State affairs for the achievement of efficiency and should take every measure to prevent and suppress corruption.

Section 59. The State should organize the system of judicial process to ensure justice to the people and to meet the requirement of expediency.

Section 60. The State should promote and support education and professional training according to the suitability and to the demand of the country.

The organization of educational system is an exclusive duty of the State. All educational establishments shall be under the control and supervision of the State.

The State should provide the indigent persons with grants and requisites in their education and occupational training.

Compulsory education in the educational establishments of the State is to be provided without charge.

As for higher education, the State should allow educational establishments to manage their own affairs within the limits provided by law.

Section 61. The State should encourage researches in arts and sciences and should promote the application of science and technology in the development of the country.

Section 62. The State should support and promote national youth development so that they may be physically, mentally and intellectually sound for the purpose of economic and social development and for the security of the State.

Section 63. The State should promote public understanding of and public belief in the democratic regime of government with the King as its Head as well as the local government.

The State should ensure the local people to enjoy the right of self-government as provided by law.

Section 64. The State should promote and conserve the national culture.

Section 65. The State should conserve the balance of environment and eliminate pollution which jeopardizes the health and hygiene of the people.

Section 66. The State should proceed to raise the economic and social status of individuals to the level of comfortable livelihood.

Section 67. The State should, by means of land reform or by other means, secure land ownership or rights in land to all farmers for engaging in agriculture.

The State should protect and preserve the interests of the farmers in the production and in the disposition of their produce by means of price guarantee, or price maintenance as well as organizing the system and control of production and disposition appropriate to the demand of the market or by other means, and should promote the assembling of farmers in the form of co-operatives or other forms.

Section 68. The State should support economic initiative in the private sector.

The State should engage in an enterprise in the nature of public utility in such a way as to be beneficial to the people as a whole. An enterprise in the nature of public utility shall be engaged in by individuals only if done by virtue of law.

The State should impose measures to prevent direct or indirect economic monopoly by individuals, which is not created by virtue of law.

Section 69. The State should have a demographic policy appropriate for natural resources, economic and social conditions, and technological progress for the purpose of economic and social development and for the security of the State.

Section 70. The State should give aid to persons suffering from performing duties for the Nation, or rendering assistance to the official service or performing a moral duty, or from natural calamities.

Section 71. The State should promote and support the State and private social works for the welfare and happiness of the people.

Section 72. The State should support the people of working age to obtain suitable employments, ensure the fair protection of labour, and provide for the system of labour relations including the settlement of fair wages.

Section 73. The State should promote public health and provide the indigent persons with free medical treatment.

The State shall prevent and suppress harmful contagious diseases in the interest of the public without charge.

---

*Published in the *Government Gazette*, Vol. 63, Part 30, dated 10 May B.E. 2489 (1946).

APPENDIX 5

CONSTITUTION FOR THE ADMINISTRATION

OF THE KINGDOM,*

B.E. 2534 (1991)

BHUMIBOL ADULYADEJ, REX.

Given on the 1st Day of March B.E. 2534;

Being the 46th Year of the Present Reign.

Phrabat Somdet Phraparamintharamaha Bhumobol Adulyadej Mahittalathibet Ramathibodi Chakkri Narubodin Sayammintharathirat Borommanatthabophit is graciously pleased to proclaim that:

Whereas the Chairman of the National Peacekeeping Command, who successfully seized and took control of the State administrative power on 23rd February 1991, has advised the King that the abrogation of the Constitution of the Kingdom of Thailand B.E. 2521 and the Amendments thereof has been carried out by the National Peacekeeping Command with a desire to have an appropriate Constitution to ensure a peaceful administration of the country and with a view to averting danger to the Nation and the institution of the King and creating peace within a short period, as well as to establish the administration of the country and which is appropriate for the condition of the country, economic and social background of the people, but the time necessary for such doing depends upon the circumstances, it is therefore expedient to have an interim Constitution of the Kingdom appropriate to the present situation and, in order to give effect to the advice of the Chairman of the National Peacekeeping Command, the King, therefore, is graciously pleased to proclaim the following provisions as the Constitution of the Kingdom to remain in force until the Constitution which will be drafted under the provisions of this Constitution is promulgated:

Section 1. Thailand is a Kingdom, one and indivisible.
The King is Head of State and holds the position of Head of the Thai Armed Forces.
Section 2. The Sovereign power emanates from the Thai people. The King who is Head of State exercises such power only in conformity with the provisions of this Constitution.
Section 3. The King exercises the legislative power through the National Legislative Assembly, the executive power through the Cabinet, and the judicial power through the Courts.
Section 4. The person of the King is in a sacred position and shall not be violated, accused or sued in any manner whatever.

Section 5. The King selects and appoints the President of the Privy Council and not more than fourteen Privy Councilors from qualified persons to constitute the Privy Council.

The Privy Council has the duty to advise the King on all matters pertaining to His functions as He may consult.

The selection and appointment of a Privy Councillor and the removal of a Privy Councillor from office shall be at the King's pleasure.

Section 6. There shall be a National Legislative Assembly having the duty to prepare the Constitution and consider bills.

In preparing the Constitution, the National Legislative Assembly shall have regard for the general election which is to be held in the year B.E. 2534.

Section 7. the National Legislative Assembly consists of not less than two hundred but not more than three hundred members to be appointed by the King from persons of Thai nationality by birth upon the advice of the President of the National Peacekeeping Council.

If there is a vacancy in the membership of the National Legislative Assembly, the King may appoint a person with qualification under paragraph one to fill it.

The President of the National Peacekeeping Council shall countersign the Royal Command appointing members of the National Legislative Assembly.

Section 8. In the case where any member of the National Legislative Assembly commits an act which brings disgrace to the membership of the National Legislative Assembly or behaves in such a way as to obstruct the performance of duty of a member of the National Legislative Assembly, members of the National Legislative Assembly of not less than twenty members have the right to present their petition to the President of the National Legislative Assembly to terminate the membership of such member.

A resolution of the National Legislative Assembly terminating the membership of a member under paragraph one shall be passed by votes of not less than two-thirds of the total number of existing members on the date thereof.

Section 9. The King, in accordance with the resolution of the Assembly, appoints one member of the National Legislative Assembly President of the Assembly and one or several members of the National Legislative Assembly Vice-Presidents of the Assembly.

The President of the National Peacekeeping Council shall countersign the Royal Command appointing the President and the Vice-Presidents of the National Legislative Assembly.

Section 10. The National Legislative Assembly shall appoint a Committee consisting of not more than twenty members having the duty to draft the Constitution for submission to the National Legislative Assembly.

The Committee under paragraph one may also consist of persons who are not members of the National Legislative Assembly.

Section 11. After having received the draft constitution from the Committee under section 10, the National Legislative Assembly shall consider it in three readings. The first and second readings shall be in accordance with the rules of procedure of the National Legislative Assembly and the third reading shall take place only after the lapse of fifteen days from the second reading.

In the third reading, the attendance of not less than three-fourths of the total number of existing members on the date thereof is required to constitute a quorum.

The voting in the third reading shall be decided by a roll call, and the promulgation of the Constitution must be approved by votes of not less than two-thirds of the total number of existing members of the date thereof.

After the resolution of approval in the third reading by the National Legislative Assembly, the President of the National Legislative Assembly shall present the draft constitution to the King for His signature for its promulgation as the Constitution.

In the promulgation of the Constitution, the President of the National Legislative Assembly shall countersign the Royal Command.

Section 12. If no votes of approval are obtained in the third reading of the draft constitution under section 11 paragraph three, the National Legislative Assembly shall prepare a new draft constitution and consider it under the provisions of this Constitution. If the Preparation and consideration of the said draft constitution should make the holding of the general election in the year B.E. 2534 impossible, the period for election shall be extended for one hundred and twenty days as from the end of the year B.E. 2534.

Section 13. If no votes of approval are obtained under section 11 in the first or third reading of the new draft constitution prepared under section 12, all members of the National Legislative Assembly shall vacate office on the data thereof, and the National Peacekeeping Council shall hold a joint sitting with the Cabinet in order to complete the revision of the draft constitution under section 10 or section 12 or any previously promulgated Constitution of the Kingdom of Thailand within thirty days as from the date thereof, and shall present it to the King for His signature for its promulgation as the Constitution.

The President of the National Peacekeeping Council shall preside over the joint sitting under paragraph one.

In proceeding under paragraph one, it shall have regard to the general election which must be held as soon as possible.

In the promulgation of the Constitution under this section, the Prime Minister shall countersign the Royal Command.

Section 14. Subject to section 11, a sitting of the National Legislative Assembly requires the attendance of not less than one-third of the total number of existing members on the date thereof to constitute a quorum.

Section 15. At a sitting of the National Legislative Assembly, words Expressed by any person in giving a statement of fact or opinion or in casting the vote are absolutely privileged. No charge or action in any manner whatever shall be brought against such person.

The privilege provided in paragraph one shall also extend to members of Committees of the Assembly, printers and publishers of minutes under the order of the President of the National Legislative Assembly.

In the case where a member of the National Legislative Assembly is detained or placed in custody or charged in a criminal case, his release or the suspension of his trial shall be ordered at the request of the President of the National Legislative Assembly.

Section 16. The National Legislative Assembly has the power to make regulations concerning the selection and performance of duties of the president and Vice-President, and Committee members, the Procedures for sitting, consideration of draft constitution, consideration of bills, introduction of a motion which is not of such nature as to require the Cabinet to give a statement or opinion on any matter, debate, adoption of resolution, maintenance of order, and other activities in the exercise of its powers and duties.

Section 17. The King enacts an Act with the advice and consent of the National Legislative Assembly.

A bill shall be introduced only by the Cabinet.

Section 18. There shall be a National Peacekeeping Council consisting of the persons under the Announcement of the National Peacekeeping Command No. 2, dated 23rd February B.E. 2534 and the Announcement of the National Peacekeeping Command No. 5, dated 23rd February B.E. 2534 as members.

The President of the National Peacekeeping Council may make additional appointment of not more than fifteen other persons to be members of the National Peacekeeping Council.

The Chairman of the National Peacekeeping Command shall be President of the National Peacekeeping Council. One of the Vice-Chairman of the National Peacekeeping Command appointed by the National Peacekeeping Council shall be Vice-President of the National Peacekeeping Council. The Secretary-General of the national Peacekeeping Command shall be the Secretary-General of the National Peacekeeping Council.

The National Peacekeeping Council shall appoint one or several persons, whether or not such person is member of the National Peacekeeping Council, to be the Deputy Secretary-General of the National Peacekeeping Council.

In the case where the President of the National Peacekeeping Council is not present or is unable to perform the duties, the Vice-President of the National Peacekeeping Council shall perform the duties of the President of the National Peacekeeping Council, and in the case where the President and Vice-President of the National Peacekeeping Council are not present or are unable to perform the duties, the members of the National Peacekeeping Council shall elect a member to perform the duties of the President of the National Peacekeeping Council.

Section 19. The National Peacekeeping Council shall have the powers and duties to jointly prescribe the policy with the Cabinet on the administration of the State affairs which the Cabinet will announce to the National Legislative Assembly, and to recommend or give opinion on any matter which is considered expedient for the Cabinet to administer the State affairs, and shall have such other powers and duties as provided in this Constitution.

The President of the National Peacekeeping Council shall preside over the joint sitting of the National Peacekeeping Council and the Cabinet.

Section 20. In the case where it is considered expedient. The President of the National Peacekeeping Council or the Prime Minister may refer any problem relating to the administration of the State affairs to a joint sitting of the National Peacekeeping Council and the Cabinet for consideration and resolution.

Section 21. The King appoints a Prime Minister upon the advice of the President of the National Peacekeeping Council and a number of Ministers upon the advice of the Prime Minister to constitute a Cabinet having the duty to administer the State affairs.

Section 22. The King has the prerogative of removing the Prime Minister from office upon the advice of the President of the National Peacekeeping Council and of removing a Minister from office upon the advice of the Prime Minister.

Section 23. The President of the National Peacekeeping Council shall countersign the Royal Command appointing the Prime Minister or removing him from office.

The Prime Minister shall countersign the Royal Command appointing a Minister or removing him from office.

Section 24. The Prime Minister and the Ministers shall neither be members of the National Legislative Assembly nor hold any position in a private undertaking which operates its business for profit.

The Prime Minister and the Ministers have the right to be present in order to announce their policy and give their opinion at the sitting of the National Legislative Assembly but are not entitled to vote, and the provisions governing privileges under section 15 shall apply *mutatis mutandis*.

Section 25. The King has the prerogative of enacting a Royal Decree which is not contrary to the law.

Section 26. In case of an emergency to maintain peace or security of the Kingdom or the public safety or the security of the national economy or to avert public calamity, or in case of necessity to have a law on taxation or currency which, in the interest of the State, requires an urgent and confidential consideration, the Prime Minister may, with the approval of the National Peacekeeping Council, advise the King to enact an Emergency Decree which shall have the force of an Act.

After the promulgation of the Emergency Decree, the Cabinet shall, without delay, submit it to the National Legislative Assembly. If the National Legislative Assembly approves it, it shall continue to have the force of an Act. If the National Legislative Assembly disapproves it, it shall lapse; provided that it shall not affect any act done during the enforcement thereof.

The approval or disapproval of an Emergency Decree shall be published in the Government Gazette. In case of disapproval, the disapproval shall be effective as from the date of its publication in the Government Gazette.

Section 27. In the case where the President of the National Peacekeeping Council or the Prime Minister deems it necessary for the prevention or suppression of an act subverting peace or security of the Kingdom, the Throne, the national economy or the State affairs, or of an act disturbing or threatening public order or good moral, or of an act destroying the natural resources or detrimental to public health, whether such act has occurred before or occurs after the day on which this Constitution is promulgated, wither within or outside the Kingdom, the President of the National Peacekeeping Council or the Prime Minister or the President of the National Peacekeeping Council and the Prime Minister shall, with the approval of the joint sitting of the National Peacekeeping Council and the Prime Minister, have the power to issue any order or take any action, and such order or action as well as acts performed in compliance therewith shall be considered lawful. After having issued any order or taken any action under paragraph one, the President of the national Peacekeeping Council or the Prime Minister, or the President of National Peacekeeping Council and the Prime Minister shall report to the President of the National Legislative Assembly in order to inform the National Legislative Assembly thereof.

Section 28. All laws, Royal Rescripts and Royal Commands relating to the State affairs must be countersigned by the Prime Minister or a Minister.

Section 29. Judges are independent in the trial and adjudication of cases in accordance with the law.

Section 30. Whenever no provision of this Constitution is applicable to any case, it shall be decided in accordance with the constitutional practices of Thailand under the democratic form of government.

In the case where a question concerning the decision of any case under paragraph one should arise in the affairs of the National Legislative Assembly or be referred by the Cabinet to the National Legislative Assembly for decision, it shall be decided by the National Legislative Assembly.

Section 31. In the case where there should be a question as to whether or not any act or performance is contrary to, inconsistent with, or not in compliance with the provisions of this Constitution, it shall be decided by the National Legislative Assembly.

Section 32. All acts, announcements or orders of the Chairman of the National Peacekeeping Command or those of the National Peacekeeping Command, done or issued before the day on which this Constitution is enacted in relation to the seizure and control of the State administrative power on 23rd February B.E. 2534, regardless of their manner or form and regardless of their legislative, executive or judicial force, including the acts performed in compliance therewith as well as the acts of any person done in relation to such seizure or control of the State administrative power, shall be considered lawful.

Section 33. Prior to the appointment of the Cabinet, the President of the National Peacekeeping Council performs the duties of the Prime Minister, and the national Peacekeeping Council performs the duties of the Cabinet.

Countersigned by:

General Sundhara Kongsompong
Chairman of the National Peacekeeping Command

Certified correct translation
Signature
(Rongphol Charoenphandhu)
Office of the Juridical Council
(Office of the Council of State)

---

*Published in the Government Gazette, Vol. 108, Part 40, Special Issue, dated 1st March B.E. 2534 (1991).

CONCLUSION

*Towards Human Rights Constitutionalism
in Asia and the United States?*

Lawrence W. Beer

The most significant development in institutions of politics and law during the twentieth century may have been the human rights revolution, a global explosion of awareness that humans of whatever size and shape, race and religion, sex and ethnic identity are all equally endowed from the womb with an inherent dignity requiring respectful response from governments and societies. The status of human rights has depended less on the instruments of force than on the elements of nobility and shame at exposure of barbarism in the human character. Human rights counterbalance unprecedented power to destroy peoples and environments, and give coherence and meaning to bewildering advances in knowledge, science, and technology, and to their worldwide diffusion.

Millennia of yearning and groping in all inhabited points on the planet for humane standards of just governance gradually issued in diverse political wisdoms, some recorded in writing, others refined and passed on by communal ritual, art, story-telling and unwritten law. Coerced world dialogue on the foundations of statehood during the recent centuries of Western colonialism and imperialism brought global attention to Western conceptions of constitutionalism, rights and law. This discourse gradually undercut the legitimacy of Western dominance with universalist doctrines calling for the freedom and equal treatment of all peoples and for democratic processes under law. These ideas also undermined in whole or in part a multitude of non-Western understandings of just rule and community life.

Efforts to institutionalize *human* rights under international law based on recognition of each human's inherent dignity began in nineteenth-century Europe's attention to the treatment of war victims and prisoners,[1] and meshed with the earlier spread of documentary constitutionalism after the revolutions of the United States and France. Comprehensive formulations of human rights did not gain serious worldwide consideration until the International Bill of Human Rights developed after 1945 in the United Nations, following the long agonies of world wars, colonialism, and regional and civil conflicts. Majoritarian democracy has failed as a sufficient basis for human rights enforcement, but until recent decades, human rights were not commonly discussed as *the* appropriate defining foundation for constitutionalist government everywhere. In public discourse and academic analysis on Asia, as on other continents, economic development, military conflict, leadership problems, and political culture preoccupied scholars and publicists, to the neglect of law and constitutions as elements of a successful civilization.[2] Yet "constitutionalizing" a right is often important for its legitimizing and institutionalization.

By 1991, 168 of 173 states had a single-document national constitution with substantial provisions about human rights, and shared for the first time in history a common understanding of a few alternative modern models of government and law. Of course, understanding among the world's opinion-makers implies precision about disagreements rather than agreement and tells us nothing about the views of a general citizenry. Discourse was still dominated by Western categories without adequate attention to non-Western varieties of constitutionalism. Old terminology--words like "liberalism," "conservatism," "communism," "socialism," "modernization," "development," "free enterprise," "individualism," and "collectivism"--does not enliven transcultural analysis of the foundations of constitutional government and human rights.[3] Usage may be particularly brittle in America's public parlance, because rhetoric and human rights realities have in many respects parted company here. In Asia and elsewhere, ethnic tribalism and religious faith often replaced secular ideology as dominant public forces, along with economic factors. But politico-legal traditions in many countries retained their relevance for the future insofar as they could accommodate the intellectual power and moral authority behind human rights imperatives. Human rights arguments gained widening acceptance as an effective response to exaggerated collectivism or individualism and amoral legal positivism,[4] and as the basis for a life with dignity in a free community.

"Mutualism" was offered in chapter 1 as a better word than "individualism" or "collectivism" to capture the ideals of human rights constitutionalism. Unlike some terms, mutualism would not posit as fact or norm a weak community composed of solipsistic selves, but rather the possibility of strong awareness of reciprocity as inherent in interpersonal relations and government-citizen relations, and the inseparability of rights and responsibilities under democratic law. Mutualism does not recognize a war of all against all in economic life; nor does it legitimize hierarchical strata determinative of unequal rights in society. Institutionalization of human rights law began in the modern West, but much more noteworthy than their geographical and historical origins, human rights have become the most widely accepted universalist, secular basis for government and law in the world.[5]

In the analytical terms used in chapter 1, human rights constitutionalism has become the most commonly shared constitutional ideal in Asia. Within the ruling and politically active elites of many countries, even in some "nonconstitutionalist" authoritarian states, an increasingly firm agreement was emerging that the primary purpose of government and law is precisely to protect and promote human rights, not for example, property rights, state rights, or military interests. Respect for individual human rights in criminal and civil justice, socio-economic rights, rights of political participation, and other civil liberties were commonly perceived to be essential to a national claim of honoring human rights in law and policy. In recent years, the practical issue for human rights constitutionalism was not simply how to limit as suspect the power of government, in general or in deference to a particular economic or social interest group, but how to channel under law as much power as possible on behalf of human rights, whether to restrain police or mobs or to gain pragmatic cooperation between the public and private sectors on economic problems. Constitutionalist government requires that power be divided and that it be limited in some contexts (for example, in regulating business and press freedom); but it is just as essential for human rights to restrict private power (for example, in giantist mass media companies, global corporations, and exploitive landholdings), to enhance a government's capacity to effectively deliver services, and to monopolize means of coercion to protect personal security rights. In the economically less prosperous countries of Asia, insufficient government resources and the limited reach of official authority beyond major cities have sometimes meshed with private denial of rights, even where government policy strongly favored rights. Government priorities and public values rather than inadequate resources seemed to explain America's major performance deficiencies in criminal and social justice.

What of trends in Asia's constitutional systems? In 1991 five themes stood out in Asia's constitutional politics: leadership succession problems; corruption based on family or patron-client favoritism; the military's diminishing role in governance; the salience of religion as a positive or negative force in constitutionalism; and human rights issues.

In the 1980s and 1990, leadership changed hands in many Asian countries, not just in the sense of one leader succeeding another--after election, assassination, natural death, popular upheaval, coup d'etat, or oligarchic selection--but in the deeper sense of a generation passing away and established modes of governance beginning to change direction. By 1991, the incidence and legitimacy of militarized and military-dominant regimes appeared to be receding in importance and civilian constitutionalism advancing. It was at least being challenged, except perhaps in Indonesia and Burma. Human rights concerns found fresh emphasis on the world scene with the diplomacy of President Jimmy Carter (1977-1981), with the spreading acceptance of United Nations and regional human rights documents, and with the growth of human rights studies and advocacy. At the fortieth anniversary of the United Nations' Declaration of Universal Human Rights on December 10, 1988, on balance, the increased rhetorical prominence of individual rights in Asia seemed to be matched by more government and private effort than in the past to institutionalize constitutional rights in law.

Religion--most widely, Islam and Buddhism--occupied a central place in the increasingly firm sense of constitutional identity that emerged in many Asian nations and subnational groupings. Christianity played a major role in the democracy revolutions of the Philippines and South Korea, and buttressed other supports for human rights in Japan, Taiwan, Indonesia and elsewhere. Religions were accorded a modicum of tolerance in China and Vietnam, while religio-ethnic intolerance was a factor in communal tensions within India, Sri Lanka, Malaysia, China, Indonesia, and other countries. Nevertheless, religion as a powerful motive force either for democratic development and tolerance or for hypernationalism and intolerance was still neglected in constitutional studies. The distinguished commentator on religious affairs, Martin Marty, explains: [6]

> Everybody, 15, 25 years ago, and for the past 200 years, was predicting that the world's future would be secular, rational, serene. The religions that would survive would be rational, tolerant, cool, ecumenical, interactive.
> To everybody's surprise, therefore, we have to cope with the fact that every hot spot in the world...is nationalist and is tribal, and usually religious, and when it's religious, it's fundamentalist or fundamentalist-like....
> Americans get much madder over the Pledge of Allegiance and burning the flag than they do about equality, justice and freedom.

A further trend was a generational change of leadership, linked in many cases with shifts in the status of military politics and human rights. One symbol of such transitions was the passing on January 7, 1989 of Emperor Hirohito of Japan. Although postwar Japan has been marked by peaceful democracy, Hirohito had continued to remind some, at home and abroad, of the aggressive militarist government which ended in September, 1945. Emperor Akihito and Empress Michiko were both educated more to peaceful internationalism and awareness of human rights than to Shinto nationalism. During U.N.-sanctioned actions against Iraq to liberate Kuwait and oil flow in 1990-91, the strong opposition in Japan to sending military aid to the U.S.-dominated "coalition forces" confirmed dramatically the seriousness of Japan's constitutional renunciation of war (Article 9); in addition, many criticized as "unconstitutional" Japan's generous financial support of the United Nations effort. A major issue for constitutional and political debate is the shape which Japan's non-military world leadership will take in the 1990s.[7]

Nepotistic succession in India's Congress Party occurred when Rajeev Gandhi followed Indira Gandhi as Prime Minister in 1984, but ended with his own tragic assassination in 1991. The sons of North Korea's Kim Il-sung and Singapore's Lee Kuan Yew also rose. A son or daughter of a national leader may have excellent credentials, as in the case of Chiang Ching-kuo (1910-1988) of Taiwan and apparently in the case of Benazir Bhutto of Pakistan, the first woman prime minister of a major Islamic country, removed prematurely by the military in 1990. Or legitimate doubts may exist about the stature of a leader's offspring, as in the case of Kim Jong-Il. The problem may be especially sensitive if, as in Thailand, the monarch (King Bhumibol Adulyadej) is of great constitutional importance and the heir apparent excites considerably less respect than the incumbent.

Restraint of abuses of family power remained a seminal constitutional problem in a number of Asian systems, due to the clash between public duties under law and ingrained tendencies toward family favoritism and patron-client loyalty. However, efforts against familistic corruption in the Philippines, South Korea and India were sometimes impressive; in most Asian countries, such corruption was not fatalistically accepted as the norm or inevitably normal behavior. For example, the Philippine Constitution bans presidential appointment of relatives to high office.[8]

Cambodia was ravaged by Pol Pot's massacre of his own people after the Vietnam War, and then by a protracted civil-international war involving Vietnam. The great exodus of refugees from Indochina (Laos, Vietnam, Cambodia) and Afghanistan after 1975 raised the world's awareness of human rights during the 1980s. Despite continuing multi-lateral efforts, peace, a viable constitutional order, and the stability essential for human rights have eluded Cambodia, a country with no experience of democratic leadership succession. For China and its Communist Party, the historic period of group leadership which began in 1935 entered its final phase when Mao Zedong and Chou Enlai died around 1975, but will not end until Deng Xiaoping passes away. Modern China has no precedent for such a generational succession, and Deng's efforts to put new leaders--most notably, Hu Yaobang and Zhao

Ziyang--into place in the 1980s proved abortive. In June, 1989, Premier Li Peng, his colleagues, and the People's Liberation Army, lost public trust and rendered the future even more problematic when they crushed the democracy movement in Tiananmen Square, Beijing. Semi-capitalism combined with harsh repression. Other Asian popular movements called, some successfully, for more freedom and more democratic governance in Bangladesh, Burma, Nepal, Pakistan, the Philippines, South Korea and Taiwan. More local autonomy was fought for in Tibet and Sri Lanka (Tamils). The Philippines and South Korea have shared in the past a major constitutional problem affecting human rights: the unwillingness of an incumbent to relinquish power after a legally set period in office, and the lack of a stable, routinized system in law and politics for passing from one leader or group of leaders to the next. Since 1961, South Korea's presidents have been former generals first chosen by their military colleagues rather than by popular vote and open processes. At the end of Roh Tae Woo's five-year term in 1993, will the military allow transition to a president of civilian background? In 1990, Burma's General Newin allowed elections, then suppressed the democratic victors. Will the pattern of military political involvement change in China, Pakistan, the Philippines, and Taiwan? If not, as in Thailand in February, 1991, will the military respect or dismiss the need for quick return to democratic civilian government? Which general will succeed President Soeharto in the 1990s?

Since the 1940s, some of Asia's military-dominated governments have had noteworthy peacetime accomplishments, and one-party civilian governments obviously can be as inimical to constitutionalism and human rights as military leaders. These points are clear from the repressive record of Asia's communist and other non-constitutionalist states, and from instances elsewhere of military leaders yielding to civilian democracy. Nevertheless, a military is an irregular center of government power accountable only to itself and prone to martial suspension of ordinary constitutionalist law. In general, military primacy in a government is as reliable an indicator of weak constitutionalism as are deficient systemic provisions for democratic leadership succession, freedom of expression, or criminal justice rights.

In sum, prescinding from their wildly varying and in some cases irrelevant levels of economic development, the accomplishments of many Asian countries since 1945 in overcoming formidable obstacles and building law, constitutionalism and human rights commitments into their state systems and policies have been impressive. Where human rights constitutionalism is not accepted, more peoples have grounds for hope (if not optimism) than have reasons for pessimism about the likelihood of humane change.

A New American Constitutionalism?

A comparative study of constitutional systems in Asia at the Bicentennial of the United States Constitution and Bill of Rights can sharpen perspective on the state of American constitutionalism. The U.S. Constitution is of course important, but public policy choices and deficient leadership, not lack of resources, explain more than the operative constitution about the appalling quality of life and criminal justice endured by tens of millions of Americans and passively accepted by a majority in government, politics and society. That acknowledged, nevertheless, as an instrument for modern and democratic governance, the U.S. Constitution, with all its amendments and judicial interpretations to date, seems defective. For example, it does not include a clear statement of human rights or American constitutional goals and values. Formal revision of the near-sacred text may not be on the near political horizon, but seems needed. More modestly, may not a constitutional consensus exist or be achievable on one or more of the following issues explicitly dealt with in one or more Asian constitutional systems discussed in this volume?

a) *a new Preamble*--A simple, eloquent formulation of what American constitutionalism and democracy stand for, drawing upon historically honored sources such as the Declaration of Independence, the U.S. Constitution, and Abraham Lincoln's major addresses. The Preamble might end with elucidation of a few key policy commitments, spelled out as "Directive Principles of State Policy".

b) *judicial review*--Formal recognition in the U.S. Constitution of the power of federal courts to determine issues of constitutionality and legality.

c) *restraints on militarization and possession of arms*--A constitutional renunciation of the use of force as a means of settling international disputes apart from carefully delimited exceptions, and a stated commitment to the development of reliance upon United Nations peace-keeping capacities. Unnecessary and excessive American use of armed forces in Grenada, Nicaragua, Panama, and the Persian Gulf region in recent years have manifested a highly militarized political culture and a sometimes lawless lack of restraint which are at odds with U.S. claims to respect peace, life, law, and constitutional government. Finally, the current serious abuse of "the right to bear arms" clause could be remedied by an amendment removing the provision and instituting restraints on the private possession and use of firearms.

d) *socioeconomic rights*--Explicit constitutional provision for:

1) The right of each person to minimum levels of food, clothing and shelter in keeping with human dignity. A mandate for remedial action on

behalf of the endemically disadvantaged.   (A world standard for local
determination of a survival wage is needed.)

2) The centrality of the family and parental-filial responsibilities in the
nurturing and education of children.

3) The right to roughly equal public education, rather than radically
unequal opportunities as at present, based on tax revenue differentials among
school districts.

4) The right of all to a modest level of publicly assured health care,
but not to all expensive medical procedures; a mixed (public + private) health
care delivery system, as in a number of democracies.

5) Employee rights to organize unions, to bargain collectively, to strike
with impunity, to work under labor conditions as safe and humane as those
of management, and to freely report employer wrongdoing to authorities
without fear of reprisal. (The latter, because in the U.S., private employers
now commonly have a legal right to dismiss an employee "at will," that is, for
any reason, even for reporting a company's crimes. Public employees are also
punished for "whistleblowing".)[9]

e) *equality rights*--The right to equal treatment under public and private
law. A ban on both negative discrimination based on race, gender, religion
or ethnic identity, and positive discrimination (for example, in criminal justice
practices) based on wealth or social position.

f) *political participation rights*--

1) The right to vote under radically simplified voter registration
requirements at all levels of government, in place of the current restrictive
and disparate requirements.

2) The right of each political party to publicly funded, limited air time
on TV and radio. A ban on TV and radio political advertisements during
election campaigns, because abuse has proven to be serious and unavoidable.

3) The right of each candidate for major national office to public
campaign funds, and a restraint on the amount that may be spent on any
campaign for national office (i.e., Congress, Senate, Presidency).

4) A limitation of the President to one six-year term.

5) Exclusion from federal appointive posts of close relatives of
elective or appointive high officials.

g) *"First Amendment rights"*--This constitutional provision seems
appropriately unchangeable, but not in its interpretation (as suggested under
d) and f), for example).   More in keeping with constitutional practice
elsewhere would be an approach to the separation of religion and the state

that, while not establishing a specific religion, is not secularist but appreciative of the general public value of religion. While U.S. law bans a few minutes of content-neutral silent meditation in public schools, many democratic states support opportunities for education in the religions of choice in a spirit of tolerance. With respect to freedom of expression, as yet only a narrow spectrum of views seems to enjoy effective sociopolitical tolerance.

Documentary changes are obviously less critical to a living constitution than the intent of the political and legal professions to honor human rights. Using again the terms in chapter 1, the United States seems more in favor of majoritarian democracy than human rights constitutionalism, with only limited constitutionalist constraints on private wealth and private power. Asians who lavishly praise American democracy are often uninformed or less interested in human rights within the United States than in discrete politeness or aid emanating from the U.S. Unless they are refugees from one of Asia's repressive regimes who have happily tasted freedom and local community kindness and have avoided urban and rural poverty pockets, the positive imagery Asians may have of America seems exaggerated. American public rhetoric about rights sometimes overstates U.S. accomplishments and rarely reflects knowledge of comparative data. In fact, the U.S. is an unusually dangerous country to live in and, from a human rights perspective, governmentally harsh.[10] One is rarely electable to public office on a strong human rights platform. The economic system is less humane to the less fortunate than other prosperous democracies and some authoritarian states, and since 1981 has fostered a widening division between the majority and a very large, endemically deprived minority. Compared to most other democracies, the U.S. plutocratically favors the extraordinary wealth of a relative few.

The American President has been elected by a small plurality of voting-age Americans; indeed, only a bare majority participated in the constitutional system's most important election in 1988. The school system has no plan to remedy the national pattern of political apathy or "disconnectedness". Many of Asia's democratic electoral systems have much more impressive records. In addition, the results of U.S. voting in some recent elections have been more affected by unrestrained spending and the manipulation of TV images in negative campaigning and deceptive use of flag symbolism than by the candidates' accomplishments or positions on issues. In this constitutionally crucial mode of corruption and in campaign spending per national candidate, perhaps no Asian (or other?) democracy rivals the United States.[11] In some respects at least, the influence of American constitutionalism abroad is more in its afterglow and abstract ideals than in its current substantive performance.

Besides slavery and its enduring aftermath, non-white immigrants--most notably Asians--were "ineligible to citizenship" from 1790 to 1952.[12] The greatness of America's living constitutionalism has not been in the country's human rights performance or its commitment to tolerance of diverse beliefs and ideas. Many have surpassed the U.S. on both scores, without the pretentious claims of superiority all too common among Americans. Some of these nations have reinforced human rights in the world by ratifying the International Bill of Human Rights, while our government has declined to ratify the major Covenants with a dismissive claim to be honoring rights more effectively than countries which do ratify.[13] With meanness of spirit, the U.S. absented itself from UNESCO, a major world forum for human rights dialogue. Domestically, only two relatively similar political parties are viable in American political culture, the Democratic Party and the Republican Party, each with interchangeable parts; while other democracies accommodate a more vibrant diversity of viewpoints in organized parties.

Rather than in the above performance categories, if there is greatness in American constitutionalism, it may be in its halting and sometimes weakly sustained, yet historically impressive effort to *welcome* to citizenship and community life *all* ethnic and religious groupings and eventually all races as *equally human*, subject to only a few conditions: a willingness to honor the constitutional system which lends a measure of coherence to American culture, a willingness to speak the English language, and a willingness to assert one's subcultural and other interests in a manner minimally respectful of good manners, fairness, and constitutional conventions. That, at least, seems the operative ideal more in keeping with the Declaration of Independence than with the 18th century constitution, as we try to leave racism behind. While sometimes caught up in arrogant imaginings that "We are the world", as the song would have it, Americans at their authentic best do, in a very large country, try to live out a dream that is appropriate in part for the whole world, a dream of respect for diverse peoples within a democratic community. That element of broad, universalist idealism about *the possibility of tolerance and respect* for each human as human is admirable. It is not indigenous to at least some Asian constitutional cultures. Tolerance of each person is more critical to human rights than tolerance of all ideas, not an American trait. Human rights constitutionalism requires both tolerance and assurance to all of basic needs and services, the goals of many Asian constitutional systems in the late twentieth century.

NOTES

1. On the Red Cross movement, and the evolution of human rights treaty law, see David Forsythe, *Human Rights and World Politics*, Lincoln, University of Nebraska Press, 1989, 7-23.
2. Vernon Bogdanor, ed., *Constitutions in Democratic Politics*, Aldershot, U.K., Gower Publishing Co., 1988, 1-13, 380-386.
3. On the theoretical importance of regional and local economic variations, on which analogies can be made regarding constitutionalism, see Benjamin Harris, *The Road Less Traveled: A Development Economist's Quest*, Canberra, National Centre for Development Studies, 1989; and Kazuko Tsurumi and Tadashi Kawata, eds., *Naihatsuteki Hatten Ron* (The Theory of Endogenous Development), Tokyo, Tokyo University Press, 1989, and the review by Ronni Alexander in *Journal of International Studies*, Sophia University, Tokyo, July, 1989, 79-83.
4. On the distinctive relativism of American legal positivism, see Mary Ann Glendon, *Abortion and Divorce in Western Law: American Failures, European Challenges*, Cambridge, Harvard University Press, 1987, 114-125.
5. Jack Donnelly, *Universal Human Rights in Theory and Practice*, Ithaca, Cornell University Press, 1989; Robert F. Drinan, *Cry of the Oppressed: History and Hope in the Human Rights Revolution*, New York, Harper & Row, 1988.
6. In 1990, Martin Marty and a multinational group were engaged in a comparative study of fundamentalism in the world; interviewed by Carol M. Ostrom, "A Study of Fundamentalism," *The Seattle Times*, March 24, 1990. On religion and public life in the U.S., see *First Things*, a monthly. On problems attendant to foreign perceptions of Islam, see Akbar S. Ahmed, "Postmodernist Perceptions of Islam: Observing the Observer," *Asian Survey*, March, 1991, 213-231.
7. See Courtney Purrington and A.K., "Tokyo's Policy Responses During the Gulf Crisis," *Asian Survey*, April, 1991, 307.
8. See *Supra*, Chapter 8, Article 7, Sec. 13, Philippine Constitution.
9. On the limited effects of whistleblowing, see R.A. Johnson and M.K. Kraft, "Bureaucratic Whistleblowing and Policy Change," *The Western Political Quarterly*, Vol. 43, No. 4, Dec., 1990, 849.
10. See David Ellwood, *Poor Support: Poverty in the American Family*, New York, Basic Books, 1988; Michael B. Katz, *The Undeserving Poor: From the War on Poverty to the War on Welfare*, New York, Pantheon Books, 1989 (1990 figures continued this trend); *The Forgotten Half: Non-College Youth in America*, Washington, D.C. William T. Grant Foundation Commission on Work, Family, and Citizenship, January, 1988. The proportion of jobs that are low paying will continue to increase rapidly in the years ahead.

Another indicator of U.S. harshness is its leadership of the world in number of citizens in jail, 426 per 100,000, well above the next two in this unenviable ranking, South Africa (333) and the Soviet Union (268). Black Americans are incarcerated at four times the rate of black imprisonment in South Africa, 3,109 to 729 per 100,000. On the Sentencing Project, see *The Christian Science Monitor*, March 8, 1991.

See also Frances Moore Lappe', *Rediscovering America's Values* (New York: Ballantine Books, 1990), and the U.S. Census Bureau Report to the House Committee on Children, Youth, and Families, Washington, D.C., March, 1990.

11. See Bingham Powell, "American Voter Turnout in Comparative Perspective," *American Political Science Review*, Vol. 80, No. 1, 1986, 35; and David Scott, *Christian Science Monitor*, May 22, 1990.

12. On the historic experience of Asian immigrants and the racist views of some of America's Founding Fathers, see Ronald Takaki, *Strangers from a Different Shore: A History of Asian Americans*, New York, Penguin Books, 1990, especially at 11-18.

13. For instances of American opposition to international human rights, see David P. Forsythe, "Human Rights in U.S. Foreign Policy," *Political Science Quarterly*, Vol. 105, No. 3, 1990, 435; and R. Brody, P. Parker, and D. Weissbrodt, "Major Developments in 1990 at the U.N. Commission on Human Rights," *Human Rights Quarterly*, Vol. 12, 1990, 559.

ABOUT THE AUTHORS

Preben A.F. Aakesson is Director of Publications, Murat Bunnag International Law Office, Bangkok, Thailand. He was educated as a social scientist in Denmark and Cornell University. He is a member of the Asian Patent Attorneys Association and the Law Association for Asian and the Pacific, for which he serves as Chairman, Standing Committee on the Law and Drugs.

Nobuyoshi Ashibe is President of both the Public Law Association and the International Human Rights Law Association in Japan. In 1990 he was elected to the Japan Academy. He is past Dean and Professor Emeritus, Faculty of Law, Tokyo University, and now teaches at Gakushuin University, Tokyo. Among his many publications are: *A Theory of Constitutional Litigation* (1973), *A Theory of Modern Human Rights* (1974), and *The Modern Development of Constitutional Litigation* (1981), all in Japanese.

Lawrence Ward Beer is Fred Morgan Kirby Professor of Civil Rights at Lafayette College, Pennsylvania. From 1966 to 1982 he taught at the University of Colorado, at Boulder. He is past Chair, Committee on Asian Law, Association for Asian Studies and Co-Chair,the World Association of Law Professors. His books include: *Freedon of Expression in Japan* (1984), *Constitutionalism in Asia: Asian Views of the American Influence* (1979 and 1988), and (with Hiroshi Itoh) *The Constitutional Case Law of Japan: Selected Supreme Court Decisions, 1961-1970* (1978).

Marut Bunnag, Barrister-at-Law, heads the Marut Bunnag International Law Office in Bangkok. He received his law degree from Thammasat University in 1947, and now teaches law at several law faculties in Thailand. He has also served the law profession as: President, Lawyers Association of Thailand; President for Australasia, World Association of Lawyers, World Peace through Law Center; founder member and President of the Law Association for Asia and the Pacific; and Councillor, International Bar Association. In the Government of Thailand, he has served as M.P., Senator, Justice Minister, Minister of Education, and Minister of Public Health.

Rujira Bunnag is Barrister-at-Law and Managing Director of the Murat Bunnag International Law Office, Bangkok. He graduated from Thammasat University in 1979, and also holds LL.M. degrees from Tulane University (Admiralty Law) and the University of Pennsylvania. He is a lecturer on Insurance Law at Assumption University. He is a member of the Law Association for Asia and the Pacific, the Asian Patent Attorneys Association, and the Asian Pacific Lawyers Association. He is now President of the Lawyers Association of Thailand.

Sung Yoon Cho is Assistant Chief, Far Eastern Law Division, Library of Congress. After graduating from Seoul National University in 1953, he earned M.A. and Ph.D. degrees from Tulane University and the M.C.L. degree from George Washington University. He was Korean Attorney from 1953 to 1955 for the United Nations Civil Assistance Command in Seoul, and has long served as a consultant on Korean and Japanese law. His scholarly work focuses principally on North Korean government and law. In 1988 he published *Law and Legal Literature of North Korea: A Guide*.

Rajeev Dhavan was educated at Allahabad, Cambridge, and London Universities. He is called to the Indian and English Bars, and is now a practicing advocate in the High Court and Supreme Court of India. He is Honorary Professor at the Inidan Law Institute and former Professor of Law, Brunel University, England. A few of his numerous publications are: *The Supreme Court of India* (1977), *Amending the Constitution* (1978), *The President's Rule in the States* (1979), *Public Interest Litigation in India: An Investigative Report* (1981), and *The Law of the Press in India* (1987).

William J. Duiker is Professor of East Asian History at the Pennsylvania State University. An ex-Foreign Service Officer who served in Vietnam in the 1960s, he is author of numerous books and articles on contemporary Vietnam. Recent publications include *Vietnam Since the Fall of Saigon* (1985) and *China and Vietnam: The Roots of Conflict* (1986).

Emma Quisumbing Fernando is a retired Attorney and teacher of constitutional law at the University of the Philippines. She is author of the commentary *The Constitution of the Philippines* (1984).

Enrique M. Fernando is retired Chief Justice of the Supreme Court of the Philippines and Professorial Lecturer on Comparative Constitutional Law, University of the Philippines. After earning law degrees at the University of the Philippines, he was the first Filipino Sterling Fellow at Yale University. While George A. Malcolm Professor of Constitutional Law at the University of the Philippines, he was advisor to Presidents, represented his country at various United Nations conferences, and chaired the Civil Liberties Union of the Philippines. He has written extensively on Philippine constitutional law.

Ahmad bin Mohammed Ibrahim is the founding Dean, Faculty of Law, International Islamic University, Selangor, Malaysia, and former Dean, Faculty of Law, University of Malaya, Kuala Lumpur. He holds the title of Shaikh Kulliyah of Laws and is among his country's most honored educators. His written works include *Toward a History of Law in Malaysia and Singapore* (1970).

Masami Ito is a retired Justice of the Supreme Court of Japan. In 1990 he was admitted to the Japan Academy and became President, Japan Scholarship Foundation. He is past Dean and Professor Emeritus of Anglo-American Law, Faculty of Law, University of Tokyo. His numerous writings, almost all in Japanese, include the prize-winning *The Freedoms of Speech and the Press* (1962) and *Constitutional Law* (1982). He is Chairman of the Board of the Science and Technology Foundation of Japan, and also heads the Japan Copyright Commission, and the Lifelong Education Commission. Justice Ito also serves as a Director of the Japan Broadcasting Corporation (NHK).

M.P. Jain has been Professor of Law, University of Malaya, Kuala Lumpur, since 1978, following a long association with the University of Delhi, as student, professor, and then Dean of the Faculty of Law. His doctoral degree is from Yale University. He was Research Director, Indian Law Institute from 1963 to 1965. He has also taught at Banaras Hindu University, Australian National University, Heidelberg University, University of Singapore, and Monash University (Melbourne). Two more recent works are *Administrative Law in Malaysia and Singapore* (1980) and *Indian Constitutional Law, 4th ed.* (1987).

William Catron Jones, Charles Nagel Professor of International & Comparative Law, at Washington University, St. Louis, has been on that faculty since 1955. He was educated in law at Harvard Law School (LL.B.) and the University of Chicago (LL.M. and J.S.D.). He has been visiting professor at Freiburg i. Br. (1967), National Taiwan University (1971), and Wuhan University, China (1982-1984). He was a Visiting Research Scholar at Tokyo University and Visiting Research Fellow at the Institute for Developing Economics in 1976-77. Many of his law review articles deal with Chinese law and legal history. In 1984 he published a translation of the *Fourth Draft of the Civil Code of the People's Republic of China*. In 1989, his *Basic Principles in Civil Law in China* appeared.

Tscholsu Kim has taught in the College of Law, Seoul National University, for over thirty years. He holds the Ph.D. degree from that school and has also conducted research at Munich University and Harvard Law School. He has served as President of the Korean Public Law Association and of The Korean Law Professors Association. Among more recent wortks are *A Comparative Study of Constitutions* (1980), *A Treatise on Constitutional Law* (1988), and *The Constitutional History of Korea* (1988), all in Korean.

Sang Dan Lee is Associate Professor of Law at Chung-Ang University in Seoul, and Editor, *The Korean Journal of Comparative Law* (in English). A graduate of Seoul National University, he also holds degrees from the University of Miami (M.C.L.) and Tulane University (LL.M. and S.J.D.). His publications include *The Constitution and the Supreme Court of the United States* (1983), in Korean.

Chi-Tung Lin is the late Grand Justice of the Judicial Yuan, Taiwan, Republic of China and Professor, College of Law, National Taiwan University. His multi-volume commentary *An Article-By-Article Interpretation of the Constitution of the Republic of China* received the highest award for academic achievement from the Ministry of Education.

Herbert Han-Pao Ma is Grand Justice of the Judicial Yuan, Republic of China and Professor of Law, National Taiwan University. He attended National Fudan University in Shanghai from 1944 to 1947 and graduated from National Taiwan University in 1950. He has been Visiting Scholar at Harvard Law School in 1976 and Visiting Professor in the Asian Law Program, University of Washington in 1971 and 1979. His publications in Chinese include: *Essays on Western Legal Thought*, and in English "American Influence on the Formation of the Constitution and Constitutional Law of the Republic of China: Past History and Future Prospects", in L. Beer, ed., *Constitutionalism in Asia* (1979).

Padmo Wahjono is Professor in the Faculty of Law, University of Indonesia, Jakarta, from which he graduated in 1958. He has served as Deputy for Development and Study Affairs in the Pancasöla Studies Agency and as a member of the staff of experts in the National Law Development Center, Department of Justice. Among his publications, all in Indonesian, are: *Sistem Hukum Nasional delam Negara Hukum Pancasila* (1983), and *Penarapan Pancasila delam Demokrasi de Indonesian* (1983).

Valentine S. Winslow is Associate Professor, Faculty of Law, National University of Singapore. He holds M.A. and LL.B. degrees from Cambridge University and is a Barrister-at-Law, Middle Temple, London. In 1973 he became Advocate and Solicitor of the Supreme Court, Singapore. He was Research Fellow at the Academy of ASEAN Law and Jurisprudence, University of the Philippines, 1984-1986, and was principal reporter for a multi-national study of the constitutional systems of countries in the Association of Southeast Asian Nations.

THE TRANSLATORS
Keiko Harada Beer (B.A., Seisen Women's College, Tokyo) resides in Bethlehem, Pennsylvania.

William B. Cleary (Ph.D., Hokkaido University, Sapporo, Japan) is a member of the Bar Associations of California, Guam, New York, and West Virginia, specializing in Japanese law; he is currently practicing law in New York with the firm of Fried, Frank, Harris, Shriver & Jackson, but intends to return to academe.

John W. Garver (Ph.D., University of Colorado) is Associate Professor of Political Science, Georgia Tech University, and author of two books and numerous articles on modern China.

Masako Kamiya (Ph.D., Tokyo University) is Associate Professor of Law, Hokkaido University, Sapporo, Japan. She has also studied at Cambridge University. She writes about Japanese, English, and American Constitutional law. In 1990 she was Visiting Professor in the Law School of Columbia University.

Joseph H. Saunders is a Ph.D. candidate in Anthropology and Southeast Asian Studies at Cornell University. In 1984-85 and 1989-90 he conducted research in West Java, Indonesia as a Fulbright Scholar affiliated with Padjadjaran University, Bandung, and the Bandung Teacher's Training College. In 1991 Mr. Saunders was studying law at New York University School of Law.

J

XYZ